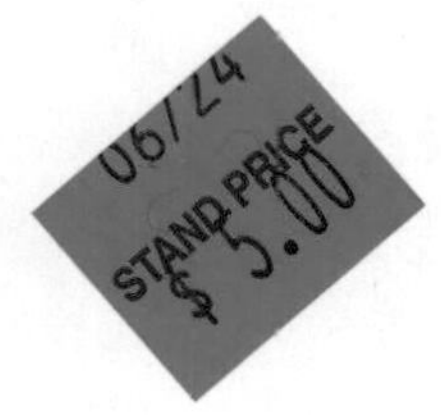
06/24
STAND PRICE
$5.00

CONCURRENCY CONTROL AND RELIABILITY IN DISTRIBUTED SYSTEMS

CONCURRENCY CONTROL AND RELIABILITY IN DISTRIBUTED SYSTEMS

Edited by

Bharat K. Bhargava
Department of Computer Science
Purdue University
West Lafayette, Indiana

VNR VAN NOSTRAND REINHOLD COMPANY
New York

Library of Congress Catalog Card Number 86-19121
ISBN 0-442-21148-1

Printed in the United States of America

Van Nostrand Reinhold Company Inc.
115 Fifth Avenue
New York, New York 10003

Van Nostrand Reinhold Company Limited
Molly Millars Lane
Wokingham, Berkshire RG11 2PY, England

Van Nostrand Reinhold
480 La Trobe Street
Melbourne, Victoria 3000, Australia

Macmillan of Canada
Division of Canada Publishing Corporation
164 Commander Boulevard
Agincourt, Ontario M1S 3C7, Canada

16 15 14 13 12 11 10 9 8 7 6 5 4 3 2 1

Library of Congress Cataloging-in-Publication Data

Concurrency control and reliability in distributed
systems.

"May 1986."
Bibliography: p.
Includes index.
1. Electronic data processing—Distributed processing.
I. Bhargava, Bharat, 1948–
QA76.9.D5C67 1987 004'.36 86-19121
ISBN 0-442-21148-1

To All the Contributors

Contributors

Bharat K. Bhargava, *Purdue University*
David Butterfield, *LOCUS Computing Corporation*
Bo-Shoe Chen, *Bell Laboratories*
Douglas E. Comer, *Purdue University*
Dean Daniels, *Carnegie-Mellon University*
Danny Dolev, *Hebrew University, Israel*
Daniel Duchamp, *Carnegie-Mellon University*
Robert English, *University of California at Los Angeles*
Jeffrey L. Eppinger, *Carnegie-Mellon University*
Hector Garcia-Molina, *Princeton University*
Cecil T. Hua, *Honeywell*
Jack Kent, *Xerox PARC*
Kane H. Kim, *University of California at Irvine*
Charles Kline, *LOCUS Computing Corporation*
Walter H. Kohler, *University of Massachusetts*
Leslie Lamport, *DEC Research Center (WRL)*
Leszek Lilien, *University of Illinois at Chicago*
Barbara Liskov, *Massachusetts Institute of Technology*
Toshimi Minoura, *Oregon State University*
J. Eliot B. Moss, *University of Massachusetts*
Susan S. Owicki, *Stanford University*
Thomas Page, *University of California at Los Angeles*
F. Panzieri, *The University of Pisa, Italy*
Randy Pausch, *Carnegie-Mellon University*
Marshall Pease, *SRI International*
Larry L. Peterson, *University of Arizona*
Gerald Popek, *University of California at Los Angeles*
Krithi Ramamritham, *University of Massachusetts*
Joylyn N. Reed, *Oxford University*
P. Rolin, *INRIA, France*
Zuwang Ruan, *Purdue University*
Robert Scheifler, *Massachusetts Institute of Technology*
Fred B. Schneider, *Cornell University*
Robert Shostak, *ANSA Software*
Santosh K. Shrivastava, *The University of Newcastle upon Tyne, UK*

Dale Skeen, *TEKNEKRON, Inc.*
Alfred Z. Spector, *Carnegie-Mellon University*
John A. Stankovic, *University of Massachusetts*
Michael Stonebraker, *University of California at Berkeley*
Greg Thiel, *LOCUS Computing Corporation*
Bruce Walker, *LOCUS Computing Corporation*
Gio Wiederhold, *Stanford University*
Raymond T. Yeh, *SYSCORP International*

Foreword

Computer users have been building distributed systems for years now, though each one has been built as a special case. Until recently, there have been few principles available to help in the design of such systems. Largely, they have been built by trial and error—mostly error.

Based on many experimental and production distributed systems, several approaches have been discarded, while a few have survived. For some issues, elegant and powerful abstractions have emerged—notably, the concepts of transaction, recovery, locking, atomicity, fail-stop, Byzantine agreement, distributed naming, distributed execution, and remote procedure calls.

This book collects the best current work on these topics, presented by active workers in the field. Taken as a whole, it presents an exciting and dynamic experimental discipline. Using the ideas presented here, one can understand and solve many of the problems encountered in the construction of distributed computer systems.

Jim Gray
Cupertino, California

Preface

Distributed systems are essential for many real-world applications, ranging from space stations to automatic teller machines. Several design principles necessary to build high performance and reliable distributed systems have evolved from conceptual research and experimentation during the eighties. This book is a compendium of these principles. It contains definitions and introductory material for the beginner, theoretical foundations and results, experiences with implementations of both real and prototype systems, and surveys of many important protocols. This book focuses on the important aspects of transaction processing, including: concurrency, commitment, and recovery as they apply to database systems, operating systems, or programming systems. The manuscript for this book has been used in a graduate course on distributed database systems at Purdue University. The book can be used in a graduate course on distributed systems and can serve as a good reference material for research. The material has been presented to demonstrate the practicality of certain successful designs and implementation choices, so as to benefit the systems programmers and those who have the responsibility for making distributed systems work.

Bharat Bhargava

Introduction

A distributed system consists of a set of computers located in different sites connected by means of a communications network. There are different programs running on each of these computers and the programs are accessing local or remote resources such as databases. The programs can be viewed as transactions which consist of atomic actions. The resources may be partially replicated or partitioned.

The major objective of a distributed system is to provide low cost availability of the resources of the system by localizing access and providing insulation against failures of individual components. Since many users can be concurrently accessing the system, it is essential that a distributed system also provide a high degree of concurrency.

In the last decade much research has been conducted to develop algorithms that provide:

- A high degree of concurrency and consistency
- Transparency to failures of individual sites and communication systems
- Treatment of Byzantine failures
- Management of replicated copy
- Commitment and termination of transactions ensuring atomicity

Many of these algorithms have been implemented in experimental prototype systems such as Argus,[1] Distributed INGRES,[2] EDEN,[3] LOCUS,[4] RAID,[5] SDD-1,[6] SYSTEM R*,[7] TABS,[8] etc. In addition, several important concepts such as transaction,[9] nested transaction,[10] and naming,[11] have been studied in depth to support the development of distributed systems.

This book is a compilation of a subset of the research contribution in the area of concurrency control and reliability in distributed systems. An attempt has been made to cover all interesting areas, including the theoretical and experimental efforts. Thirty-nine computer scientists contributed their research papers for the nineteen chapters that constitute this book.

SUMMARY OF CHAPTERS

The first chapter contains a review of various reliability issues in distributed database systems. It contains definitions of most terms used in this area of research, and identifies the various problems that arise in the operations of a distributed database system.

First of all, the integrity of the database must be maintained. A transaction may be incorrect and may violate this integrity. Concurrent transactions may not be serializable or may produce different updates on different sites. The messages from one site may not reach the other sites in the order they were sent or may arrive too late. In addition, due to a hardware/software malfunction or failure, a site may crash or a set of sites may not be able to communicate with other sites. A failure may cause the loss of certain actions of a transaction, or destroy the contents of the memory and other storage media. Each of these problems can be handled by a subsystem. Six subsystems have been identified: external data integrity control, program (transaction) correctness control, atomicity control, concurrency control, site crash/partition treatment, and internal data integrity control. A survey of algorithms for each subsystem is given and approximately one hundred and seventy-five references are given for further studies.

The second chapter contains the specifications and analysis of concurrency control algorithms for distributed database systems. An event order based model has been used to represent casual relations among actions of a concurrency controller. The model is used as a tool to study the correctness, degree of concurrency, freedom from deadlocks, and robustness properties of a concurrency control algorithm.

The third chapter presents the fundamental concepts used in the design of the experimental system, Argus, that is being developed at MIT. The system provides support for constructing and maintaining distributed programs. A module called **Guardian** is introduced for dealing with concurrency and site failures.

The fourth chapter presents the architecture of the experimental distributed operating system LOCUS implemented at UCLA. LOCUS is UNIX compatible and connects 17 VAX/750's via Ethernet. It provides a distributed file system, distributed (remote) process execution, support for nested transactions and distributed database systems, and high reliability features to deal with recovery of files and network partitioning. The system supports a certain level of heterogeneity.[12]

The fifth chapter describes an experimental distributed database system called SIRIUS-Delta that has been implemented in INRIA, France. The use of principles such as two phase locking, two phase commit, and maintenance of journals to deal with failures are included.

The sixth chapter presents an experimental facility being developed at Carnegie-Mellon University, TABS, that provides operating system-level support for distributed transactions that operate on shared abstract types. The objects in this system are instances of abstract data types and are encapsulated in processes called *data servers*. Data servers also support the synchronization requirements of transactions by using type-specific locking. The system provides extensive support for atomic objects via write-ahead logging.

There are two basic types of communication primitives: message passing and remote procedure call (RPC). While LOCUS and TABS use primitives such as send and receive, Argus uses the remote procedure call (RPC) as the basic means of interprocess communications. Chapter 7 discusses the remote procedure call (RPC) and the functionality of the underlying interprocess communication facility. It discusses the call semantics and exceptions handling, orphans handling, and robust atomic action. Performance results of initial tests for data transfer rates as seen by the user for local and remote operations are compared.

Chapter 8 discusses practical mechanizations based on the monitor approach to interprocess communications. The coordination of the detection and recovery activities of cooperating processes is discussed. This work contributes towards the design of fault-tolerant concurrent programming.

A formal model for commit protocols for a distributed database systems is given in Chapter 9. The commit protocol is specified as a collection of nondeterministic finite state automata—one for each site. A local state transition consists of reading one or more messages, performing some local processing, and sending zero or more messages. Independent site recovery and network partitions are modelled and conditions are specified for correct recovery and termination of transactions. It is concluded that there exists no protocol using independent recovery that is resilient to arbitrary failures by two sites and there exists no protocol resilient to multiple partitions.

It is essential that concurrency control and reliability mechanisms support each other. Chapter 10 discusses an optimistic approach to concurrency control and demonstrates how it lends itself naturally towards the design of a reliable distributed database system. Optimistic concurrency control is based on the validation of conflicting transactions just before commit rather than the locking of database objects. The optimistic approach has been found to provide good performance when there is a mix of large and small transactions.[13] The optimistic approach is also good for network partition treatment protocols.

In a distributed system, sites may be up, down, or recovering. The basic idea for correct recovery is that a user transaction must have a consistent view of the status (up or down) of the sites at the time of reading and writing any physical copy. This problem becomes very interesting when the databases are replicated over several sites. Chapter 11 deals with the problem of replicated copy control and transaction processing when failed sites are recovering. A global view of the status is represented by a nominal session vector which contains the session number (incarnation number) of each operational site. The identification of out-of-date data items for the recovering site is done by using fail-locks on the operational sites.

The Byzantine Generals problem has drawn much attention from many researchers since it deals with not only clean failures of components of a distributed system but also malfunctions that give conflicting information to different parts of the system. The fundamental problem is the agreement on a piece of data based on the cooperation among several processes. Chapter 12 presents algorithms to ensure that all correctly functioning processors reach an agreement. It is shown that, with unforgeable written messages, the algorithms are possible for any number of processors and possible malfunctioning components. Applications of the solutions to the Byzantine Generals problem to reliable computer systems are discussed.

Many applications do not require a perfect system that must tolerate an arbitrary number of failures within a certain time interval. In the fail-stop processor approach presented in Chapter 13, it is possible to build systems that can tolerate well-defined failures. The operating characteristics of a fail-stop processor, programming fail-stop processors, illustrative examples, and the implementation issues have been presented in this chapter. Convincing arguments for studying the fail-stop processor are given.

Nested transactions can model user's programs in a much more natural way. A typical transaction for travel plans may involve three subtransactions: get a seat on a plane, reserve a rental car, and book a room in a hotel. Similarly, an update on an object with several copies may be issued as a nested transaction with three subactions corresponding to each update. Chapter 14 presents the model of a nested transaction and gives a nested transaction management algorithm for distributed systems. Convincing arguments are given to justify the concept of nested transactions for reliable distributed software. Algorithms for deadlock detection, avoidance, and resolution are given.

Chapter 15 presents the true-copy token scheme for concurrency and reliability control in a distributed database system. True-copy tokens are used to designate the most up-to-date physical copies. This chapter presents the regeneration of lost tokens (or true copies). This research contributed towards the management of replicated copies in the presence of site failures and network partitions.

Chapter 16 deals with the issue of performance evaluation of the reliability of a distributed system. A collection of models and measures have been proposed and then used to obtain sample results on commit protocols, numbers of blocked sites, numbers of backed out transactions, etc.

A distributed system provides users with access to a variety of objects such as files, processing agents, devices, etc. The users identify objects in the same manner, whether they are available locally or remotely. This transparency to location allows software to migrate both before and during its execution. The name resolution mechanism performs the mapping of names (as defined by users) to objects as they exist in the system. Chapter 17 presents a survey of naming mechanisms supported by several experimental distributed systems. It presents a model that describes the underlying principles and concepts of naming and investigates the role of name servers in name resolution. The model views names to be purely syntactic entities and name resolution to be a syntax-directed operation.

Chapter 18 describes a specification and verification technique for concurrent distributed systems. Specification refers to a concise mathematical characterization of the functionality of programs actually implemented with code. The technique is used to study liveness properties of concurrent programs. The technique is illustrated with communicating sequential processes. Illustrative examples that use this technique have been included.

The last chapter contains a survey of current efforts in distributed systems software and in distributed database systems.

In the area of operating systems software, three classes have been identified: network operating systems, distributed operating systems, and distributed processing operating systems. Most experimental systems have been classified in these classes. The choices for structuring distributed systems have been discussed next. Other issues such as addressing distributed processes, communication primitives, decentralized control, and distributed file systems have been discussed.

In the area of distributed database systems, the transaction model, data replication, deadlock resolution, and recovery have been summarized and several test-beds have been identified. Once again, over two hundred references (some of which overlap with those in the first chapter) have been listed.

FUTURE RESEARCH ISSUES

The research in concurrency control for distributed systems appears to be maturing while there is great activity in the area of reliability. The failure treatment in replicated copy management needs further studies. Site failure and network partition treatment protocols that include detection and recovery from failures need to be developed. There has been good research in the area of clock synchronization, but the incorporation of these algorithms into experimental systems is still awaited. One of the primary applications of distributed systems is high performance transaction processing systems. The system level support to process up to one thousand transactions per second will be needed. Hopefully, the research in parallel processing will help. Still, the distributed systems which appear more like distributed file systems need to incorporate more of such notions as a global process and shared memory. Transparency to location needs to be built into the system itself. We are still waiting for commercially available distributed systems.

Fortunately, the research is proceeding at a fast pace. This is evident from specialized symposiums (e.g., the IEEE Computer Society's Symposiums on

Reliability in Distributed Software and Database Systems), workshops, and special issues of journals devoted to concurrency and reliability problems. We look forward to the work of our colleagues in academia, industry, and government.

ACKNOWLEDGMENTS

This book is possible only due to the brilliant research of the contributors of all the chapters. I am indebted to them for providing me with the opportunity to produce this book. Their research ideas will benefit the research of the readers. Graduate students in particular will find this work of great interest.

REFERENCES

1. Liskov, B. and R. Scheifler, On linguistic support for distributed programs, *IEEE Trans Software Eng.*, vol. SE-8, pp. 203–210, May 1982.
2. Stonebraker, M. The design and implementation of distributed INGRES, in *The INGRES Papers*, (M. Stonebraker, ed.), Reading, MA: Addison Wesley, 1985.
3. Jessop, W. H., J. D. Noe, D. M. Jacobson, J. L. Baer, and C. Pu, The Eden transaction-based file system, in *Proc. 2nd IEEE Symp. on Reliability in Distributed Software and Database Systems*, Pittsburgh, PA, July 19–21, 1982.
4. Walker, B., G. Popek, R. English, C. Kline and G. Thiel, The LOCUS distributed operating system, in *Proc. 9th ACM Symp. on Operating Systems Principles*, Bretton Woods, NH, Oct. 10–13, 1983.
5. Bhargava, B. and J. Riedl, The design of an adaptable distributed system, *Proc. IEEE COMPSAC*, Chicago, IL, Oct. 1986.
6. Rothnie, J., P. A. Bernstein, S. Fox, N. Goodman, M. Hammer, T. A. Landers, C. Reeve, D. W. Shipman, and E. Wong, Introduction to a system for distributed databases (SDD-1), *ACM Trans. Database Systems*, pp. 1–17, March 1980.
7. Lindsey, B. G., L. M. Haas, C. Mohan, P. F. Wilms, and R. A. Yost, Computation and communication in R*; A distributed database manager, *ACM Trans. Computer Systems*, pp. 24–38, Feb. 1984.
8. Spector, A., J. Butcher, D. S. Daniels, D. J. Duchamp, J. L. Eppinger, C. E. Fineman, A. Heddaya, and P. M. Schwartz, Support for distributed transactions in the TABS prototype, *IEEE Trans. Software Eng.*, vol. SE-11, June 1985.
9. Gray, J. N., *The transaction concept: Virtues and limitations*, Very Large Database Conference, pp. 144–154, Sept. 1981.
10. Moss, J. E. B., Nested transactions and reliable distributed computing, *Proc. 2nd IEEE Symp. on Reliability in Distributed Software and Database Systems*, pp. 33–39, July 1982.
11. Comer, D. and L. Peterson, *A name resolution model for distributed Systems, Proc. 6th IEEE Int. Conference on Distributed Computing Systems*, Cambridge, MA, May 19–23, 1986.
12. Popek, G. and B. Walker, *The LOCUS Distributed System Architecture*, Cambridge, MA: MIT Press, 1986.
13. Bhargava, B., Performance evaluation of the optimistic concurrency control approach to distributed database systems and its comparison with locking, *Proc. 2nd IEEE Int. Conference on Distributed Computing Systems*, Miami, FL, October 18–22, 1982.

Contents

CONCURRENCY CONTROL AND RELIABILITY IN DISTRIBUTED SYSTEMS

1. A Review of Concurrency and Reliability Issues in Distributed Database Systems

BHARAT BHARGAVA

and

LESZEK LILIEN

ABSTRACT

Database reliability is defined as accuracy, consistency, and timeliness of data. A reliable distributed database management system must maintain database reliability and allow continuous access to the database. A functional structure of a system—called database reliability control—for achieving the above goal is proposed.

Database reliability control is divided into six subsystems: external data integrity control, transaction correctness control, transaction atomicity control, concurrency control, reconfiguration control, and internal data integrity control. Failures endangering database reliability and their impact on different functional subsystems of database reliability control are considered.

Database reliability control at any moment can be in 1) the normal mode, or 2) an adaptation mode, or 3) a degradation mode, or 4) a recovery mode. Research on the operation of the database reliability control system in these modes is surveyed.

This work has been supported in part by the U.S. Department of Transportation grant DTRS 5680-C-00026.

1. INTRODUCTION

1.1. Preliminary Remarks

1.1.1. Statement of the Problem and the Goal of the Chapter

Correct data and continuous access to data are essential elements of reliable data processing and decision making. Access to data is governed by a *database system.*

Database system reliability is the ability of the system to maintain the data values as they were intentionally placed in the database and to allow non-stop access to the data. The importance of database system reliability grows with the size and complexity of databases, and the trend in the development of database systems is towards larger and more complex databases.

The goal of this chapter is a presentation of basic notions, system structures, methods, and algorithms for improving the reliability of distributed database systems.

1.1.2. Outline of the Chapter

The chapter consists of three parts. The first part, this Section, gives definitions of the basic notions used in the discussion. Many of these terms are widely accepted in the field of database systems, but some have been introduced here due to the lack of a proper term, or due to confusing inconsistencies in the usage of the existing terms. The second part of the chapter, contained in Section 2, proposes a functional structure of a system for improving reliability of database systems. The third part, in Sections 3–8, includes a survey of the methods and algorithms that can be used to implement the proposed structure.

1.2. Basic Definitions

1.2.1. Database

All data objects stored more-or-less permanently in a computer constitute a *database*. A database can be divided into two parts: the *memory-resident database*, also called the *volatile database*, and the *storage-resident database*, also called the *stable database*. The latter resides on the secondary and lower levels of storage hierarchy.

In our model, we assume that the volatile database only temporarily holds data that are to be written to the stable database. In other words, the volatile database is a buffer for the stable database.

1.2.2. Database Management System and Database System

User access to database is facilitated by the software system called a *database management system* (*DBMS*). DBMS, together with an operating system (OS)

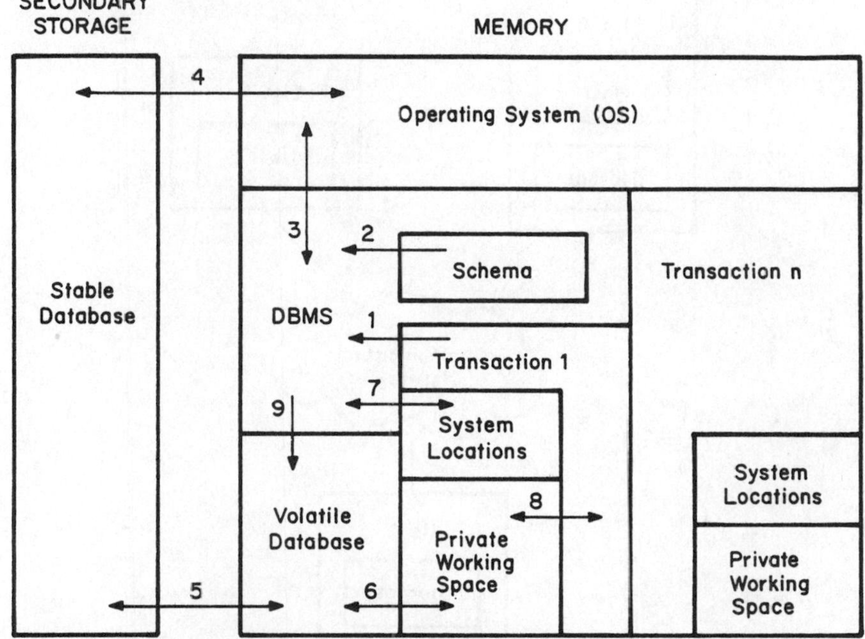

1 — write/read request by the transaction,
2 — DBMS supplements the request with schema information (schema describes structure of the database),
3 — DBMS requests I/O operations from the OS,
4 — the OS interacts with the stable database,
5 — the OS transfers data between the stable and the volatile database,
6 — DBMS transfers data between the volatile database and the private working space,
7 — DBMS provides status information to the transaction,
8 — data in the private working space are manipulated by the transaction,
9 -- DBMS administers the volatile database.

Fig. 1.1. Operation of a database system.[6]

and hardware underlying both DBMS and OS (CPU, memory, disks, etc.), constitutes a *database system.* Operation of a database system is depicted in Fig. 1.1.[6]

1.2.3. Centralized and Distributed Database System

A *centralized database system* can access any data under its control without using external communication links (such as dedicated telephone links). In a *distributed database system* there are several autonomous computers dispersed throughout space and connected by some communication medium. In between centralized and distributed systems lie *centralized control database systems* which

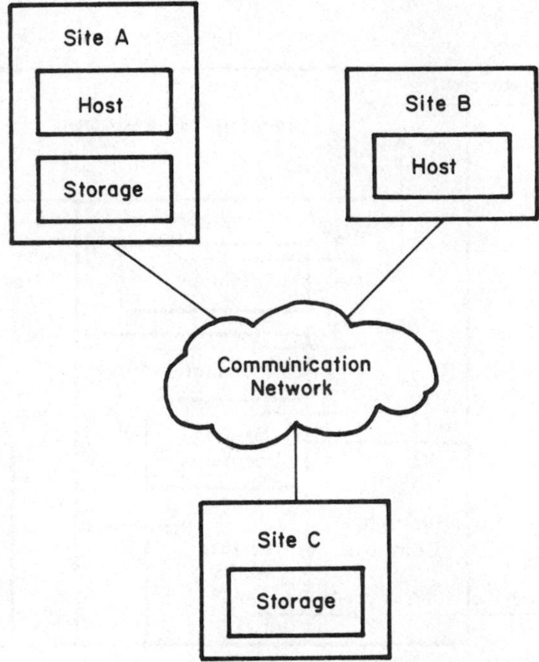

Fig. 1.2. A distributed database system.

consist of several computers dispersed in space and controlled by a single *central computer*.

Each group of hardware elements, residing at a location removed from other groups of hardware elements, together with the associated software, constitutes a *site*. Hence a centralized system has only one site and a distributed system has two or more sites. A site may include *storage*, comprising secondary storage and lower levels of storage hierarchy, and the *host*, comprising the remaining elements of the site, in particular its processors and memory.

As shown in Fig. 1.2, it is possible that a site will include only one of these elements. For example, a site without a host can be controlled by a distant host. In the case that a host controls storage residing at a distant site, we might be using the term ''site'' to refer to both host and its storage.

1.2.4. Entity, Action, and Transaction

A *database state* is a function from names of database objects to values of database objects. Each ⟨name, value⟩ pair is called an *entity*. In a distributed database system an entity (a *logical entity*) can have numerous *physical copies* at different sites. An entity which has multiple copies is called a *replicated entity.* If an entity has a copy at all storage sites, it is called *fully replicated.* A distributed database system with (fully) replicated entities is called a (*fully*) *replicated database system.*

A DBMS provides *read* and *write operations,* which manipulate one or more entities. The execution of an operation is called an *action.*[77] Write actions *update* the database, that is, modify values of entities or insert/delete entities. Read actions or computation actions do not change database contents at all.

Actions are grouped into transactions. A *transaction* (a process or a group of processes) consists of an ordered sequence of actions. A computer program is a static description of a transaction. A transaction submitted by a user is called a *user transaction,* in contrast to a *system transaction.*

Transactions can be divided into *update transactions,* including write operations, and *read-only transactions* (*retrieval transactions*), without any write operation. For a given transaction, the collection of entities read from the database constitutes its *readset* and the collection of entities updated (modified, inserted, deleted) by the transaction constitutes its *writeset.* (The writeset of a retrieval transaction is empty.)

In certain circumstances, it may be necessary to *undo* (*back out, rollback*) a transaction, that is, to ensure that no results of the transaction survive in the database. This goal can be attained by undoing all actions of the transaction. Undoing a transaction before it is completed is called an *abort.* Undoing or abort of a transaction may be necessary due to the decision of a user or due to system reasons (e.g., deadlock resolution).

Transactions can be executed serially or concurrently. During *serial execution,* the next transaction may be started only after the previous one has been completed. This implies that, for any two transactions, the last action of one of the transactions must precede the first action of another. *Concurrent execution* allows for two or more transactions to be under execution at the same moment. In other words, the actions of concurrent transactions can be interleaved.

In a distributed system, different parts of a transaction can be run at different hosts. Each of these parts is called a *subtransaction.*

1.2.5. Correctness and Acceptability

Absolute correctness of a database or of a transaction is an ideal and unobtainable goal, since there are no means of ensuring that the whole database and all transactions are perfect (faultless). As a consequence, only *acceptability,*[137] enforcing some lower, imperfect standard of behavior, is a practical notion.

There are two criteria for expressing the acceptability of a database state. The first, based on the dynamic characteristics of the system, is called transaction-consistency. The second, based mainly on the static properties of the database, is called integrity.

1.2.6. Transaction-Consistency of a Database

Ignoring the issue of transaction correctness, we arrive at the first criterion of database acceptability: transaction-consistency.[58] A *transaction-consistent database state* (also simply called a *consistent database state*) can be defined recursively: an initial database state is transaction-consistent; any state obtained from a transaction-consistent state through its transformation by a serially executed transaction is transaction-consistent.* Alternatively, we can say that, given an initial transaction-consistent database state DBS_0, a database state DBS is transaction-consistent if and only if there exists a serial *history* (a sequence of transaction actions) which transforms DBS_0 into DBS.

1.2.7. Serializability

Transaction-consistency can be trivially achieved by the serial execution of transactions. However, this solution seriously impairs system performance, since any transaction has to wait for completion of the previous one. A criterion that allows for concurrent execution of transactions and at the same time preserves transaction-consistency of the database is called serializability. *Serializability* allows only for such interleaving of actions of different transactions as results in the same effects on the database as a serial execution of the transactions.[166, 173]

EXAMPLE:

Let us assume that three accounts X, Y, Z have the balances 200, 400, and 600 dollars, respectively. Consider the standard example with two transactions which transfer funds from one account to another: T1 transfers 100 dollars from account X to account Y, and T2 transfers 200 dollars from account Y to account Z. Any serial execution of these transactions preserves the value of the sum X + Y + Z (because each transaction run by itself preserves X + Y + Z).

Three different executions of T1 and T2 are shown in Fig. 1.3. The balances of accounts X, Y, Z after both the serial and serializable executions of T1 and T2 are the same: X = 100, Y = 300, Z = 800. In both these executions the sum X + Y + Z is preserved. The nonserializable execution gives the final balances: X = 100, Y = 500, Z = 800. These balances violate the requirement that the value of X + Y + Z be preserved. If this is not clear, trace each of the executions. Remember that change of the value of a local copy of a database entity does not affect the database value. For example, X = X − 100 in T1 changes only the value of the local copy of X (that is, the value of X in the private working space of T1); only WRITE X writes the updated local value to the database.

*This definition explains the notion of a transaction as a unit of consistency.

Time	T1	T2	T1	T2	T1	T2
		READ Y		READ Y	READ X	
		Y=Y−200	READ X		X=X−100	
		WRITE Y		Y=Y−200	WRITE X	
		READ Z	X=X−100			READ Y
		Z=Z+200		WRITE Y		Y=Y−200
		WRITE Z	WRITE X		READ Y	
	READ X			READ Z		WRITE Y
	X=X−100		READ Y		Y=Y+100	
	WRITE X			Z=Z+200	WRITE Y	
	READ Y		Y=Y+100			READ Z
	Y=Y+100			WRITE Z		Z=Z+200
↓	WRITE Y		WRITE Y			WRITE Z
	Serial Execution		Serializable Execution		Nonserializable Execution	

Fig. 1.3. Serial, serializable, and nonserializable executions of two transactions.

Since the order of transaction execution is arbitrary, an execution is serializable if it is equivalent to any serial execution of the same transactions. The serializable execution shown in Fig. 1.3 is equivalent to the serial execution of T2 followed by T1. Another serializable execution could be equivalent to the serial execution of T1 followed by T2. Both are acceptable.

1.2.8. Integrity Assertions and Database Integrity

Database integrity is specified by a set of *integrity assertions,* which are basically predicates on database values that prohibit some incorrect combinations of database values. The term "database integrity," or briefly "integrity," is used in the chapter only in this narrow sense.

There are two types of integrity assertions. The first type is based on *structural constraints,* such as functional dependencies, among attributes in the database. The second type deals with the actual values stored in the database and is referred to as *semantic integrity assertions.* We consider semantic integrity assertions only and refer to them simply as "integrity assertions."

1.2.9. Integral Database State

We call a database state *integral* if all integrity assertions defined for the database evaluate to TRUE for this state. A compromise between the number of integrity assertions and the verification cost makes the verification procedure practically viable. In contrast, verification of transaction-consistency of a given database state is NP-complete.[30, 117] In other words, no practical algorithms for verification of transaction-consistency of a given database state are known and possibly no such algorithms exist.

1.2.10. Rollback

During system operation it may be necessary to "return" to—or restore—a database state S that existed in the past. The actions of the system restoring the state S are referred to as *rollback*. Rollback is only possible if a past database state has been recorded and stored in some form within the system. Three basic alternative implementations of rollback are based on using checkpoints, snapshots, or on utilization of a system log.

A *checkpoint* enables us to restore a past database state, without being a copy of an entire database state: for example, it records only updated database entities. A checkpoint exists and can be used to restore a past database state only in conjunction with the database. Different implementations of checkpoints are discussed in Section 7.3.1. A *snapshot* records *in extenso* the entire database state at a certain moment. Once created, it exists independently of the database (even if the database is lost). One may argue that a snapshot is a special case of a checkpoint. In this chapter, snapshots are regarded as means for the restoration of a past database state only, but snapshots can also have other applications. Different applications and implementations of snapshots are discussed in references 2, 11, 60, and 141.

A *system log* does not record a state of a database system. Instead, it records all of the relevant system actions, that is, the history of the system operation. To restore a past state S, every action following the state S has to be undone (backed out). The order of undoing the actions is the reverse of the order of their execution (last done, first done).

Different kinds of information can be recorded on the log. The following are the basic alternatives:[173]

1. *Request logging:* The update or retrieval requests issued by transactions are recorded on the log. Retrieval requests do not change the state of the system, but show whether updates of another transaction have or have not influenced the readset and hence the execution of the retrieving transaction;
2. *Logging of entity changes:* When an entity is updated, the old entity value is recorded on the log. The old value and the new value of an entity are referred to as *before-image* and *after-image,* respectively; and
3. *Transaction logging:* Every read or write action of a transaction is recorded on the log. This method records the progress of a logged transaction by linking all entities affected by the transaction.

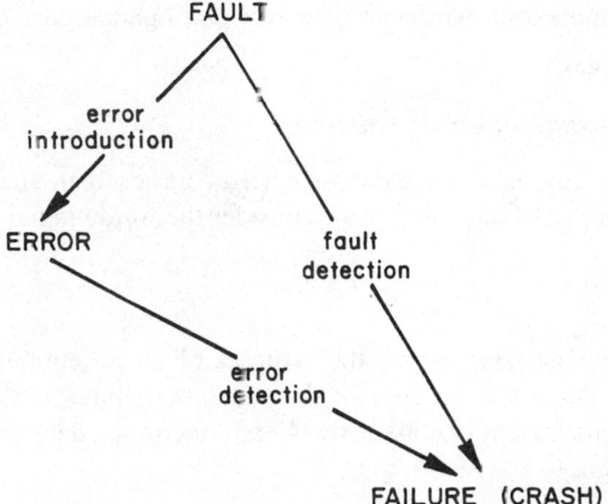

Fig. 1.4. Causal relation among faults, errors, and failures (crashes).

1.2.11. Faults, Errors, and Failures

A *fault* is defined as a malfunction in a hardware, software, or human component of the system (e.g., design faults) that may cause failures or introduce errors into the system. *Errors* are incorrect entities or pieces of program stored or transmitted within the system, or lost entities or pieces of program. Alternatively, an error can be defined as a state of the system which, in the absence of any corrective actions could lead to a failure which would not be attributed to any event subsequent to the error.* A fault causes, directly or through the errors it introduces, a failure (crash). A *failure* (*crash*) is the cessation of a normal (prescribed by the specification), timely operation by all or a part of the system, or delivery to the outside world of incorrect data.[8, 13, 71]

We interpret a detection of a fault or an error at instant *t* as a failure at instant *t:* the moment it is detected, the system must take some special actions and its normal operation is disrupted. Note that some failures will become manifest directly through detection of faults and not through detection of errors introduced by these faults (Fig. 1.4). For example, in the case of a major hardware fault, the fault detection and the failure are simultaneous.

A *fault* (*an error*) is *diagnosable* if its origin can be traced, and *undiagnosable* otherwise. *Faults* can be either *permanent* or *transient.* The former type is represented by program logic faults or many hardware faults. The latter type is represented by faults due to timing conditions that produce rare system states,

*For a classification of errors see, e.g., references 8 and 13.

or due to malfunctioning hardware elements that operate correctly most of the time.

1.2.12. A Classification of Failures

There are many reasons why a database system can reach an unacceptable state. Using the criterion of fault causes, we consider the following classes of failures (see Fig. 1.5):

1. *Data failure:*
   Inconsistent writeset, when the writeset of an acceptable transaction is unacceptable; a special case of this class of failures is the system input failure, when a transaction "transfers" incorrect data from the system environment to its own output,

   Database failure, when faults or errors are detected in the database;
2. *Transaction failure:*
   Internal transaction failure, when, due to faulty transaction code, there is

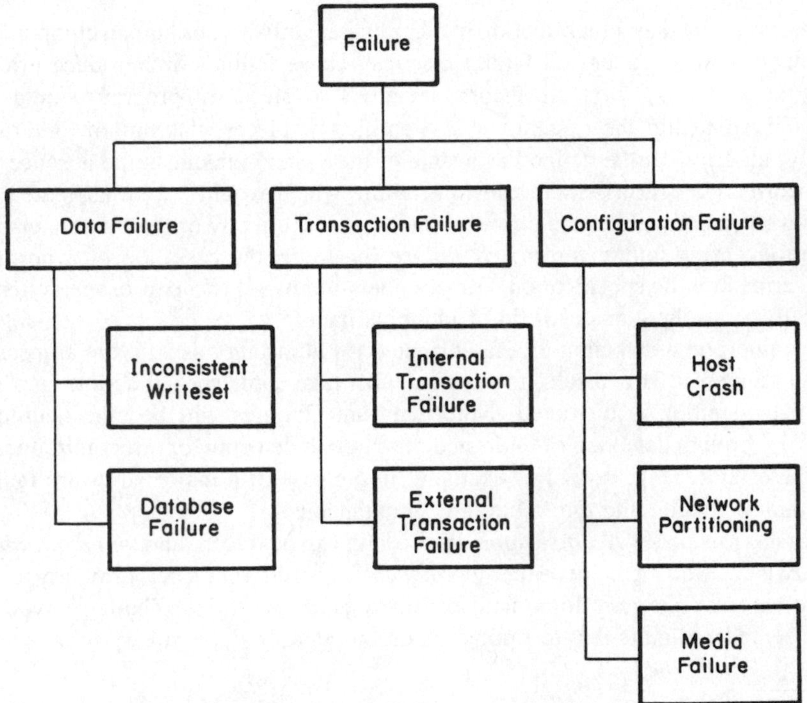

Fig. 1.5. A classification of failures.

a contradiction between the planned and the performed activities of a transaction,

External transaction failure, caused by mishandling of an acceptable transaction by the database management system; for example, a transaction abort due to a deadlock, or a bad classification of transactions into SDD-1[143] classes;*

3. *Configuration failure:*

Host crash (system failure), when the volatile database (database buffers) is lost (e.g., due to power failure, memory failure, processor failure, software fault),

Network partitioning, when communication line failures break all connections between two or more subsets of system sites;** communication line failures that do not cause partitionings are ignored,

Media failure (storage crash), when the stable database or its part is lost due to media (e.g., disk) malfunction.

1.2.13. Modes of Computer System Operation

A computer system operates in one of the following modes (Fig. 1.6):

- The *normal mode,* in which no faults/errors are present in the system;
- *Abnormal modes,* characterized by the presence of faults/errors in the system; three different abnormal modes are discriminated:

A *degradation mode,* in which the number of failed system elements and/or errors increases,

An *adaptation mode* in which the number of failed system elements is constant (equal at least to one) and the number of errors decreases,

A *recovery mode,* in which the number of failed system elements decreases and the number of errors may decrease.

The adaptation mode of operation consists of bypass and restart phases. *Bypass* is the ability of the system to react to a failure by either 1) reduction of its functional capabilities or slowing down its operation, or 2) replacement of

*Suppose that a transaction contains an identification of a class to which it belongs. Based on this identification, the concurrency controller schedules the transaction, avoiding incorrect interleaving of transaction actions. Incorrect identification, that is, external transaction fault, results in scheduling the transaction as if it were from another class.

**The term "*partitioning*"[153] is used to denote a state of the system, and the term "*partition*" is used to denote a maximal subset of sites that can communicate with each other.

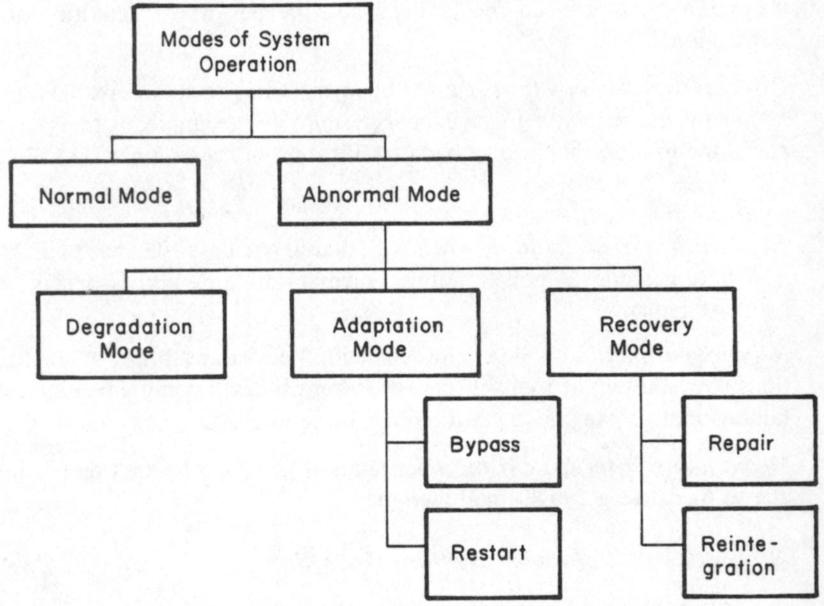

Fig. 1.6. Modes of system operation.

the failed element by a stand-by element. In the former case, some functions of the failed elements are dispensed with. In the latter case, some functions are passed to other elements substituting for the functions of these failed elements.[150] From the moment of bypass of a faulty element until completion of its recovery, the element is eliminated from the system. *Restart* is the resumption of (possibly degraded) operation of the system following a bypass.

The adaptation mode of operation may be caused by multiple failures. Different adaptation modes of operation are identified by specifying a set of failures existing in a given adaptation mode. For example, the adaptation mode with Host A crashed is different from the adaptation mode with transaction T_j incorrect.

The recovery mode contains repair and reintegration phases. *Repair* is the restoration of a damaged system element to a sound condition after its failure. A special case of repair is *replacement,* when the failed element is replaced by an intact element of the same or similar kind.* After repair is completed, the repaired element should be *reintegrated* into the system to regain the original level of system performance.

*Note that replacement by a stand-by constitutes the bypass phase of the adaptation mode, while replacement by an element which is not a stand-by constitutes the repair phase of the recovery mode.

1.2.14. Backward and Forward Bypass

There are two basic alternatives for a bypass in a computer system:[104] a forward bypass and a backward bypass (Fig. 1.7). A *forward bypass* does not try to locate the fault responsible for the failure, but only corrects errors caused by the fault. Forward bypass is fast and can be very effective for certain classes of failures. Assuming that the fault which caused the failure is permanent, a *backward bypass* consists of: 1) rollbacking (backing out) to a state S which—it is hoped—precedes the instant when the fault occurred; 2) location of the fault responsible for the failure to the smallest replacement unit; and 3) elimination of the faulty unit or its replacement by a stand-by unit. Bypass of transient faults omits steps 2 and 3. In this case, restart initiates a *retry* of operations following the state *S*.

1.2.15. Backward and Forward Reintegration and Recovery

For a given crash, a *backward reintegration* restores a past state preceding the instant of the crash. By contrast, a *forward reintegration* leaves the system in

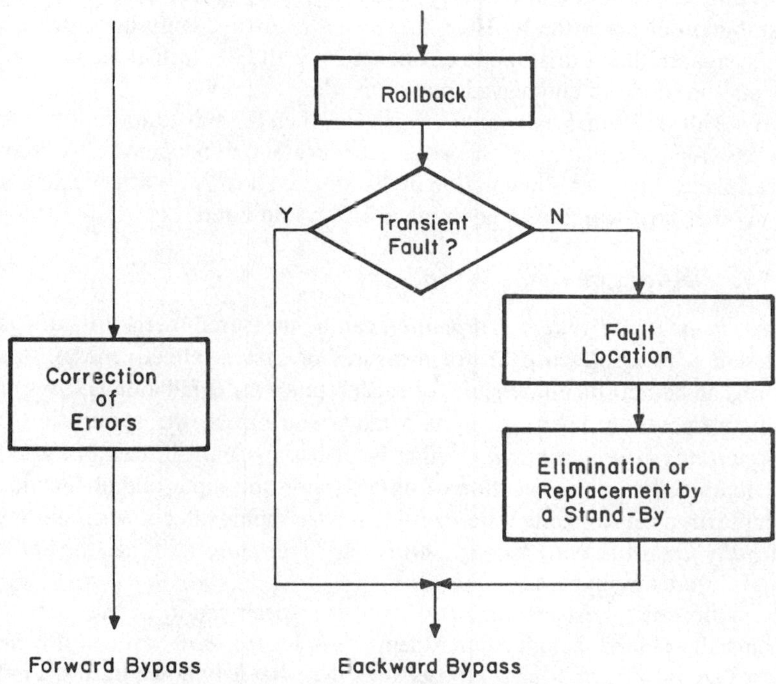

Fig. 1.7. Forward and backward bypass.

a state that did not exist before the crash but could have been achieved if the crash did not occur.

If the reintegration phase of a recovery is a backward (forward) reintegration, then the recovery is called a *backward* (*forward*) *recovery*.

1.2.16. Degradation, Adaptation, and Recovery

The terms "degradation," "adaptation," and "recovery" are not only used in conjunction with the term "mode." A *degradation* is a transition from the normal or an abnormal mode into an abnormal mode with a larger number of failures and/or errors. An *adaptation* is a transition between modes characterized by a constant number of failed system elements and a decreasing number of errors. A *recovery* is a transition which results in a decreased number of failed system elements. Let us explain these terms by an example.

EXAMPLE:

Assuming initially the normal mode of operation of a distributed system with three hosts named A, B, and C, a crash of Host A is a degradation. So is a crash of Host B while Host A is down. Now, resumption of the normal operation by Host B is a recovery, even if Host A is still down. Subsequent resumption of operation by Host A is also a recovery. Only the latter returns the system to the normal mode of operation, while the former leads from one adaptation mode to another adaptation mode.

If we allow a stand-by host in the system, then the substitution of the stand-by host for the failed host A is not a recovery but an adaptation. A recovery takes place only after reintegration of the repaired host A (or after reintegration of another host which was not a stand-by and now replaces A).

1.2.17. Degrees of Degradation

Degree (*intensity*) *of system degradation* can be measured by the loss of system effectiveness (see reference 88 for measures of system effectiveness). A degradation can be transparent, visible, or catastrophic. A degradation is *transparent* to system operation when, for certain faults and errors, the system is (*fully*) *fault-tolerant* (*fail-operational*),[36] that is, it has the built-in capability to preserve continued correct execution of its programs and input/output functions.[12]

Degradation causes some *visible* but non-catastrophic effects when the system is *partially fault-tolerant* (*fail-soft*, *gracefully degrading*):[12] it has the ability to react to failures by bypass.

The notion of *n*-host resiliency[5] is a further specification of the term "fail-soft" in a distributed system environment: a service is *n-host resilient* if it cannot be provided only when at least *n* hosts are simultaneously down during a critical phase of the service. (It may be possible for *n* or more hosts to fail outside of such a critical phase without disrupting the service.)

Finally, degradation is *catastrophic*, when it disrupts system operation completely.

1.3. Limitations of the Scope of the Chapter

The most visible limitations of the scope of this chapter can be summarized as follows. First, the focus is on fault tolerance methods for improving reliability of database systems, and fault avoidance methods are ignored. The goal of the *fault avoidance*[137] (*fault intolerance*)[12] methods is assuring system reliability by *a priori* elimination of faults. For example, careful design, testing, and validation of a computer system before its release represent fault avoidance.[3,92] Since no fault avoidance methods can guarantee absence of faults in a system, the need for *fault tolerance* (*robustness*)[176] methods arises. The goal of this category of methods is assuring system reliability by a proper reaction to errors caused by faults present in the system or its environment.[12,87,137] For example, in aviation and space applications, redundant computers working in parallel are often used and the output of the system is the output of the majority of the computers. The system reacts to a failure of any minority of its computers by simply ignoring their outputs and relying on the remaining consistent outputs of the majority of the computers.

Fault avoidance methods and fault tolerance methods complement each other, and ignoring the former does not mean that their critical importance is denied: it is simply beyond the scope of this chapter.

Second, hardware reliability problems[101,158] are considered only marginally since software is becoming the most critical element of highly reliable systems[169] and hardware reliability is comparatively well understood.

Third, primarily permanent failures are considered. Treatment of the transient failures involves rollback and retry operations.

Fourth, the scope of our considerations does not include *security* problems,[166] such as malicious data errors or transaction faults, as well as less frequent maliciously caused host crashes or communication link failures. However, some of the techniques discussed can be applied to combat these forms of misuse and crime. For example, given that the input data control mechanism has the necessary information, it is quite simple to treat unauthorized user requests as incorrect input and reject them.

2. A FUNCTIONAL STRUCTURE OF A HIGHLY RELIABLE DATABASE SYSTEM

2.1. System Structure

A functional structure of a fault-tolerant database system can be derived by analyzing the dangers that impend over database reliability.

A transaction may introduce data from the environment (human users, sensors, etc.) into the database. If all these input data are indiscriminately written into the database, there is no barrier against incorrect data and the database can easily be contaminated. Hence the need for the *external data integrity control* (*XDIC*) subsystem, which could oppose this threat.

A transaction, using external or database data as its input, produces a result that is written into the database or acts upon the environment. A transaction is sometimes incorrect itself—it does not perform as intended. The system should try to detect faults of this nature and eliminate the faulty transactions. Hence the need for the *transaction correctness control* (*TCC*) subsystem.

A transaction is a unit of consistency[118]—if completely executed, it transforms a consistent database state into another consistent database state. If only a part of the transaction updates is executed and the rest is lost, then a database state left by the incomplete transaction might be inconsistent. To prevent this situation, the *transaction atomicity control* (*TAC*) subsystem is needed. TAC ensures transaction *atomicity*, that is, ensures that either none or all actions of a transaction are executed.

Each transaction consists of a number of actions. To improve the performance of a database system, concurrent execution of transactions is permitted. But not every possible interleaving of actions can be allowed. The need to ensure correct concurrent execution of transactions is realized by the *concurrency control* (*CC*) subsystem.

When we move from centralized to distributed database systems, the problem of synchronization of system-wide decisions appears. Synchronization—based on message switching—is no longer "for free." Message switching introduces considerable delays; execution of a process synchronization primitive on a single host could be on the order 0.1 to 1 milliseconds while network message delay could be on the order of 100 milliseconds.[5]

So far, we have not considered the possibility of host crashes or partitionings, which have a negative impact on database reliability. For example, an inability to access a given site could make data integrity control or transaction correctness control impossible, if the data needed for such a verification are stored only at the inaccessible site. Similarly, destroyed synchronization among hosts could result in completing a subtransaction at one host while rejecting another subtransaction of the same transaction at another host and thus compromising transaction atomicity. Destroyed synchronization also causes incorrect scheduling of concurrent transactions running at different hosts, compromising concurrency control. Maintenance of correct operation of a database system in spite of host crashes and partitionings is primarily the task of the *reconfiguration control* (*RC*) subsystem (cf. the auditor subsystem in reference 101).

Assuming that the above control mechanisms and hardware are perfect, the database system would always maintain consistency and integrity of the database. Since this is only an ideal goal which cannot be reached, we need one more mechanism—the *internal data integrity control* (*IDIC*) subsystem. IDIC tries to mend errors in the database produced or overlooked by other subsystems or caused by hardware faults. An internal data control is used: 1) to check integrity of data from the database before these data are used by a transaction, which is the domain of the *transaction input control* mechanism, 2) to validate integrity of data to be written to the database by a transaction, which is done by the *transaction output control* mechanism, 3) to check periodically, or on demand, integrity of the database or its parts, which is performed by the *database audit* mechanism.

The above discussion suggests the functional structure of the *database reliability control* (*DRC*) system, as shown in Fig. 1.8. The functional elements of the system—called the *reliability subsystems*—are discussed in more detail in the following sections.

At this point, the scope of the domains of the transaction correctness control (TCC) and the internal data integrity control (IDIC) subsystems must be made clear. TCC monitors, first of all, whether an "intention" of a transaction has been fulfilled by the data processing part of the transaction. This intention can be represented by *acceptance checks* or *tests*, which are predicates on local transaction variables and values of database entities. For example, TCC can control if a given transaction has really sorted a set of positive numbers in ascending order. TCC also monitors whether input and/or output data of a transaction do or do not conflict with its "intention." For instance, in a transaction sorting a set of positive numbers, the TCC should reject any negative

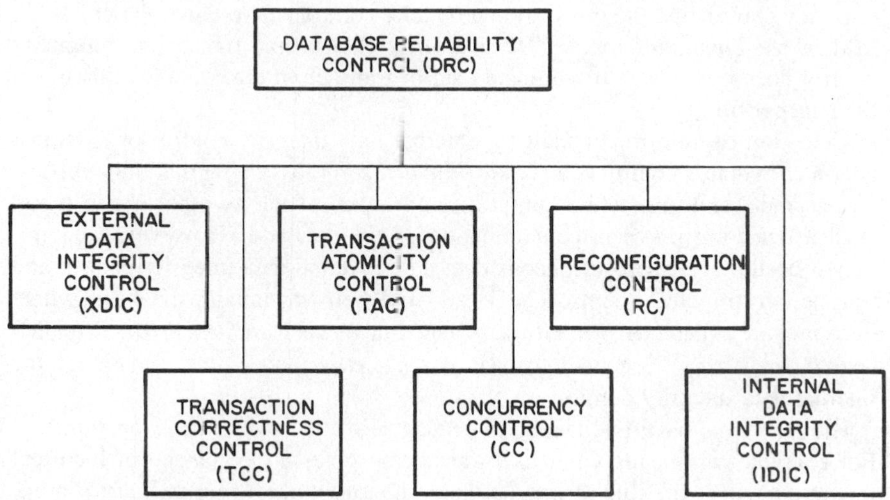

Fig. 1.8. The functional structure of the database reliability control system.

input data. The task of IDIC is control of entity values only, ignoring transaction intentions completely.

Summarizing, one can characterize TCC as a monitor of transaction semantics and IDIC as a monitor of database semantics. The former can be more precise, but operates in the restricted context of a single transaction, while the latter operates in the more general context of the entire database.

2.2. Identification of the Mode of Operation

The reliability system at a given moment, may be unable to determine its mode of operation.[8] For example, an error in the database may remain undetected. Such a situation is allowed. But it is necessary that it does not produce a complete system breakdown as a consequence. In other words, it is imperative that there exist a recovery for each degradation.

2.3. Immediate and Delayed Detection in Database Reliability Control

If ideal external data integrity control, concurrency control, and transaction atomicity control could be implemented, together with a faultless transaction set, there would be no need for the transaction correctness control and the internal data integrity control subsystems. However, only a part of system input errors are detected by external data integrity control before they penetrate the system. Similarly, faults in transactions happen and only some of them are detected by the transaction correctness control subsystem. The remaining, unrecognized faulty transactions can update the database or compromise the concurrency control and the transaction atomicity control subsystems, which results in database *contamination*.[18,54] Concurrency control and transaction atomicity control do not even try to eliminate data or transaction errors, since this is not their responsibility.

Detection of an error or fault by external data integrity control or by transaction correctness control is an *immediate detection*; assuming that only verified system input and transaction output data are made visible to other transactions, such a detection prevents contamination of the database. However, contamination occurs in reality—erroneous data pass external data integrity control and transaction correctness control checks and find their way into the database, where they remain undetected for a time. Detection of such *hidden errors*[26] (called also *latent errors*[151]) constitutes *delayed detection* and is the domain of the internal data integrity control.

Hidden errors have a tendency to propagate, causing *data deterioration*.[1,146] For example, erroneous input to a transaction gives an avalanche of incorrect output data. It is the role of internal data integrity control to reduce error propagation to manageable proportions by error confinement[51] and detect errors before data deterioration exceeds the critical point of no return.

2.4. Chapter Structure Revisited

We have defined four modes of system operation: 1) the normal mode, 2) an adaptation mode, 3) a degradation mode, and 4) a recovery mode. In this and the following sections, the operation of each reliability subsystem in the normal mode, an adaptation mode, and a recovery mode are discussed in turn. For the adaptation and recovery modes, we consider the reaction of the reliability subsystem under discussion to each of the considered failures (see Fig. 1.5), assuming that: 1) a given class of failures is relevant, and 2) either the subject has been discussed in the literature (to the best of our knowledge), or, we propose a new approach or classification scheme. There is no discussion of a degradation mode, since it is viewed as an unintended and rapid transition from the normal, an adaptation, or a recovery mode into an adaptation mode. Since the transition is instantaneous, no system actions can be performed within its duration.

As we have mentioned, it is not always possible to discriminate clearly among different modes of operation for a given reliability subsystem. However, focusing on one mode of operation at a time can be an abstraction useful for perceiving more distinctly the functions of the reliability subsystems. The discussion revolves around the functional structure of the database reliability control (DRC).

The review of the functions of external data integrity control, transaction correctness control, transaction atomicity control, concurrency control, reconfiguration control, and internal data integrity control is presented in Sections 3 through 8.

3. EXTERNAL DATA INTEGRITY CONTROL (XDIC)

Input errors are a special case of inconsistent writeset errors, since system data input is just a transmission of data from environment to transaction writeset. But protection against system input errors is a distinctly different issue, since the system input steps over the barrier between the system and its environment. In such a case, it is no longer adequate to consider only the system factors; the environmental ones should also be investigated. In particular, those factors that define kinds and frequency of the probable input errors require special attention. Prevention of certain erroneous inputs in the environment may be more efficient than their detection by input checking.

These "environmental" considerations are beyond the scope of this chapter. As an illustration of the range of issues involved, the book by Gilb and Weinberg,[73] dealing extensively with the alphanumeric input, can be studied.

Some of the techniques discussed for inconsistent writeset errors might be useful for input checking, but only to the extent that the "environmental" factors do not render these techniques inappropriate. With this reservation, the system input problems and the XDIC subsystem are not discussed any further.

4. TRANSACTION CORRECTNESS CONTROL (TCC)

4.1. Transaction Correctness Control in the Normal Mode

An analysis of causes of program errors is given in, e.g., reference 55.

4.1.1. Monitoring Against Internal Transaction Failures

Transaction Intent Checks. The basic function of TCC is to ensure the consistency of intentions of a transaction with the actions the transaction actually performs. The intention of a transaction is expressed within the program of the transaction by *checks*, also called *tests*.[137] Checks are predicates on the old/new values of the local program variables and database entities.

Completeness, Independence, and Consistency of Checks. An important issue is *completeness* of checks—whether checks cover all aspects of transaction specifications. The problem of deriving specifications is beyond the scope of our considerations (for more detail see the study by Bhargava and Hua.)[28] A methodology for the specification of checks against erroneous transaction input is proposed in reference 18.

Another issue is the *independence* of checks from the transaction they monitor. A rule for general detection systems says that, ideally, the checks should be based only on the specification of the function that the transaction is supposed to perform, and be independent of the transaction itself. Otherwise, there is a possibility of a single fault affecting both the transaction and the check, and so preventing transaction error detection.[137]

Additionally, *consistency* of checks with transaction semantics should be assured. Due to the limited scope of a transaction, this task seems much easier than the analogous task of ensuring consistency of checks with database contents.[57] Sometimes, the less stringent requirement of *mutual consistency of checks* replaces this requirement.

Since completeness of checks and independence of checks cannot be absolute,[137] the checks which can be designed are the ones that attempt to enforce *acceptability*. Acceptability checks provide a reasonably high degree of confidence that a transaction fault will be detected.

Classes of Checks. Different classes of checks can be distinguished. For the criterion of *check placement* we discriminate between (a) *internal checks*, that are embedded in a transaction, and (b) *external checks*, that monitor and correlate transaction input and output. An example of the latter class is the majority voting scheme, where outputs of different transactions supposed to be identical functionally are checked for consistency.

For the criterion of the *check activation moment* we discriminate between a) *immediate checks*, that are performed as soon as the data structure to be tested is produced, and b) *delayed checks*, which are periodic checks separated by periods when no checking is performed.

Many other types of checks are distinguished without a common classification frame. *Checks by replication*[137] might involve execution of two or more independent and supposedly functionally equivalent transactions, followed by testing of consistency of their outputs. *Reversal checks*[137] involve processing the results of a transaction or its part in order to determine corresponding inputs and check them against actual inputs. *Watchdog timers*[85,87,109] implement the timeout scheme to monitor whether a specific event occurs within a defined interval. *Validity of use checks*[137] verify whether an attempted use of a component is allowed. Examples of checks of this class are *data tests*—checking whether a process is intended to process certain data, *call tests*—checking whether a procedure (subroutine) is intended to be called in a given way, and *output tests*—checking the input-output data correlation and checking whether a process is intended to produce given output.[87] The validity of use checks are also the basis of the *capability mechanism*.[51]

Costs of Check Enforcement. The problem of efficient implementation of checks while preserving their effectiveness is of primary concern. To achieve one goal without the other is easy, but reaching a compromise between the two is challenging.

A simple measure for the estimation of the verification costs could ignore all but the costs of searching data files.[61] Another measure of check verification cost is the number of stable database accesses, that is, accesses to the secondary storage.

Checks can be evaluated at different costs at compile, run, and post-execution times. The selection of one of these methods as minimizing the number of database accesses relies on implementation-dependent assumptions.[14,27] *Compile time validation* means that a transaction is allowed to execute only after its checks are evaluated and all found satisfied. The values, which the database would have had if the transaction had been executed, are derived by a simulation of the transaction. Simulation of a transaction is any procedure which answers the question "Is the transaction acceptable?" with less read accesses than necessary for the actual execution of the transaction. Any method decreasing the number of read accesses increases the efficiency of the compile time validation.[35,84] The validation procedure tests the values derived by the simulation.

Run time validation means that the check validation is concurrent with transaction execution, but the actual update (writing into the database) is not performed until the transaction validation is completed without a violation of the checks.

Post-execution validation requires that a transaction is first executed and then its results are validated. The results of the validation decide whether corrective actions are necessary.

''*Mixed*'' *evaluation* methods perform parts of check enforcement at compile time, run time, or after execution. For example, run time and post-execution methods[14] or compile time and run time validation[123] can be combined.

Another method for minimizing check enforcement costs maintains automatically *redundant aggregate information* (such as average, minimum, and maximum values) on certain data sets in the database.[22] For a class of checks using aggregates, checks are tested using these redundant data rather than all individual values in the data set. This gives important speed up of the verification of these checks.*

EXAMPLE:
Let us suppose that a database redundantly stores the value v of the length of the shortest route between two cities, A and B. The check which verifies that no route between the cities is shorter than their physical distance d has only to check whether v is not smaller than d. In the case when no minimal value v is stored redundantly, the verification of the same check would require testing lengths of all routes between A and B.

4.1.2. Monitoring Against External Transaction Failures

The category of external transaction faults includes transaction faults that produce failures indirectly. One example is ''cheating'' concurrency control—for instance, when a transaction has bad SDD-1 class specification. Another example is ''cheating'' transaction atomicity control, for instance, when the ''TRANSACTION_END'' declaration, to be used for a proper transaction termination, is misplaced.

Checks used for monitoring against external faults have to be derived not only from transaction specifications but also from requirements for other subsystems. For example, to guard against incorrect declaration of SDD-1 transaction classes,[143] one needs to know the specification of these classes.

4.2. Transaction Correctness Control in an Adaptation Mode

4.2.1. Adaptation of TCC to Data Errors

Blocking of Transactions by Inaccessibility of Data. Transactions may be blocked by the inaccessibility of data due to data failures, host crashes, or partitionings. Blocking of transactions due to data failures is more probable in

*A generalization of this method is proposed in reference 102.

nonreplicated database systems,* that is, database systems where every entity has a single copy. No transaction in need of inaccessible data can succeed. Clearly, adaptation can be achieved more easily in replicated databases,[38] that is, databases with multiple copies of entities.

TCC blocked by data inaccessibility must decide how to treat the transaction: wait for data recovery, bypass the block, or abort the transaction.

Wait-or-Abort Strategy for Transactions Blocked by Failures. Let us consider two of the above three strategies.[170] First, a transaction can wait until recovery from the failure blocking the data, and none of the resources it controls are released before this recovery—this is a *waiting strategy*. Second, an affected transaction can be aborted, and its resources released—this is an *aborting strategy* (originally called a restructuring strategy).

Obviously, if recovery is fast, the waiting strategy is cheaper than the aborting strategy. If recovery takes a longer time, resource blocking by the affected transaction may become more expensive than aborting the transaction, since the blocking of resources reduces system throughput. There exists an algorithm for deciding which of the two strategies to follow—either for *all* transactions the waiting strategy is applied or for *all* transactions the aborting strategy is applied.[171]

4.2.2. Adaptation of TCC to Transaction Failures

TCC is able to bypass failures only in transactions that are still not committed. A committed transaction can be undone (compensated) by internal data integrity control (see Section 8.3.1). Bypass can be as simple as an abort, but sometimes a more ambitious bypass goal is desirable.

Paradigm for the Bypass of Transaction Failures. Process failures can be classified into a) expected, b) unexpected but manageable, and c) unexpected and unmanageable failures.[76] A failure is expected if special provisions for bypass of failures of its type exist. An unexpected failure can be handled if there exists a general adaptation mechanism that can handle failures of this type without being tailored specifically for adaptation to failures of this type.

If a transaction failure is expected, or if the failure is unexpected but can be handled, then forward or backward bypass, respectively, is made. If a transaction failure is unexpected and cannot be handled, then the transaction is aborted (see Fig. 1.9). Incidentally, an abort is a special case of a backward bypass.

*We use the term "nonreplicated" instead of "partitioned" to avoid the use of the latter for two meanings: 1) to denote a nonreplicated database system, and 2) to denote a partitioned database system—where partitions cannot communicate with each other.

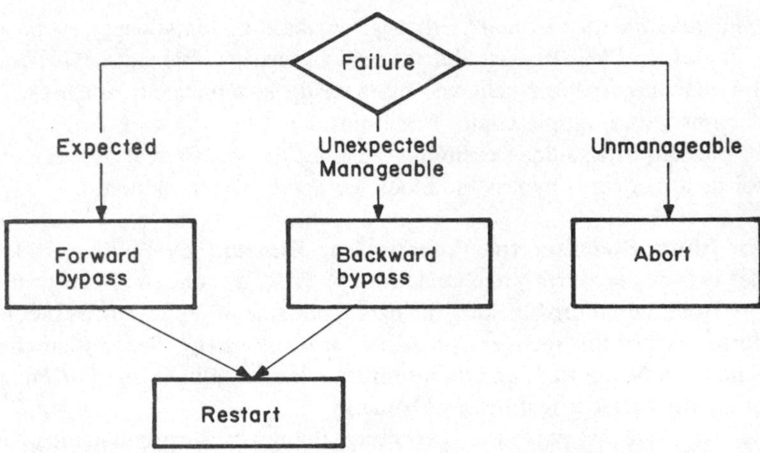

Fig. 1.9. Paradigm for the bypass of transaction failures.

Forward Bypass of Transaction Failures. Bypass in the case of expected transaction failures takes on a form of *exception handling*.[45,46,137,177] A transaction can contain statements which cause particular exceptions—such as arithmetic overflow, end of tape, array bound check—to ''hold,'' and statements indicating what is to be done when each of these exceptions occurs. Exceptions can be organized into hierarchies,[76] so that if a lower level of the hierarchy fails to handle a failure, it is passed on to a higher level of the hierarchy.

Backward Bypass of Transaction Failures. A method based on the principle of retry can be used to bypass transient faults. Within a transaction, a number of *save points*[79] (called also *backup points*[48]) is specified. A save point stores information necessary for a transaction restart from this point. In case of a transaction failure, a restart from its last save point is performed.

A more general adaptation method for unexpected transaction failures relies on implementing transactions as recovery blocks,* which comprise not only backward bypass, but also restart actions. Each *recovery block*[136] (Fig. 1.10) comprises a predicate, called an *acceptance test*, and a collection of alternative procedures, called *alternates*. The procedures are basically functionally identical but independently implemented; for instance, they can use different algorithms or merely be written by different programmers. However, in some cases the primary procedure could realize a given function exactly, while each alternate could produce only approximate, but still acceptable, results.**

*The name should rather be ''adaptation block,'' since no repair of the faulty transaction is performed.

**Recovery blocks can also be used for hardware fault-tolerance.[112]

ENSURE <acceptance test>
BY <primary procedure>
ELSE-BY <first alternate>
...
ELSE-BY <n-th alternate>
ELSE <failure> ;

Fig. 1.10. Structure of a recovery block.

On an entry to a recovery block, the primary alternate is tried. If it succeeds, that is, passes the acceptance test, a normal block exit follows. If it fails, all variables are restored to their values as of entry to the recovery block, then the second alternate is tried, and so on. In general, an acceptance test has a limited ability to detect errors, so it is possible that erroneous results will pass the test.

Recovery blocks can include a watchdog timer that monitors availability of an output within a specified interval; now acceptance test includes a timing condition required for real-time applications.[87] A further modification of the recovery block for real-time systems led to the construction of the *deadline mechanism*,[172] which contains a high-quality primary procedure and an approximate alternate producing acceptable result in a known, fixed, length of time. The deadline mechanism ensures that, if not the primary, then the alternate will complete before the specified deadline (in the latter case, even if some time has been lost in trying the primary first).

If a transaction implemented as a recovery block uses values updated by uncommitted transactions, an adaptation mechanism for interacting recovery blocks ("conversation") has to be used.[99,136,151]

Implementation of the recovery block scheme involves the problems of a) defining suitable acceptance tests,[43] b) maximization of the reliability/cost ratio by manipulation of the number of alternates* and the granularity (size) of the recovery blocks,[25,28] and c) efficient restoration of the state as of entry to the recovery block, which is necessary for trying the next alternate.[6]

Recovery block is a mechanism internal to a transaction. Other adaptation techniques for unexpected failures could involve mechanisms external to transactions. An example is the *majority voting* scheme (*N-version programming*),[13] selecting a consistent output produced by a majority of concurrently run transactions, while ignoring an inconsistent minority.

---

*It has been argued[72] that producing two alternates should cost only about 10 percent more than producing a single procedure version.

Bypass of* A Priori *Suspected Transactions. A transaction can be suspected as faulty from a past history of its executions. A recently modified or added transaction is more likely to be faulty than an "old" one.[168, 169] If the suspicion is sufficiently strong, the transaction should be eliminated from the system. If the system cannot remain operational without the transaction, recovery of the transaction is necessary before the system can resume its operation (see Section 4.3.1).

Otherwise, the ability to eliminate some noncritical transactions lends a degree of fault tolerance to a system with a) "simple" transactions, not implemented as recovery blocks, or b) failed recovery blocks, that is, recovery blocks in which all of the alternates failed.[87]

4.3. Transaction Correctness Control in a Recovery Mode

4.3.1. Recovery of TCC from Transaction Faults

If transaction repair cannot be done automatically, human intervention is required. An empirical study[168] finds some support for the claim that the extent of the repair maintenance increases as a program is modified more frequently. Only weak support exists for the claims that 1) more complex programs experience more repair maintenance, and 2) structured programs will experience less repair maintenance than modular programs and the latter experience less repair maintenance than unstructured programs. There is *no* support for the hypotheses that 1) higher quality programmers will produce programs requiring less repair maintenance, and 2) as the program gets older, less maintenance is required. The anomalous results might reflect the need to develop better operational measures of program complexity, programming style, and programmer quality. In another study,[80] for the program sample studied, size (the number of lines of code) was found to be the best predictor of the number of errors remaining in a program after its release.

5. TRANSACTION ATOMICITY CONTROL (TAC)

5.1. Transaction Atomicity Control in the Normal Mode

5.1.1. The Goals of TAC

The need for TAC was first perceived in the context of a system with host crashes. In a pioneer paper,[109] transaction atomicity is defined as the guarantee that, after recovery from a host crash, for each transaction either all or none of its updates are executed.

Even with the assumption that a system is failure-free, TAC is needed. First,

TAC must exist in distributed database systems where a transaction might be aborted, even if it is correct, for a reason such as deadlock resolution. In this case, some coordination among all subtransactions is necessary to prevent inconsistencies. For example, the situation where Host A aborts one subtransaction of a transaction T while Host B commits the updates of another subtransaction of T is inadmissible. To ensure atomicity of a transaction, all of its subtransactions should be terminated uniformly—either all aborted or all committed.[76,118,143] Second, the need to preserve the *autonomy* of each host[119] requires that each host be free to abort its subtransactions. Third, if more than one software system that manages its own recoverable resources (e.g., the DB2 database management system and the CICS/OS/VS system) is involved in processing an application, it is necessary to coordinate the recovery activities of these systems.[47]

5.1.2. Prelude and Commitment

Each transaction consists of a number of actions, some of which can be canceled without difficulty. The first action of a transaction which cannot be easily canceled is called a *commit action.* All actions of a transaction preceding its commit action constitute a *prelude*, and the remaining ones—a *commitment*. A transaction can be easily stopped and aborted at any time during its prelude, but not during or after its commitment.[77]*

5.1.3. Undoability and Logging

Actions that can be easily canceled are called *undoable*.[77] Once the consequences of an action have filtered to the environment, the action might be difficult or impossible to undo.[137] For example, a cancellation of an erroneous payment may require legal actions.

For implementing undoability of transactions, a *log* (also called a *journal*[141] or *audit trail*[41]) of important system events is kept. Specifically, all system updates are recorded on the *UNDO log*[77]—for example as a pair: old value/new value for each updated entity. Now, an uncommitted transaction can be undone by setting entities to their old values.

There are two types of logging.[118] *Logical logging* requires that the log records logical database operations performed. For example, a logical log record for a record insertion would simply describe the file, record type, and field values of the new record. Insertion of the record into the access paths (such as indices)

*The term "commitment" is used with two different meanings: (1) as the commitment phase, (2) as the act of committing.

defined for the record type is implied by the logical log record. On the other hand, *physical logging* records addresses and changes of all pages modified by database operations. For example, this may include index or hash table pages modified to support accesses to a new record. Summarizing, physical logging tends to require that more information be recorded on the log, and logical logging leads to more complex undo procedures.

5.1.4. Commit Deferment

Commitment is an impediment to transaction abort. A solution widely used for reducing the necessity of undoing committed transactions is containment of transaction commitment[48] that is, *deferring the commit action* of a transaction,[76] which extends the prelude phase and shrinks the commitment phase of the transaction.

One popular implementation uses a private working space for each updating transaction. All updated data are kept in this space during transaction execution. At the end of the transaction all updates kept in the working space are either made visible in the database (commitment) or backed out (abort). Backing out is done simply by erasing the working space.[24, 132]

5.1.5. Commit Protocols

Protocols used by TAC for synchronous commitment are called *commit protocols*. If only the uniformity of termination and not host autonomy is required, a simple protocol is sufficient. One of the subtransactions of a transaction, the central subtransaction, is given the decision power. This subtransaction decides for itself and for all the remaining subtransactions how to terminate the whole transaction. Only one round of messages is necessary in this case: the central subtransaction sends the decision to all of its companions and collects all of the acknowledgements. We call such a protocol—by analogy to the protocol introduced below—a *one-phase commit* (*1PC*) protocol.

The 1PC protocol deprives all of the cooperating hosts—except the one running the central subtransaction—of their autonomy. No schemes which both guarantee complete autonomy and maintain transaction atomicity are known. But there are protocols which allow participating hosts to abandon a transaction at any time up to the moment when the host starts to participate in the making of the abort-or-commit decision.[118] The best known and simplest representative of these protocols is the two-phase commit (2PC) protocol.[15, 33, 76, 109, 118, 142, 157]

5.1.6. Two-Phase Commit (2PC) Protocols

The *two-phase commit* (*2PC*) protocol is based on the two-phase communication principle.[170] During Phase 1, all hosts are queried as to whether they can commit a transaction. All hosts agreeing to commit are equally prepared either to commit or to abort the transaction. All disagreeing hosts send abort messages. Using these votes, a decision to commit or to abort the transaction is reached. There are different versions of the protocol depending on how this decision is made. In Phase 2, the decision is communicated to all other hosts, which uniformly abort or commit the transaction.

Different versions of 2PC are known. One classification[118] identifies linear, centralized, and mixed 2PC protocols, and another [33] identifies linear, centralized, and decentralized 2PC protocols.

5.2. Transaction Atomicity Control in an Adaptation Mode

5.2.1. Adaptation of TAC to Host Crashes

Durability. All actions of a prelude must be undoable, but all actions of a commitment must be *durable* (*redoable*): once a transaction commits, all of its effects must persist[79] even in presence of host crashes. Committed transactions can be *redone*,[77,79] using new values recorded on the *REDO log* (which is a part of the system log).

Durability (redoability) is needed only for adaptation while undoability of an uncommitted transaction is important in both the normal and adaptation modes—an abort can happen in any of these modes. Thus, we can say that, in the normal mode "atomicity = synchronization − undoability," and in an adaptation mode with a crashed host "atomicity = synchronization + undoability + redoability."

Nested Transactions. Because of the "all-or-nothing" property of transactions, a substantial amount of processing power might be lost when a "long" transaction fails. *Nested transactions*[131,138,140,154,161] solve this efficiency problem by forming a tree structure of atomic actions. When a transaction not at the root of the tree terminates, its results survive all local crashes. However, the results are not made permanent until the outermost transaction (at the root of the tree) commits. Each subtree of transactions is recoverable individually.[161]

Robust Commit Protocols. It should be noted that the 2PC protocol is a paradigm, and in its pure form it can be used only in systems without host crashes or partitionings. Different implementations of the robust 2PC protocols guarantee recovery in case of host crashes.

The centralized 2PC protocol is compromised by a crash of the central process controlling commitment. To assure adaptation of the protocol, redundant processes backing up the central one can be added, making it the *four-step proto-*

col.[85] The problem of crashed hosts, with processes other than the central one, can be solved by the very nature of the communication mechanism used. For example, if the Reliable Network (RelNet) mechanism[85] is used, the protocol collects acknowledgements of RelNet and not of the participating hosts. RelNet guarantees delivery of each message it acknowledges, not only to the operational hosts, but even—during their recovery—to the failed ones.

The *four-step centralized commitment*[68] puts together an update strategy using local locking and timestamps on lock tables with a commitment protocol. The host originating a transaction is the central one in the process of committing this transaction. All noncentral failed hosts can be ignored by the protocol. No provisions are made to back up the central host. Instead, two critical actions of the commitment algorithm are assumed to be atomic.

The 2PC protocol can be blocked, and thus prevented from termination, in the case when not all hosts of a system are operational.[85, 155] This happens because the protocol requires answers from all hosts to terminate. A *three-phase commit* (*3PC*) protocol of two varieties, centralized and decentralized, assures nonblocking of the commitment process in the case of host crashes.[155] There exists an even more robust commit protocol,[52] based on the Byzantine Agreement (that is, the solution to the Byzantine Generals Problem).[111]

Termination Protocols. The broad view of a commit protocol includes in it rules of operation in the normal mode and in adaptation modes. However, it has been proposed[156] that only the rules of operation in the normal mode be called a commit protocol, while the rules of operation in an adaptation mode with crashed hosts be called a termination protocol. From this point of view, a *termination protocol* is an adaptation procedure for a commit protocol. Still, it is the responsibility of a commit protocol to always leave transaction processing in a state allowing a termination protocol to proceed.

Termination protocols are used in conjunction with nonblocking commit protocols. A termination protocol is invoked when occurrences of host crashes render the continued execution of a commit protocol impossible. The purpose of a termination protocol is to identify the operational hosts and move them toward a commit decision which is consistent with both operational and failed hosts.[156]

6. CONCURRENCY CONTROL (CC)

6.1. Concurrency Control in the Normal Mode

The goal of the CC subsystem is to ensure a correct (e.g., serializable) concurrent execution of transactions. The thorough survey of the operation of CC in the normal mode is beyond the scope of the chapter. Furthermore, there are many published basic theoretical results[19,93,106,133] and extensive surveys.[23,33,118,174]

A general classification of concurrency control mechanisms[33] identifies three classes using as the basic criterion the type of update synchronization. Synchronization can be based on a) transaction wait, or b) assigning timestamps to transactions, or c) transaction undoing. Another classification[118] divides update strategies used in distributed database systems into the following groups: a) unanimous agreement strategy, b) single primary update strategy, c) moving primary update strategy, d) majority vote update strategy, and e) majority read update strategy. The next classification[20] discriminates update synchronization by locking, by majority consensus, and by pre-analysis (e.g., SDD-1 approach).[143] A number of both qualitative and quantitative criteria for comparison of concurrency control algorithms are given in.[174]

The common criterion of correct synchronization of concurrent transactions is their serializability. However, weaker criteria, allowing for a higher degree of concurrency control algorithms are given in reference 174.

6.2 Concurrency Control in an Adaptation Mode

6.2.1. Adaptation of CC to Host Crashes

Strategies for the adaptation of CC to host crashes (for example, see Appendix A1) can be classified as follows:

- Ignore the possibility of host crashes; if such a crash occurs, it causes a *host crash catastrophe*—which destroys database consistency.
- Stop updates as soon as reconfiguration control detects a host crash and informs CC about it.
- Continue updates in a degraded mode; for example, do not allow read or write accesses to entities that have copies in the stable database managed by the crashed host.
- Continue updates without restrictions; in this case reconfiguration control should be able to restore consistency or the CC algorithm itself should be robust (e.g., the majority consensus algorithm[164] works correctly as long as the majority of the hosts are operational).

The selection of a given adaptation strategy for CC depends on the robustness of the concurrency control algorithm itself, as well as on the ability of the reconfiguration control subsystem to recover to a consistent state after a host crash (see Section 7.3.1).

6.2.2. Adaptation of CC to Partitionings

Internal and Mutual Consistency. As long as the distributed system is fully connected, CC maintains mutual consistency of all database copies. After partitioning splits the system, each partition can be kept internally consistent by using the same techniques. The following example illustrates that internal consistency does not imply mutual consistency, that is, transactions allowed in separate partitions can be incorrect in the context of a fully connected system.[5, 142]

EXAMPLE:
Imagine a naive automatic bank teller system. In a connected system, nobody can overdraw an account. Now suppose that a partitioning occurs and two partitions result. None of the partitions allows a customer to withdraw more cash than is on deposit, but nevertheless double the amount of the balance can be withdrawn by withdrawing the full balance from both partitions.

Assuming that general updating operations are permitted, it is impossible to keep any two partitions mutually consistent. At the same time, in many situations it is essential that updates are not interrupted.[142]

General Remarks. Since it is impossible to run transactions that require any data not available in the local partition, we are concerned only with transactions using exclusively local data.

Read-only transactions do not endanger mutual consistency. Also, there is no problem if transactions update nonreplicated data.[153] However, if a transaction T updates some replicated data, or if it uses values written by transactions which update replicated data, it may still be necessary to undo the transaction T, due to the *domino effect*.[136]

EXAMPLE:
Let us suppose that Transaction T1 updated a nonreplicated entity B and a replicated entity A, and then Transaction T2 read the entity B. If, during recovery from partitioning, T1 must be undone due to a conflict on the entity A, T2 has to be undone also.

For a majority of applications, operation in a partitioned state consists of providing a very degraded service. The service in this case depends heavily on the application, as well as the frequency and duration of partitionings, and can easily span the entire spectrum from doing nothing—which is a complete degradation—to only slightly impaired operation.[5]

A Classification of Adaptation Strategies. Adaptation protocols for CC in a partitioned system can be divided into two categories: a) ''pessimistic'' protocols that preserve mutual consistency among partitions at all times, and b) ''optimistic'' protocols, which temporarily violate mutual consistency. Clearly, the former result in more degraded performance during partitioning, while the latter require more complex recovery capabilities.

Protocols for adaptation of CC to partitionings must be complemented by recovery protocols (Recovery to a consistent state after *reconnection*—that is, the resumption of communication among partitions—is the domain of reconfiguration control and is discussed in Section 7.3.2.). The selection of a given adaptation strategy for CC depends on the ability of its complementary recovery protocol to reach a consistent state once partitions are reconnected.

Extending the classifications available in the literature,[29,49,153] we classify the adaptation protocols as shown in Fig. 1.11.(For examples of protocols see Appendix A2.)

- Partitioning avoidance.
- Update avoidance.
  - Update prohibition.
  - Update retraction.
- Update permissiveness.
  - Update conflict prevention.
    - Permit updates if only one live partition exists.
    - Permit updates in one partition only.
    - Permit updates of different entities in more than one partition.
    - Permit updates of some entities in more than one partition.
  - Update conflict reconciliation.
    - Limited conflict reconciliation.
    - Unlimited conflict reconciliation.
- Hybrid solutions.

Fig. 1.11. A classification of CC adaptation protocols for partitioning.

Partitioning Avoidance. Partitioning avoidance relies on increasing reliability of the system to the point where the probability of system partitioning is arbitrarily small. The SDD-1 system[85] is an example of such an approach. The primary factor limiting the effectiveness of this approach is its cost.

Systems assuming partitioning avoidance as the only means of solving the problem are subject to a *partitioning catastrophe* when a partitioning occurs.

Update Avoidance. Techniques for update avoidance ensure that even if updates are made during a partitioning, none survive the merge of partitions. By *merge* we mean the reintegration phase of the recovery from a partitioning.

UPDATE PROHIBITION. The update prohibition approach stops all updates at the instant when a partitioning occurs, and, hence, requires instantaneous detection of partitionings. Practically, instantaneous detection means detection of any partitioning occurring between any two updates; two sites differing on a single entity cannot be in conflict—just one of them is not up-to-date.

Updating in a partitioned system—resulting, for example, from an insensitive partitioning detection mechanism—leads to a catastrophe. The possibility of a catastrophe in the case of a late partitioning detection, and system unavailability during partitioning, are disadvantages of this approach.

UDATE RETRACTION. In the update retraction approach updating is stopped, as before, at the moment of partitioning detection, but this time detection does not have to be instantaneous. Recovery to a consistent state relies on saving a database state preceding the moment of partitioning (methods for saving database states are discussed in Section 7.3.1).

Update Permissiveness. In the update permissiveness approach some updates performed during partitioning survive the merge of partitions. The approach contains a number of alternatives.

UPDATE CONFLICT PREVENTION. Only mutually nonconflicting updates in a partitioned system are allowed for solutions based on the update conflict prevention. We have identified four approaches here:

- permit updates if there is only one *live partition*,*
- permit updates in one partition only,
- permit updates of a given entity in one partiton only, and
- permit updates of some entities in more than one partition.

*A *partition* is *live* if not all of its hosts are failed.

In all of these cases, any transaction that cannot access data it requires for successful completion is blocked and must wait for the reintegration of the hosts that return the needed data to its partition.

PERMIT UPDATES IF ONLY ONE LIVE PARTITION EXISTS. Since in this case we must be sure that there is only one live partition, the nontrivial ability to distinguish crashed hosts from partitions is critical.

PERMIT UPDATES IN ONE PARTITION ONLY. In this case, more than one partition can exist. But updates are permitted in only one of the partitions. The main problem is identification of the single privileged partition. A general solution is based on ascertaining before each update that the host at which the update originates belongs to the priviledged partition. The privileged partition may be identified as follows:

- The partition contains a majority of the sites of the system. A consensus of a majority of sites has to be reached before any update can be made. This approach is used in the majority consensus algorithm[164] for completely replicated database systems. The disadvantage of this approach is that it allows for situations when none of the partitions has a majority of sites. It should be noted that robustness of the algorithm is achieved as a side effect of the normal operation, without additional costs.
- The partition contains a statically selected site; for example, the site with the highest numerical identifier. The selected site could reflect the priority of sites in the system. A slight modification of this scheme adds robustness: a lower priority site is chosen when all higher priority sites are down.
- The partition contains a dynamically selected site; for example, the site possessing a working-partition token. The selected site can reflect a dynamically changing priority of sites. Multiple tokens of different priorities could be used to enhance robustness of this scheme in a manner similar to the one for the case above. A robust mechanism for passing tokens is required.[37]
- The sum of weights assigned statically to the sites of the partition exceeds half of the total sum of weights assigned to all system sites. The weights can reflect the priority of sites in the system.* To increase robustness, the weights of crashed sites are not added to the total sum of the weights.
- The sum of weights assigned dynamically to the sites of the partition exceeds half of the total sum of the weights. Dynamic weights can reflect a dynamically changing priority of sites. Robustness of the scheme can be enhanced by ignoring

*For example, the weight of a site can reflect the number of database entities at the site. Then the selected partition is the partition with more than half of the database entities.

weights of crashed sites. A reliable and "atomic" mechanism for reassignment of weights is required.

PERMIT UPDATES OF A GIVEN ENTITY IN ONE PARTITION ONLY. This scheme allows the system to process updates in more than one partition and, simultaneously, avoids conflicts. The scheme should guarantee that once an entity is updated by some transaction in one partition, it is never updated in any other partition as long as partitioning persists. In other words, updating an entity in one partition "locks" it for the exclusive use by that partition.

The problems to be solved are: how to pass to all other partitions the information that an update of an entity has occurred in one partition and how to avoid simultaneous "first" updates of an entity in different partitions.

Pseudo-partitioning. One group of solutions relies on a limited-bandwidth backup link (for example, a dial-up phone link) for passing this vital information. Of course, it is no longer a true partitioning, but rather a pseudo-partitioning (Fig. 1.12). The limited-bandwidth link is not used for supporting a regular transaction processing, but for passing concise messages, such as:

1. "A"—to indicate that entity A is to be updated;
2. "OK A"—to indicate that a receiver of the previous message allows its sender to update A; this message is used to prevent simultaneous "first" updates; and
3. "NO A"—to indicate that a receiver of the message "A" does not allow its sender to update A.

The problem of two or more partitions sending the message "A" simultaneously can be resolved by algorithms based on static or dynamic priority of sites.

The above solution is a general one. The assumption of a fixed transaction set allows for the reduction of the volume of messages.

EXAMPLE:
Suppose the following system is considered. There are two sites and the database contains fully replicated entities A, B, C, and D. There are only three types of transactions that can arrive at the system. Transactions of Type 1 arrive at Site 1 only and they update values of A and B. Transactions of Type 2 arrive at Site 2 only and they update values of C only. Transactions of Type 3 can arrive at any of the sites and update value of the entity D. Clearly, transactions of Types 1 and 2 can be allowed without any message exchange. The first transaction of Type 3 executed during partitioning requires a message when it arrives for the first time at some site i ($i = 1$ or $i = 2$).

a) System before partitioning

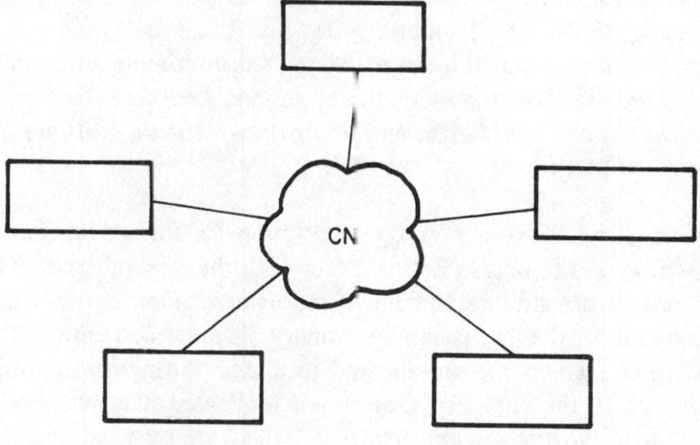

b) System after partitioning

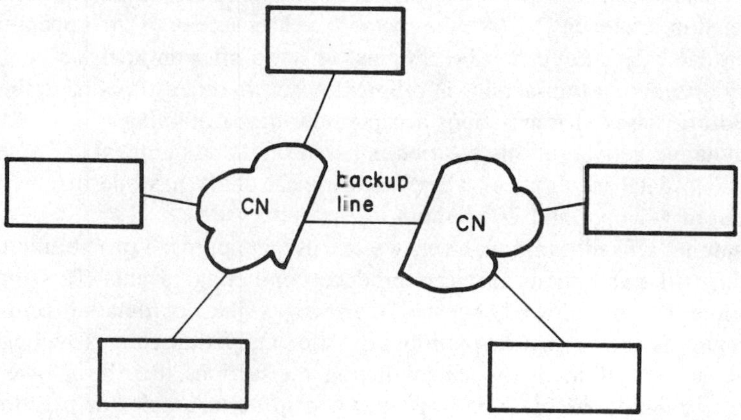

CN—Communication Network

Fig. 1.12. Pseudo-partitioning.

Later this transaction may be allowed only at the site *i* (but no more messages are required). In that manner instead of four message exchanges—one for each entity—only one is required (for D).

Notice that a transaction set with just one transaction not known *a priori* destroys this message reduction method. Any unknown transaction could create a conflict if not all access information is broadcast. For instance, for the system described in the above example, a transaction updating A at Site 2 during partitioning introduces conflicts if its originating site does not receive a message from a transaction of Type 1 ''locking'' A for Site 1.

If only a part of the transaction set is known, the following solution can be proposed: the fixed (known) transactions are pre-analyzed and allowed if they guarantee update conflict avoidance, and no unknown transactions are allowed when the system is partitioned.

Real Partitioning. Another group of solutions is for *real partitionings*, that is, not pseudo-partitionings. Let us begin with the general case. The first solution is based on a static assignment of mutually disjoint ''own'' database subsets to each site or, dually, assigning primary sites to each entity. Transactions originating at a given site are allowed to update during partitioning only the entities owned by the site. For example, a replicated database {A, B, C, D} in a partitioned two-site system, where A and C are own entities of Site 1 and B and D are own entities of Site 2, allows updates of A and C only at Site 1 and updates of B and D only at Site 2. An implementation of this solution is presented in reference 127 (see the protocol of Menasce *et al.* in Appendix A2).

Own database subsets can be assigned to hosts after an analysis of the frequency of different transactions at different hosts, in order to optimize the number and/or classes of transactions accepted during partitioning.

A dynamic version of this solution is based on the assignment of ''true-copy tokens'' to database entities, where each logical entity has one token (see the protocol of Minoura and Wiederhold in Appendix A2).[129]

Assuming a fixed transaction set, we can use an approach prohibiting unconditionally all transactions that can produce conflicting results. This time, no exceptions can be allowed, because there is no link coordinating transaction processing as in the pseudo-partitioning case. Only transactions belonging to one of the sets of mutually nonconflicting transactions may be allowed. For instance, transactions of Type 3 as specified in the example for pseudo-partitioning must be prohibited.

PERMIT UPDATES OF SOME ENTITIES IN MORE THAN ONE PARTITION. Again, we consider pseudo-partitioning and real partitioning.

Pseudo-partitioning. The role of the backup line here is the same as the role of the primary line: it is used to resolve conflicts as they appear.

EXAMPLE:

Let us assume that a fully replicated two-site database system is partitioned. Suppose that an update tries to change the value of X at Site 2 (denoted X_2). The update is blocked until the value X_1 of entity X at Site 1 arrives. Even if Site 2 has the newest version of the logical entity, it is necessary to assure that by an exchange of messages with Site 1.

If the conflicts are to be resolved, a concurrency control mechanism is required. This mechanism should be tailored to the pseudo-partitioned environment by minimizing the volume of messages it passes. One idea is to assure *consistency on demand* rather than to assure *instantaneous consistency* (the latter is guaranteed by the regular consistency control mechanisms working in the normal mode of operation). For instance, X_1 and X_2 from the above example could remain with different values as long as no next update of X comes. A normal, instantaneous consistency replaces the "emergency" consistency on demand only after the merge of the partitions restores the mutual consistency. This solution works for an arbitrary transaction set.

A fixed transaction set allows for reduction of the number of messages during partitioning. For example, if transaction T1 originates always at Site 1 and it is the only transaction which updates entity Y, this transaction (and this entity) could be ignored by the "emergency" concurrency control mechanism. Hence, no messages to coordinate T1 with other transactions are ever sent during partitioning.

Real Partitioning. Solutions for real partitionings require knowledge of the semantics of both the transaction set and of the database, that is, solutions are application-dependent, and hence difficult to generalize. The following example illustrates this case.[153]

EXAMPLE:

The copies of seat assignment information are kept at several sites within a ten-site airline reservation system. Suppose that the system is partitioned into a seven-site and a three-site partition. The protocol could state that the larger partition is allowed to allocate up to $\frac{7}{10}$ of the remaining seats on any flight, while the smaller partition is allowed to allocate up to $\frac{3}{10}$ of the remaining seats. For an integrity assertion stated simply as "No flight is overbooked," mutual consistency is preserved.

UPDATE CONFLICT RECONCILIATION. For the solutions based on the update conflict reconciliation approach, some conflicting updates are allowed in a partitioned system. We have identified two approaches to conflict reconciliation: a limited conflicts reconciliation, and an unlimited conflicts reconciliation. Again, any transaction which cannot access the data it requires for successful completion is blocked.

LIMITED UPDATE CONFLICT RECONCILIATION. This is a less general case.

Paradigm of Mutually Reconcilable Transactions. The basis for considerations on limited conflict reconciliation is the paradigm of *mutually reconcilable transactions*. We distinguish a subset of transactions—called a *reconcilable transaction subset* (*RTS*)—such that all transactions from the subset can be processed in the partitioned system with the guarantee that the merge of the partitions incurs constant costs, independently of the number of reconcilable transactions executed in a partitioned system. Let us consider an example.

EXAMPLE:

We assume a two-site database system, with a single logical entity X fully replicated (X_1 at Site 1 and X_2 at Site 2). Suppose that all transactions update entities irrespective of their old values by a constant, and that a partitioning occurs at instant t_p when $X_1(t_p) = X_2(t_p) = 125$. In a partitioned system, transactions arrive at both sites: Site 1 processes four transactions which add 10, add 80, subtract 15, and add 25 respectively; Site 2 processes five transactions which subtract 10, add 25, add 15, add 30, and subtract 10, respectively. At the instant t_r when the partitions are reconnected $X_1(t_r) = 125 + 10 + 80 - 15 + 25 = 225$ and $X_2(t_r) = 125 - 10 + 25 + 15 + 30 - 10 = 175$. To find a mutually consistent database state of the reconnected system, the following application-dependent "reconciliation formula" is used:

$$X = X_1(t_r) + [X_2(t_r) - X_2(t_p)] =$$
$$= 225 + (175 - 125) = 275$$

This value of X is given to both physical copies of X.

The example shows the simplest case: transactions perform "blind" additions and subtractions, updating old values by a constant. As a consequence, the reconciliation formula is simple. But the example illustrates the idea well.

The advantages of using reconcilable transaction subsets (RTSs) include the following: a) none of the reconcilable transactions is blocked during partitioning, and b) read-only transactions—which are always allowed, since they do not introduce conflicts—access more up-to-date values.

EXAMPLE:

Let us consider the same example again. Suppose that the conflict avoidance approach allows no updates at Site 2. Thus any retrieval at that site would read the value $X_2(t_p) = 125$, frozen at the moment of partitioning. Allowing the reconcilable transactions to update entities at Site 2, the value of X_2 changes from 125 through 115, 140, 155, 185, to 175. Retrievals following any update see a value which is more up-to-date. (The value is still not quite up-to-date since the updates made at Site 1 are not passed to Site 2.)

The choice of the reconcilable transaction subset has an effect on system performance measures such as throughput, response time, etc. Hence, the set could be optimized with the goal of improving some of these measures. Let us now discuss the solutions proposed.

Pseudo-Partitioning. In the pseudo-partitioning case, a backup line can be used to pass information on all updates. Only transactions from the same *reconcilable transaction subset* (*RTS*), which "lock" a given entity for their private use, are allowed to update the entity. (Notice that different reconcilable transaction sets can be allowed to update different entities.)

The decision as to which RTS can update a given entity could be made dynamically. For instance, the first transaction updating a given entity A "locks" this entity (using brief messages sent via the backup line) for the exclusive use by transactions of its own RTS. In general, a transaction can belong to more than one RTS. In that case, it "locks" the entity for the exclusive use by transactions from the sum of all its RTSs. Next, incoming transactions updating the entity A can further narrow down the sum, until finally a single RTS could be identified. For example, if the first transaction locks A for RTSs R_1, R_2, R_5, and the next transaction locks A for RTSs R_1, R_3, and R_5, the entity A is locked for $\{R_1, R_2, R_5\} \cap \{R_1, R_3, R_5\} = \{R_1, R_5\}$.

For an arbitrary transaction set, we must require that a transaction declare its type or that the type of the transaction is automatically identified, so that the transaction can be classified as a member of some RTS (or RTSs). For instance, a transaction could declare that it is a "blind subtraction" transaction. As such, it is classified as an element of (among others) "blind addition and subtraction" RTS.

We assume that membership to any given RTS is clear for any transaction in the case when the transaction set is fixed. As shown before, the assumption of a fixed transaction set reduces the number of messages required.

Real Partitioning. The specification of entities that can be updated by a given RTS during a real partitioning must be made statically before partitioning occurs.

UNLIMITED UPDATE CONFLICT RECONCILIATION. This is the most general approach to adaptation of concurrency control to partitionings.

Pseudo-Partitioning. This time, a backup line is not used to reduce the number of conflicts or the type of conflicts which occur in the partitioned system. Instead, it is used to merge partitions even during pseudo-partitioning. The narrower the bandwidth of the backup line the larger a lag of the merge behind the conflicts—actually the merge ''creeps'' behind conflicts. The main advantage of the *creeping merge* is that the work still remaining to be done after reconnection is diminished by the amount of work already done by the creeping merge.

Real Partitioning. For real partitionings, the *optimistic protocol* can be applied. The idea of the optimistic approach—though not its name—has been around for some time.[5] The approach allows execution of all transactions in all partitions. Of course, some transactions will be blocked if data they need is not in the partition in which they run. Optimistic protocols maintain the highest possible operational power during partitioning. The costs of eliminating inconsistencies are paid during merge.[50]

This approach is more useful if conflicts rarely occur. In the worst case, all transactions executed in all but one partition have to be backed out and then reexecuted (or redone) after system reconnection. In the best case, it is possible that, for a relatively large database and a relatively short-lived partitioning, no conflicts whatsoever occur.

For a fixed transaction set, the decision to allow the optimistic approach may be based on the analysis of the frequency of conflicts. For an arbitrary transaction set, optimism is completely blind.

Hybrid Approaches. Hybrid solutions to the partitioning problem include a combination of the ''simple'' approaches enumerated above. There is a multitude of possible methods here. For example, the update retraction method can be combined with the optimistic unlimited update conflict reconciliation: after partitioning is detected, only conflicting updates on some entities are backed out, while the processing of other entities is unrestricted.

7. RECONFIGURATION CONTROL (RC)

7.1. Reconfiguration Control in the Normal Mode

7.1.1. The Role of RC

The role of RC in the normal mode of operation is the detection of host crashes and partitionings. If the underlying network is able to perform this detection, RC merely passes information about the configuration failures to other subsystems.

7.1.2. Detection of Host Crashes

Each host can be in one of the following states:[85]

1. DOWN: that is, not operating;
2. SLOW: running, but slow to respond to messages, that is, not acknowledging messages within a specified timeout interval;
3. FAULTY: running, responding to messages within the timeout interval, but operating incorrectly, that is, producing erroneous messages; and
4. UP: running correctly, and responding to messages within the timeout interval.

It is impossible to distinguish accurately among all four states. A remote host cannot determine whether another host is failing to respond because it is DOWN or merely because it is SLOW. It is also not always possible to distinguish whether a tested host is FAULTY or UP.

A remote host may suspect that another host has failed in several ways. It may receive an incorrect message from that host, or it may fail to receive an expected message within a reasonable time. In some communication network architectures it may also be possible to detect that a remote host has failed to accept a message—indicating overload or failure of that host.[130] A host may also set failure watches on other hosts by probing them with periodic messages. If a probed host fails to respond within a timeout interval, it is assumed to have failed.[85]

One solution[85] to the uncertainty regarding the state of a remote host is to consider both states SLOW and FAULTY as DOWN. Merging the state SLOW into the state DOWN results in regarding any host that fails to respond to a message that demands a response within a timeout interval as being in the DOWN state. However, the system must recognize the possibility that the host may merely be SLOW and takes appropriate action by sending to the host "YOU'RE_DOWN" message. Upon receiving such a message the host is forced to crash. Merging FAULTY into DOWN requires a procedure (called Crashsite) to explicitly crash a host that is *believed* to be FAULTY. Another way of merging FAULTY into DOWN[147,148] relies on the implementation of "fail-stop processors" (hosts) which halt in response to any internal failure, and do so before the effects of these failures become visible to remote hosts.

More powerful algorithms for testing a foreign host could distinguish among all four states of the host. This issue is the topic of the research on system diagnosability.[16,44,82,91] Alternatively, the system must be able to achieve a decision even with (a bounded number of) failed components behaving unpredictably; for example, sending conflicting information to different parts of the system. This problem is known as the *Byzantine Generals Problem.*[111]

7.1.3. Detection of Partitionings

In general, detection of a partitioning might not occur until *reconnection*, that is, when different partitions start to communicate again.[127]

7.1.4. Discriminating Between Host Crashes and Partitionings

Adaptation/recovery procedures for partitionings can also be used for host or crash adaptation/recovery, but are more complex and expensive. The reason is that any crashed host ceases processing, and therefore it cannot introduce inconsistencies with regard to another host, whereas this can happen when the system is partitioned. Hence the ability to distinguish between host crashes and partitionings is important. This problem is non-trivial. For example, Host H1 in Fig. 1.13 may be unable to infer whether Host H2 has crashed or is in another partition.

A solution to the problem depends on how much information about failures is returned by the communication system.[5] If the system distinguishes between ''I was unable to deliver the message to the destination host'' (indicating a partitioning) and ''Message delivered to the destination host, but the host is not servicing the interface'' (indicating a host crash), then it is possible to classify some configuration failures as host crashes. If the communication network does not make the distinction, every host crash has to be treated pessimistically as a partitioning, and a more expensive adaptation/recovery procedure has to be used.

Until its status is known, a host should be treated as a *live host*,[129] which continues operation in another partition. The status of a partition, where a crashed host is viewed as a ''dead'' partition, can be communicated to other partitions by one of many methods. For example, the following approaches are possible:[128] a) a message port attached to a host may detect its failure and generate the failure notification message; b) for a local-area network, special highly reliable transmission lines carrying status information may be laid; c) the system operator may supply status information about other hosts; or d) a host is treated as live only if the partition to which it belongs forms a majority of the hosts in the system; all hosts of other partitions cease processing.

7.2 Reconfiguration Control in an Adaptation Mode

7.2.1. Adaptation of RC to Host Crashes

Causes of Host Crashes. A host crash, also called a *soft crash*,[74] a *(volatile) memory loss*,[164, 170] or a *host failure*,[95] can be caused by errors in critical tables, wild branches by trusted processes, operating system failures, other software failures which compromise the database management system as a host,* or

*If a site is halted without a warning, the volatile database can be left in an inconsistent state since transaction atomicity is violated.

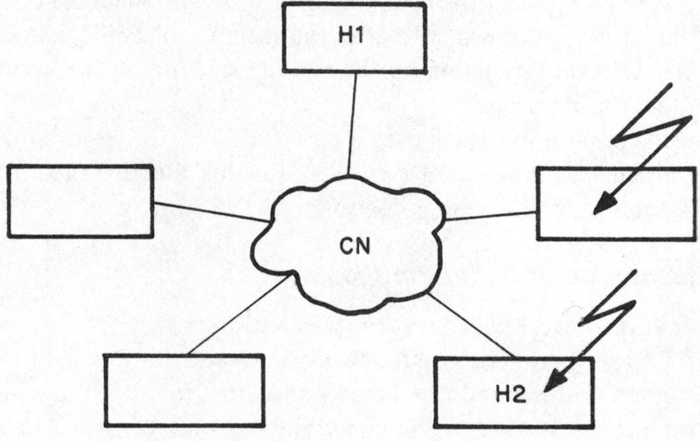

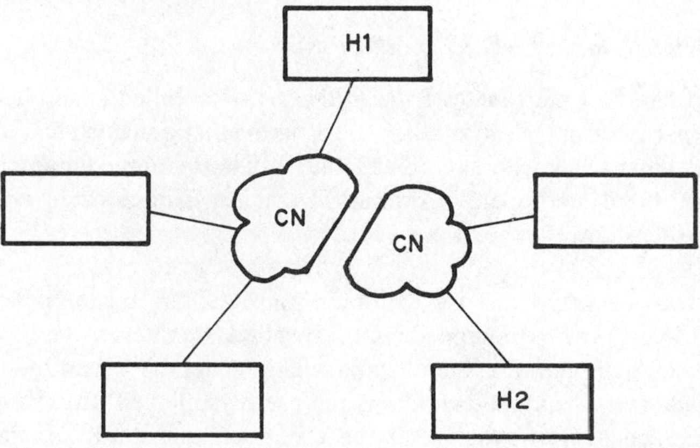

CN—Communication Network

Fig. 1.13. Discriminating between host crashes and partitionings.

hardware (CPU, memory) crashes.[76,118] Host crashes generally occur with the frequency of several per month.[79]

Functions of RC. A new function of RC in a system with a crashed host is the *reintegration watch*:[85] finding out whether reintegration of a host should be attempted. For example, after a host crashes due to a failure of its only CPU, RC should set the reintegration watch on the host to be able to initiate reintegration of the host as soon as its CPU is repaired.

The operation of a distributed system can be continued even without the recovery of the crashed host. Adaptation actions can eliminate the unoperational host from the system. Performance after the restart will be degraded, with the degree of degradation depending on the number of hosts in the system and on the method of data replication.

If any of the system functions uses a centralized control algorithm and if the crashed host acted as the central controller for this function, RC is burdened with the *election* of a new central controller.[65,68]

7.2.2. Adaptation of RC to Partitionings

Communication Line Failures versus Partitionings. As long as message re-routing[5,130] can guarantee communication between any pair of sites, communication line failures should be made transparent to other reliability subsystems. Re-routing can be done by an underlying network (in which case it is also transparent to RC) or, if the network is dumb, by RC. A proper network topology aids this task.

7.2.3. Adaptation of RC to Media Failures

Causes of Media Failures. *Media failures*,[79] also called *hard crashes*,[74] are caused by parity errors, head crashes, dust on magnetic media, lost tapes, software errors which make storage unreadable or distort storage data, catastrophes such as fire, flood, and operator errors.[76] Database failures occur with the frequency on the order of several per year.[79]

EXAMPLE OF ADAPTATION TO MEDIA FAILURES. In the reliable network (RelNet)[85] every site is equipped with so-called *stable storage*,* which can survive some media failures. Stable storage can be approximated by using hardware redundancy. A simple example is the use of duplexed disks. This kind of masking protects against a disk head crash, but not against a fire in the machine room.[79] Other methods of masking use redundant data structures.[163]

7.3. Reconfiguration Control in a Recovery Mode

7.3.1. Recovery of RC from Host Crashes

General Remarks. In this and the following sections, we assume that the effects of a host crash are limited to a single site, that is, host recovery can be achieved without compensation (undoing) of committed transactions at other sites. (Transactions that are not committed can easily be aborted.) This assumption is realized through the use of commit protocols. Further, we assume

*Do not mistake stable storage for stable database—these are two different notions.

that data is transferred between the memory and stable database in pages and that implementation guarantees *strong atomic property for page transfer.*[109] The property requires that the transfer of a page from memory to secondary storage can never be partial and may have only one of the following outcomes: either the page is not transferred at all, or the page is transferred successfully. This assumption is realized by the underlying file system primitives.

The Goals of Host Recovery. Host recovery is needed to achieve consistency of the entire database, not only to achieve consistency of the volatile database. The reason is that a host crash might leave the stable database in an inconsistent state. For example, if a transition from an old consistent stable database state to a new one requires the transfer of two pages from memory to storage and a host crash occurs when the first page is already in the stable database but the second is not, the stable database is left in an inconsistent state.

Procedures for Host Recovery. Only the reintegration phase of the recovery, which follows repair (for permanent faults) or ''self-repair'' (for transient faults) of the crashed host, is discussed next. The reintegration has to 1) restore a consistent database state of the site, and 2) assure that the updates delayed during a host crash are performed to bring the local database up-to-date. (For examples of host recovery protocols see Appendix A3.)

Restoration of a Consistent Database State. Since we have assumed that the effects of a crash are limited to a single site, only local information available at the recovering host is used in the restoration of database consistency. The techniques for the restoration of a consistent database state can be classified as shown in (Fig. 1.14).

Log-only restoration: This restoration requires that 1) all transactions that were uncommitted at the instant of the crash are undone, and 2) all transactions that were committed at the instant of the crash are redone.

There are two problems with log-only restoration. First, to undo all uncommitted transactions, the system must go back to the oldest undo log entry re-

- Log-only restoration.
- Snapshot and log restoration.
- Checkpoint and log restoration.

Fig. 1.14. A classification of RC protocols for the restoration of a consistent database state.

corded for any uncommitted transaction. Long transactions will force the system to go back a long way. However, in many systems long transactions are very rare, and this problem disappears. Second, to redo all committed transactions, the system must go back to the oldest redo log entry recorded for any committed transaction. This means going back almost to the beginning of the log. Since a log may be weeks or months old, this solution is clearly unacceptable.

Snapshot and log restoration: This technique solves the problem with the redoing of committed transactions. In addition to maintaining the system log, periodically a snapshot of a database state is made. Since each snapshot is preceded by the flushing of all database buffers, it records the state of the entire database, not just that of the stable database. To restore a consistent database state 1) undo each transaction that was started before the most recent snapshot but was uncommitted at the instant of the crash, and 2) for each transaction that was committed after the most recent snapshot, redo all of its updates performed after this snapshot.

Notice that there is *no* need to redo transactions committed before the most recent snapshot. This solves the more urgent of the two problems with log-only restoration: to redo the identified committed transactions the system must go back only to the oldest redo log entry *following* the most recent snapshot (instead of going to the oldest redo log entry, period). Similarly, there is *no* need to undo transactions started after the most recent snapshot. This will somewhat reduce the costs of undoing transactions. The problem of long transactions is not yet solved, however.

The snapshot and log restoration technique introduces a significant disadvantage. For all but very small databases, the cost of making a copy of the entire database is substantial.

Checkpoint and log restoration: This technique solves the problem of overly costly snapshots by replacing them with checkpoints. Since the checkpoints do not record the whole database,* the overhead of preparing checkpoints is much lower. It should be mentioned that this approach introduces some minor inefficiencies in the process of undoing uncommitted transactions.

For a more detailed discussion of these restoration techniques, see the study cited in reference 81.

For the checkpoint and log recovery, efficient implementation of checkpoints plays an essential role. The techniques for implementing checkpoints include the following:

1. *Audit trail:*[47,79,167,173] All updates of the database, with an indication of the transaction that made them, are recorded on the system log. The *"write ahead log" (WAL) protocol*[79] assures that, in all but catastrophic cases, the log is complete, since all update records are saved on the log *before* the correspond-

*In this case, a snapshot is *not* considered a special case of a checkpoint.

ing update is performed on the database. If the system log is complete, it can be used for the restoration of the consistent state: committed updates performed by completed transactions can be redone[77,79] by using the redo records from the log (a faster implementation uses a *change accumulation log* or a *compacted log*,[97] which is constructed from the redo records of the log by its compression). To limit the size of the log, special records, called *checkpoint records* (or *save points*),* are written to the log. Checkpoint records indicate that all preceding updates recorded on the log have already been saved in the stable database. As far as host crashes are considered, all redo log records preceding the last checkpoint record can be erased.

2. *Backup/current versions (shadowing):*[32,121,126,167] Copies of updated entities of the database are maintained in parallel with the unchanged "originals." Once a copy of an entity is made, only the copy is accessed by the transactions. The "originals" constitute a backup version used, if necessary, in the recovery process. The current version (containing all copies) replaces the backup version after a number of transactions that have updated the copy are completed.

3. *Complete database dump:*[60,141,145] If a complete dump is performed in such a manner that a consistent database state is recorded periodically, reloading the latest dump restores the consistent state. Please note that this technique creates snapshots.

4. *Differential files:*[4,149,167] The main file (the database itself) stores the most recent consistent database state, and the differential file records all changes in the database following this state. If the updates made by incomplete transactions and recorded in the differential file are ignored, then the merge of the differential file with the main file creates a new consistent state.

5. *Incremental database dump:*[10,167] This is a more efficient version of the complete database dump technique. Only entities of the database updated since the previous incremental dump are recorded by the next incremental dump. Reloading an initial (or periodic) complete dump and "updating" it with the entities recorded by the incremental dumps restores a database state. If the moments when incremental dumps are made are selected as the instants for complete dumps before, the consistent state is restored.

6. *Multiple copies:*[32,167] More than one copy of each entity is permanently maintained in the database. An efficient implementation uses two copies, and each copy has an "update-in-progress" flag. The flag indicates that the associated copy is under update, and thus possibly in an inconsistent state. Only one copy at a time can be updated by a group of transactions. After the first copy is updated to a consistent state, the updates are applied to another copy. (In a quiescent database state, both copies converge to an identical state.)

---

*Save points of the log have nothing in common, except the name, with save points embedded in transactions.

Updating a Database to the Current System-Wide State. Updating a database to the current system-wide state can be based on obtaining lost information, such as update and synchronization data, from other hosts of a (partially) replicated database system.[38]

Sometimes, a host under reintegration cannot—because of failures of other hosts—obtain information necessary for the update. In this case, it can only allow read operations on its database, with a warning that the data might be obsolete.[132] Updates under these conditions lead to inconsistencies; after other hosts recover, two different versions of the same data exist, and neither is correct.

EXAMPLE:
Assume a fully replicated two-host database system. Consider the following scenario. Host A crashes while Host B continues its operation—Transaction T1 reads an entity X and updates its value from X to $X_B = f_1(X)$. Next, Host B crashes. Later, Host A recovers but does not learn about the update of X. Host A resumes its operation—Transaction T2 reads Item X and updates its value from X to $X_A = f_2(X)$. Next, Host B recovers. At this moment, there are two values of X in the system: $X_B = f_1(X)$ and $X_A = f_2(X)$. The correct value of X is $f_2(f_1(X))$ or $f_1(f_2(X))$, that is, the one equivalent to a serial execution of T1 and T2. Neither of the hosts records such a value.

Note that if a serial history can be derived from X_A and X_B by a simple operation (e.g., by applying a reconciliation formula), the situation is rectified. But this is not always possible, and then it is necessary to undo one of the transactions T1 and T2. If, instead of a single transaction Ti (i = 1, 2) in the above scenario, there is a set of transactions $Ti_1, \ldots, Ti_n$, all transactions run at one of the hosts have to be undone.

To increase the availability of the recovery information when a host needs it, the guaranteed delivery mechanism[85] can be used. *Guaranteed delivery* ensures that a message sent to a failed host is received by that host upon its reintegration, even if the sending host is down at the time the destination host is under reintegration. To resume the operation, a recovering host needs to process only update messages received while it was unoperational. These messages are stored redundantly at a few neighboring sites until the recovering host updates its database during reintegration.

Since obtaining the information for host reintegration from other hosts is not instantaneous, certain timing conditions have to be fulfilled to guarantee that a recovering host can obtain the information it needs from other hosts before these hosts crash.[110]

If the host crash was relatively short, the most efficient update procedure is to obtain lost updates from the log of another host. Otherwise, the best approach is to acquire the entire database from a nearby site. This alternative is not viable if the database is very large compared to the spare communications bandwidth available.[38] An implementation of the latter alternative in completely replicated database systems, given in reference 11, consists of three steps: 1) turn on the concurrency control algorithm at the host under reintegration; 2) tell all other hosts to begin updating the data in the database controlled by the recovering host (the host and the database it controls can be, in general, at different sites); and 3) do not let any transaction to read an entity X from the database controlled by the recovering host until X has been updated at least once.

Two steps are taken to speed up the availability of data from the database controlled by the recovering host. First, special *copier transactions* are run, which read data values at remote sites and write them into the database controlled by the recovering host. Copiers must be synchronized by the concurrency control algorithms exactly like other transactions. Second, only those entities that were updated while the host was unoperational need to be updated during its reintegration.

One can imagine an extension of this method for non-replicated data, but then restoration of a non-replicated entity X would rely on the assumption that there is a transaction which reads replicated data and, based on their values, computes a new value for X.

The Costs of Host Recovery. A significant amount of time is required for preparatory actions such as making snapshots, checkpoints, maintaining logs or multiple copies, and for restoration processes.[32,41,97] These time costs can be divided into a) *fixed costs*, independent of the number of host crashes, and b) *variable costs*, incurred only if a host crash occurs. Also, hardware costs for storing different snapshots or copies have to be considered. On the other hand, an effective automatic recovery system saves some unquantifiable costs that come from a) the use of invalid data, and b) expenditure of efforts by individual users for protecting their data against error and manually recreating them after host crashes.

Different implementations of checkpoints result in different costs of making a single checkpoint, as discussed above. In addition, for restoration methods based on checkpoints, time costs can be minimized by selecting checkpointing moments which maximize system availability or minimize its response time.[40,69,70,120,162] If the inter-checkpoint interval is too small, too much time is spent on making checkpoints, and if this time is too large, restoration lasts too long.

For real-time systems, still another model is used.[39] Each program run by the system is partitioned into several tasks. Checkpoints must be scheduled in between tasks so that, at every point during program execution, the maximum recovery time does not exceed the real-time constraints. The objective of checkpoint scheduling is to minimize the maximum (or worst case) time that may be spent in preparing system checkpoints.

The above optimization criteria might be too insensitive to justify the introduction of checkpoints:[105] a numerical example demonstrates a case when use of the criteria would lead to the recommendation that there be no checkpoints at all. At the same time, a more sensitive criterion (the ratio between the marginal gain accrued to users who suffer system failure and the presumably slight loss suffered on average by all users) indicates the advantage of introducing checkpoints. The new criterion does not address the issue of user-perceived delays.

Implementation of checkpoints (as discussed earlier) is a critical factor. The cost analysis in references 32 and 117 looks for the checkpointing technique that minimizes the time required for restoration of a transaction-consistent database state and selects the differential file technique as the optimal one.

Robustness of Host Recovery Procedures. Failures during restoration of a consistent database state include a failure during reprocessing the log.[40] If this failure is not caused by a loss of the log, execution can simply be resumed from the after-crash state or the state known to be restored. The condition is that operations recorded on the log are *idempotent*[79, 109] (*repeatable*)[76]—that is, doing these operations several times produces the same result as doing them once. Then the database restoration process itself is idempotent.

Different means of assuring robustness of the update phase of host reintegration are discussed in references 42, 85, 127, and 164. The method proposed in the paper by Chou and Liu[42] requires that hosts buffer messages sent to a crashed host H0. Every recovering host H0 has to acknowledge execution of actions ordered by each message sent to it by any of the other hosts before the sender may delete the message sent from its buffer. This guarantees that none of the messages sent to H0 during its recovery are lost, even in the case where H0 crashes again during this recovery.

7.3.2. Recovery of RC from Partitionings

General Remarks. Repair of a partitioning ends with the resumption of communication among partitions, that is, *reconnection*. Mutual reintegration of reconnected partitions, called *merge*, has as its goal reconciliation of all inconsistencies among reconnected partitions. Correct merge actions may depend on the semantics of the database, the topology of partitions, and transactions run during partitioning.[142]

If the merged partitions are not mutually consistent, they cannot be reconciled by simply taking the newest versions of each entity. As the following example shows,[132] there could be no newest version.

EXAMPLE:

Suppose that there are two copies, X_1 and X_2, of the entity X. At the moment when partitioning separates X_1 from X_2, both copies are consistent. If the updates to X are allowed in both partitions, X_1 is modified into X_1' and X_2 into X_2' before merge is attempted. X_1' and X_2' are two different versions of the same entity, and no one is the new or the old one: neither was X_1' derived from X_2' (that is, X_1' is not newer than X_2') nor was X_2' derived from X_1' (that is, X_2' is not newer than X_1').

A Classification of Merge Protocols. Merge protocols and concurrency control protocols for adaptation to a partitioning are independent. In general, the smaller the degradation in the operation of concurrency control in a partitioned system, the higher the complexity of the merge protocol of RC. Merge protocols can be classified as shown in Fig. 1.15. In parentheses, we specify for which category of CC adaptation protocols (see Section 6.2.2) a given merge protocol applies. (For examples of merge protocols see Appendix A4.)

Empty Merge. When the update prohibition protocol is used for concurrency control in an adaptation mode, no updates are performed during partitioning. The system state at the moment of reconnection is the same as it was immediately before partitioning, and the system can simply resume operation without any merging actions.

Merge by Update Retraction. In this approach, updates are retracted and the database state is rollbacked to some state (not necessarily consistent) preceding the moment of partitioning. The requirements are that an instant t preceding the partitioning be defined and a system state prior to t be saved. Time between the instant t and the moment of partitioning defines the "distance" from the saved state.

The first condition can be satisfied by periodic checking of the accessibility

- "Empty" merge (for update prohibition protocols of CC).
- Merge by update retraction (for update retraction protocols).
- Merge by compensation of lost updates (for update conflict prevention protocols).
- Merge by partition reconciliation (for update conflict reconciliation protocols).
- Hybrid techniques (for hybrid solutions).

Fig. 1.15. A classification of RC merge techniques.

of all hosts. (The duration of the inter-checking period defines the upper bound on the interval between the instant *t* and the instant of partitioning.) A system state can be saved by any of the methods described for host recovery (Section 7.3.1) or storage recovery (Section 8.3.1).

Merge by Compensation of Lost Updates. This merge protocol can be applied under the assumption that no conflicting updates were allowed during partitioning. It is possible that, at reconnection, certain copies of entities in certain partitions have more up-to-date values than other copies. The goal of the merge is to propagate the up-to-date values of each entity to all of its physical copies. After all copies have the up-to-date value, the merge is completed and regular database processing can be resumed.

Merge is more complex if non-conflicting updates were permitted in two or more partitions. The entities updated during partitioning and their up-to-date values can be identified, for example, by the system log or by timestamps on physical copies of entities.

Merge by Partition Reconciliation. Since no reconciliation is necessary for entities that have preserved their mutual consistency, an efficient merge process requires detecting these entities of different partitions that are (or, pessimistically, could be) mutually inconsistent. A detection method for the case when entities are files is given in reference 134.

For the limited update conflict reconciliation approach, the technique using the reconcilable transaction subsets (RTSs) and reconciliation formulas or other semantic-dependent methods[66] can be used.

For the unlimited update conflict reconciliation, RC must be able to reconcile any detected update conflicts. Since it is impossible to predict which transactions will have to be undone, each transaction executed while the system is partitioned must be either uncommitted or compensable[29,49,50] (see protocols of Davidson and Garcia-Molina and Bhargava in Appendix A4).

7.3.3. Recovery of RC from Media Failures

General Recovery Procedures. Recovery from a media failure is needed if a part of the stable database is lost or if a log is lost. Recovery relies on the existence of the following redundant copies of the database and the log: 1) An *archive snapshot*, which records the entire state of the database at a certain instant in the relatively distant past; 2) the *archive log*, which is a copy of the log up to a certain moment; and 3) *incremental dumps*, which are copies of the changed parts of the database.

Redundancy inherent in the archive snapshot, archive log, and incremental dumps allows the system to limit the media recovery to a single site. Incremental dumps are periodically merged off-line with the archive snapshot to produce a newer version of the archive snapshot. Media recovery requires reloading the database from the archive snapshot, merging with it all incremental dumps not merged with the archive log so far, and updating the resulting database state with the entries from the archive log (and the ''main'' log if the archive log is not completely up-to-date). For details, see reference 81.

Backup Mechanism. For additional protection, redundant copies of snapshots can be maintained off-line, for example, on tapes stored in a vault. Maintenance of redundant off-line snapshots is the task of a *backup mechanism*[144] which must have failure modes independent of the on-line media recovery mechanism. In the case where on-line media recovery fails, the backup mechanism is used.

A special type of a backup mechanism is an *archival system*,[75] which stores copies of data for very long or indefinite periods, and guarantees random access to old copies of data.

Cold Start. In a worst possible case, due to the loss of all archive snapshots, no useful database state can be restored. In this case, *cold start*[76, 137] is an uncomfortable necessity. The database system should be cold started only once: when its first version is created. Even a system update to a new version should not cause a cold start.[169]

8. INTERNAL DATA INTEGRITY CONTROL (IDIC)

8.1. Internal Data Integrity Control in the Normal Mode

8.1.1. The Structure of IDIC

There is a need for database validation as means of maintaining data reliability at some required level.[61] Recall that IDIC fulfills three functions: transaction input control, transaction output control, and database audit. The difference between the three lies in the timing of their activation—whether data are verified immediately before a transaction uses its readset, before a transaction writeset is recorded in the database, or at another moment, respectively. There is also a difference in the scope between, on one side, transaction input/output control, and, on the other side, database audit. Transaction input(output) control checks only the part of the database interdependent with a readset (a writeset) of a transaction, while database audit verifies the entire database.

Database audit is a form of diagnostic checking,[137] with all its shortcomings—the major one is an unchecked propagation of errors between the audits. Shorter inter-audit periods contain this propagation, but increase costs.

8.1.2. Integrity Assertions

To distinguish checks used by IDIC from checks used by transaction correctness control, we call the former integrity assertions. Comprehensively defined, an *integrity assertion* (*integrity constraint*) contains:[59]

1. the identifier of the object (entity) *o* to which the integrity assertion applies (for example, *o* is an air track in a flight plan database);
2. identification *t* for what type of database update (modification/insertion/deletion) the integrity assertion applies to;
3. a predicate *p* stating a semantic constraint which must be true for an occurrence of the object *o* (for example: "Air track is XYZ or YZW");
4. a condition *c* expressing a prerequisite for applying the semantic constraint *p* to object *o* (for example, the predicate "Air track is XYZ or YZW" with the condition "Flight number equals 300" will force air tracks for Flight 300 to be limited to the enumerated ones); and
5. an enforcement type *e* that specifies the action that should be taken by the system if *p* is not true (for example, reject the requested modification or insertion).

In applications where any of *o*, *t*, *c*, and/or *e* are obvious, they can be omitted. This explains why sometimes integrity assertions are defined simply as "predicates."

8.1.3. Mechanisms for Database Integrity Validation

Mechanisms for database auditing, that is, for validation of the integrity of database-resident data, are primarily implemented by one of three generic approaches:[56] a) by a *special code* built into programs that access the database, b) by *special procedures* auditing database contents periodically or on demand, or c) by a *semantic integrity subsystem*.

The first approach causes redundancy of code, and forces each transaction to trust other transactions not to violate the integrity of data. This approach is too risky.

One technique representing the second approach is *manual auditing*. It can be effective only when the database is very small and has a simple structure.[63] As the database size increases, it is necessary to switch to *automatic auditing*.[61,160] A program for the automatic auditing of data integrity[63] can print a "condition report" which lists: a) errors, b) discrepancies, that is, possible errors, c) exception notes, that is, conditions which should be called to a user's attention, d) counts, that is, frequencies of occurrence of user-defined conditions. The report has three parts: the first part identifies every entity in which a reportable condition—such as an error, discrepancy, or note—has been detected, the second part is a condition-to-entity cross-reference, and the third part is a condition report summary, providing a concise history of the condition of database files. The error-discrepancy statistics provide a useful facility for diagnosing software as well as hardware faults.

Still, serious drawbacks with the second validation approach remain: when an auditing program detects an error, its exact diagnosis is difficult; the auditing programs are complex, may be implementation-dependent, and lack data independence (they might be severely impacted by any reorganization of data).[56]

The third approach—integrity enforcement by some form of a semantic integrity subsystem—is widely represented in the literature.[22,56,57,59,62,108,115,116,117,159,160] A semantic integrity subsystem could consist of five principal components:[83]

1. *high level nonprocedural languages* to express a set of integrity assertions;
2. *processors for the nonprocedural languages*, which translate high level integrity assertions into an internal form;
3. an *integrity assertion enforcer* (*checker*) to determine which integrity assertions need to be checked after one or more database changes occur, and to perform that checking;
4. a *violation-action processor*, which takes appropriate action when an integrity assertion violation is detected by the enforcer; and
5. an *integrity assertion compatibility checker*, which is responsible for ensuring that the current set of integrity assertions for a database is free from conflicts and other undesirable properties.

Both automatic audits by special programs and semantic integrity subsystems are based on the use of integrity assertions on database contents.

8.1.4. Types of Integrity Assertions

Different types of integrity assertions can be distinguished. For example,[78] the assertions can be defined on: 1) a record, 2) a set of records,[139] 3) a transformation of a record, 4) a set of transformations on a set of records (these assertions are called "transaction constraints").

Using the criterion of timing of their enforcement, integrity assertions can be divided into *immediate assertions*, checked immediately after each database action or after each database transaction, and *delayed assertions*, checked periodically.[56]

Further, we can distinguish between static and dynamic integrity assertions.[56] *Static assertions* (*state assertions*) characterize integral database states. *Dynamic assertions* (*transition assertions*) characterize the valid transitions between integral database states. For example, a dynamic integrity assertion could require that a change in the altitude of a plane not exceed 70 meters per second.

In the context of the relational database model, we can discriminate between a) *domain assertions*, that are predicates on domains, and b) *relation assertions*, that specify properties or relationships that are to hold for one or more relations or their parts.[83]

Other classifications of integrity assertions are based 1) on the syntactic structure of assertions,[160] or 2) on the view on which the assertions are defined.[135]

8.1.5. Integrity Assertion Activation

So far, selection of the moment of activation of integrity assertions has not been discussed. An integrity assertion can be enforced after a primitive database change, after some logical group of changes, or upon user or system demand.[83] We can specify types of database access—such as insertion, modification, or deletion—for which an assertion is to be invoked[59] and classify the assertions as *insertion rules*, *change rules*, or *deletion rules*, respectively.[62]

A *trigger subsystem*,[57] used for the implementation of integrity assertions, invokes execution of the body (a program) of a *trigger* whenever an event specified by a trigger condition takes place. A trigger may be activated: a) before or after execution of a statement expressed in a data sublanguage, or b) after an occurrence of a specific database state, or c) after an occurrence of a specific transition between states.

For a special database type—large design databases—the maintenance is delayed until strictly necessary, and integrity violations are temporarily tolerated. Integrity assertions are pre-compiled procedures included in entity definitions and automatically activated by the system. The temporary existence of simultaneous alternative values for entities, which is important in systems for decision making, is allowed.[53,108]

Subsets of integrity assertions to be activated for a given database state can be specified by the condition of applicability c given in the definition of each assertion.

8.1.6. Costs of Integrity Enforcement

Although the importance of semantic integrity control in database systems is well known, only limited forms of integrity control, involving only the simplest forms of integrity assertions, have been incorporated into existing database systems due to the high cost of integrity assertion checking. The costs of achieving a high degree of database consistency may be prohibitive.[62] Hence, as in case of transaction correctness control, efficiency/effectiveness compromise for IDIC is critical. Our considerations of the costs of checks for transaction correctness control also apply for integrity assertions. Further, numerous query optimization techniques[94] can be applied to integrity verification. Additionally, other improvements discussed below are available.

Specifically, for transaction output control, the approach called query modification[159] is applicable. *Query modification* requires that each interaction with the database is immediately modified, by appending to it integrity assertions (at the query language level), to one guaranteed to have no database integrity violations. It is argued that appending integrity assertions at this high level increases update efficiency and allows for enforcing complex integrity checking, which is difficult to enforce at lower levels. The scheme also allows the user to demand the enforcement of integrity assertions (using the RETRIEVE command), instead of checking them at each update.

For many updates, only *partial evaluation* of integrity assertions is necessary. For example, an integrity assertion verifying that maximum allowed plane altitude is not exceeded cannot change its value from TRUE to FALSE if the plane is descending. Lengthy recomputation of assertions should not be required to determine that the update could not violate database integrity. There is a method[35]—working not only for trivial cases, such as the one described—that reduces the work necessary for determining that an update could not falsify an integrity assertion. For a certain class of updates, no database accesses are necessary to determine that an integrity assertion could not change its value. For other classes of updates, a partial evaluation of assertions is required to determine this fact.

Statistical methods for integrity analysis[160] drastically reduce verification costs, at the price of lower effectiveness of error detection. These methods can be used for a) estimating the reliability of data if the exact audition of database contents is not required, or b) between regular, exact verifications of database contents.

Another efficient strategy for integrity verification—*ordered batch verification*[116]—is particularly attractive for delayed integrity assertions when integrity assertions are verified in batches. Proposed heuristics define a proper order of verification of the integrity assertions that results in a substantial decrease of the I/O costs, as compared to an arbitrary order of verification.

EXAMPLE:

Integrity assertions IA_1, IA_2, and IA_3 are to be verified (Fig. 1.16). IA_1 needs pages 1, 5, 7 for verification, IA_2 needs pages 2, 4, 8, and IA_3 needs pages 1, 3, 5. Assume a volatile database size of three pages and assume that, at the time of verification, none of the needed pages is in the volatile database. If the integrity assertions are verified in the order IA_1–IA_2–IA_3, then $3 + 3 + 3 = 9$ pages have to be transferred to the memory. If the assertions are checked in order IA_1–IA_3–IA_2, then only $3 + 1 + 3 = 7$ page transfers are needed, since IA_3 uses pages 1 and 5 already in the memory after verification of IA_1.

Specialized hardware allows for further efficiency improvements. For example, in a cellular-logic device with an array of cells, each containing rotating

PAGES REQUIRED FOR VERIFICATION:

IA_1: 1,5,7 IA_2: 2,4,8 IA_3: 1,3,5

"NATURAL" ORDER (1-2-3)

101	102	103	C=0
1	5	7	C=3
2	4	8	C=6
1	3	5	C=9

AN OPTIMAL ORDER (1-3-2)

101	102	103	C=0
1	5	7	C=3
+1	+5	3	C=4
2	4	8	C=7

C - CUMULATIVE VERIFICATION COST

Fig. 1.16. Ordered batch IA verification.

memory and a special-purpose processor, verification can be performed independently of the host at the place where data are stored.[90]

8.2. Internal Data Integrity Control in an Adaptation Mode

8.2.1. Adaptation of IDIC to Database Failures

IDIC must block access to erroneous storage-resident data and it may be able to make some data errors transparent to other subsystems. For example, for transactions accepting highly correlated numerical data as input, detection of an input data error can be followed by the generation of estimated data to replace the wrong or unexpected data.[175]

8.3. Internal Data Integrity Control in a Recovery Mode

8.3.1. Recovery from Database Failures

Goal of Database Recovery. The goal of *database recovery*, that is, recovery from database failures, is restoring the semantic integrity of the database, with minimal loss of work already performed by the system. It can be shown that recreating an integral database state ''closest'' to a given nonintegral database state is an NP-hard problem,[117] even if only a single site is involved. This explains why the solutions proposed in the literature use the simpler paradigm of backward recovery, which relies on the restoration of a pre-recorded integral database state.

Database recovery attempts to remove errors that were caused by faults undetected by all of the reliability subsystems discussed so far. Attempts to locate the underlying undiagnosable faults would be futile, and we must treat the database itself as the source of errors. Therefore, we will refer to the process of removing these errors as repair. Database reintegration, which follows, requires simply opening the database for transaction access.

Our aim is to repair the database automatically, by restoring its integrity. The repair is performed by the violation-action processor of the semantic integrity subsystem.

Database Repair Procedures. A classification of database repair procedures is shown in Fig. 1.17. The distinguished types of database repair procedures are discussed next in more detail.

Database Repair After Limited and Diagnosable Errors. If error propagation is limited and can be traced, there is a method, called here database patching, which can be used. *Database patching*[48] (cf. the backtracking algorithm in reference 173) consists of three steps, following the detection of an error. First, the original erroneous data are diagnosed and corrected, and the transaction that has written these data is determined by using the log. Next, the extent of the exposure resulting from the original error is determined. This is accomplished by identifying values and transactions that depended upon the error—that is, upon a value that was wrong and is now right or thought to be right. Third, for each transaction that had different input, it must be decided whether the difference affected the outcome of that transaction. If so, then it must be decided whether to undo the old transaction and rerun it to generate differences, or merely to compensate by means of another transaction. The results of the third step are examined to see which output data would have been different, and the second and third steps are repeated until no more transactions are affected.

If patching involves not a single site but a number of sites, a careful synchronization of repair actions at different sites is necessary to preserve their mutual consistency. Whether one or more sites are involved in the repair, the database entities to be patched should be locked for the duration of the repair process.

- Database Repair After Limited and Diagnosable Errors.
- Database Repair After an Extensive Damage or Undiagnosable Errors.
    - Local Database Repair.
    - Global Database Repair.

Fig. 1.17. A classification of IDIC procedures for database repair.

Database Repair After Extensive Damage or Undiagnosable Errors. Database patching is possible only if erroneous data can be identified, and requires that the database update history be recorded on the log in sufficient detail. Algorithms for database patching lose their appeal if the advantage of undoing only suspected transactions, and transactions depending on them, is outweighed by the long duration time of the restoration process. For example, certain errors can propagate widely throughout the database before they can be detected. In such cases, database patching is impossible, and the methods described next have to be used.

LOCAL DATABASE REPAIR. Database repair after damage to the database at a single site,* localized to this site, that is, using only information available at the site, is called local database repair. Non-local hosts could be required, at most, to abort uncommitted transactions involving the host under repair. This can be easily achieved if the two-phase commit protocol is used.[146] The goal of a local database repair is restoration of an integral (and consistent) database state. The techniques for restoration include the following:

1. *Rollback and recovery* (*RR*) *procedure:***[41] Rollback and recovery is defined as the process of periodically creating checkpoints of the database, reestablishment of the database, and reprocessing the log from the checkpoint to the point of error detection.

The rollback and recovery procedure records a checkpoint of the database without verification of whether the recorded state is acceptable or not. This can lead to restoration of an unacceptable state after a crash, which results in "re-creating" exactly the same crash a moment after database reintegration. Reintegration may fail if the restored checkpoint contains errors. In this case, the system might rollback once more to the second most recent checkpoint, and if the error persists, to earlier checkpoints.

2. *Database integrity block* (*DIB*) *scheme:*[115,116,117] In the DIB scheme, a checkpoint of a database state is recorded only after this state is verified as integral. Clearly, an integral checkpoint can still be erroneous. However, restoration of an unacceptable state happens less frequently with this scheme than for the rollback and recovery procedure. The DIB scheme relies on efficient implementations of checkpoints (see Section 7.3.1).

GLOBAL DATABASE REPAIR. If hidden errors have propagated over two or more sites, or when local restoration of an integral state at a site does not guarantee mutual consistency of all database sites, local repair is impossible. In

---

*Recall that a host, together with the remote storage it controls, is viewed as a single site.

**The term "rollback and recovery" is sometimes used in the literature in the broad sense as referring to any backward recovery mechanism.

this case, the mutual consistency of all sites can be ensured only by a synchronization of all checkpoints of local integral states. This solution is much more expensive.

The simplest solution to the checkpoint synchronization problem is the coordination of all local checkpoints so that all are taken in a period of time when no transaction is active, that is, in a quiescent system state. This *strongly synchronized solution* is extremely expensive.

There are two more efficient classes of solutions:[146] loosely synchronized solutions, which also require global checkpoints, but obtain them more efficiently, and nonsynchronized solutions, where global checkpoints are no longer necessary. The *loosely synchronized solutions* involve a slight modification of the transaction management system. For each transaction, its primary subtransaction is defined as the subtransaction running at the host when the transaction originated. The primary subtransaction assigns to each secondary subtransaction, that is, a subtransaction sent to another host, checkpoint number i of the last checkpoint performed locally. Host Y executing a secondary subtransaction checks to determine whether its local checkpoint number is equal to, less than, or greater than i, and starts the transaction, or puts it asleep until checkpoint number of host Y equals i, or rejects the transaction, respectively. This procedure guarantees that a set of all local checkpoints with the same number represents a global checkpoint.

The class of *nonsynchronized solutions* requires a more complex procedure. Let us suppose that a host A can only restore a checkpoint c_A. Given local restoration of c_A, the database is in a mutually consistent state if all global transactions for which A executed subtransactions after c_A are undone. The undoing of a transaction T implies the undoing of each transaction T' dependent on T. The set of transactions to be undone can be identified if special rules are followed.[125,146]

It is clear from this description that nonsynchronized solutions allow for the domino effect. Conditions for avoiding it can be specified,[96,98] but since the conditions require a loose synchronization, effectively the solution is reduced to a loosely synchronized class.

In another approach,[165] checkpoints are not synchronized most of the time, and synchronized only periodically, after the number of transactions that could be involved in the domino effect in case of a database failure exceeds a predefined limit.

For nonsynchronized solutions, each host is perfectly free to decide when to write its checkpoints, and hence not slowed down by synchronization. This advantage is paid for by a more complex restoration process and the necessity to undo uncommitted transactions and, sometimes, even canceling (via compensation—see below) committed ones. If the restoration is needed rarely and the real-time constraints are not critical, then the advantages of better performance in the normal mode could prevail.

The Costs of Database Repair. Database repair can be expensive even if it is automatic, especially if data deterioration is substantial. Thus, the problem of cost efficiency is critical. One way of reducing the costs relies on finding optimal intervals between database checkpoints and optimal checkpoint implementations (see Section 7.3.1).

Another attempt to optimize database reintegration costs tries to minimize the cost of restoration of a past integral database state, not by tuning the periods between checkpoints, but by making the integrity verification and repair techniques themselves more efficient.[115,117]

Canceling Committed Transactions. Database patching or restoration of a past integral database state may require undoing committed transactions. The only way of canceling the effects of a committed transaction is *compensation*—a new transaction is run to offset these effects.[79,118] Compensation of a transaction is possible if a reverse operation for each of its actions exists.[9] Many real-life actions seem to naturally come in pairs with reverse actions, e.g., deposits and withdrawals, credits and debits, issues and receipts, which makes compensation of these actions easy. But in most real-time systems, such as nuclear power plant control, monitoring intensive-care patients, etc. there are also cases of actions which are difficult to compensate or—even worse—irreversible.[86,113]

9. THE STATE OF THE ART AND DIRECTIONS FOR FURTHER WORK

During the last several years, research in this field has concentrated on the design of efficient algorithms for concurrency control in distributed database systems. We propose that concurrency control be considered as a part of a total reliability control system,[31] and supplemented with integrity control, transaction correctness control, transaction atomicity control, and reconfiguration control. This will lead toward robust distributed database systems that can provide non-stop transaction processing.

We believe that the following problems need attention in the next stage of research leading to the above goal:

1. *Integrity control:* Although some work has been done in specifying and monitoring integrity assertions, there is a further need to express the semantics of information represented by the database. In most applications, it is desirable to limit the cost of verifying integrity assertions to about 15% of the cost of normal processing. Research is needed to decrease such costs. We may have to look into hardware solutions, rather than purely software ones, to achieve this goal.

We will need to find algorithms and procedures to repair the database if its integrity is lost. Old versions may not be easily available and it is necessary to assign values to database entities that are compatible with integrity assertions. In general, this problem is NP-complete,[117] but we must find solutions that are based on heuristics and approximation.

2. *Transaction correctness control:* Beyond the mechanisms for verifying and testing a transaction, the system must depend on functionally equivalent alternate transactions and fair acceptance tests. Though this problem has been discussed in reference 28, the design of alternates and acceptance tests as well as the bypassing of transaction faults in an efficient manner still remain a challenge. In addition, minimization of partial undo/restart of a transaction based on the semantics of transaction processing needs further study.

3. *Transaction atomicity control:* To ensure the atomicity of a transaction at one site, the proposals of redo and undo logs are interesting. But writing on logs is expensive, and efficient mechanisms to save storage and access cost should be explored further. Empirical data on design alternatives for transaction logging are needed.

To ensure that a transaction is committed or aborted at all sites, a two-phase commit protocol has been proposed. This protocol has been extended[155] for handling host crashes. But the number of messages is increased by each additional phase of commitment. The reduction of message volume and its impact on the overall system performance require further studies.

4. *Concurrency control:* There is a need to study the performance of various concurrency control approaches. Though certain simulation and analytic results have appeared in the literature, it is necessary to obtain some empirical evidence on the viability of different approaches.

Moreover, our goal is to ensure robustness of the overall system. Certain concurrency control algorithms, such as the optimistic algorithm,[29] have nice resiliency features. Concurrency control algorithms that provide robustness in a natural way and can be integrated with other subsystems of the reliability control system should be investigated further. Also, ''special'' concurrency control protocols, such as consistency on demand protocols and creeping merge protocols for pseudo-partitioned systems, need to be studied.

5. *Reconfiguration control:* There is much research to be done on this subject. First of all, the operation of a host in an environment in which sites may fail arbitrarily has not been studied enough. We need to develop and compare the alternatives for robust adaptation/recovery protocols for host crashes in order to present system designers with a spectrum of choices. This study will require a more detailed classification of types of failures causing host crashes, so that the most efficient adaptation/recovery method can be selected for a given type of failure.

The research on partitioning should focus on robust adaptation/recovery protocols that will reduce the blocking of transaction processing. The design of compensating transactions and undo actions, in case optimistic commitment protocols are used, requires further study.

We believe that research on reliability in distributed database systems is at its most fertile stage. Questions of the level of availability of the system for transaction processing and the performance issues related to various subsystems of the reliability control system are of the utmost concern. We hope that the increased awareness of such issues, which have concerned practitioners for a long time, will bring about much needed theoretical and empirical studies. The words "The system is down" should not be heard too often.

Acknowledgment. We wish to thank Mr. Robert Amendola for drawing figures for this chapter.

GLOSSARY

Abort. Undoing a transaction before it is completed.

Acceptability. A practical standard for system behavior, lower than the ideal standard of correctness.[137] There are two criteria for expressing acceptability of a database state: transaction-consistency and integrity.

Acceptance check. A predicate on local transaction variables and database values, used to verify transaction acceptability.

Action. Execution of an operation.[77]

Attribute. The name of a domain of a relation (i.e., the name of a column in the table representing a relation).

Backing out a transaction. See: Undoing a transaction.

Backward recovery. Recovery based on restoration of a state that has preceded the crash (cf. Forward recovery).

Bypass. The first phase of adaptation. The ability of the system to react to a failure by either 1) reduction of its functional capabilities, or 2) slowing down its operation, or 3) replacement of the failed element by a stand-by element. In the first case, some functions of the failed elements are dispensed with. In the second case, some functions are passed to other elements substituting for the functions of these failed elements. Bypass is followed by a restart (cf. Restart).

Centralized control database system. A database system which consists of several computers, possibly dispersed in space, but controlled by a single central computer (cf. Centralized database system, Distributed database system).

Centralized database system. A database system which can access any data under its control without using external communications media (such as dedicated telephone links) (cf. Centralized control database system, Distributed database system).

Checkpoint. A mechanism that enables a system to restore a pre-defined past database state without using a copy of the entire database. For example, a checkpoint may record only database entities updated since the previous checkpoint. A checkpoint does not exist independently of the database (cf. Snapshot).

Commit action. The first action of a transaction which cannot be easily undone.

Commitment. a) Execution of the commit action by a transaction; b) The sequence of actions containing the commit action and all subsequent actions of a transaction.

Concurrency control. A subsystem responsible for correct (e.g., serializable) scheduling of concurrent transactions.

Concurrent execution of transactions. A schedule which allows two or more transactions to be under execution at the same moment. Actions of concurrent transactions are interleaved (cf. Serial execution of transactions).

Consistent database state. See: Transaction-consistent database state.

Correctness of a database/transaction. Absolute certainty that the database/transaction is perfect (faultless).

Crash. See: Failure.

Data acceptability. A practical standard of data quality (as opposed to the ideal correctness).

Data independence. A property of a program achieved when database reorganization does not make the program unusable.

Database. A collection of mutually related data stored more-or-less permanently in a computer.[166, 173]

Database generation. A version of the database created by a reorganization of the physical structure of its data.

Database integrity. A property of a database achieved when all integrity assertions defined for the database are satisfied.

Database management system. The software system facilitating user access to a database.

Database state. A function from names of database objects to values of database objects.[77]

Database system. A computer system constituted by DBMS together with an operating system and hardware underlying both DBMS and the operating system (CPU, memory, disks, etc.)

DBMS. See: Database management system.

Delayed assertion. An assertion that needs not be enforced immediately after an entity verified by it is updated.

Dependent transaction. A transaction whose writeset is affected by the writeset of a given transaction.

Diagnosable error. An error whose origin can be traced.

Diagnosable fault. A fault whose origin can be traced.

Distributed database system. Database system with several autonomous computers dispersed throughout space and connected by some external communication media (cf. Centralized control database system, Centralized database system).

Domain. A set of values for an attribute of a relation.

Entity. An element of a database state, i.e., the pair ⟨name of database object, value of database object⟩.[77]

Error. An incorrect entity or a piece of a program stored or transmitted within the system, or a lost entity or a piece of a program.[71]

Failure. The cessation of normal, timely operation by all or a part of the system, or delivery to the outside world of incorrect data. Detection of a fault or an error is viewed as a failure.[71]

Fault. A malfunction in a hardware, software, or human component of the system that may introduce errors or allow errors to be introduced. A fault causes a failure (a crash) either directly or through the errors it introduces.[71]

Fault-tolerant system. A system in which certain faults and errors are transparent to system operation.

Forward recovery. A recovery based on the restoration of a state that did not exist before the crash and could have been achieved if the crash did not occur (cf. Backward recovery).

History. The execution of a set of transactions by the system starting from some distinguished database state (e.g., the initial state).[77]

Host. The part of the system comprising all of the elements of the site except its secondary and lower levels of storage hierarchy. In particular, a host includes processors and memory.

Immediate assertion. An assertion that must or should be enforced immediately, as soon as an entity verified by the assertion is updated.

Integrity. See: Database integrity.

Integrity assertion. Basically, a predicate on database values that prohibits some combinations of database values. There are two types of assertions, structural and semantic (cf. Semantic integrity assertion and Structural integrity assertion).

Integral database state. A database state for which all integrity assertions defined on the database evaluate to TRUE.

Log. See: System log.

Memory. A fast memory.

Memory-resident database. A database that holds only temporarily data which are to be stored in the stable database. A memory-resident database is a buffer for the stable database.

Operation. Manipulation, such as reading or updating, of one or more entities.[77]

Permanent fault. A fault that cannot be avoided by the repetition of the failed operation. Faults of this nature are represented by program logic faults or many hardware faults (cf. Transient fault).

Read-only transaction. A transaction with no write operations. The writeset of a read-only transaction is empty (cf. Update transaction).

Readset. The collection of entities read from the database by a transaction (cf. Writeset).

Reintegration. The second phase of recovery. Actions to upgrade the level of system performance by returning a repaired element to the system. Reintegration follows repair (cf. Repair).

Relation. A subset of the Cartesian product of a list of domains (can be viewed as a two-dimensional table where rows are tuples and columns are named by attributes).

Repair. The first phase of recovery. Restoration of a damaged system element to a sound condition. A special case of repair is replacement, when the failed element is replaced by an intact element of the same or similar kind, which is not a stand-by (replacement by a stand-by constitutes bypass rather than repair). Repair is followed by reintegration (cf. Reintegration).

Restart. The second phase of adaptation. Resumption of (possibly degraded) system operation following a bypass (cf. Bypass).

Retrieval transaction. See: Read-only transaction.

Rollback. Actions of the system restoring a system state that has existed in the past. Rollback is possible only if a past state has been recorded and stored within the system. The three basic alternative implementations of rollback use snapshots, checkpoints, or a system log.

Rollbacking a transaction. See: Undoing a transaction.

Semantic integrity assertion. An integrity assertion which deals with the actual values stored in the database and enforces the semantics of the application universe (cf. Structural integrity assertion).

Serial execution of transactions. A schedule in which a next transaction may be started only after the previous one has been completed. This implies that, for any two transactions, the last action of one of the transactions must precede the first action of another (cf. Concurrent execution of transactions).

Serial history. A history in which transactions are executed serially.

Serializability. An operational criterion of correctness for a concurrency controller. The criterion allows for concurrent execution of transactions, but at the same time permits only such interleaving of their actions which results in the same effects on the database as a serial execution.

Serializable history. A history in which actions of transactions are serializable, i.e., a history equivalent in its effects on the database to a serial history.

Site. Each group of hardware elements residing at a location removed from the other groups of hardware elements, together with the associated software. A site may contain only a host, or only storage, or both. In case a host controls storage residing at a distant site, the term "site" may be used to refer to both the host and its storage.

Snapshot. A mechanism that enables the system to restore a pre-defined past database state using a copy of the entire database. A snapshot records *in extenso* this past database state. Once created, the shapshot exists independently of the database (cf. Checkpoint).[2, 141]

Stable database. See: Storage-resident database.

Storage. A part of the system comprising secondary storage and the lower levels of storage hierarchy.

Storage-resident database. The database residing on the secondary and the lower levels of storage hierarchy.

Structural integrity assertion. An assertion enforcing formal, structural constraints, such as functional dependencies, which follow from the data model used and are independent of the application universe (cf. Semantic integrity assertion).

Subtransaction. The part of a transaction executed in a distributed environment, which is run at a single host.

System log. A recording of actions that change database states. Restoration of a past state S can be achieved by using the log to undo every action following the state S. The order of undoing of the actions is the reverse of the order of their execution (last done, first undone).[77]

Transaction. An ordered sequence of actions (a process or a group of processes). A computer program is a static description of a transaction.

Transaction atomicity. A transaction property that guarantees that either all or none of the actions of a transaction are performed.

Transaction-consistent database state. The notion is defined recursively: an initial database state is transaction-consistent; any state obtained from a transaction-consistent state through its transformation by a serially executed transaction is transaction-consistent. In other words, given an initial transaction-consistent database state DBS_0, a database state DBS is transaction-consistent if and only if there exists a serial history which transforms DBS_0 into DBS.[57]

Transient fault. An abnormal condition represented by faults due to coincidences that produce rare system states, or due to malfunctioning hardware elements that operate correctly most of the time. Repetition of the operation that has failed due to a transient fault gives correct results with high probability (cf. Permanent fault).

Tuple. A member of a relation. A row in a relation represented as a table.

Undiagnosable error. An error of unknown origin.

Undiagnosable fault. A fault of unknown origin.

Undoing a transaction. Erasing all effects of the transaction from the database.

Update. Result of a write action, i.e., modification of values of entities or insertion/deletion of entities.

Update transaction. A transaction that includes write operations, i.e., a transaction with a non-empty writeset (cf. Read-only transaction).

Volatile database. See: Memory-resident database.

Writeset. The collection of entities updated by a transaction (cf. Readset).

APPENDIX: EXAMPLE PROTOCOLS

A1. EXAMPLES OF CC ADAPTATION PROCEDURES FOR HOST CRASHES

A1.1. Protocol of Kaneko et al. The protocol of Kaneko *et al.*[95] guarantees that a crash of a host or of communication lines adjacent to a host, occurring at logical time k, blocks logical time for all other hosts at $k + 1$. A physical-time timer limits the duration of a logical time unit, and simultaneously supports detection of host and communication line crashes. Once a configuration failure is detected, a "*degradation procedure*" is entered. An adaptation procedure is initialized when a failure of Host i is detected by Host j at logical time k. The list of all the up hosts is then circulated by Host j. All transactions that, at logical time k, were running at Host i are backed out to their respective latest checkpoints and all other transactions are backed out to logical time $k - 1$. Now the system resumes processing from the logical instance $k - 1$.

A1.2. Protocol of Thomas (Majority Consensus Algorithm). The majority consensus algorithm[164] adapts to host crashes in a completely replicated database by relying on the *persistent communication* mechanism and on distributed control that is more crash-resistant than centralized control. Only a majority of hosts is required for proper system operation, and hosts necessary for a majority consensus need not be simultaneously available. It is advantageous that the robust behavior of the algorithm does not require detection of host crashes and switching into a special adaptation mode of operation.

A1.3. Protocol of Menasce, Popek, and Muntz (Centralized Locking Protocol). In the *Centralized Lock Controller* protocol,[127] the central lock manager—called the *lock controller* (*LC*)—maintains control data, among them the *up list*. The up list contains identifiers of all sites that are seen as accessible by the LC. Note that a site can already be inaccessible but still be on the up list. Every time a site is found to be inaccessible, it is dropped from the up list and simultaneously all transactions that have at least one active lock on the data of the crashed site are aborted and the locks are released. Thus, for a blocked transaction, the question "wait or abort?" is answered "abort."

A2. EXAMPLES OF CC ADAPTATION PROTOCOLS FOR PARTITIONINGS

A2.1. Protocol of Thomas (Majority Consensus Algorithm). Treatment of a partitioning in the *majority consensus algorithm*[164] for a completely replicated database relies on the need for a majority consensus before any update can be committed. Hence, partitions with less than a majority of hosts cannot accept any request.

The disadvantage of this approach is that it allows for situations when none of the partitions has a majority of sites and hence none of them is operational.

A2.2. Protocol of Hammer and Shipman (RelNet Scheme). The possibility of partitioning is ignored in the *RelNet scheme*.[85] However, it is indicated that the violation of this assumption results in a RelNet catastrophe, known as *partitioning catastrophe*.

A2.3. Protocol of Menasce, Popek, and Muntz (Centalized Lock Controller). Menasce *et al.*[127] propose *centralized locking protocol* for concurrency control. Each partition has a single central manager, the *lock controller* (*LC*), that survives partitioning in one of the partitions and is regenerated in the other. The basic idea of the adaptation algorithm is that of *entities local* to a partition, that is, entities that have all of their physical copies within the partition. *Transactions* that are *local* to a partition, that is, access only local data, continue to be serviced as if no partitioning has occurred. Other transactions are blocked. LCs in each partition are responsible for maintaining internal consistency.

The most severe shortcoming of this protocol seems to be that the higher the replication of a database, the worse system performance is during partitioning. In the extreme, for fully replicated databases, the protocol is completely useless during partitioning—no data are then local to any partition and all transactions are blocked.

A2.4. Protocol of Minoura and Wiederhold (True-Copy Token Scheme). The partitioning problem in the *true-copy token scheme*[129] is solved by the use of so-called *true-copy tokens*. Among multiple copies of an entity, only one—called *true copy*—owns the token. During normal system operation, a transaction may access only true copies. The rule does not change when the system is partitioned. The only difference is that some transactions are blocked if true copies they need are not accessible within their partition (a similar case can occur in a fully connected system in which some hosts have crashed). In that way, no entity can be accessed in more than one partition. This prevents any conflicts among partitions.

A3. EXAMPLES OF RC HOST RECOVERY PROTOCOLS

A3.1. Protocol of Kaneko *et al.* Kaneko *et al.*[95] use the notion of logical time. Suppose that a host crash is detected at logical time k. First, all transactions that have made updates only at the crashed host before its crash are backed out to their respective latest checkpoints, and all transactions running at the crashed host, that made updates also at other hosts, are backed out to the logical time $k - 1$. Next, the logical time of a working host is obtained. All working hosts are ordered to stop at logical time t, where t is selected in such a way that the message with the order is guaranteed to reach each host before t. After halting the system, the log of all updates since logical time $k - 1$ until logical time t is obtained from a working host. The log is used to update and to correct the data of the recovering host. Last, all working hosts are identified and regular processing is restarted at logical time t.

A3.2. Protocol of Thomas (Majority Consensus Algorithm). *Memory loss recovery* for the majority consensus concurrency control algorithm[164] in the completely replicated database environment is tailored to its specifics. Memory recovery procedure requires that a recovering host must 1) recover all updates which the whole distributed database system has accepted, and has not forgotten since the point of its memory loss, and 2) recover all *unresolved update requests*, that is, requests still under voting, which it has voted on since the point of its memory loss. In general, a recovering host must interact with every other host in order to guarantee that all of the information it has lost is obtained again.

Let us discuss the recovery protocol in more detail. A host has "lost memory" if it has forgotten updates that have been accepted, or if it has forgotten how it has voted on currently unresolved update requests, that is, requests neither accepted nor rejected. Memory loss can result in malfunctioning of the majority consensus algorithm if: 1) a host votes for accepting a request that conflicts with accepted updates it has forgotten, or 2) when asked to vote on an unresolved request it has previously voted on and forgotten, a host votes differently.

It is assumed that, by itself, a host M has no way of determining whether it has lost memory, that memory loss occurs as a result of some catastrophic event at the host, and that in such a case, information critical to host operation is restored by a human operator from a backup tape. Whenever information is backed up in this way, Host M is signaled that it has lost memory. Host M can determine the point of memory loss by reading the timestamp of, for instance, the last update accepted at any other host that is recorded on its backup copy.

The recovery procedure consists of two passes. On the first pass, Host M informs every host that it is trying to recover from a memory loss. Each host acknowledges this message. Recovery can proceed only after all hosts answer. (This requirement makes the recovery procedures not robust.) Then, every host temporarily stops forwarding to other hosts unresolved requests that have been voted on by Host M.

On the second pass, Host M requests from each other host in turn information concerning updates accepted since the point of memory loss of M and unresolved update requests voted on by M. If, on the second pass, M encounters a host that is unaware that M is engaged in memory recovery, then this host has lost its memory since the first recovery pass. Should M encounter such a host, it must abort the second pass of recovery and restart its memory recovery. Otherwise, a pathological system behavior can occur, namely, an unresolved request voted on by M can remain active in the system without ever being recovered by M. When M successfully completes the second pass, it can participate as a voting member of the system. A disadvantage of this host recovery procedure is that it requires human intervention to restore critical information after a memory loss.

A3.3. Protocol of Menasce, Popek, and Muntz (Single Node Recovery). Menasce *et al.*[126] specify a host recovery procedure—called *single node recovery* (*SNR*)—in the context of centralized locking update strategy. SNR logically connects a recovering host to the system or to a partition. The first step encompasses finding out the identity of the central manager—called the *lock controller* (*LC*)—of the system or partition that keeps the up list. The LC is informed that the recovery host is alive again. If the LC can be found, it sends to the recovering host all the lock or lock release requests for which not all acknowledgments have been received—the LC knows that some hosts could miss these messages. (We assume that all remote updates covered by the lock being released are passed piggyback with the lock release request.) It is the task of the LC, and not of the host of the origin, to ensure execution of all these remote updates. No request can be blocked by a crashed host, unless this host is still on the up list, which increases protocol robustness. We need to consider the following two cases now:

1. The recovering host is still on the up list.
   In this case, no lock request can be granted as long as the recovering host, believed to be up, does not respond; thus no update can be executed by any other host since an update must follow lock granting. Also, any lock release request, together with all of the remote updates it carries, is blocked as long as the recovering host does not respond. Hence, no updates are possible when a recovering host that is down—but still on the up list—does not respond.
2. The recovering host is not on the up list.
   In this case, some updates can be processed by other hosts while this host is down. During recovery, these updates have to be communicated, to restore the mutual consistency of the recovering host with the other hosts. That requirement is fulfilled by sending to the recovering host all lock release messages (carrying piggyback update information), for which not all acknowledgements have been received.

After these actions, the recovering host becomes a part of the system again.

If no LC can be found by the recovering host, then the recovering host becomes a partition on its own; an LC is started at the host.

A3.4. Protocol of Bhargava (Optimistic Approach). In the protocol of Bhargava,[29] each transaction goes through a validation phase to ensure both the correctness of concurrent execution and integrity. After successful verification, a transaction is considered to be in a *semi-commit state*. The updates of semi-committed transactions are kept in a private working space.

A *dynamic conflict graph* (*DCG*), whose nodes represent transactions and edges represent serializability conflicts, is maintained. Correct concurrency control is ensured by maintaining acyclicity of the DCG. The integrity of its update is checked using the assertions of IDIC.

A transaction is sent to all hosts for validation. If the validation is successful at all hosts, the transaction is committed, otherwise it is aborted.

If a host crashes, all semi-committed transactions are considered aborted unless they have been saved on the log. On host recovery, committed transactions are obtained from other hosts.

A3.5. Protocol of Minoura and Wiederhold (True Copy Token Scheme).

Presentation of a host recovery procedure in the *true-copy token scheme*[129] must be preceded by the definition of a few notions. A set of physical entities that covers the complete set of logical entities in the system and is always updated atomically constitutes an *atomic update set* (*AUS*). Multiple AUSs are provided. In general, AUSs are not disjoint—for example, a single physical entity representing a logical entity could belong to all AUSs—and their member physical entities can reside at different hosts.

A *merge* operation on a collection of AUSs is defined as the function that associates with each logical entity its newest version found in this collection of AUSs. The scheme uses *version numbers* which facilitates merging.

A host crash is treated as a crash of an AUS containing entities residing at the host (for simplicity, we will not consider the case when more than one AUS is impaired by a single host crash). When a host is to be reintegrated (and no other hosts of the atomic update set are failed), its complete AUS has to be restored. An AUS is restored by inserting it into the system or a working partition after restoring all values of its physical entities by a merge of the AUSs in the system. Also, a more efficient method can be employed: values of physical entities are copied from one working AUS.

A4. EXAMPLES OF RC MERGE PROTOCOLS

A4.1. Protocol of Kaneko *et al.*

In the protocol of Kaneko *et al.*,[95] recovery erases all updates done in one of the partitions being merged. Only the updates executed in the other partition survive the merge. Thus, this approach allows updating effectively in one partition only, but at the cost of backing out all the updates of the other partition, which is not cost efficient.

A4.2. Protocol of Menasce, Popek, and Muntz (Logical Component Merge).

Menasce *et al.*[127] propose a recovery mechanism called the *logical component merge* (*LCM*). Merge of partitions is always done pairwise between partitions. Each partition has a central manager—the *lock controller* (*LC*). The LC keeps the up list. The list can lag behind the list of hosts which are actually reachable because of delayed detection of configuration failures. The subsystem indicated by the up list constitutes a *logical partition*. Recall that the transactions that need to access entities, such that all the physical copies of these entities are stored at hosts included in the up list, are called *local transactions*.

In the merge process, the LC of one of the partitions plays an active role while the other is passive. The LCM is divided into two phases, namely a *reconnection phase* and a *merge phase*.

In the reconnection phase, each LC periodically sends a message to every host not on its up list to detect the existence of hosts that were not reachable before but were up. If such a host is detected by the message, its corresponding LC is identified by the message sender. Without considering all the details of the protocol, let us focus our attention on a potentially dangerous situation. Let us suppose that two logical partitions to be merged are P1 and P2 with LCs denoted LC1 and LC2 and with up lists U1 and U2, respectively. There is a possibility that the set U2′ = U2 ∩ U1 is not empty, that is, LC2 has not sensed yet that some hosts in U2′ are claimed to belong to another partition—meaning that, if the claim is true, the up list of LC2 is not an actual up list. All the locks active in LC2 recorded in the lock table of LC2, that are not local with respect to the up list U2 − U1, are released and the corresponding transactions are aborted. Next, the up list U2 is sent to LC1, which releases all the locks in its lock table that are not local with respect to the up list U1 − U2.

The protocol is pessimistic when it releases all locks held on hosts U1 ∩ U2. Let us explain this statement.

EXAMPLE:

Suppose that U1 ∩ U2 = {H1, H2} and that actually H1 belonged to U1 and H2 to U2. Neither transactions run in Partition P1 and using H1, nor transactions run in Partition P2 and using H2 violate consistency—they are local to their respective partitions.

As shown in the example, the solution of Menasce *et al.* satisfies sufficient but more than necessary conditions for mutual consistency. The main disadvantage, beyond lowered efficiency, of the protocol is that it may require aborts of already committed transactions. To be sure, no transaction "using" a host actually not reachable within a partition can be finished, because the inaccessibility of the host is always detected prior to the receipt of any message from this host. But this does not prevent a transaction using a host actually within a partition and on the up list of another partition (as with H1 of P1 in the above example) from committing.

The only gain of this approach seems to be avoiding the necessity to identify to which partition elements of U1 ∩ U2 actually belong. And the identification is not too difficult for hosts which were used by at least one transaction during partitioning. The "unused" hosts can be ignored—even if they are dropped from both up lists, this does not cause any transaction aborts.

Summarizing, the protocol erases all conflicts between a pair of partitions by aborting transactions thought to be local but actually not local—pessimistically, even some local transactions are aborted. Thus, only the results of transactions actually local to a partition, but not all local transactions, survive recovery.

After the logical connection is established between two LCs, they do not accept any new requests from hosts in their own partitions and complete all outstanding ones. In the second phase—*merge*—the union of the lock tables at both partitions is constructed. There is no need for circulating surviving updates executed in the partitioned state, as only local updates are allowed during partitionings and consistently recorded in each "old" partition of the "new" partition. Now, the LC that played an active role during LCM becomes the LC of the new logical partition and normal processing is resumed.

A4.3. Protocol of Davidson and Garcia-Molina (Optimistic Protocol). Davidson and Garcia-Molina[49] in their *optimistic protocol* also designate exactly one host per partition as the coordinator. When a host in a partition P1 discovers that it can communicate with a host in another partition P2, coordinators in P1 and P2 are notified, and local processing in each partition ceases. The coordinator in each group examines the local histories of each host in its group and forms an equivalent serial partition-global history. This history summarizes transactions performed and their relative order within a partition. (The serial partition-global history is guaranteed to exist under the assumption of correctness of the update protocol within each partition—correct protocol guarantees serializability, that is, equivalence to a serial history.)

Next, a so-called *precedence graph* is constructed from the serial partition-global histories h1 of P1 and h2 of P2. In this graph, nodes represent transactions and conflicts are represented by cycles. By undoing certain transactions, the graph can be made acyclic, thus resolving all conflicts between the partitions. The partitions P1 and P2 are then merged by sending update messages of "surviving," that is not undone, transactions of P1 to P2 and vice versa. A new coordinator is elected for the merged partition. This restores consistency in the single, larger partition P1 $\cup$ P2. The regular transaction processing is resumed.

Minimization of the number of transactions to be undone can be achieved by intelligent selection of transactions.

A4.4. Protocol of Bhargava (Optimisitic Approach). In the protocol of Bhargava[29] (for a description see A3.4), during partitioning transactions in each partition can reach a semi-commit state. Some of these transactions are committed by using the true-copy token mechanism. If a transaction can be undone or compensated, it is committed but a warning is given to users accessing its results.

On a merge of the partitions, all semi-committed transactions are sent for validation to the hosts from "foreign" partitions. If a cycle in the DCG appears on any host, some of the semi-committed transactions are undone in such a manner that the cost of reprocessing of transactions is minimized.

A4.5. Protocol of Minoura and Wiederhold (True-Copy Token Scheme). The adaptation mode of the scheme given by Minoura and Wiederhold[129] ensures that no logical entity is accessed in more than one partition, which makes a merge simple. When reconnection among partitions is restored, all physical entities within the new partition are set to a consistent state defined by the newest values of data from the old partitions. This effectively performs remote updates delayed during partitioning.

REFERENCES

1. Adiba, M., et al., Issues in distributed data base management systems: A technical overview, *Proc. 4th Int. Conf. on Very Large Data Bases*, West Berlin, Sept. 1978, pp. 89–105.
2. Adiba, M. E. and B. G. Lindsay, *Database Snapshots*, IBM Res. Rep. RJ2772, IBM Res. Lab., San Jose, CA, March 1980.
3. Adrion, W. R., M. A. Branstad, and J. C. Cherniavsky, Validation, verification, and testing of computer software, *ACM Comput. Surveys*, Vol. 14, pp. 159–192, June 1982.
4. Aghili, H. and D. G. Severance, A practical guide to the design of differential files for recovery of on-line databases, *ACM Trans. Database Syst.*, Vol. 7, pp. 540–565, Dec. 1982.

5. Alsberg, P. A. and J. D. Day, A principle for resilient sharing of distributed resources, *Proc. 2nd Int. Conf. Software Eng.*, San Francisco, CA, Oct. 1976, pp. 562–570.
6. Anderson, D. R., Data base processor technology, *Proc. AFIPS National Computer Conf. 1976*, New York, NY, June 1976, pp. 811–818.
7. Anderson, T. and R. Kerr, Recovery blocks in action: A system supporting high reliability, *Proc. 2nd Int. Conf. on Software Eng.*, San Francisco, CA, Oct. 1976, pp. 447–457.
8. Anderson, T. and J. C. Knight, A framework for software fault tolerance in real-time systems, *IEEE Trans. Software Eng.*, Vol. SE-9, pp. 355–364, May 1983.
9. Archer, Jr., J. E., R. Conway, and F. B. Schneider, User recovery and reversal in interactive systems, *ACM Trans. Programming Languages and Syst.*, Vol. 6, pp. 1–19, January 1984.
10. Astrahan, M. M. et al., System A: A relational data base management system, *IEEE Computer*, Vol. 12, pp. 42–48, May 1979.
11. Attar, A., P. A. Bernstein, and N. Goodman, Site initialization, recovery, and backup in a distributed database system, *IEEE Trans. Software Eng.*, Vol. SE-10, pp. 645–650, Nov. 1984.
12. Avizienis A. Fault-tolerant systems, *IEEE Trans. Computers*, Vol. C-25, pp. 1304–1312, Dec. 1976.
13. Avizienis, A. and J. P. J. Kelly, Fault tolerance by design diversity: Concepts and experiments, *IEEE Computer*, Vol. 17, pp. 67–80, Aug. 1984.
14. Badal, D. Z. and G. J. Popek, Cost and performance analysis of semantic integrity validation methods, *Proc. ACM-SIGMOD Int. Conf. on Management of Data*, Boston, MA, May–June 1979, pp. 109–115.
15. Balter, R. Selection of a commitment and recovery mechanism for a distributed transactional system, *Proc. Symp. on Reliability in Distributed Software and Database Syst.*, Pittsburgh, PA, July 1981, pp. 21–26.
16. Barsi, F., F. Grandoni, and P. Maestrini, A theory of diagnosability of digital systems, *IEEE Trans. Computers*, Vol. C-25, pp. 585–593, June 1976.
17. Bayer, R., H. Heller, and A. Reiser, Parallelism and recovery in database systems, *ACM Trans. Database Syst.*, Vol. 5, pp. 139–156, June 1980.
18. Bellon, C. and A. G. Saucier, Protection against external errors in a dedicated system, *IEEE Trans. Computers*, Vol. C-31, pp. 311–317, April 1982.
19. Bernstein, P. A., D. W. Shipman, and W. S. Wong, Formal aspects of serializability in database concurrency control, *IEEE Trans. Software Eng.*, Vol. SE-5, pp. 203–216, May 1979.
20. Bernstein, P. A. and N. Goodman, Approaches to concurrency control in distributed data base systems, *Proc. AFIPS National Computer Conf. 1979*, New York, NY, June 1979, pp. 813–820.
21. Bernstein, P. A., D. W. Shipman, and J. B. Rothnie Jr., Concurrency control in a system for distributed databases (SDD-1), *ACM Trans. Database Syst.*, Vol. 5, pp. 18–51, March 1980.
22. Bernstein, P. A., B. T. Blaustein, and E. M. Clarke, Fast maintenance of semantic integrity assertions using redundant aggregate data, *Proc. 6th Int. Conf. on Very Large Data Bases*, Montreal, Canada, Oct. 1980, pp. 126–136.
23. Bernstein, P. A. and N. Goodman, Concurrency control in distributed database systems, *ACM Comput. Surveys*, Vol. 13, pp. 185–221, June 1981.
24. Bhargava, B., An optimistic concurrency control algorithm and its performance evaluation against locking, *Proc. Int. Computer Symp.*, Taipei, Republic of China, Dec. 1980, pp. 314–327.
25. Bhargava, B., Software reliability in real-time systems, *Proc. AFIPS National Computer Conf. 1981*, Chicago, IL, May 1981, pp. 297–309.

26. Bhargava, B. and L. Lilien, Feature analysis of selected database recovery techniques, *Proc. AFIPS National Computer Conf. 1981*, Chicago, IL, May 1981, pp. 543-554.
27. Bhargava, B. and L. Lilien, On optimal scheduling of integrity assertions in a transaction processing system, *Int. J. Computer and Inform. Sci.*, Vol. 10, pp. 315-330, Oct. 1981.
28. Bhargava, B. and C. Hua, Cost analysis of a recovery block scheme and its implementation issues, *Int. J. Computer and Inform. Sci.*, Vol. 10, pp. 359-382, Dec. 1981.
29. Bhargava, G., Resiliency features of the optimistic concurrency control approach for distributed database systems, *Proc. 2nd Symp. on Reliability in Distributed Software and Database Syst.*, Pittsburgh, PA, July 1982, pp. 19-32.
30. Bhargava, B. and L. Lilien, Time complexity of database verification and recovery, *Proc. Int. Computer Symp. ICS 82*, Taichung, Republic of China, vol. 1, pp. 229-238, Dec. 1982.
31. Bhargava, B., Guest editorial: Reliability issues in distributed systems, *IEEE Trans. Software Eng.*, Vol. SE-8, pp. 165-167, May 1982.
32. Bhargava, B. and L. Lilien, Cost analysis of selected database restoration techniques, in *Entity-Relationship Approach to Software Engineering*, ed. C. G. Davis et al., pp. 783-805, New York, NY: North-Holland, 1983.
33. Bhargava, B., Performance evaluation of reliability control algorithms for distributed database systems, *J. Systems and Software*, Vol. 4, pp. 239-264, July 1984.
34. Bhargava, B., Concurrency control and reliability in distributed database systems, in *Software Engineering Handbook*, ed. C. V. Ramamoorthy and C. Vick. New York, NY: Van Nostrand and Reinhold, 1984.
35. Buneman, O. P. and E. K. Clemons, Efficiently monitoring relational databases, *ACM Trans. Database Syst.*, Vol. 4, pp. 368-382, Sept. 1979.
36. Burrow, L. D., The 'Fail Soft' design of complex systems, *Proc. Int. Conf. on Distributed Computer Control Syst.*, University of Aston, Birmingham, U.K., 1977, pp. 151-156.
37. Bux, W. et al., *A reliable token-ring system for local-area communication*, IBM Res. Rep. RZ 1095, IBM Zurich Res. Lab., Ruschlikon, Switzerland, Sept. 1981.
38. Champine, G. A., Current trends in data base systems, *IEEE Computer*, Vol. 12, pp. 27-41, May 1979.
39. Chandy, K. M. and C. V. Ramamoorthy, Rollback and recovery strategies for computer programs, *IEEE Trans. Computers*, Vol. C-21, pp. 546-556, June 1972.
40. Chandy, K. M., J. C. Browne, C. W. Dissly, and W. R. Uhrig, Analytic models for rollback and recovery strategies in data base systems, *IEEE Trans. Software Eng.*, Vol. SE-1, pp. 100-110, March 1975.
41. Chandy, K. M., A survey of analytic models of rollback and recovery strategies, *IEEE Computer*, Vol. 8, pp. 40-47, May 1975.
42. Chou, C. and M. T. Liu, A concurrency control mechanism and crash recovery for a distributed database system (DLDBS), in *Distributed Data Bases*, ed. C. Delobel and W. Litwin, pp. 201-214, Amsterdam, Holland: North-Holland, 1980.
43. Chuang, H. Y. H., Analysis of recovery block scheme with internal error detection, *Proc. Int. Computer Symp.*, Taipei, Republic of China, Dec. 1980, pp. 724-730.
44. Chwa, K-Y. and S. L. Hakimi, On fault identification in diagnosable systems, *IEEE Trans. Computers*, Vol. C-30, pp. 414-422, June 1981.
45. Cristian, F., Exception handling and software fault-tolerance, *IEEE Trans. Computers*, Vol. C-31, pp. 531-539, June 1982.
46. Cristian, F., Correct and robust programs, *IEEE Trans. Software Eng.*, Vol. SE-10, pp. 163-174, March 1984.
47. Crus, R. A., Data recovery in IBM Database 2, *IBM Systems J.*, Vol. 23, pp. 178-188, 1984.
48. Davies, C. T., Data processing spheres of control, *IBM Systems J.*, Vol. 17, pp. 179-198, 1978.

49. Davidson, S. B. and H. Garcia-Molina, Protocols for partitioned distributed database systems, *Proc. Symp. on Reliability in Distributed Software and Database Syst.*, Pittsburgh, PA, July 1981, pp. 145–149.
50. Davidson, S. B., Optimism and consistency in partitioned distributed database systems, *ACM Trans. Database Syst.*, Vol. 9, pp. 456–481, Sept. 1984.
51. Denning, P. J., Fault-tolerant operating systems, *ACM Comput. Surveys*, Vol. 8, pp. 359–389, Dec. 1976.
52. Dolev, D. and H. R. Strong, Distributed commit with bounded waiting, *Proc. 2nd Symp. on Reliability in Distributed Software and Database Syst.*, Pittsburgh, PA, July 1982, pp. 53–60.
53. Eastman, C. M. and G. M. E. Lafue, *Semantic Integrity Transactions in Design Databases*, Tech. Rep. LCSR-TR-20, Lab. for Comput. Sci., Rutgers–The State University of New Jersey, New Brunswick, N.J., October 1981.
54. Edelberg, M., Data base contamination and recovery, *Proc. of ACM SIGMOD Workshop on Data Description, Access and Control*, Ann Arbor, MI, May 1974, pp. 419–430.
55. Endres, A., An analysis of errors and their causes in systems programs, *IEEE Trans. Software Eng.*, Vol. SE-1, pp. 140–149, June 1975.
56. Eswaran, K. P. and D. D. Chamberlin, *Functional Specifications of a Subsystem for Data Base Integrity*, IBM Rep. RJ 1601, IBM Res. Lab., San Jose, CA, June 1975.
57. Eswaran, K. P., *Specifications, Implementations, and Interactions of a Trigger Subsystem in an Integrated Database System*, IBM Rep. RJ 1820, IBM Res. Lab., San Jose, CA, August 1976.
58. Eswaran, K. P., J. N. Gray, R. Lorie, and A. Traiger, The notions of consistency and predicate locks in a database system, *CACM*, Vol. 19, pp. 624–633, Nov. 1976.
59. Fernandez, E. B. and R. C. Summers, Integrity aspects of a shared data base, *Proc. AFIPS National Computer Conf. 1976*, pp. 819–827, New York, NY, June 1976.
60. Fischer, M. J., N. D. Griffeth, and N. A. Lynch, Global states of a distributed system, *IEEE Trans. Software Eng.*, Vol. SE-8, pp. 198–202, May 1982.
61. Florentin, J. J., Consistency auditing of databases, *Computer J.*, Vol. 17, pp. 52–58, Feb. 1974.
62. Fong, E. and S. R. Kimbleton, Database semantic integrity for a network data manager, *Proc. AFIPS National Computer Conf. 1980*, Anaheim, CA, May 1980, pp. 261–268.
63. Fried, R., Monitoring data integrity, *Datamation*, Vol. 24, pp. 176–181, June 1978.
64. Galtieri, C. A. *Architecture for a Consistent Decentralized System*, IBM Res. Rep. RJ2846, IBM Res. Lab., San Jose, CA, June 1980.
65. Garcia-Molina, H., Elections in a distributed computing system, *IEEE Trans. Computers*, Vol. C-31, pp. 48–59, Jan. 1982.
66. Garcia-Molina, H., Using semantic knowledge for transaction processing in a distributed database, *ACM Trans. Database Syst.*, Vol. 8, pp. 186–213, June 1983.
67. Gardarin, G., Integrity, consistency, concurrency, reliability in distributed database management systems, in *Distributed Data Bases*, ed. C. Delobel and W. Litwin, pp. 335–351, Amsterdam, Holland: North-Holland, 1980.
68. Gardarin, G. and W. W. Chu, A distributed control algorithm for reliably and consistently updating replicated databases, *IEEE Trans. Computers*, Vol. C-29, pp. 1060–1068, Dec. 1980.
69. Gelenbe, E. and D. Derochette, Performance of rollback recovery systems under intermittent failures, *CACM*, Vol. 21, pp. 493–499, June 1978.
70. Gelenbe, E., On the optimum checkpoint interval, *J. ACM*, Vol. 26, pp. 259–270, April 1979.
71. Gibbons, T., *Integrity and Recovery*, Rochelle Park, NJ: Hayden Book Company, 1976.

72. Gilb, T., *Software Metrics*, Cambridge, MA: Winthrop Publishers, 1977.
73. Gilb, T., and Weinberg, *Humanized Input*, Cambridge, MA: Winthrop Publishers, 1977.
74. Giordano, N. J. and M. S. Schwartz, Data base recovery at CMIC, *ACM SIGMOD Int. Conf. on Management of Data*, Washington, D.C., 1976, pp. 33–42.
75. Gravina, C. M., National Westminster Bank mass storage archiving, *IBM Systems J.*, Vol. 17, pp. 344–358, 1978.
76. Gray, J., Notes on data base operating systems, in *Lecture Notes in Computer Science 60. Operating Systems, an Advanced Course*, ed. R. Bayer et al., pp. 393–481, New York, NY: Springer-Verlag, 1978.
77. Gray, J. N., *A Transaction Model*, IBM Res. Rep. RJ 2895, IBM Res. Div. San Jose Lab., San Jose, CA, Feb. 1980.
78. Gray, J. N., Review of the paper "The application of data types to database semantic integrity," *Computing Rev.*, Vol. 22, p. 162, April 1981.
79. Gray, J., et al., The recovery manager of the System R database manager, *ACM Comput. Surveys*, Vol. 13, pp. 223–242, June 1981.
80. Gremillion, L. L., Determinants of program repair maintenance requirements, *CACM*, Vol. 27, pp. 826–832, Aug. 1984.
81. Haerder, T. and A. Reuter, Principles of transaction-oriented database recovery, *ACM Comput. Surveys*, Vol. 15, pp. 287–317, Dec. 1983.
82. Hakimi, S. L. and K. Nakajima, On adaptive system diagnosis, *IEEE Trans. Computers*, Vol. C-33, pp. 234–240, March 1984.
83. Hammer, M. M. and D. J. McLeod, Semantic integrity in a relational data base system, *Proc. Int. Conf. on Very Large Data Bases*, Framingham, MA, Sept. 1975, pp. 25–42.
84. Hammer, M. and S. K. Sarin, Efficient monitoring of database systems, *Proc. ACM-SIGMOD Int. Conf. on Management of Data*, Austin, TX, May–June 1978, p. 159.
85. Hammer, M. and D. Shipman, Reliability mechanisms for SDD-1: A system for distributed databases, *ACM Trans. Database Syst.*, Vol. 5, pp. 431–466, Dec. 1980.
86. Hebalkar, P. G., Application specification for distributed data base systems, *Proc. 4th Int. Conf. on Very Large Data Bases*, West Berlin, Sept. 1978, pp. 442–449.
87. Hecht, H., Fault-tolerant software for real-time applications, *ACM Comput. Surveys*, Vol. 8, pp. 391–407, Dec. 1976.
88. Hecht, H., Effectiveness measures for distributed systems, *Proc. Symp. on Reliability in Distributed Software and Database Syst.*, Pittsburgh, PA, July 1981, pp. 185–188.
89. Hecht, H. and J. D. Gabbe, Shadowed management of free disk pages with a linked list, *ACM Trans. Database Syst.*, Vol. 8, pp. 503–514, Dec. 1983.
90. Hong, Y. C. and S. Y. W. Su, Associative hardware and software techniques for integrity control, *ACM Trans. Database Syst.*, Vol. 6, pp. 416–440, Sept. 1981.
91. Hosseini, S. H., J. G. Kuhl, and S. M. Reddy, A diagnosis algorithm for distributed computing systems with dynamic failure and repair, *IEEE Trans. Computers*, Vol. C-33, pp. 223–233, March 1984.
92. Howden, W. E., Validation of scientific programs, *ACM Comput. Surveys*, Vol. 14, pp. 193–227, June 1982.
93. Hua, C. T. *Verification of Concurrency Control Algorithms for Distributed Database Systems*, (Ph.D. Diss.) University of Pittsburgh, Pittsburgh, PA, 1981.
94. Jarke, M. and J. Koch, Query optimization in database systems," *ACM Comput. Surveys*, Vol. 16, pp. 11–152, June 1984.
95. Kaneko, A., Y. Nishihara, K. Tsuruoka, and M. Hattori, Logical clock synchronization method for duplicated database control, *Proc. 1st Int. Conf. on Distributed Computing Syst.*, Huntsville, AL, Oct. 1979, pp. 601–611.
96. Kant, K. and A. Silberschatz, Error recovery in concurrent processes, *Proc. Computer Software and Applications Conf. COMPSAC 80*, Chicago, IL, Oct. 1980, pp. 608–614.

97. Kaunitz, J. and L. Van Ekert, Audit trail compaction for database recovery, *CACM*, Vol. 27, pp. 678–683, July 1984.
98. Kim, K. H., An implementation of a programmer-transparent scheme for coordinating concurrent processes in recovery, *Proc. Computer Software and Applications Conf. COMPSAC 80*, Chicago, IL, Oct. 1980, pp. 615–621.
99. Kim, K. H., Approaches to mechanization of the conversation scheme based on monitors, *IEEE Trans. Software Eng.*, Vol. SE-8, pp. 189–197, May 1982.
100. Kim, W., Auditor: A framework for high availability of DB/DC systems, *Proc. 2nd Symp. on Reliability in Distributed Software and Database Syst.*, Pittsburgh, PA, July 1982, pp. 76–84.
101. Kim, W., Highly available systems for database applications, *ACM Comput. Surveys*, Vol. 16, pp. 71–98, March 1984.
102. Koenig, S., *A Transformational Framework for Automatic Derived Data Control and Its Applications in an Entity-Relationship Data Model*, Tech. Rep. LCSR-TR-23 (Ph.D. Diss.), Lab. for Comput. Sci. Res., Rutgers University, New Brunswick, NJ, Dec. 1981.
103. Kohler, W., A survey of techniques for synchronization and recovery in decentralized computer systems, *ACM Comput. Surveys*, Vol. 13, pp. 149–183, June 1981.
104. Kopetz, H., Software design for fault tolerance, *Proc. Computer Software and Applications Conf. COMPSAC 80*, Chicago, IL, Oct. 1980, pp. 591–595.
105. Krishna, C. M., K. G. Shin, and Y.-H. Lee, Optimization criteria for checkpoint placement, *CACM*, Vol. 27, pp. 1008–1012, Oct. 1984.
106. Kung, H. T. and C. H. Papadimitriou, An optimality theory of concurrency control for databases, *Proc. ACM-SIGMOD Int. Conf. on Management of Data*, Boston, MA, May–June 1979, pp. 116–126.
107. Kung, H. T. and J. T. Robinson, On optimistic methods for concurrency control, *ACM Trans. Database Syst.*, Vol. 6, pp. 213–226, June 1981.
108. Lafue, G. M. E., An approach to automatic maintenance of semantic integrity in large design data bases, *Proc. AFIPS National Computer Conf. 1979*, New York, NY, June 1979, pp. 713–715.
109. Lampson, B. and H. Sturgis, *Crash Recovery in a Distributed Data Storage System*, Tech. Rep. Xerox Palo Alto Res. Center, Palo Alto, CA, 1976.
110. Lamport, L., The implementation of reliable distributed multiprocess systems, *Computer Networks*, Vol. 2, pp. 95–114, 1978.
111. Lamport, L., R. Shostak, and M. Pease, The Byzantine generals problem, *ACM Trans. Programming Languages and Syst.*, Vol. 4, pp. 382–401, July 1982.
112. Lee, Y.-H. and K. G. Shin, Design and evaluation of a fault-tolerant multiprocessor using hardware recovery blocks, *IEEE Trans. Computers*, Vol. C-33, pp. 382–401, Feb. 1984.
113. Leveson, N. G. and P. R. Harvey, Analyzing software safety, *IEEE Trans. Software Eng.*, Vol. SE-9, pp. 569–579, Sept. 1983.
114. Lian, R. C., *Design of a Fault-Tolerant Distributed Operating System Based on Nested Atomic Actions*, (Ph.D. Diss.) Dep. Comput. and Inform. Sci., The Ohio State University, Columbus, OH, 1984.
115. Lilien, L., *Integrity in Database Systems*, (Ph.D. Diss.) Dep. Comput. Sci., University of Pittsburgh, Pittsburgh, PA, 1983. Available from University Microfilms International, Ann Arbor, MI 48106.
116. Lilien, L. and B. Bhargava, A scheme for batch verification of integrity assertions in a database system, *IEEE Trans. Software Eng.*, Vol. SE-10, pp. 664–680, Nov. 1984.
117. Lilien, L. and B. Bhargava, Database integrity block construct: Concepts and design issues, *IEEE Trans. Software Eng.*, Vol. SE-11, pp. 865–885, Sept. 1985.
118. Lindsay, B. G., *Notes on Distributed Databases*, IBM Tech. Rep. RJ 2571, IBM Res. Div., San Jose Lab., San Jose, CA, July 1979.

119. Lindsay, B. and P. G. Selinger, *Site Autonomy Issues in R*: A Distributed Database Management System*, IBM Res. Rep. RJ2927, IBM Res. Lab., San Jose, CA, Sept. 1980.

120. Lohman, G. M. and J. A. Muckstadt, Optimal policy for batch operations: Backup, checkpointing, reorganization, and updating, *ACM Trans. Database Syst.*, Vol. 2, pp. 209–222, Sept. 1977.

121. Lorie, A. A., Physical integrity in a large segmented database, *ACM Trans. Database Syst.*, Vol. 2, pp. 91–104, March 1977.

122. Lynch, N. A., Multilevel atomicity—A new correctness criterion for distributed databases, *ACM Trans. Database Syst.*, Vol. 8, pp. 484–502, Dec. 1983.

123. Malvestuto, F. M., On an optimal policy for the data base integrity checking, *Proc. Symp. on Reliability in Distributed Software and Database Syst.*, Pittsburgh, PA, July 1981, pp. 200–204.

124. March, S. T. and G. D. Scudder, On the selection of efficient record segmentation and backup strategies for large shared databases, *ACM Trans. Database Syst.*, Vol. 9, pp. 409–438, Sept. 1984.

125. Menasce, D. A., R. R. Muntz, and G. J. Popek, A formal model of crash recovery in computer systems, *Proc. 12th Hawaii Int. Conf. on System Sciences*, pp. 28–35, Jan. 1979.

126. Menasce, D. A. and O. E. Landes, *On the Design of a Reliable Storage Component for Distributed Database Management Systems*, Tech. Rep. DB 038002, Departamento de Informatica, Pontificia Universidade Catolica do Rio de Janeo, Rio de Janeiro, Brazil, March 1980.

127. Menasce, D. A., G. J. Popek, and R. R. Muntz, A locking protocol for resource coordination in distributed databases, *ACM Trans. Database Syst.*, Vol. 5, pp. 103–138, June 1980.

128. Minoura, T., *Resilient Extended True-Copy Token Algorithm for Distributed Database Systems*, Tech. Rep. TR-197 (Ph.D. Diss.), CSL, Stanford University, Stanford, CA, 1980.

129. Minoura, T. and G. Wiederhold, Resilient extended true-copy token scheme for a distributed database system, *IEEE Trans. Software Eng.*, Vol. SE-8, pp. 173–189, May 1982.

130. Morgan, D. E., D. J. Taylor, and G. Custeau, A survey of methods for improving computer network reliability and availability, *IEEE Computer*, Vol. 10, pp. 42–50, Nov. 1977.

131. Moss, J. E. B., *Nested Transactions: An Approach to Reliable Distributed Computing*, (Ph.D. Diss.), TR-260, Lab. for Comput. Sci., Massachusetts Institute of Technology, 1981.

132. Munz, R., Realization, synchronization and restart of update transactions in a distributed database system, in *Distributed Data Bases*, ed. C. Delobel and W. Litwin, pp. 173–182. Amsterdam, Holland: North-Holland, 1980.

133. Papadimitriou, C. H., The serializability of concurrent database updates, *J. ACM*, Vol. 26, pp. 631–653, Oct. 1979.

134. Parker, D. S. et al., Detection of mutual inconsistency in distributed systems, *Trans. Software Eng.*, Vol. SE-9, pp. 240–247, May 1983.

135. Prakash, N., N. Parimala, and N. Bolloju, Specifying integrity constraints in a network DBMS, *Computer J.*, Vol. 27, pp. 209–217, Aug. 1984.

136. Randell, B., System structure for software fault tolerance, *IEEE Trans. Software Eng.*, Vol. SE-1, pp. 220–232, June 1975.

137. Randell, B., P. A. Lee, and P. C. Treleaven, Reliability issues in computing system design, *ACM Comput. Surveys*, Vol. 10, pp. 123–165, June 1978.

138. Reed, D. P., Implementing atomic actions on decentralized data, *ACM Trans. Computer Syst.*, Vol. 1, pp. 3–23, Feb. 1983.

139. Reiter, R., *On the Integrity of Typed First Order Data Bases*, Tech. Rep. 80-6, Dep. Comput. Sci., The University of British Columbia, Vancouver, Canada, April 1980.

140. Ries, D. R. and G. C. Smith, Nested transactions in distributed systems, *IEEE Trans. Software Eng.*, Vol. SE-8, pp. 167–172, May 1982.

141. Rosenkrantz, D. J., Dynamic database dumping, *Proc. ACM SIGMOD Int. Conf. on Management of Data*, Austin, TX, May–June 1978, pp. 3–8.

142. Rothnie, J. B. and N. Goodman, A survey of research and development in distributed database management, *Proc. 3rd Int. Conf. on Very Large Data Bases*, Tokyo, Japan, Oct. 1977, pp. 48–62.
143. Rothnie, J. B. et al., Introduction to a system for distributed databases (SDD-1), *ACM Trans. Database Syst.*, Vol. 5, pp. 1–17, March 1980.
144. Ryan, T. M., *Backup and Recovery for Distributed Interactive Computer Systems*, IBM Tech. Rep. G320-2133, IBM Cambridge Scientific Center, Cambridge, MA, Nov. 1980.
145. Sayani, H. H., Restart and recovery in a transaction-oriented information processing system, *Proc. ACM SIGMOD Workshop on Data Description, Access and Control*, Ann Arbor, MI, May 1974.
146. Schlageter, G. and P. Dadam, Reconstruction of consistent global states in distributed databases, in *Distributed Data Bases*, ed. C. Delobel and W. Litwin, pp. 191–200. Amsterdam, Holland: North-Holland, 1980.
147. Schlichting, R. D. and F. B. Schneider, Fail-stop processors: An approach to designing fault-tolerant computing systems, *ACM Trans. Comput. Syst.*, Vol. 1, pp. 222–238, Aug. 1983.
148. Schneider, F. B., Byzantine generals in action: Implementing fail-stop processors, *ACM Trans. Comput. Syst.*, Vol. 2, pp. 145–154, May 1984.
149. Severance, D. G. and G. M. Lohman, Differential files: Their application to the maintenance of large databases, *ACM Trans. on Database Syst.*, Vol. 1, pp. 256–267, Sept. 1976.
150. Seifert, M., Reconfiguration and recovery of multiprocess systems in fault-tolerant distributed systems, *Proc. COMPSAC 80 Comput. Software and Applications Conf.*, Chicago, IL, Oct. 1980, pp. 596–602.
151. Shin, K. G. and Y.-H. Lee, Error detection process—Model, design, and its impact on computer performance, *IEEE Trans. Computers*, Vol. C-33, pp. 529–540, June 1984.
152. Shin, K. G. and Y.-H. Lee, Evaluation of error recovery blocks used for cooperating processes, *IEEE Trans. on Software Eng.*, Vol. SE-10, pp. 692–700, Nov. 1984.
153. Shipman, D., Handling network partitioning in distributed databases, *IEEE Database Eng.*, Vol. 3, pp. 3–8, April 1979.
154. Shrivastava, S. K. and J.-P. Banatre, Reliable resource allocation between unreliable processes, *IEEE Trans. on Software Eng.*, Vol. SE-4, pp. 230–241, May 1978.
155. Skeen, D., Nonblocking commit protocols, *Proc. ACM SIGMOD 1981 Int. Conf. on Management of Data*, Ann Arbor, MI, April–May 1981, pp. 133–142.
156. Skeen, D., A decentralized termination protocol, *Proc. Symp. on Reliability in Distributed Software and Database Syst.*, Pittsburgh, PA, July 1981, pp. 27–32.
157. Skeen, D. and M. Stonebraker, A formal model of crash recovery in a distributed system, *IEEE Trans. Software Eng.*, Vol. SE-9, pp. 219–228, May 1983.
158. Special Issue: Fault-Tolerant Computing, *IEEE Computer*, Vol. 17, Aug. 1984.
159. Stonebraker, M., Implementation of integrity constraints and views by query modification, *Proc. ACM SIGMOD Conf.*, San Jose, CA, 1975, pp. 188–194.
160. Svanks, M. I., *Integrity Analysis: A Methodology for EDP Audit and Data Quality Control*, Tech. Rep. #131 (Ph.D. Diss.), Dep. Comput. Sci., University of Toronto, Toronto, Canada, 1981.
161. Svobodova, L., "Resilient distributed computing," *IEEE Trans. Software Eng.*, Vol. SE-10, pp. 257–268, May 1984.
162. Tantawi, A. N. and M. Ruschitzka, Performance analysis of checkpointing strategies, *ACM Trans. Computer Syst.*, Vol. 2, pp. 123–144, May 1984.
163. Taylor, D. J., D. E. Morgan, and J. P. Black, Redundancy in data structures: Improving software fault tolerance, *IEEE Trans. Software Eng.*, Vol. SE-6, pp. 585–594, Nov. 1980.
164. Thomas, R. H., A majority consensus approach to concurrency control for multiple copy databases, *ACM Trans. Database Syst.*, Vol. 4, pp. 180–209, June 1979.
165. Tsuruoka, K., A. Kaneko, and Y. Nishihara, Dynamic recovery schemes for distributed

processes, *Proc. Symp. on Reliability in Distributed Software and Database Syst.*, Pittsburgh, PA, July 1981, pp. 124–130.

166. Ullman, J. D., *Principles of Database Systems*, Potomac, Maryland: Computer Science Press, 1980.
167. Verhofstad, J. S. M., Recovery techniques for database systems, *ACM Comput. Surveys*, Vol. 10, pp. 167–195, June 1978.
168. Vessey, I. and R. Weber, Some factors affecting program repair maintenance: An empirical study, *CACM*, Vol. 26, pp. 128–134, Feb. 1983.
169. Wallace, J. J. and W. W. Barnes, Designing for ultrahigh availability: The Unix RTR operating system, *IEEE Computer*, Vol. 17, pp. 31–39, Aug. 1984.
170. Walter, B., Concepts for a robust distributed data base system, in *Distributed Data Bases*, ed. C. Delobel and W. Litwin, pp. 161–171. Amsterdam, Holland: North-Holland, 1980.
171. Walter, B., Strategies for handling transactions in distributed data base systems during recovery, *Proc. 6th Int. Conf. on Very Large Data Bases*, Montreal, Canada, Oct. 1980, pp. 384–389.
172. Wei, A. Y. and R. H. Campbell, *Construction of a Fault-Tolerant Real-Time Software System*, Tech. Rep. UIUCDCS-R-80-1042, Dep. Comput. Sci., University of Illinois at Urbana-Champaign, Urbana, IL, Dec. 1980.
173. Wiederhold, G., *Database Design*, New York, NY: McGraw-Hill, 1983.
174. Wilms, P., Qualitative and quantitative comparison of update algorithms in distributed databases, in *Distributed Data Bases*, ed. C. Delobel and W. Litwin, pp. 275–294. Amsterdam, Holland: North-Holland: 1980.
175. Yee, J. G. and S. Y. H. Su, A scheme for tolerating faulty data in real-time systems, *Proc. 2nd Int. Computer Software and Application Conf. COMPSAC 1978*, Chicago, IL, Nov. 1978, pp. 663–667.
176. Yeh, R. T., Guest Editorial, *ACM Comput. Surveys*, Vol. 8, pp. 301–303, Sept. 1976.
177. Yemini, S., An axiomatic treatment of exception handling, *Proc. 7th Symp. on Principles of Programming Languages*, 1982.

2. A Causal Model for Analyzing Distributed Concurrency Control Algorithms

BHARAT BHARGAVA

and

CECIL T. HUA

ABSTRACT

An event order based model for specifying and analyzing concurrency control algorithms for distributed database systems has been presented. An expanded notion of history that includes the database access events as well as synchronization events is used to study the correctness, degree of concurrency, and other aspects of the algorithms such as deadlocks and reliability. The algorithms are mapped into serializable classes that have been defined based on the order of synchronization events such as lock points, commit point, the arrival of a transaction, etc.

1. INTRODUCTION

Several algorithms for concurrency control or synchronization in distributed database management systems have been proposed in the literature and have been surveyed in references 3 and 5. Special proofs of correctness for individual algorithms have appeared in references 2, 18, and 25. This chapter presents a general approach for analyzing algorithms. This analysis is used to study several desirable properties of the algorithms, such as proof of correctness, the allowable degree of concurrency, deadlock freedom, and robustness. A simple hypothetical concurrency control algorithm has been used to illustrate the approach. In reference 12, the majority consensus approach[25] has been analyzed as an example.

In reference 4, examples of the analysis of locking algorithms and other types of algorithms have been included. The notion of serializability[19] is used to establish the degree of concurrency and as the correctness criterion. The deadlock freedom refers to the absence of an infinite delay of either the transaction or the system processing. The robustness refers to the capability of an algorithm in handling certain hardware/software failures and/or lost messages.

The basic approach used in this discussion contains the following steps: 1) Identify all events that occur due to the processing of the transactions or the concurrency control algorithm. 2) Establish an order (causal relationship) among all events. This gives a causal graph. 3) Derive subgraphs representing event ordering for the transaction and the concurrency control algorithm. The subgraphs are like a template representing generic processing for a transaction or a node. 4) Using the transaction and node subgraphs, determine the conditions for the allowable histories generated by the concurrency control algorithm. 5) Check to see if these conditions are satisfied by a subclass of all possible serializable histories. The classes of the serializability for distributed database systems have been established in reference 6. If the conditions are satisfied, the degree of concurrency and correctness are verified; otherwise the algorithm produces nonrecognizable histories. 6) Study to see if there exists a sequence of events that lets the processing of a transaction or a concurrency controller to proceed from an initial event to the terminal (final) event. If so, deadlock freedom is guaranteed. 7) Check whether the occurrence of some event transition is based on certain processing on another node or certain message transmissions. If so, the algorithm is not robust with respect to the failure of such processing or message transmission. 8) Identify events that are necessary for deadlock freedom and robustness and add them to the original set of events. Establish relationships among these new events and other existing algorithms. This gives a new causal graph. From this improved causal graph, obtain a new modified algorithm.

The above steps are also shown in Fig. 2.1. In this study, only the first seven steps as discussed above have been presented. The last step is the topic for future research.

In Section 2, the causal model has been presented. In Section 3, the mechanism of the analysis of concurrency control algorithms with an illustrative algorithm has been presented. The basic terminology has been presented in the Appendix. The classes of serializable histories for distributed database systems have been presented in reference 6, and the semantic information used in analyzing certain classes of algorithms has been included in reference 13. Finally, a brief comparison of the causal model to other models, such as Petri nets and path expressions, has been included.

2. THE CAUSAL MODEL

In this section, a causal model for representing concurrency control algorithms is introduced. The model is based on the identification of events in an algorithm

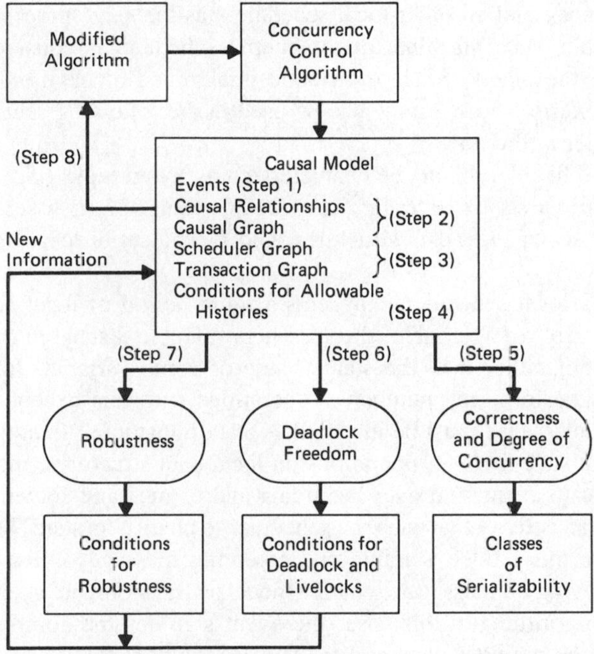

Fig. 2.1. Steps for analyzing and modifying concurrency control algorithms.

and the causal relationship among the events.[4, 16] The purpose is to map the specification of algorithms to the classes of serializable histories.

The first section describes a model for concurrency control algorithms. The model specifies the states and the events of concurrency control algorithms. The second section explains the causal rules which represent the causal relationship among the events. The third section describes the causal graph and node/transaction subgraphs to represent possible ordering of events. A hypothetic concurrency control algorithm is used for illustration.

2.1. A Model for Concurrency Control Algorithms

A *distributed concurrency control algorithm* Φ can be modeled as a collection of *local schedulers* $\{\Phi_n\}$ such that Φ_n is the local scheduler running at node n. The local schedulers represent the distributed components of the overall concurrency control algorithm.

Each local scheduler acts like a finite state machine, and has independent state and event specifications, as well as local data structures. All local schedulers are not necessarily homogeneous. For example, a synchronization algorithm with centralized control may have one local scheduler running on a central (controlling) node and all other local schedulers as the slave processes. In such a case, the finite state machine for the central scheduler is considerably more complex than the others. Since each node is assumed to have only one local scheduler, the term "node" may also be used in the following sections to refer to the scheduler at the node.

Each local scheduler Φ_n can be characterized by a quintuple $\langle S_n, E_n, M_n, D_n, L_n \rangle$ where S_n is a set of states, E_n is a set of events, M_n is a set of message types, D_n is a set of local data structures, and L_n is a set of local operations on M_n and D_n.

A *state* of a local scheduler represents a finite period of local computation. Unlike the "state" of a variable, the state here refers to a stage in the execution of the algorithm rather than the status value of some variable. In a state, an algorithm can perform any number of operations with one exception: sending and receiving messages must be modeled as state transitions. Examples of legal operations in a state include: operations on local data structures, message preparation, predicate evaluation over local data and/or message contents, etc.

An *event* is an activity that causes a scheduler to change its state. For example, as required by this model, sending and receiving messages constitute events. An event involving no message exchange models a transition between processing stages of an algorithm. In this case, the event signifies the completion of the processing in the previous state and the start of the next state.

Since each event is associated with a state transition of a local scheduler and vice versa, the set of events for a local scheduler can be viewed as the state transition function of the scheduler. An event is a member of the set $S_n \times S_n$. Also, messages can be identified by remote events since the act of sending a message must be modeled as an event.

In a schematic representation of an algorithm, events are represented by directed edges connecting states. Message sending will be shown as the message is embedded in the edge representing the sending event. Message reception will be denoted by tagging the message id or the sending event just beside the state from which the receiving event starts. For example, in Fig. 2.2, event *e* causes the scheduler to change from state *S*1 to state *S*2. Message MESS is sent when event *f* takes place (from state *S*3 to state *S*4). The receiving node changes state

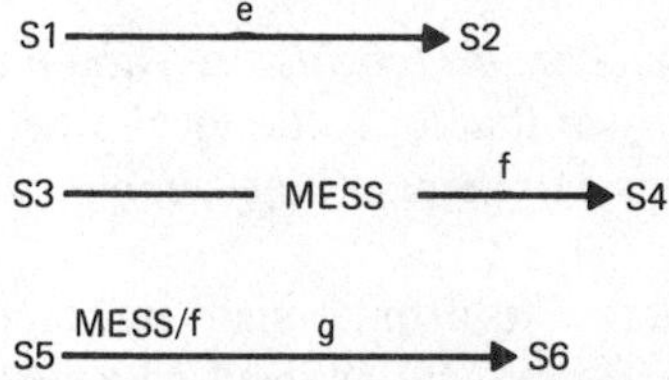

Fig. 2.2. The schematic representation of states and events.

(event g) from state $S5$ to state $S6$ upon receiving the message MESS. Since MESS is sent in event f, the tag beside state $S5$ can also be f instead of MESS.

The *message types* M_n specify message id's and the message formats.

The *local data structures* D_n contain all local variables accessible only by Φ_n. The database at a node is considered as a part of the local data structure, since it is accessible only by a local scheduler.

The *local operations* of Φ_n, L_n, are defined over M_n and D_n. Computational details are specified in L_n.

A concurrency control algorithm achieves synchronization by coordinating updates on local nodes, and the process of coordination is done through proper message exchanges among nodes. These message exchanges are events. The database accesses are associated with particular events in the algorithm. Hence, an output history of an algorithm can be viewed as a sequence of scheduler events embedded between the events associated with access operations. The read and write operations are associated to special events of a scheduler. The sequence of system events, thus, represents a detailed description of the synchronization process by a concurrency control algorithm. This is the notion of *expanded history*, i.e., a history of atomic operations plus embedded scheduler events. Each event can be associated to a transaction and/or to a node. The node and transaction projections of an expanded history can be defined. This expanded notion of the "history" of a system will be used in the following discussions.

The notation $e(i, j)$ is used to designate an event e for transaction i at node j. We would avoid the subscripts whenever possible and represent $e(i, j)$ by e. The subscript will be necessary when the identification of the transaction and the node for an event is important in the context of other events.

The notion of events and states is further illustrated by the state transition diagram of a hypothetical concurrency control algorithm in Fig. 2.3. The sending of a message is represented by embedding the message id in the transition arrow; each transition is also marked with corresponding events ei, $0 \leq i \leq 5$.

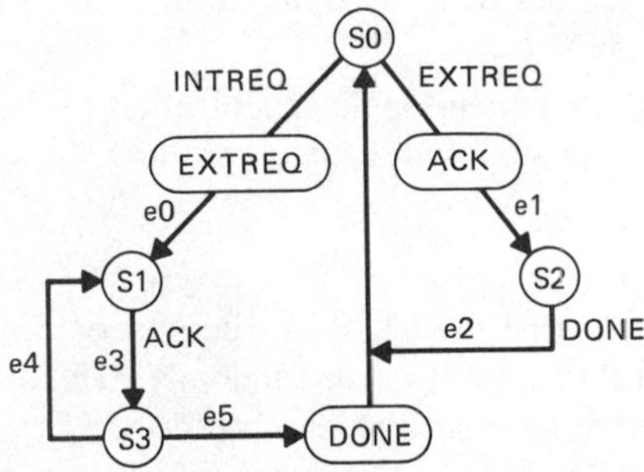

Fig. 2.3. The state transition diagram of a hypothetical algorithm.

The algorithm works as follows. A local scheduler waits for incoming transactions in the state $S0$ (the idle state). Upon receiving the request from a transaction (INTREQ), the local scheduler broadcasts a message EXTREQ to every other node (event $e0$) to obtain locks. The scheduler must initialize the counter and lock X_n. The scheduler then waits for acknowledgment (ACK) from all other nodes before proceeding to execute the transaction. This is implemented by local operations A_n^+ on the local variable A_n. Event $e4$ represents the waiting loop for acknowledgments. A DONE message will be broadcasted to inform schedulers at other nodes that the transaction has been completed. If a scheduler is in the idle state and receives an EXTREQ message, it will send back an ACK message to acknowledge the request for locking and hold the lock for that transaction until a DONE message is received.

The local variables used by the local scheduler in this hypothetical algorithm include a simple counter for registering the acknowledgment messages and a lock variable for the data item Y (one data item assumed). Let $\Phi_n = \langle S_n, E_n, M_n, D_n, L_n \rangle$ be the local scheduler. Then

S_n: states = $\{S0, S1, S2, S3\}$;
E_n: events = $\{e0, e1, e2, e3, e4, e5\}$;
M_n: message types = {INTREQ, EXTREQ, ACK, DONE};
D_n: local data structures =
- A_n: a counter for ACK responses;
- X_n: a variable indicating whether the lock is held currently by some transaction;
- Y_n: the database at node n;

L_n: local operations =
- A_n^+: increase the counter by 1;
- X_n^+: increase X_n by 1, indicating the locking;
- A_n^-: initialize the counter to zero;
- X_n^-: unlock by resetting X_n to zero;
- $W_i^n[Y]$: local accesses to Y_n by transaction i.

The causal model requires reasonable specification of the operational aspects of an algorithm before the analysis of the algorithm.

2.2. Causal Rules

From the basic computational model, it can be observed that events of a concurrency control algorithm do not occur randomly. There are certain relationships among them. These relationships can be specified by causal rules.

1. *Definitions of Causal Rules.* A *causal rule* U is a quintuple $\langle u, @, v, L, P \rangle$ where u, v are events, and @ is one of the *causal relationships* $\{\rightarrow, \Rightarrow, \twoheadrightarrow\}$.

The causal relationship $\rightarrow$ specifies the ordering of non-message-related events. $\langle u, \rightarrow, v, L, P \rangle$ is a causal rule if there are states $x, y, z \in S_n$ such that $u = \langle x, y \rangle$, $v = \langle y, z \rangle$, the local operation L is performed in state y, P is a Boolean condition for v to occur, and no messages are involved in activating v. In other words, the algorithm of Φ_n must have the following state transition.

$$x \overset{u}{\rightarrow} y \overset{v}{\rightarrow} z.$$

Intuitively, event u precedes event v on node n, and Φ_n executes event v following the occurrence of u without waiting for messages. Between these two events, the local operation L will take place. The predicate P must be defined over D_n and M_n (it can test the contents of previous messages). If $\langle u, \rightarrow v, L, P \rangle$ is a causal rule for some L and P, then event u is said to *precede* event v (or v *follows* u).

The other two causal relationships, $\Rightarrow$ and $\twoheadrightarrow$, describe the ordering between message-related events. $\langle u, \Rightarrow, v, L', P \rangle$ and $\langle w, \twoheadrightarrow, v, L'', Q \rangle$ are causal rules iff there are states $x, y, z \in S_n$, $t, s \in S_k$, $k \neq n$, such that $u = \langle x, y \rangle$, $v = \langle y, z \rangle$, $w = \langle t, s \rangle$, w is the event that node k sends a message to node n, and node n responds with event v at state y. L' is the local operation of node n in state y, which is independent of the message sent by the remote event w. L'' is the local operation of node n in state y that can be performed only after the message is received. P is the predicate that node n chooses to wait for messages after the event u, and Q is the condition that the message of event w will be recognized by node n. Schematically, nodes n and k must have the following state transitions.

$$\text{node } k\text{:} \quad t \overset{w}{\rightarrow} s$$

$$\text{node } n\text{:} \quad x \underset{u}{\rightarrow} y \overset{w}{\underset{v}{\rightarrow}} z.$$

It denotes that node n, while waiting at state y, receives a message sent by event w of node k, and then executes event v in response. Event w is said to *cause* event v if $\langle w, \twoheadrightarrow, v, L, Q \rangle$ is a causal rule for some L and Q. Note that the causal rules $\langle u, \Rightarrow, v, L', P \rangle$ and $\langle w, \twoheadrightarrow, v, L'', Q \rangle$ are related to each other; no causal rules $\langle u, \Rightarrow, v, L', P \rangle$ should exist without the corresponding $\langle w, \twoheadrightarrow, v, L'', Q \rangle$ causal rules.

Either L or P in the above causal rules can be null. A null L signifies that no local operation is associated with the events involved, and a null P indicates that the causal relationships are unconditional, i.e., independent of local data values or messages.

The predicate P of a causal rule $\langle u, \twoheadrightarrow, v, L, P \rangle$ can also be used to specify the sites receiving the message generated in event u. Hence, either message broadcasting or daisy-chain transmission can be described by a proper predicate P. The detailed semantics, such as the exact node id to which a message is sent, are not critical, in general, to the causal relationship $\twoheadrightarrow$.

The following notation is used in this chapter to designate a causal rule $\langle u, @, v, L, P \rangle$:

$$u \mathbin{@} v + L \text{ if } P.$$

For example, the following causal rules are derived from the hypothetical algorithm in Fig. 2.3. In the listing, i, m designates transactions, and j, k designates nodes. $W_i^j[Y]$ represents the database access by transaction i to item Y at node j. Let $\text{INIT}(i)$ be the originating node of transaction i and N be the set of nodes.

$$e0(i, j) \twoheadrightarrow e1(i, k) + X_k^+, \forall k \neq j;$$

$$e1(i, j) \twoheadrightarrow e3(i, k) + A_k^+, k = \text{INIT}(i), k \neq j;$$

$$e3(i, j) \rightarrow e4(i, j) \text{ if } A_j < |N| - 1;$$

$$e3(i, j) \rightarrow e5(i, j) + W_i^j[Y] + X_j^- \text{ if } A_j = |N| - 1;$$

$$e5(i, j) \twoheadrightarrow e2(i, k) + W_i^k[Y] + X_k^-, k \neq j;$$

$$e0(i, j) \Rightarrow e3(i, j) + A_j^- + X_j^-;$$

$$e4(i, j) \Rightarrow e3(i, j);$$

$$e1(i, j) \Rightarrow e2(i, j);$$

$$e5(i, j) \Rightarrow e0(m, j), m \neq i;$$

$$e5(i, j) \Rightarrow e1(m, j), m \neq i;$$

$$e2(i, j) \Rightarrow e0(m, j), m \neq i;$$

$$e2(i, j) \Rightarrow e1(m, j), m \neq i.$$

In the rule $e0(i, j) \twoheadrightarrow e1(i, k)$, the predicate "$\forall k \neq j$" indicates the broadcasting of messages, whereas in the rule $e1(i, j) \twoheadrightarrow e3(i, k)$, k is uniquely specified. The local access to the database is associated with the event $e5$; this is indicated by the rule $e3(i, j) \rightarrow e5(i, j)$. The update by a remote transaction is associated with the event $e2$, which is initiated by a message from a remote $e5$ event. Notice that in the rule $e0(i, j) \Rightarrow e3(i, j)$, the local operations of initializing A_j and X_j are included, since they are independent of the response message. The last four rules indicate that the event $e0$ or $e1$ after the event $e5$ or $e2$ refers to a different transaction.

2. *Inference of Causal Rules.* In an effective model for distributed concurrency control algorithms, causal rules should be easily derivable from common descriptions of an algorithm. An informal description of the mapping procedure follows.

Consider the examples in Fig. 2.4. They are sample flow diagrams of an algorithm. Case (a) represents the processing of a scheduler in state S; the scheduler activates $e2$ after entering state S via event $e1$. Case (b) represents the receipt of a message MESS when the scheduler is in state S, and the response is event $e5$. Assume that the message MESS is associated with a remote event $e4$. It follows from the definition that

$$\text{Case (a):}\quad e1 \rightarrow e2;$$

$$\text{Case (b):}\quad e3 \Rightarrow e5;\ e4 \twoheadrightarrow e_5.$$

Cases (c) and (d) represent conditional branches in the flow of an algorithm. In case (c), the scheduler consults the local data values for selecting one of $e2$ and $e3$. It can be translated into the following causal rules:

$$\text{Case (c):}\quad e1 \rightarrow e2 \text{ if } P_{12};\ e1 \rightarrow e3 \text{ if } P_{13};$$

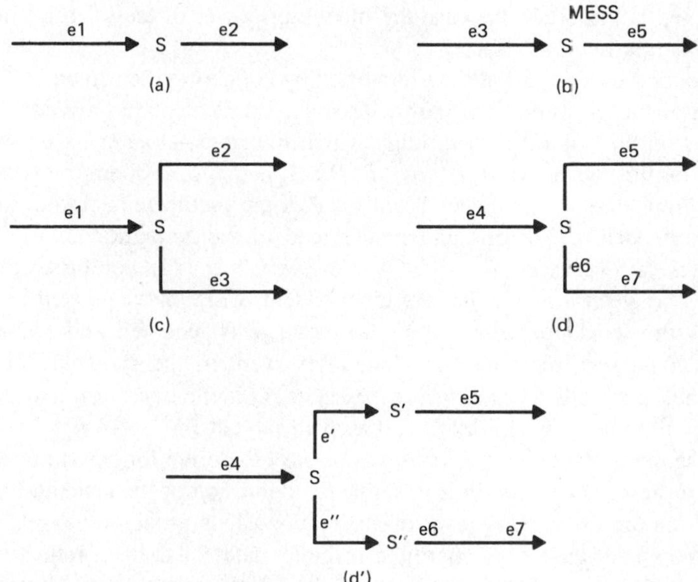

Fig. 2.4. Sample flow diagrams of an algorithm.

where P_{12} and P_{13} are predicates over the local data structure. They are not necessarily mutually exclusive, and the result can be nondeterministic execution. Case (d) stands for conditional processing depending on the presence or absence of messages. State S will choose $e7$ if a message is received, otherwise it will continue with $e5$. The definition of the relationships does not prohibit such behavior, which can be represented by

$$\text{Case (d):} \quad e4 \rightarrow e5 \text{ if } P;\ e4 \Rightarrow e7;\ e6 \twoheadrightarrow e7;$$

where P is a predicate indicating the absence of message $e6$. However, case (d) can be alternatively represented as case (d′), where

$$\text{Case (d}'\text{):} \quad e4 \rightarrow e' \text{ if } P;\ e4 \rightarrow e'' \text{ if } \neg P;$$

$$e' \rightarrow e5;\ e'' \Rightarrow e7;\ e6 \twoheadrightarrow e7.$$

The decomposition of state S of case (d) into the states S, S', and S'', of case (d′) may also reduce the complexity of deriving semantic conditions for causal rules.

So far, only the procedure for identifying the type of causal relationships between events has been discussed. To specify the local operation and the predicate part of a causal rule, the semantics within a state must be examined, and this step is important because the modeling power of causal rules depends on the semantic interpretation.

Local operations can usually be identified by collecting the semantics of each statement or the primitive in a particular state. Predicates are derived from the conditions on the control path through which the state activates an event. Specifically, for the causal rule $\langle u, \rightarrow, v\, L, P \rangle$, L is the local operation performed in the intermediate state between u and v. P is the predicate such that the state will perform local operations and finally lead to the activation of v. For the causal rules $\langle u, \Rightarrow, v, L', P \rangle$ and $\langle w, \twoheadrightarrow, v, L'', Q \rangle$, L' comprises the local operations between u and v that are independent of the message sent by w; L'' comprises the local operations after the message is received and recognized. Predicate P denotes the condition that, after event u, the state will choose a control path that leads to waiting for messages. Q is the condition that the state recognizes the message sent by w and activates event v.

These semantic specifications may not be easy to derive for certain operations and control flow. One solution is to refine the definition of the state and identify events which are on a lower level of abstraction. This process is similar to the process shown for case (d), where the original state S has been refined further to include extra states S' and S'' in case (d′). With a finer level of states and events, semantic inference is easier. The semantics of concurrency control algorithms is usually not difficult to specify as exemplified by the above hypothetical algorithm and as shown in reference 12.

The set of causal rules is not large. If the local schedulers are homogeneous, their causal rules are identical. In this case, the only difference between the specifications of two schedulers is in identifying the receiving node of a message for the relationship $-\!\!\gg$. However, the semantics of selecting the receiving node is fixed and can be represented by suitable quantifiers to the predicate. For example, broadcasting a message can be represented by the following causal rule:

$$u(i, j) -\!\!\gg v(i, k) \ \forall\, k \neq j, j, k \in N,$$

instead of repeating the rule for different nodes (N is the set of nodes). Hence, only one set of relationships for the scheduler needs be specified and others can be "folded" onto the set.

For heterogeneous schedulers, the number of specifications is also relatively small. For instance, only two graphs are necessary for the centralized control algorithm, one for the central scheduler and the other representing all other nodes.

2.3. Causal Graph

A *causal graph* $G = \langle V, E \rangle$ for a set of causal rules of an algorithm is a labeled diagraph with vertices $V = \{e \mid \text{events}\}$ the edges $E = \{\langle e, f \rangle \mid$ there exists a causal relationship @, local operation L, and predicate P such that $\langle e, @, f, L, P \rangle$ is a causal rule$\}$. The vertices and the edges are labeled with their corresponding events and causal relationships. The edges in a causal graph are referred to as $\rightarrow$ edges, $\Rightarrow$ edges, or $-\!\!\gg$ edges, according to their labels. The paths in a causal graph represent possible event sequences in the execution history.

The *node subgraph* consists of those paths containing only $\rightarrow$ and $\Rightarrow$ edges. These paths represent the possible execution history of each local scheduler at one node. A path in the node subgraph is called a *node path*.

The *transaction subgraph* consists of those paths containing $-\!\!\gg$ edges. A path in the transaction subgraph is called a *transaction path*. Events on transaction paths of the transaction subgraph are events for a single transaction. Transaction paths represent the message switching behavior of the schedulers concerning transaction synchronization. The derivation procedures of these subgraphs are explained below.

For concurrency control algorithms, there is one initial or wait state. In the wait state, say $S0$, a scheduler waits for a new transaction. All the events ending at $S0$ will have $\Rightarrow$ edges to all the events starting from $S0$. This implies that it is possible to have many cycles formed by these $\Rightarrow$ edges in the causal graph.

The events returning to state $S0$ are not critical in the processing of the transactions. For example, new requests from a user are processed by starting the scheduler from the initial state $S0$. Thus, a scheduler returning to $S0$ without completing the processing of an older transaction must be able to resume the processing some time later. This is often done through local data structures such as a waiting list. As far as the local scheduler is concerned, the current processing of the older transaction at this node is complete. Events entering the idle state $S0$ represent the termination of a node's current processing of a transaction and are called *terminal node events*. Similarly, the events starting from $S0$ are called *initial node events*.

To find the node subgraph from a causal graph, first remove from the causal graph all $\twoheadrightarrow$ edges, and then remove all $\Rightarrow$ edges from the terminal node events to the initial node events. The remaining $\rightarrow$ and $\Rightarrow$ edges are meaningful for processing at a single node. The $\twoheadrightarrow$ edges can be removed because they relate events at different nodes. The $\Rightarrow$ edges from terminal node events to initial node events can be removed because of the arguments about the initial state $S0$. They are not related to the transaction processing at a node. Their presence is implied when the terminal and the initial node events are identified.

To find the transaction subgraph, it is necessary to identify the initial and the terminal events for transaction processing. An *initial transaction event* neither follows any event nor is caused by any event. It represents spontaneous activities such as user requests. An event $e(i, j)$ is a *terminal transaction event* if no further processing for transaction i at node j is needed. For concurrency control algorithms, terminal transaction events signify the final decision of the acceptance or the rejection of a transaction.

The following steps are used to find the transaction subgraph.

1. Remove all $\Rightarrow$ edges from the causal graph.
2. For any event which is not a transaction terminal and has no outgoing edges, include all outgoing $\Rightarrow$ edges that are related to the processing of the same transaction.
3. For any event with incoming $\Rightarrow$ edges (generated by the previous step), also include all outgoing $\Rightarrow$ edges that are related to the processing of the same transaction.

The intuition behind step 1 is based on the assumption that messages are necessary for concurrency control in the distributed environment. When a local scheduler is waiting for a message, it is the remote event of sending the message that carries most of the control information. In other words, the control flow for processing a transaction can be viewed as moving from node to node along with message transmission. Note that by "advancing" it does not necessarily mean that transactions are forwarded from node to node or remote procedures are invoked one by one. For example, the broadcasting of locking requests represents that the control flow for processing the transaction has forked simultaneously at all other remote nodes; the control flow will not return to the initial node until a response message is received. Hence, the ⇒ edge between the message broadcasting event to the message receiving event does not carry any semantic significance for the transaction processing. The ⇒ edge, however, does carry important ordering information for the node processing. It is therefore included in the node subgraph, as explained previously in the procedure for generating node subgraphs. The → edges are not removed because they represent the order between local events (events involving no messages). Both node processing and transaction processing have to follow the order depicted by the → edges.

The intuition behind step 2 is that nonterminal transaction events without outgoing → or —≫ edges (called *halting transaction events*) represent a temporary halt in the control flow of processing transactions. A typical example is a pending transaction waiting for the release of locks held by, say, a higher priority transaction. No messages can be generated and no further local processing is possible for that transaction. Hence the local scheduler may put the transaction in a local waiting list and resume normal processing. The transaction will be awakened by later messages. Hence, there are only outgoing ⇒ edges from this event. In this case, the flow of processing for this transaction will be represented by these ⇒ edges, and such edges should be included in the transaction subgraph. Complication arises in selecting which outgoing ⇒ edges are to be included. Because a local scheduler usually resumes normal processing after a halting transaction event, outgoing ⇒ edges from the event may lead to events that are not related to the halted transaction. In this case, semantics expressed by the predicate part of the causal rules for those ⇒ edges have to be examined. Only the ⇒ edges leading to those events related to the processing of the same halted transaction should be included.

Step 3 follows the same intuition as in step 2. It deals with the case that an awakened transaction may be asked to wait again. The awakening message may generate further messages that are associated with other transactions; this is represented by the outgoing —≫ edges from the event of receiving the awakening message. However, if the awakened transaction should be put to wait again, its processing flow cannot follow the outgoing —≫ edges, which is for messages of other transactions. Hence, the outgoing ⇒ edges are included to indicate the fact that the halted transaction must be processed locally. As in step 2, semantics have to be examined to determine which edge is related to processing the same transaction.

The causal graph of the hypothetical algorithm of Fig. 2.3 is shown in Fig. 2.5. To simplify the drawing, the ⇒ edges are represented by dotted arrows. The transaction subgraph is shown in Fig. 2.6 and the node subgraph is shown

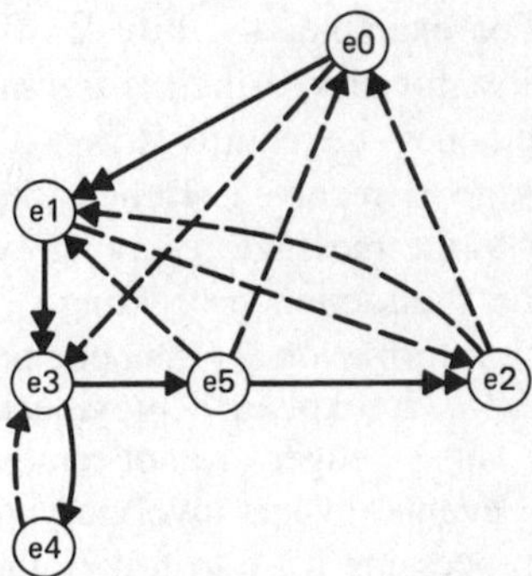

Fig. 2.5. The causal graph for the hypothetical algorithm.

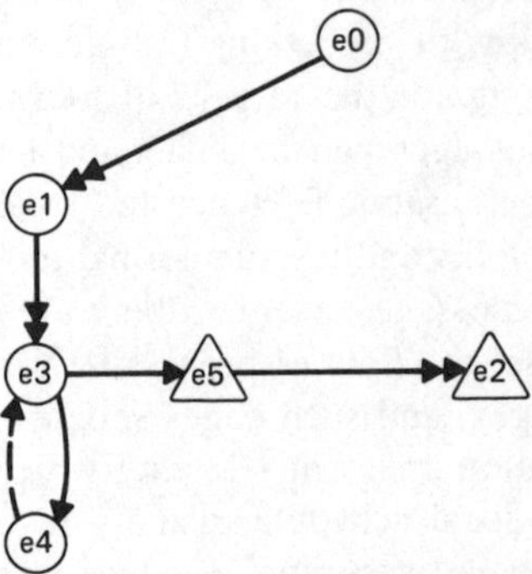

Fig. 2.6. The transaction subgraph for the hypothetical algorithm.

in Fig. 2.7. The initial transaction event is *e*0, and the terminal transaction events are *e*5 and *e*2. The initial node events are *e*0 and *e*1, and the terminal node events are the same as the terminal transaction events. The terminal events are represented by a triangle rather than a circle.

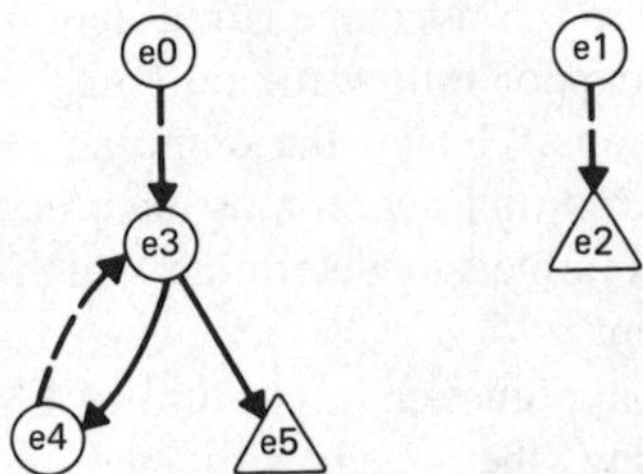

Fig. 2.7. The node subgraph for the hypothetical algorithm.

The node subgraph is derived by removing all $\twoheadrightarrow$ edges and all $\Rightarrow$ edges from the terminal node events to the initial node events. The transaction subgraph is derived by first removing all $\Rightarrow$ edges, then including the $\Rightarrow$ edge between $e4$ and $e3$. The $\Rightarrow$ edge from $e4$ to $e3$ is included because $e4$ is a nonterminal transaction event without outgoing $\rightarrow$ or $\twoheadrightarrow$ edges and the $\Rightarrow$ edge is related to the same transaction (see the corresponding causal rule in Section 2.2.1.).

2.4. Summary of the Causal Model

The causal model proposed in this chapter is intended for verifying concurrency control algorithms of distributed database systems. An algorithm is modeled as a set of local schedulers; each scheduler is associated with a node in a distributed database system. The scheduler is first represented by a state transition diagram, where a state represents a finite period of local processing. Messages are modeled as state changes, and each state change constitutes an event. Then the causal relationships between these events are described by causal rules. A graphical representation of the causal rules, the causal graph, is constructed to assist in determining the possible event ordering. By considering events related to a single node and events related to a single transaction, two subgraphs can be derived from the causal graph. The paths in these two subgraphs and the semantic conditions related to each edge will be used in the final verification process.

3. ANALYSIS OF CONCURRENCY CONTROL ALGORITHMS USING THE CAUSAL MODEL

In our model for distributed database systems, the notion of history is used to model system behavior. The concurrent read/write activities of the transactions are modeled as a sequence of atomic operations. The events related to a particular scheduler or a transaction can be described by subsequences called node projections and transaction projections. This sequence (either the overall history or the projections) represents the order of those atomic operations in real time. The basic terminology and formal definitions of transaction, history, and serializability are included in the Appendix.

The performance of a concurrency control algorithm can be measured by several parameters, e.g., average response time, average throughput, number of messages required to correctly synchronize, the degree of concurrency allowed, etc. Some of these measures are dependent on the types of transactions arriving in the system while some others are based on the particular characteristics of the system parameters, e.g., a secondary storage access I/O cost, CPU processing cost, data structures employed to broadcast messages, etc.

The degree of concurrency allowed by a concurrency control algorithm is a measure that is independent of the particular system parameters, and has been used by Kung[14] and Papadimitriou.[19] A synchronization algorithm is viewed as a scheduler which observes the sequence of operations requested by different transactions. If a particular sequence (or part of the history) is recognized by the scheduler to be acceptable, the scheduler allows further processing. If the scheduler cannot recognize a particular history, it will change the execution sequence of some operations so as to map the current history into one that is accepted by the scheduler. This may require delaying the operations of some transactions. If an algorithm recognizes more histories to be serializable, to a lesser extent, it will interfere with them. Thus, by studying the class of serializable histories recognized by the algorithms, we can compare their degree of concurrency. This measure is a qualitative comparison of algorithms rather than a quantitative comparison.

The problem of testing any arbitrary history for serializability has been shown to be NP-complete.[19] Several subsets of the serializable histories, however, have been identified for fast serializability test. These subsets, called *classes*, are defined by histories acceptable to a scheduler. We have extended the definitions of these classes for histories generated in a distributed database system. In reference 6, five classes are defined: global two-phase locking (G2PL), local two-phase locking (L2PL), distributed conflict preserving (DCP), distributed serializable in time-stamp order (DSTO), and distributed strictly serializable (DSS).

To prove the correctness of an algorithm, the recognizable histories of the algorithm are tested against these classes. If the histories of an algorithm are contained within a known class, then the correctness of the algorithm is guaranteed and the relative power of this algorithm with respect to the algorithms whose histories are contained in other classes can also be decided.[14]

This section is further organized as follows. In the first subsection, the link between the order of events in a history and the causal rules is shown. In the second subsection, the mechanisms to check the semantic conditions in the causal rules are discussed. The steps for verifying an algorithm for the serializability of its output histories are described in the third subsection. Comments on the usage of causal graphs for investigation of other aspects of the algorithm, such as deadlock possibility and reliability, are included in the fourth subsection.

3.1. Event Ordering and Causal Rules

In the causal model, event sequences are represented by paths in the causal graph. A path in the causal graph defines the partial order for the events of the path in the history. The synchronization process of the schedulers can be traced by traversing the causal graph. An event A will precede another event B in the history if a path from A to B can be found in the causal graph.

We introduce two sets of events $Q(e)$ and $R(e)$ that are reachable from an event e in the causal graph. Formally they are defined as follows.

Let $Q(e) = \{ f \mid f$ is an event and there exists local operation L, predicate P such that $\langle e, \twoheadrightarrow, f, L, P \rangle$ is a causal rule$\}$, and $R(e) = \{ f \mid f$ is an event and there exists local operation L, predicate P such that $\langle e, \Rightarrow, f, L, P \rangle$ or $\langle e, \rightarrow, f, L, P \rangle$ is a causal rule$\}$.

The predicate part of each causal rule represents the condition that the specified causal relation between the two events will appear in the execution history of the system. For an event $e(i, m)$ in the history, the local scheduler at node m will execute an event $f(k, m)$, $i, k \in T$, as the very next event if 1) there is either $\Rightarrow$ or $\rightarrow$ causal relation between $e(i, m)$ and $f(k, m)$, and 2) the predicate for that causal relation has been satisfied. In other words, $f \in R(e)$. For a message-sending event $e(i, j)$, some remote nodes will subsequently execute an event $f(k, m)$, $i, k \in T$, $j, m \in N$, $j \neq m$ if 1) there is $\twoheadrightarrow$ causal relation between $e(i, j)$ and $f(k, m)$, and 2) the predicate for that causal relation has been satisfied. Hence $f \in Q(e)$. If e is a halting transaction event, i.e., an event with no outgoing $\rightarrow$ or $\twoheadrightarrow$ edges in the transaction paths, the next event for the halted transaction will be one of the events reachable from e via $\Rightarrow$ edges. Hence, $f \in R(e)$. In all cases, the event $f(k, m)$ can be viewed as *selected* by the predicate from the corresponding set $R(e)$ for node processing or $R(e) \cup Q(e)$ for transaction processing. The following proposition summarizes the above discussion and relates the partial ordering of scheduler events in an execution history to the causal graph.

Proposition 3.1:

1. $\pi^i(f(k, j)) = \pi^j(e(i, j)) + 1$ for some $i, k \in T, j \in N$, $e, f \in E_j$ iff $f(k, j)$ is selected from $R(e)$.
2. If $e(i, j)$ is an event for transaction i and $f(i, k)$ is selected from $R(e) \cup Q(e)$ for the same transaction i, $j, k \in N$, then $\pi_i(f(i, k)) > \pi_i(e(i, j))$.
3. An event $f \in R(e)$ iff f is adjacent to e in the node subgraph.
4. For events e, f of the same transaction, $f \in R(e) \cup Q(e)$ iff f is adjacent to e in the transaction subgraph.

The proof for Proposition 3.1 is intuitive and straightforward. Proposition 3.1.1 states that any event which occurred immediately after event e in a node history must be one of the events in $R(e)$, since otherwise the local scheduler Φ_n could not possibly have advanced from e to f. Proposition 3.1.2 states that the next event of the same transaction selected from $R(e) \cup Q(e)$ should occur after e. Proposition 3.1.3 relates the set $R(e)$ to the node subgraph. The set $R(e)$ can be derived from the node subgraph, since all $\Rightarrow$ and $\rightarrow$ edges are in the node subgraph. Proposition 3.1.4 relates the events of the same transaction in $R(e) \cup Q(e)$ to the transaction subgraph.

The permutation order of a node projection is related to the node subgraph in Proposition 3.1 by 3.1.1 and 3.1.3. The set of possible next events for an event e at the same node are identified as those in the set $R(e)$. The exact selection of the next event depends on the semantics and the predicate part of the causal rule. If the selection is not unique, then nondeterministic choice is possible.

If some of the events in $R(e)$ can never be selected, they become useless events because they can never be activated. The algorithm can be redesigned to remove such events, and the resulting algorithm will have the same behavior as the original one. If no events in $R(e)$ can be selected, then the scheduler will be deadlocked after event e, unless e is the last event of the history. Hence, it follows from Proposition 3.1.1 that there exists at least one event from $R(e)$ for any event e in a history such that $\pi^j(f) = \pi^j(e) + 1$, unless e is the last event or a deadlock has occurred at node j. We assume that an algorithm is free from useless events before it is analyzed.

The permutation order of a transaction projection is related to the transaction subgraph in Proposition 3.1 by 3.1.2 and 3.1.4. One event f in the set $R(e)$ or $Q(e)$ must occur after e if both e and f are events of the same transaction. The event f may not occur immediately after e in the transaction projection because, for example, the event e may be a message broadcasting event and f is one of the responses. Then, the event f by a particular scheduler may not immediately follow e, since this f may not be the first response to e.

If an event e is a terminal transaction event, then the events in $R(e)$ must be associated with another transaction (from the definition of terminal transaction events). If a nonterminal transaction event e cannot select from $R(e)$ or $Q(e)$ a next event for the transaction, then the transaction is deadlocked. Hence, for a nonterminal and nondeadlocked transaction event e, there exists at least one event f from either $R(e)$ or $Q(e)$ such that f is for the same transaction and $\pi_i(f) > \pi_i(e)$. Proposition 3.1.3 and 3.1.4 indicate that the selected events can be determined from examining the node and the transaction paths.

From the above proposition, the following theorem can be proven.

Theorem 3.1: Let $e(i, j), f(k, m)$ $i, k \in T, j, m \in N$, be events in a history corresponding to events e, f of the causal graph. If $f(k, m)$ is selected from $R(e) \cup Q(e)$ then $\pi(f(k, m)) > \pi(e(i, j))$.

Proof: From the definitions of the node and the transaction projections, $\pi(e) < \pi(f)$ iff $\pi^j(e) < \pi^j(f)$, and $\pi(e) < \pi(f)$ iff $\pi_i(e) < \pi_i(f)$ for events e, f. If $f(k, m)$ is selected from $R(e) \cup Q(e)$, it is related to either the node processing or the transaction processing. If $f(k, m)$ is selected from $R(e)$

(node processing), then $m = j$ and $\pi^j(f(k, j)) = \pi^j(e(i, j)) + 1 > \pi^j(e(i, j))$ from Proposition 3.1.1. If $f(k, m)$ is selected from $Q(e)$ (transaction processing), then $k = i$ and $\pi_i(f(i, m)) > \pi_i(e(i, j))$ from Proposition 3.1.2. It follows from the above mentioned properties of π_i and π^j and $\pi(f(k, m)) > \pi(e(i, j))$.

Theorem 3.1 says that any event from $R(e) \cup Q(e)$ selected by some predicate for an event e must follows e in the history. More than one event can be selected by different predicates, but all selected events must follow Theorem 3.1.

3.2. Checking the Semantic Conditions of Causal Graphs

In a causal graph, the edges reflect the ordering defined by the causal rules; the semantic information is captured by local operations and the predicate associated with the corresponding causal rule. The local operations and the predicate are defined over local data structures. Hence, it is necessary to examine the value of local data structures for checking the semantic conditions for the paths in the causal graphs. The following theorem tells us about the conditions for effectively checking the semantic conditions.

Theorem 3.2: The semantic conditions necessary for a path from one event to another in a causal graph can be effectively decided if the causal rules contain only first-order predicates and primitive recursive functions.

Proof: The proof is presented by considering two cases for the paths in the causal graph as discussed in the following.

Case 1—A Single Edge in the Causal Graph: Let D_n be the local data structure at node n, and let $(D_n)^u$ be the value of D_n just after the occurrence of an event u. For the causal rule

$$u \rightarrow v + L \text{ if } P$$

and the corresponding edge in the causal graph, the data value after v, $(D_n)^v$, can be characterized as

$$(D_n)^u \; P\{L\}.$$

It means that L is applied to $(D_n)^u$ if the predicate P is true over $(D_n)^u$. The above expression can be viewed as a small program, which evaluates the predicate P on the given input $(D_n)^u$ and performs the operation L. Given $(D_n)^u$ and simple P, L such as first-order predicates for P and primitive recursive functions for L, $(D_n)^v$ can be effectively determined. Once $(D_n)^v$ can be decided, the semantic conditions for any events which are reachable from v via $\rightarrow$ edges can also be determined. Let v be followed by some other events as in

$$v \rightarrow e + L_1 \text{ if } P_1;$$

$$v \rightarrow f + L_2 \text{ if } P_2;$$

then P_1 and/or P_2 can be effectively decided, and

$$(D_n)^e = (D_n)^v\ P_1\{L_1\} = (D_n)^u\ P\{L\}\ P_1\{L_1\};$$
$$(D_n)^f = (D_n)^v\ P_2\{L_2\} = (D_n)^u\ P\{L\}\ P_2\{L_2\}.$$

In this manner, given the initial value of D_n, the semantic conditions for any $\rightarrow$ edges in the causal graph can be checked.

Similarly, the semantics of $\Rightarrow$ and $-\!\!\gg$ relations can be represented as follows:

$$u \Rightarrow v + L' \text{ if } P';$$

$$w -\!\!\gg v + L'' \text{ if } P''.$$

Let n be the node at which the events u and v occur, then $(D_n)^v$ can be characterized as

$$(D_n)^u\ P'\{L'\}\ P'' \wedge (w \text{ occurred})\ \{L''\}.$$

The data value of D_n after u, $(D_n)^u$, is tested for P', then L' is applied to D_n. L'' will not be applied unless the condition $P'' \wedge (w \text{ occurred})$ is satisfied. The first part of the above notation for $(D_n)^v$, $P'\{L'\}$, represents the semantic interpretation of the causal rule

$$u \Rightarrow v + L' \text{ if } P';$$

where P' is independent of the message content from the event w. The second part has a predicate "w occurred," which represents the semantics for the occurrence of the event w. How to check this predicate is the major task in checking semantic conditions of causal graphs.

Let m be the node where the event w occurred. There are two aspects in representing the semantics of "w occurred."

The data value $(D_m)^w$. This will characterize the local operations associated with the event w at node m. Predicates on $(D_m)^w$ can be determined by the same inference rules as described here.

The temporal order of the event w. The temporal relationship between the event w and other events can be inferred as follows. If there are causal rules

$$e \rightarrow w;$$

$$f \rightarrow w;$$

then "w occurred" implies that "e or f occurred." Exactly which of the events e and f occurred depends on the semantic conditions of the two causal rules. To infer these conditions, the same procedure described in this section can be used. If there are causal rules

$$e \Rightarrow w;$$

$$f -\!\!\gg w;$$

then "w occurred" implies that "e and f occurred." The semantic conditions for "e and f occurred" can again be inferred recursively using the procedure in this section.

Case 2—A Loop in the Causal Graph: A loop in the causal graph represents possible repetitions of a set of events, and an important semantic condition for a loop is the *exit condition* of that loop. The exit condition refers to any semantic condition that can stop the cyclic repetitions of the events on a loop. The cyclic processing is stopped either by a terminal event or by the invocation of some other events which are not on the loop. A loop containing terminal events will not cause endless repetitions because the terminal events signify the completion of the processing; the edges coming out of the terminal events are either referring to different transactions or are not semantically significant (see the discussions on generating node/transaction subgraphs). Hence, in general, the exit conditions are the predicates that enable an event which is not on the loop.

For example, consider the following causal rule

$$u \rightarrow v + L \text{ if } P,$$

where u is involved in a loop which does not involve v. Assume that n is the node at which the events u and v occurred. An exit condition for that loop is established when P is satisfied by $(D_n)^u$. Another situation for an exit condition is represented by the following causal rules

$$u \Rightarrow v + \mathrm{L}' \text{ if } P';$$

$$w -\!\!\gg v + L'' \text{ if } P''.$$

Let the events u and v occur at node n, the event w at node m. If u is involved in a loop which does not involve v, then an exit condition for the loop is established when "w occurred" and P'' is true over the data value

$$(D_n)^u \; P'\{L'\}$$

(Compare this exit condition to the second part of the notation designating the value $(D_n)^v$). Note that if in the above case w is also on a loop in which v is not involved, then the above exit condition for the loop involving u is also a possible exit condition for the loop involving w. The loop involving w is broken when "w occurred" and P'' allows the responding event v to occur.

From the previous discussions on inferring the semantic conditions about a single edge, the exit conditions of the loops can also be effectively decided.

EXAMPLE

To illustrate the inference procedure described above, consider the following causal rules for the hypothetical algorithm.

$$e0(i,j) \twoheadrightarrow e1(i,k) + X_k^+, \; \forall \, k \neq j;$$

$$e1(i,j) \twoheadrightarrow e3(i,k) + A_k^+, \; k = \mathrm{INIT}(i), \; k \neq j;$$

$$e3(i,j) \rightarrow e4(i,j) \text{ if } A_j < |N| - 1;$$

$$e3(i,j) \rightarrow e5(i,j) + W_i^j[Y] + X_j^- \text{ if } A_j = |N| - 1;$$

$$e0(i,j) \Rightarrow e3(i,j) + A_j^- + X_j^+;$$

$$e4(i,j) \Rightarrow e3(i,j).$$

From the third and the fourth causal rules, $(D_j)^{e3}$ will be tested against two predicates to determine which of the events $e4$ and $e5$ will follow. The two predicates, "if $A_j < |N| - 1$" and "if $A_j = |N| - 1$," can exclusively choose one of $e4$ and $e5$. $(D_j)^{e4}$ is identical to $(D_j)^{e3}$, since no local operations are involved in the third causal rule. $(D_j)^{e5}$ will be

$$(D_j)^{e3} \; \text{``}A_j = |N| - 1\text{''} \; \{W_i^j[Y] + X_j^-\},$$

where the update of transaction i will be performed and X_j will be initiated to zero. Note that the predicate "$A_j = |N| - 1$" will be true for both $(D_j)^{e3}$ and $(D_j)^{e5}$, since no operations on A_j are involved in the fourth causal rule. The acknowledgement count A_j will be initialized in the fifth causal rule.

The first and the second causal rules represent the message switching behavior for a transaction request. If $j = \mathrm{INIT}(i)$, the initial node of transaction i, then the second rule can be restated as

$$e1(i,k) \twoheadrightarrow e3(i,j) + A_j^+, \; k \neq j,$$

where k is some remote node having received the message by $e0(i, j)$ (the first rule). If node j has local data value $(D_j)^{e0}$, then the second and the fifth rule will produce

$$(D_j)^{e3} = (D_j)^{e0} \{A_j^- + X_j^-\} \text{``}e1(i, k) \text{ occurred''} \{A_j^+\}.$$

If node j has local data value $(D_j)^{e4}$, then the second and the sixth causal rules will produce

$$(D_j)^{e3} = (D_j)^{e4} \text{``}e1(i, k) \text{ occurred''} \{A_j^+\}.$$

The predicate "$e1(i, k)$ occurred" can be characterized by the data value $(D_k)^{e1}$ and the temporal ordering of events which leads to the occurrence of $e1(i, k)$. From the causal rules (the complete list of causal rules for the hypothetical algorithm), "$e1(i, k)$ occurred" implies that "$e0(i, j)$, j = INIT(i), occurred."

In the transaction subgraph of the hypothetical algorithm (Fig. 2.6), there is only one cycle formed by $e3$ and $e4$. The exit condition is specified in the fourth causal rule. Although the exit condition is "$A_j = |N| - 1$," the semantic condition for the sixth causal rule has to be considered, since the loop involves this $\Rightarrow$ edge. From the above discussion, the increment to A_j will occur only after $e1(i, k)$ occurred, and $e1(i, k)$ occurred only because $e0(i$, INIT$(i))$ occurred. From the quantifiers on k in the first and the second rule, only one $e1(i, k)$ at any node $k \neq$ INIT(i) can respond to $e0(i$, INIT$(i))$. Hence, the exit condition "$A_j = |N| - 1$" is equivalent to "$e1(i, k)$, $\forall k \neq j$, occurred." Since the database update $W_i^j[Y]$ is associated with the occurrence of the event $e5(i, j)$, from the exit condition, the database update will not occur until "$e1(i, k)$, $\forall k \neq j$, occurred." This demonstrates how the event ordering semantics can be inferred from the exit condition and the local data values.

Important semantics for each class have been identified in Hua.[13]

3.3. Verification Strategies

In this section, the procedure for verifying the serializability of the output histories of an algorithm is informally presented. The basic idea is to view the causal graph and the subgraphs as specifications for the order of system events. Using Theorem 3.2 and Proposition 3.1, all possible permutations of system events can be derived from the node/transaction paths. Hence an examination of the paths and the order of events specified by them can decide whether all implied histories are serializable.

Three possible strategies are discussed below. The first strategy is for verifying algorithms based on locking. The second strategy is for verifying algorithms based on time stamps. The third strategy is for verifying algorithms which output DCP histories.

The procedure for finding whether a given set of causal rules of an algorithm will generate a known class of serializable histories can be characterized as follows. First, examine the algorithm for obvious synchronization mechanisms such as locks, time stamps, etc. If the algorithm uses locks, the strategy for verifying locking algorithms can be applied. If time stamps are used, the strategy for time-stamp-based algorithms is applicable. The hierarchy of the classes of serializability for distributed database systems is shown in Fig. 2.8. It is recommended that the verification process should start from a smaller class (G2PL or DSTO). The larger classes should be attempted if the algorithm cannot be shown to generate the smaller class. In this way, the characteristics of the histories which are allowed by the algorithm but not in the smaller class can usually be observed during the verification procedure, which can assist in finding sample histories for showing the hierarchical relationship between the algorithm's output and other classes. If none of the strategies for DSTO/DSS and G2PL/L2PL is applicable, the strategy for the class DCP should be applied. However, the class DCP lacks a general strategy and the verification procedure proposed here is based on heuristics.

1. *Strategy for Verifying Locking Algorithms.* Algorithms based on locking are expected to generate either G2PL or L2PL histories. Let the event α_i represent the first database access for transaction i, and let the event ω_i represent the last database access (read or write) to an entity never accessed before by the transaction i or a write access to an entity never written before by the transaction.

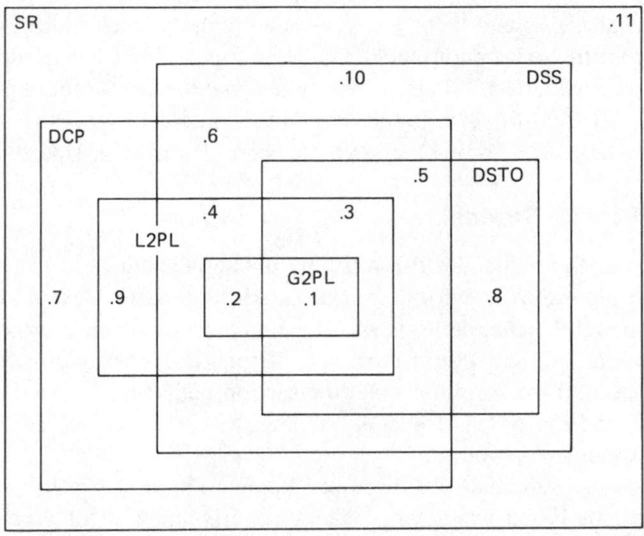

Fig. 2.8. The hierarchy of the classes SR, DCP, L2PL, G2PL, DSTO, and DSS based on the degree of concurrency.

Intuitively, the ω_i signifies the committment of a transaction. For more details, refer to reference 6.

Definition G2PL: A history h is in the *global two-phase locking* (G2PL) class iff there exists a set of global lock points $\{L_i \mid i \in T\}$ such that for transactions i and j:

i) $\pi(\alpha_i) \leq L_i \leq \pi(\omega_i) \; \forall \; i \in T$.

ii) If σ_i and σ_j conflict, and $\pi(\sigma_i) < \pi(\sigma_j)$ then a) $L_i < L_j$, and b) $\pi(\sigma_i) < L_j$.

Definition L2PL: A history is in the *local two-phase locking* (L2PL) class iff there exists a set of local lock points $\{L_i^j \mid i \in T, j \in N\}$ such that for transactions i and j:

i) $\forall \; i \in T \; L_i^k \leq \pi^k(\sigma_i)$ if $\pi(\omega_i) \leq \pi(\sigma_i)$, and $\pi^k(\alpha_i) \leq L_i^k$ if α_i is on node k.

ii) If σ_i and σ_j conflict on node k, and $\pi^k(\sigma_i) < \pi^k(\sigma_j)$ then a) $L_i^k < L_j^k$, and b) $\pi^k(\sigma_i) < L_j^k$,

iii) $L_i^k < L_j^k \Leftrightarrow L_i^m < L_j^m \; \forall \; k, m \in N$.

Note that mutual exclusion, and conventional class of synchronization in the operating systems, is just a special case of the class G2PL. For mutually exclusive accesses, consider the case $L_i = \alpha_i$. The conflicting accesses will be forced to execute serially. In other words, accesses are mutually exclusive since $\pi(\sigma_i) < L_j = \alpha_j$ for conflicting transactions i and j.

The verification strategy for locking algorithms has the following steps:

1. Identify in the transaction subgraph the event(s) which represent the lock points;
2. Identify in the node subgraph all events where the read/write atomic operations can occur. These events are called *access events*. Consider all possible pairs of these access events. For each pair call the first event of each pair σ_i and the second σ_j;
3. Find all necessary events on the node subgraph from σ_i to σ_j. "Necessary" means that these events are on all the paths from σ_i to σ_j in the node subgraph;*
4. For every event e identified in step 3), find in both transaction and node subgraphs the corresponding lock point event(s) which either precede or follow the event e;
5. By Proposition 3.1 and Theorem 3.2, infer the order between those events identified in 3) and 4);
6. Test whether the order in part ii) of the definitions G2PL or L2PL is satisfied.

---

*It is understood that there are implied $\Rightarrow$ edges between the terminal node events and the initial node events. These edges are usually not important semantically, but are considered here because they are useful in determining the events between σ_i and σ_j.

7. If all the event pairs meet the required order, then the algorithm only produces histories in the class G2PL or L2PL.

Step 2 considers only node subgraph since σ_i and σ_j in part ii) of the definitions that are on the same node. Step 3 traces the node subgraph to identify the events which can decide the order between σ_i and σ_j. Such identified events will be the pivot points in the subgraph for inferring the order. Step 4 uses the transaction subgraph to determine the order between the lock point event and the access event since they both belong to the same transaction. If necessary, node paths will also be used. Step 5 is the major step. It has to infer all possible ordering for identified events. Steps 6 and 7 test the conditions for G2PL or L2PL and lead to conclusions.

In step 5, the inference process may be quite involved since cycles are possible. Cycles in the causal graph and the subgraphs represent events that are executed repeatedly in the actual history. The number of repetitions must be shown to be finite to exclude the presence of an infinite loop. The cycles may also cause inconsistent ordering. For example, if both the α event and the access event σ are in a cycle, then both orderings $\pi(\alpha) < \pi(\sigma)$ and $\pi(\sigma) < \pi(\alpha)$ are possible. Careful examination of the semantics are described in the previous sections will be necessary to decide the proper order.

In step 1 the events representing the global or the local lock points of a transaction must be identified. It may not be possible to identify this event in a straightforward manner. However, some useful heuristics are listed below.

1. This event must be an event with local locking operations since the lock point is reached when a transaction acquires all the necessary locks.
2. This event should precede an access event due to the fact that a lock point must precede the ω_i access event and that accesses can only be done after the lock has been granted.
3. This event may be the converging point of $\twoheadrightarrow$ edges in the transaction paths for G2PL algorithms. Since synchronization by global locking often involves broadcasting request and acknowledgment messages, this event may be activated by the receipt of messages.

2. *Strategy for Verifying Time-Stamp-Based Algorithms.* For classes based on the locking approach such as G2PL, there are identifiable events and specific ordering rules. For classes such as DSTO, only the final serialization order is specified. The serialization order is defined by time stamps. The definitions of two classes DSTO and DSS that are based on time stamps are listed below.

Definition DSTO: The class DSTO contains all histories that are *distributed serializable in the time-stamp order*. A history $h = \langle D, T, \Sigma, \pi \rangle$ is in DSTO iff there exists a serial history $g = \langle D, T, \Sigma, \rho \rangle$ such that:

i) $h^j \equiv g^j \; \forall j \in N$, and
ii) $\forall i, j \in T, i \neq j, \pi(\alpha_i) < \pi(\alpha_j)$ implies $\rho(\alpha_i) < \rho(\alpha_j)$.

Definition DSS: The class DSS contains all histories that are *distributed strictly serializable*. A history $h = \langle D, T, \Sigma, \pi \rangle$ is in DSS iff there is a serial history $g = \langle D, T, \Sigma, \rho \rangle$ such that:
i) $h^j \equiv g^j \; \forall j \in N$, and
ii) $\forall i, j \in T, i \neq j, \pi(\omega_i) < \pi(\alpha_j)$ implies $\rho(\omega_i) < \rho(\alpha_j)$.

The histories in these classes rely on the order of the α event and/or the ω event to decide the final serialization order. Time stamps can be viewed as a means to register the order of α events for transactions.

The verification strategy for time-stamp-based algorithms has the following steps:

1. Identify the event(s) defining the final serialization order. In the case of DSTO, it is the event α for each transaction; for the class DSS, the ω_i event must also be considered.
2. Infer the order of access events for two conflicting transactions at each node and its relation to the order of the event(s) that define the serialization order.
3. Prove that the equivalent effect of accesses by conflicting transactions conforms to the order of the α / ω events.

Step 3 relies on the semantic interpretation and the ordering information obtained from Step 2. Step 2 is a general statement about a process that involves examining detailed semantics of each causal rule. Normally the process will trace the node/transaction subgraphs in both directions from the event(s) α / ω to determine other access events and their relationship to conflicting accesses.

3. *Strategy for Verifying Algorithms Producing DCP Histories.* The histories in the class DCP have acyclic dynamic conflict graphs (DCG). The definition for DCG is given below.

Definition DCG: A dynamic conflict graph (DCG) for a history $h = \langle D, T, \Sigma, \pi \rangle$ is a digraph $\langle V, E \rangle$: V is the set of vertices which is the same as T, the set of transactions. E is the set of edges, where $\langle i, j \rangle$ is an edge if and only if there exist atomic operations σ_i for transaction i, σ_j for transaction j such that σ_i, σ_j conflict and $\pi(\sigma_i) < \pi(\sigma_j)$.

From the definition, a DCG of a history is a graph structure that reflects the order among conflicting database accesses of several transactions. An acyclic DCG implies consistent ordering between the accesses from any two conflicting transactions. An acyclic DCG guarantees that the history is serializable. This provides a test for whether a history is in class DCP or not.

To maintain acyclic DCG distributively in an algorithm, however, is not easy. One technique is to associate the order of database accesses to the order of a special event. Since the order of any particular event in processing each transaction is necessarily acyclic, i.e., the special event for one transaction cannot possibly precede and follow the special event for another transaction simultaneously due to the natural law of time, associating the order of accesses to a special event guarantees acyclic DCG. The technique, of course, can only permit a subset of the DCP histories. As far as the authors know, no general algorithms which implement the whole DCP class have been proposed. The verification strategy below is geared toward this technique, but extensions of the verification strategy for general DCP algorithms are possible.

The verification strategy is as follows:

1. Identify the special event that decides the order of conflicting database accesses.
2. Infer the relationship between the temporal order of the events representing conflicting database accesses and the temporal order of the special events.

In step 2 the inference procedure can use the techniques for inferring the relationship between the access events and the lock point events in the strategy for locking algorithms. Step 1 may involve heuristics to determine the special event. A good guess is when the first write access of a transaction is accepted since that instance will make the effect of a transaction visible to other transactions.

EXAMPLE:

To illustrate how to use the strategy for locking, we now analyze the hypothetical algorithm for mutual exclusion. In reference 12, we have analyzed the majority consensus algorithm.[25] Recall that mutual exclusion is a special case of G2PL; the global lock point is the first access event, α. In the algorithm, database access activities are associated with two events, $e5$ and $e2$. The event $e5$ represents the global lock point since it is the first access activity, the α event, during transaction processing.

Lemma 3.1: The hypothetical algorithm only produces mutually exclusive accesses.

Proof: To prove the lemma, first, the event $e5$ is identified as the α event of this algorithm, since all $e2$ events must follow $e5$ ($e2$ is only reachable from $e5$ in the transaction subgraph). Then, the event $e5$ of this algorithm is identified as the global lock point defined in Definition G2PL. The proof will follow the strategy for verifying locking algorithms. Consider two conflicting transactions i, j and $\pi(\sigma_i) < \pi(\sigma_j)$ for accesses σ_i, σ_j, at node k. Then their accesses to the database on node k are either $e5$ or $e2$ in this algorithm. There are four cases.

1. Both $e5$. It is obvious that the condition of Definition G2PL is satisfied.
2. $\sigma_i = e5(i, k)$ and $\sigma_j = e2(j, k)$. $\pi(e5(i, k)) < \pi(e2(j, k))$. Since $e2$ is reachable only from $e1$ in the node subgraph (Fig. 2.7), the local scheduler at node k must execute $e1(j, k)$ immediately before $e2(j, k)$ (Proposition 3.1). Hence, $\pi(e5(i, k)) < \pi(e1(j, k)) < \pi(e2(j, k))$. In the transaction subgraph in Fig. 2.6, there is a path from $e1$ to $e5$; hence $\pi(e1(j, k)) < \pi(e5(j, m))$ for some node m (Theorem 3.2). This is the only possible ordering between $e1(j, k)$ and $e5(j, m)$ since $e1$ and $e5$ are not on a cycle. Therefore $\pi(e5(i, k)) < \pi(e5(j, m))$, which satisfies Definition G2PL.
3. $\sigma_i = e2(i, k)$ and $\sigma_j = e5(j, k)$. Again, from the transaction subgraph (Fig. 2.6), $\pi(e5(i, m)) < \pi(e2(i, k))$ for some node m. Hence, $\pi(e5(i, m)) < \pi(e5(j, k))$.
4. Both $e2$. Since $e2$ is the only member in $R(e1)$ from the node subgraph (Fig. 2.7), $\pi_k(e2(i, k)) = \pi_k(e1(i, k)) + 1$ by Proposition 3.1.1. Hence $\pi(e1(i, k)) < \pi(e2(i, k)) < \pi(e1(j, k)) < \pi(e2(j, k))$ due to the fact that $\pi(e2(i, k)) < \pi(e2(j, k))$ and the properties of π_k. Since $\pi(e5(i, m)) < \pi(e2(i, k))$ and $\pi(e1(j, k)) < \pi(e5(j, n))$ for some node m, n (the requirement from the transaction subgraph), $\pi(e5(i, m)) < \pi(e2(i, k)) < \pi(e5(j, n))$.

Since $e5$ satisfies the condition of global lock point and it is also the α event (see the transaction subgraph), this algorithm will produce mutually exclusive accesses.

3.4. Other Aspects of Verification

Two operational aspects of an algorithm are the deadlock possibility and the reliability. The use of the causal model for the analysis of these aspects is presented in the following.

1. *Deadlock Possibility.* Both deadlock and livelock will delay a transaction indefinitely. The term "deadlock" will be used to refer to the indefinite delay of processing for the sake of simplicity.

The emphasis here is to analyze whether a deadlock is possible for an algorithm. The following proposition is based upon the observation in Section 3.1.

Proposition 3.2: A concurrency control algorithm is deadlock free if and only if: 1) the processing of a transaction starting from initial transaction events can reach the terminal transaction events in a finite number of events in the transaction projection; and 2) every local scheduler starting from initial node events can reach terminal node events in a finite number of events in the node projection.

The justification for this proposition is intuitive.

Since event ordering in the node (transaction) projection is closely related to the node (transaction) subgraph, the following list of conditions are used to verify the deadlock possibility of an algorithm.

1. Every nonterminal event must be on a path leading to terminal node/ transaction events.
2. For every nonterminal event u, there is at least one event v in $R(u) \cup Q(u)$ such that v can be selected as the next event after u.
3. Events on the cycles in the transaction/node subgraphs can only be selected finitely many times for the same transaction.

   Condition 1 guarantees that there exists a possible sequence of events which can take a local scheduler or a transaction to termination after the occurrence of a nonterminal event. Condition 2 requires that no events can lead to a dead-end situation without any possible next event. Condition 3 limits the number of times a transaction can execute the events on a cycle.

Theorem 3.3: Conditions 1, 2, and 3 are satisfied if and only if a concurrency control algorithm has the properties 1) and 2) in Proposition 3.2.

Proof:

The sufficient condition. Recall the assumption that an algorithm does not have "useless" events (events which will never be selected). Then it is clear that the processing of an algorithm will not be guaranteed to reach terminal events if condition 3 is not satisfied. If an event cannot select a next event [violation of condition 2], the algorithm is deadlocked once its processing reaches this event. If an event is not on any path which may lead to terminal events, the processing of an algorithm will not be able to reach terminal events after this event no matter what next event it selects. Hence condition 1 is also necessary for the properties in Proposition 3.2.

The necessary condition. There are two aspects: the processing must end in terminal events and the processing must reach there via a finite number of events. Assume that some transaction (node) processing stops at a nonterminal event. It directly violates condition 2. Assume that some transaction (node) processing has incurred an infinite number of events. Since there are only a finite number of transactions and a finite number of events in the transaction (node) subgraphs there must be a cycle such that the processing can repeatedly select events from the events on the cycle. This is a violation of condition 3.

Since many deadlock or livelock situations can be examined only through semantic information, the complete analysis of the deadlock possibility cannot be performed by testing merely the ordering of system events.

2. *Reliability.* A complete analysis of the reliability aspects of a distributed concurrency control algorithm is beyond the scope of this chapter. In what follows is an informal description of how to utilize the causal graph and event ordering to infer some characteristics of the reliability of an algorithm.

One way to interpret the causal rules, or the edges in the causal graph, is to view them as ordering specifications. This is the approach used in Section 3.1. Another interpretation, however, is to view them as dependency specifications. If a causal relation exists between events u and v, i.e., $\langle u, @, v, L, P \rangle$ is a causal rule for some @, L, and P, then the occurrence of v is dependent on the occurrence of u. For example, if $u \twoheadrightarrow v$, then v depends on the occurrence of u. Further, it implies that v also depends on the reliable transmission of the message by event u. Hence, studying the effect generated by assuming that one of the causal rules failed to occur can reveal the reliability of an algorithm, especially the dependency of an algorithm or certain events.

A possible scenario of the analysis is as follows.

1. Assume that some causal rule is not fulfilled, which indicates a failure situation.
2. Infer how many events are going to be affected: are they altered or prohibited?
3. Examine the corresponding effects on the node and the transaction projections, respectively.

The types of failures that can be modeled by step 1 are node failures (e.g., $u \rightarrow v$ is nullified), and lost messages (e.g., $u \twoheadrightarrow v$ is nullified). This type of analysis is at best qualitative in nature, but should be adequate in identifying possible consequences of failures.

EXAMPLE:

To illustrate the above concepts, the hypothetical algorithm is analyzed for its deadlock possibility and reliability. To test whether a node will deadlock, the paths between initial node events and the terminal node events must be shown not to block the local scheduler [Proposition 3.2.1].

From the node subgraph (Fig. 2.7), event $e0$ is followed only by $e3$ and the only condition for $e3$ to occur is the occurrence of event $e1$. Also, the terminal node event $e5$ can be reached if and only if all other nodes have performed $e1$ (from the transaction subgraph in Fig. 2.6). Hence, a node cannot be guaranteed to complete processing of a transaction unless all other nodes execute $e1$. It can happen if the two local schedulers simultaneously execute the event $e0$. Neither of them can execute $e1$ before executing $e5$, which can be executed only if the other executes $e1$. Thus, deadlock is possible in this algorithm.

The deadlock possibility can also be shown in another way. In the node subgraph (Fig. 2.7), there is only one path from $e1$ to the terminal event $e2$. Hence, only when a DONE message is received can a node finish the processing of a remote lock request. Any node which performs $e1$ cannot terminate unless the transaction is finished. However, the completion of a transaction depends on the global consensus; two nodes which simultaneously perform the event $e1$ for different transactions will create a deadlock because no transactions can get the global consensus.

The reliability of this algorithm can be determined by examining the node subgraphs and the $\twoheadrightarrow$ causal rules for the events on a node subgraph. There are only three types of messages in this algorithm; they are represented by $e0$, $e1$, and $e5$. When an $e0$ message (EXTREQ) from one node to another is lost, i.e., $e0 \twoheadrightarrow e1$ is nullified, no corresponding $e1$ is possible, since $e0$ is the only cause for $e1$. No global consensus is possible for the transaction and the transaction is deadlocked. A lost $e1$ (ACK) will have the same effect. Since $e5$ (DONE) is the only cause for $e2$, which is the terminal event for the node path $e1 \Rightarrow e2$, a node will not be able to finish if an $e5$ message is lost. Hence, any lost message causes deadlock, and this fact is indicated by the structure of the transaction subgraph (Fig. 2.6): Any loss of messages in one of the events $e0$, $e1$, and $e5$ effectively breaks all the paths from the transaction initial event ($e0$) to the transaction terminal events.

Any node failure will cause the algorithm to halt. As indicated by the node subgraph in Fig. 2.7, any local scheduler starting from event $e0$ can reach the terminal node event $e5$ only if $e1$ is responded to by all other nodes. If one of the nodes failed to respond, the node that initiates $e0$ will be kept waiting, and no other transactions can proceed. On the other hand, if the node initiating $e0$ fails to complete $e5$, all other nodes cannot proceed either, since the only possible way to start $e1$ is after the node completes $e5$.

The algorithm is faulty because it allows deadlock to occur, and is not reliable since deadlock will occur when the messages are lost or a node fails.

4. COMPARISON TO OTHER MODELS

We compare the causal model to three other modeling mechanisms: Petri nets, *L* systems, and path expressions. The comparisons are based on the descriptive capability for synchronization schedulers. Neither the exhaustive list of the modeling mechanisms nor the descriptive capability of the three for other modeling purposes is included. The comparison is presented for discussion and to show the specific advantage of our approach rather than to make a general claim on its merits. For more details, see reference 13.

4.1. Petri Nets

Petri nets, surveyed in Peterson,[20] are abstract formal models for information and control in systems exhibiting concurrent and asynchronous behavior. They consist of places where one or more tokens can reside and the places are connected via transitions. A transition is enabled (fired) when all of its input places have tokens. The firing of a transition causes tokens to be moved from their input places to their output places. The modeling of distributed processing is done by associating logical interpretations to places, token, and firing rules. For example, places can be thought of as different programs, such as producers and consumers, where tokens are resources to be produced and consumed. Firing transitions can be used to model the process of producing and consuming the resources. By properly connecting places, transitions into a net, and placing the initial marking of tokens, the producer-consumer problem can be represented. Petri nets can be used to model two aspects of systems: events and conditions, and their relationships.

To prove the correctness of schedulers, we have to express the scheduler in the nets. To model a synchronization algorithm, the capability of representing value-dependent semantics is required. The Petri nets in their original form are not quite able to do this without increased complexity. The predicate/transition nets represent an extension of the Petri nets and are obtained by adding predicates and semantics interpretation. A detailed comparison of a distributed concurrency control algorithm using the causal model and predicate/transition nets[10,26] has been done in reference 13. From this study, we observe that the transformation from parallel processes to the modeling Petri nets is nontrivial. Even if a net could be constructed, some problems about the net such as the reachability problem, i.e., whether a target marking can be reachable from a given marking, have an exponential lower bound of complexity. Other problems, such as the equivalence of reachable marking sets, are even undecidable. The complexity bounds as well as the large number of places and transitions needed to model indicate that, although some analysis questions may be decidable using Petri nets, in a general case the cost of deciding may make such analysis unfeasible.

Another limitation of nets seems to be the difficulty in specifying the correctness condition for concurrency control such as serializability. It is easy to associate the condition of mutual exclusion with the exclusive presence of tokens in one place but the specification of the serializability condition is not obvious since it is necessary to know the ordering of events in the history. The conditions over place markings prescribe a set of configuration of tokens in places. These conditions seem to be memoryless in nature, i.e., how the tokens arrive at the prescribed configuration is not specified.

The causal model can easily represent value-dependent semantics through local data structures and local operations in the causal rules. The very general form of predicates for causal relations enables us to express the semantic interpretation of an algorithm. The purpose of the causal graph model is to concentrate on the global picture of event ordering. Events and their causal relations are also natural extensions from the descriptions of algorithmic state transitions, which increase the descriptive power of our model.

Another advantage of expressing read/write requests as events is that the transformation from serializability conditions to event ordering information is straightforward. Not only can problems such as mutual exclusion be modeled by the causal graph model, more complex synchronization policy like the two-phase locking protocol can also be described as event ordering constraints.

4.2. Linguistic Models

Ellis introduced the modeling of synchronization schedulers in distributed database by *L* systems.[8] *L* systems, originally studied in Rosenberg,[22] are similar to phrase structure grammars but with no terminal symbols and with simultaneous replacement rules selected from an arbitrary finite set of tables. Ellis expresses the synchronization algorithm in terms of evaluation nets, a modified form of Petri nets, and then translates the evaluation net semantics into a set of *L* system tables. The rules mimic the operation of each node's state transition and the changes of local variables by manipulating a string of symbols assembled from the state symbols of each node and the local variables. The message switching is modeled by letting one node examine/change other nodes' states and variables, i.e., the *L* system grammar is context sensitive. The algorithm's properties such as mutual update exclusion, and deadlock avoidance capability are expressed as membership problems of the language generated by the *L* grammar.

Analyzing *L* system models for algorithms is relatively easy because the membership problem of a context sensitive grammar can be automated. However, the translation from evaluation nets to *L* system grammars lacks a well-defined methodology, and the context sensitivity of the *L* grammars makes the rule tables extremely complex if the message switching is of arbitrary configuration.

The expression of high level synchronization policies is also a problem with *L* system models. In Ellis' example, the analysis is done by testing the membership of a string of local variables and local scheduler's state variables. The algorithm is shown "incorrect" by showing that a string of variables with two different nodes simultaneously having the same lock and the update is a member of the language. However, an algorithm is not necessarily correct if the above strings are absent, because the serializability is not simply the state of local variables or the local program counters. To show an algorithm correct with L system models, we need to prove that members of the language are produced in correct sequences of derivation steps.

4.3. Path Expressions

Path expressions[7,17,23] follow the event ordering notion and specify the behavior of concurrent program operations. A path expression is a formal definition of some ordering constraint on the way in which occurrences of events in a system are to relate. The set of all path expressions for a system is an abstract description of the system and can be viewed as a set of grammar rules for generating strings representing system histories. From these path expressions, characteristics such as deadlock avoidance capability can be analyzed by expressing them in path expressions, then verifying whether the description of the algorithm implies such characteristics or not.

For example, the synchronization aspect for a version of the producer/consumer problem can be described in path expressions[7] in forms like

path { read }, { write } **end**
path write **end**.

The first path means that if the read procedure begins to execute, all reading requests are accepted. The same is the case with writes. A read and a write may not overlap, but a read can overlap with other reads. The second path ensures that the actions of writing are mutually exclusive. Thus, executions of write are synchronized with respect to read in the first path expression, the synchronization among writes is expressed in the second path.

Path expressions were originally proposed as synchronization tools rather than as verification models. Sometimes the description can be too abstract to leave any indication for implementation. The paths describe the desired ordering of operations but give little indication for implementation, as we can see from the example. Although procedures for translating path expressions into P's and V's are given in Campbell and Habermann,[7] no translations to message switching algorithms are known.

Path expressions can be used as the verification tool by viewing them as conditions that an algorithm has to satisfy. In other words, path expressions can be viewed as behavior descriptions of the operations in an algorithm. The problem of proving that a set of path expressions for describing a system really represents the system is difficult.[23] Contrary to the causal graph model, the originally proposed path expressions do not contain semantic as well as history information about the system's behavior. This makes the process of deducing/transforming path expressions from/to an algorithm difficult. An attempt of adding predicates to path expressions[1] is similar to our construct of causal rule predicates, but its emphasis is still on using path expressions as programming specification for synchronization. Andler presented an implementation of predicate path expressions through shared monitors for abstract object types; the applicability of such construct in distributed environment needs further research work.

APPENDIX
BASIC TERMINOLOGY

A *distributed database management system* (DDBMS) is a database system distributed among a set of *nodes* N connected by communication links. Each node has its own independent computing resources.

The database is modeled by a set of *logical database entities* which may have one or more *physical copies of data value*. The database entities are accessed by unique names; how this naming is maintained is insignificant to this study. The database may be either completely or partially replicated, or it may be partitioned on different nodes.

A distributed database is *consistent* if it satisfies some predefined assertions about the intrinsic characteristics of the data values. For a replicated distributed database, it is necessary for the physical copies of the same database entity on different nodes to remain identical.

The user actions on a distributed database consist of a sequence of atomic operations. An *atomic operation* is represented by $\sigma_i = A_i^j[x]$ where i is a unique identification for a transaction, j is a unique identification for a node, A is either R or W, representing a read or write operation, and x is one or more logical database entities. As far as the DDBMS is concerned, these read/write operations constitute indivisible (or atomic) operations to the database.[11] The atomic operations are grouped into logical units called *transactions* that will preserve the database consistency if executed alone. A transaction can be viewed as a quantum change for the database from one consistent state to another; however, the consistency assertions may be temporarily violated during the execution of a transaction but must be satisfied when there are no incomplete transactions or the system is quiescent. The purpose of the concurrency control is to guarantee that the concurrent execution of a set of transactions does not result in an inconsistent database state.

The *transaction set* T represents all user transactions, and the *atomic operation set* Σ contains all the atomic operations specified by the transaction set. A transaction has to read only one copy of a replicated data entity but has to update all copies.

Two atomic operations σ_i, σ_j *conflict* if a) they belong to different transactions, b) both access the same database entity at the same node, and c) at least one of them is a write operation. In particular, conflicting atomic operations σ_i and σ_j have i) *WR-conflict* if σ_i is a write operation and σ_j is a read operation, ii) *RW-conflict* if σ_i is a read operation and σ_j is a write operation, and iii) *WW-conflict* if both σ_i and σ_j are write operations.

There are two special atomic operations in a transaction that are important. The *last* *new atomic operation* ω_i of transaction i is its last atomic operation such that the access is to a new database entity or the access is at a higher level* than before for a previously accessed entity. Every atomic operation after ω_i either accesses some used entity or repeats a lower level access. The *earliest new atomic operation* α_i for a transaction i is the first atomic operation which starts accessing new entities. Since each atomic operation accesses some database entities, α_i is simply the first atomic operation in a transaction.

For example, ω_i of the following transaction

$$R_i^1[x]\ W_i^2[y]\ W_i^2[z]\ W_i^3[y]\ W_i^3[z]$$

is $W_i^2[z]$ since z is the last new entity being accessed. The ω_i of the following transaction

$$R_i^1[x]\ W_i^2[y]\ W_i^2[z]\ W_i^3[y]\ W_i^3[z]\ W_i^1[x]\ R_i^2[z]\ R_i^1[x]$$

is $W_i^1[x]$ since it is the latest higher level access to any entity (x in this case).

The concurrent activities of a distributed database system can be modeled as a sequence of all atomic operations. This sequence is called the *history* of the system, and is represented by a quadruple $h = \langle D, T, \Sigma, \pi \rangle$ where D is a distributed database, T is the transaction set, Σ is the atomic operation set, and π is a *permutation function* which gives the permutation indices for atomic operation σ in $h(\sigma \in \Sigma)$. For example, if a history h is the following sequence

$$\alpha\beta\gamma \cdots \omega$$

then $\pi(\alpha) = 1$, $\pi(\beta) = 2$, $\cdots$, $\pi(\omega) = |\Sigma|$. A *serial history* is one in which each transaction runs to completion before the next one starts. In other words, in a serial history the atomic operations of different transactions are not interleaved.

Although the system's activities can be modeled as a string of atomic operations, the activity at one node is potentially independent of those at other nodes. Each node records its own history. To capture this notion of local activities, *the node projection* $h^j = \langle h, \Sigma^j, \pi^j \rangle$ of a history h is defined as the subsequence of h containing only those operations pertaining to node j where $\Sigma^j = \{\sigma \mid \sigma \in \Sigma$ and σ is performed at node $j\}$ is a subset of Σ, and π^j is the permutation function for h^j, i.e., $\pi^j(\sigma_1) < \pi^j(\sigma_2)$ iff $\pi(\sigma_1) < \pi(\sigma_2)$ for $\sigma_1, \sigma_2 \in \Sigma^j$. The order of the atomic operations in h is retained in π^j.

The activities of a transaction in a distributed database system can be modeled by a sequence of operations on the database related to this transaction. This sequence is called *the transaction projection* $h_i = \langle h, \Sigma_i, \pi_i \rangle$ where $\Sigma_i = \{\sigma \mid \sigma \in \Sigma$ and σ belongs to transaction $i\}$ is a subset of Σ, and π_i is the permutation function of h_i, i.e., $\pi_i(\sigma_1) < \pi_i(\sigma_2)$ iff $\pi(\sigma_1) < \pi(\sigma_2)$ for every $\sigma_1, \sigma_2 \in \Sigma_i$.

From the above definitions, it is clear that a serial history h has the form

$$h_{i_1}\ h_{i_2}\ h_{i_3} \cdots h_{i_t} \text{ for } i_k \in T,\ k = 1, \cdots, t$$

*For the transaction model used here, the read operation is considered a lower level access when compared to the write operation.

where $t = |T|$ and $i_1\ i_2\ i_3 \cdots i_t$ is a permutation of transaction id's (h_{i_1}, say, is the transaction projection for transaction i_1 from the serial history h). Note that each node projection of a serial history is essentially a sequential execution of transactions following the same permutation order $i_1\ i_2 \cdots i_t$ of the serial history.

Each operation in a history transforms one database state into another one. Two histories are *equivalent* or indistinguishable if they transform a given initial state to the same final database state. The notation $\equiv$ denotes the equivalence relation between histories. A history h is *serializable* iff there exists a serial history g such that $h^j \equiv g^j$ for every node j.

If every transaction when executed alone preserves the database consistency, then each node projection of a serializable history will also preserve the consistency. Since a serial history produces node projections with the same serial transaction order, a serializable history necessarily generates a consistent database. An algorithm is considered correct if all its allowed histories are serializable.

The use of serializability as a correctness criterion is popular among researchers.[2,9,19,21] Although nonserializable histories can be consistent when semantic information is available,[15,24] we still consider serializability to be the correctness criterion. It has been shown in reference 14 that concurrency control algorithms with only syntactic information can, at best, produce serializable histories.

REFERENCES

1. Andler, S., *Predicate Path Expressions: A High-level Synchronization Mechanism*, Tech. Rep. CMU-CS-79-134 (Ph.D. Dis.), Dep. Comput. Sci., Carnegie-Mellon Univ., 1979.
2. Bernstein, P. A., D. W. Shipman, and W. D. Wong, Formal aspects of serializability in database concurrency control, *IEEE Trans. Software Eng.*, vol. SE-5, pp. 203–216, May 1979.
3. Bernstein, P. A. and N. Goodman, Concurrency control in distributed database systems, *ACM Comput. Surveys*, vol. 13, pp. 185–222, June 1981.
4. Bhargava, B. and C. T. Hua, The causal graph model for distributed database synchronization algorithms, *IEEE Proc. 4th Int. Comput. Software Applications Conf.* (*COMPSAC*), Chicago, IL, Oct. 1980, pp. 444–452.
5. Bhargava, B., Concurrency control and reliability in distributed database system, in *Software Engineering Handbook*, C. V. Ramamoorthy and C. R. Vick, eds., pp. 331–358, Princeton, NJ: Van Nostrand Reinhold, 1983.
6. Hua, C. and B. Bhargava, Classes of serializable histories and synchronization algorithms in distributed database systems," *Proc. IEEE Int. Conf. Distributed Comput. Syst.*, Miami, FL, Oct. 18–22, 1982, pp. 438–446.
7. Campbell, R. H. and A. N. Habermann, The specification of process synchronization by path expressions, in *Lecture Notes in Computer Science*, vol. 16, W. Berlin-Springer-Verlag, 1974, pp. 89–102.
8. Ellis, C. A., Consistency and correctness of duplicate database systems, *Proc. 6th ACM Symp. Operating Syst.*, Nov. 1977.
9. Eswaran, K. P., J. N. Gray, R. Lorie, and A. Traiger, The notions of consistency and predicate locks in a database system, *CACM*, vol. 19, pp. 624–633, Nov. 1976.
10. Genrich, H. J. and K. Lautenbach, The analysis of distributed systems by means of predicate/transition nets, *Proc. Int. Symp. Semantics Concurrent Computation* (*Lecture Notes in Computer Science 70*). New York: Springer-Verlag, 1979, pp. 123–146.

11. Gray, J. N., A transaction model, IBM Res. Rep. RJ2895, IBM Res. Div., San Jose Laboratory, CA, Feb. 1980.
12. Hau, C. T. and B. Bhargava, Analysis of the majority consensus algorithm for correctness and performance using the event ordering approach, *IEEE Proc. Int. Conf. Inform. and Commun.*, San Diego, CA, Apr. 1983.
13. Hua, C. T., *Verification of Concurrency Control Algorithms for Distributed Database Systems* (Ph.D. diss.), Dep. Comput. Sci., Univ. Pittsburgh, PA, 1981.
14. Kung, H. T. and C. H. Papadimitriou, An optimality theory of concurrency control for databases, *Proc. ACM SIGMOD 1979*, May 1979, pp. 116–126.
15. Lamport, L., Towards a theory of correctness for multi-user data base systems, Tech. Rep. CA-7610-0712, Massachusetts Computer Associates, Inc., Oct. 1976.
16. Lamport, L., Time clocks, and the ordering of events in a distributed system, *CACM*, vol. 21, pp. 558–564, July 1978.
17. Lauer, P. E. and R. H. Campbell, Formal semantics for a class of high level primitives for coordinating concurrent processes, *Acta Informatica*, vol. 5, pp. 297–332, 1975.
18. Menasce, D. A., G. Popek, and R. Muntz, A locking protocol for resource coordination in distributed databases, ACM *Trans. Database Syst.*, vol. 5, pp. 103–138, June 1980.
19. Papadimitriou, C. H., The serializability of concurrent database updates," *J. Ass. Comput. Mach.*, vol. 26, pp. 631-653, Oct. 1979.
20. Peterson, J. L., Petri nets, *Comput. Surveys*, vol. 9, pp. 223–252, ACM, Sept. 1977.
21. Rosenkrantz, D. L., R. E. Stearns, and P. M. Lewis II, System level concurrency control for distributed database systems, *ACM Trans. Database Syst.*, vol. 3, pp. 178–198, June 1978.
22. G. Rozenberg, *L Systems*. New York: Springer-Verlag, 1974.
23. Shields, M. W., Adequate path expressions, *Proc. Int. Symp. Semantics Concurrent Computation* (*Lecture Notes in Computer Science 70*). New York: Springer-Verlag, 1979, pp. 249–265.
24. Silberschatz, A. and Z. Kedem, Consistency in hierarchical database systems, *J. Ass. Comput. Mach.*, vol. 27, pp. 72–80, Jan. 1980.
25. Thomas, R. H., A majority consensus approach to concurrency control, *ACM Trans. Database Syst.*, vol. 4, pp. 180–209, June 1979.
26. Voss, K., Using predicate/transition nets to model and analyze distributed database systems, *IEEE Trans. Software Eng.*, vol. SE-6, pp. 539–544, Nov. 1980.

3. Guardians and Actions: Linguistic Support for Robust, Distributed Programs

BARBARA LISKOV

and

ROBERT SCHEIFLER

ABSTRACT

This chapter presents an overview of an integrated programming language and system designed to support the construction and maintenance of distributed programs: programs in which modules reside and execute at communicating, but geographically distinct, nodes. The language is intended to support a class of applications concerned with the manipulation and preservation of long-lived, on-line, distributed data. The language addresses the writing of robust programs that survive hardware failures without loss of distributed information and that provide highly concurrent access to that information while preserving its consistency. Several new linguistic constructs are provided; among them are atomic actions, and modules called guardians that survive node failures.

1. INTRODUCTION

Technological advances have made it cost-effective to construct large systems from collections of computers connected via networks. To support such systems, there is a growing need for effective ways to organize and maintain *distributed*

This research was supported in part by the Advanced Research Projects Agency of the Department of Defense, monitored by the Office of Naval Research under contract N00014-75-C-0661, and in part by the National Science Foundation under grant MCS79-23769.

programs: programs in which modules reside and execute at communicating, by geographically distinct, locations. In this chapter we present an overview of an integrated programming language and system, called Argus, that was designed for this purpose.

Distributed programs run on *nodes* connected (only) via a communications network. A node consists of one or more processors, one or more levels of memory, and any number of external devices. Different nodes may contain different kinds of processors and devices. The network may be longhaul or shorthaul, or any combination, connected by gateways. Neither the network nor any nodes need be reliable. However, we do assume that all failures can be detected, as explained in Lampson and Sturgis.[16] We also assume that message delay is long relative to the time needed to access local memory, and therefore access to non-local data is significantly more expensive than access to local data.

The applications that can make effective use of a distributed organization differ in their requirements. We have concentrated on a class of applications concerned with the manipulation and preservation of long-lived, on-line data. Examples of such applications are banking systems, airline reservation systems, office automation systems, database systems, and various components of operating systems. In these systems, real-time constraints are not severe, but reliable, available, distributed data is of primary importance. The systems may serve a geographically distributed organization. Our language is intended to support the implementation of such systems.

The application domain, together with our hardware assumptions, imposes a number of requirements:

1. Service. A major concern is to provide continuous service of the system as a whole in the face of node and network failures. Failures should be localized so that a program can perform its task as long as the particular nodes it needs to communicate with are functioning and reachable. Adherence to this principle permits an application program to use replication of data and processing to increase availability.
2. Reconfiguration. An important reason for wanting a distributed implementation is to make it easy to add and reconfigure hardware to increase processing power, decrease response time, or increase the availability of data. It also must be possible to implement logical systems that can be reconfigured. To maintain continuous service, it must be possible to make both logical and physical changes *dynamically*, while the system continues to operate.
3. Autonomy. We assume that nodes are owned by individuals or organizations that want to control how the node is used. For example, the owner may want to control what runs at the node, or to control the availability of services provided at the node. Further, a node might contain data that

must remain resident at that node: for example, a multinational organization must abide by laws governing information flow among countries. The important point here is that the need for distribution arises not only from efficiency considerations, but from political and sociological considerations as well.

4. Distribution. The distribution of data and processing can have a major impact on overall efficiency, in terms of both responsiveness and cost-effective use of hardware. Distribution also affects availability. To create efficient, available systems while retaining autonomy, the programmer needs explicit control over the placement of modules in the system. However, to support a reasonable degree of modularity, changes in location of modules should have limited, localized effects on the actual code.
5. Concurrency. Another major reason for choosing a distributed implementation is to take advantage of the potential concurrency in an application, thereby increasing efficiency and decreasing response time.
6. Consistency. In almost any system where on-line data is being read and modified by on-going activities, there are consistency constraints that must be maintained. Such constraints apply not only to individual pieces of data, but to distributed sets of data as well. For example, when funds are transferred from one account to another in a banking system, the net gain over the two accounts must be zero. Also, data that is replicated to increase availability must be kept consistent.

Of the above requirements, we found consistency the most difficult to meet. The main issues here are the coordination of concurrent activities (permitting concurrency but avoiding interference), and the masking of hardware failures. Thus, to support consistency we had to devise methods for building a reliable system on unreliable hardware. Reliability is an area that has been almost completely ignored in programming languages (with the exception of references 22, 24, and 27). Yet our study of applications convinced us that consistency is a crucial requirement: an adequate language must provide a modular, reasonably automatic method for achieving consistency.

Our approach is to provide *atomicity* as a fundamental concept in the language. The concept of atomicity is not original with our work, having been used extensively in data base applications.[4,5,6,8,9,10] However, we believe the integration into a programming language of a general mechanism for achieving atomicity is novel.

The remainder of the chapter is organized as follows. Atomicity is discussed in the next section. Section 3 presents an overview of Argus. The main features are *guardians*, the logical unit of distribution in our system, and atomic *actions*. Section 4 illustrates many features of the language with a simple mail system. The final section concludes with a discussion of what has been accomplished.

2. ATOMICITY

Data consistency requires first of all that the data in question be resilient to hardware failures, so that a crash of a node or storage device does not cause the loss of vital information. Resiliency is accomplished by means of redundancy. We believe the most practical technique using current technology is to keep data on stable storage devices.[16] Of course, stable storage, in common with any other technique for providing resiliency, cannot guarantee that data survive all failures, but it can guarantee survival with extremely high probability.*

Data resiliency only ensures data survival in a quiescent environment. Our solution to the problem of maintaining consistent distributed data in the face of concurrent, potentially interfering activities, and in the face of system failures such as node crashes and network disruptions while these activities are running, is to make activities *atomic*.

The state of a distributed system is a collection of data objects that reside at various locations in the network. An activity can be thought of as a process that attempts to examine and transform some objects in the distributed state from their concurrent (initial) states to new (final) states, with any number of intermediate state changes. Two properties distinguish an activity as being atomic: indivisibility and recoverability. By *indivisibility*, we mean that the execution of one activity never appears to overlap (or contain) the execution of any other activity. If the objects being modified by one activity are observed over time by another activity, the latter activity will either always observe the initial states or always observe the final states. By *recoverability*, we mean that the overall effect of the activity is all-or-nothing: either all of the objects remain in their initial state, or all change to their final state. If a failure occurs while an activity is running, it must be possible either to complete the activity, or to restore all objects to their initial states.

2.1. Actions

We call an atomic activity an *action*. An action may complete either by *committing* or *aborting*. When an action aborts, the effect is as if the action had never begun: all modified objects are restored to their previous states. When an action commits, all modified objects take on their new states.

One simple way to implement the indivisibility property is to force actions to run sequentially. However, one of our goals is to provide a high degree of concurrency. The usual method of providing indivisibility in the presence of concurrency, and the one we have adopted, is to guarantee *serializability*,[6]

*We need merely assume that stable storage is accessible to every node in the system; it is not necessary that every node have its own local stable storage devices.

namely, actions are scheduled in such a way that their overall effect is as if they had been run sequentially in some order. To prevent one action from observing or interfering with the intermediate states of another action, we need to synchronize access to shared objects. In addition, to implement the recoverability property, we need to be able to undo the changes made to objects by aborted actions.

Since synchronization and recovery are likely to be somewhat expensive to implement, we do not provide these properties for all objects. For example, objects that are purely local to a single action do not require these properties. The objects that do provide these properties are called *atomic objects*, and we restrict our notion of atomicity to cover only access to atomic objects. That is, atomicity is guaranteed only when the objects shared by actions are atomic objects.

Atomic objects are encapsulated within *atomic abstract data types*. An abstract data type consists of a set of objects and a set of primitive operations; the primitive operations are the only means of accessing and manipulating the objects.[17] Atomic types have operations just like normal data types, except the operations provide indivisibility and recoverability for the calling actions. Some atomic types are built-in while others are user-defined. Argus provides, as built-in types, atomic arrays, records, and variants, with operations nearly identical to the normal arrays, records, and variants provided in CLU.[18] In addition, objects of built-in scalar types, such as characters and integers, are atomic, as are structured objects of built-in immutable types, such as strings, whose components cannot change over time.

Our implementation of (mutable) built-in atomic objects is based on a fairly simple locking model. There are two kinds of locks: read locks and write locks. Before an action uses an object, it must acquire a lock in the appropriate mode. The usual locking rules apply: multiple readers are allowed, but readers exclude writers and writer excludes readers and other writers. When a write lock is obtained, a *version* of the object is made, and the action operates on this version. If, ultimately, the action commits, this version will be retained, and the old version discarded. If the action aborts, this version will be discarded, and the old version retained. For example, atomic records have the usual component selection and update operations, but selection operations obtain a read lock on the record (not the component), and update operations obtain a write lock and create a version of the record the first time the action modifies the record.

All locks acquired by an action are held until the completion of that action, a simplification of standard two-phase locking.[8] This rule avoids the problem of *cascading* aborts: if a lock on an object could be released early, and the action later aborted, any action that had observed the new state of that object would also have to be aborted.

Within the framework of actions, there is a straightforward way to deal with hardware failures at a node: they simply force the node to crash, which in turn forces actions to abort. As was mentioned above, we make data resilient by storing it on stable storage devices. Furthermore, we do not actually copy information to stable storage until actions commit. Therefore, versions made for a running action and information about locks can be kept in volatile memory. This volatile information will be lost if the node crashes. If this happens, the action must be forced to abort. To ensure that the action will abort, a standard two-phase commit protocol[9] is used. In the first phase, an attempt is made to verify that all locks are still held, and to record the new state of each modified object on stable storage. If the first phase is successful, then in the second phase the locks are released, the recorded states become the current states, and the previous states are forgotten. If the first phase fails, the recorded states are forgotten and the action is forced to abort, restoring the objects to their previous states.

Turning hardware failures into aborts has the merit of freeing the programmer from low-level hardware considerations. It also reduces the probability that actions will commit. However, this is a problem only when the time to complete an action approaches the mean time between failures of the nodes. We believe that most actions will be quite short compared to realistic mean time between failures for hardware available today.

It has been argued that indivisibility is too strong a property for certain applications because it limits the amount of potential concurrency.[15] We believe that indivisibility is the desired property for most applications, *if* it is required only at the appropriate levels of abstraction. Argus provides a mechanism for *user-defined* atomic data types. These types present an external interface that supports indivisibility, but can offer a great deal of concurrency as well. We will not present our mechanism here; user-defined atomic types are discussed in Weihl and Liskov.[29]

2.2. Nested Actions

So far, we have presented actions as monolithic entities. In fact, it is useful to break down such entities into pieces; to this end we provide hierarchically structured, *nested* actions. Nested actions, or subactions, are a mechanism for coping with failures, as well as for introducing concurrency within an action. An action may contain any number of subactions, some of which may be performed sequentially, some concurrently. This structure cannot be observed from outside; i.e., the overall action still satisfies the atomicity properties. Subactions appear as atomic activities with respect to other subactions of the same parent. Subactions can commit and abort independently, and a subaction can abort without forcing its parent action to abort. However, the commit of a subaction is conditional: even if a subaction commits, aborting its parent action will abort it. Further, object versions are written to stable storage only when top-level actions commit.

Nested actions aid in composing (and decomposing) activities in a modular fashion. This allows a collection of existing actions to be combined into a single, higher-level action, and to be run concurrently within that action with no need for additional synchronization. For example, consider a database replicated at multiple nodes. If only a majority of the nodes need to be read or written for the overall action to succeed, this is accomplished by performing the reads or writes as concurrent subactions, and committing the overall action as soon as a majority of the subactions commit, even though some of the other subactions are forced to abort.

Nested actions have been proposed by others[5,10,25]; our model is similar to that presented by Moss.[23] To keep the locking rules simple, we do not allow a parent action to run concurrently with its children. The rule for read locks is extended so that an action may obtain a read lock on an object provided each action holding a write lock on that object is an ancestor. An action may obtain a write lock on an object provided every action holding a (read or write) lock on that object is an ancestor. When a subaction commits, its locks are inherited by its parent; when a subaction aborts, its locks are discarded.

Note that the locking rules permit multiple writers, which implies that multiple versions of objects are needed. However, since writers must form a linear chain when ordered by ancestry, and actions cannot execute concurrently with their subactions, only one writer can ever actually be executing at one time. Hence, it suffices to use a stack of versions (rather than a tree) for each atomic object. On commit, the top version becomes the new version for the parent; on abort the top version is simply discarded. Since versions become permanent only when top-level actions commit, the two-phase commit protocol is used only for top-level actions. A detailed description of locking and version management in a system supporting nested actions is presented in reference 23.

In addition to nesting subactions inside other actions, it is sometimes useful to start a new top action inside another action. Such a ''nested'' top action, unlike a subaction, has no special privileges relative to its parent; for example, it is not able to read an atomic object modified by its parent. Furthermore, the commit of a nested top action is not relative to its parent; its versions are written to stable storage, and its locks are released, just as for normal top actions. Nested top actions are useful for benevolent side effects. For example, in a naming system, a name look-up may cause information to be copied from one location to another, to speed up subsequent look-ups of that name. Copying the data within a nested top action ensures that the changes remain in effect, even if the parent action aborts.

2.3. Remote Procedure Call

Perhaps the single most important application of nested actions is in masking communication failures. Logical nodes (described in the Section 3) in Argus communicate via messages. We believe that the most desirable form of communication is the paired send and reply: for every message sent, a reply message is expected. In fact, we believe the form of communication that is needed is *remote procedure call*, with *at-most-once* semantics, namely, that (effectively) either the message is delivered and acted on exactly once, with exactly one reply received, or the message is never delivered and the sender is so informed.

The rationale for the high-level, at-most-once semantics of remote procedure call is presented Liskov[20] (also see Spector[28]). Briefly, we believe the system should mask from the user low-level issues, such as packetization and retransmission, and that the system should make a reasonable attempt to deliver messages. However, we believe the possibility of long delays and of ultimate failure in sending a message cannot and should not be masked. In such a case, the communication would fail.* The sender can then cope with the failure according to the demands of the particular application. However, coping with the failure is much simpler if it is guaranteed that in this case the remote procedure call had no effect.

The all-or-nothing nature of remote procedure call is similar to the recoverability property of actions, and the ability to cope with communication failures is similar to the ability of an action to cope with the failures of subactions. Therefore, it seems natural to implement a remote procedure call as a subaction: communication failures will force the subaction to abort, and the caller has the ability to abort the subaction on demand. However, as mentioned above, aborting the subaction does not force the parent action to abort. The caller is free to find some other means of accomplishing its task, such as communicating with some other node.

2.4. Remarks

In our model, there are two kinds of actions: subactions and top-level actions. We believe these correspond in a natural way to activities in the application system. Top-level actions correspond to activities that interact with the external environment, or, in the case of nested top actions, to activities that should not be undone if the parent aborts. For example, in an airline reservation system, a top-level action might correspond to an interaction with a clerk who is entering a related sequence of reservations. Subactions, on the other hand, correspond

*For example, the system would cause the communication to fail if it is unable to contact the remote node. We believe the system, and not the programmer, should take on this kind of responsibility, because the programmer would find it very difficult to define reasonable timeouts.

to internal activities that are intended to be carried out as part of an external interaction; a reservation on a single flight is an example.

Not all effects of an action can be undone by aborting that action, since a change to the external environment, e.g., printing a check, cannot be undone by program control alone. But as long as all effects can be undone, the user of our language does not need to write any code to undo or compensate for the effects of aborted actions.

Before doing something like printing a check, the application program should make sure that printing the check is the right thing to do. One technique for ensuring this is to break an activity into two separate, sequential top-level actions. All changes to the external environment are deferred to the second action, to be executed only if the first action is successful. Such a technique will greatly decrease the likelihood of actions having undesired effects that cannot be undone.

The commit of a top-level action is irrevocable. If that action is later found to be in error, actions that compensate for the effects of the erroneous action (and all later actions that read its results) must be defined and executed by the user. Compensation must also be performed for effects of aborted actions that cannot be undone. Note that in general there is no way that such compensation could be done automatically by the system, since extra-system activity is needed (e.g., cancelling already issued checks).

Given our use of a locking scheme to implement atomic objects, it is possible for two (or more) actions to *deadlock*, each attempting to acquire a lock held by the other. Although in many cases deadlock can be avoided with careful programming, certain deadlock situations are unavoidable. Rather than having the system prevent, or detect and break, deadlocks, we rely on the user to time out and abort top-level actions. These timeouts generally will be very long, or will be controlled by someone sitting at a terminal. Note that such timeouts are needed even without deadlocks, since there are other reasons why a top action may be too slow (e.g., contention).

A user can retry a top action that aborted because of a timeout or crash, but Argus provides no guarantee that progress will be made. Argus will be extended if needed (e.g., by raising the priority of a top action each time it is repeated[26] or by using checkpoints[10]).

3. LINGUISTIC CONSTRUCTS

In this section we describe the main features of Argus. The most novel features are the constructs for implementing guardians, the logical nodes of the system, and for implementing actions, as described in the previous section. To avoid rethinking issues that arise in sequential languages, we have based Argus on an existing sequential language. CLU[18,21] was chosen because it supports the construction of well-structured programs through abstraction mechanisms, and because it is an object-oriented language, in which programs are naturally thought of as operating on potentially long-lived objects.

3.1. Overview

In Argus, a distributed program is composed of a group of *guardians*. A guardian encapsulates and controls access to one or more resources, e.g., databases or devices. A guardian makes these resources available to its users by providing a set of operations called *handlers*, which can be called by other guardians to make use of the resources. The guardian executes the handlers, synchronizing them and performing access control as needed.

Internally, a guardian contains data objects and processes. The processes execute handlers (a separate process is spawned for each call) and perform background tasks. Some of the data objects, e.g., the actual resources, make up the *state* of the guardian; these objects are shared by the processes. Other objects are local to the individual processes.

A guardian runs at a single node, but can survive crashes of this node (with high probability). Thus, the guardians themselves are resilient. A guardian's state consists of *stable* and *volatile* objects. Resiliency is accomplished by writing the stable objects to stable storage when a top action commits; only those objects that were modified by the committing action need be written. The probability of loss of volatile objects is relatively high, so these objects must contain only redundant information if the system as a whole is to avoid a loss of information. Such redundant information is useful for improving efficiency, e.g., an index into a data base for fast access.

After a crash of the guardian's node, the language support system re-creates the guardian with the stable objects as they were when last written to stable storage. A process is started in the guardian to re-create the volatile objects. Once the volatile objects have been restored, the guardian can resume background tasks, and can respond to new handler calls.

Guardians allow a programmer to decompose a problem into units of tightly coupled processing and data. Within a guardian, processes can share objects directly. However, direct sharing of objects between guardians is not permitted. Instead, guardians must communicate by calling handlers, and the arguments to handlers are passed by value: it is impossible to pass a reference to an object in a handler call. This rule ensures that objects local to a guardian remain local, and thus ensures that a guardian retains control of its own objects. It also provides the programmer with a concept of what is expensive: local objects are close by and inexpensive to use, while non-local objects are more expensive to use. A handler call is performed using a message-based communication mechanism. The language implementation takes care of all details of constructing and sending messages (see reference 11).

Guardians are created dynamically. The programmer specifies the node at which a guardian is to be created; in this way individual guardians can be placed at the most advantageous locations within the network. The (name of the) guardian and (the name of) its handlers can be communicated in handler calls. Once (the name of) a guardian or one of its handlers has been received, handler calls can be performed on that guardian. Handler calls are location independent, however, so one guardian can use another without knowing its location. In fact, handler calls will continue to work even if the called guardian has changed its location, allowing for ease of system reconfiguration.

Guardians and handlers are an abstraction of the underlying hardware of a distributed system. A guardian is a logical node of the system, and inter-guardian communication via handlers is an abstraction of the physical network. The most important difference between the logical system and the physical system is reliability: the stable state of a guardian is never lost (to a very high probability), and the at-most-once semantics of handler calls ensures that the calls either succeed completely or have no effect.

3.2. Guardian Structure

The syntax of a guardian definition is shown in Fig. 3.1.* A guardian definition implements a special kind of abstract data type whose operations are handlers. The name of this type, and the names of the handlers, are listed in the guardian header. In addition, the type provides one or more creation operations, called *creators*, that can be invoked to create new guardians of the type; the names of the creators are also listed in the header. Guardians may be *parameterized*, providing the ability to define a class of related abstractions by means of a single module. Parameterized types are discussed in references 18 and 21.

The first internal part of a guardian is a list of abbreviations for types and constants. Next is a list of variable declarations, with optional initializations,

name = **guardian** [*parameter-decls*] **is** creator-names
                                        handles handler-names
    { *abbreviations* }
    { [**stable**] *variable-decls-and-ints* }
    [**recover** *body* **end**]
    [**background** *body* **end**]
    { *creator-handler-and-local-routine-definitions* }
    end *name*

Fig. 3.1. Guardian structure.

*In the syntax, optional clauses are enclosed with [ ], zero or more repetitions are indicated with {}, and alternatives are separated by |.

defining the guardian state. Some of these variables can be declared as **stable** variables; the others are volatile variables.

The stable state of a guardian consists of all objects *reachable* from the stable variables; these objects, called stable objects, have their new versions written to stable storage by the system when top-level actions commit. Argus, like CLU, has an object-oriented semantics. Variables name (or refer to) objects residing in a heap storage area. Objects themselves may refer to other objects, permitting recursive and cyclic data structures without the use of explicit pointers. The set of objects reachable from a variable consists of the object that variable refers to, any objects referred to by that object, and so on.*

Guardian instances are created dynamically by invoking **creators** of the guardian type. For example, suppose a guardian type named *spooler* has a creator with a header of the form:

create = **creator** (dev: printer) **returns** (spooler).

When a process executes the expression

spooler$create(pdev),

a guardian object is created at the same physical node where the process is executing and (the name of) the guardian is returned as the result of the call.** Guardians can also be created at other nodes. Given a variable *home* naming some node,

spooler$create(pdev) @ home

creates a guardian at the specified node.

When a creator is invoked, a new guardian instance is created, and any initializations attached to the variable declarations of the guardian state are executed. The body of the creator is then executed; typically, this code will finish initializing the guardian state and then return the guardian object. (Within the guardian, the expression **self** refers to the guardian object.)

Aside from creating a new guardian instance and executing state variable initializations, a creator has essentially the same semantics as a handler, as described in the next section. In particular, a creator call is performed within a new subaction of the caller, and the guardian will be destroyed if this subaction or some parent action aborts. The guardian becomes permanent (i.e., survives

*In languages that are not object-oriented, the concept of reachability would still be needed to accommodate the use of explicit pointers.

**As in CLU, the notation *t$op* is used to name the *op* operation of type *t*.

node crashes) only when the action in which it was created commits to the top level. A guardian cannot be destroyed from outside the guardian (except by aborting the creating action). Once a guardian becomes permanent, only the guardian can destroy itself, using a destroy primitive.

The **recover** section runs after a crash. Its job is to re-create a volatile state that is consistent with the stable state. This may be trivial, e.g., creating an empty cache, or it may be a lengthy process, e.g., creating a data base index.

After a crash, the system re-creates the guardian and restores its stable objects from stable storage. Since updates to stable storage are made only when top-level actions commit, the stable state has the value it had at the latest commit of a top-level action before the guardian crashed. The effects of actions that had executed at the guardian prior to the crash, but had not yet committed to the top level, are lost and the actions are aborted.

After the stable objects have been restored, the system creates a process in the guardian to first execute any initializations attached to declarations of volatile variables of the guardian state and then execute the **recover** section. This process runs as a top-level action. Recovery succeeds if this action commits; otherwise the guardian crashes and recovery is retried later.

After the successful completion of a creator, or of the **recover** section after a crash, two things happen inside the guardian: a process is created to run the **background** section, and handler invocations may be executed. The **background** section provides a means of performing periodic (or continuous) tasks within the guardian; examples are given in Section 4. The **background** section is not run as an action, although generally it creates top-level actions to execute tasks, as explained in Section 3.4.*

3.3. Handlers

Handlers (and creators), like procedures in CLU, are based on the termination model of exception handling.[19] A handler can terminate in one of a number of conditions: one of these is considered to be the "normal" condition, while others are "exceptional," and are given user-defined names. Results can be returned both in the normal and exceptional cases; the number and types of results can differ among conditions. The header of a handler definition lists the names of all exceptional conditions and defines the number and types of results in all cases. For example,

```
files_ahead_of = handler (entry_id: int) returns (int)
                                         signals (printed(date))
```

*A process that is not running as an action is severely restricted in what it can do. For example, it cannot call operations on atomic objects or call handlers without first creating a top-level action.

might be the header of a spooler handler used to determine how many requests are in front of a given queue entry. Calls of this handler either terminate normally, returning an integer result, or exceptionally in condition *printed* with a date result. In addition to the named conditions, any handler can terminate in the *failure* condition, returning a string result; failure termination may be caused explicitly by the user code, or implicitly by the system when something unusual happens, as explained further below.

A handler executes as a subaction. As such, in addition to returning or signalling, it must either commit or abort. We expect committing to be the most common case, and therefore execution of a **return** or **signal** statement within the body of a handler indicates commitment. To cause an abort, the **return** or **signal** is prefixed with **abort.**

Given a variable x naming a guardian object, a handler h of the guardian may be referred to as $x.h$. Handlers are invoked using the same syntax as for procedure invocation, e.g.,

$$x.h(\text{``read''}, 3, \text{false})$$

However, whereas procedures are always executed locally within the current action, and always have their arguments and results passed *by sharing*,* handlers are always executed as new subactions, usually in a different guardian, and always have their arguments and results passed by value.

Let us examine a step-by-step description of what the system does when a handler is invoked:

1. A new subaction of the calling action is created.
2. A message containing the arguments is constructed. Since part of building this message involves executing user-defined code (see reference 11), message construction may fail. If so, the subaction aborts and the call terminates with a *failure* exception.
3. The system suspends the calling process and sends the message to the target guardian. If that guardian no longer exists, the subaction aborts and the call terminates with a *failure* exception.
4. The system makes a reasonable attempt to deliver the message, but success is not guaranteed. The reason is that it may not be sensible to guarantee success under certain conditions, such as a crash of the target node. In such cases, the subaction aborts and the call terminates with a *failure* exception. The meaning of such a failure is that there is a very low probability of the call succeeding if it is repeated immediately.
5. The system creates a process and a subaction (of the subaction in step 1)

*Somewhat similar to passing by reference. See Liskov *et al.*[21]

at the receiving guardian to execute the handler. Note that multiple instances of the same handler may execute simultaneously. The system takes care of locks and versions of atomic objects used by the handler in the proper manner, according to whether the handler commits or aborts.

6. When the handler terminates, a message containing the results is constructed, the handler action terminates, the handler process is destroyed, and the message is sent. If the message cannot be sent (as in step 2 or 4 above), the subaction created in step 1 aborts and the call terminates with a *failure* exception.
7. The calling process continues execution. Its control flow is affected by the termination condition as explained in reference 19. For example,

```
count: int := spool.files_ahead_of(ent) % normal return
      except when printed (at: date): ... % exceptional returns
    when failure (why: string): ...
    end
```

Since a new process is created to perform an incoming handler call, guardians have the ability to execute many requests concurrently. Such an ability helps to avoid having a guardian become a bottleneck. Of course, if the guardian is running on a single-processor node, then only one process will be running at a time. However, a common case is that in executing a handler call, another handler call to some other guardian is made. It would be unacceptable if the guardian could do no other work while this call was outstanding.

The scheduling of incoming handler calls is performed by the system. Therefore, the programmer need not be concerned with explicit scheduling, but instead merely provides the handler definitions to be executed in response to the incoming calls. An alternative structure for a guardian would be a single process that multiplexes itself and explicitly schedules the execution of incoming calls. We think our structure is more elegant, and no less efficient, since our processes are cheap: creating a new process is only slightly more expensive than calling a procedure.

As was mentioned above, the system does not guarantee message delivery; it merely guarantees that, if message delivery fails, there is a very low probability of the call succeeding if it is repeated immediately. Hence, there is no reason for user code to retry handler calls. Rather, as mentioned earlier, user programs should make progress by retrying top-level actions, which may fail because of node crashes even if all handler calls succeed.

3.4. Inline Actions

Top-level actions are created by means of the **enter** statement:

enter topaction *body* **end**

This causes the *body* to execute as a new top-level action. It is also possible to have an inline subaction:

enter action *body* **end**

This causes the *body* to run as a subaction of the action that executes the **enter.**

When the body of an inline action completes, it must indicate whether it is committing or aborting. Since committing is assumed to be most common, it is the default; the qualifier **abort** can be prefixed to any termination statement to override this default. For example, an inline action can execute

leave

to commit and cause execution to continue with the statement following the **enter** statement; to abort and have the same effect on control, it executes

abort leave

Falling off the end of the *body* causes the action to commit.

3.5. Concurrency

The language as defined so far allows concurrency only between top actions originating in different guardians. The following statement form provides more concurrency:

coenter { *coarm* } **end**

where

coarm :: = *armtag* [**foreach** *decl-list* **in** *iter-invocation*]
body

armtag :: = **action** | **topaction.**

The process executing the **coenter,** and the action on whose behalf it is executing, are suspended; they resume execution after the **coenter** is finished.

A **foreach** clause indicates that multiple instances of the coarm will be activated, one for each item (a collection of objects) yielded by the given iterator invocation.* Each such coarm will have local instances of the variables declared in the *decl-list*, and the objects constituting the yielded item will be assigned to them. Execution of the **coenter** starts by running each of the iterators to com-

*An iterator is a limited kind of coroutine that provides results to its caller one at a time.[18,21]

pletion, sequentially, in textual order. Then all coarms are started simultaneously as concurrent siblings. Each coarm instance runs in a separate process, and each process executes within a new top-level action or subaction, as specified by the *armtag*.

A simple example making use of **foreach** is in performing a write operation concurrently at all copies of a replicated database:

```
coenter
    action foreach db: db_copy in all_copies(. . .)
        db.write(. . .)
    end.
```

This statement creates separate processes for the guardian objects yielded by *all_copies*, each process having a local variable *db* bound to a particular guardian. Each process runs in a newly created subaction and makes a handler call.

A coarm may terminate without terminating the entire **coenter** either by falling off the end of its *body* or by executing a **leave** statement. As before, leave may be prefixed by **abort** to cause the completing action to abort; otherwise, the action commits.

A coarm also may terminate by transferring control outside the **coenter** statement. Before such a transfer can occur, all other active coarms of the **coenter** must be terminated. To accomplish this, the system forces all coarms that are not yet completed to abort. A simple example where such early termination is useful is in performing a read operation concurrently at all copies of a replicated database, where a response from any single copy will suffice:

```
coenter
    action foreach db: db_copy in all_copies(. . .)
        result := db.read(. . .)
        exit done
    end except when done: . . . end
```

Once a read has completed successfully, the **exit** will commit the read and abort all remaining reads. The aborts take place immediately; in particular, it is not necessary for the handler calls to finish before the subactions can be aborted. (Such aborts can result in *orphan* handler processes that continue to run at the called guardians and elsewhere. We have developed algorithms for dealing with orphans, but they are beyond the scope of this chapter.)

There is another form of **coenter** for use outside of actions, as in the **background** section of a guardian. In this form the *armtag* can be **process** or **topaction.** The semantics are as above, except that no action is created in the **process** case.

3.6. Program Development and Reconfiguration

Argus, like CLU, provides separate compilation of modules with complete type checking at compile time (see Liskov *et al.*[21]). Separate compilation is performed in the context of a program library, which contains information about abstractions (e.g., guardian types).

Before creating a guardian at a node, it is first necessary to load the code of that guardian at that node. Once the code image has been loaded, any number of guardians of that type can be created at that node. It is also possible to load a different code image of the same guardian type at the node, and then create guardians that run that code.

To build a code image of a guardian definition, it is necessary to select implementations for the data, procedural, and iteration abstractions that are used, but not for other guardian abstractions. In other words, each guardian is linked and loaded separately. In fact, each guardian is independent of the implementation of all other guardians, because our method of communicating data values between guardians is implementation-independent (see reference 11). A guardian is also independent of all abstractions except for those it actually uses. New abstractions can be added to the library, and new implementations can be written for both old and new abstractions, without affecting any running guardian.

Guardians are constrained to communicate with other guardians only via handlers whose types were known when the guardian was compiled. Communication via handlers of unknown type is not sensible; the situation is exactly analogous to calling a procedure of unknown type. Of course, a guardian or handler argument of known type but unknown value can be very useful. We *do* provide this: guardians and handlers can be used as arguments in local procedure calls and in handler calls.

Compile-time-type-checking does *not* rule out dynamic reconfiguration. By receiving guardians and handlers dynamically in handler calls, a guardian can communicate with new guardians as they are created or become available. For example, the Argus system contains a distributed *catalog* that registers guardians and handlers according to their type. The catalog would respond to a request for printer guardians by returning all guardians of type "printer" that previously had been registered.

In many applications, it will be necessary to change the implementations of running guardians. We are investigating a replacement strategy that permits new implementations to be provided for running guardians without affecting the users of these guardians.[2] This system also allows for certain kinds of changes in guardian type (e.g., additional handlers).

4. A SIMPLE MAIL SYSTEM

In this section, we present a simple mail system, designed somewhat along the lines of Grapevine.[1] This is a pedagogical example: we have chosen inefficient or inadequate implementations for some features, and have omitted many necessary and desirable features of a real mail system. However, we hope it gives some idea of how a real system could be implemented in Argus.

The interface to the mail system is quite simple. Every user has a unique name (*user_id*) and a mailbox. However, mailbox locations are hidden from the user. Mail can be sent to a user by presenting the mail system with the user's user_id and a *message*; the message will be appended to the user's mailbox. Mail can be read by presenting the mail system with a user's user_id; all messages are removed from the user's mailbox and are returned to the caller. For simplicity, there is no protection on this operation: any user may read another user's mail. Finally, there is an operation for adding new users to the system, and operations for dynamically extending the mail system.

All operations are performed within the action system. For example, a message is not really added to a mailbox unless the sending action commits, messages are not really deleted unless the reading action commits, and a user is not really added unless the requesting action commits.

The mail system is implemented out of three kinds of guardians: mailers, maildrops, and registries. *Mailers* act as the front end of the mail system: all use of the system occurs through calls of mailer handlers. To achieve high availability, many mailers are used, e.g., one at each physical node. All mailers would be registered in the catalog for dynamic lookup. A *maildrop* contains the mailboxes for some subset of users. Individual mailboxes are not replicated, but multiple, distributed maildrops are used to reduce contention and to increase availability, in that the crash of one physical node will not make all mailboxes unavailable. The mapping from user_id to maildrop is provided by the *registries.* Replicated registries are used to increase availability, in that at most one registry need be accessible to send or read mail. Each registry contains the complete mapping for all users. In addition, registries keep track of all other registries.

Two built-in atomic types are used in implementing the mail system: *atomic_array* and *struct.* Atomic arrays are one-dimensional, and can grow and shrink dynamically. Of the array operations used in the mail system, *new* creates an empty array, *addh* adds an element to the high end, *trim* removes elements, *elements* iterates over the elements from low to high, and *copy* makes a complete copy of an array. A real lock on the entire array is obtained by new, elements, and copy, and a write lock is obtained by addh and trim. Structs are immutable (hence atomic) records: new components cannot be stored in a struct object once it has been created. However, the fact that a struct is immutable does not prevent its component objects from being modified if they are mutable.

The mailer guardian is presented in Fig. 3.2. Each mailer is given a registry when created; this registry is the mailer's stable reference to the entire mail system. The mailer also keeps a volatile reference, representing the "best"

```
mailer = guardian is create
                    handles send_mail, read_mail, add_user,
                            add_maildrop, add_registry, add_mailer

reg_list  = atomic_array[registry]
msg_list = atomic_array[message]

stable some: registry   % stable reference to some registry
best: registry          % volatile reference to some registry

recover
    best := some        % reassign after a crash
    end
background
    while true do
        enter topaction
            regs: reg_list := best.all_registries( )
            coenter
                action foreach reg: registry in reg_list$elements(regs)
                    reg.ping( )     % see if it responds
                    best := reg     % make it best
                    exit done       % abort all others
                end except when done: end
            end except when failure (*): end
        sleep(. . .)  % some amount of time
        end
    end

create = creator (reg: registry) returns (mailer)
    some := reg
    best := reg
    return(self)
    end create

send_mail = handler (user: user_id, msg: message) signals (no_such_user)
    drop: maildrop := best.lookup(user)
        resignal no_such_user
    drop.send_mail(user, msg)
    end send_mail

read_mail = handler (user: user_id) returns (msg_list) signals (no_such_user)
    drop: maildrop := best.lookup(user)
        resignal no_such_user
    return(drop.read_mail(user))
    end read_mail

add_user = handler (user: user_id) signals (user_exists)
    drop: maildrop := best.select(user)
```

Fig. 3.2. Mailer guardian.

```
        resignal user__exists
    regs: reg__list := best.all__registries( )
    coenter
        action
            drop.add__user(user)
        action foreach reg: registry in reg__list$elements(regs)
            reg.add__user(user, drop)
        end
    end add__user

add__maildrop = handler (home: node)
    drop: maildrop := maildrop$create( ) @ home
    regs: reg__list := best.all__registries( )
    coenter
        action foreach reg: registry in reg__list$elements(regs)
            reg.add__maildrop(drop)
        end
    end add__maildrop

add__registry = handler (home: node)
    new: registry  := best.new__registry(home)
    regs: reg__list := best.all__registries( )
    coenter
        action foreach reg: registry in reg__list$elements(regs)
            reg.add__registry(new)
        end
    end add__registry

add__mailer = handler (home: node) returns (mailer)
    m: mailer := mailer$create(best) @ home
    return(m)
    end add__mailer

end mailer
```

Fig. 3.2. (*Continued*)

access path into the system. The **background** code periodically polls all registries; the first to respond is used as the new best registry.

A mailer performs a request to send or read mail by first using the best registry to look up the maildrop for the specified user, and then forwarding the request to that maildrop. A mailer adds a new user by first calling the registry *select* handler to make sure the user is not already present and to choose a maildrop; then concurrently the new user/maildrop pair is added to each registry and the new user is added to the chosen maildrop. A maildrop (or registry) is added by creating the maildrop (or registry) and then concurrently adding it to all registries. A new mailer is created with the current best registry for its stable reference.

Fig. 3.3 shows the registry guardian. The state of a registry consists of an atomic array of registries together with a *steering list* associating an array of users with each maildrop. When a registry is created, it is given the current steering list, and an array of all other registries, to which it adds itself. The *lookup* handler uses linear search to find the given user's maildrop. The *select* handler uses linear search to check if a user already exists, and then chooses some existing maildrop. The *add_user* handler uses linear search to find the specified maildrop, and then appends the user to the associated user list. The *add_user*, *add_maildrop*, and *add_registry* handlers perform no error-checking because correctness is guaranteed by the mailer guardian.

```
registry = guardian is create
                     handles lookup, select, all_registries, ping,
                            add_user, add_maildrop, new_registry, add_registry

reg_list   = atomic_array[registry]
steer_list = atomic_array[steering]
steering   = struct[users: user_list,   % users with mailboxes
                    drop: maildrop]     % at this maildrop
user_list  = atomic_array[user_id]

stable regs: reg_list        % all registries
stable steers: steer_list    % all users and maildrops

create = creator (rlist: reg_list, slist: steer_list) returns (registry)
   reg_list$addh(rlist, self)   % add self to list
   regs := rlist
   steers := slist
   return(self)
   end create

lookup = handler (user: user_id) returns (maildrop) signals (no_such_user)
   for steer: steering in steer_list$elements(steers) do
      for user: user_id in user_list$elements(steer.users) do
         if usr = user then return(steer.drop) end
         end
      end
   signal no_such_user
   end lookup

select = handler (user: user_id) returns (maildrop) signals (user_exists)
   for steer: steering in steer_list$elements(steers) do
```

Fig. 3.3. Registry guardian.

```
            for usr: user_id in user_list$elements(steer.users) do
                if usr = user then signal user_exists end
                end
            end
        return(. . .) % choose, e.g., maildrop with least users
        end select

    all_registries = handler ( ) returns (reg_list)
        return(regs)
        end all_registries

    ping = handler ( )
        end ping

    add_user = handler (user: user_id, drop: maildrop)
        for steer: steering in steer_list$elements(steers) do
            if steer.drop = drop
                then user_list$addh(steer.users, user) % append user
                        return
                end
            end
        end add_user

    add_maildrop = handler (drop: maildrop)
        steer: steering := steering${users: user_list$new( ),
                                     drop: drop}
        steer_list$addh(steers, steer)
        end add_maildrop

    new_registry = handler (home: node) returns (registry)
        reg: registry := registry$create(regs, steers) @ home
        return(reg)
        end new_registry

    add_registry = handler (reg: registry)
        reg_list$addh(regs, reg)
        end add_registry

    end registry
```

Fig. 3.3. *(Continued)*

The maildrop guardian is given in Fig. 3.4. The state of a maildrop consists of an atomic array of mailboxes; a mailbox is represented by a struct containing a user_id and an atomic array of messages. A maildrop is created with no mailboxes. The *add_user* handler is used to add a mailbox. Note that this handler does not check to see if the user already exists since the mailer will

```
maildrop = guardian is create
                        handles send_mail, read_mail, add_user

box_list   = atomic_array[mailbox]
mailbox    = struct[mail: msg_list,   % messages for
                    user: user_id]    % this user
msg_list   = atomic_array[message]

stable boxes: box_list := box_list$new( )

create = creator ( ) returns (maildrop)
   return(self)
   end create

send_mail = handler (user: user_id, msg: message)
   for box: mailbox in box_list$elements(boxes) do
      if box.user = user
         then msg_list$addh(box.mail, msg)   % append message
              return
         end
      end
   end send_mail

read_mail = handler (user: user_id) returns (msg_list)
   for box: mailbox in box_list$elements(boxes) do
      if box.user = user
         then mail: msg_list := msg_list$copy(box.mail)
              msg_list$trim(box.mail, 1, 0)   % delete messages
              return(mail)
         end
      end
   end read_mail

add_user = handler (user: user_id)
   box: mailbox := mailbox${mail: msg_list$new( ),
                            user: user}
   box_list$addh(boxes, box)
   end add_user

end maildrop
```

Fig. 3.4. Maildrop guardian.

have already performed this check. The *send_mail* and *read_mail* handlers use linear search to find the correct mailbox. When the mailbox is found, *send_mail* appends a message to the end of the message array; *read_mail* first copies the array, then deletes all messages, and finally returns the copy. Both handlers assume the user exists; again, the mailer guarantees this.

Now that we have all of the pieces of the mail system, we can show how the initial configuration of the mail system is created:

```
reg: registry := registry$create(reg_list$new( ), steer_list$new( ))
                 @ home1
m: mailer := mailer$create(reg) @ home2
```

where *reg_list* and *steer_list* are defined as in the registry. The resulting mailer can then be placed in the catalog, and used to add maildrops and users, as well as more registries and mailers.

Finally, we show a simple use of the mail system, namely, sending a message to a group of users, with the constraint that the message be delivered either to all of the users or to none of them:

```
enter action
    coenter
        action foreach user: user_id in user_group(''net'')
            m.send_mail(user, msg)
        end except when no_such_user, failure (*):
                                  % ignore failure string
                                  abort leave
                  end
    end.
```

The message is sent to all users simultaneously. A non-existent user or a failure to send a message transfers control outside the **coenter,** forcing termination of all active coarms; the outer action is then aborted, guaranteeing that none of the messages are actually delivered.

4.1. Remarks

One obvious problem with the mailers as implemented is that if the best registry for a mailer goes down, the mailer effectively goes down as well, since every task the mailer performs (including choosing a new *best* registry) requires communication with that registry. A better implementation might be for each mailer to have stable and volatile references to multiple registries, and for mailer handlers to try several registries (sequentially) before giving up.

Close examination of the mail system will reveal places where the particular choice of data representation leads to less concurrency than might be expected. For example, in the maildrop guardian, since both *send_mail* and *read_mail* modify the message array in a mailbox, either operation will lock out all other operations on the same mailbox until the executing action commits to the top level. Even worse, since both *send_mail* and *read_mail* read the mailbox array, and *add_user* modifies that array, an *add_user* operation will lock out all operations on all mailboxes at that maildrop. In the registry guardian, an *add_user* operation will lock out lookup operations on all users with mailboxes at the given maildrop, and an *add_maildrop* operation will lock out all lookup operations.

In a traditional mail system, this lack of concurrency might be tolerable, but there are other, similar systems where it would not be acceptable. What is needed are data types that allow more concurrency than atomic arrays. For example, an associative memory that allowed concurrent insertions and lookups could replace the mailbox array in maildrops and the steering list in registries; a queue with ''first-commit first-out'' semantics, rather than ''first-in first-out'' semantics, could replace the message arrays in maildrops. Such types can be built as user-defined atomic types, although we will not present implementations here.

The concurrency that is built into the mail system can lead to a number of deadlock situations. For example, in the registry guardian, any two concurrent *add_user* or *add_registry* requests will almost always deadlock, and two *add_maildrop* requests can deadlock by modifying registries in conflicting orders. Some of these deadlocks would disappear if data representations allowing more concurrency were used. For example, the use of a highly concurrent associative memory for the steering list would allow all *add_maildrop* requests to run concurrently, as well as all *add_user* requests for distinct users. Other deadlocks can be eliminated simply by reducing concurrency. To avoid deadlocks between *add_registry* requests, all *new_registry* calls could be made to a distinguished registry, and *new_registry* could obtain a write lock on the registry list before creating the new registry.

It may be argued that the strict serialization of actions enforced by the particular implementation we have shown is not important in a real mail system. This does not mean that actions are inappropriate in a mail system, just that the particular granularity of actions we have chosen may not be the best. For example, if an action discovers that a user does (or does not) exist, it may not be important that the user continues to exist (or not to exist) for the remainder of the overall action. It is possible to build such ''loopholes'' through appropriately defined abstract types. As another example, it might not be important for all registries to have the most up-to-date information, provided they receive all updates eventually. In particular, when adding a user, it may suffice to guarantee that all registries eventually will be informed of that user. This could be accomplished by keeping appropriate information in the stable state of one of the registries, and using a background process in that registry to (eventually) inform all other registries.

5. SUMMARY AND CONCLUSIONS

Argus has two main concepts: guardians and actions. Guardians maintain local control over their local data. The data inside a guardian is truly local; no other guardian has the ability to access or manipulate the data directly. The guardian provides access to the data via handler calls, but the actual access is performed inside the guardian. It is the guardian's job to guard its data in three ways: by synchronizing concurrent access to the data, by requiring that the caller of a handler have the authorization needed to do the access, and by making enough of the data stable so that the guardian as a whole can survive crashes without loss of information.

While guardians are the unit of modularity, actions are the means by which distributed computation takes place. A top-level action starts at some guardian. This action can perform a distributed computation by making handler calls to other guardians; those handler calls can make calls to still more guardians, and so on. Since the entire computation is an atomic action, it is guaranteed that the computation is based on a consistent distributed state, and that when the computation finishes, the state is still consistent, assuming in both cases that user programs are correct.

Argus is quite different from other languages that address concurrent or distributed programs.[3,7,13,14] These languages tend to provide modules that bear a superficial resemblance to guardians, and some form of communication between modules based on message passing. For the most part, however, the modules have no internal concurrency and contain no provision for data consistency or resiliency. Indeed, the languages completely ignore the problem of hardware failures. In the area of communication, either a low-level, unreliable mechanism is provided, or reliability is ignored, implying that the mechanism is completely reliable, with no way of actually achieving such reliability.

Although a great many details have been omitted, we hope that enough of the language has been described to show how Argus meets the requirements stated in the introduction. Consistency, service, distribution, concurrency, and extensibility are all well-supported in Argus. However, there are two areas that are not well-supported. One is protection. Guardians could check for proper authorization before performing requests, for example by requiring principle ids as arguments to handler calls. But, there is no way within the language to express constraints as to where and when guardians may be created. For example, the owner of a node may wish to allow a particular guardian to be created at that node but disallow that guardian from creating other guardians at the node. These kinds of protection issues are under investigation.

Another area that may need work is support for scheduling. Within a guardian a separate process is automatically created for each handler call. This structure provides no direct support for scheduling incoming calls. If one wanted to give certain incoming calls priority over others, this could be done explicitly (by means of a shared monitor-like[12] object.) If one wanted certain incoming calls to take priority over calls currently being executed, this could be done (very awkwardly) by programming handlers to periodically relinquish control. However, if one wanted to make priorities global to an entire node, rather than just within a single guardian, there would be no way to accomplish this in Argus. We are not convinced that priorities are required frequently enough to justify any additional mechanism. We prefer to adopt a "wait and see" attitude, although we are investigating priority mechanisms.

Supporting atomic activities as part of the semantics of a programming language imposes considerable implementation difficulties. We have completed a preliminary, centralized implementation of the language, ignoring difficult problems such as lock propagation and orphan detection. We are now working on a real, distributed implementation. At this point it is unclear how efficient such an implementation can be.

The approach to resiliency taken in Argus represents an engineering compromise given the current state of hardware. If ultra-reliable hardware does become practical, it may no longer be necessary to compensate for hardware failures in software. This would simplify the structure of guardians since stable objects and the recover section would no longer be needed. Furthermore, the implementation of Argus would become more efficient.

However, regardless of advances in hardware, we believe atomic actions are necessary and are a natural model for a large class of applications. If the language/system does not provide actions, the user will be compelled to implement them, perhaps unwittingly reimplementing them with each new application, and may implement them incorrectly. For some applications, actions simply may be a convenient tool, not a strictly necessary one. We believe that actions can be implemented efficiently enough that they will be used in applications even when they are not strictly necessary. We expect to get a much more realistic idea of the strengths and weaknesses of the language once the distributed implementation is complete and we can run applications.

ACKNOWLEDGMENTS

The authors gratefully acknowledge the contributions made by members of the Argus design group, especially Maurice Herlihy, Paul Johnson, and Bill Weihl.

REFERENCES

1. Birrell, A., R. Levin, R. Needham, and M. Schroeder, Grapevine: An exercise in distributed computing, *CACM*, vol. 25, pp. 260–274, Apr. 1982.
2. Bloom, T., *Dynamic Module Replacement in a Distributed Programming System* (Ph.D. diss.), Tech. Rep. MIT/LCS/TR-303, MIT Lab. for Comput. Sci., Cambridge, MA, 1983.

3. Brinch Hansen, P., Distributed processes: A concurrent programming concept, *CACM*, vol. 21, pp. 934–941, Nov. 1978.
4. Davies, C. T., Recovery semantics for a DB/DC system, *Proc. 1973 ACM National Conf.*, 1973, pp. 136–141.
5. Davies, C. T., Data processing spheres of control, *IBM Systems J.*, vol. 17, pp. 179–198, 1978.
6. Eswaren, K. P., J. N. Gray, R. A. Lorie, and I. L. Traiger, The notion of consistency and predicate locks in a database system, *CACM*, vol. 19, pp. 624–633, Nov. 1976.
7. Feldman, J. A., High level programming for distributed computing, *CACM*, vol. 22, pp. 353–368, June 1979.
8. Gray, J. N., R. A. Lorie, G. F. Putzolu, and I. L. Traiger, Granularity of locks and degrees of consistency in a shared data base, in *Modeling in Data Base Management Systems*, ed. G. M. Nijssen, Amsterdam, Holland: North-Holland, 1976.
9. Gray, J. N., Notes on data base operating systems, in *Lecture Notes in Computer Science*, vol. 60, eds. Goos and Hartmanis, Berlin: Springer-Verlag, pp. 393–481, 1978.
10. Gray, J. N., *et al.* The recovery manager of the System R database manager, *ACM Comput. Surveys*, vol. 13, pp. 223–242, June 1981.
11. Herlihy, M. and B. Liskov, A value transmission method for abstract data types, *ACM Trans. Programming Languages and Syst.*, vol. 4, pp. 527–551, Oct. 1982.
12. Hoare, C. A. R., Monitors: An operating system structuring concept, *CACM*, vol. 17, pp. 549–557, Oct. 1974.
13. Hoare, C. A. R., Communicating sequential processes, *CACM*, vol. 21, pp. 666–677, Aug. 1978.
14. Ichbiah, J. D. *et al.*, Preliminary ADA reference manual, *SIGPLAN Notices*, vol. 14, June 1979.
15. Lamport, L., *Towards a Theory of Correctness for Multi-User Data Base Systems*, Report CA-7610-0712, Massachusetts Computer Associates, Wakefield, MA, Oct. 1976.
16. Lampson, B. and H. Sturgis, *Crash Recovery in a Distributed Data Storage System*, Xerox PARC, Palo Alto, CA, Apr. 1979.
17. Liskov, B. and S. N. Zilles, Programming with abstract data types, Proc. ACM SIGPLAN Conf. on Very High Level Languages, *SIGPLAN Notices*, vol. 9, pp. 50–59, Apr. 1974.
18. Liskov, B., A. Snyder, R. R. Atkinson, and J. C. Schaffert, Abstraction mechanisms in CLU, *CACM*, vol. 20, pp. 564–576, Aug. 1977.
19. Liskov, B. and A. Snyder, Exception handling in CLU, *IEEE Trans. Software Eng.*, vol. 5, pp. 546–558, Nov. 1979.
20. Liskov, B., On linguistic support for distributed programs, *IEEE Trans. Software Eng.*, vol. 8, pp. 203–210, May 1982.
21. Liskov, B. *et al.*, *CLU Reference Manual*, Berlin: Springer-Verlag, 1984.
22. Lomet, D., Process structuring, synchronization, and recovery using atomic actions, Proc. ACM Conf. on Language Design for Reliable Software, *SIGPLAN Notices*, vol. 12, pp. 128–137, March 1977.
23. Moss, J. E. B., *Nested Transactions, An Approach to Reliable Distributed Computing*, Cambridge, Ma.: The MIT Press, 1985.
24. Randell, B., System structure for software fault tolerance, *IEEE Trans. Software Eng.*, vol. 1, pp. 220–232, June 1975.
25. Reed, D. P., *Naming and Synchronization in a Decentralized Computer System*, (Ph.D. diss.), Technical Report MIT/LCS/TR-205, MIT Lab. for Comput. Sci., Cambridge, MA, 1978.
26. Rosenkrantz, D., R. Stearns, and P. Lewis, System level concurrency control for distributed database systems, *ACM Trans. Database Syst.*, vol. 3, pp. 178–198, June 1978.

27. Shrivastava, S. K. and J. P. Banatre, Reliable resource allocation between unreliable processes, *IEEE Trans. Software Eng.*, vol. 4, pp. 230–240, May 1978.
28. Spector, A., Performing remote operations efficiently on a local computer network, *CACM*, vol. 25, pp. 246–260, April 1982.
29. Weihl, W. and B. Liskov, Implementation of resilient, atomic data types, *ACM Trans. Programming Languages and Syst.*, vol. 7, pp. 244–269, Apr. 1985.

4. Functionality and Architecture of the LOCUS Distributed Operating System

GERALD POPEK, BRUCE WALKER, DAVID BUTTERFIELD, ROBERT ENGLISH,
CHARLES KLINE, GREG THIEL, and THOMAS PAGE

ABSTRACT

LOCUS is a highly reliable distributed operating system which supports transparent access to data through a network-wide filesystem, permits automatic replication of storage, supports transparent distributed process execution, supplies a number of high reliability functions such as atomic transactions, and is upward compatible with Unix. Partitioned operation of subnets and their dynamic merge is also supported.

The system has been operational for about four years at UCLA and extensive experience in its use has been obtained. The complete system architecture is outlined in this chapter, and that experience is summarized.

1. INTRODUCTION

LOCUS is a Unix compatible, distributed operating system in operational use at UCLA on a network of 30 PCs, VAX/750s, and 370s connected by a standard Ethernet.* The system supports a very high degree of *network trans-*

This research was supported by the Advanced Research Projects Agency under research contract DSS-MDA-903-82-C-0189.

This chapter is primarily a compilation of previously published papers: 1. Walker, B., G. Popek, R. English, C. Kline, and Greg Thiel, The LOCUS Distributed Operating System, *Proc. 9th ACM Symp. on Operating Systems Principles*, Bretton Woods, NH, 10–13 October, 1983, and is used by permission of the Association for Computing Machinery under copyright © ACM 0-89791-115-6/83/010/0049. 2. Butterfield, D. and G. Popek, Network Tasking in the LOCUS Distributed Unix System, *Proc. USENIX Assoc. Summer Conf.*, Salt Lake City, UT, 12–15 June, 1984.

*Initial work was done on DEC PDP-11/45's and VAX 750's using both 1 and 10 megabit ring networks.

parency, i.e. it makes the network of machines appear to users and programs as a single computer; machine boundaries are completely hidden during normal operation. Both files and programs can be moved dynamically with no effect on naming or correct operation. Remote resources are accessed in the same manner as local ones. Processes can be created locally and remotely in the same manner, and process interaction is the same, independent of location. Many of these functions operate transparently even across heterogeneous CPUs.

High reliability and availability are key to applications envisioned for Locus. Many applications themselves demand a high level of reliability and availability. For example, the effect of a machine failure for an office system user is the equivalent of randomly locking that user out of his office at a random point for an unknown duration, an unacceptable situation. The distributed environment presents serious new sources of failures and complex partial failures. Mechanisms needed to cope with failures in distributed systems are more difficult to construct than in single machine systems. To require each application to solve these problems is a considerable burden. LOCUS provides advanced facilities for maintaining high reliability and availability in both the local and distributed environment.

Mechanisms in LOCUS to enhance reliability include flexible and automatic replication of storage at the file level, a full implementation of distributed atomic transactions,[6, 14] and a substantially more robust data storage facility than conventional Unix systems. The automatic replication of data insures that loss of a copy of a replicated file does not affect continued operation, and the system insures that the old version will be atuomatically brought up to date when it becomes available. The LOCUS *commit* mechanism guarantees that, in the face of all manner of failures, files will remain in a consistent state, either completely updated or unchanged, even if alterations were in progress at the time of the failure. This facility involves no additional I/O and so performs very well. All of the functions reported here have been implemented, and most are in routine use.

This chapter provides an overview of the basic LOCUS system architecture. The file system, especially its distributed naming catalog, plays a central role in the system structure, both because file system activity typically predominates in most operating systems and so high performace is critical, and because the generalized name service provided is used by so many other parts of the system. Therefore, the file system is described first. Remote processes are discussed next, including discussions of process creation, inter-process functions, and error handling.

An important part of the LOCUS research concerns recovery from failures of parts of the system, including partition of a LOCUS system into separated but functioning subnetworks. The next sections of this chapter discuss the several LOCUS facilities dedicated to recovery. First is the merging of the catalog; the hierarchical directory system. The handling of other object types in the file system is also briefly considered. These recovery algorithms are designed to permit normal operation while resources are arriving and departing. Last, the protocols which LOCUS sites execute in order to maintain and define the accessible members of a network, i.e. the network topology, are discussed. These protocols are designed to assure that all sites converge on the same answer in a rapid manner.

The chapter concludes with a set of observations regarding the use of LOCUS in production settings, especially the value of its network transparent interface.

2. DISTRIBUTED FILESYSTEM

2.1. Filesystem Overview

The LOCUS filesystem presents a single tree structured naming hierarchy to users and applications. It is functionally a superset of the Unix tree structure naming system. There are three major areas of extension. First, the single tree structure in LOCUS covers all objects in the filesystem on all machines. LOCUS names are fully transparent; it is not possible from the name of a resource to discern its location in the network. Such location transparency is critical for allowing data and programs in general to move or even be executed from different sites. The second direction of extension concerns replication. Files in LOCUS can be replicated to varying degrees, and it is the LOCUS system's responsibility to keep all copies up to date, assure that access requests are served by the most recent available version, and support partitioned operation.

To a first approximation, the pathname tree is made up of a collection of filegroups, as in a conventional Unix environment.* Each group is a wholly self-contained subtree of the naming hierarchy, including storage for all files and directories contained in the subtree. Gluing together a collection of filegroups to construct the uniform naming tree is done via the *mount* mechanism. Logically mounting a filegroup attaches one tree (the filegroup being mounted) as a subtree within an already mounted tree. The glue which allows smooth path traversals up and down the expanded naming tree is kept as operating system state information. Currently this state information is replicated at all sites. To scale a LOCUS network to hundreds or thousands of sites, this "mount" information would be cached.

A substantial amount of the LOCUS filesystem design, as well as implementation, has been devoted to appropriate forms of error and failure management. These issues will be discussed throughout this chapter. Further, high performance has always been a critical goal. In our view, solutions to all the other

*The term filegroup in this chapter corresponds directly to the Unix term filesystem.

problems being addressed are really not solutions at all unless their performance is suitable. In LOCUS, when resources are local, access is no more expensive than on a conventional Unix system. When resources are remote, access cost is higher, but dramatically better than traditional layered file transfer and remote terminal protocols permit. Measured performance results are presented in Goldberg and Popek.[1]

2.2. File Replication

2.2.1. Motivation for Replication

Replication of storage in a distributed filesystem serves multiple purposes. First, from the users' point of view, multiple copies of data resources provde the opportunity for substantially increased availability. This improvement is clearly the case for read access, although the situation is more complex when update is desired, since if some of the copies are not accessible at a given instant, potential inconsistency problems may preclude update, thereby decreasing availability as the level of replication is increased.

The second advantage, from the user viewpoint, concerns performance. If users of the file exist on different machines, and copies are available near those machines, then read access can be substantially faster compared to the necessity of having one of the users always make remote accesses. This difference can be substantial; in a slow network, it is overwhelming, but in a high speed local network it is still significant.*

In a general purpose distributed computing environment, such as LOCUS, some degree of replication is essential in order for the user to be able to work at all. Certain files used to set up the user's environment must be available even when various machines have failed or are inaccessible. The start-up files in Multics, or the various Unix shells, are obvious examples. Mail aliases and routing information are others. Of course, these cases can generally be handled by read-only replication, which in general imposes fewer problems.†

From the system point of view; some form of replication is more than convenient; it is absolutely essential for system data structures, both for availability and performance. Consider a file directory. A hierarchical name space in a distributed environment implies that some directories will have entries which refer to files on different machines. There is strong motivation for storing a copy of all the directory entries in the backward path from a file at the site where the

*In the LOCUS system, which is highly optimized for remote access, the CPU overhead of accessing a remote page is twice local access, and the cost of a remote open is significantly more than the case when the entire open can be done locally.

†The problems which remain are present because few files are strictly read-only; it is just that their update rate is low. When an update is done, some way to make sure that all copies are consistent is needed. If the rate is low enough, manual methods may suffice.

file is stored, or at least "nearby." The principal reason is availability. If a directory entry in the naming path to a file is not accessible because of network partition or site failure, then that file *cannot be accessed*, even though it may be stored locally.

Second, directories in general experience a high level of read access compared to update. As noted earlier, this characteristic is precisely the one for which a high degree of replicated storage will improve system performance. In the case of the file directory hierarchy, this improvement is critical. In fact, the access characteristics in a hierarchical directory system are, fortunately, even better behaved than just indicated. Typically, the top of the hierarchy exhibits a very high level of lookup, and a correspondingly low rate of update. This pattern occurs because the root of the tree is heavily used by most programs and users as the starting point for name resolution. Changes disrupt programs with embedded names, and so are discouraged. The pattern permits (and requires) the root directories to be highly replicated, thus improving availability and performance simultaneously. By contrast, as one moves down the tree toward the leaves, the degree of shared use of any given directory tends to diminish, since directories are used to organize the name space into more autonomous subspaces. The desired level of replication for availability purposes tends to decrease as well. Further, the update traffic to directories near the leaves of the naming tree tends to be greater, so one would have less directory replication to improve performance.

The performance tradeoffs between update/read rates and degree of replication are well known. However, there are other costs as well. For example, concurrency control becomes more expensive. Without replication the storage site can provide concurrency control for the object since it will know about all activity. With replication some more complex algorithm must be supported. In a similar way, with replication, a choice must be made as to which copy of an object will supply service when there is activity on the object. This degree of freedom is not available without replication. If objects move, then, in the no replication case, the mapping mechanism must be more general. With replication a move of an object is equivalent to an add followed by a delete of an object copy.

2.2.2. Mechanism Supporting Replication

File replication is made possible in LOCUS by having multiple physical containers for a logical filegroup. A given file belonging to logical filegroup X may be stored at any subset of the sites where there exist physical containers corresponding to X. Thus the entire logical filegroup is not replicated by each physical container as in a "hot shadow" type environment. Instead, to permit substantially increased flexibility, any physical container is incomplete;* it stores only a subset of the files in the subtree to which it corresponds.

*The exception to this rule is the Primary Copy, which must be complete.

To simplify access and provide a basis for low level communication about files, the various copies of a file are assigned the same file descriptor or inode number within the logical filegroup. Thus a file's globally unique lowlevel name is:

⟨logical filegroup number, file descriptor (inode) number⟩

and it is this name which most of the operating system uses. The high-to-low-level name translation need happen only once in a file access.

2.2.3. File Replication and Partitioned Operation

To simplify the protocols necessary to maintain filesystem consistency in a dynamic network environment, the system allows file modification at only one copy of the filegroup (the primary pack).* The modifications can originate from any using site, but must use the primary site as the storage site. This approach eliminates the possibility of conflicting updates to a file, simplifying the general problem of update reconciliation to one of update detection and propagation. While this approach limits availability somewhat (the primary pack must be in the user's partition for a file to be modified), it works well for filegroups like the system root, where updates are rare and universal readability essential. The commit and update propagation protocols keep the packs synchronized during normal operation.

2.3. Accessing the Filesystem

There were several goals directing the design of the network-wide file access mechanism. The first was that the system call interface should be uniform, independent of file location. In other words, the same system call with the same parameters should be able to access a file whether the file is stored locally or not. Achieving this goal of transparency would allow programs to move from machine to machine and allow data to be relocated.

The primary system calls dealing with the filesystem are *open, create, read, write, commit, close,* and *unlink*. After introducing the three logical sites involved in file access and the file access synchronization aspect of LOCUS, these system calls are considered in the context of the logical tasks of file reading, modifying, creating and deleting.

2.3.1. LOCUS Logical Sites for Filesystem Activities

LOCUS is designed so that every site can be a full function node. As we saw above, however, filesystem operations can involve more than one host. In fact,

*It is sometimes more convenient to refer to the copies of a filegroup as packs to distinguish a copy of the filegroup from a copy of a file.

there are three logical functions in a file access and thus three logical sites. These are:

1. the *using site*, (US), which issues the request to open a file and to which pages of the file are to be supplied,
2. the *storage site*, (SS), which is the site at which a copy of the requested file is stored, and which has been selected to supply pages of that file to the using site, and
3. the *current synchronization site*, (CSS), which enforces a global access synchronization policy for the file's filegroup and selects SSs for each open request. A given physical site can be the CSS for any number of filegroups but there is only one CSS for any given filegroup in any set of communicating sites (i.e. a partition). The CSS need not store any particular file in the filegroup, but in order for it to make appropriate access decisions it must have knowledge of which sites store the file and what the most current version of the file is.

There are three possible independent roles a given site can play (US, CSS, SS). A particular site can therefore operate in one of eight modes. LOCUS handles each combination, optimizing some for performance.

2.3.2. Synchronization

As soon as one introduces data replication, synchronization becomes a necessity. One must also address the issue of operation when not all copies of a file are accessible.

Since all open requests for a file go through the CSS function, it is possible to implement a large variety of synchronization policies. The LOCUS synchronization policy is upward compatible with the total lack of synchronization in standard Unix. In particular, the default locking policy is called *Unix mode*, which implements on multiple machines exactly what Unix has on a single machine. Processes can concurrently read and modify the same files from one or more sites.

In standard Unix, the system guarantees that each successive operation sees the effects of the ones that precede it. This is fairly easy to achieve as, in a single site environment, the processes access the same operating system data structures and data cache, simple locks on data structures can serialize requests.

In the multiple-site LOCUS environment, concurrent file activity must be supported by more complex mechanisms. Information about open files is cached at each US, but the cached information may be marked invalid at certain times, as the file is being actively modified by processes on other sites. A *token* mechanism ensures that cached information is kept up to date.

In order to maintain total Unix compatibility, the default policy in LOCUS is to allow an arbitrary assortment of reading and writing processes on various sites in the network. However, LOCUS does include a distributed implementation of *lockf*- the /usr/group standard for file and record synchronization. Records or files can be locked by a process if not already locked by a different process. Locking can be advisory or enforced. Processes may choose to either fail upon denial of a lock request or to queue waiting for the record to be unlocked. Processes waiting for locks are interruptible.

In LOCUS, so long as there is a copy of the desired resource available, it can be accessed. If there are multiple copies present, the most efficient one to access is selected. Other copies are updated in background, but the system remains responsible for supplying a mutually consistent view to the user. Within a set of communicating sites, synchronization facilities and update propagation mechanisms assure consistency of copies, as well as guaranteeing that the latest version of a file is the only one that is visible.

2.3.3. Strategy for Distributed Operation

LOCUS is a procedure-based operating system—processes request system service by executing system calls, which trap to the kernel. The kernel runs as an extension to the process and can sleep on behalf of the process. In general, application programs and users cannot determine if any given system call will require foreign service. In fact, most of the high level parts of the system service routines are unaware of the network. At the point within the execution of the system call that foreign service is needed, the operating system packages up a message and sends it to the relevant foreign site. Typically the kernel then sleeps, waiting for a response, much as it would after requesting a disk i/o to be performed on behalf of a specific process.

This flow of control structure is a special case of remote procedure calls. Operating system procedures are executed at a remote site as part of the service of a local system call. Figure 4.1 traces, over time, the processing done at the requesting and serving site when one executes a system call requiring foreign service.

2.3.4. Reading Files

To read a file, an application or system supplied program issues the *open* system call with a filename parameter and flags indicating that the open is for read. As in standard Unix, pathname searching (or directory interrogation) is done within the operating system open call.* After the last directory has been interrogated, the operating system on the requesting site has a ⟨ logical flegroup number,

*Pathname searching is described in the next section.

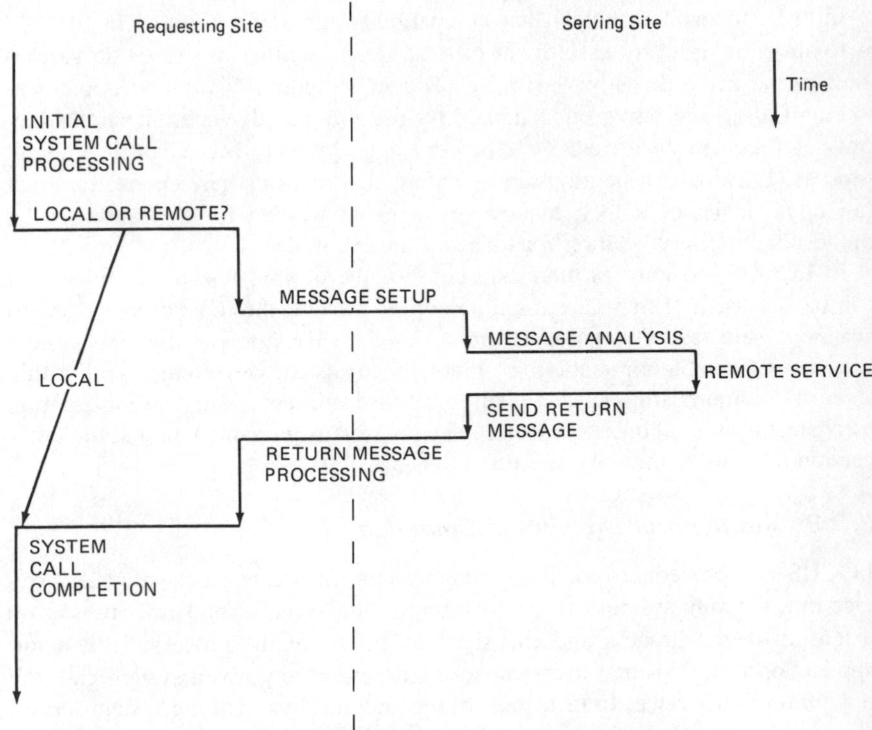

Fig. 4.1. Processing a system call.

inode number⟩ pair for the target file that is about to be opened. If the inode information is not already in an incore inode structure, a structure is allocated. If the file is stored locally, the local disk inode information is filled in. Otherwise very little information is initially entered.

Next, the CSS is interrogated. If the local site is the CSS, only a procedure call is needed. If not, the CSS is determined by examining the logical mount table, a message is sent to the CSS, the CSS sets up an incore inode for itself, calls the same procedure that would have been called if the US were the CSS, packages the response, and sends it back to the US. The CSS is involved for several reasons. One is to enforce synchronization controls. Enough state information is kept incore at the CSS to support those synchronization decisions. For example, if the policy allows only a single open for modification, the site where that modification is ongoing would be kept incore at the CSS. Another reason for contacting the CSS is to determine a storage site. The CSS stores a copy of the disk inode information whether or not it actually stores the file. Consequently, it has a list of packs which store the file. Using that information and mount table information, the CSS can select potential storage sites. The potential sites are polled to see if they will act as storage sites.

Besides knowing the packs where the file is stored, the CSS is also responsible for knowing the latest version number. This information is passed to potential storage sites so they can check it against the version they store. If they do not yet store the latest version, they refuse to act as a storage site.

Two obvious optimizations are done. First, in it's message to the CSS, the US includes the version number of the copy of the file it stores, if it stores the file. If that is the latest version, the CSS selects the US as the SS and just responds appropriately to the US. Another simple case is when the CSS stores the latest version and the US doesn't. In this case the CSS picks itself as SS (without any message overhead) and returns this information to the US.

The response from the CSS is used to complete the incore inode information at the US. For example, if the US is not the SS then all the disk inode information (eg. file size, ownership, permissions) is obtained from the CSS response. The CSS in turn had obtained that information from the SS. The most general open protocol (all logical functions on different physical sites) is:

US --> CSS	OPEN request
CSS --> SS	request for storage site
SS --> CSS	response to previous message
CSS --> US	response to first message.

Figure 4.2 displays this general message sequence.

After the file is open, the user level process issues read calls. All such requests are serviced via kernel buffers, both in standard Unix and in LOCUS. In the local case, data is paged from external storage devices into operating system buffers and then copied from there into the address space of the process. Access

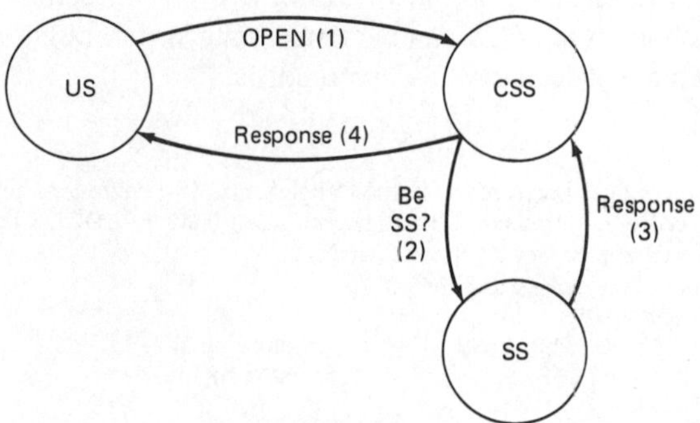

Fig. 4.2. Open protocol.

to locally stored files is the same in LOCUS as in Unix, including the one page readahead done for files being read sequentially.

Requests for data from remote sites operates similarly. Instead of allocating a buffer and queueing a request for a page from a local disk, however, the operating system at the US allocates a buffer and queues a request to be sent over the network to the SS. The request is simple. It contains the ⟨logical filegroup, inode number⟩ pair, the logical page number within the file and a guess as to where the incore inode information is stored at the SS.

At the SS, the request is treated, within the operating system, as follows:

1. The incore inode is found using the guess provided;
2. The logical page number is translated into a physical disk block number;
3. A standard low-level operating system routine is called to allocate a buffer and get the appropriate page from disk (if it is not already in a buffer); and
4. The buffer is queued on the network i/o queue for transmission back to the US as a response to a read request.

The protocol for a network read is thus:*

US → SS	request for page *x* of file *y*
SS → US	response to the above request.

As in the case of local disk reads, read ahead is useful in the case of sequential behavior, both at the SS, as well as across the network.

One of several actions can take place when the *close* system call is invoked on a remotely stored file, depending on how many times the file is concurrently open at this US. If this is not the last close of the file at this US, only local state information need be upadated in most cases. However, if this is the last close of the file, the SS and CSS must be informed so they can deallocate incore inode structures and so the CSS can alter state data which might affect it's next synchronization policy decision. The protocol is:**

---

*There are *no* other messages involved; no acknowledgements, flow control, or any other underlying mechanism. This specialized protocol is an important contributor to LOCUS performance, but it implies the need for careful higher level error handling.

**The original protocol for close was simply:

US → SS	US close of file *y*
SS → US	SS close of file *y*

However, we encountered a race condition under this scheme. The US could attempt to reopen the file before the CSS knew that the file was closed. Thus the responses were added.

US → SS	US close
SS → CSS	SS close
CSS → SS	response to above
SS → US	response to first message.

Closes of course can happen as a result of error conditions like hosts crashing or network partitions. To properly effect closes at various logical sites, certain state information must be kept in the incore inode. The US of course must know where the SS is (but then it needed that knowledge just to read pages). The CSS must know all the sites currently serving as storage sites so if a certain site crashes, the CSS can determine if a given incore inode slot is thus no longer in use. Analogously, the SS must keep track, for each file, of all the USs that it is currently serving.

The protocols discussed here are the lowest level protocols in the system, except for some retransmission support. Because multilayered support and error handling, such as suggested by the ISO standard, is not present, much higher performance has been achieved.

2.3.5. Pathname Searching

In the previous section we outlined the protocol for opening a file given the ⟨ logical filegroup number, inode number ⟩ pair. In this section we describe how that pair is found, given a character string name.

All pathnames presented to the operating system start from one of two places, either the root (/) or the current working directory of the process presenting the pathname. In both cases an inode is incore at the US for the directory. To commence the pathname searching, the ⟨ logical filegroup, inode number ⟩ of the starting directory is extracted from the appropriate inode and an internal open is done on it. This is the same internal open that was described at the start of the previous section, but with one difference. A directory opened for pathname searching is not open for normal READ but instead for an internal unsynchronized read. The distinction is that no global locking is done. If the directory is stored locally and there are no propagations pending to come in, the local directory is searched without informing the CSS. If the directory is not local, the protocol involving the CSS must be used but the locking is such that updates to the directory can occur while interrogation is ongoing. Since no system call does more than just enter, delete, or change an entry within a directory and since each of these actions are atomic, directory interrogation never sees an inconsistent picture.

Having opened the initial directory, protection checks are made and the directory is searched for the first pathname component. Searching of course will require reading pages of the directory, and if the directory is not stored locally these pages are read across the net in the same manner as other file data pages. If a match is found, the inode number of that component is read from the directory to continue the pathname search. The initial directory is closed (again internally), and the next component is opened. This strategy is continued up to the last component, which is opened in the manner requested by the original system call. Another strategy for pathname searching is to ship partial pathnames to foreign sites so they can do the expansion locally, avoiding remote directory opens and network transmission of directory pages. Such a solution is being investigated but is more complex in the general case because the SS for each intermediate directory could be different.

2.3.6. File Modification

Opening an existing file for modification is much the same as opening for read. The synchronization check at the CSS is different and the state information kept at all three logical sites is slightly different.*

The act of modifying data takes on two forms. If the modification does not include the entire page, the old page is read from the SS using the read protocol. If the change involves an entire page, a buffer is set up at the US without any reads. In either case, after changes are made, the page is sent to the SS via the write protocol, which is simply**

US → SS   Write logical page *x* in file *y*.

The action to be taken at the SS is described in the next section in the context of the commit mechanism.

The close protocol for modification is similar to the read case. However, at the US all modified pages must be flushed to the SS before the close message is sent. Also, the mechanism at the SS interacts with the commit mechanism, to which we now turn.

2.3.7 File Commit

The important concept of atomically committing changes has been imported from the database world and integrated into LOCUS. All changes to a given file are handled atomically. Such a commit mechanism is useful both for database work and in general, and can be integrated without performance degrada-

---

*Opening a file for modification in a replicated filesystem requires a little more mechanism. The primary copy of the filesystem must be available, and all processes that are currently reading this file must now use the primary copy so that changes will be immediately visible. This will be discussed in more detail.

**There are low level acknowledgements on this message to ensure that it is received. No higher level response is necessary.

tion. No changes to a file are permanent until a commit operation is performed. *Commit* and *abort* (undo any changes back to the previous commit point) system calls are provided, and closing a file commits it.

To allow file modifications to act like a transaction, it is necessary to keep both the original and changed data available. There are two well-known mechanisms to do so: a) logging and b) shadow pages or intentions lists.[3] LOCUS uses a shadow page mechanism, since the main advantage of logs, namely the ability to maintain strict physical relationships among data blocks, is not valuable in Unix-style systems where file modifications tend to overwrite entire files. Further, high performance shadowing is very much easier to implement.

The US function never deals with actual disk blocks but rather with logical pages. Thus the entire shadow page mechanism is implemented at the SS and is transparent to the US. At the SS, then, a new physical page is allocated if a change is made to an existing page of a file. This is done without any extra i/o in one of two ways: if an entire page is being changed, the new page is filled in with the new data and written to the storage medium; if the change is not of the entire page, the old page is read, the name of the buffer is changed to the new page, the changed data is entered and this new page is written to the storage medium. Both these cases leave the old information intact. Of course it is necessary to keep track of where the old and new pages are. The disk inode contains the old page numbers. The incore copy of the disk inode starts with the old pages but is updated with new page numbers as shadow pages are allocated. If a given logical page is modified multiple times it is not necessary to allocate different pages. After the first time the page is modified, it is marked as being a shadow page and reused in place for subsequent changes.

The atomic commit operation consists merely of moving the incore inode information to the disk inode. After that point, the file permanently contains the new information. To abort a set of changes rather than commit them, one merely discards the incore information since the old inode and pages are still on disk, and free up page frames on disk containing modified pages. Additional mechanism is also present to support large files that are structured through indirect pages that contain page pointers.

As is evident by the mechanism above, we have chosen to deal with file modification by first committing the change to one copy of a file. Via the centralized synchronization mechansism, changes to two different copies at the same time is blocked, and reading an old copy while another copy is being modified is prevented.* As part of the commit operation, the SS sends messages to all the other SS's of that file as well as the CSS. At a minimum, these

*Simultaneous read and modification requests, even when initiated at different sites, are allowed. Page-valid tokens are managed by the kernels for this purpose. Only one storage site can be involved, unlike the case when there are only multiple readers.

messages identify the file and contain the new version vector. Additionally, for performance reasons, the message can indicate: a) whether it was just inode information that changed and no data (eg. ownership or permissions) or b) which explicit logical pages were modified. At this point, it is the responsibility of these additional SS's to bring their version of the file up to date by propagating in the entire file or just the changes. A queue of propagation requests is kept by the kernel at each site and a kernel process services the queue.

Propagation is done by ''pulling'' the data rather than ''pushing'' it. The propagation process which wants to page over changes to a file first internally opens the file at a site which has the latest version. It then issues standard read messages either for all of the pages or just the modified ones. When each page arrives, the buffer that contains it is renamed and sent out to secondary storage, thus avoiding copying data into and out of an application data space, as would be necessary if this propagation mechanism were to run as an application level process. Note also that this propagation-in procedure uses the standard commit mechanism, so if contact is lost with the site containing the newer version, the local site is still left with a coherent, complete copy of the file, albeit still out of date.

Given this commit mechanism, one is always left with either the original file or a completely changed file but never with a partially made change, even in the face of local or foreign site failures. Such was not the case in the standard Unix environment.

2.3.8. File Creation and Deletion

The system and user interface for file creation and deletion is just the standard Unix interface, to retain upward compatibility and to maintain transparency. However, due to the potential for replicated storage of a new file, the create call needs two additional pieces of information—how many copies to store and where to store them. Adding such information to the create call would change the system interface, so instead defaults and per process state information are used, with system calls to modify them.

For each process, an inherited variable has been added to LOCUS to store the default number of copies of files created by the process. A new system call has been added to modify and interrogate this number. Currently the initial replication factor of a file is the minimum of the user settable number-of-copies variable and the replication factor of the parent directory.

Initial storage sites for a file are currently determined by the following algorithm: 1. all such storage sites must be a storage site for the parent directory; 2. the local site is used first if possible; and 3. then follow the site selection for the parent directory, except that sites which are currently inaccessible are chosen last. This algorithm is localized in the code and may change as experience with replicated files grows.

As with all file modification, the create is done at one storage site and propagated to the other storage sites. If the storage site of the created file is not local, the protocol for the create is very similar to the remote open protocol, the difference being that a placeholder is sent instead of an inode number. The storage site allocates an inode number from a pool which is local to that physical container of the filegroup. That is, to facilitate inode allocation and allow operation when not all sites are accessible, the entire inode space of a filegroup is partitioned so that each physical container for the filegroup has a collection of inode numbers that it can allocate.

File delete uses much of the same mechanism as normal file update. After the file is open for modification, the US marks the inode and does a commit, which ships the inode back to the SS and increments the version vector. As part of the commit mechanism, pages are released and other sites are informed that a new version of the file exists. As those sites discover that the new version is a delete, they also release their pages. When all the storage sites have seen the delete, the inode can be reallocated by the site which has control of that inode (i.e. the storage site of the original create).

2.4. Other Issues

The LOCUS name service implemented by the directory system is also used to support interprocess communication and remote device access, as well as to aid in handling heterogeneous machine types in a transparent manner. We turn to these issues now.

2.4.1. Site and Machine Dependent Files

There are several aspects to the hardware heterogeneity problem, such as number representation, byte ordering, instruction set differences, and special hardware constraints (eg. floating point availability). Strong file typing and conversions during transmission can help some of these problems. Here we address only the file naming problem.

While globally unique user visible file naming is very important most of the time, there can be situations where an uttered filename wants to be interpreted specially, based on the context under which it was issued. The machine-type context is a good example. In a LOCUS net containing both Motorola M68000s and DEC VAX750s, a user would want to type the same command name on either type of machine and get a similar service. However, the load modules of the programs providing that service could not be identical and would thus have to have different globally unique names. To get the proper load modules executed when the user types a command, then, requires using the context of which machine the user is executing on. A discussion of transparency and the context issue is given in Popek and Walker.[10] Here we outline a mechanism implemented

in LOCUS which allows context-sensitive files to be named and accessed transparently.
The scheme consists of four parts:

1. Make the globally unique name of the object in question refer to a special kind of directory (hereafter referred to as a *hidden directory*) instead of the object itself.
2. Inside this directory put the different versions of the file, naming them based on the context with which they are associated. For example, have the command */bin/who* be a hidden directory with the file entries *68K* and *vax* that are the respective load modules.
3. Keep a per-process inherited context for these hidden directories. If a hidden directory is found during pathname searching (see Section 2.3.4 for pathname searching), it is examined for a match with the process's context rather than the next component of the pathnames passed to the system.
4. Give users and programs an escape mechanism to make hidden directories visible so they can be examined and specific entries manipulated.

As we shall see, not only does this naming scheme allow us to store and name load modules for different sites, but allows us to transparently run a requested command on the site for which a load module exists.

2.4.2. Other Filesystem Objects

In LOCUS, as in Unix, the name catalog also includes objects other than files; devices and interprocess communication (ipc) channels are the best known.

LOCUS provides for transparent use of remote devices in most cases.* This functionality is exceedingly valuable, but involves considerable care. The implementation architecture is beyond the scope of this chapter.

Interprocess communication (ipc) is often a controversial subject in a single machine operating system, with many differing opinions. In a distributed environment, the requirements of error handling imposes a number of additional requirements that help make design decisions, potentially easing disagreements.

In LOCUS, the initial ipc effort was further simplified by the desire to provide a network-wide ipc facility which is fully compatible with the single machine functions that were already present in Unix. Therefore, in the current LOCUS system release, Unix *named pipes* and *signals* are supported across the network. Their sematics in LOCUS are identical to those seen on a single machine Unix

*The only exception is remote access to raw, non-character devices and these can be accessed by executing processes remotely.

system, even when processes are resident on different machines in LOCUS. Just providing these seemingly simple ipc facilities was non-trivial, however. Details of the implementation are given in Walker.[12]

3. INTRODUCTION TO NETWORK TASKING

There were two very strong considerations in choosing a user model of network tasking for LOCUS. One of these considerations was that LOCUS is a Unix system, and as such it should be compatible with other Unix systems. This means that portable C programs from other Unix systems should run unmodified in the LOCUS network environment. It was considered desirable for these programs to be able to take some advantage of the network, even if they were naive about its existence. It was also considered desirable that it be easy to add minimal code to an existing program which would allow it to make extensive use of the network.

The other major consideration was the overall LOCUS philosophy of *network transparency,* which requires that processes operate and interact with files and other processes across the network in the same way and with the same effect as locally. Adhering to this philosophy allows the user model to be considerably simpler than it might otherwise be, makes development of distributed algorithms easier, and allows graceful reconfiguration or degradation of distributed groups of cooperating processes when some nodes of the network are unavailable. (References to more complete discussions of various aspects of network transparency may be found in the Bibliography.)

Thus, the major considerations when choosing a network model were that it fit well into the Unix model, providing compatibility, and that it allow local and remote processes to be manipulated in the same ways, providing network transparency. Other important desirable characteristics were ease of user control, high performance, and retention of local autonomy of individual nodes in the network.

3.1. Network Tasking in LOCUS

The major Unix process control functions *fork* and *exec* have extended in an upward compatible way. Recall that *fork* creates a new process, running the same program image as the caller, and that *exec* replaces the code and data of a running process with a new program and data image. In LOCUS, both of these calls have been extended for the network. For compatibility, the system calls look the same as in Unix, but under certain circumstances they operate over the network. *Fork* can cause a new process to be created locally or remotely. *Exec* has been extended to allow a process to migrate to another site as it replaces its image.

The decision about where the new process or new image will execute is made by examining a list of preferred execution sites specified by information associated with the calling process. This information is inherited by child processes when a process forks, and can be set dynamically by a *setxsites* system call. By issuing *setxsites*, a running program can specify where its subprocesses and future images will execute. An interactive user can set the site of execution of subsequent programs by giving a command to his shell, which will issue the *setxsites* call.

Use of an additional system call to set execution site information was chosen rather than adding arguments to the process calls for two reasons. First, by not changing the existing system call interfaces, programs written without knowledge of the network continue to work, and in fact may have their execution sites selected by their parents. This aspect is especially valuable when a source code is not available. Second, it was considered desirable to separate those functions which affect the semantics of a program from those functions which are performance optimizations. With few exceptions, the site where a process runs does not have any effect on the results that the process computes.

A new system call, *migrate*, has been added to permit a process to change its site of execution while in the midst of execution. A long-running process might choose to do this, for example, if it received a signal telling it that the current site was about to be taken down.

Another application for process migration is load leveling. Process migration can be induced externally by sending a new signal whose default action is to migrate the process. If the user code of the process does not catch or ignore the signal, then the process will move to a new site. Using this mechanism, a load leveling daemon can monitor loads on various machines on the network and cause long-running CPU-intensive processes to move to less loaded sites.

3.2. Local Autonomy of Sites

In some LOCUS networks, it may be desirable to restrict the use of various machines in the network for use only by certain users. For instance, some machines may be reserved only for a particular group. The LOCUS network tasking protocols are designed so that each site in the network makes the final decision about whether to accept a process which is attempting to migrate to that site, and whether to create a process when a fork to that site has been requested. The site can implement whatever permission checking it deems necessary. In this way, the local autonomy of the site is preserved with respect to CPU resources expended upon user processes.

In addition to the Unix limitation on the number of processes a user may have on a site, LOCUS associates a site permission mask with each process (inherited by children) which specifies to which sites the process may perform network process creation or migration operations. This permission mask is set at sign-on time by *login*, on an individual user basis.

3.3. Integrated Fork/Exec Call

In typical Unix programs which create subprocesses, very often the *fork* call is quickly followed by an *exec* call. In LOCUS, another new system call, *run*, has been added. *Run* is intended to achieve the effect of a combination of *fork* and *exec*. *Run* creates a new process and invokes a new program image in it before returning to the user code of the child process. In this way, the costly overhead of the *fork* system call can be avoided, without sacrificing machine independence.

To be useful in most situations, *run* takes as an argument a structure specifying certain operations to be performed by the kernel in the child process before the new program image begins execution. The permitted operations are those found between the *fork* and the *exec* in typical Unix programs. These include operations which close or duplicate file descriptors and change signal actions.

Run can create the child process locally or remotely, just as *fork*, and since it invokes a new image, may operate across different CPU types.

3.4. Network Tasking Applications

One application of remote tasking is load leveling. As was noted in a previous section, load leveling can be performed automatically by a daemon process which looks for CPU-bound processes and unloaded sites, and asks the processes to migrate there.

A simpler form of load leveling may be performed by the shell. If the user has requested this option, the shell can keep track of the load on various sites and automatically execute the user's commands on the least loaded site. The mechanisms required to implement load leveling were almost trivial to construct under LOCUS.

Another application of remote tasking is the distribution of programs which have inherent parallelism. The *make* program is an example. *Make* has been modified so that multiple machines may simultaneously participate in making a final target which requires several intermediate targets. With two machines participating, the compile time of a major program is cut nearly in half. The changes required to *make* were quite simple.

3.5. Implementation Challenges

Implementing transparent remote tasking presented several difficulties. A major difficulty was *process tracking*. It is sometimes necessary to find a process in the network to deliver signals. To do this without having to search the entire network requires that the system keep track of processes when they migrate about. The process tracking code must be extremely careful when processes are moving around while delivery of a signal is being attempted, so that the signal is delivered reliably.

Another major effort was the code which implements file sharing among related processes on different sites. Unix file-sharing semantics require inherited file descriptors to share read/write pointers among the processes involved. LOCUS implements these semantics across the network; the most common cases execute as fast with the processes distributed as when they are collected on a single site.

3.6. Network Tasking Experience

Our experience with transparent tasking has been an unqualified success, from the user's point of view. As illustrated above, the job of building software to execute in a distributed environment has been substantially eased, and the simplification of the user interface has been found to be quite valuable. As a further example, some time ago, a demonstration of LOCUS on a 6800 workstation connected to a larger VAX LOCUS network was being given. The demonstrator edited a program source file for a given language, and then compiled and ran it, piping the results to another program running on his workstation. Only afterward did he realize that there was no compiler for the language on the workstation; this compilation and subsequent program execution took place, transparently, elsewhere, on a VAX.

However, from the LOCUS implementors' point of view, the design and development of transparent tasking required considerably more effort than had been originally contemplated. Of course, the existence of a very high degree of transparency in the basic LOCUS system was an essential prerequisite. Without it, transparent tasking is obviously not feasible. Nevertheless, transparency still had to be extended to process relevant issues, such as shared file descriptors, signals, and so on. Also, given how much had already been accomplished, the opportunity to further extend the LOCUS transparency mechanism to heterogeneous CPUs was especially attractive. Although heterogeneity presents significant additional problems, and complete solutions are not feasible, nevertheless a great deal can be accomplished, and the result so obviously frees the user from so much unnecessary complexity in his environment that the cost of development has clearly been justified.

LOCUS tasking greatly simplifies the development of software for a distributed environment. Load leveling is simple to accomplish. Automatic selection of the site of execution as a function of needed resources, including CPU characteristics, is also done automatically. Execution of programs with inherent parallelism, such as *make*, can be done on multiple machines simultaneously with little change to the original, single machine program. Transparent support for remote processes requires a facility to create a process on a remote machine, initialize it appropriately, support cross-machine, inter-process functions with the same semantics as were available on a single machine, and reflect error conditions across machine boundaries. Each of these is discussed below.

3.6.1. Remote Process Creation

LOCUS permits one to execute programs at any site in the network, subject to permission control, in a manner just as easy as executing the program locally. In fact, one can dynamically, even just before process invocation, select the execution site. No rebinding or any other action is needed. The mechanism is entirely transparent, so that existing software can be executed either locally or remotely, with no change to that software.

The decision about where the new process is to execute is specified by information associated with the calling process. That information, currently a structured advice list, can be set dynamically. Shell commands to control execution site are also available.

Processes are typically created by the standard Unix *fork* call. Both fork and *exec,* the Unix call which installs a load module into a process and starts execution, are controlled by site information in the process environment. If exec is to occur remotely, then the process is effectively moved at that time. By doing so, it is feasible to support remote execution of programs intended for dissimilar CPU types.

In both cases, a process body is allocated at the destination site following a message exchange between the calling site and the new process site. More significant, it is necessary to initialize the new process' environment correctly. This requires, for Unix compatibility, that the parent and child process share open file descriptors (which contain current file position pointers*), a copy of other process state information.

In the case of a fork, the process address space, both code and data, must be made a copy of the parents'. If the code is reentrant, and a copy already exists on the destination machine, it should be used. In any case, the relevant set of process pages are sent to the new process site.

For optimization purposes, a *run* call has been added that is similar to the effect of a fork followed by a exec. If the run is to execute remotely, the effect is a local fork and a remote exec. However, run is transparent as to where it executes. Run avoids the copy of the parent process image which occurs with

*To implement this functionality across the network we keep a file descriptor at each site, with only one valid at any time, using a token scheme to determine which file descriptor is currently valid.

fork, and includes parameterization that permits the caller to set up the environment of the new process, be local or remote.

3.6.2. Inter-process Functions

The semantics of the available functions by which processes interact determines, to a large extent, the difficulty involved in supporting a transparent process facility. In Unix, there are explicit functions such as signals and pipes (named or not), but there are also implicit mechanisms; shared open files are the most significant. The most difficult part of these functions' semantics is their expectation of shared memory. For example, if one process sharing an open file reads or writes a character, and then another does so, the second process receives or alters the character following the one touched by the first process. Pipes have similar characteristics under certain circumstances.

All of these mechanisms are supported in LOCUS, in part through a token mechanism which marks which copy of a resource is valid; access to a resource requires the token. This concept is used at various levels within the system. While in the worst case, performance is limited by the speed at which the tokens and their associated resources can be flipped back and forth among processes on different machines, such extreme behavior is exceedingly rare. Virtually all processes read and write substantial amounts of data per system call. As a result, most collections of Unix processes designed to execute on a single machine run very well when distributed on LOCUS.

3.6.3. Error Handling

In LOCUS, process errors are folded into the existing Unix interface to the degree possible. The new error types primarily concern cases where either the calling or called machine fails while the parent and child are still alive. When the child's machine fails, the parent receives an error signal. Additional information about the nature of the error is deposited in the parent's process structure, which can be interrogated via a new system call. When the parent's machine fails, the child is notified in a similar manner. Otherwise, the process interface in LOCUS is the same as in Unix.

4. DYNAMIC RECONFIGURATION

4.1. Introduction

Transparency in LOCUS applies not only to the static topology of the network, but to the configuration changes themselves. The system strives to insulate the users from reconfigurations, providing continuing operation with only negligible delay. Requiring user programs to deal with reconfiguration would shift the network costs from the operating system to the applications programs.

This section discusses the concept of transparency as it relates to a dynamic network environment, gives several principles that the operating system should follow to provide it, and presents the reconfiguration protocols used in LOCUS. The protocols make use of a high-level synchronization strategy to avoid the message overhead of two-phased commits or high-level ACKs, and are largely independent of the specific architecture of LOCUS.

The high-level protocols of LOCUS assume that the underlying network is fully connected. By this we mean that if site A can communicate with site B, and site B with site C, then site A can communicate with site C. In practice, this may be done by routing messages from A to C through B, although the present implementation of LOCUS runs on a broadcast network where this is unnecessary. The assumption of transitivity of communication significantly simplifies the high-level protocols used in LOCUS.

The low-level protocols enforce that network transitivity. Network information is kept internally in both a high-level status table and a collection of virtual circuits.* The two structures are, to some extent, independent. Membership in the partition does not guarantee the existence of a virtual circuit, nor does an open virtual circuit guarantee membership in the partition. Failure of a virtual circuit, either on or after open, does, however, remove a node from a partition. Likewise, removal from a partition closes all relevant virtual circuits. All changes in partitions invoke the protocols discussed later in this chapter.

The system attempts to maintain file access across partition changes. If it is possible, without loss of information, to substitute a different copy of a file for one lost because of partition, the system will do so. If, in particular, a process loses contact with a file it was reading remotely, the system will attempt to reopen a different copy of the same version of the file.

The ability to mount filegroups independently gives great flexibility to the name space. Since radical changes to the name space can confuse users, however, this facility is rarely used for that purpose, and that use is not supported in LOCUS. The reconfiguration protocols require that the mount hierarchy be the same at all sites.

4.2. Requirements for the Reconfiguration Protocols

The first constraint on the reconfiguration protocol is that is maintain consistency with respect to the internal system protocols. All solutions satisfying this constraint could be termed correct. Correctness, however, is not enough. In addition to maintaining system integrity, the solution must insulate the user from the underlying system changes. The solution should not affect program development, and it should be efficient enough that any delays it imposes are negligible.

*The virtual circuits deliver messages from *site* A to *site* B (the virtual circuits connect sites, not processes) in the order they are sent.

As an example of a "correct" but poor solution to the problem, the system could handle only the boot case, where all machines in the network come up together. Any failures would be handled by a complete network reboot. Such a solution would easily satisfy the consisistency constraint; however, one might expect murmurs of complaint from the user community.

Similarly, a solution that brings the system to a grinding halt for an unpredictable length of time at unforeseeable intervals to reconstruct internal tables might meet the requirement of correctness, but would clearly be undesirable.

Optimally, the reconfiguration algorithms should not affect the user in any manner whatsoever. A user accessing resources on machine A from machine B should not be affected by any activity involving machine C. This intuitive idea can be expressed in several principles:

1. User activity should be allowed to continue without adverse affect, provided no resources are lost.
2. Any delay imposed by the system on user activity during reconfiguration should be negligible.
3. The user should be shielded from any transient effects of the network configuration.
4. Any activity initiated after the reconfiguration should reflect the state of the system after the reconfiguration.
5. Specialized users should be able to detect reconfigurations if necessary.
6. No user should be penalized for increased availability of resources.*

All these principles are fairly intuitive. They merely extend the concept of network transparency to a dynamic network and express a desire for efficiency. They do, however, give tight constraints on the eventual algorithms. For example, those operations with high delay potential must be partitioned in such a way that the tasks relevant to a specific user request can be run quickly, efficiently, and immediately.

The principles have far-reaching implications in areas such as file access and synchronization. Suppose, for example, a process were reading from a file replicated twice in its partition. If it were to lose contact with the copy it was reading, the system should substitute the other copy (assuming, of course, that it is still available).

4.3. Protocol Structure

As noted before, the underlying LOCUS protocols assume a fully-connected network. To insure correct operation, the reconfiguration strategy must guarantee this property. If, for instance, a momentary break occurs between two

*This last point may cause violations of synchronization policies, as discussed below.

sites, all other sites in the partition must be notified of the break. A simple scan of available nodes is insufficient.

The present strategy splits the reconfiguration into two stages: first, a *partition* protocol runs to find fully connected subnetworks; then a *merge* protocol runs to merge several such subnetworks into a full partition. The partition protocol affects only those sites previously thought to be up. It divides a partition into subpartitions, each of which is guaranteed to be fully-connected and disjoint from all other subpartitions. It detects all site and communications failures and cleans up all affected multisite data structures, so that the merge protocol can ignore such matters. The merge protocol polls the set of available sites, and merges several disjoint subpartitions into one.

After the new partition is established, the recovery procedure corrects any inconsistencies brought about either by the reconfiguration code itself, or by activity while the network was not connected. Recovery is concerned mainly with file consistency. It detects modifications and schedules update propagation.

All reconfiguration protocols are controlled by a high-priority kernel process. The partition and merge protocols are run directly by that process, while the recovery procedure runs as a privileged application program.

4.4. The Partition Protocol

Communication in a fully-connected network is an equivalence relation. Thus, the partitions we speak about are partitions, in the strict mathematical sense of the set of nodes of the network. In normal operation, the site tables reflect the equivalence classes: all members of a partition agree on the status of the general network. When a communication break occurs, for whatever reason, these tables become unsynchronized. The partition code must re-establish the logical partitioning that the operating system assumes, and synchronize the site tables of its member sites to reflect the new environment.

In general, a communication failure between any two sites does not imply a failure of either site. Failures caused by transmission noise or unforeseen delays cannot be detected directly by foreign sites, and will often be detected in only one of the sites involved. In such situations, the partition algorithm should find maximum partitions: a single communications failure should not result in the network breaking into three or more parts.* LOCUS implements a solution based on iterative intersection.

A few terms are helpful for the following discussion. The *partition set*, P_α is the set of sites believed up by site α. The *new partition set*, P'_α, is the set of sites known by α to have joined the new partition.

Consider a partition P after some set of failures has occurred. To form a new

*Breaking a virtual circuit between two sites aborts any ongoing activity between those two sites. Partition fragmentation must be minimized to minimize the loss of work.

partition, the sites must reach a consensus on the state of the network. The criterion for consensus may be stated in set notation as: for every $\alpha,\beta \in P$, $P_\alpha = P_\beta$. This state can be reached from any initial condition by taking successive intersections of the partition sets of a group of sites.

When a site α runs the partition algorithm, it polls the sites in P_α. Each site polled responds with its own partition set $P_{pollsite}$. When a site is polled successfully, it is added to the new partition set P'_α, and P_α is changed to $P_\alpha \cap P_{pollsite}$. α continues to poll those sites in P_α but not in P'_α until the two sets are equal, at which point a consensus is assured, and α announces it to the other sites.

Translating this algorithm into a working protocol requires provisions for synchronization and failure recovery. These two requirements are antagonistic—while the algorithm requires that only one active site poll for a new partition, and that other sites join only one new partition, reliability considerations require that sites be able to change active sites when one fails. Since the details of the protocol are not relevant to the overall discussion, they are not included in this document.

4.5. The Merge Protocol

The *merge* procedure joins several partitions into one. It establishes new site and mount tables, and reestablishes CSS's for all the file groups. To form the largest possible partition, the protocol must check all possible sites, including, of course, those thought to be down. In a large network, sequential polling results in a large additive delay because of the timeouts and retransmissions necessary to determine the status of the various sites. To minimize this effect, the merge strategy polls the sites asynchronously.

The algorithm itself is simple. The site initiating the protocol sends a request for information to all sites in the network. Those sites which are able respond with the information necessary for the initiating site to build the global tables. After a suitable time, the initiating site gives up on the other sites, declares a new partition, and broadcasts its composition to the world.

The algorithm is centralized and can only be run at one site, and a site can only participate in one protocol at a time, so the other sites must be able to halt execution of the protocol. To accomplish this, the polled site sends back an error mesage instead of a normal reply:

```
IF ready to merge THEN
        IF merging AND actsite == locsite THEN
                IF fsite < locsite THEN
                        actsite := fsite;
                        halt active merge;
                ELSE decline to merge
                FI
```

```
        ELSE actsite := fsite;
        FI
    ELSE decline to merge
    FI.
```

If a site is not ready to merge, then either it or some other site will eventually run the merge protocol.

The major source of delay in the merge procedure is in the timeout routines that decide when the full partition has answered. A fixed length timeout long enough to handle a sizable network would add unreasonable delay to a smaller network or a small partition of a large network. The strategy used must be flexible enough to handle the large partition case and the small partition case at the same time.

The merge protocol waits longer when there is a reasonable expectation that further replies will arrive. When a site answers the poll, it sends its partition information in the reply. Until all sites believed up by some site in the new partition have replied, the timeout is long. Once all such sites have replied, the timeout is short.

4.6. The Cleanup Procedure

Even before the partition has been reestablished, there is considerable work that each node can do to clean up its internal data structures. Essentially, each machine, once it has decided that a particular site is unavailable, must invoke failure handling for all resources which its processes were using at the site, or for all local resources which processes at that site were using. The action to be taken depends on the nature of the resource and the actions that were under way when failure occurred. The cases are outlined in the table below.

Once the machines in a partition have mutually agreed upon the membership of the partition, the system must select, for each mounted filegroup, a new synchronization site (CSS). This is the site to which the LOCUS file system protocols direct all file open requests. Once the synchronization site has been selected, that site must reconstruct the lock table for all open files from the information remaining in the partition.

4.7. Protocol Synchronization

The reconfiguration procedure breaks down into three distinct components, each of which has already been discussed. What remains is a discussion of how the individual parts are tied together into a robust whole. At various points in the procedure, the participating sites must be synchronized, and control of the protocol must be handed to a centralized site. Those sites not directly involved in the activity must be able to ascertain the status of the active sites to insure that no failures have stalled the entire network.

Table 4.1. Failure Handling cases.

Local Resource in Use Remotely

Resource	Failure Action
File (open for update)	Discard pages, close file and abort updates
File (open for read)	Close file

Remote Resource in Use Locally

Resource	Failure Action
File (open for update)	Discard pages, set error in local file descriptor
File (open for read)	Internal close, attempt to reopen at other site

Interacting Processes

Failure Type	Action
Remote Fork/Exec, remote site fails	return error to caller
Fork/Exec, calling site fails	notify process
Distributed Transaction	abort all related subtransactions in partition

One way to synchronize the sites would be to require each site to signal its readiness before beginning a new phase. This approach increases both the message traffic and the delay, both critical performance quantities. It also requires careful analysis of the critical sections in the protocols to determine where synchronization is required. If a site fails during a synchronization stage, the system must still detect and recover from that failure.

LOCUS reconfiguration uses an extension of its failure detection mechanism to handle synchronization control. Whenever a site takes on a passive role in a protocol, it checks periodically on the active site. If the active site fails, the passive site can restart the protocol.

As the various protocols execute, the states of both the active and the passive sites change. An active site at one instant may well become a passive site the next, and a passive site could easily end up waiting for another passive site. Without adequate control, this could lead to circular waits and deadlocks.

One solution would be to have passive sites respond to the checks by returning the site that they themselves are waiting for. The checking site would then follow that chain and make sure that it terminated. This approach could require several messages per check, however, and communications delays could make the information collected obsolete or misleading.

Another alternative, the one used in LOCUS, is to order all the stages of the protocol. When a site checks another site, that site returns its own status information. A site can wait only for those sites who are executing a portion of the protocol that precedes its own. If the two sites are in the same state, the ordering is by site number. This ordering of the sites is complete. The lowest ordered site has no site to legally wait for; if it is not active, its check will fail, and the protocol can be re-started at a reasonable point.

5. EXPERIENCE

Production LOCUS has now been operating for over four years at UCLA, and has been installed at a few other sites. Most of the experience with a large network configuration has occurred at UCLA. The host facility consists of 6 VAX-11/750s, a VAX-11/780, 2 IBM 370s, and 20 PC/ATs connected by an Ethernet network. Typically, 150–200 people are using the network at a given time. The LOCUS system is used for virtually all the interactive computing in the UCLA Computer Science Department. Most of the user experience with Locus has been acquired on a version of the system that did not support replication of user files or the transaction facility. The following observations largely reflect the experience at UCLA.

First, it is clearly feasible to provide high performance, transparent distributed system behavior for file and device access, as well as remote, interprocess interaction. Measurements consistently indicate the Locus performance equals Unix in the local case, and that remote access in general, while somewhat slower than when resources are local, is close enough that no one typically thinks much about resource location because of performance reasons. For example, user's decisions about where to login or where to run a process are most often based on CPU load rather than file location. This ability to provide a substantial degree of *performance transparency* was surprising. There is still no indication that the Ethernet bandwidth is any significant limitation. It is, however, difficult to swap load images across the network with high perfomrance because of the software cost of packet disassembly and reassembly for the current hardware and low level protocols. Much larger configurations clearly cannot share the same broadcast cable of that bandwidth.

Most of the problems which were encountered by users resulted from those situations where transparency was not completely supported, either because the implementation was not finished, or because explicit decision to make exceptions were made. Experience with transparency has been very positive; giving it up, once having had it, would be nearly unthinkable.

LOCUS executes programs locally as the default. We found that the primary motivation for remote execution was load balancing. Remote process execution is also used to access those few peripheral devices which are not remotely transparent. The remote processing facility is also heavily used when the LOCUS network is composed of heterogeneous CPUs.

User experience with replicated storage was limited at the time this chapter was written, so few firm conclusions can be drawn, except that we certainly cursed its absence.

However, automatic replication of the system files has been an invaluable asset for the operations staff as it makes a large part of the system management problem no more difficult than the single machine case.[2] For example, a changed piece of software need be installed only once rather than 30 times, even though, for reliability reasons, a copy is stored on each machine. System management in a large distributed system would be unreasonably difficult without automatic replication of some system files.

As usual, the tasks involved in providing a reasonably production quality environment were far more extensive and much more painful than anyone had anticipated, even though we held university standards for "production quality," and we all knew to expect this phenomenon.

We estimate that, from the project inception in 1979 till early 1983, about 50 man-years were spent on LOCUS. This effort included almost a year in the conceptual phase (transparency was only a vague idea at that time, for example), an extensive design phase that lasted almost a year, initial construction on PDP-11s, multiple ports to the Vax and Ethernet, development of the general-use, development and testing configuration at UCLA, extensive debugging, some redesign and reimplementation to more fully maintain Unix compatibility, and a significant number of masters and Ph.D. theses. Continuing work is now being done in a commercial environment rather than by a university research project.

6. CONCLUSIONS

The most obvious conclusion to be drawn from the LOCUS work is that a high performance, network transparent, distributed file system which contains all of the various functions indicated throughout this chapter, is feasible to design and implement, even in a small machine environment.

Replication of storage is valuable, both from the user and the system's point of view. However, much of the work is in recovery and in dealing with the various races and failures that can exist.

Nothing is free. In order to avoid performance degradation when resources are local, the cost has been converted into additional code and substantial care in implementation architecture. LOCUS is approximately one-third bigger than Unix and certainly more complex.

The difficulties involved in dynamically reconfiguring an operating system are both intrinsic to the problem, and dependent on the particular system. Rebuilding lock tables and synchronizing processes running in separate environments are problems of inherent difficulty. Most of the system-dependent problems can be avoided, however, with careful design.

The fact that LOCUS uses specialized protocols for operating system to operating system communication made it possible to control message traffic quite selectively. The ability to alter specific protocols to simplify the reconfiguration solution was particularly appreciated.

The task of developing a protocol by which sites would agree about the membership of a partition proved to be surprisingly difficult. Balancing the needs of protocol synchronization and failure detection while maintaining good performance presented a considerable challenge. Since reconfiguration software is run precisely when the network is flaky, those problems are real, and not events that are unlikely.

Nevertheless, it has been possible to design and implement a solution that exhibits reasonably high performance. Further work is still needed to assure that scaling to a large network will successfully maintain that performance characteristic, but our experience with the present solution makes us quite optimistic.

In summary, however, use of LOCUS indicates the enormous value of a highly transparent, distributed operating system. Since file activity is often the dominant part of the operating system load, it seems clear that the LOCUS architecture, constructed on a distributed file system base, is rather attractive.

ACKNOWLEDGMENTS

The authors would like to thank all those members of the research contract who have helped, over the years, in the design, implementation, and support of LOCUS. In addition, special recognition should be given to Terry Gray, who is responsible for keeping the LOCUS facility running at UCLA.

REFERENCES

1. Goldberg, A., and G. Popek, *Measurement of the Distributed Operating System LOCUS*, UCLA Tech. Rep. 1983.
2. Gray, T. E., *UCLA Comput. Sci. Dep.* Qtrly. vol. 13, *Two years of network transparency: Lessons learned from LOCUS* pp. 2–12, Apr. 1985.
3. Lampson B. W., *Atomic Transactions,* Distributed Systems—Architecture and Implementation (Lecture Notes in Computer Science 105), New York: Springer-Verlag, 1981, pp. 246–264.
4. Lampson B. W., *Ethernet, Pub and Violet,* Distributed Systems—Architecture and Implementation (Lecture Notes in Computer Science 105), New York: Springer-Verlag, 1981, pp. 446–484.
5. Menasce, D. A., G. J. Popek, and R. R. Muntz, *A Locking Protocol for Resource Coordination in Distributed Systems*, Tech. Rep. UCLA-EG-7808, Dept. of Compu. Sci., UCLA, Oc. 1977.
6. Mueller E., J. Moore, and G. Popek, *A Nested Transaction System for LOCUS*, SOSP '83.
7. Parker, D. Stott, Gerald J. Popek, G. Rudisin, A. Stoughton, B. Walker, E. Walton, J. Chow D. Edwards, S. Kiser, and C. Kline, *Detection of Mutual Inconsistency in distributed systems,* IEEE Trans. Software Eng. May 1983.

8. Popek, G., B. Walker, J. Chow, D. Edwards, C. Kline, G. Rudisin, and G. Thiel, LOCUS: A network transparent, high reliability distributed system, *Proc. Symp. on Operating Systems Principles*, Pacific Grove, CA., Dec. 1981.
9. Popek, G. J. and B. Walker, *The Locus Distributed System Architecture*, Cambridge, MA: The MIT Press, 1985.
10. Popek, Gerald J., and Bruce J. Walker, *Network Transparency and its Limits in a Distributed Operating System*, Submitted for Publication.
11. Popek, G. J., *et al.*, *LOCUS System Architecture*, LOCUS Computing Corporation Tech. Rep., 1983.
12. Walker, B. J., *Issues of Network Transparency and File Replicatioan in Distributed Systems: LOCUS* (Ph.D. Diss.), Comput. Sci. Dep., University of California, Los Angeles, 1983.
13. Walker, B. J., G. Popek, R. J. English C. Kline, and G. Thiel, *The LOCUS Distributed Operating System*, *Proc. 9th ACM Symp. on Operating Systems Principles*, Bretton Woods, New Hampshire, 10–13 October, 1983.
14. Weinstein, M., T. W. Page, Jr., B. Livezey, and G. Popek, Transactions and synchronization in a distributed system, *Proc. 10th ACM Symp. on Operating Systems Principles*, Orcas Island, Eastsound, Washington, 1–4 December, 1985.

5. Modeling of the Data Allocation Algorithm in SIRIUS-Delta

P. ROLIN

ABSTRACT

The realization of a distributed data base system requires a data allocation mechanism. This chapter describes the techniques used in SIRIUS-Delta to reach this goal. We describe the principles used: two-phase locking, conflict avoidance, two-phase commitment, and journals. We assume failures are possible and the developed algorithms maintain the database consistency in such situations. An inquiry mechanism is used to finish transactions. Journals are maintained to recover from any type of failure. Partial destruction of journals is studied and a general roll-back mechanism proposed. Proposals for evaluation are described. All the algorithms are modeled using Nutt's net formalism.

1. INTRODUCTION

The current development of systems in which the information is distributed requires a system kernel able to perform the classical operating systems functions. This work describes the solutions to data allocation and failure problems in the SIRIUS-Delta prototype. In Section 2 we will describe the context of this work and define the hypotheses which are made about the transport level. We shall use Nutt's net formalism in the descriptions, which is quite powerful in formalizing these types of problems.

To reach the previously stated objective, we follow five principles: total ordering of the transactions, decentralized locking, temporary files, two-phase commitment, and journals. We use the virtual ring mechanism to obtain a unique and ordered set of names. In Section 3 we will describe how this is used to manage a quite simple locking strategy and to prevent deadlocks by using a roll-back mechanism. All of these mechanisms are completely decentralized, and each site has complete control of its local data. Such a mechanism requires the capability to undo any part of a running transaction. Since we write immediately on the data base (DB), a copy of the object value is made in a "before-image" file before any write.

In Section 4 we study the two-phase commitment protocol and show that this mechanism is fault-tolerant. In case of the failure of a site where a transaction has been initiated, we describe how the involved sites are able to finish this transaction properly, with the help of an inquiry mechanism. The information about a running transaction is written on a journal in order to be able to reconstruct the transaction context after a crash has occurred.

The employment (or use) of this journal for a recovery operation is studied in Section 5. In the case of a catastrophic crash, including a partial destruction of the journal, it must be possible to come back to a mutually consistent state for the whole distributed system. We define a mechanism providing global recovery lines on the journals and we describe how to use them. We indicate ways to improve this mechanism in order to undo only the strictly useful transactions.

Measurements of the distributed data base system (DDBS) are needed to determine the evolution and the cost of the base. An *a priori* evaluation is made using the formal model. Then this formal model is used to place traces in the prototype software. Measurements giving elapsed time spent for a specific function are given. Since elapsed time is load-dependent, a measurement project has been conducted with a hardware monitor. Results are provided as the number of instructions per function. In Section 6, we also propose some criteria for evaluating the distributed system.

2. SIRIUS-Delta: A French DDBS System

2.1. General Objectives

The general objectives may be expressed in terms of transparencies[8]:

- Distribution/replication transparency: The user is not aware of data and process distribution.
- Concurrency transparency: A global control mechanism mediates concurrent DDBS access.
- Failure transparency: The replication of data, programs, and processors allows high resiliency. A failure detection and reconfiguration system provides a high degree of failure transparency.

2.2. Architecture

Here, we are interested only in the distributed functions. Using the ISO model,[6] we can say that SIRIUS-Delta uses four levels as shown in Fig. 5.1. We make

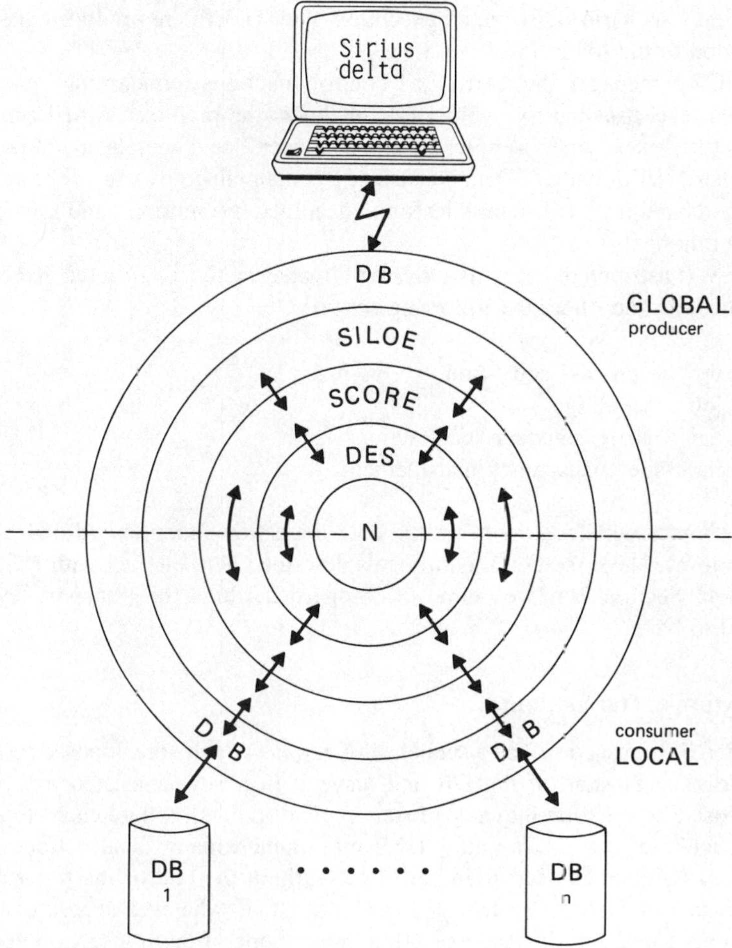

Fig. 5.1. SIRIUS-Delta Architecture.

a distinction between the global level (producer) which implements the user interface, and the local level (consumer) which manages the data base accesses. We then find the four service levels at the global and local sides.

From the user to the transport level:

- DBMS is the DB software offered by Intertechnique on Realite 2000 machines.
- SILOE handles data distribution, and decomposes the user request into several scenarios (several possible execution strategies), selecting the

"best" scenario. Distributed execution plans (DEP) are produced and submitted to the lower level.[5]

- SCORE manages the distributed control functions (concurrency control). This level uses the following three methods: the producer virtual ring, the control token, and the circulating sequencer,[9] to generate a unique and ordered set of names. Data consistency is maintained by use of the following techniques: two-phase locking, deadlock prevention, and two-phase commitment.[15]
- DES (Distributed Executive System) manages the distributed execution functions and offers the following services:[16]

  1. remote process activation,
  2. job scheduling,
  3. data transfer between local actions, and
  4. inter-site concurrency management.

This chapter will focus only on the data allocation functions offered by the SCORE level. Nevertheless, the protocols described here interact with DES and SILOE. In Section 2.4, we define the properties which the transport level is assumed to have.

2.3. Atomic Transactions

We define a "transaction" as a sequence of actions which are supposed to begin with a consistent state of the DB and leave it in a new consistent one.[3] We decompose a transaction into steps (user recovery points), where each step may involve with several DEPs and a DEP may launch many local actions (Fig. 5.2). Locks are set as needed and are freed only at the end of the transaction. SCORE data allocation mechanisms guarantee that, whatever access conflicts and failures happen during the execution, all or none of the transaction updates are performed. Therefore, the transaction is seen by the user as an atomic action.

2.4. Transport Functions

We assume that the underlying transport level has the following properties:[6]

- Message sequencing and flow control.
- Error free delivery (via retransmission as necessary).
- Site inaccessibility signalled by the message CLinac(x) (Close link inaccessible site x).
- Link control between pairs of processes.
- The communication network is assumed to have routing that adapts to changes in topology.

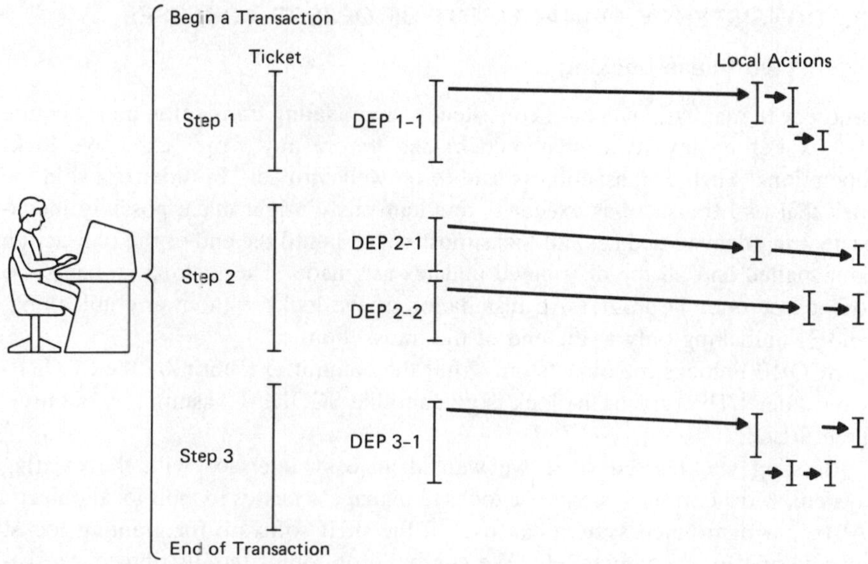

Fig. 5.2. Transaction schemata.

Adaptive routing allows us to state that, if a site x is connected with a site y, the relation $C(x, y)$ is said to be satisfied, and that C is a reflexive relation. C is also transitive: $C(x, y)$ and $C(y, z)$ implies $C(x, z)$.

In the protocols we will be informed of a link closure only if this event, denoted $\text{CLinac}(x)$, concerns a transaction site, x being the remote site name.

2.5. Nutt's Net Formalism

Evaluation nets are a modified form of Petri nets. They are convenient for description of solutions to our problem since they are graphical, unambiguous, and applications-oriented.[2] Circles (places) denote possible states of the process, squares (message locations) denote incoming messages, and horizontal lines denote actions. Transition schemata allow token flow via the net (fork, join, and select transitions). A transition may be fired if and only if the preceding place is occupied by at least one token and there is a message in the square symbolizing the entry queue. Message transmission and broadcast are denoted with an arrow and dots after a transition line.

$\longrightarrow .$ $\quad TR_{Dest}$ (message)
Transmit a message to the destination

$\longrightarrow \ldots$ $\quad BRD_{list}$ (message)
Broadcast this message to the members of the list.
Of course, if the list is empty nothing is done.

3. CONSISTENCY MANAGEMENT OF OBJECT ACCESSES

3.1. Two-Phase Locking

In order to maintain data base consistency, an updating transaction must acquire a lock before any read (shared lock) and before any write (exclusive lock) operations. Such a transaction is said to be well formed.[3] In order to avoid the risk that two transactions executed simultaneously might make possibly inconsistent interleaved updates, all locks must be held until the end of the transaction is signalled and all the distributed updates are made. The locking strategy is a two-phase one: 1) progressive installation of the locks without any unlocking, and 2) unlocking only at the end of the transaction.

SCORE unlocks the objects only after the commit execution by the SCORE-Consumer.[1] The type of the lock is given to the SCORE-Consumer by the user, here SILOE.

Locking was chosen since we wanted an easy interface with the existing system. Most current systems use locks to manage accesses to their local objects. Also, our distributed system can use off-the-shelf software for granting locks, discovering local conflicts, etc. We can build on top of the distributed consistency management software for each local site, using primitives of the existing software. This results in minimal coding, and compatibility with different operating systems.

3.2. Deadlock Prevention

Each SCORE-Consumer treats access requests independently from the other consumers, and access requests to objects may be generated at any time during the execution of a transaction (dynamic locking). Therefore, simultaneous transaction execution can result in deadlock, as shown in a later figure. To solve this problem, we associate a ticket with each transaction[11] (circulating sequencer). Remember that a ticket belongs to a set of unique and ordered numbers in the whole distributed system. Each consumer maintains (virtually) one waiting queue per object. Action requests are queued according to increasing ticket order. For each request, the following information is maintained:

- Current object state: free, or locked in share (R), or exclusive (W) mode.
- When in locked exclusive mode, the transaction's name, and when in share mode, the transactions' names.
- For each transaction, the step during which the lock was set.

Remember, each SCORE-Consumer involved in a transaction knows if this transaction is in its ending phase. All of the lock requests are managed according to the following rules:

Requested lock \ Object locked in	NO LOCK	READ	WRITE
READ	YES	YES	NO
WRITE	YES	NO	NO

Fig. 5.3. Locks rules.

1. Any lock allocation request compatible with the current lock on the object is accepted (Fig. 5.3).
2. Any lock allocation request incompatible with the actual lock, coming from:

- a transaction with a ticket younger than at least one of the transactions owning the object, is put in the waiting queue (example: Fig. 5.4c, T_2, W, 3 on object a);
- a transaction with a ticket older than all the transactions accessing the object, will issue a roll-back request to all these transactions. The lock request waits until all the roll-back requests have been performed (Figs. 5.4c and 5.4d). If a transaction owning the object is in the commit phase, the roll-back request is only memorized, and will be executed only if an abort is received from the SCORE-Producer (A transaction which is in the commit phase has got all its resources, there is no deadlock risk, since the object will be released at the end of commit).

The reader will notice that:

- The step concept allows us to undo only the strictly needed parts.
- Roll-back may be requested even if a conflict does not lead to a deadlock situation (it is an avoidance protocol).
- The ticketing strategy precludes the starvation (tickets are always increasing), and priority is given to older transactions. A rolled-back transaction keeps its ticket.

It is easy to see that if two transactions have conflicts at different consumers, the conflicts will be resolved identically at each consumer, and the decision will be immediate (tickets define a total ordering on any set of actions).

According to Rosenkrantz taxonomy, this is the Wait–Die policy. The choice for it has been made according to three criteria:

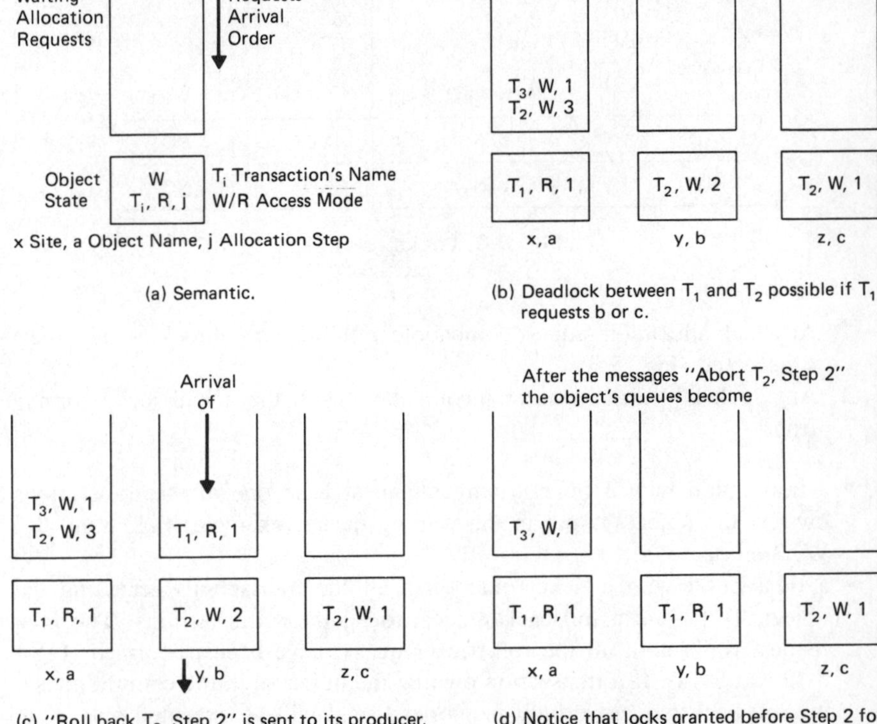

Fig. 5.4. Deadlock avoidance.

1. User response time is constant. This means that there is no sudden change in user waiting time for the same request. Variation around the average response time is low. This protocol does not give the best response time when compared to others by simulation, but maintains the lowest variation around the average.
2. Minimize the communications overhead (compare to deadlock detection).
3. The protocol is simple to implement. Each site makes decisions by itself.

3.3. Modeling of Step Submission and the Distributed Executive Plan

We have shown in Section 2.3 that a transaction is composed of successive steps (user recovery points), and that each step is made up of one or more distributed executive plans (DEP). The net of Fig. 5.5 describes the SCORE-Producer step and DEP treatment, and Fig. 5.6 describes the corresponding SCORE-Consumer part.

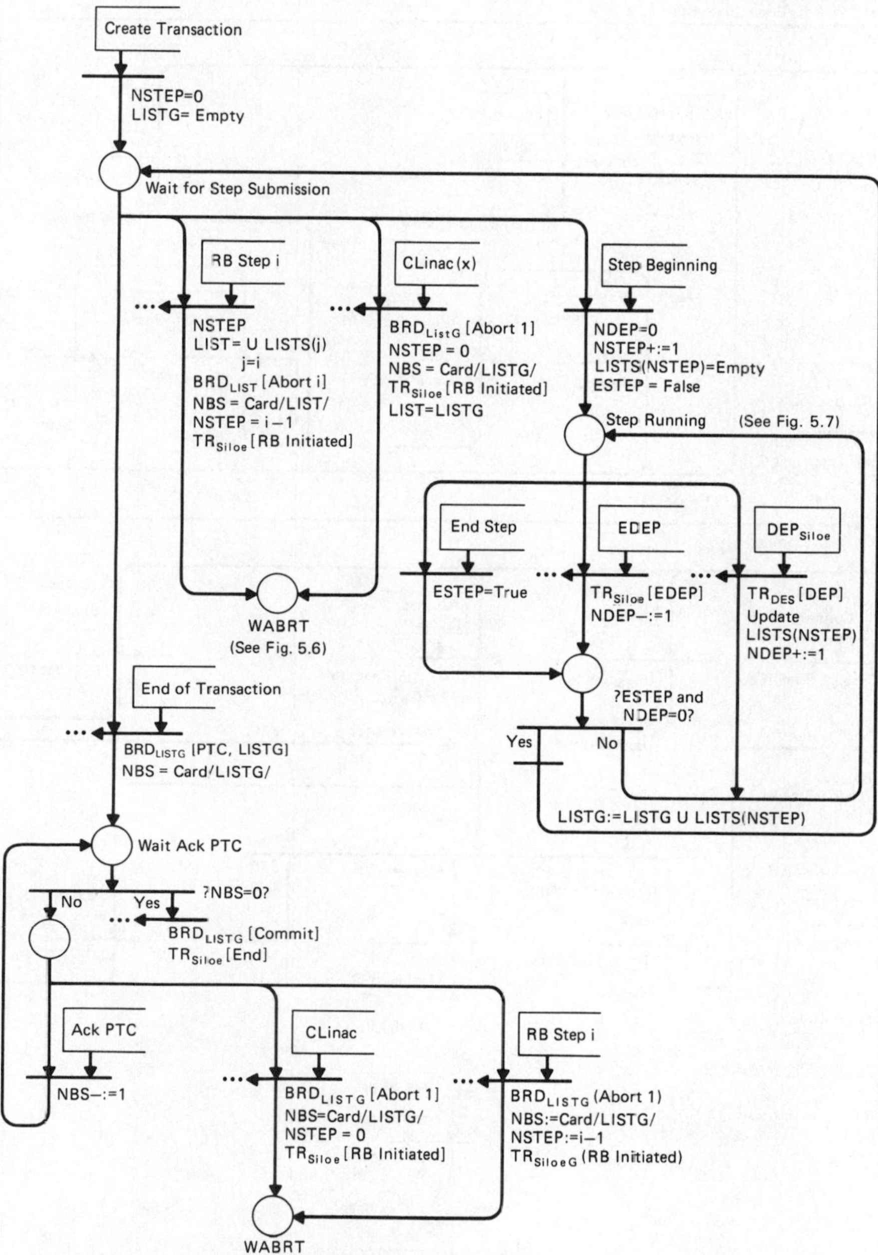

Fig. 5.5 SCORE Producer step and DEP treatment.

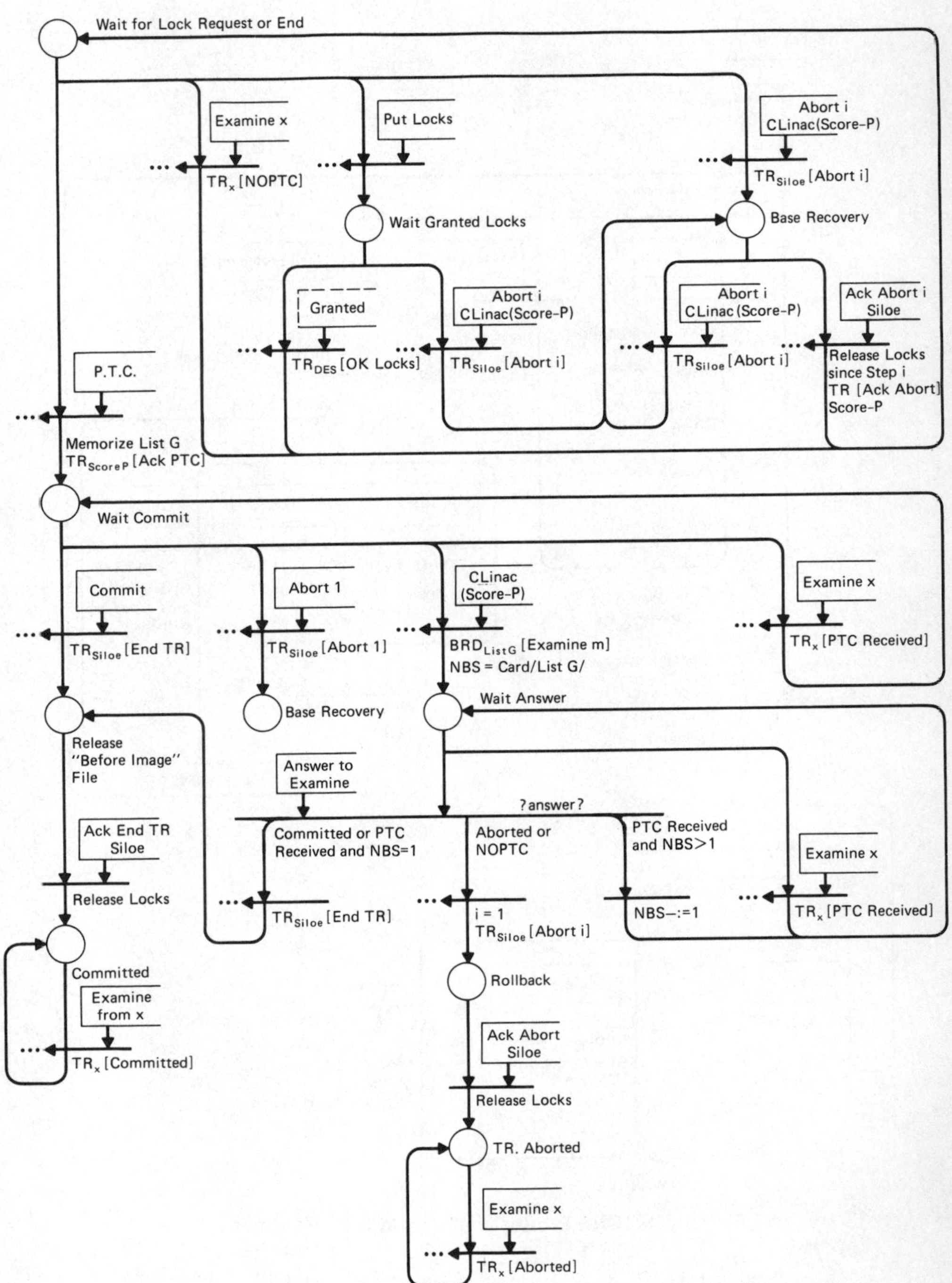

Fig. 5.6. SCORE Consumer step and DEP treatment.

For a new transaction, the user (SILOE) requests a ticket from the SCORE-Producer (circulating sequencer) before starting transaction execution. The net (Fig. 5.5) describing the running transaction is initialized by a ''create transaction'' message. The variable ''NSTEP'' is zeroed; it will give the current transaction's step name. Another variable (''LISTG''), which will maintain the list of the sites involved in this transaction, is set to empty. Then the automaton waits for a step to be submitted.

- Upon the reception of the message ''Step beginning'', the SCORE-Producer:

  1. Sets the DEP counter to zero (NDEP),
  2. increments NSTEP, and uses its value as the step name,
  3. sets the boolean ESTEP to false,
  4. sets the list of local sites needed by the step (LISTS(NSTEP)) to empty, and
  5. changes the state to ''Step running''. Now DEPs can be submitted.

- Upon reception of a DEP, SCORE-Producer updates LISTS(NSTEP) with the local sites specified for each local action, and increments the DEP counter. Then the DEP is transmitted to DES level. The automaton state remains ''Step running''.
- Upon reception of the end of a DEP (EDEP) from DES, the SCORE-Producer decrements NDEP and signals the end of DEP to SILOE. State remains ''Step running''.
- Upon receiving an ''End Step'' from SILOE, the SCORE-Producer sets ESTEP to true. If NDEP is not 0, the automaton remains ''Step running''.

These concurrent steps finish when NDEP=0 and ESTEP=true, then the SCORE-Producer updates LISTG (LISTG=LISTG U LISTS(NSTEP)) and changes the state to ''Wait for step submission''.

On the SCORE-Consumer, only requests for locks will arrive from DES, with the message ''Put locks'' (Fig. 5.6). The automaton remains in ''Wait granted locks'', and that state can be exited only when the locks are granted. It is in this state that the allocation algorithm (Section 3.2) is executed and ''roll-back'' messages may be issued to the requesting SCORE-producer for preemption. We have denoted the granting of locks by the event ''granted'', since there is not a real message because everything happens in the same level. As soon as all the locks are granted, DES is alerted by the message ''OK locks'', and one reenters to the state ''wait for lock request or end''. In fact, this part is related to each local action: DES may make from SCORE-Consumer many lock requests for different local actions. It is obvious that these requests will be treated in parallel.

When an object is accessed in write mode, then each time a write is performed on the object, a copy of its old value is made in a "before-image" file. Most existing systems do the opposite: they use a temporary file to write, and perform actual writes on the DB only at the end of the transaction. This choice is implementation-dependent based on the properties of the manufacturer's software. Our method implies that writes are made directly on the DB, therefore they must be undone in the case of Roll-Back or transaction abortion using "before-image" file information.

3.4. Roll-Back Management and Failures before the End of the Transaction

Two events may happen at any time in the life of a transaction: a failure or inaccessibility of an involved site (producer or consumer), or a request for a roll-back (RB) to step *i*. We can see that these events may happen in the state "Wait for step submission" (Fig. 5.5) or "Step running" (Fig. 5.7).

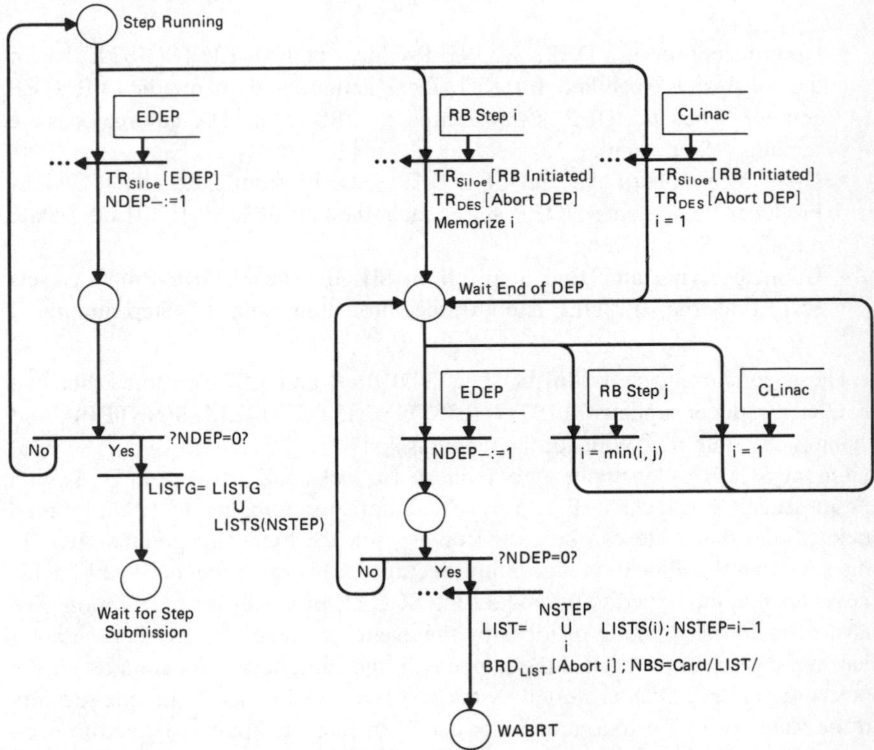

Fig. 5.7. Treatment of roll-back and failures occurring during a step execution. Details of state "Step running" of Fig. 5.5.

The reception of a message "CLinac(x)" at a SCORE-Producer (site x inaccessible, where x belongs to LISTG or LISTS(NSTEP)), is equivalent to the reception of a "R.B. step i" with $i = 1$, followed by the transaction disappearing from the executive system.

On the reception of "R.B. step i", the SCORE-Producer warns SILOE with a message "R.B. Initiated". The messages coming from SILOE will now be ignored, except for "Ack Abort step i".

If the automaton is in the position "Step running" (Fig. 5.7) SCORE must make sure that all local actions of the transaction are terminated or aborted before release of the locks. So the SCORE-Producer, if NDEP is not 0, orders SER to cancel all the local actions of the running DEPs. The automaton remains "Wait end of DEP". When all messages "EDEP" are received one comes to the following case.

If the automaton is in the state "Wait for step submission", NDEP = 0, (Fig. 5.5), the SCORE-Producer computes the list of the involved sites:

$$\text{LIST} = \bigcup_{j=i}^{\text{NSTEP}} \text{LISTS}(j).$$

Then a message "Abort i" is broadcast to all the sites of LIST, NBS is set to the number of sites in LIST, and the automaton changes to state "Wait Ack Abort i". (WABRT Fig. 5.8).

The reception of the message "RB Step j" with $j < = i$ will carry along the same treatment, but if $j > i$ the message is ignored.

For the SCORE-Consumer (Fig. 5.6), the treatment of the message "Abort i" (come back to step i included), is the same no matter what the state is before the end of the transaction.

The message "CLinac(x)" where x is the producer of the transaction, will be treated as an "Abort i" with $i = 1$.

Upon reception of "Abort i" the SCORE-Consumer asks SILOE-Local to restore the DB to a consistent state equal to the beginning of step i using the "before-image" file. The automaton changes to state "Base Recovery".

When receiving a message "Ack Abort i" from SILOE-Local, the SCORE-Consumer releases the locks set at steps $> = i$, sends an "Ack Abort i" to the SCORE-Producer, and returns to the state "Wait for lock request or end".

A message "Abort j" may be received during all this treatment and if $j < i$, the same work must be executed.

The SCORE-Producer, upon reception of an "Ack Abort i" (Fig. 5.8) with i equal to the last abort ordered, decrements NBS (number of asked Acks). If NBS = 0 (all the Acks received or List empty) SCORE-P notifies the execution of the Roll-Back step i to SILOE. SILOE has to acknowledge the message before the start of a new step.

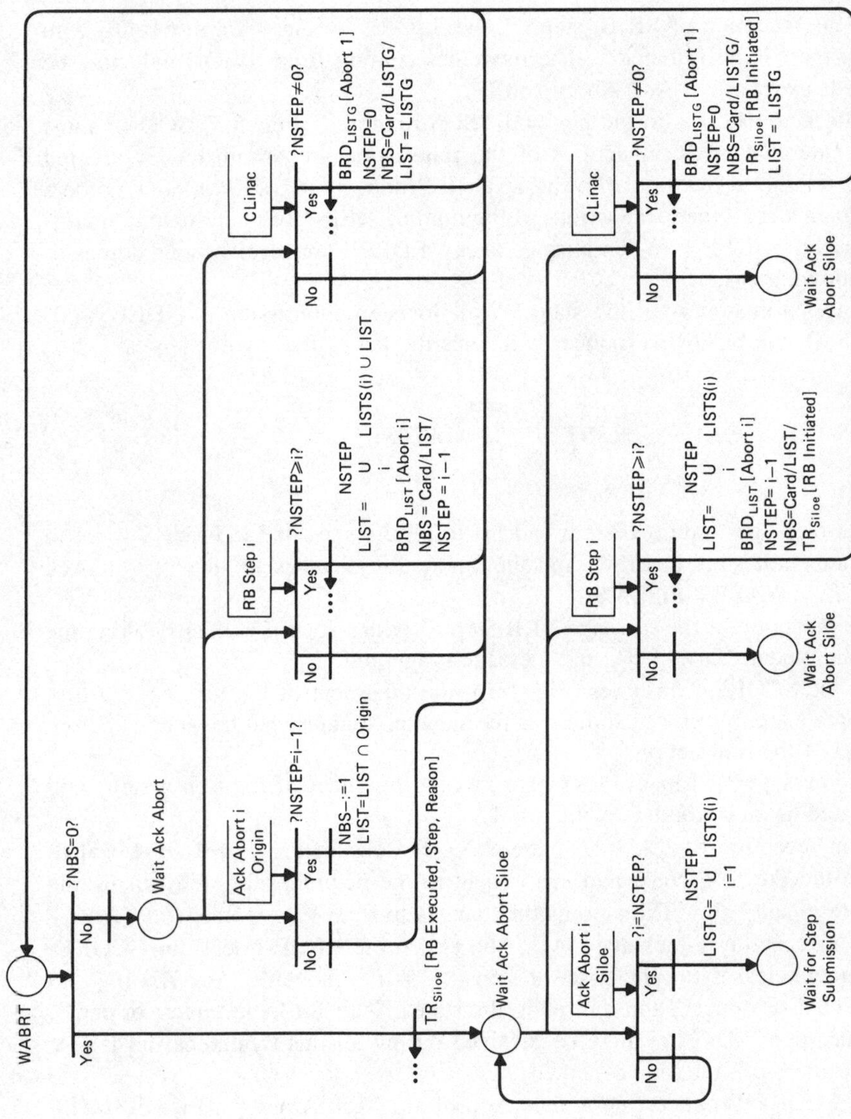

Fig. 5.8. Producer roll-back management. Details of state "WABRT" of Fig. 5.5.

When receiving the "Ack Abort *i*" from SILOE (Fig. 5.8), the SCORE-Producer reinitializes LISTG

$$\text{LISTG} = \bigcup_{i=1}^{\text{NSTEP}} \text{LISTS}(i),$$

sets NSTEP to $i - 1$ and then returns to the state "Wait for step submission" and a new step can be submitted.

3.5. Special Functions

The user may wish to cancel all of the transaction, or only some of the steps. These functions are treated as "RB Step 1" or "RB Step *i*". In the case of a dropped transaction, the SCORE-Producer, after receiving all "Ack Abort" messages from SCORE-C, acknowledges the request to SILOE-G, and the transaction disappears from the system. These facts are not shown on the nets since they are not vital functions.

4. TRANSACTION COMMITMENT AND FAILURE RESILIENCY

We have shown that a transaction must be an atomic action to maintain data base consistency. All of the actions must be executed, or none of them. Since these local actions may be executed at different sites, a site failure after the beginning of the broadcasting of the message "End of Transaction" by the score-producer can destroy consistency. Indeed, a local site could have received this message and committed the local updates of this transaction. Conversely, another site may not have received the message, and aborts the transaction. In order to avoid this danger we use a two-phase commitment protocol.

4.1. Two-Step Commitment Protocol

As soon as the user has finished a transaction, the message "End of Transaction" is sent to SCORE-P. SCORE-P carries out this order only in the state "Wait for step submission". In this state, SCORE-P knows in LISTG the names of all of the involved local sites and can initialize the commitment protocol. Fig. 5.9 shows the net of this protocol without any failures.

Step 1: SCORE-P broadcasts a message "Prepare to Commit" (PTC) to all the sites in LISTG. This message includes LISTG.

Upon reception of this message, SCORE-C is supposed to be in the state "Wait for lock request or end"; if not, the message is ignored. SCORE-C writes a PTC item in the journal, including the locks held by the transaction, the updated data, and the value of LISTG. Then an acknowledgment is sent

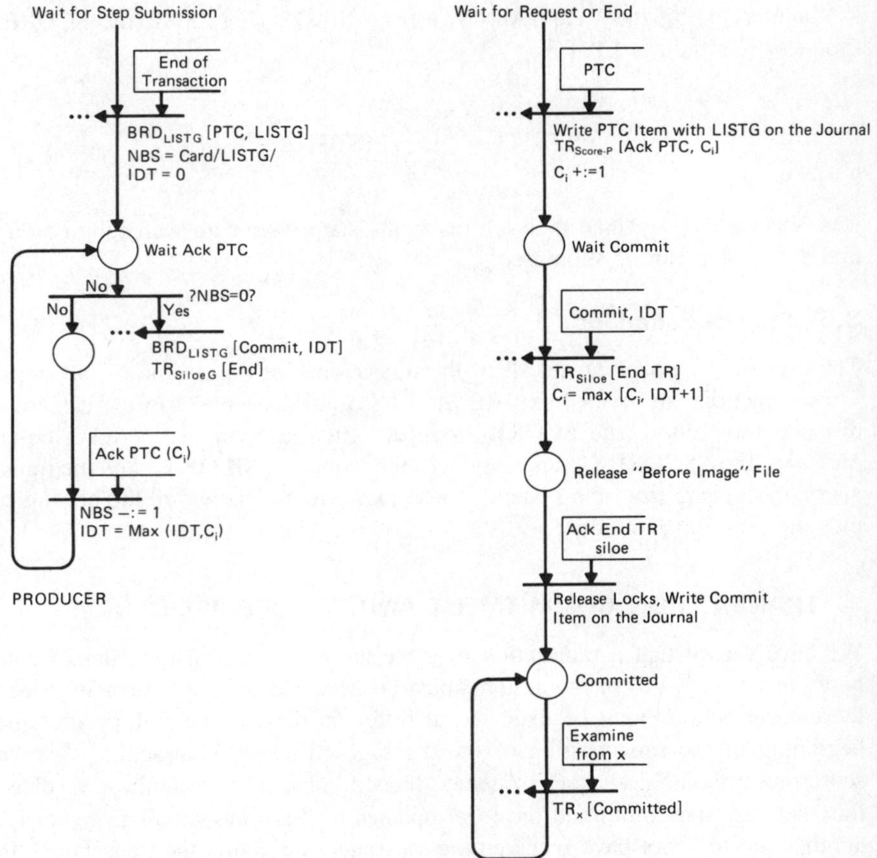

Fig. 5.9. Two-step commitment protocol schemata.

back to SCORE-P and the state "Wait commit" is entered. After this point, no roll-back request for conflicting access will be executed for this transaction, and the request is only memorized.

Step 2: As soon as SCORE-P has received all the PTC acknowledgments from SCORE-Cs, Step 2 is initiated. SCORE-P broadcasts the "Commit" message to the sites of LISTG, notifies the user (SILOE-G) of the execution of the transaction, and destroys its transaction context.

On the reception of the "Commit" message, each SCORE-C asks SILOE-L to free the "before-image" file. Upon acknowledgment, SCORE-C writes a commit item in the journal, releases the locks held by the transaction, and enters the state "Committed".

When SCORE-P is in the state "Wait ack PTC", a roll-back request can be received from SCORE-C. This message is accepted and the commitment cancelled. SCORE-P carries out the roll-back as in the state "Wait for step submission" (Section 3.4). Then SCORE-C can receive an "Abort *i*" in the state "Wait Commit". SCORE-C executes that order, writes an abort item on the journal, and allows the roll-back. The roll-back memorized at the state "Wait Commit" will be now performed.

4.2. Consumer Inaccessibility Detection by the Producer

When SCORE-P (see Fig. 5.5) receives a "CLinac(x)" in the state "Wait ack PTC", two cases arise:

- SCORE-P has received a PTC acknowledgment from x; then the commitment protocol can continue.
- SCORE-P has not received the PTC acknowledgment from x, so as it is no longer possible to know if x has received the "PTC" or not, the transaction must be cancelled. SCORE-P interrupts the commitment protocol, and the "CLinac(x)" is treated as in the state "Wait step submission" (Section 3.4). The message "Abort *i*" is broadcast to SCORE-C.

4.3. Inquiry Protocol: Producer Inaccessibility Detection by a Consumer

When SCORE-C (see Fig. 5.6) receives a "CLinac(x)" in the state "Wait commit" (where x is the name of the producer where the transaction has been initialized), the treatment must be different from the treatment of "Abort *i*".

Some SCORE-C may have committed or cancelled the transaction. The SCORE-C must ask the other consumers what decision they have taken. SCORE-C has knowledge of all of the involved sites (in the message "PTC"), and so can broadcast to them (except itself) a message "Examine m" (where m stands for my name). A variable LISTS set to LISTG -$\{m\}$ will maintain the list of the sites which are supposed to answer. The state "Wait answer" is entered, and three events are possible:

1. One SCORE-C answers "I have received the commit": for this site the transaction is or will be committed. Therefore, locally, the receiving SCORE-C must treat the answer as the reception of a "Commit" in the state "Wait commit".

2. One SCORE-C answers "I have received an Abort 1": for this consumer the transaction is or will be cancelled. Therefore, locally, the receiving SCORE-C must treat the answer as the reception of an "Abort 1" in the state "Wait commit".

3. One SCORE-C answers "I am in the state 'Wait commit' and I had SCORE-P inaccessible": in this case one removes this site from LISTS. When

LISTS is empty, SCORE-C knows that all of the involved sites are in the state ''Wait commit'' and takes the decision to commit the transaction. The treatment is just as if a message ''commit'' is received in the state ''Wait commit''.

Special cases: if a single site is involved in the transaction the SCORE-Consumer can commit immediately; or some SCORE-C may be unreachable during the ''Examine'' message broadcast. This problem is solved by periodically retransmitting the message to the members of LISTS (non-answering sites).

5. RECOVERY FROM A CRASH

Data consistency can be destroyed for many other reasons:

- User handling error or malicious access,
- machine crash,
- network partition, or
- partial destruction of the data base.

In all of these cases, it must be possible to come back to a previous consistent state. In order to minimize the consequences of such catastrophes, journals are maintained[7] in which all data modifications are logged. Using the journal, it is possible to do or undo any part of the database history. We will show how and what one must write in the journal; a formal proof is given in reference 4. Whatever precautions are taken (multiples copies, etc.), a journal can be partially destroyed, and an algorithm is required to recover a consistent DB state.

We have chosen to write the updates on the database immediately after having written the objects' old value on a ''before-image'' file. This choice minimizes modifications to the manufacturer's software, since there is no modification for a read; the writes are trapped to store the ''before-image'' value. For a transaction, access to modified data does not imply any overhead. Of course, the ''before-image'' file must be in stable memory.

On the other hand, this choice alters database consistency as soon as a write is performed. In case of a roll-back or crashes, one must recover the old values of objects. In such situations, the recovery mechanism is a bit more complicated. In case a consumer site fails, the SCORE-Producer and the other consumers know how to recover the DB (State ''base recovery'' of the SCORE-C automaton). In case a producer fails, each SCORE-Consumer will receive a CLinac (producer) and recover the DB for the transactions issued by this site.

5.1. DB Recovery without Journal or ''Before-Image'' File Destruction

If there is no journal or ''before-image'' file destruction, a user may: 1. recover all of the database using the ''before-image'' files and release the objects; or 2.

recover, for each committing transaction we find in the journal with the PTC item: the SCORE-Consumer context, the list of locks, the modified data, and the list of involved sites.

After these transactions' contexts have been recreated, the site can be inserted in the DDBS, and for these transactions the inquiry mechanism is initiated, the same as after the reception of a CLinac(SCORE-P).

5.2. DB Recovery When the DB is Destroyed and the Journal is Safe

To recover from a point where the DB is destroyed and the journal is safe, a user must: 1. restart from an older DB copy; 2. execute sequentially the committed writes from the journal; 3. execute step 2 of the previous subsection.

5.3. Recovery After a Crash with the Journal Partially Lost

This local site does not have enough information to come back into the system without endangering DDB consistency. It is a catastrophic case: all of the DDB has to be Rolled-Back to a previous consistent state. This state requires journal recovery lines.

5.3.1. Transaction Termination Identifier

When a two-phase commit is executed, a transaction termination identifier (*IDT*) is computed. Each consumer maintains a private counter (Fig. 5.9) *Ci*. Before sending the message "PTC", the variable *IDT* is zeroed at the producer site. SCORE-C sends, in the PTC acknowledgment, its current counter value and increments it. The SCORE-P computes *IDT* as the maximum of the *Ci* received and sends it with the commit message. SCORE-C writes this value on the commit item and executes $Ci = \max(IDT + 1, Ci)$. The *Ci* computation, upon receiving the commit message, ensures that a transaction not in the commit phase will have a greater *IDT* than the last committed one. Then, if a transaction *Tj* depends on *Ti* (*Tj* reads a value written by *Ti*) we have $IDT(Tj) > IDT(Ti)$. The transactions which are already in the commit phase may have an *IDT* less than or equal to the *IDT* of the last committed one. This means that the transactions are independent.

5.3.2. Global Roll-Back to a Consistent State

In Fig. 5.10, we can see that the order of the commit items in the journals may differ from one site to another. A roll-back to (T2, 20) requires that this site reads all of its journal to be sure to have undone all of the transactions which have $IDT > 20$. In order to optimize this mechanism, one writes in the journal with each commit item the last maximal *IDT* (MAX*i*) of transactions already committed by this consumer. When a roll-back(TRANSID, *IDT'*) is required, the journal will be read until $MAXi < IDT'$ (Fig. 5.11).

Consumer C1		*Consumer C2*	
Received Order	Data Write on the Journal	Received Order	Data Write on the Journal
PTC T1	10 PTC T1	PTC T2	20 PTC T2
PTC T2	11 PTC T2	PTC T1	21 PTC T1
Commit T1	21 Commit T1	Commit T2	20 Commit T2
Commit T2	20 Commit T2	Commit T1	21 Commit T1
IDT.C1 = 22	time ↓	IDT.C2 = 22	

Fig. 5.10. Order and value of the PTC and Commit items on the journal.

IDT	Item	Ti	MAXi	LPTCi
1	PTC	T1		
2	PTC	T2		
5	Commit	T1	5	T2
6	PTC	T3		
8	Commit	T3	8	T2
9	PTC	T4		
10	PTC	T5		
9	Commit	T4	9	T2 T5
. . . .				
9	Commit	T4	9	T2 T5
. . . .				

Journal not readable

Fig. 5.11. Information on the C' journal.

In order to simplify the recovery at a site where the journal has been damaged, we add the list of the transactions which are in the commit phase (LPTC). When the consumer reads the last correct commit item of its journal, LPTC will inform it of all transactions to be restored to the "wait commit" state. For each of them, if a PTC item has an $IDT > IDT'$ the transaction is cancelled; otherwise the inquiry mechanism is initiated. On Fig. 5.11, C' will start recovery at (T4,9). The IDT of the PTC.T5 item is greater than 9, so T5 is cancelled. C' inquires about T2. This recovery mechanism guarantees that transaction atomicity is maintained.

6. ALGORITHMS EVALUATION AND MEASURES

The existence of the prototype raises questions about performance: Is the implementation efficient? What is the cost of the primitives? How is concurrency used? Are the effects significantly profitable or are they obscured by system overhead?

Here, we will give only the results obtained for the SCORE layer. The interested reader may find more complete information in references 12 and 14. Three types of results are obtained: information about complexity using the nets, the number of executed instructions, and elapsed time on the prototype.

6.1. Complexity

From the nets, we can give the number of states and messages used. These two values are an approximation of the algorithm's complexity. The number of messages exchanged in a step execution gives an idea of the transmission cost. The number of states of the SCORE-Producer automaton is 6 and of the SCORE-Consumer automaton is 9 (2 are posttransaction states). Fig. 5.12 summarizes

Destination

Origin	SILOE global	SCORE Producer	DES	Transport	SCORE Consumer	SILOE local
SILOE global		6 Create TR End TR Ack abort i Step begin DEP Estep				
SCORE Producer	4 RB init RB exec EDEP End TR		2 DEP Abort DEP		3 PTC Commit Abort i	
DES		1 EDEP			1 Put locks	
Transport		1 CLinac			1 CLinac	
SCORE Consumer		3 Ack PTC RB step i Ack Abort i	1 OK locks		2 Examine x Answer	2 Abort i End TR
SILOE local						2 Ack Abort Ack End TR

Fig. 5.12. Messages exchanged between levels.

the number of messages exchanged between the different levels. These numbers do not increase when adding the special functions (Section 3.5); there are only two new messages from SILOE to the SCORE-Producer.

6.2. Cost in Executed Instructions

Our point of view is that the number of instructions needed to perform a function is the most useful measure, since it is easy to use in the analytic model for different classes of computers. It is also less machine-dependent than elapsed time, which varies widely according to machine load and speed. For instance, our minicomputers are very slow (40 microseconds per instruction), and so are nearly always overloaded.

The first operation of a transaction is to get a ticket from the virtual ring. This includes the management of a context for SCORE at the global site. The cost observed for that primitive is 110,000 instructions.

The two-phase commitment protocol cost consists of both: a global cost for n involved sites which is: n*12,000 instructions. This cost is mainly due to the messages used by the protocol; a cost at each local site of about 90,000 instructions. This cost is important, since two items have to be written in the journal. This cost does not depend strongly of the number of accessed data objects.

The cost for locking objects in this measure includes the releasing phase. The observed cost is 30,000 instructions. This does not include the "before image" processing.

The cost for a single call to the "before image" procedure is about 2,000 instructions, but there is an initialization cost of 30,000 instructions.

The costs of the different aspects of SCORE are rather moderate. Locks are expensive if the granularity is small. We didn't measure the cost of roll-backs, since it is very difficult to repeat them systematically.

6.3. Cost in Elapsed Time

The nets have been used to set probes for a software monitor. Probes are installed in the net's places (or states). The time of entering and leaving each state is recorded, so that we can compute elapsed time for: each transition computation, waiting time in a state, and waiting time between two states. Extensive measurements have been taken on the prototype; we will only discuss here the results for setting locks and two-phase commitment. Elapsed time includes, of course, time spent for other concurrent processes sharing the CPU. Since scheduling is unpredictable, it is not possible to eliminate the time spent for them.

6.3.1. Time to Set Locks

This corresponds to the time spent between the messages "Put locks" and "granted" in Fig. 5.6. Results are presented in Fig. 5.13. For each local action

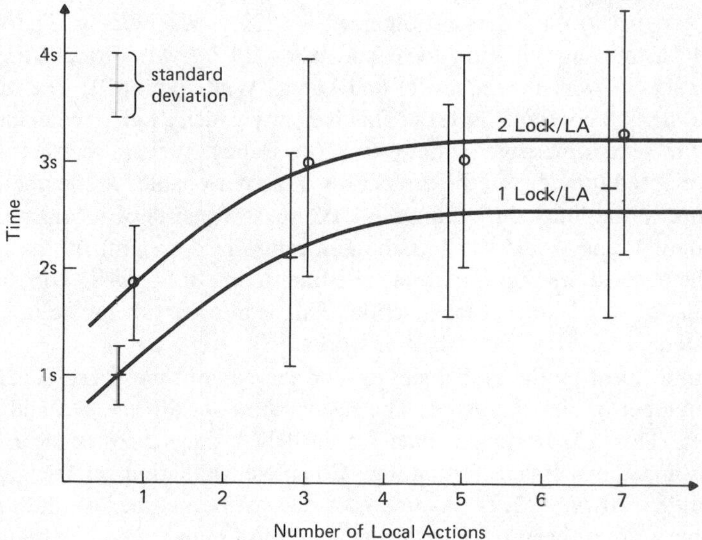

Fig. 5.13. Elapsed time to set locks.

only one message is sent, whatever the number of locks requested. The result shows that the number of the LA on the local site influences the response time (due to the load involved). The limit is about 3.25s for two locks and 2.75s for one lock in each request. For this measurement, the objects were always available. Also, there is no waiting time due to another transaction owning the object. Since the two curves are very similar, the difference between them is due to the locking process itself. It seems to be about 0.5s for each lock. A large amount of time is spent for message analysis, program initialization, table loading, etc.

6.3.2. Two-Phase Commitment

Measurements in the global system are made according to two criteria: The number of sites involved and number of locks requested by the transaction. Time spent between the states "wait for step submission or end" and "Wait ack PTC" is 0.25s ± 0.06 for a transaction involving one site, and 0.43 s ± 0.12s for a transaction with two sites. This is not very relevant, since only in this elapsed time is the time to post the message to the communications queue measured. It will be the same as the time spent to execute the transition where the commit is broadcast.

The time spent receiving the entire "ack PTC" message depends upon the number of locks. Let *Nbli* be the number of locks requested at site *i*. Note that it is the union of the locks requested by the LA executed at site *i*. The number of locks which is important is the value *MNbl* (being the maximum among

(*Nbl*1, . . . , *Nblj*)). The result obtained is .98s**MNbl* + 2.3s. The handling of the PTC message at each local site takes 0.98s**Nbl* + 1.2s (time spent between states ''wait for request or end'' and ''Wait commit''). The difference between the two constants is 1.1s. This is nearly exactly twice the elapsed time required to send a message (0.6s ± 0.2s/message). We can see that the overhead in elapsed time due to the protocol is quite reasonable. Remember that the work done at the local site during the PTC phase consists of recording an item in the journal, and would be the same in a centralized system. In this measurement, the elapsed time for a multiple site transaction disappears. The remaining time consists of the longest local action. This is a major advantage in a distributed system; Fig. 5.14 shows how it works.

The time spent by the global site to send the commit messages depends only on the number of sites involved. The results are 0.4s for one site and 0.6s for two sites. This is a bit longer than for the PTC, since there is the *IDT* computation and the message formatting. Complete validation on the global site gives: 0.98s**MNbl* + 2.9s. A time cost due to the number of sites involved exists, but has not been obtained because of the limited number of sites in the

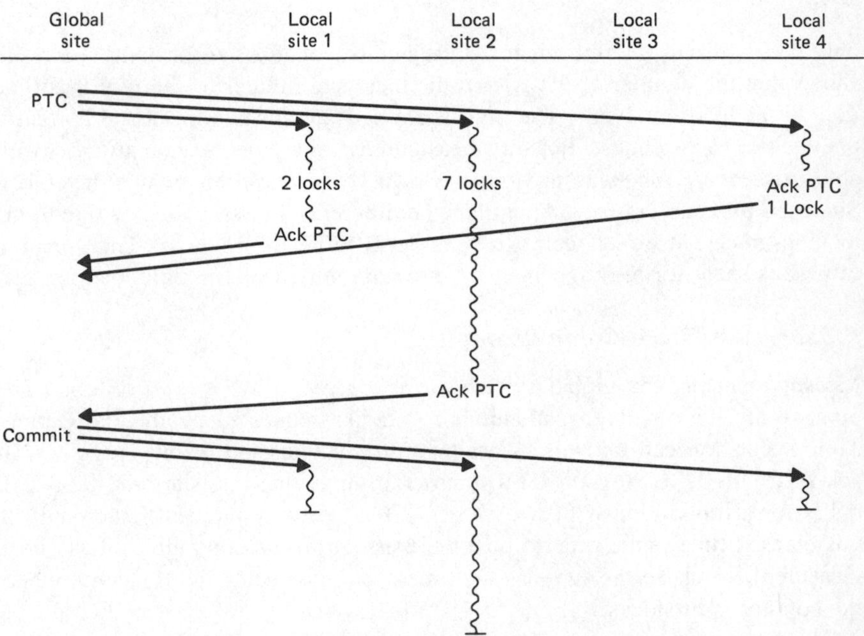

Fig. 5.14. Example of two-phase commit synchronization in a transaction involving three sites.

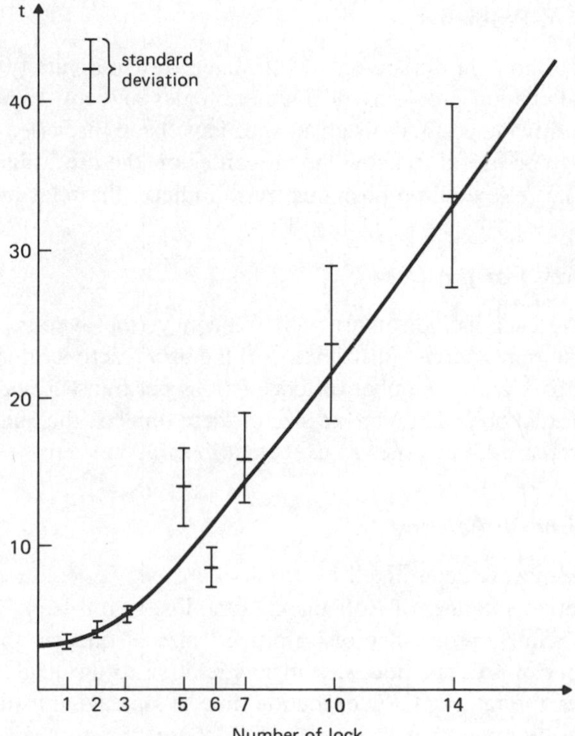

Fig. 5.15. Elapsed time for the commit treatment on a local site.

prototype. Commitment on the local site is quite different, since time spent here in the state "Wait commit" depends strongly on the complexity of the local part of the transaction. It will be long if the site had local action with a few locks and at least one other local site had a more complex treatment. It is obvious in Fig. 5.14 that sites 1 and 3 will wait for completion at site 2.

The time spent between states "Wait commit" and "Committed" depends mainly on the number of locks. The work consists of writing a commit item on the journal, the release of the "before image" file, and finally the release of the locks. The results obtained are shown in Fig. 5.15. Obviously, this is not a linear curve, possibly as a consequence of the CPU load. Nevertheless, the reader should remember that this cost is not specific to a distributed system; it is the same in a centralized system except for two facts: 1) the number of locks would be the union of all locks set by the transaction. This seems to be quite bad considering this exponential curve; and 2) each local site computes in parallel with others.

6.4. Evaluation Problems

Some implementations in the area of DDBS have shown a variety of solutions to distributed allocation problems, locking strategies and roll back, optimistic strategies, etc. Advantages and disadvantages have been discussed by their authors. It seems to be useful to know the properties of: the user, algorithms, and the network. The following propositions try to indicate the relevant issues.

6.4.1. Properties of the User

Properties of the user include transaction frequency (the average interval between read, write transactions), distribution of the user's activity during the day, transaction complexity, the number of local actions per transaction, the average number of requested objects, the mean size of these objects, the quantity of data transferred between different sites to execute a local action, etc.

6.4.2. Algorithm Efficiency

Algorithm efficiency is determined by the locking policy, conflict frequency, conflict localization, number of Roll-Backs, time lost in roll-back, average service time, the frequency of usage of primitives, size of queues, the CPU load (by site), number of I/O operations, statistics relative to the load produced by the local actions, the ratio of CPU execution time to message transfer time, cost of the two-phase commitment protocol in CPU time, the number of messages exchanged for a transaction, efficiency in case of a failure, elapsed time to reconfigure, elapsed time to recover, etc.

6.4.3. Network Performance

Network performance is measured by the average block transfer time, average access time, failure rate, probability that access is denied, probability of link failure, probability of message loss average, retransmission probability, time lost before signalling a failure to the upper level, etc.

6.5. Conclusions about Measurements

The elapsed times obtained are very long. This is mainly due to our very slow minicomputer (40 microsecond/instruction or 25 Kips). The operating system used was not devised for this type of application. Also, the reader should keep in mind the ratio of visible distributed protocol overhead to centralized work. A comparison on the results obtained in the number of instructions and elapsed time helps in building and refining analytic models.

7. CONCLUSION

We have presented the design details of our data allocation mechanism and the recovery techniques used in an unreliable environment. The development of the prototype SIRIUS-Delta shows the practicality of DDBS's in an industrial context. We believe that many of our techniques will be used in future products.

ACKNOWLEDGMENT

This design has been developed and implemented by the SCORE team in SIRIUS-Delta, namely P. Boichot, J. Boudenant, G. Ferran, G. Le Lann, P. Rolin, and S. Sedillot.

REFERENCES

1. Boudenant, J., SIRIUS-DELTA un cas concret: cohérence de bases de données réparties, partitionnées et répliquées JIIA Paris, juin 1980.
2. Ellis, C. A robust algorithm for updating duplicate data bases, *2nd Berkeley Workshop on Distributed Data Management and Computer Networks*, Aug. 1977, pp. 531–544.
3. Eswaran, K. P., et al., On the notions of consistency and predicate locks in a data base system, *CACM*, vol. 19, pp. 624–633, Nov. 1976.
4. Gardarin, G., J. L. Baer, C. Girault, and C. Roucairol, *The Two-step Commitment Protocol, Modeling, Specification and Proof Methodology*, Institut de Programmation, Université Pierre et Marie Curie, 75230 Paris, Cedex 05.
5. Glorieux, A. M., Decomposition d'une requete dans SIRIUS-DELTA Type de répartition et méthodologie, JIIA Paris, juin 1980.
6. International Standard Organization, *Open System Interconnection* (ISO/TC97/SC16).
7. Lampson, B. and H. Sturgis, *Crash Recovery in a Distributed System*, Xerox Res. Rep., Xerox Palo Alto Research Center, 1977.
8. Le Bihan, J., C. Esculier, G. Le Lann, and L. Treille, SIRIUS-DELTA: A distributed data base system prototype, *Sixth Berkeley Workshop*, 1981.
9. Le Lann, G., Algorithms for distributed data-sharing systems which use tickets, *Third Berkeley Workshop*, INRIA, Aug. 1978, pp. 259–272.
10. Le Lann, G., Consistency and concurrency control in distributed data base systems, EEC course ''Distributed data base'' Sheffield (U.K.), INRIA, 1979.
11. Le Lann, G., An experimental fault-tolerant distributed data-sharing system, INRIA, 1980 (Doc SIRIUS CTR-I-025).
12. Litwin, W., et al., SIRIUS: system for distributed data management,'' in *Distributed Data Bases*, H. J. Schneider, ed. Amsterdam, Holland: North Holland Publishing Company, 1982, pp. 311–366.
13. Rolin, P., Using Petri-nets in measurements of a distributed data base system. *2nd Int. Workshop on theory and application of Petri-nets*, Strasbourg, 1980.
14. Rolin, P., Rapport sur la campagne de mesure de performance du prototype SIRIUS-Delta, Rapport INRIA, 1982.
15. Sedillot, S. and G. Sergeant, The consistency and execution control systems for a distributed data base in SIRIUS-DELTA, 1980 (Doc SIRIUS SCH-I-076).
16. Treille, L., and G. Sergeant, SER: A system for distributed execution based on decentralized control techniques. Intl. Conf. on Computers and Communications, 1980 Atlanta, GA.
17. Wilms, P., Etude et comparaison d'algorithmes de maintien de la coherence dans les BD reparties, (Ph.D. diss.), *IMAG*, Grenoble, France.

6. Distributed Transactions for Reliable Systems

ALFRED Z. SPECTOR, DEAN DANIELS, DANIEL DUCHAMP, JEFFREY L. EPPINGER, and RANDY PAUSCH

ABSTRACT

Facilities that support distributed transactions on user-defined types can be implemented efficiently and can simplify the construction of reliable distributed programs. To demonstrate these points, this chapter describes a prototype transaction facility, called TABS, that supports objects, transparent communication, synchronization, recovery, and transaction management. Various objects that use the facilities of TABS are exemplified and the performance of the system is discussed in detail. The chapter concludes that the prototype provides useful facilities, and that it would be feasible to build a high performance implementation based on its ideas.

1. INTRODUCTION

General purpose facilities that support distributed transactions are feasible to implement and useful in simplifying the construction of reliable distributed applications. To justify this assertion, this chapter describes the design, implementation, use, and performance of TABS,[57] a prototype facility that supports transactions on user-defined abstract objects. We attempt to generalize from our experiences with the prototype, particularly in the sections on the usage and performance of TABS.

This work was supported by IBM and the Defense Advanced Research Projects Agency, ARPA order no. 3597, monitored by the Air Force Avionics Laboratory under contract F33615-81-K-1539, and by graduate fellowships from the National Science Foundation and the Office of Naval Research. The views and conclusions contained in this document are those of the authors and should not be interpreted as representing the official policies, either expressed or implied, of any of the sponsoring agencies or the US government.

We define a *distributed transaction facility* as a distributed collection of components that supports not only such standard abstractions as processes and interprocess communication, but also the execution of transactions and the implementation of objects on which operations can be performed. Although there is room for diversity in its exact functions, a distributed transaction facility must make it easy to initiate and commit transactions, to call operations on objects from within transactions, and to implement abstract types that have correct synchronization and recovery properties.

Transactions provide three properties that should make them useful in a variety of distributed applications.[36,41,56] Synchronization properties, such as serializability, guarantee that concurrent readers and writers of data do not interfere with each other. Failure atomicity simplifies the maintenance of invariants on data by ensuring that updates are not partially done. Permanence provides programmers with the luxury of knowing that only catastrophic failures will corrupt or erase previously made updates.

Certainly, these properties of transactions are useful in database applications.[13,22] Database applications are typically characterized by the need for absolute data integrity, permanent updates, and careful synchronization between processes that access large quantities of shared data. When considering the application of transactions to other domains, such as the construction of distributed operating systems and real time systems, there are questions pertaining to what transaction facilities should be provided, how they should be implemented to achieve adequate performance, and where they should be used. For example, a typical question is whether the recovery and synchronization techniques that are suitable for database systems have sufficient performance and flexibility to support transactions on user-defined shared abstract types in other applications. Quite a few research projects in addition to our own are considering these issues.[1,5,15,28,39]

The next section surveys the underlying models and techniques on which this research is based and provides necessary background into the function, implementation, and use of transaction facilities. The reader who is expert in distributed transaction processing may be able to skip most of this section and read only the summary in Section 2.1.4. Following this survey, Section 3 describes the interface and implementation of TABS.

Section 4 shows how the TABS prototype is used to support various abstract data types including arrays, queues, directories, replicated directories, and reliable terminal displays. Although these objects do not constitute user-level applications, they represent rather important building blocks. The primary goal of this section is to show how the TABS interface is used and thereby highlight its strengths and weaknesses.

Section 5 describes the performance of the TABS prototype on a variety of benchmarks, both in terms of execution time and in terms of primitive operations. This performance evaluation permits us to predict the effect of changes to the system (e.g., combining certain TABS processes or reducing message passing times) and conclude that high performance general purpose transaction facilities based on the ideas of TABS are feasible. Section 6 contains a brief comparison of TABS with two important related systems, R*[63] and Argus.[40] Section 7 contains the conclusions of this research project and directions for future work.

2. BACKGROUND

This section surveys the research and development that has influenced this work and identifies many of the algorithms and paradigms that we have used. The discussion is divided into two parts. The first discusses the fundamental issues in *implementing* distributed transactions on abstract objects focusing on the objects themselves, distribution, and transaction processing. The second part discusses the *use* of distributed transactions.

2.1. Distributed Transactions on Abstract Objects

2.1.1. Abstract Objects

Abstract objects are data or input/output devices, having distinct names, on which collections of *operations* have been defined. Access to an object is permitted only by these operations. A queue object having operations such as **Enqueue, Dequeue,** or **EmptyQueue** is a typical data object, and a CRT display having operations such as **WriteLine** and **ReadLine** is a typical I/O object. Objects vary in their lifetimes and their implementation. The notion of object presented here is similar to the *class* construct of Simula,[10] *packages* in ADA,[14] and the abstract objects supported by operating systems such as Hydra.[64] The operating system work has tended to emphasize authorization—an issue not addressed here.

Many models exist for implementing abstract objects that are shared by multiple processes. In one model, objects are encapsulated in protected subsystems and accessed by protected procedure calls or capability mechanisms.[19,51] TABS uses another model, called the *client/server* model, as a basis for implementing abstract objects.[61] Servers encapsulate one or more data objects. They accept request messages that specify operations and a specific object. To implement operations, they read or modify data they directly control and invoke operations on other servers. After an operation is performed, servers typically send a response message containing the result. Servers that encapsulate data objects are called *Data Servers* in TABS, *Resource Managers* in R*,[35] and *Guardians* in Argus.[40]

Message transmission mechanisms and server organizations differ among implementations based upon the client/server model. In these aspects, TABS is substantially influenced by the Accent operating system kernel on which it was developed.[48] Accent provides heavyweight processes with 32-bit virtual address spaces and supports messages that are arbitrarily long vectors of typed information, addressed to *ports*. Many processes may have send rights to a port, but only one has receive rights. Send rights and receive rights can be transmitted in messages along with ordinary data. Large quantities of data are efficiently conveyed between processes on the same machine via copy-on-write mapping into the address space of the recipient process. This message model differs from that of Unix 4.2[30] and the V Kernel[8] in that messages are typed sequences of data which can contain port capabilities, and that large messages can be transmitted with nearly constant overhead.

The programming effort associated with packing and unpacking messages is reduced in TABS through the use of a remote procedure called facility called *Matchmaker*.[29] (We use the term *remote procedure call* to apply to both intra-node and inter-node communication.) Matchmaker's input is a syntactic definition of procedure headers and its outputs are client and server stubs that pack data into messages, unpack data from messages, and dispatch to the appropriate procedures on the server side.

Servers that never wait while processing an operation can be organized as a loop that receives a request message, dispatches to execute the operation, and sends a response message. Unfortunately, servers may wait for many reasons: to synchronize with other operations, to execute a remote operation or system call, or to page-fault. For such servers, there must be multiple threads of control within a server, or else the server will pause or deadlock when it need not.

One implementation approach for servers is to allocate independently schedulable processes that share access to data. With this approach, a server is a class of related processes—in the Simula sense of the word "class." An alternative approach is to have multiple lightweight processes within a single server process. Page-faults still cause all lightweight processes to be suspended, but a lightweight process switch can occur when a server would otherwise wait. Although this approach does not permit servers to exploit the parallelism of a multiprocessor, it was easy to implement on Accent, and TABS uses it. The topic of server organization has been clearly discussed by Liskov and Herlihy.[38]

Before leaving the topic of abstract objects, it is necessary to discuss how objects are named. Certainly, a port to a server and a *logical object identifier* that distinguishes between the various objects implemented by that server are sufficient to name an object. The dissemination of these names can be done in many ways. A common method is for servers to register objects with a well known server process on their node, often called a *name server,* and for the name server to return one or more <port, logical object identifier> pairs in response to name lookup requests. Name servers can cooperate with each other to provide transparent naming across a network.

2.1.2. Distribution

Replicated and partitioned distributed objects are feasible to implement in the client/server model. For example, there may be many servers that can respond identically to operations on a replicated object. However, servers must contain the replication or partitioning logic. The TABS project hypothesizes that the availability of transaction support substantially simplifies the maintenance of distributed and replicated objects.

Transparent inter-node message passing can simplify access to remote servers. In the Accent environment, inter-node communication is achieved by interposing a pair of processes, called Communication Managers, between the sender of a message and its intended recipient on a remote node.[48] The Communication Manager supplies the sender with a local port to use for messages addressed to the remote process. Together with its counterpart at the remote node, the Communication Manager manages the network and implements the mapping between the local port used by the sender and the corresponding remote port belonging to the target process.

There has been considerable research aimed at providing high-performance interprocess communication mechanisms. Local and inter-node message facilities can be optimized with the use of simplified protocols, machine registers, microcode, and careful coding.[6,9,44,54] The TABS Project assumes that high performance communication systems can be constructed, but it has not invested the effort to build one for the prototype. However, TABS has been careful to use datagrams for communication during transaction commit; more costly communication based on sessions is used only for the remote procedure calls that implement operations on remote data objects. R* also uses both datagram and session-based communication.[35]

2.1.3. Transactions

Although the concept of a transaction has been defined precisely in the literature,[18,23] TABS does not require that objects enforce serializability, failure atomicity, or permanence. Certainly, support exists for the standard notions, but transactions are permitted to interfere with each other and to show the effects of failure—if this is useful. In other words, TABS provides basic facilities for supporting many different types of objects and lets the implementors choose how they want to use them.

Many techniques exist for synchronizing the execution of transactions. Locking, optimistic, timestamp, and many hybrid schemes are frequently discussed; these are surveyed by Bernstein and Goodman.[4] TABS has chosen to use locking.[13] To obtain synchronized access to an object, a transaction must first obtain a *lock* on all or part of it. A lock is granted unless another transaction already holds an incompatible lock.

TABS chose to use locking for two reasons. First, locking is an efficient synchronization mechanism that has been used successfully in many commercial data management systems. Second, because servers implement locking locally, they can tailor their locking mechanism to provide better performance. With *type-specific* locking, implementors can obtain increased concurrency by defining type-specific lock modes and lock protocols.[31,52,53] Type-specific locking requires the use of a specialized compatibility relation to determine whether a lock may be acquired by a particular transaction.

Locking restricts the flow of information between transactions by delaying operations on shared data, even if that delay leads to a deadlock. Some systems implement local and distributed deadlock detectors that identify and break cycles of waiting transactions.[35,45] However, TABS, like many other systems, currently relies on time-outs, which are explicitly set by system users.[59]

Recovery in TABS is based upon *write-ahead logging,* rather than *shadow paging.*[22,24,25,32,34,42,52] To discuss write-ahead logging, it is first necessary to discuss the three-tiered storage model on which it depends. Storage consists of volatile storage—where portions of objects reside when they are being accessed, nonvolatile storage—where objects reside when they have been accessed recently, and stable storage—memory that is assumed to retain information despite failures. The contents of volatile storage are lost after a system crash, and the contents of nonvolatile storage are lost with lower frequency, but always in a detectable way.

In recovery techniques based upon logging, stable storage contains an append-only sequence of records. Many of these records contain an undo component that permits the effects of aborted transactions to be undone, and a redo component that permits the effects of committed transactions to be redone. Updates to data objects are made by modifying a representation of the object residing in volatile storage and by spooling one or more records to the log. Logging is called ''write-ahead'' because log records must be safely stored (forced) to stable storage before transactions commit, and before the volatile representation of an object is copied to nonvolatile storage. Because of this strategy, there are log records in stable storage for all the changes that have been made to nonvolatile storage, and for all committed transactions. Thus, the log can be used to recover from aborted transactions, system crashes, and nonvolatile storage failures.

The advantages of write-ahead logging over other schemes have been discussed elsewhere and include the potential for increased concurrency, reduced I/O activity at transaction commit time, and contiguous allocation of objects on secondary storage.[24,50,60] All objects in TABS use one of two coexisting write-ahead logging techniques and share a common log.

The simpler technique is *value* logging, in which the undo and redo portions of a log record contain the old and new values of at most one page of an object's representation. During recovery processing, objects are reset to their most recently committed values during a one pass scan that begins at the last log record written and proceeds backward. If this value logging algorithm is used, only one transaction at a time may modify any individually-logged component of an object that is to be failure atomic and permanent.

The other technique is called *operation* (or *transition*) logging. With it, data servers write log records containing the names of operations and enough information to invoke them. Operations are redone or undone, as necessary, during recovery processing to restore the correct state of objects. An important feature of this algorithm is that operations on multipage objects can be recorded in one log record. The operation-based recovery algorithm also permits a greater degree of concurrency than the value based recovery algorithm and may require less log space. However, it is more complex, and it requires three passes over the log during crash recovery, instead of the single pass needed for the value-based algorithm. The TABS recovery algorithms are similar to other previously published write-ahead log-based algorithms,[22,34] and are fully described by Schwarz.[52]

Both value and operation logging algorithms require that periodic system *checkpoints* be taken. Checkpoints serve to reduce the amount of log data that must be available for crash recovery and shorten the time to recover after a crash.[25] At checkpoint time, a list of the pages currently in volatile storage and the status of currently active transactions are written to the log. Some systems also force certain pages to nonvolatile storage and abort transactions that have been running for a long time. To reduce the cost of recovering from disk failures, systems infrequently *dump* the contents of nonvolatile storage into an off-line archive.

Recently, researchers have begun to discuss high performance recovery implementations that integrate virtual memory management with the recovery subsystem and use higher performance stable storage devices.[3,15,17,58,60] Section 3 discusses how virtual memory management and recovery are integrated in TABS.

The most important component of a transaction facility not yet discussed is the one that commits and aborts transactions. Commit algorithms vary in their efficiency and robustness.[16,34] TABS uses a tree-structured variant of the two-phase commit protocol, in which each node serves as coordinator for the nodes that are its children. Though two-phase commit is simple and efficient, it does have failure modes in which nodes participating in a distributed transaction must restrict access to some data until other nodes recover from a crash. TABS could use one of the other commit algorithms that do not have this deficiency.

As a final point in the implementation of transactions, the increased interest in building nested abstractions using transactions has led to the investigation and implementation of facilities for supporting nesting.[40,43,49] These facilities limit the concurrency anomalies that can occur within a single transaction that has simultaneous threads of control, and they permit portions of a transaction to abort independently.

TABS has a limited subtransaction facility, which was very easy to implement. It can be characterized by its synchronization and commit policies. With respect to synchronization, a subtransaction behaves as a completely separate transaction. This provides protection between simultaneous threads of control, but may cause intra-transaction deadlock if two subtransactions update the same data. With respect to commit, a subtransaction is not committed until its top-level parent transaction commits, but a subtransaction can abort without causing its parent transaction to abort. Subtransactions that can abort independently permit their parent to tolerate the failure of some operations.

2.1.4. Summary of Implementation Issues

The major points of this development can be tersely summarized: TABS supports transactions on abstract objects. Objects are implemented within server processes, and operations on objects are invoked via messages with a remote procedure call facility to reduce the programming effort of packing, unpacking, and dispatching. Inter-node communication uses both sessions and datagrams. Inter-transaction synchronization is done via locking, with time-outs used to resolve deadlock. Write-ahead logging is the basis of recovery and transaction commit is done via the tree structured two-phase commit protocol. A limited subtransaction model is implemented.

2.2. Use of Transactions

Currently, transactions are primarily used to support the hierarchical, relational, and networked abstract types used in database systems. Date surveys these abstract types and describes some aspects of their implementation.[13] The literature contains many descriptions of more general types, and there are some implementations of these. For example, Lomet, Weihl and Liskov, and Schwarz and Spector have written about buffer, directory, queue, and mailbox types,[41,53,62] and there have been a few experimental transactional file systems, such as the one described by Paxton.[46]

The properties provided by these transactional types simplify abstractions that are built on them. For example, the invariants needed for the replicated objects described by Bloch *et al.*, Gifford, and Herlihy[7,21,26] are easier to maintain. The availability of distributed transactions makes it easier to generate R*'s query execution plans.[11] The integrity guarantees of a mail system, such as one sketched by Liskov, are also simplified. More collections of abstract types, combined into larger and more diverse applications, will undoubtedly be developed as general purpose transactions facilities become more prevalent (See Section 4 for a discussion of abstract types that we have built.).

3. AN EXPERIMENTAL DESIGN—THE TABS PROTOTYPE

The TABS Prototype is implemented in Pascal on a collection of networked Perq workstations[47] running a modified version of the Accent operating system. At each node, there is one instance of the TABS facilities and one or more user-programmed data servers and/or applications. Data servers are programmed with the aid of system-supplied libraries for doing synchronization and recovery, and for performing a data server's role during two-phase commit. Applications initiate transactions and call data servers to perform operations on objects. The library interfaces to TABS are described in detail in Section 3.1.

The TABS facilities are made up of four processes that run on Accent (see Fig. 6.1). The processes, called Name Server, Communication Manager, Recovery Manager, and Transaction Manager, perform name dissemination, net-

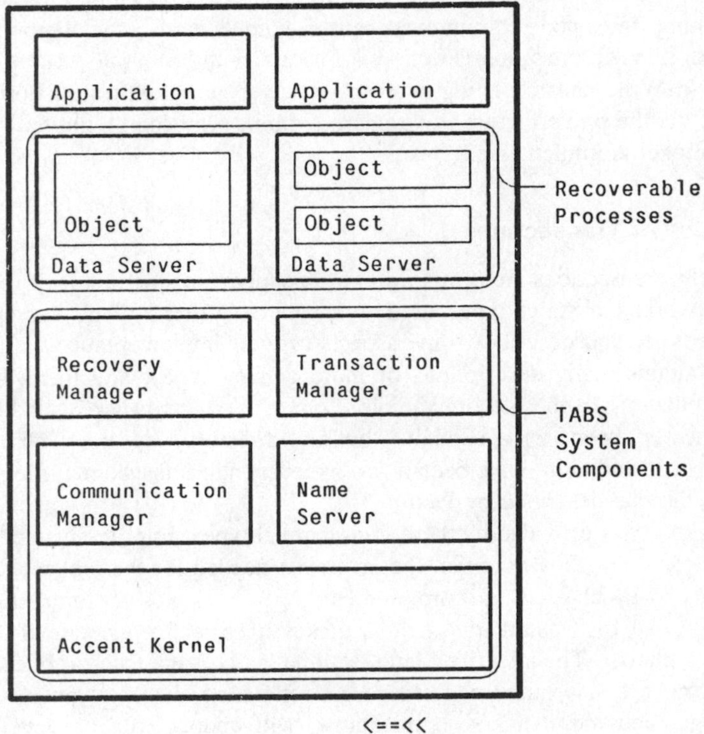

Fig. 6.1. The basic components of a TABS node.

work communication, recovery and log management, and transaction management, respectively. Section 3.2 briefly describes the implementation of these TABS processes and our modifications to Accent.

TABS began to operate in the Fall of 1984, and all of its facilities are operational with one exception. Operation-based recovery and the necessary type-specific locking are not supported in the TABS libraries, though the operation-based algorithm has been tested and integrated with the value-based algorithm. The system contains about 51,000 lines of Matchmaker, Pasmac macro language,[33] and Pascal sources. This count includes one data server and application that we use in testing releases, but it does not include the changes we have made to the Accent kernel.

3.1. The Tabs Programming Interface

The interface to TABS is provided by three libraries. The server library, used only by data servers, supports shared/exclusive locking, value logging, and miscellaneous utilities. The transaction management library provides routines for controlling the execution of transactions. The name server library provides access to TABS name dissemination services. The use of many routines from these libraries is illustrated in Section 4.

3.1.1. The Server Library

The functions that make up the server library fall into six broad categories. These categories are listed beside the procedure headers of the library routines in Table 6.1.

Four procedures are used to initialize the data server. **InitServer** initializes server library data structures, and **ReadPermanentData** maps the data server's recoverable data into virtual memory (see Section 3.2.1.). **RecoverServer** accepts the log records that the Recovery Manager reads from the log. This procedure understands the format of the log records written by the server library routines during forward processing, and calls the server library's undo/redo code to restore the data to a transaction-consistent state. Once the virtual memory copy of the recoverable data is consistent, the data server calls **AcceptRequests.** This routine takes a procedure argument that dispatches on operation request messages.

Since a programmer works with virtual addresses, but the log manager works with disk addresses contained in ObjectIDs, data servers must do address translation. The routines **CreateObjectID** and **ConvertObjectIDtoVirtualAddress** perform these conversions.

Three routines support locking. **LockObject** attempts to acquire a lock, and waits if the lock is not available. **ConditionallyLockObject** also attempts to acquire a lock, but it returns immediately if the lock is unavailable. **Is-**

Table 6.1. The complete TABS server library.

Routine	Purpose
InitServer(ServerID)	Startup
ReadPermanentData(DiskAddress) returns(VirtualAddress, DataSize)	Startup
RecoverServer	Startup
AcceptRequests(DispatchFunction)	Startup
CreateObjectID(VirtualAddress, length) returns(ObjectID)	Address Arithmetic
ConvertObjectIDtoVirtualAddress(ObjectID) returns(VirtualAddress)	Address Arithmetic
LockObject(ObjectID, LockMode)	Locking
ConditionallyLockObject(ObjectID, LockMode) returns(Boolean)	Locking
IsObjectLocked(ObjectID) returns(Boolean)	Locking
PinObject(ObjectID)	Paging Control
UnPinObject(ObjectID)	Paging Control
UnPinAllObjects	Paging Control
PinAndBuffer(ObjectID)	Paging Control, Logging
LogAndUnPin(ObjectID)	Logging, Paging Control
LockAndMark(ObjectID, LockMode)	Locking
PinAndBufferMarkedObjects	Paging Control, Logging
LogAndUnPinMarkedObjects	Paging Control, Logging
ExecuteTransaction(TransactionProcedure)	Transaction Management

This table summarizes the library routines used by data servers. The routine names have been made as explicit as possible; a description of their function may be found in the accompanying prose. The types of the parameters and return values are shown as well as the general purpose of each routine. Routines used both by data servers and applications are shown in Tables 6.2 and 6.3.

ObjectLocked returns true if and only if a lock is set. All unlocking is done automatically by the server library at commit or abort time.

Paging control operations prevent the kernel from paging an object to secondary storage. They are used to ensure that an object's permanent representation is not changed before all modifications to it have been logged. **PinObject** prevents the kernel from paging an object to secondary storage until **UnPinObject** or **UnPinAllObjects** is called.

The paging control operations are usually performed as side effects of logging routines. **PinAndBuffer** pins the specified object and then copies the existing (old) value of the object into a buffer in anticipation of a modification. After the modification is made, **LogAndUnPin** sends the (buffered) old value and the existing (new) value to the Recovery Manager and unpins the object.

The checkpoint protocol requires that data servers not wait (e.g., for a lock) while objects are pinned. One approach to meeting this requirement is to set all locks before any modifications are performed. The server library facilitates this by providing three routines: **LockAndMark** locks the specified object and enqueues a reference to the object on a "to be modified" queue. **PinAndBufferMarkedObjects** pins every object on the queue and copies each object's current (old) value into buffers. **LogAndUnPinMarkedObjects** sends to the Recovery Manager the (buffered) old value and existing (new) value for each object on the queue. When all the old and new values are logged, **LogAndUnPinMarkedObjects** unpins all the objects and deletes the queue.

The remaining routine, **ExecuteTransaction,** takes a procedure argument and executes that procedure within a new top-level transaction.

Lightweight processes use a coroutine mechanism embedded within every data server. The server library treats each incoming request as a separate coroutine invocation. A coroutine switch is performed only when an operation waits, e.g., for a lock or for starting a transaction. The server library contains additional code that automates a data server's participation in transaction commit, abort, and checkpoint.

3.1.2. The Transaction Management Library

The routines in the transaction management library provide a standard interface to transaction management functions (see Table 6.2). **BeginTransaction** creates a *subtransaction* of the specified transaction. To create a new top-level transaction, a special null **TransactionID** is given as the argument. **EndTransaction** and **AbortTransaction** initiate commit and abort of the specified transaction, respectively. The **TransactionIsAborted** exception is raised in the application process if the specified transaction has been aborted by some other process.

3.1.3. The Name Server Library

The abstractions represented by data servers are permanent entities that must persist despite node failures, even though the ports through which they are accessed change. The TABS name server implements an interface that allows a single name to be mapped to one or more **⟨port, logical-object-identifier⟩** pairs. A data server has the option of servicing operation requests for several

Table 6.2. The TABS transaction management library.

Routine
BeginTransaction(TransactionID) returns(NewTransactionID)
EndTransaction(TransactionID) returns(Boolean)
AbortTransaction(TransactionID)
TransactionIsAborted(TransactionID) [*exception*]

Table 6.3. The TABS name server library.

Routine
Register(Name, Type, Port, ObjectID)
DeRegister(Name, Port, ObjectID)
LookUp(Name, NodeName, DesiredNumberOfPortIDs, MaxWait) returns(ArrayOfPortIDPairs, ReturnNumberOfPortIDs)

objects on the same port, and independent data server processes can together implement replicated objects. The most important routines in the name server library are summarized in Table 6.3.

3.2. Implementation of TABS

Most of the operations TABS libraries provide to data servers and applications are implemented by the TABS System components and the Accent kernel. The modifications to the kernel and the TABS System components are summarized in this section and described in more detail in a recent paper.[57]

3.2.1. The Accent Kernel

The failure atomic and/or permanent data stored by data servers are stored in disk files that are mapped into virtual memory. These files are called *recoverable segments*. When mapped into memory, the kernel's paging system updates a recoverable segment directly instead of updating paging storage.[17]

To support the write-ahead algorithms used by TABS, the kernel sends three types of messages to the Recovery Manager. The first message indicates that a page frame that is backed by a recoverable segment has been modified for the first time. The second message indicates that the kernel wants to copy a modified page back to its recoverable segment. The kernel does not write the page until it receives a message from the Recovery Manager indicating that all log records that apply to this page have been written to nonvolatile storage. The third and final message indicates whether the contents of a page frame have been successfully copied to a recoverable segment.

In addition to the special messages that support the write-ahead log algorithms, the Accent Kernel also implements the paging control primitives of the server library.

A final modification to Accent has been made to support the TABS operation logging recovery algorithm. This algorithm requires that the kernel atomically write a sequence number each time it copies a page of a recoverable segment to nonvolatile storage. This sequence number (currently, 39 bits) is stored in header space that is available on a Perq disk sector. The Recovery Manager sends the sequence number to the kernel in the message that indicates that the page can be written to disk. During crash recovery, the Recovery Manager sends a request to the kernel when it wishes to read a page's sequence number.

3.2.2. Recovery Manager

The Recovery Manager coordinates access to the log. The log should be on *stable storage;* but, because of our Perq hardware restrictions (only one disk), the nonvolatile storage used for the log is not stable. Hence, we do not consider disk failures in this work.

The Recovery Manager writes log records in response to messages sent by data servers, the Transaction Manager, and the Accent kernel. Log records written in response to kernel messages help to identify (at recovery time) the pages that were in memory at crash time. All log records are written into a volatile buffer until the buffer fills or until the buffer is forced to nonvolatile storage by either the write-ahead log or commit protocols. Upon transaction abort, the recovery manager follows the backward chain of log records that were written by the transaction and sends messages to the servers instructing them to undo their effects.

After a node crash, the Recovery Manager scans the log one or more times. It directly interprets the recovery log records, but it must pass transaction management records back to the Transaction Manager. The Recovery Manager then queries the Transaction Manager to discover the state of the transaction. Based on this information, the Recovery Manager gives each data server instructions to redo or undo previously performed operations. In this way, the Recovery Manager assures that objects in recoverable segments reflect only the operations of committed and prepared transactions.

The last function of the Recovery Manager is to coordinate checkpoints. After a crash, the Recovery Manager must read the portion of the log written after the last checkpoint. Depending on the contents of the checkpoint record, earlier sections of the log may also be read, but the most recent checkpoint record contains enough information to determine when crash recovery will be complete. In our system, checkpoints are performed at intervals determined by the transaction manager or when the system is close to running out of log space. In the latter instance, the Recovery Manager runs a reclamation algorithm that attempts to reclaim log space. Log reclamation may force pages back to disk before they would otherwise be written.

3.2.3. Transaction Manager

The Transaction Manager's major responsibilities are implementing commit protocols and allocating globally unique transaction identifiers. Application processes and data servers send the Transaction Manager messages to begin a transaction, to attempt to commit a transaction, or to force a transaction to be aborted. The tree-structured two-phase commit protocol used by the Transaction Manager is based on a spanning tree, where a node A is a parent of another node B if and only if A were the first node to invoke an operation on behalf of the transaction on B. The information about a node's relation to the nodes directly above and below it in the spanning tree is kept by its Communication Manager.

There are two messages that processes send to inform the Transaction Manager of the progress of a transaction. The first is sent by a data server the first time it is asked to perform an operation on behalf of a particular transaction; doing so enables the Transaction Manager to know which servers it must inform when the transaction is being terminated. The other message is sent by the Communication Manager the first time an inter-node message is sent or received on behalf of a particular transaction. This message indicates that there are remote sites that have servers active on behalf of the given transaction. At this point, the Transaction Manager becomes aware that remote sites are involved in the transaction, but it cannot yet identify these sites. The complete site list is obtained from the Communication Manager during commit processing.

The existence of subtransactions in the TABS model does not complicate transaction management. The same messages that are used to inform the Transaction Manager about top-level transactions are used for subtransactions. The only regard in which transaction processing differs is that subtransactions can be aborted without requiring the parent transaction to abort. Subtransactions, however, may not be committed before their parents. When a parent transaction commits or aborts, its subtransactions are committed or aborted as well.

3.2.4. Communication Manager

The Communication Manager is the only process that has access to the network. It implements three forms of network communication: datagrams for the distributed two-phase commit; reliable *session* communication for implementing remote procedure calls; and broadcasting for name lookup by the Name Server.

For session communication, two Communication Managers cooperate to provide at-most-once, ordered delivery of arbitrary-sized messages. The Communication Manager detects permanent communication failures and, thereby, aids in the detection of remote node crashes. The Communication Manager also scans any transaction identifiers included in messages and is responsible for constructing the local portion of the spanning tree that the Transaction Manager uses during two-phase commit. In particular, the Communication Manager records the node's parent, whether the transaction was initiated by a remote node, and the list of all the node's children. It also records a small amount of additional information that is used for detecting some types of node crashes.

3.2.5. Name Server

In TABS, the Name Server process on each node maintains a mapping of object names to one or more ⟨**port, logical-object-identifier**⟩ pairs for all the objects managed by data servers on that node. Whenever the Name Server is asked about a name it does not recognize, it broadcasts a name lookup request to all other Name Servers. If the broadcast is successful, the Communication Managers on the local and the remote machines automatically establish a session between the requesting node and the data server implementing the named object.

4. THE TABS PROTOTYPE IN USE

This section presents five of the data servers we have implemented with the TABS prototype: The integer array server, the weak queue server, the IO server, the B-tree server, and the replicated directory object. The integer array server, B-tree server, and replicated directory object all preserve the serializability, failure atomicity, and permanence of the transactions that invoke them. The IO server provides a permanent, nonfailure atomic object, and the weak queue server provides a permanent, failure atomic object that is not serializable.

4.1. The Integer Array Server

The integer array server maintains an array of (one word) integers, and provides the following abstract operations:

```
FUNCTION   GetCell(cellNum: integer): integer;
PROCEDURE SetCell(cellNum: integer; value: integer);
```

The two operations supported by the integer array server are simple enough that the best description is the Pascal code that implements one of them. Note that the virtual address of a cell is obtained by adding the proper offset to the base of the recoverable segment.

```
FUNCTION   SetCell(arrayPort:port;   { needed for RPC }
                   transaction:tid;
                   cellNum:integer;
                   value:integer): GeneralReturn;

{ SetCell sets array[cellNum] to contain 'value' }

VAR
  obj: ObjectID; { object for the cell }
  size: integer; { the size of a cell }
```

```
BEGIN

IF (cellNum >= 1) AND (cellNum <= maxCell) THEN
        BEGIN
        size := WordSize(integer);
        obj := CreateObjectID(baseOfArray +
                                        (cellNum-1) * size, size);
        LockObject(obj, Write);
        PinAndBuffer(obj);
        obj.ptr↑ := value; { do actual assignment }
        LogAndUnPin(obj);
        SetCell := Success;
        END
ELSE SetCell := IndexOutOfRange;

END;
```

The implementation of **GetCell** is very similar, and the combined code for both operations requires 50 lines of Pascal. The balance of the 140 lines of code in the integer array server performs module imports and initialization. The integer array server is a very straightforward data server; it uses only the two-phase locking and value logging techniques found in many transaction-based systems. The data servers described below take more advantage of the flexibility of TABS.

4.2. The Weak Queue Server

The weak queue server provides access to a weak queue, sometimes called a semi-queue.[53,62] In a weak queue, items in the queue are not guaranteed to be dequeued strictly in the order that they were enqueued. Relaxing the strict FIFO nature of the queue allows greater concurrency, while retaining failure atomicity. The weak queue server provides the following abstract operations:

```
PROCEDURE Enqueue(data: integer);
FUNCTION  Dequeue: integer;
FUNCTION  IsQueueEmpty: boolean;
```

The queue is implemented as an array of individually lockable elements, with head and tail pointers bounding the currently used section of the array. Because gaps may exist in the range between the head and tail pointers, each element in the array contains both its contents and an extra boolean, **InUse,** indicating whether that element actually contains a value that is currently stored in the queue. **Enqueue** and **Dequeue** set and clear this **InUse** bit, and if they abort, this bit is restored along with the previous contents of the element. The head pointer is a permanent, failure atomic object. The tail pointer can be recomputed after crashes by examining the head pointer and **InUse** bits, so it is kept in volatile storage.

To add a new item to the queue, **Enqueue** places the item in the element below the tail pointer, sets that element's **InUse** bit to true, and sets the tail pointer to the new element. If the **Enqueue** later aborts, this will leave a gap in the array when the **InUse** bit is reset to false. Because the tail pointer is not locked, the weak queue server relies on the monitor semantics of TABS co-routines to ensure that only a single transaction at a time can update the tail pointer.

Dequeue is more complex, because elements in the array may not be legally dequeued for either of two reasons: If an element is locked, another operation is still manipulating it; if an element's **InUse** bit is False, the **Enqueue** of that element is aborted or the element has already been successfully removed. **Dequeue** scans elements starting at the head pointer, using the **IsObjectLocked** primitive, and then testing the **InUse** bit. When an unlocked element whose **InUse** bit is True is found, **Dequeue** locks it and returns its contents.

Enqueue and **Dequeue** both read the head pointer to check for a full queue. **Dequeue** does not alter the head pointer because this would restrict concurrency. The head pointer must eventually be moved, however, or the queue will fill. Abstractly, one imagines a ''garbage collection'' operation that gets randomly invoked and moves the head pointer past any elements that are not locked, and whose **InUse** bits are False. The current implementation does the garbage collection as a side effect of **Enqueue.**

The weak queue server is 380 lines of Pascal code. Its design prompted the addition of the **ConditionallyLockObject** and **IsObjectLocked** primitives to the server library. Much of the work that went into creating the weak queue server dealt with mapping the logical operations on the queue into manipulations of data with the value logging mechanisms. For this reason, we believe that certain abstract data types are more suited to operation logging than value logging.

4.3. The Input/Output Server

The IO server extends the domain of TABS to include the bitmap display by restoring the screen contents after a failure, and by giving the user a comfortable model of transaction-based input/output. The current implementation uses character input/output in a standard typescript fashion. Recovering the screen is straightforward; TABS runs within a window manager that provides overlapping, rectangular windows. Restoring the screen requires keeping track of a window's contents and location in a recoverable segment.* Providing a good user model of transaction-based IO is more complex. Writing to a terminal is often cited as the canonical nonrecoverable action. An obvious approach is to buffer all output and only display it if the transaction commits, but this technique fails for conversational transactions. The IO server displays all output as it occurs, in a style that indicates the current state of the transaction that performed the output. While a transaction is in progress, the output is displayed in gray, to indicate its tentative nature. If the transaction commits, the output is redrawn in black, to indicate that the operation really occurred. If the transaction aborts, lines are drawn through the output. This is preferable to making the output disappear, which is disconcerting to the user. Users know that an operation has not really happened until its output is displayed in black. See Fig. 6.2.

Multiple input/output areas are maintained on the screen, to allow for concurrent interaction with the user. The abstract operations are:

```
FUNCTION    ObtainIOarea:      ioAreaID;
PROCEDURE DestroyIOarea       (ioArea: ioAreaID);
PROCEDURE WriteToArea         (ioArea: ioAreaID; data:String);
PROCEDURE WritelnToArea       (ioArea: ioAreaID; data:String);
FUNCTION    ReadCharFromArea  (ioArea: ioAreaID): Char;
FUNCTION    ReadLineFromArea  (ioArea: ioAreaID): String;
```

To display output even after a client transaction later aborts, the IO server maintains permanent, nonfailure atomic data in an array of characters for each area. Rather than having the client transaction modify this array, the IO server uses **ExecuteTransaction** to invoke a new top-level transaction to write the data for each operation. If the client transaction aborts, the characters stored via the **ExecuteTransaction** will not be altered.

In order to display the output of a transaction, the IO server needs to determine the status (aborted, committed, or in progress) of the transaction. The Transaction Manager cannot provide this facility, because doing so would require retaining an infinite amount of log data. When a transaction establishes ownership of an area, the IO server uses **ExecuteTransaction** to write *aborted* into a state object in the data structure for the area. The IO server then has the client transaction lock the state object and set it to contain *committed.* This causes an old value/new value pair of *aborted/committed* to be written in the log for the client transaction. The IO server can now determine the transaction's current state by using the **IsObjectLocked** primitive. If the state object is locked, the client transaction is still in progress. If the object is no longer locked, then the

*The easiest way to test whether windows are restored to the correct location is to mark display screens with grease pencils. This leads to research on chemicals that remove grease pencil markings from display screens . . . .

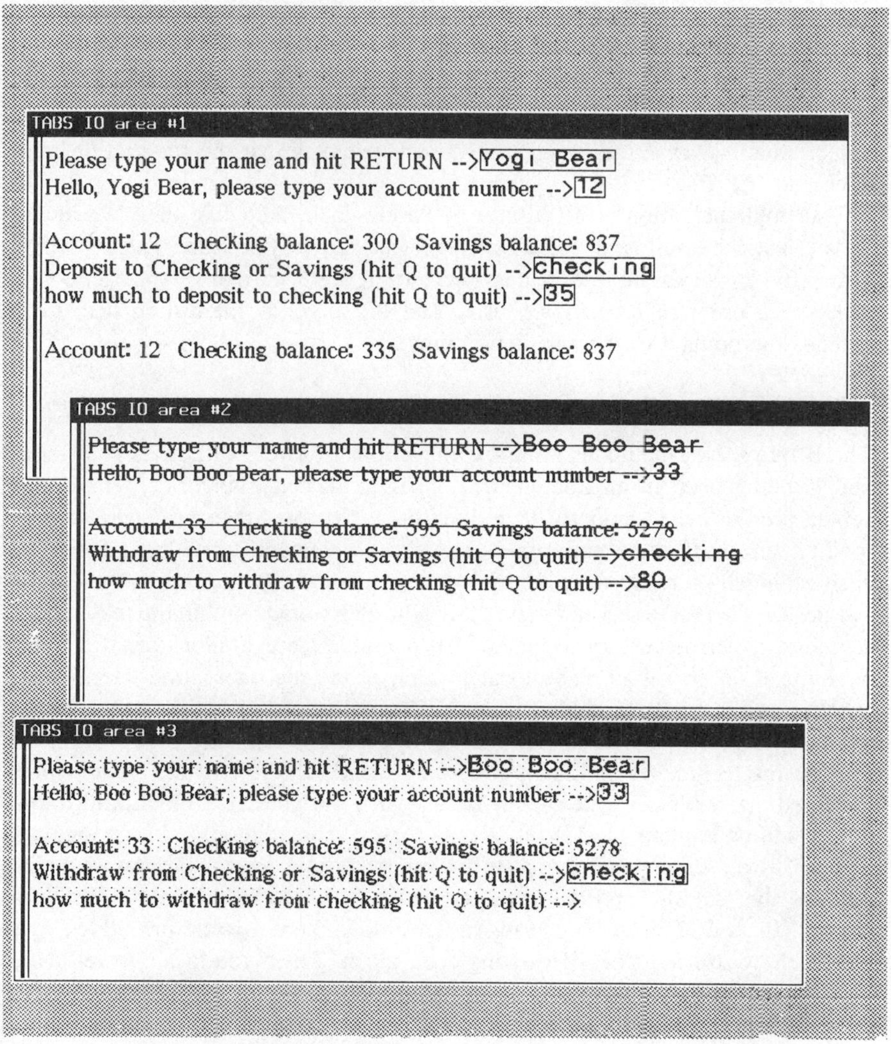

TABS IO area #1

Please type your name and hit RETURN -->Yogi Bear
Hello, Yogi Bear, please type your account number -->12

Account: 12 Checking balance: 300 Savings balance: 837
Deposit to Checking or Savings (hit Q to quit) -->checking
how much to deposit to checking (hit Q to quit) -->35

Account: 12 Checking balance: 335 Savings balance: 837

TABS IO area #2

~~Please type your name and hit RETURN -->Boo Boo Bear~~
~~Hello, Boo Boo Bear, please type your account number -->33~~

~~Account: 33 Checking balance: 595 Savings balance: 5278~~
~~Withdraw from Checking or Savings (hit Q to quit) -->checking~~
~~how much to withdraw from checking (hit Q to quit) -->80~~

TABS IO area #3

Please type your name and hit RETURN -->Boo Boo Bear
Hello, Boo Boo Bear, please type your account number -->33

Account: 33 Checking balance: 595 Savings balance: 5278
Withdraw from Checking or Savings (hit Q to quit) -->checking
how much to withdraw from checking (hit Q to quit) -->

Fig. 6.2. Sample display screen. This is an actual snapshot of the current IO server running a trivial bank implementation. This example exhibits the IO server; the bank application also uses the integer array server to store its information. In area one, the user successfully deposited 35 dollars to a checking account. The user knew that the action had occurred (committed), because its output was displayed in black. In area two, the user attempted to withdraw 80 dollars from a checking account, but the node failed during the transaction, causing it to abort. The IO server restored the screen when the system became available, and the user is currently trying again in area three, where the transaction is still in progress. The rectangles drawn around user input indicate that the characters have been read by the application.

transaction has finished. If the state object contains *aborted,* the transaction aborted, and the object was reset by the recovery mechanisms. Otherwise, the object contains *committed,* and the IO server knows that the transaction must have committed.

The implementation is 2500 lines of Pascal code, and, like the weak queue server, uses the ability to test if an object is currently locked. The IO server also provides an example of a data server that needs to invoke transactions of its own in order to process requests. The IO server is interesting because it extends the domain of the transaction model.

4.4. The B-Tree Server

The B-tree server maintains arbitrary collections of directory entries in B-trees, and is being used in an implementation of replicated directories. The B-tree server provides the standard operations on multikey directories: add, delete, modify, etc. Indices on nonprimary keys are implemented as separate B-trees, each of which points to the primary key B-tree's leaves which contain the data.

Because the B-tree server dynamically allocates storage within the recoverable segment, it was necessary to create a recoverable storage allocator. If a transaction uses an operation that allocates storage, and the transaction later aborts, the memory is made available for reuse. The B-tree server maintains a separate storage pool for each size object that it allocates, and allocates blocks from the pool, using techniques similar to the weak queue server. This technique works for fixed sized blocks, but cannot be used for variable size block allocation, which will be implemented in future data servers using operation-based logging.

The B-tree server was orginally implemented as a Pascal program running outside the TABS environment. By using the **LockAndMark, PinAndBufferMarkedObjects,** and **LogAndUnPinMarkedObjects** primitives, we were able to use most of the existing code intact. These routines allowed us to avoid bracketing every assignment in the original program with **PinAndBuffer** and **LogAndUnPin** calls, in order to avoid having data pinned when requesting other locks. The total modifications, including initialization and storage allocation changes, increased the size of the B-tree server from 4500 to 5000 lines of Pascal code.

4.5. A Replicated Directory Object

The replicated directory object provides an abstraction identical to a conventional directory but stores its data in multiple *directory representative servers* on different nodes. The replicated directory uses our variation of Gifford's weighted voting algorithm for global coordination.[7,12,21] Each of the directory representative servers uses a B-tree server to actually store the data, and requires another 2700 lines of code to perform localized functions for the voting algorithm. The interface to client programs is provided by a module that does global coordination of the voting, and is implemented as 1100 lines of code that are linked in with the client program.

The replicated directory object demonstrates many of the facilities of the TABS prototype: Aborting transactions that use the replicated directory requires recovery on multiple nodes, and committing transactions requires the global coordination protocols for multiple node commit. Our tests involved three nodes, which permitted one node to fail and have the data remain available.

4.6. Evaluation of Data Servers

The data servers that have been created cover a good range of the design space, although we have currently restricted our data servers to use standard read/write locking and value logging. Most of the advantages of the system are easy to overlook because they involve simply having a system in the first place. For example, recovery, synchronization, and communication mechanisms exist as tools that are relatively easy to use. Moreover, these tools are not mechanically imposed, which has made it possible to add new primitives easily, and to build several data servers that use these tools in novel ways.

These flexible tools underscore our major claim: Many interesting data servers are difficult, if not impossible, to build using traditional read/write locking. In support of this claim, we note that all the data servers except the integer array server required the addition of primitives to circumvent the locking mechanism, and that even with these additions, the implementors were required to use unnecessarily complex algorithms and/or unprotected reads of data. We intend to explore the type-specific locking capability of TABS with future data servers.

Our second claim is: Value logging is inconvenient for non-array implementations. The implementors of the weak queue server, the IO server, and the B-tree server storage allocator initially sketched simple designs that used operation-based logging. The eventual implementations were complicated by the use of value logging. The use of operation-logging, type-specific locking, and value logging where appropriate will provide a rich environment for reimplementing existing data servers, and creating new ones.

5. ANALYSIS OF TABS PERFORMANCE

This section presents analytical and experimental evidence supporting our hypothesis that it is possible to implement efficient general purpose facilities that support distributed transactions. This evaluation permits us to describe the performance and limitations of the current implementation, and it permits us to predict how well TABS would work if it used more efficient underlying primitives and were more tightly integrated. The analysis presented in this chapter is an application of a performance evaluation methodology for predicting the cost of transaction execution (latency and resource utilization) under conditions of no load.[55]*

The section continues by describing a collection of benchmarks and characterizing them in terms of the repeated execution of primitive operations. We use both this characterization and an empirical performance study to describe the performance of TABS and to predict how it would perform if improvements were made.

5.1. A Microscopic Approach to Transaction System Performance Evaluation

The performance of a commercial transaction processing system can be described macroscopically by its performance on standard work loads.[2] This approach is not sufficient for our evaluation of TABS for two reasons. First, the work loads encountered by a general purpose facility supporting abstract types are not easily characterizable. Second, throughput rates or latencies, by themselves, do not lead to an understanding of how individual algorithms and implementation decisions have affected system performance. Hence, we need to understand more microscopic effects to critique our system and to predict the effects of algorithmic or structural changes.

To describe TABS performance, we have chosen to measure the performance of a collection of benchmarks, from which it is possible to deduce the performance of other transactions. To illustrate this deduction process, consider two benchmarks: one is a read-only transaction that performs one remote read operation on data in primary memory, and the other is a similar transaction that performs five remote read operations on data in primary memory. From these two transactions, it is possible to deduce the amount of time to perform an incremental nonpaging, remote read operation. The benchmarks, which are described below, are as simple as possible consistent with their forming a basis for estimating the performance of other transactions.

The execution times of benchmarks, while useful for predicting the performance of other transactions, do not explain how transaction performance changes as a function of algorithmic or underlying system changes. Nor do the execution times of benchmarks shed light on the resources that they use. To provide this additional information requires a more complex analysis. The analysis that we propose is based on the notion that each benchmark is substantially made up of the repetitious execution of a collection of primitive operations, such as disk reads or inter-node datagrams. These primitives have counterparts in all transaction systems and collectively account for much of the execution time of a transaction.

---

*This methodology does not address the effects of concurrent transaction execution on performance, even though TABS fully supports the necessary synchronization.

The primitive operations we use are the following:

- **Data Server Calls** in TABS are remote procedure calls between applications and data servers on a single node. Servers instantiate a coroutine for each call. We measure the time for the Data Server Call primitive by measuring the time for a TABS application process to call a null procedure in a TABS data server process.
- **Inter-Node Data Server Calls** are implemented and measured analogously to single node Data Server Calls. These calls use sessions implemented by the Communication Manager.
- **Datagrams** are used for inter-node transaction management messages.
- Accent interprocess messages are used for communication between TABS applications, data servers, and TABS system processes on one node. Because message performance depends on the size of messages and on the method by which data is transferred from one process to another, three different message types are counted: 1) A **Small Contiguous Message:** small messages typically contain less than 100 bytes, but in all cases have less than 500 bytes; 2) a **Large Contiguous Message:** we use 1100 bytes for the average size of these messages; and 3) a **Pointer Message:** contains a pointer to data that is transmitted by copy-on-write remapping of processes' virtual memory.
- In TABS, all disk reads and writes, other than those for the log, are performed by Accent as part of its demand paging of virtual memory. Pages are 512 bytes. In Accent, random access reads and writes take about the same time, so we report only one (combined) **Random Access Paged** I/O primitive. Because our Perqs have only a single disk, log writing breaks up sequential access disk writes, so sequential access writes do not occur. **Sequential Reads** do occur in our benchmarks, and this primitive is also reported separately.
- The **Stable Storage Write** primitive is the elapsed time required for the Recovery Manager to force a page of log data to nonvolatile storage.

The costs of the primitives were estimated by repeatedly calling the appropriate Accent and TABS functions. For example, we determined demand-paged I/O costs by instrumenting a program that repeatedly read (or wrote) individual pages in a large array that is mapped into virtual memory. This experiment measures the average cost of a read (or a read/write pair). Table 6.4 shows the measured performance of the primitive operations on a Perq T2 computer.[47] The Data Server Call primitive time is high due to an inefficient implementation of coroutines. As background, we note that the speed of a Perq executing Pascal is approximately 20 to 25% of the speed of a Vax-11/780 executing C.[20]

After determining the appropriate primitives and measuring their performance,

Table 6.4. Primitive operation times (in milliseconds).*

Primitive	Average Time
Data Server Call	26.1
Inter-Node Data Server Call	89.0
Datagram	25.0
Small Contiguous Message	3.0
Large Contiguous Message	4.4
Pointer Message	18.3
Random Access Paged I/O	32.0
Sequential Read	18.0
Stable Storage Write	79.0

*These primitive times are used to predict system time in Table 6.7.

the next step in our analysis is to define a set of benchmarks and to express the latency of each benchmark as a function of primitive operation times. The benchmarks are among the simplest that can be designed to produce the desired system behavior. There are four dimensions of system behavior that the benchmarks exercise. First, some benchmarks are read-only, while others modify data. Second, benchmarks either cause no page faults, cause random page faults, or read pages sequentially. Third, benchmarks either perform a single data server operation on each node or perform multiple data server operations on one of the nodes in the benchmark. Finally, benchmarks perform operations on one, two, or three nodes.

There are four read-only benchmarks in which both the application and data server processes are located on the same machine. The simplest is a transaction that reads an identical element of a recoverable array of integers. The second benchmark is similar, but is a transaction that reads the same array element five times. This permits the determination of the costs of individual read operations on data servers. The third is similar to the first, but is modified to measure the performance of the demand paging of recoverable data. It is a transaction that reads an element from successive pages of a large array. This array is 5000 pages, which is more than three times the available physical memory on a Perq with TABS running. The final test reads random elements from the array and demonstrates the effect of random I/O times on TABS performance.

The performance of the system for transactions that modify recoverable data is measured by benchmarks that write the array instead of reading it. Because there is only one disk on our system, there should be no significant difference between the random-access case and the sequential-access case because of the intervening seeks required by paging writes. Hence, we include only a sequential paging test.

To study the performance effects of inter-node communications, there are similar benchmarks that use two data servers, one on the same node as the application and one on a remote node. Read tests have one local nonpaging read and one remote nonpaging read; one local nonpaging read and five remote nonpaging reads; and one local sequential paging read and one remote sequential paging read. Two additional tests measure two node write transactions: one test with one local nonpaging write and one remote nonpaging write, and one test with one local paging write and one remote paging write. These remote write tests reflect the cost of the more complex two-phase commit protocol. We do not include a benchmark that measures five-write operations remotely, as this can be deduced from other benchmark times.

To show how the cost of transaction commit increases as a function of the number of nodes, benchmarks that read or write the same cell on three nodes are included. The performance of these benchmarks must be adjusted for the number of operations to show the incremental commit cost directly.

The time in each benchmark attributable to primitive operations can be expressed as a function of primitive operation times. Potentially, this analysis involves complicated stochastic models, but our benchmarks have a simple approximate analysis. In our transaction model, all operations prior to commitment execute sequentially. Hence the pre-commit latency of a transaction that is due to the execution of primitive operations is a sum of the primitive operation times weighted by the numbers of primitive operations performed. The benchmarks are deterministic in the steady state, so determining the primitive counts is fairly easy. For the random read benchmark, it is simpler to count page reads during the test than to measure the available buffer memory and estimate what fraction of references will be to pages in the buffer. These formulas are reported in Table 6.5, the *Pre-commit primitive count table.*

The latency of the commit portion of a transaction is sequential in the local case, but involves parallel processing in the distributed case. For each type of transaction commit protocol, we estimate the execution path of longest duration through the distributed system. This path is used as the basis of the benchmark counts that are incorporated in Table 6.6, the *Commit primitive count table.* Because different transactions use the same commit protocol, there are fewer entries in this table than in Pre-commit primitive count table (Table 6.5). Commit times for the three node benchmarks are longer than commit times for the two node benchmarks by a one-half datagram time for read-only transactions and by 2 one-half datagram times for update transactions. This is due to the estimated cost of sending datagrams in parallel to different nodes.

5.2. The Performance of TABS

The sum of the primitive operation times in Table 6.4, as weighted by the counts of Tables 6.5 and 6.6, accounts for a significant portion of the latency of each

Table 6.5. Pre-commit primitive counts.

Benchmark	Data Server Calls	Remote Data Server Calls	Small Local Msg	Large Local Msg	Sequential Page Reads	Random Page I/O
1 Local Read, No Paging	1		4			
5 Local Read, No Paging	5		4			
1 Local Read, Seq. Paging	1		4		1	
1 Local Read, Random Paging	1		4			.86
1 Local Write, No Paging	1		6	1		
5 Local Write, No Paging	5		14	5		
1 Local Write, Seq. Paging	1		10	1		2
1 Lci Rd, 1 Rem Rd, No Paging	1	1	8			
1 Lci Rd, 5 Rem Rd, No Paging	1	5	8			
1 Lci Rd, 1 Rem Rd, Seq. Paging	1	1	8		2	
1 Lci Wr, 1 Rem Wr, No Paging	1	1	12	2		
1 Lci Wr, 1 Rem Wr, Seq. Paging	1	1	20	2		4
1 Lci Rd, 1 Rem Rd, 1 Rem Rd, NP	1	2	11			
1 Lci Wr, 1 Rem Wr, 1 Rem Wr, NP	1	2	17	3		

This table shows the number of primitive operations each benchmark is expected to perform before starting commit. The primitive operations are listed in Table 6.4. The number .86 is the measured number of page I/O's per transaction. Blank entries denote zero values.

benchmark. This sum is shown in the first column of Table 6.7, labeled "System Time Predicted by Primitives."

Benchmarks times were measured by counting the number of transactions executed in 20 or 30 second time intervals and averaging these rates over 20 to 30 minutes of testing. Transients at the beginning and ending of tests were

Table 6.6. Commit primitive counts.

Protocol	Remote Datagram Msg	Small Local Msg	Large Local Msg	Local Pointer Msg	Stable Storage Writes
1 Node, Read Only		5			
1 Node, Write		8	1		1
2 Node, Read Only	2	11	1		1
2 Node, Write	4	17	5	1	4
3 Node, Read Only	2.5	11	1		1
3 Node, Write	5	17	5	1	4

This table shows the number of primitive operations in the longest estimated execution path for various commit protocols. The one-half datagram time in the 3 Node, Read Only case is an approximation for the time required to immediately send a "Prepare" datagram to the second remote node. The 3 Node, Write case contains two one-half datagram times, because there is also a "Commit" datagram that is sent to the second remote node. Blank entries denote zero values.

Table 6.7. Benchmark times (in milliseconds).

Benchmark	Sys Time Predicted by Primitives	Measured TABS Proc Time	Measured Elapsed Time	Improved TABS Architecture	New Primitive Times
1 Local Read, No Paging	53	41	110	107	67
5 Local Read, No Paging	157	41	217	213	80
1 Local Read, Seq. Paging	71	41	126	123	75
1 Local Read, Random Paging	81	41	140	137	98
1 Local Write, No Paging	156	83	247	228	136
5 Local Write, No Paging	302	119	467	424	225
1 Local Write, Seq. Paging	232	104	371	345	249
1 Lcl Rd, 1 Rem Rd, No Page	306	223	469	459	228
1 Lcl Rd, 5 Rem Rd, No Page	662	368	829	819	268
1 Lcl Rd, 1 Rem Rd, Seq. Page	341	226	514	504	257
1 Lcl Wr, 1 Rem Wr, No Page	697	407	989	775	442
1 Lcl Wr, 1 Rem Wr, Seq. Page	864	441	1125	873	539
1 Lcl Rd, 1 Rem Rd, 1 Rem Rd, NP	416	381	621	611	282
1 Lcl Wr, 1 Rem Wr, 1 Rem Wr, NP	831	670	1200	968	534

This table shows predicted, average measured, and projected improved times for the benchmarks. The "System Time Predicted by Primitives" is computed by summing the primitive operation times for each benchmark from Tables 6.4, 6.5, and 6.6. "Measured TABS Process Time" is the sum of TABS system process times on all nodes. "Measured Elapsed Time" is the *average* measured time of the benchmark over a long run, including all points except starting and ending transients. For the single node tests, the "System Time Predicted" plus "Measured TABS Process Time" should approximately yield "Measured Elapsed Time," as they do. As described in the text, the TABS architecture could be improved and the primitive times reduced. The "Improved TABS Architecture" column shows the projections of elapsed time based on algorithmic and structural changes to TABS. The "New Primitive Times" column shows how the times in the preceding column would improve if primitive operations times were as in Table 6.8. Multinode write tests used one or two Perq 2 computers, which have average disk seek times about 15 milliseconds slower than the Perq T2 used for the primitive time measurements of Table 6.3. The "System Time Predicted by Primitives" for these tests have been increased by 30 or 45 milliseconds. Projected times always assume the use of Perq T2 disks.

discarded. The column labeled "Measured Elapsed Time" in Table 6.7 shows the average elapsed time for each benchmark. The column labeled "Measured TABS Process Time" reports the sum of average measured CPU time of the TABS Communication, Recovery, and Transaction Manager processes on all nodes in the test.

Rather than reiterating numbers in the tables, we present more details about the performance of the system instead. We account for the latency of a local, single operation, nonpaging read transaction. We also show where the additional time is spent in a single node, nonpaging write transaction. Finally, we show how to reconcile "System Time Predicted by Primitives," "Measured TABS Process Time," and "Measured Elapsed Time" for two-node transactions. This discussion uses execution time data for individual processes, which are not included in Table 6.7.

The measured elapsed time for processing a transaction that performs a single node, nonpaging read operation is 110 msec. This is 57 msec greater than predicted by primitive operations alone. Of this additional time, 41 msec is accounted for by TABS system processes: 36 msec in the Transaction Manager and 5 msec in the Recovery Manager. (TABS system process times remain constant in all local read-only transactions.) By a complex deduction, we determined that the application and data server require about 3 msec and 4 msec, respectively, to initiate and commit a transaction. Our analysis does not account for the remaining 9 msec.

The difference in measured times between the simplest read and simplest update transactions is 137 msec, of which 78 msec is the time for the Stable Storage Write. The data server uses an additional 5 msec to do a write, rather than a read. This time is used to format and send log data to the Recovery Manager. The Recovery Manager uses an extra 10 msec to spool this data to the log. The more complex commit protocol for an update-transaction requires an additional 8 msec in the Recovery Manager, 24 msec in the Transaction Manager, and 4 msec in the data server. Together, these times with the additional message primitives executed (see Tables 6.5 and 6.6) sum to 155 msec. This is 18 msec more than measured, which may be partially due to double counting some Recovery Manager time included in the Stable Storage Write time.

Two-node distributed transactions involve little parallel execution, so we might expect "System Time Predicted by Primitives" plus "Measured TABS Process Time" to equal "Measured Elapsed Time." This is not true, however, because communication time is counted in both the "Measured TABS Process Time" and the "System Time Predicted by Primitives." If the Communication Manager time were subtracted, the sum of the remaining TABS Process time and Predicted times is within 4% of elapsed time for read transactions and within 10% for write transactions. Three-node transactions involve considerable parallel processing during commit, so this simple reconciliation is not applicable.

5.3. Improving TABS Performance

In this section, we use the primitive operation analysis to project the performance of different implementations of TABS. Two projections are given here. The first projection is based on the measured times of primitive operations reported above, but assumes feasible architectural and implementation changes to TABS. The second projection is based on the first, but also assumes new primitive operation times, which are described and justified below. In neither case are we counting on a faster processor or better compiler; thus, projected times are higher than measured TABS Process Time except for benchmarks having parallelism or high communication costs.

For the first projection, labeled "Improved TABS Architecture" in Table 6.7, we assume that the Recovery Manager and Transaction Manager processes are merged with the Accent kernel. This eliminates message passing between these three components, and also allows one prepare message sent from a data server to the modified kernel to perform the function of two messages in the current implementation. We have previous experience with the integration of functions implemented by separate processes into the kernel and believe that this is a simple process. Additionally, we assume optimized commit algorithms that eliminate unnecessary messages and permit some of the processing for commit of distributed write transactions to occur in parallel with the execution of succeeding transactions. The projections based on these changes are derived by reducing the measured elapsed times by the times for primitive operations that would not be performed. Remote write transactions show the biggest performance increase, because of the elimination of considerable commit processing from the critical execution path of the transaction.

The second performance projection, labeled "New Primitive Times" in Table 6.7 is derived from the "Improved TABS Architecture" projections by setting the primitive operation times to those given in Table 6.8. The costs of these new primitives are based on our estimates of the applicability to the Perq/Accent environment of published techniques for efficient implementation of these primitives. Accent random I/O times already approach the performance of the disk, so we do not assume any improvement here, though we hypothesize a small improvement in sequential read time.

Intraprocessor message times have been reported as low as 0.77 msec on hardware that is (roughly) similar in performance to the Perq.[9] However, Accent processes have completely separate virtual address spaces, and context switching times are greater for Accent than for other operating systems, and so we chose times of 1.0 and 1.25 msec for our projections. The implementation of pointer messages is fairly complex and we therefore assume only small improvement. Careful implementation or the use of lazy evaluation should substantially eliminate the high costs of coroutine allocation in the Data Server Call primitive.

Table 6.8. Achievable primitive operation times (in milliseconds).

Primitive	Average Time
Data Server Call	2.5
Inter-Node Data Server Call	9.0
Datagram	2.0
Small Contiguous Message	1.0
Large Contiguous Message	1.25
Pointer Message	15.0
Random Access Paged I/O	32.0
Sequential Read	10.0
Stable Storage Write	32.0

This table shows primitive times achievable by tuning software and adding disks.

Considerable work has been devoted to efficient inter-processor message passing.[6,54] We feel that times of 9 msec for remote data server calls, and 2 msec for datagram messages allow reasonable overheads, compared with times reported for similar hardware.[44]

If the existence of small (disk track size) quantities of zero latency stable storage (e.g. battery backup CMOS primary memory) and dedicated logging disks are assumed, then log writing costs could approach main memory copy costs. However, to lend more credence to our projections we estimate that log writing can be performed for the same cost as paged disk writes. This estimate assumes dedicated logging disks and off-line archival of the log.

With these improvements, the projected performance of local transactions ranges from 67 msec for nonpaging, read-only transactions to 249 msec for paging write transactions. The performance of multinode benchmark transactions ranges from 228 msec to 539 msec. Of course, these numbers could be reduced further by improving the code in the TABS system components and by using a faster CPU. TABS system process times dominate the costs in these projections, and their execution time would decrease on a faster CPU.

6. RELATIONSHIP TO R* AND ARGUS[35,37,40,63]

TABS is similar in many ways to R* and Argus. R* is a distributed database management system, developed at IBM San Jose Research, that supports transactions on relational database servers. Argus is a programming language, developed at the MIT Laboratory for Computer Science, that supports transactions and user-defined types on which they can operate.

The transaction facility of R* is implemented by a combination of the underlying operating system, CICS,[27] and a component called TM*. This logically unified facility permits servers to register themselves and their operations when they are ready to receive requests, and performs routing of operation requests to local servers. The facility also issues transaction identifiers, oversees transaction commitment and aborting, and does deadlock detection.

Servers in R* have two types of interfaces. The first type includes operations specific to a server. The second type includes operations required for transaction management, deadlock detection/resolution, and remote access by other servers. In R*, requests are never directly issued to remote servers. Instead, they are passed to local servers, which then interact with remote ones.

Broadly, TABS is very similar to R* in that both systems make available transportation facilities for applications and servers. However, they differ in many ways. For example, TABS, its applications, and its servers are implemented as a collection of processes that communicate via messages, rather than via the protected procedure calls, which R* uses. Another major difference is that remote servers in TABS can be directly invoked in a transparent way. Also, TABS servers retain little context between operations and use a common log and recovery algorithms provided by the system; servers in R* must utilize the same context for each operation within a transaction, and each server must provide for its own recovery. Some of these differences are relatively minor, but some affect performance or usability. For example, the common log and transparent inter-node communication provide efficiency and flexibility respectively; but, on the other hand, protected procedure calls on the IBM 370 are very fast.

Internally, Argus contains many facilities that are analogous to those of TABS and R*, but it has the more ambitious goal of making those facilities very easy to use. Some objects can be implemented without the type implementor having to consider synchronization or recovery issues. However, types needing highly concurrent access require explicit attention paid to synchronization and recovery. For these high concurrency types, synchronization and recovery are done with the aid of a specialized object, called a *mutex*, rather than via explicit locking and logging.

Argus is certainly easier to use than TABS for constructing simple objects. However, it is difficult to compare the amount of work needed to use mutex objects versus that of explicitly setting locks and writing log records. We have not considered the performance differences between the approaches.

7. CONCLUSIONS

Our use of TABS has convinced us that its facilities for supporting transactions and data servers are useful for both local and distributed abstractions. Specialized distributed database systems, file systems, mail systems, spoolers, editors, etc. could be based on the implementation techniques that our existing servers use. In our view, the use of location-transparent operation invocation, locking within data servers, write-ahead logging with a common log, and the implementation of permanent objects in virtual memory were good design choices. We must give due credit to the Accent kernel, which implements many of the facilities that TABS uses or provides, and which has proven invaluable for supporting distributed computation.

Because TABS uses nearly the minimum number of expensive primitive operations such as disk I/O's, log writes, inter-node messages, and datagrams, TABS performance is sufficient for many applications in an interactive workstation environment. Transactions considerably more complex than the benchmarks of Section 5 take less than a few seconds of elapsed time. For example, our analysis indicates that about two seconds are required for a local transaction that invokes five operations, each of which updates two pages that are not in memory. The same transaction would require about one-half second if the data were in main memory. If the operations were performed on one or more remote nodes, these transactions would take only about one second longer.

Certainly, TABS can be substantially improved. To simplify programming simple data servers, the calls to TABS synchronization and recovery facilities should be hidden in a language run-time system, such as that of Argus. For more complex servers that need greater flexibility, the server library should provide a better set of primitives, including some for operation logging and type-specific locking. Thought should also be given to providing better debugging support for data servers.

Functionally, TABS should be extended to permit the recovery of a single server without the recovery of the entire node. In addition, TABS should use stable storage for the log and support media recovery. Finally, TABS should probably have a more complete subtransaction model, particularly for the implementation of replicated objects.

In its implementation, TABS loses performance because of the division of the Recovery Manager, Transaction Manager, and Accent into separate processes. The TABS coroutine, logging, and internode communication facilities need reimplementation or tuning. If these changes were made and TABS used more modern hardware, one would expect transaction times that are four to ten times faster than the currently measured ones.

We are continuing to enhance the system and study its use. For example, we plan to empirically compare the relative merits of value and operation logging. We are also continuing to investigate architectures and algorithms that will provide increased transaction throughput. In addition, we would like to develop a performance methodology for measuring and predicting throughput. Though much work remains, our experiences to date have convinced us that general purpose distributed transaction facilities are feasible and useful for a wide variety of systems.

ACKNOWLEDGMENTS

Jacob Butcher, Charles Fineman, Sherri Menees, and Peter Schwarz made major design and programming efforts; their work was essential to the underlying TABS prototype and the data servers that use it. Maxwell Berenson constructed the distributed performance monitor that permitted us to obtain accurate performance measurements of distributed transactions. Sherri Menees provided editorial assistance for this chapter, and Maurice Herlihy, David Nichols, and Rick Rashid provided helpful comments.

REFERENCES

1. Allchin, J. E. and M. S. McKendry, Synchronization and recovery of actions, in *Proc. 2nd Annual Symp. on Principles of Distributed Computing*, Montreal, Canada, ACM, pp. 31–44, 1983.
2. Anonymous, A measure of transaction processing power, *Datamation*, vol. 31, Apr. 1985. Also available as Tech. Rep. TR 85.2, Tandem Corporation, Cupertino, CA, Jan. 1985.
3. Banatre, J. P., M. Banatre, and F. Ployette, Construction of a distributed system supporting atomic transactions, in *Proc. 3rd Symp. on Reliability in Distributed Software and Database Systems*, Clearwater Beach, FL, IEEE, Oct. 1983.

4. Bernstein, Philip A. and Nathan Goodman, Concurrency control in distributed database systems, *ACM Comput. Surveys*, vol. 13, pp. 185–221, June 1981.
5. Birman, K. P., D. Skeen, A. El Abbadai, W. C. Dietrich, and T. Raeuchle, *Isis: An Environment for Constructing Fault-Tolerant Distributed Systems*, Tech. Rep. 83-552, Cornell University, Ithaca, NY, 1983.
6. Birrell, Andrew D. and Bruce J. Nelson, Implementing remote procedure calls, *ACM Trans. Computer Syst.*, vol. 2, pp. 39–59, Feb. 1984.
7. Bloch, Joshua J., Dean S. Daniels, and Alfred Z. Spector, *A Weighted Voting Algorithm for Replicated Directories*, Tech. Rep. CMU-CS-86-132, Carnegie-Mellon University, Pittsburgh, PA, June 1986.
8. Cheriton, David R., The V kernel: A software base for distributed systems, *IEEE Software*, vol. 1, pp. 186–213, Apr. 1984.
9. Cheriton, David R., An experiment using registers for fast message-based interprocess communication, *Operating Syst. Rev.*, vol. 18, pp. 12–20, Oct. 1984.
10. Dahl, O. J. and C. A. R. Hoare, Hierarchical program structures, in *A.P.I.C. Studies in Data Processing, vol. 8: Structured Programming*, C. A. R. Hoare, ed. London and New York: Academic Press, 1972, pp. 175–220.
11. Daniels, Dean S., *Query Compilation in a Distributed Database System* (Master's thesis), Massachusetts Institute of Technology, Cambridge, MA, 1982.
12. Daniels, Dean S. and Alfred Z. Spector, An algorithm for replicated directories, in *Proc. 2nd Annual Symp. on Principles of Distributed Computing*, Montreal, Canada, ACM, pp. 104–113, Aug. 1983.
13. Date, C. J., *The System Programming Series: An Introduction to Database Systems*, vol. 2, Reading, MA: Addison-Wesley, 1983.
14. Department of Defense, *Reference Manual for the Ada Programming Language, July 1982 edition*, Department of Defense, Ada Joint Program Office, Washington, DC, 1982.
15. Diel, Hans, Gerald Kreissig, Norbet Lenz, Michael Scheible, and Bernd Schoener, Data management facilities of an operating system kernel, in *Sigmod '84*, pp. 58–69, June, 1984.
16. Dwork, Cynthia and Dale Skeen, The inherent cost of nonblocking commitment, in *Proc. Annual Symp. on Principles of Distributed Computing*, Montreal, Canada, ACM, pp. 1–11, Aug. 1983.
17. Eppinger, Jeffrey L. and Alfred Z. Spector, *Virtual Memory Management for Recoverable Objects in the TABS Prototype*, Tech. Rep. CMU-CS-85-163, Carnegie-Mellon University, Pittsburgh, PA, Oct. 1985.
18. Eswaran, K. P., James N. Gray, Raymond A. Lorie, and Irving L. Traiger, The notions of consistency and predicate locks in a database system. *CACM*, vol. 19, pp. 624–633, Nov. 1976.
19. Fabry, R. S., Capability-based addressing. *CACM*, vol. 17, pp. 403–411, July 1974.
20. Fitzgerald, Robert P. and Richard F. Rashid, The integration of virtual memory management and interprocess communication in Accent. *ACM Trans. Computer Syst.*, vol. 4, May 1986. Also *Proc. 10th Symp. on Operating System Principles*, Orcas Island, WA, Dec. 1985.
21. Gifford, David K., Weighted voting for replicated data, in *Proc. 7th Symp. on Operating System Principles*, Pacific Grove, CA, ACM, pp. 150–162, Dec. 1979.
22. Gray, James N., Notes on database operating systems, in *Lecture Notes in Computer Science, vol. 60: Operating Systems—An Advanced Course*, R. Bayer, R. M. Graham, and G. Seegmuller, eds., Berlin: Springer-Verlag, 1978, pp. 393–481. Also available as Tech. Rep. RJ2188, IBM Res. Lab., San Jose, CA 1978.
23. Gray, James N., *A Transaction Model*, Tech. Rep. RJ2895, IBM Res. Lab., San Jose, CA, Aug. 1980.
24. Gray, James N., *et al.*, The recovery manager of the system R database manager, *ACM Comput. Surveys*, vol. 13, pp. 223–242, June 1981.

25. Haerder, Theo and Andreas Reuter, Principles of transaction-oriented database recovery, *ACM Comput. Surveys*, vol. 15, pp. 287–318, Dec. 1983.
26. Herlihy, Maurice P., *General Quorum Consensus: A Replication Method for Abstract Data Types*, Tech. Rep. CMU-CS-84-164, Carnegie-Mellon University, Pittsburgh, PA, Dec. 1984.
27. IBM Corporation, *Customer Information Control System/Virtual Storage*, *Introduction to Program Logic* SC33-0067-1 edition, IBM Corporation, 1978.
28. Jensen, E. D. and N. Pleszkoch, ArchOS: A physically dispersed operating system, *IEEE Distributed Processing Technical Committee Newsletter*, June, 1984.
29. Jones, Michael B., Richard F. Rashid, and Mary R. Thompson, Matchmaker: An interface specification language for distributed processing, in *Proc. 12th Annual Symp. on Principles of Programming Languages*, New Orleans, LA, ACM, pp. 225–235, Jan. 1985.
30. Joy, William, Eric Cooper, Robert Fabry, Samuel Leffler, Kirk McKusick, and David Mosher, *4.2 BSD System Interface Overview*. Tech. Rep. CSRG TR/5, University of California at Berkeley, July, 1983.
31. Korth, Henry F., Locking primitives in a database system. *JACM*, vol. 30, pp. 55–79, Jan. 1983.
32. Lampson, Butler W., Atomic transactions, in *Lecture Notes in Computer Science*, *vol. 105: Distributed Systems—Architecture and Implementation: An Advanced Course*, G. Goos and J. Hartmanis, eds., Berlin: Springer-Verlag, 1981, pp. 246–265.
33. Lansky, Amy L., *Pasmac—A Macro Processor for Pascal*, Tech. Rep. CSL-TN-174, Stanford University Computer Systems Laboratory, Apr. 1980.
34. Lindsay, Bruce G., *et al.*, *Notes on Distributed Databases*, Tech. Rep. RJ2571, IBM Res. Lab., San Jose, CA, July, 1979. Also appears in *Distributed Databases*, Droffen and Poole eds., Cambridge University Press, 1980.
35. Lindsay, Bruce G., Laura M. Haas, C. Mohan, Paul F. Wilms, and Robert A. Yost, Computation and communication in R*: A distributed database manager, *ACM Trans. Computer Syst.*, vol. 2, pp. 24–38, Feb. 1984.
36. Liskov, Barbara, On linguistic support for distributed programs, *IEEE Trans. Software Eng.*, vol. SE-8, pp. 203–210, May 1982.
37. Liskov, Barbara, *Overview of the Argus Language and System*, Programming Methodology Group Memo 40, MIT Lab. for Comput. Sci., Feb. 1984.
38. Liskov, Barbara and Maurice Herlihy, Issues in process and communication structure for distributed programs, in *Proc. 3rd Symp. on Reliability in Distributed Software and Database Systems*, Tampa, FL, Oct. 1983.
39. Liskov, Barbara and Robert Scheifler, Guardians and actions: Linguistic support for robust, distributed programs, in *Proc. 9th Annual Symp. on the Principles of Programming Languages*, ACM, pp. 7–19, Jan. 1982.
40. Liskov, B., M. Herlihy, P. Johnson, G. Leavent, R. Scheifler, and W. Weihl, *Preliminary Argus Reference Manual*, Programming Methodology Group Memo 39, MIT Lab. for Comput. Sci., Oct. 1983.
41. Lomet, David B., Process structuring, synchronization, and recovery using atomic actions, *ACM SIGPLAN Notices*, vol. 12, March, 1977.
42. Lorie, Raymond A., Physical integrity in a large segmented database. *ACM Trans. Database Syst.*, vol. 2, pp. 91–104, March 1977.
43. Moss, J. Eliot B., *Nested Transactions: An Approach to Reliable Distributed Computing* (Ph.D. diss.), Massachusetts Institute of Technology, Cambridge, MA, 1981.
44. Nelson, Bruce Jay, *Remote Procedure Call* (Ph.D. diss.), Carnegie-Mellon University, Pittsburgh, PA, 1981. Available as Tech. Rep. CMU-CS-81-119a, Carnegie-Mellon University.
45. Obermarck, Ron, Distributed deadlock detection algorithm, *ACM Trans. Database Syst.*, vol. 7, pp. 187–208, June 1982.

46. Paxton, William H., A client-based transaction system to maintain data integrity, in *Proc. 7th Symp. on Operating System Principles*, ACM, pp. 18–23, Dec. 1979.
47. Perq Systems Corporation, *Perq System Overview*, March 1984 edition, Perq Systems Corp., Pittsburgh, PA, 1984.
48. Rashid, Richard and George Robertson. Accent: A communication oriented network operating system kernel, in *Proc. 8th Symp. on Operating System Principles*, ACM, pp. 64–75, Dec. 1981.
49. Reed, David P., *Naming and Synchronization in a Decentralized Computer System* (Ph.D. diss.), Massachusetts Institute of Technology, Cambridge, MA, 1978.
50. Reuter, Andreas, Performance analysis of recovery techniques, *ACM Trans. Database Syst.*, vol. 9, pp. 526–559, Dec. 1984.
51. Saltzer, Jerome H., Protection and the control of information in multics, *CACM*, vol. 17, July 1974.
52. Schwarz, Peter M., *Transactions on Typed Objects* (Ph.D. diss.), Carnegie-Mellon University, Pittsburgh, PA, Dec. 1984. Available as Tech. Rep. CMU-CS-84-166, Carnegie-Mellon University.
53. Schwarz, Peter M. and Alfred Z. Spector, Synchronized shared abstract types, *ACM Trans. Computer Syst.*, vol. 2, pp. 223–250, Aug. 1984. Also available as Tech. Rep. CMU-CS-83-163, Carnegie-Mellon University, Pittsburgh, PA, Nov. 1983.
54. Spector, Alfred Z., Performing remote operations efficiently on a local computer network, *CACM*, vol. 25, pp. 246–260, Apr. 1982.
55. Spector, Alfred Z. and Dean S. Daniels, *Performance Evaluation of Distributed Transaction Facilities*, presented at the Workshop on High Performance Transaction Processing, Asilomar, Sept. 1985.
56. Spector, Alfred Z. and Peter M. Schwarz, Transactions: A construct for reliable distributed computing, *Operating Syst. Rev.*, vol. 17, pp. 18–35, Apr. 1983. Also available as Tech. Rep. CMU-CS-82-143, Carnegie-Mellon University, Pittsburgh, PA, Jan. 1983.
57. Spector, Alfred Z., Jacob Butcher, Dean S. Daniels, Daniel J. Duchamp, Jeffrey L. Eppinger, Charles E. Fineman, Abdelsalam Heddaya, and Peter M. Schwarz, Support for distributed transactions in the TABS prototype. *IEEE Trans. Software Eng.*, vol. SE-11, pp. 520–530, June 1985. Also available in *Proc. 4th Symp. on Reliability in Distributed Software and Database Systems*, Silver Springs, MD, IEEE, Oct. 1984 and as Tech. Rep. CMU-CS-84-132, Carnegie-Mellon University, Pittsburgh, PA, July 1984.
58. Stonebraker, Michael, Virtual memory transaction management. *Operating Syst. Rev.*, vol. 18, pp. 8–16, Apr. 1984.
59. Tandem Computers, Inc., *ENCOMPASS Distributed Data Management System*, Tandem Computers, Inc., Cupertino, CA, 1982.
60. Traiger, Irving L., *Virtual Memory Management for Database Systems*. Tech. Rep. RJ3489, IBM Res. Lab., San Jose, CA, May 1982.
61. Watson, R. W., Distributed system architecture model, in *Lecture Notes in Computer Science, vol. 105: Distributed Systems—Architecture and Implementation: An Advanced Course*, B. W. Lampson, ed., Springer-Verlag, 1981, pp. 10–43.
62. Weihl, W. and B. Liskov, Specification and implementation of resilient, atomic data types, in *Sympos. on Programming Language Issues in Software Systems*, San Francisco, CA, June 1983.
63. Williams, R., *et al.*, *R*: An Overview of the Architecture*, IBM Res. Rep. RJ3325, IBM Res. Lab., San Jose, CA, Dec. 1981.
64. Wulf, W. A., E. Cohen, W. Corwin, A. Jones, R. Levin, C. Pierson, and F. Pollack, HYDRA: The kernel of a multiprocessor operating system. *CACM*, vol. 17. pp. 337–345, June 1974.

7. Reliability Aspects of Remote Procedure Calls

S. K. SHRIVASTAVA

and

F. PANZIERI

ABSTRACT

A number of reliability issues are involved that must be resolved during the design and implementation of a remote procedure call mechanism. An overview of these issues together with various ways of dealing with them are discussed. In particular, we discuss (i) the functionality of the interprocess communications facility over which the mechanism is to be constructed; (ii) protocol design considerations; (iii) call semantics and exception handling; (iv) the problem of orphans; and (v) robust atomic actions. Finally, a working example of a remote procedure call mechanism is presented.

1. INTRODUCTION

A very convenient means of arranging communication between client and server processes in a distributed system is to make use of remote procedure calls (RPC's), enabling clients to invoke services offered by remote servers and obtain appropriate results. Conceptually, a very simple client-server protocol is needed to implement an RPC mechanism: the client sends its service request as a **call** message to the server, and waits for a reply; on the other hand, the server receives the **call** message, performs the service, and sends the result as a **reply** message to the client. Desite the apparent simplicity of such a protocol, a number of reliability issues are involved that require careful analysis during the design phase. In this chapter, we review these reliability issues and discuss how they can be dealt with. We also present a case study that illustrates many of our ideas. We begin by presenting an overview of some of the issues in RPC design.

2. RELIABILITY ISSUES

An adequate RPC mechanism should cope effectively with any unreliabilities of the underlying message facility and also with problems arising out of client or server node crashes. Figure 7.1 depicts message exchanges for a call between a client and a server.

We assume a protocol whereby a client can re-send its call request whenever a loss of message is suspected (alternatively, or in addition, the send primitive itself could contain a message retransmission facility). As a result, it is possible that a server can occasionally receive multiple call messages for a single invocation by a client, thereby causing—unless preventive measures are employed—superfluous and undersirable executions (referred to as *orphan* executions).

The above problem of orphans can be avoided altogether if the underlying message system offers a service such that a message is delivered reliably without duplication. Then there is no need to include message retries in the RPC protocol. We therefore ask the question: what should the functionality of the underlying message system be? The answer to this question is presented in Section 3.

Orphans can occur due to node crashes as well. For example, assume that a client crashes in the middle of a call (see Fig. 7.2) and resumes that call after recovery by resending the call. If the work performed by a server is idempotent (i.e., multiple executions are equivalent to a single one), then the orphans de-

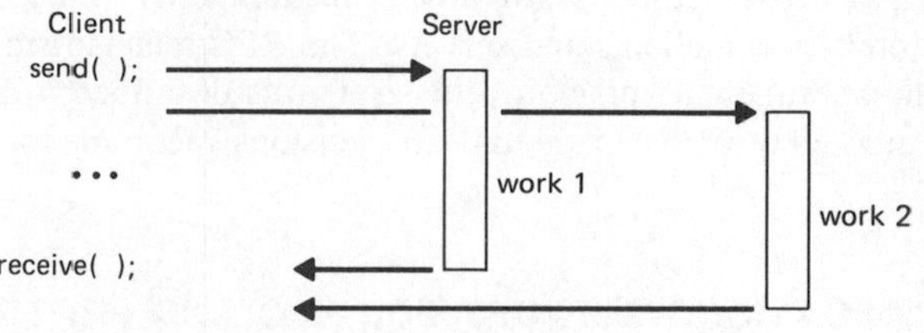

Fig. 7.1. Message orphan.

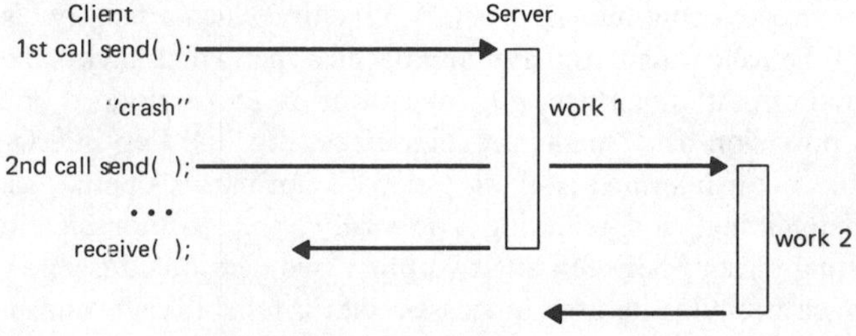

Fig. 7.2. Crash orphan.

picted in Figs. 7.1 and 7.2 need not pose any semantic problems. This raises the possibility of choosing RPC semantics that permits one or more executions per call. We will discuss orphans and RPC semantics issues in Sections 4 and 5, respectively.

Network protocols typically employ time-out mechanisms to prevent indefinite (or long) waiting by a process expecting a reply. Suppose that a server crashes in the middle of a call and does not resume that call after recovery, in which case the client will never receive a reply. If the client has a timer set, then a time-out exception will eventually be signaled. In Section 6, we discuss exception handling aspects of remote procedure calls. It is interesting to note here that, in general, a time-out exception could indicate either of the following four possibilities: (a) the server crashed during the call; or (b) the server did not receive the request; or (c) the server's reply did not reach the client; or (d) the server is still performing the work (so the time-out interval was not long enough). If the client simply retries the call, then we again have the possibility of orphans. Such orphans-related issues are also discussed in Section 6.

A particularly vexing reliability problem is to do with guaranteeing clean termination of user programs in the presence of failures such as node crashes. It is now well known that robust atomic actions (atomic transactions) provide a suitable framework for achieving this objective.[7] In Section 7 we shall discuss how remote procedure calls integrate with such actions.

At Newcastle, we have designed and constructed a distributed UNIX* system over a local area network that uses remote procedure calls as the only means of communication between clients and servers. The RPC mechanism implemented to support an experimental version of this system is described in Section 8 as a case study embodying many of the design decisions recommended in previous sections.

3. COMMUNICATIONS SUPPORT FOR RPC AND PROTOCOL DESIGN ISSUES

The implementation of RPC's requires that the underlying level provide some kind of interprocess communications (IPC) facility. Such a facility can be based on either of the following two major approaches: that which favors the provision of a "virtual circuit" interface, e.g. that of an X.25 network,[13] or that which favors the provision of a "datagram" interface, e.g. the Pup interface.[2]

A virtual circuit interface is characterized by primitive operations for establishing, maintaining, and releasing a logically direct communication channel (i.e., a virtual circuit) between any two processes distributed over a network.[20] This interface provides its user processes with a reliable data transport service

*UNIX is a trademark of Bell Laboratories.

which "guarantees" delivery of data (messages) exchanged between these processes. The software supporting a virtual circuit interface generally implements features such as end-to-end acknowledgements, flow control, and detection and recovery from various errors which may occur over an established virtual circuit; in addition, this software guarantees that messages are kept in sequence in that they are delivered in the same order as they were sent.

A datagram interface, instead, provides its user processes with primitive operations for transmitting and receiving individually addressed messages of variable size, up to some fixed maximum. Processes using the datagram interface can transmit and receive messages at network addresses maintained by that interface. Each message is encapsulated as a distinct data object, termed a datagram, by the software implementing the datagram interface. A datagram consists, in general, of a header containing some control and addressing information used by the datagram software itself (e.g., **start of datagram,** and the **destination** and **source** addresses), the user message, and a trailer (e.g. a checksum field). Each datagram is transmitted and received independently of other datagrams; that is to say, the datagram software does not guarantee sequencing and ordered delivery of distinct datagrams. Hence, processes using a datagram interface may receive messages not in the same order as they were sent. Flow control and end-to-end acknowledgements are also not implemented by the datagram software and, in general, the software does not provide the facility of guaranteed delivery of datagrams (in a well-designed system, however, datagrams are transported with a reasonably high probability of success).

At a superficial level, it may appear reasonable to base an implementation of RPC over a virtual circuit based interface, since a reliable IPC facility would obviously simplify RPC protocol implementation. However, it is necessary to point out that the implementation of virtual circuits requires that a considerable amount of state information be maintained at the end points of each established virtual circuit; in addition, a (potentially large) number of messages may have to be exchanged both to establish a virtual circuit and to implement flow control and end-to-end acknowledgements over it.[18] The maintenance of state information and the message exchanges needed to implement flow control and end-to-end acknowledgements introduce overheads, not to mention complexity, in the software supporting the virtual circuit interface. These overheads may well result in a considerable reduction of the communication bandwidth available on the network; this bandwidth may be utilized more effectively by the application software instead.

In view of the above observations, let us investigate whether the functionality offered by a simple datagram service could be adequate (note that the provision of such an interface generally entails considerably less reduction in communications bandwidth than the previous case). We note that, as far as a client is concerned, the acknowledgement that is really required is not that its call message has been delivered but that the requested service has been performed. This is implicit in the reply message from the server. Further, it is relatively easy to cope with the occasional loss of messages by retries. We thus see that datagrams certainly provide an attractive alternative to virtual circuits.

Our experience with RPC's implemented over a local area network (Cambridge Ring)[21] bears out this fact.[12] On a local area network, it is relatively easy to construct a datagram service such that datagrams are sent with a high probability of success. Further, datagrams on most local area networks are delivered in the order sent. These factors simplify the implementation of RPC's.

The choice over a wide area network (where the just-mentioned properties need not hold true) is not so clear. If RPC's are used for transmitting small amounts of data (a few hundred bytes) then datagrams still provide a better alternative.[8] However, if a large amount of data is to be transferred frequently, then the facility offered by a virtual circuit would typically be desired.

We conclude this section by briefly discussing some RPC protocol design aspects, considering first the datagram-based approach. When messages are confined to a local network, the protocol can be very simple indeed: the client sends its call request with a sequence number and waits for a reply (any exceptions during the send are typically dealt with by retransmission with the same sequence number); the server, on the other hand, receives a call request (discarding further requests with the same sequence number), performs the work, sends the result (i.e., a reply message) and forgets about the call. The reply message is sent with the same sequence number as the call message, so a client is in a position to accept the right message. The RPC implementation described in Section 8 uses this protocol. A further refinement is required to effectively cope with the following situation: the reply message is lost, therefore the client times out and then retries the call. If the server maintains the state information regarding the most recent executions for its clients then it can simply resend the appropriate reply message (and thereby avoiding an orphan execution). When should a server discard state information maintained for a call? Two approaches are possible: (i) as soon as the server receives a new call from the client, or (ii) an explicit third message is introduced in the protocol whereby the client sends an acknowledgement message to the server.

If datagrams travel over a wide area network or an internet (thus the probability of lost messages is higher than in the previous case), then a more sophisticated version than the two-message protocol will probably be required at the outset. When datagrams travel less reliably, it is appropriate to introduce message acknowledgements to eliminate the situation that would occur when a client waits for results even though the server did not receive the request. This will result in a four-message protocol (standard optimization techniques can be employed whereby acknowledgements can piggyback on call and reply messages).

The last issue we will consider regarding a datagram-based RPC implementation has to do with fragmentation and reassembly of data. If the size of data to be sent is larger than the maximum datagram size, then the RPC protocol should contain facilities for fragmenting the data into datagrams, and similarly for reassembling the arriving datagrams into meaningful data. Such facilities are relatively easy to implement on a typical local area network. However, on a wide area network or on an internet, the possibility of out-of-order arrival of datagrams may impose some additional complexity in the implementation. In a well-engineered system, the maximum allowable size of a datagram should be chosen such that the probability of fragmentation and reassembly is kept to a minimum, so that some very simple (and perhaps not very efficient) strategy can be employed without much performance penalty.

Lastly, we consider some protocol issues for virtual circuit based RPC's. A simple approach would consist of opening a connection between the client and the server, so that call and reply messages can be transported, and then closing the connection. The protocol need not be concerned about the problems of lost messages and those of fragmentation and reassembly—those problems being the responsibility of the underlying virtual circuit protocol. In order to minimize the overheads of opening and closing connections, an optimization is certainly possible whereby a connection is kept opened over a sequence of calls. The remote procedure call protocol **Courier**[22] is an example of a virtual circuit based implementation.

4. ORPHANS

Let us consider a simple execution model for remote calls: for every request received, a server creates a worker process that performs the work, sends the reply, and then the worker destroys itself. This may be regarded as a *maximally concurrent* model, in that most implementations will either follow the execution strategy of the model or will be *less concurrent* versions of it (for example, an implementation could involve a server serially executing incoming requests). In terms of our model, we see that a single call can give rise to computations that interfere with each other (in Fig. 7.1, the two processes executing work 1 and work 2 could interfere). Such interference is clearly undesirable, and what we require is that computations invoked by remote calls at a server be free from interference (i.e., be logically serializable.[1]) Consider now the execution of a single sequential program containing RPCs; it has been shown elsewhere[16] that it is necessary and sufficient for a server to follow the two implementation rules stated below:

IR1: Once the execution of a call starts, requests belonging to other calls must not be honored and, in particular, requests belonging to prior calls must never be scheduled (i.e., all the orphans of prior calls must precede this call);

IR2: Computations performed by worker processes for a single call must not interfere with each other.

Note that we admit the possibility of workers themselves making remote calls. These two conditions are easier to meet in a serial implementation mentioned earlier (in particular, no special measures are necessary to meet IR2).

5. RPC SEMANTICS

The presence of orphans in a computation can cause semantic consistency problems. For example, suppose the work requested by a client involves the server making an increment operation, then clearly more than one execution would be inconsistent. On the other hand, more than one execution can be tolerated if the requested operation has the idempotency property. In view of this, we identify two types of semantics for RPC's,[11] namely *at least once* and *exactly once* (a finer classification is presented in reference 17). We assume that a call made by a client can terminate in one of the following three possible ways: (i) normal termination (the client process receives a reply; this may include an exceptional response from the server); (ii) abnormal termination (a time-out exception is raised); and (iii) crashed termination (client crashes after making a call but before receiving reply or time-out exceptions; note that, for the sake of simplicity, we are assuming that a call does not survive client crashes).

A few words regarding abnormal termination are in order. For conventional procedure calls, an abnormal (or exceptional) termination implies that the called module has provided an exceptional service.[4] For a remote call, however, it is helpful to distinguish between the case that represents *no* response from the server (case (ii)) and those that represent some response from the server (case (i)), since it is the former situation that raises the possibility of orphans.

5.1. *At Least Once* Semantics

As the name suggests, a normally terminated call implies that one or more executions have taken place. Further, abnormal or crashed termination implies zero, one, or more executions at the server. This semantics may be viewed as the *least demanding*, since normal calls are supposed to tolerate orphans. Many distributed systems containing file servers have opted for this semantics,[10] in view of the fact that file server operations—with some care and imposing certain restrictions—can be made idempotent. In subsequent discussions, we will assume the idempotency property for such calls.

5.2. *Exactly Once* Semantics

A normally terminated call results in one and only one execution at a server. if a call gives rise to nested calls, then they must also be *exactly once* calls. Thus, a normally terminated call implies that no orphan executions have taken place (for nested calls, this must hold for every call). An abnormal or crashed termination implies zero or one execution at the server.

In either of the above two cases, orphans are permitted when calls do not terminate normally. We have taken the view that it is the responsibility of exception handlers and crash recovery procedures of a node to cope with orphans in an application-dependent manner (see the next Section). On the other hand, if robust atomic actions are employed for the construction of user applications, then recovery measures of such actions can be exploited as discussed in Section 7.

6. EXCEPTION HANDLING AND ORPHAN TREATMENT

In this section, we will discuss ways of meeting requirements IR1 and IR2, bearing in mind any additional requirements posed by a particular call semantics.[16] We will assume, for this discussion, the execution model introduced in Section 4. Orphans can be *killed*, *prevented*, *or tolerated*; we will examine the relevance of these measures for the two types of call semantics.

6.1. *At Least Once* Calls

First, we will investigate any problems due to orphans for the three termination cases of remote calls of the *at least once* variety. Let us consider the simple case whereby the work performed by a server is local and atomic (e.g., the server performs atomic disk page read and write operations). In such a case, requirement IR2 is met implicitly and it is only necessary to make sure that executions pertaining to different calls do not interleave (requirement IR1). A rather ingenious way of ensuring this is to design a protocol in which the client accepts results from the *lastest* execution (the 'last of many' semantics.[11]) Such an RPC protocol will ensure that normally terminated calls do not leave outstanding worker processes (thus, orphans can be tolerated).

Next consider the situation depicted in the program fragment below (where *t* indicates a time-out exception, and a pair of angular brackets encloses an exception handler):

```
rpc(. . .) ⟨ t: retry(n) ⟨ t: clean_up ⟩ ⟩;
```

The above program has the provision for retrying the remote call up to *n* times (where $n > 0$). What if all these attempts still result in a time-out exception? Ideally, we would like some *clean_up* operation that essentially undoes any side effects produced by this call.[4] The least that is required is to make sure that any orphan executions still in progress will not interleave with executions due to subsequent calls. If the underlying message system is such that the order in which messages are sent does not resemble the received order, then a safe way of meeting this requirement is for *clean_up* to include measures for terminating any orphans in existence (orphan killing techniques will be discussed shortly). If, however, messages are delivered in sequence, then it is reasonable to assume that the server's executions are in the same order as the order of call messages, in which case *clean_up* need do nothing. For crashed calls, we need a similar requirement and one that can be met by ensuring that (for an out-of-order message system) crash recovery involves killing any orphans.

We consider now the more general case where a server's work is some arbitrary computation (including calls on other servers). It is now necessary to have some explicit measure for meeting requirement IR2 (in addition to IR1). For such calls, it is very difficult to design a *last of many* protocol, and therefore tolerating orphans for normally terminated calls is no longer an attractive proposition; thus, *at least once* semantics should be abandoned in favor of *exactly once* semantics.[16]

6.2. *Exactly Once* Calls

We assume that a server's work is some arbitrary computation such that a crash of a server can leave orphans on other nodes. In view of the fact that a normally terminated call implies no orphan executions, we will make the following design choice: *exactly once* calls need not incorporate means of tolerating server crashes (robustness in the presence of crashes is better achieved within the framework of robust atomic actions). So, a crash of a server in the middle of a call should result in an abnormal termination.

In the absence of server crashes, it is relatively easy to prevent orphans—a straightforward sequence numbering scheme will do. However, a server after a crash must be initialized so as to reject precrash requests, thus guaranteeing abnormal termination for those callers. This requires that the sequence numbers be monotonically increasing despite the occurrence of crashes. The remote procedure call implementation described in Section 8 meets this requirement by making use of synchronized clocks for generating sequence numbers.

Consider now the exception handling situation depicted in the program fragment above. What we require is to maintain the semantics in the presence of retries. A simple means of achieving this is to make sure that all the call messages (those due to the original call and subsequent retries) contain the same sequence number. The clean-up program should at least ensure that any orphans are killed before further calls are made.

6.3. Orphan Killing

By orphan killing we mean aborting any server executions in progress (i.e. in terms of our model, killing worker processes). We may require this facility under two conditions: after an abnormal termination or after a crash (of a client's node). For the former, a selective abort facility is required. Let us assume a server primitive abort_call that can be invoked by a client. Consider a typical case:

rpc(· · ·) ⟨t: retry(n) ⟨t: rpc(abort_call) ⟨t: retry(m) ⟨t: wait(T)⟩⟩⟩⟩;

After n retries have failed, the abort_call is invoked (a maximum of m times). What if this also fails? A sensible strategy is to ignore this exception and proceed (thus taking a small risk of interference). If this is unacceptable, then it is necessary to rely on some orphan killing measure.

There can be several reasons for an abort_call not succeeding: (i) the server has crashed (note that this could have created orphans on nodes not known to the original caller); or (ii) the physical communications path between the client and the server has broken down; or (iii) a combination of these two events during the execution of the abort_call. If we assume some external (to the client) mechanism that regularly (say every d seconds) detects and kills orphans, then the client should wait for T seconds ($T > d$) to ensure the absence of orphans. To keep down overheads, the duration d will typically be large (seconds to minutes), hence that mechanism should be used as a last resort measure as indicated by the program.

A more powerful abort facility is needed when a client node crashes, since all outstanding calls from that node need attention. Orphan killing can be made a part of a client's node crash recovery procedure. What is required is that a list of all nodes to which calls have been made be kept in stable storage. The crash recovery procedure of a node then involves making abort requests to these nodes. A shortcoming of this method is that crash recovery can not complete if the called node is down or can not be reached due to some communication failure, and again we must rely on some other mechanism that kills orphans. One such mechanism, described elsewhere,[16] works as follows: every node maintains a ''down'' list indicating nodes that are either in a crashed state or can not be reached. This list is updated regularly, say every d seconds. Then, during an update, if a node encounters a new down node, its calls (if any) are aborted. A number of other techniques are described in references 6 and 11.

7. ROBUST ATOMIC ACTIONS

Robust atomic actions (or atomic actions for short) possess the following failure atomicity property: either the action terminates, producing the normal intended results, or no results are produced if failures such as node crashes are encountered. In view of the fact that remote procedure calls are the most widely used primitives for constructing atomic actions, it is reasonable to enquire how reliability requirements of RPC's relate to those of such actions. There appear to be two approaches concerning the implementation of RPC's and atomic actions. The first approach regards remote procedure calls as a general tool for constructing distributed programs (with atomic actions representing a special class of programs). The second approach integrates RPC's and atomic actions closely. This is, however, not a fundamental distinction and it is possible to construct atomic actions using the former approach[7, 14] or the latter approach[9, 19] with equal ease (note that the RPC mechanism described in the next Section is intended as a general tool for distributed programming). In the following discussion we will thus ignore this distinction.

Given the provision for atomic actions, it is possible to do away with any need for specific orphan killing measures and rely entirely on the recovery capability of atomic actions, if the following rule is observed: the action is aborted whenever there is the possibility of orphan creation. If, however, it is desired that atomic actions should complete normally in the presence of abnormal returns of remote calls and node crashes, then some orphan killing measures will generally be required.

8. CASE STUDY

In this section we describe the design and implementation of an RPC mechanism intended for the Cambridge Ring local area network.[12, 15] This exercise was carried out to investigate the suitability of RPCs as the basic primitive for distributed computing. The performance figures obtained (reported in Section 8.4) were very encouraging and, as a result, this design formed the basis for the RPC's as used in the distributed UNIX system built at Newcastle.[3] A number of salient points regarding this RPC mechanism was listed below.

1. Datagrams are used as the underlying communications system.
2. The simple two-message protocol is employed (note: in the protocol as used by the experimental distributed UNIX system, a server also maintains the state information for the most recent call to cope with retries).
3. The execution model used is the serial one mentioned in Section 4: a client has an agent process (at a remote node) that acts as a server for all calls by the client at that node.
4. The RPC mechanism implements the *exactly once* semantics.
5. Sequence numbers survive crashes; a node after a crash is initialized to generate sequence numbers and accept messages with sequence numbers greater than the precrash ones. A convenient means of achieving this

objective—used in this implementation—is to maintain global time in the distributed system by means of synchronized clocks (a simpler, but less secure way is to rely on operators to initialize crashed nodes with the correct time).

8.1. RPC Implementation

This Section describes the user interface supported by the RPC mechanism and certain aspects of its implementation. The implementation of this RPC mechanism has been performed in the C language; however, for the sake of readability, the algorithms given below are described in a Pascal-like language ({and} stand for **begin** and **end** and comments are enclosed within quotes). But first, a few remarks of general interest are in order:

1. The message-passing system employed by the RPC mechanism uses a naming scheme based on *port* numbers (integer values). A message is delivered to a given port at a given node; so the process that is *attached* to that port becomes the recipient of the messages directed at that port. Some higher level *name server* will typically be required through which various servers can publish their port numbers for receiving requests. The following two primitive operations are available:

```
send__msg(destination: . . . ;
          message: . . . ;
          var msg__status: . . .) ;
```

where msg__status is of type:

```
status = (OK, absent, not-done, unable);
```

destination is a record containing the node number (each node has a unique number) and the port number, and *message* is an array of 512 bytes maximum size. The response *OK* implies that the message has been delivered to the appropriate port; while the response *absent* means that the node is not connected to the ring. The response *not-done* indicates that the message was rejected—possibly because the recipient is busy (so the sender can certainly retry). The response *unable* indicates a ring malfunction during the transmission: the message may or may not have reached the destination.

```
receive__msg(at: port__number;
             var node: source;
             var message: . . . );
```

This procedure receives in *message* a message directed at port *at* from the specified source *node*. If source = *any*, then messages from any node directed at *at* are accepted (in any case, *node* will contain the node number of the sender).

2. The sequence number (sn) used in a message is derived by concatenating the current value of the local clock of the node and the node number (⟨clock value, code number⟩); a function get_sn(. . .) has been implemented that returns a sequence number.
3. The formats of call and return messages are shown in Fig. 7.3. The caller-supplied information includes the port number for receiving the reply, the server operation and the necessary parameters. The maximum length of a message has been fixed to that necessary to return a page of data as a result.

The interface maintained by the RPC mechanism to the client processes consists of the operation remote_call(. . .) described below (the time-out parameter specifies how long the client is willing to wait for a response):

```
remote_call(server : . . ;
            service: . . ;
            var result: . . ;
            var r_stat: . . ;
            time-out: . . );
```

where 'r_stat' is of type 'status':
status=(OK,not-done,absent,unable);
and parameters and results are passed by value.

The meaning of the call under various responses is given below:

status = *OK:* The service specified has been performed exactly once by the server and the answers are encoded in *result.*

status = *not-done:* The server has not performed the service because it is currently busy (so the client can certainly reissue the call in the hope of getting an *OK* response).

status = *absent:* The server is not available (so it is pointless for the client to retry).

status = *unable:* The parameter *result* does not contain the answers; whether the server performed the service is not known (this response can be obtained when the time-out expires).

The remote__call(. .) operation transfers an array of bytes (parameter *service*) to the named server (i.e., to the appropriate port) and returns an array of bytes (parameter *result*). It is left to servers and clients to view these byte arrays as structured objects. A client's view of the call message is the portion P2 of Fig. 7.3(a); the remote__call software constructs the portion P1 of the message, thus hiding unnecessary details of sequence numbering and reply port from the client. Similarly, a client only sees the portion P2 of the returned message (Fig. 7.3(b)). A number of *pack* procedures have been provided for packing simple typed variables (integers, strings, etc.) onto an array of bytes; a complementary set of *unpack* procedures are also available for constructing typed variables from an array of bytes.

In addition to the remote__call(. . .) operation available to clients, two operations—to be employed by servers—are also provided by the RPC interface: (i) the operation get__work(. . .) is used by a server to receive a call request, and (ii) the operation send__result(. . .) is used by a server to send the results of the executed call.

Our RPC mechanism meets the above specification provided the following conditions are met: (i) a node's hardware components (e.g., CPU, clock, ring interface) are working according to their specifications; (ii) the ring is working according to specifications; and (iii) the UNIX system of a node is also working according to specifications. If the failure modes of these three subsystems were clean (working or not working) then a failure of subsystem (i) or (iii) will constitute a node crash, and has the net effect of all of the ongoing calls on that

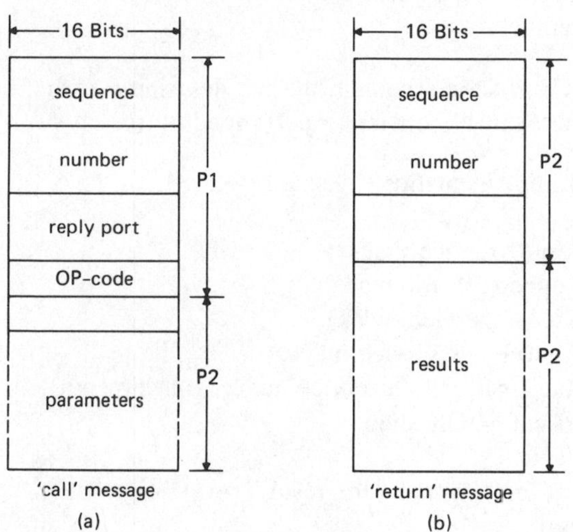

Fig. 7.3. Call and return message formats.

node not succeeding and any services provided by that node becoming unavailable; a failure of the Ring has the effect of all of the nodes becoming disconnected (so a node will be unable to obtain remote services). In practice, of course, failures are rarely clean, nor are precise system specifications available. So, if it is suspected that a subsystem is not working properly, the best strategy is to convert that failure to a clean node or ring failure by switching off appropriate power supply or by stopping the operating system as the case may be. In the case of a crashed node, once it has been repaired, it can be inserted in the system dynamically: there is no need either to stop the entire system to accommodate the new node or to inform the live nodes explicitly that a new node has been added to the system.

A rather simplified description of how a client can perform a remote read operation is given below (assume that the client knows the node number and the port number of the file server).

In UNIX, a file read operation must specify the file descriptor (an integer value), the address of the buffer for storing the data, and the number of bytes to be read. The client needs the following variables:

```
var
   where : ''server address''
      fd : integer;
    buff : array[. . .] of char;
   index : integer;
  nbytes : integer;
 service : array[. . .] of char;
  r_stat : status;
```

where the variable *fd* should contain the file descriptor of the remote file (as a result of a remote open file operation performed by the client).

```
remote_read implementation
          ---
        packint(0,service,index);
          ''opcode 0: file read''
        packint(fd,service,index);
        packint(nbytes,service,index);
        remote_call(where,service,buff,r_stat,timeout);
        if r_stat = OK then
           begin
              ''buff contains the result''
           end
        else
          ---
```

Thus a **remote_read** operation can be provided which is as easy to use as a local read. On the server's side, the server uses the **get_work**(. . .) operation to receive an array of bytes; this array is suitably unpacked and then the requested operation is performed. The server then packs the results into an array of bytes, which is then sent to the client's port using **send_result**(. . .) operation.

8.1.1. Some Implementation Details

The program below shows those details of the **remote_call**(. . .) that have to do with the provision of fault tolerance and mapping of message responses onto the status return of the call:

```
begin     ''remote_call(. . .) implementation''
  . . .
  sn := get_sn(. . .);
  at := get_port(. . .); ''get port number''
  construct the message of Fig. 7.3(a);
  retry := 0;
  done := false;
  repeat          ''call request to server''
  {   send_msg(server,msg,msg_status);
      case msg_status of
  ok        : { done := true }
  absent    : { r_stat := absent; return }
  not_done: { retry := retry + 1;
              if retry = MAXTRY then
                { r_stat := not_done; return }
            }
  unable    : { retry := retry + 1;
              if retry = MAXTRY then
                { r_stat := unable; return }
            }
      end     ''case''
  } until done;
  within time_out do
  { repeat
      receive_msg(at,server_node,result);
    until result. sn = sn
  } ⟨EXPIRED ? (r_stat := unable; return)⟩
  r_stat := OK
end;
```

In the current implementation, MAXTRY has been set to 10. A typical time-out period for a file read operation should be set by the user to a value ranging between 1 and 2 seconds, depending on the system load.

A server has to maintain certain global data which is initialized at the node start-up time. This data is the last largest sequence number (llsn) received from a given node, and is initialized to the current clock value of the server's node:

```
var llsn : array[. . .] of sn;
    for i = 1 to maxnode do
     llsn(i) : = get__sn(. . .);
```

Thereafter, the above data structure is utilized by the get__work(. . .) procedure to accept a valid request. The send__result(. . .) operation uses a similar technique to that of remote__call(. . .) for transmitting the result.

```
procedure get__work(. . .);
   . . .
begin
   repeat
        src := any;
        receive__msg(port,src,msg);
        sn := seq. no. in msg
   until sn > llsn(src);
   llsn(src) := sn;
   . . .
end;
```

8.1.2. Clock Management

As stated before, a sequence number at a given node is constructed out of the current clock value and the unique node number. All of the clocks of the system are kept loosely synchronized with each other so that they represent roughly the same physical time.[5] A simple way to achieve this objective has been described elsewhere.[15] All that is necessary is for each node to maintain two processes: (i) a broadcaster process that regularly (say once every few minutes) sends its current time to the rest of the nodes; and (ii) a synchronizer process whose task is to receive the time sent by others and to advance its clock if it is behind that of a given sender.

Three practical problems were faced in the implementation of the above scheme:

1. A client with a slow clock can experience difficulty in obtaining services from a server if the server relies on its own clock for deciding whether to accept or reject a request.

2. For the sake of efficiency, we would prefer that a broadcaster need only send its time to those nodes that are currently up. The Cambridge Ring can accommodate up to 255 nodes, though our ring is currently rather sparsely populated. This suggests the need for a dynamically maintained uplist at every node, such that if a new node is inserted in the ring, the broadcasters of the other nodes eventually discover this fact (and thus can start sending their times to the new node) and, similarly, if a node is removed from the ring, this fact is also discovered by the rest of the up nodes.
3. The fact that clocks are always advanced implies that ''fast'' clock errors will accumulate and, in particular, a runaway clock can advance the network time far ahead of the physical time. This suggests that a facility for setting clocks back is needed. Of course, this must be performed without compromising the security offered by the sequence numbering scheme.

The only way of avoiding problem 1 was to maintain the clock values of the other nodes at the server's node (the 'llsn' array mentioned in the last section). The solutions adopted to solve the remaining two problems will now be described. The solution adopted for setting back the clocks is quite practical, providing this operation is not invoked frequently. When the clocks are being set back, users are likely to encounter some difficulty in obtaining remote services; however, the system quickly stabilizes (within a few minutes). The authority for setting clocks back is vested in the broadcaster of one node only—this special broadcaster will be referred to as the Time Lord. The Time Lord can send three types of messages: *synch:* this is the normal message containing the current time; *goback:* this message is a ''get prepared to set time backwards'' message; and *set:* this message contains the new time.

All the other broadcasters can only send the *synch* message. The algorithms for a broadcaster (not a Time Lord) and a synchronizer of a node are as shown. Two shared variables *dir* and *uplist* are maintained and protected by a mutex semaphore.

```
        ''shared variables''
var
                    dir: (forward,backward);
                 uplist: array[1 . . maxnode]of(UP,DOWN);
                 mutex: semaphore; ''initially 1''

        ''BROADCASTER ALGORITHM''
var retry: integer; done: boolean;
begin
   P(mutex);
   dir := forward;
```

```
    V(mutex);
    set_clock(0);      ''initialize clock''
    for i := 1 to max_node do
    begin
       retry := 0; done := false;
       repeat ''send 'I am alive' synch message''
          send_msg(. . .,0,msg_status);
          P(mutex);
          case msg_status of
       ok : { uplist(i) := UP; done := true }
       absent: { uplist(i) := DOWN; done := true }
       unable,notdone: { retry := retry + 1;
                         if retry = max then
                         uplist(i) := DOWN }
          end      ''end case''
          V(mutex)
       until retry = max or done
    end ''end of broadcaster initialization program''
    cycle
       delay(t);       ''wait for a minute''
       P(mutex);
       if dir = forward then
       { get_sn(. . .);
         send the sequence number as synch messages
         to all 'UP' nodes }
         V(mutex)
    end     ''end cycle''
 end;   ''end broadcaster''

       ''SYNCHRONIZER ALGORITHM''
       ---- local variables ----
 cycle
       receive_msg(prt,src,message);
       P(mutex);
       case message_type of
    goback: dir := backward;
    synch: { if dir = forward then
                 { advance clock if necessary;
                   if uplist(src) = DOWN then
                       uplist(src) := UP }
           }
```

```
set   : { if dir = backward then
              { set_clock(message.time + 1tick);
                dir := forward }
        }
    end     ''end case''
        V(mutex)
end;    ''cycle''
```

When a node comes up, the broadcaster of that node sends "I am alive" messages to all the possible nodes in the system. The responses received from the send message operations are used for the construction of the uplist. We have assumed that all of the synchronizers have got the same port number, so a broadcaster's messages always go to synchronizers. Also, note that the synch message with time 0 will not affect local time at any node. A broadcaster only broadcasts its time if it is going forwards.

The synchronizer's task is to analyze the messages directed to it and act accordingly. The algorithm for the Time Lord is given below (the synchronizer at the Time Lord's node is identical to other synchronizers). The user at the Time Lord's node has to supply a **GOBACK** command which is caught by the Time Lord who then sends **goback** messages to all the up nodes. This has the net effect of stopping all the broadcasters. When the Time Lord gets the user-supplied new time, it broadcasts it. This has the net effect of initializing all the clocks. Note that no special action is needed for a node to initialize its clock when it comes up—its synchronizer will get a clock value that will result in the update of the clock.

```
    ''TIME LORD ALGORITHM''
    ---- ''initialization part,
            same as a BROADCASTER'' ----
cycle
  if GOBACK command from the user then
  {  send 'goback' messages to all 'up' nodes,
     including own synchronizer;
     get a new clock value from the user;
     send 'set' messages to all the 'up' nodes,
     including own synchronizer
  } else { same as a BROADCASTER }
end;
```

Finally, all of the servers must also discover the fact that clocks have been set back—so that they can adjust their llsn arrays, mentioned previously; otherwise requests will continue to be rejected until such time as the "new" time catches up. A simple means of performing this task is shown below—a slight modification to the get_work(. . .) procedure is needed. A *reject* count is maintained and whenever this count exceeds a given value, (say 5), it is suspected that clocks have been put back, so the llsn array is initialized.

```
"modified get_work( ) algorithm"

procedure get_work(. . .);
begin
   ---
   reject := 0;
   repeat
      src := any;
      receive_msg(port,src,msg);
      sn := seq. number in msg;
      if sn <= llsn(src) then
         reject := reject + 1
   until sn>llsn(src) or reject=MAX;
   if reject=MAX then
   {  sn := get_sn(. . .);
      for i := 1 to maxnode do
         llsn(i) := sn }
   else
      { llsn(src) := sn;
         reject := 0 }
   ---
end;
```

A few remarks regarding the actual UNIX implementation are perhaps in order. In UNIX, only files can be shared between unrelated processes; so the shared variables of our algorithms are kept in a file. This has not caused any performance problems, since both the broadcaster and the synchronizer have very little active processing to perform. The maintenance of uplists and the facility of putting clocks back certainly add complications. Nevertheless, the resulting algorithms are still fairly simple, with very little message and computation overheads.

The following three aspects of the clock management scheme are worth noting: (i) let d seconds be the maximum clock difference between any two nodes, then the minimum crash recovery time of any crashed node must be greater than d to guarantee that the sn's after a crash are greater than sn's before the crash; (ii) a crash of the Time Lord's node cannot be tolerated when clocks are being put back; (iii) the minimum amount by which clocks can be put back must exceed *d*. If crash recovery time is known, then the observation (i) indicates how much drift between clocks is tolerable, which in turn can be used to calculate how often clocks need be synchronized. Although we have not made a detailed study of clock drift, sending synchronizing messages once every few minutes (say 5 minutes) is quite acceptable.

9. PERFORMANCE MEASUREMENTS

This Section presents some of the results obtained from initial tests carried out to assess the performance of the RPC mechanism. Our aim was to compare the data transfer rates as seen by the user for local and remote operations. The measurements were carried out between two PDP 11/45 computers and involved (for the distributed case) a program on one CPU to read 50 Kbytes of data from an already opened file on the other CPU. Various block sizes for the transfer were utilized: from 16 bytes to 512 bytes (one page). The standard *time* facility of UNIX was used for obtaining the times, which are accurate to a millisecond. The graph of Fig. 7.4 shows the results obtained, where *local* figures refer to the results obtained when only one CPU was utilized.

From this graph it is seen that, when the unit of transfer is a page of data, the intermachine transfer rate is about 40% slower than the local transfer rate. This degradation is tolerable since initial user experience indicates that most users have been unable to differentiate between a local file operation and a remote one. Some additional performance data are presented in Table 7.1 (a block size of 512 bytes was used and the same file was used for the first test).

As a matter of interest, the data transfer rate obtained by utilizing a high level virtual circuit based protocol (Byte Stream Protocol) was also measured; the

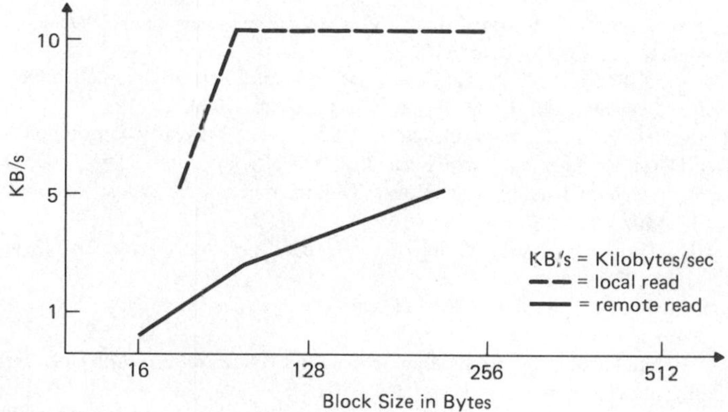

Fig. 7.4. Data transfer rate.

Table 7.1. Additional Performance Data.

Test	Local	Remote RPC	Remote BSP
open; read; close	9.12 KB/s	5.36 KB/s	1.46 KB/s
process to process (Unix pipe)	41.0 KB/s	7.4 KB/s	—
open or close file	18 msec	60 msec	—

result obtained—1.46 KB/s as against 5.36 KB/s—confirms the opinion expressed in reference 11, that sophisticated protocols are often undesirable. The process to process data transfer rate (involving no disc accesses) for the distributed case appears to be rather small if one takes into account the fact that the Ring bandwidth is 1.25 Mbytes/sec! The reason for this is that the Ring itself transmits two bytes of data at a time and our Ring interfaces are interrupt driven. So transmission of a block of data involves considerable interrupt handling overheads (the maximum raw data transfer rate of the message passing system is about 8 Kbytes/sec).

The only part of the RPC mechanism that appears a bit complex is the clock management scheme. However, as the clocks are only loosely synchronized (a node sends its time to the other up nodes once every few minutes), processing overheads for keeping clocks approximately the same are not appreciable.

Note added in proof: Since the original publication of this material, a new RPC mechanism incorporating effective orphan killing measures has been developed by the authors and is described in: Rajdoot: An RPC mechanism supporting orphan detection and killing, *IEEE Trans. on Software Eng.* (to appear).

REFERENCES

1. Best, E. and B. Randell, A formal model of atomicity in asynchronous systems, *Acta Informatica*, vol. 16, pp. 93–124, Aug. 1981.
2. Boggs, D. R., J. F. Shoch, E. A. Taft, and R. M. Metcalfe, Pup: An internetwork architecture, *IEEE Trans. Commun.*, vol. COM-28, pp. 612–624, Apr. 1980.
3. Brownbridge, D. R., L. F. Marshall, and B. Randell, The Newcastle connection or UNIXes of the World Unite!, *Software Practice and Experience*, vol. 12, pp. 1147–1162, Dec. 1982.
4. Cristian, F., Exception handling and software fault tolerance, *IEEE Trans. Computers*, vol. C-31, pp. 531–540, June 1982.
5. Lamport, L., Time, clocks and ordering of events in a distributed system, *CACM*, vol. 21, pp. 558–565, July 1978.
6. Lampson, B., Remote procedure calls, in *Lecture Notes in Computer Science*, vol. 105, Berlin: Springer Verlag, 1981, pp. 365–370.
7. Lampson, B. and H. Sturgis, Atomic transactions, in *Lecture Notes in Computer Science*, vol. 105, Berlin: Springer Verlag, 1981, pp. 365–370.
8. Larus, J. R., *On the Performance of Courier Remote Procedure Calls under 4.1c BSD*, Tech. Report UCB/CSD 83/123, EECS CSD University of California, Berkeley, Aug. 1983.

9. Liskov, B., On linguistic support for distributed programs, in *Proc. 1st Symp. on Reliability in Distributed Software and Database Systems* (IEEE Computer Society), pp. 53–60, Pittsburgh, PA, July 1981.
10. Mitchell, J. G. and J. Dion, A comparison of two network-based file servers, *CACM*, vol. 25, pp. 233–245, Apr. 1982.
11. Nelson, B. J., *Remote Procedure Call*, Tech. Report CMU-CS-81-119, Dept. Computer Science, Carnegie-Mellon University, Pittsburgh, PA, 1981.
12. Panzieri, F. and S. K. Shrivastava, Reliable remote calls for distributed UNIX: An implementation study, in *Proc. 2nd Symp. on Reliability in Distributed Software and Database Systems* (IEEE Computer Society), pp. 127–133, Pittsburgh, PA, July 1982.
13. Rybczynski, A., Packet switched network layer, in *Computer Network Architectures and Protocols*, P. E. Green, Jr., ed., New York: Plenum Press, 1982.
14. Shrivastava, S. K., Structuring distributed systems for reliability and crash resistance, *IEEE Trans. on Software Eng.*, vol. SE-7, pp. 436–447, July 1981.
15. Shrivastava, S. K. and F. Panzieri, The design of a reliable remote procedure call mechanism, *IEEE Trans. on Computers*, vol. C-31, pp. 692–697, July 1982.
16. Shrivastava, S. K., On the Treatment of Orphans in a Distributed System, in *Proc. 3rd Symp. on Reliability in Distributed Software and Database Systems* (IEEE Computer Society), pp. 155–162, Adam's Mark Caribbean Gulf Resort, Clearwater Beach, FL, Oct. 1983.
17. Spector, A. Z., Performing remote operations efficiently on a local computer network, *CACM*, vol. 25, pp. 246–260, Apr. 1982.
18. Sunshine, C. A. and Y. K. Dalal, Connection management in transport protocols, *Computer Networks*, vol. 2, pp. 454–473, North-Holland Publishing Company, 1978.
19. Svobodova, L., Resilient distributed computing, *IEEE Trans. on Software Eng.*, vol. SE-10, pp. 257–268, 1984.
20. Tanenbaum, A. S., *Computer Networks*, Englewood Cliffs, NJ: Prentice-Hall, 1981.
21. Wilkes, M. V. and D. J. Wheeler, The Cambridge communication ring, *Proc. Local Area Network Symp.* (National Bureau of Standards), Boston, MA, May 1979.
22. Xerox., *Courier: The Remote Procedure Call Protocol*, Tech. Report XSIS 038112, Xerox Corporation, Stamford, CT, Dec. 1981.

8. Approaches to Mechanization of the Conversation Scheme Based on Monitors

K. H. KIM

ABSTRACT

A basic problem in designing error detection and backward recovery capabilities into concurrent programs is to coordinate the detection and recovery activities of cooperating processes. As an aid to such design, Randell proposed a language construct called conversation in an abstract form. Practical mechanization of the conversation scheme, i.e., selection of a well-structured syntax and associated semantics, is the issue dealt with in this chapter. Four different mechanizations based on the monitor approach to interprocess communication are presented. They are presented as feasible extensions of Concurrent Pascal in order to enable visualization of their full implementation details in at least one type of concurrent programming environment. They are presented in the increasing order of the amount of effort that they require for extending Concurrent Pascal. They offer different degrees of assistance to the programmer in proper structuring of recoverable process interactions.

1. INTRODUCTION

The steadily growing complexity of computer systems and the increasing exploitation of computational parallelism with small-scale computers are two of the trends firmly established in 1970s. One natural consequence of this is the increasing demand for "hardened" concurrent programs, especially those capable of overcoming unexpected erroneous situations encountered at run time

This work was supported in part by the National Science Foundation under grant MCS-8012906. An earlier version of this chapter was presented as a paper at the IEEE Symposium on Reliability in Distributed Software and Database Systems, Pittsburgh, PA, July 21–22, 1981.

without interruption in producing acceptable results. However, design of such programs, often called *fault-tolerant concurrent programming*, is still an immature branch of software engineering.

A fundamental problem in designing error detection and recovery capabilities into a concurrent program, structured in the form of a collection of cooperating asynchronous processes, arises from the possibility of erroneous process interaction.[6,11,13] A process in an erroneous state may cause other processes to be in error. Therefore, recovery should be a cooperative effort by all of the processes involved. Here we consider the systems in which *backward recovery*, also called *rollback and retry*, is used by a process as the basic means to recover itself from an erroneous state.[2–4,10–12] To enable the backward recovery, a process saves its state at various points in execution, called *recovery points* (RP's). The fundamental problem in fault-tolerant concurrent programming is, then, the coordination of interacting processes for error detection and recovery. For example, the rollback of a process to its most recent RP nullifies the interactions that the process has had with other processes after establishing the RP. Therefore, other processes involved in the recalled interactions also have to roll back. If the RP's of interacting processes are not properly coordinated, then an intolerably long sequence of rollback propagations, called a *domino effect*,[11] can occur.

As an aid to the structuring of properly coordinated error detection and backward recovery actions of interacting processes, an abstract language construct termed *conversation* was proposed by Randell.[11] The conversation is a conceptual extension of the *recovery block* (RB), which is a concrete language construct designed to support structuring the error detection and backward recovery actions of a single process.[4,9,11] In the original proposal of the conversation scheme, only the abstract semantics was provided. Although the abstract semantics is clear and the underlying program structuring concept is a natural extension of that of the RB scheme, its *mechanization*, which involves selecting a well-structured syntax and associated precise semantics, is by no means straightforward. It still remains a subject for much more study in the future. An effective mechanization of the conversation should be easy to use and amenable to efficient execution. It should also enable a rigorous compile-time check for compliance of a given program to the program structuring rules of the conversation scheme.

An earlier attempt at developing a mechanization of the conversation scheme was made in reference 13. There two possible mechanizations were considered at an abstract level, i.e., without assuming any particular approach to interprocess communication. In this chapter, we explore four different mechanizations based on the monitor approach to interprocess communication.[1] In fact, in order to make the discussion specific and ease the visualization of the implementation details, Concurrent Pascal[1] is used as base language; the mechanizations presented can be viewed as feasible extensions of Concurrent Pascal to support the structuring rules of the conversation as specified in reference 11. Of the four, one mechanization which requires the least amount of (Concurrent Pascal) extension effort but provides the least amount of help to the programmer, is the same as one of the two mechanizations discussed in reference 13. The three new mechanizations presented in this chapter provide more help to the programmer in proper structuring of recoverable process interactions. (The other mechanization discussed in reference 13 is not considered here because its development/description is incomplete and an interpretation under which the mechanization becomes attractive could not be made. The authors of reference 13 themselves posed open questions on the unspecified details of the mechanization.)

The basic program structuring rules of the conversation scheme are first reviewed in Section 2 before the four mechanizations are presented in Section 3. Some possible extensions are dealt with in the final summary in Section 4.

2. BASIC PROGRAM STRUCTURING RULES OF THE CONVERSATION SCHEME

Since the conversation scheme is a natural extension of the RB scheme, a brief review of the latter seems useful here. The syntactic structure of RB is in Fig. 8.1. In this figure, T denotes the *acceptance test*, B_1 the *primary try block*, and B_k, $2 \leqslant k \leqslant n$, the *alternate try blocks*. All the try blocks are designed to produce the same or similar computational results. The acceptance test is a logical expression representing the criterion for determining the acceptability of the execution results of the try blocks. A try (i.e., execution of a try block) is thus always followed by an acceptance test. In a sense, RB is an enclosure of some recoverable activities of a single process.

The conversation is a two-dimensional enclosure of recoverable activities of multiple interacting processes, in short, a *recoverable interacting session*. It is thus a two-dimensional RB, i.e., an RB which spans two or more processes and creates a "boundary" which process interactions may not cross. The concept is depicted in Fig. 8.2. In this figure, processes progress downward. The bound-

```
ensure T
by B1
else by B2
. . . .
else by Bn
else error.
```

Fig. 8.1. Recovery block.

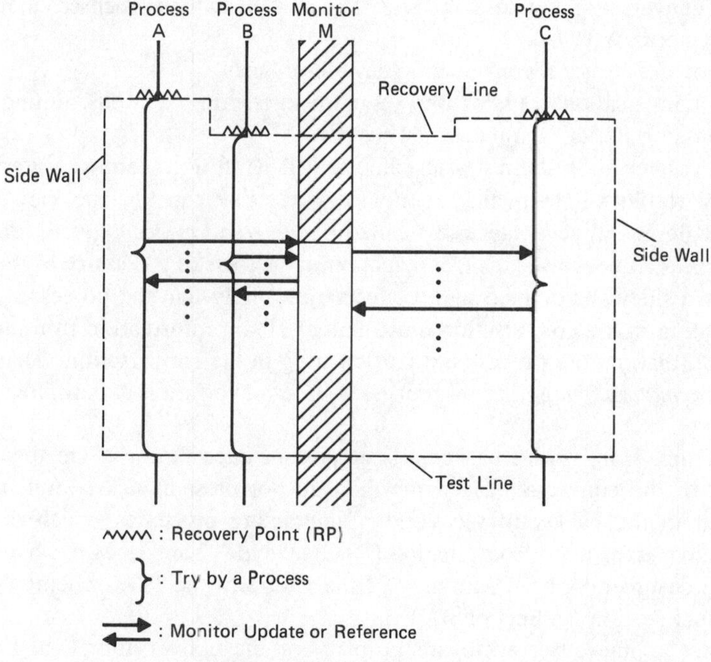

Fig. 8.2. Conversation.

ary of a conversation consists of a *recovery line*, a *test line*, and two side walls. A recovery line is a coordinated set of the RP's of interacting processes that are established (possibly at different times) before interactions begin. When all the processes roll back to the recovery line, there cannot be any further propagation of rollbacks among processes. A test line is a correlated set of all the acceptance tests of the interacting processes. A conversation is successful only if all the interacting processes pass their acceptance tests forming the test line. If any of the acceptance tests fail, all the processes roll back to the recovery line and retry with their alternate try blocks. These alternate try blocks collectively define an *alternate interacting session*, whereas the set of primary try blocks executed first after the processes enter the conversation define the *primary interacting session*. Conversations must be strictly nested in two dimensions. That is, when conversation C.nest is nested within conversation C, the set of processes that participate in nested conversation C.nest must be a subset of the processes that participate in C, the entire recovery line of C.nest must be established after the entire recovery line of C, and the entire test line of C.nest must be set before the entire test line of C.

The basic program structuring rules of the conversation scheme can thus be summarized as follows:

1. A conversation defines a recovery line as a line which processes in rollback cannot cross.
2. Processes enter a conversation asynchronously.
3. A conversation contains one or more interacting sessions aiming at the same or similar computational results.
4. A conversation defines a test line which is an acceptability criterion for the results of interacting sessions. A test line can thus be viewed as a single global acceptance test called a *conversation acceptance test*.
5. Processes cooperate in error detection, regardless of the source of the error.
6. Two sidewalls defined by a conversation imply that the processes participating in the conversation must neither obtain information from nor leak information to a process not participating in the conversation. That is, no *information smuggling* by processes in a conversation is permitted.

Properties 3 and 5 are particularly important because these are the unique features of the conversation scheme that are not present in a complementary approach to the backward recovery of interacting processes which is called programmer-transparent coordination (PTC) scheme[6,8] and does not burden the program designer. A brief summary of the nature of the PTC scheme is given in the final section (in Section 4).

Because of the strict enclosure property of the conversation which forces group activities upon participating processes, a defection by a process could result in a system crash. To be more specific, care must be taken at design time to prevent the following situations.

1. A process expected to participate in a conversation chooses not to enter the conversation. Such a *deserter process* creates a system deadlock because the processes which enter the conversation will wait forever at or before the test line.
2. A process inside a conversation smuggles information. This renders a rollback and retry by the processes in the conversation useless.

A desirable mechanization of the conversation scheme should enable the compiler to provide substantial help in preventing the situations mentioned above.

3. MECHANIZATIONS OF THE CONVERSATION SCHEME

Four different mechanizations of the conversation scheme are discussed in this Section. They are presented as feasible extensions of programming language Concurrent Pascal. This has been motivated by the fact that Concurrent Pascal is a relatively simple and extensively tested concurrent programming language and also by the belief that the presentation as feasible extensions would enable those familiar with Concurrent Pascal to visualize implementation details in full. It has also been assumed that many of the insights obtained through successful mechanization of the conversation scheme on the basis of Concurrent Pascal could still be useful in finding mechanizations based on different concurrent programming languages. The four mechanizations are presented in the increasing order of the amount of effort that they require for extending Concurrent Pascal.

3.1. Named-Linked Recovery Block

This was discussed in reference 13 and is the simplest extension of Concurrent Pascal among the four mechanizations discussed in this chapter. The idea is to extend the RB construct with a conversation identifier field, as shown in Fig. 8.3. In this figure, C is a conversation identifier. The set of name-linked RB's, each executed by a different process but having the same conversation identifier, compose a conversation construct.

When this name-linked RB is incorporated into Concurrent Pascal, the RB's forming a conversation construct appear scattered in the program text. An illustration is given in Fig. 8.4. This mechanization of the conversation suffers from the following deficiencies:

1. It is difficult to detect at design time the possibility of a process becoming a deserter and thus difficult to prevent a system deadlock, especially when each name-linked RB belonging to a conversation construct is inside a loop. For example, consider the program in Fig. 8.4. The condition COND-A1 of PROCESSA and COND-B1 of PROCESSB should be the same at the expected instants. Otherwise, only one of them will enter the conversation C1 while the other becomes a deserter. Similarly, COND-A2 and COND-B2 must be the same at the expected instants.
2. It is difficult to ensure proper nesting of conversations.
3. It is difficult to check at design time the possibility of information smuggling by processes participating in a conversation, partly because the rights of processes for access to monitors are fixed on system initialization and

[conv C:]
ensure T
by B_1
else by B_2
. . . .
else by B_n
else error.

Fig. 8.3. Name-linked recovery block.

```
type PROCESSA =
. . . . . . . .
begin
    . . . . . . . .
    cycle
        . . . . . . . .
        if COND-A1 then
        [conv C1:]
        ensure . . . .
        . . . . . . . .
        else error;
        . . . . . . . .
        while COND-A2 do
        [conv C2:]
        ensure . . . .
        . . . . . . . .
    end "cycle"
end "type"

type PROCESSB =
. . . . . . . .
begin
    . . . . . . . .
    cycle
        . . . . . . . .
        if COND-B1 then
        [conv C1:]
        . . . . . . . .
        . . . . . . . .
        while COND-B2 do
        begin . . .
            [conv C2:]
            . . . . . . . .
        end "while"
    end "cycle"
end "type"

type PROCESSC =
. . . . . . . .
```

Fig. 8.4. A concurrent program containing name-linked recovery blocks.

remain unchanged regardless of processes' participation in conversations. Suppose the remainder of the program in Fig. 8.4 contains a monitor M that can be accessed by PROCESSA, PROCESSB, and PROCESSC. Only PROCESSA and PROCESSB participate in conversations C1 and C2. However, while PROCESSA and PROCESSB communicate through M inside conversations C1 and C2, the malfunctioning PROCESSC can access M and interfere with the two processes in a conversation.

4. The conversation acceptance test is specified in the form of a scattered set of acceptance tests, each associated with a name-linked RB belonging to the conversation. This cumbersome specification makes it often difficult to understand the nature of the conversation acceptance test.
5. Similarly, alternate interacting sessions are difficult to read because of their scattered appearance in the program text.

3.2. Conversation-Monitor

Another possible mechanization of the conversation scheme is based on the use of a special monitor, termed *conversation-monitor* or *c-monitor*, within the RB's belonging to a conversation construct. The RB extension containing c-monitor has the syntactic structure shown in Fig. 8.5. The following rules are associated with this RB extension using a c-monitor.

1. The c-monitor name plays the role of a conversation identifier. Therefore, there is a unique c-monitor provided for each conversation construct. This means that access to a c-monitor can be specified only within one RB in the program text of a process.
2. When a process enters a conversation (i.e., enters an RB belonging to a conversation construct), the process loses all the monitor access rights which it has possessed. In return, the process gains an access right for the c-monitor associated with the conversation. Therefore, the c-monitor is the only mechanism available to the process for communication with other processes until the process exits from the conversation. On exit, the process regains the access right that it lost on entry to the conversation, and loses the access right for the c-monitor.
3. When a process enters a nested conversation C.nest from the enclosing conversation C, it again loses the access right for the c-monitor of C and gains the access right for the c-monitor of C.nest. On exit from C.nest, the process regains the access right for the c-monitor of C.

ensure T
using-cm CM
by B_1
else by B_2
. . . .
else by B_n
else error.

Fig. 8.5. Recovery block with a conversation monitor.

4. Once all the participating processes pass their acceptance tests and thus become ready to exit, the c-monitor is reinitialized, i.e., restored to the state that existed at the beginning of the conversation.

Storage allocation for a c-monitor used in a conversation can be performed at its initialization time or when the conversation is entered by the first entering process. In the latter case, the storage allocated to the c-monitor is returned to the free pool when the conversation acceptance test has succeeded.

This approach to mechanization of the conversation scheme still suffers from most of the deficiencies mentioned in the preceding section of the name-linked RB approach. However, there is one significant improvement. That is, this approach makes it easy to prevent information smuggling by a process participating in a conversation. This is due to the fact that a c-monitor is the only means of communication available to the processes participating in the corresponding conversation and cannot be accessed by any process outside the conversation.

The restriction on the number of c-monitors used in a conversation (to one) may be relaxed. It is still required, however, that a set of c-monitors are used exclusively within one and only one conversation construct.

3.3. Abstract Data Type

Much of the shortcomings of the previous two approaches, i.e., the name-linked RB and the c-monitor approaches, stem from the scattered appearance of the constituent RB's of a conversation construct in the program text. One approach to solving this problem is to structure the conversation construct in the form of an abstract data type.[1] A possible syntactic structure is shown in Fig. 8.6.

Basically the abstract data type *conversation* consists of c-monitors and one or more interacting sessions. Each interacting session consists of procedures which are executed by the processes participating in the conversation. The following rules are associated with this conversation construct.

1. A process enters a conversation by calling a procedure, say CONV1.PROCA, of which the name and the formal parameters are listed in the *participant* declaration area.
2. The initialization section of a conversation consists of initializations of c-monitors. That is, the initial process initializes conversations, which involves initializing the c-monitors of the conversations.
3. On entry to a conversation, a process loses access rights that it has had for (regular) monitors. It gains the access rights on exit from the conversation.

```
type C=
conversation(. . .''nested conversations''. . .)
participants
    PROCA(. . .''formal parameters''. . .);
    PROCB(. . . . . . . . . . . . . . . . . . . . . . . . . .);
    . . . . . . . .
var
    CM1: c-monitor-type1;
    CM2: c-monitor-type2;
    . . . . . . . .
ensure CAT          ''Conversation acceptance test''
by begin            ''Primary interacting session''
        PROCA: . . . . . . . .
        PROCB: . . . . . . . .
        . . . . . . . .
    end
else by begin        ''Alternate interacting session''
        PROCA: . . . . . . . .
        PROCB: . . . . . . . .
        . . . . . .
    end
. . . . . . .
else error

begin               ''Initialization''
    init CM1, CM2(. . .), . . .
end

var CONV1: C;
```

Fig. 8.6. Abstract data type conversation.

4. Once the execution of the conversation acceptance test results in a pass, the c-monitors are reinitialized.
5. The only system components that can appear in the access rights field of a conversation are nested conversations.

Fig. 8.7(a) is an example system configuration containing nested conversations. In this figure, an arc connecting two components, one positioned below the other, indicates that the component at the lower position has a right of access to the other component. Of the processes participating in conversation CONV1, some may participate in conversation CONV2 or CONV3. However, a process cannot participate in both CONV2 and CONV3 concurrently, although a process can be designed to participate in the two conversations at two different times.

Fig. 8.7(b) illustrates a violation of the rule of conversation nesting. Of the processes participating in conversation CONV3 in Fig. 8.7(b), some may have entered CONV3 directly from CONV1, whereas some others have entered CONV3 from CONV2. An execution history of processes in such illegal conversations is illustrated in Fig. 8.7(c). From CONV1 process I enters CONV2 and then CONV3 whereas process J directly enters CONV3. Once process I and process J pass the conversation acceptance test of CONV3, they discard the information saved to enable their rollback to the recovery line of CONV3. If the conversation acceptance test of CONV2 results in a failure later, then process I's retry will require a reentry into CONV3 for which process J cannot cooperate. Therefore, CONV3 may be *directly* nested within CONV2 or within CONV1, but not both.

Again, storage allocation for c-monitors used in a conversation can be performed at their initialization time or when the conversation is entered by the first entering process.

The conversation acceptance test is specified in terms of the parameters listed in the participant's declaration. There are two options in executing the conversation acceptance test. One is to make the compiler to decompose the conversation acceptance test into segments, each executed by a different participating process. The other is to have one process execute the entire conversation acceptance test. The process selected for this job is the last one that completes its procedure execution; this is to ensure that all the participating processes have completed their executions of procedures before the execution of the conversation acceptance test starts. Implementation costs of these options are dependent upon several system parameters, such as the number of processors and the interprocessor communication mechanism used.

The abstract data type approach has a number of advantages over the name-linked RB approach.

1. It is easy to prevent information smuggling by a process participating in a conversation. This is again due to the fact that c-monitors are the only means of communication available to the processes participating in the corresponding conversation and cannot be accessed by any process outside the conversation.
2. It is easy to ensure proper nesting of conversations.
3. The conversation acceptance test takes a more abstract, concise, and natural form than in the previous two approaches.
4. Each interacting session is presented as a single (continuous) unit in the program text and is thus easier to read than when its components are scattered throughout the program text.

The approach shares one deficiency with the name-linked RB approach in that it does not provide much help in preventing a system deadlock due to a deserter process. An attempt to remove this deficiency is the subject of the next section.

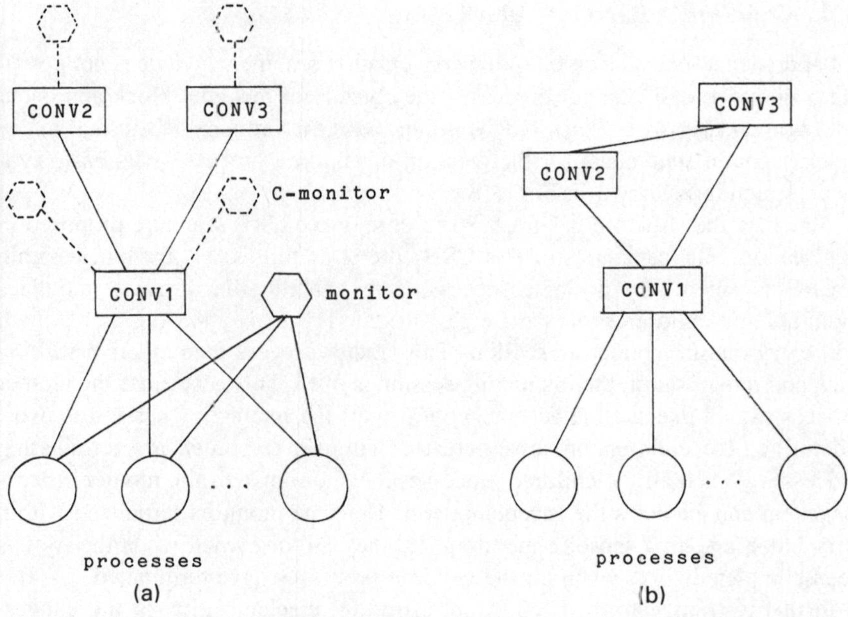

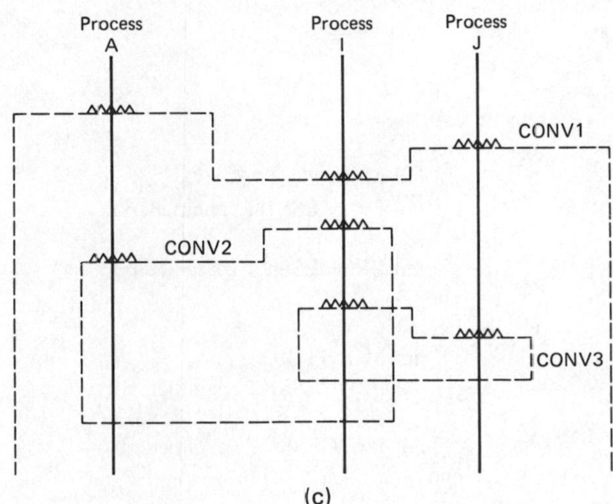

Fig. 8.7. (a) A proper nesting of conversations. (b) An illegal nesting of conversations. (c) An execution history of processes in illegal conversations.

3.4. Concurrent Recovery Block

An approach to mechanization of the conversation scheme which does not permit the occurrence of a deserter process is the concurrent recovery block approach. A *concurrent recovery block* (CRB) differs from the ordinary RB in that its try blocks contain statements for the creation of children processes. Its basic syntactic structure is shown in Fig. 8.8.

Actually, the structure in Fig. 8.8 is a core of the CRB structure proposed in this section. The semantics of this CRB core is as follows. A try block within a CRB is entered by a single process, and thereafter the process initializes monitors and children processes, e.g., PROCESS1.1, · · · , PROCESSn.1, which will carry out an interacting session. The mother process then enters a waiting state and remains until the interacting session is over. This is because the mother process cannot execute the acceptance test until the interacting session is over. Therefore, the children processes created within a try block are terminating processes. When all the children processes have terminated, the mother process wakes up and executes the acceptance test. Here the monitors initialized within a try block are, in a sense, c-monitors and they are discarded when the try has been completed, i.e., when all the children processes have terminated.

In this restrictive form, CRB is not a truthful mechanization of the conversation scheme. The deviation is in the extra synchronization imposed on initiation of an interacting session. That is, it does not enable asynchronous initialization of the participants of an interacting session. A CRB is entered by a single process and all the participants of an interacting session are initialized in a fixed sequence.

```
ensure CAT
by      begin
            init MONITOR.1;
            init PROCESS1.1 (parameters);
            . . . . . . . . . . . . .
            init PROCESSn.1 (parameters)
        end
else by begin
            init MONITOR.2;
            init PROCESS1.2 (parameters);
            . . . . . . . . . . . . .
            init PROCESSn.2 (parameters)
        end
. . . . . . . . . . . . .
else error
```

Fig. 8.8. A restrictive version of the concurrent recovery block (CRB).

In order to facilitate asynchronous initialization of the participants of an interacting session, the CRB approach incorporates a lookahead execution rule and tools for the specification of data dependency among statements.

Data dependency among statments is specified in the form of the relaying of access rights for *permanent variables* among statements. Permanent variables are "workspace" variables that are passed between mother and children processes and remain intact through creation and termination of children processes. Permanent variables are declared as shown in Fig. 8.9, and data dependency is specified by use of the using-pv construct, as illustrated in Fig. 8.10(a). Symbols "[" and "]" in Fig. 8.10 represent begin and end, respectively.

The 'using-pv V1, · · · , Vn do S' construct, where S is a staement, specifies that 1) V1, · · · , Vn are the only permanent variables that can be accessed during execution of S, and 2) the execution of S will begin only when V1, · · · , Vn are reserved exclusively for execution of S.

Moreover, the using-pv field, used as a prefix to a child process initialization statement, specifies that access rights for the permanent variables listed are given away to the child process and will be exclusively processed by the child process during its lifetime.

The following rules are applied to permanent variables and the using-pv construct.

1. The allocation of permanent variables to processes is subject to the *hierarchical allocation rule*. At the beginning, the initial process is the owner of

```
const . . . .
type . . . . .

permvar          "Permanent variables"
    PV1: record
            . . . . .
         end;
    PV2: . . . . .
    . . . . .
var

begin            "Main body of the initial process"
    init . . . . . .
    begin init . . . . . end   "Dynamic creation of"
    . . . . . .                "children processes"
    begin init . . . . . end
    . . . . . .
end
```

Fig. 8.9. A Concurrent-Pascal-based program structure extended with permanent variables and dynamic process creation.

```
Permvar
   PVPROD : record . . . . . .;
   PVCONX : record . . . . . .;
   PVCONY : record . . . . . .;
var
   MONITORa.1: monitor . . . .; MONITORa.2: monitor . . . .;
   MONITORb.1: monitor . . . .; MONITORb.2: monitor . . . .;
   PRODUCERa   : process using-pv . . . .;
   PRODUCERb.1: process . . . .; PRODUCERb.2: process . . . .;
   PRODUCERc   : process . . . .;
   PRODUCERd.1: process . . . .; PRODUCERd.2: process . . . .;
   CONSUMERXa   : process . . . .;
   CONSUMERXb.1: process . . . .; CONSUMERXb.2: process . . . .;
   CONSUMERYa   : process . . . .;
   CONSUMERYb.1: process . . . .; CONSUMERYb.2: process . . . .;
begin
   using-pv PVPROD do init PRODUCERa;
   using-pv PVCONX do init CONSUMERXa;
   using-pv PVCONY do init CONSUMERYa;
   cycle
      "CONV1" ensure CAT1
      by      [init MONITORa.1;
               using-pv PVPROD do init PRODUCERb.1 (MONITORa.1);
               using-pv PVCONX do init CONSUMERXb.1 (MONITORa.1)]
      else by [init MONITORa.2; . . . .]
      else error;

      using-pv PVPROD do init PRODUCERc;
      using-pv PVCONX do init CONSUMERXc;

      "CONV2" ensure CAT2
      by      [init MONITORb.1;
               using-pv PVPROD do init PRODUCERd.1 (MONITORb.1);
               using-pv PVCONY do init CONSUMERYb.1 (MONITORb.1)]
      else by [init MONITORb.2; . . . .]
      else error;

      using-pv PVPROD do init PRODUCERa;
      using-pv PVCONX do init CONSUMERYc;
   end "cycle"
end
```

(a)

Fig. 8.10. (a) A concurrent program based on CRB's for a system of a producer and two consumer processes. (b) A snapshot of the execution schedule taken when the lookahead of the initial process in (a) has progressed past the primary try block of CONV2. (c) A concurrent program which is logically equivalent to (a) and based on conversations mechanized as abstract data types. (d) A modified version of process PRODUCER in (c).

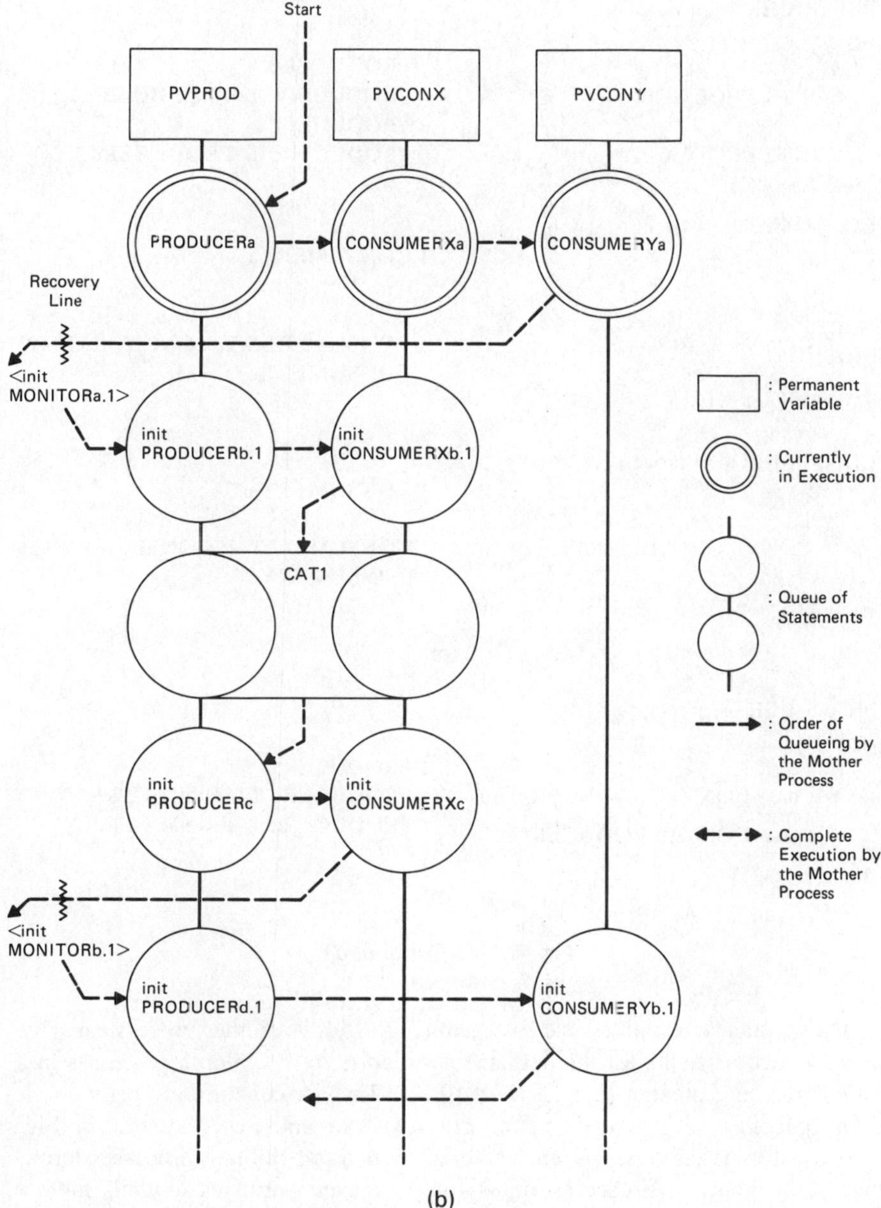

(b)

Fig. 8.10. (*Continued*)

```
PRODUCER = process;
[cycle
   . . . . . .                          "PRODUCERa"
   CONV1.PRODUCER;                      "PRODUCERb.1, PRODUCERb.2"
   . . . . . .                          "PRODUCERc"
   CONV2.PRODUCER                       "PRODUCERd.1, PRODUCERd.2"
 end "cycle"]

CONSUMERX = process;
[ . . . . . .                           "CONSUMERXa"

   cycle
      CONV1.CONSUMERX;                  "CONSUMERXb.1, CONSUMERXb.2"
      . . . . . .                       "CONSUMERXc"
   end "cycle"]

CONSUMERY = process;
[ . . . . . .                           "CONSUMERYa"
   cycle
      CONV2.CONSUMERY;                  "CONSUMERYb.1, CONSUMERYb.2"
      . . . . . .                       "CONSUMERYc"
   end "cycle"]
```

(c)

```
PRODUCER = process;
[cycle
   . . . . . .                          "PRODUCERa"
   if B then CONV1.PRODUCER             "PRODUCERb.1, PRODUCERb.2"
        else CONV2.PRODUCER             "PRODUCERd.1, PRODUCERd.2"
 end "cycle"]
```

(d)

Fig. 8.10. (*Continued*)

all the permanent variables in the system (Fig. 8.9). A mother process can give away its access rights for the permanent variables to its children processes in a nonoverlapping manner [e.g., Fig. 8.10(a)]. That is, concurrently active children processes, e.g., PRODUCERa, CONSUMERXa and CONSUMERYa in Fig. 8.10(a), do not share permanent variables. When the children processes terminate, they return their access rights for permanent variables to their mother process. Therefore, the 'using-pv V do S' construct plays a role of selecting a subset V of the currently accessible permanent variables as the set of permanent variables that should be made exclusively available during execution of the following statement S or during the lifetime of a process if S is the process initialization statement. In a sense, 'using-pv . . .' has the meaning of "after obtaining . . ." and thus can be used to specify data dependency among statements.

2. A permanent array cannot be partitioned for the purpose of distribution among children processes. It can only be given away to a single child process in its entirety. Therefore, array components cannot be used in the using-pv field. This restriction is needed to ease the compile-time check for nonoverlapped distribution of permanent variables to children processes.

The lookahead execution rule associated with the CRB and designed to exploit data dependency specifications is the following.

1. A mother process may encounter a child process initialization statement prefixed with a 'using-pv V' field when the permanent variables V are still held by the child process. In this case, the mother process simply puts the initialization statement into a queue associated with the permanent variable. Each queue contains statements which need the permanent variable associated with the queue for their execution. For example, the 'init PRODUCERb.1' statement in Fig. 8.10(a) is inserted into the queue associated with permanent variable PVPROD as shown in Fig. 8.10(b). The mother process then continues to the next statement for a lookahead.

2. The queueing rule in 1. also applies to 'using-pv V do S' statements where S is a statement other than a process initialization statement. Once the turn for execution of the statement comes, permanent variables V are held exclusively for execution of S.

3. If a statement S1 which is not a process initialization statement is queued, any other such statement S2 (i.e., a nonprocess-initialization statement) encountered by the mother process should not be *executed* before execution of S1. S2 should be merely scheduled (i.e., queued) for execution after completion of S1. Therefore, once a nonprocess-initialization statement is queued, all subsequent nonprocess-initialization statements should also be queued. In other words, lookahead used here does not involve difficult exploitation of implicit data dependency between statements. It utilizes only the dependency expressed in terms of permanent variables.

4. A mother process can look ahead past a CRB. For example, Fig. 8.10(b) shows a snapshot of the queues, i.e., the "execution schedule," taken when the lookahead of the initial process in Fig. 8.10(a) has progressed past the primary try block of conversation CONV2 and three children processes PRODUCERa, CONSUMERXa, and CONSUMERYa, are still active. If conversation acceptance test CAT1 of CONV1 results in a failure later, then all of the statements queued after CONSUMERYa will be taken off the execution schedule and the initial process will restart from the alternate try block of CONV1. If CAT1 results

in a pass, then the next two statements in the execution schedule, 'init PRODUCERC' and 'init CONSUMERXC', will be executed.

Therefore, asynchronous initialization of the participants of an interacting session can be facilitated by exploiting a) the lookahead execution rule and b) the explicit specifications of dependency among children processes in terms of permanent variables.

Note in Fig. 8.10(b) that 'init CONSUMERYb.1' can be executed as soon as child process CONSUMERYa terminates, regardless of whether children processes PRODUCERa and CONSUMERXa have terminated or not. The program in Fig. 8.10(a) is actually an adaptation of the program in Fig. 8.10(c), which is for a system of a producer and two consumer processes and uses conversations mechanized as abstract data types. Under the lookahead execution rule, execution of the CRB-based program in Fig. 8.10(a) can exploit all of the concurrency potential in the program of Fig. 8.10(c). However, this is not always the case. For example, if the PRODUCER process in Fig. 8.10(c) is changed to that in Fig. 8.10(d), then it is not feasible to obtain an equivalent CRB-based program without losing a certain amount of concurrency. The question of how significant such a loss of concurrency will be in many practical applications, requires further study.

Therefore, the CRB approach trades execution efficiency for easy prevention of deserter processes. Once a conversation begins, all the participants are bound to be initialized. It does not provide any room for introducing a deserter process, but it requires a lookahead execution rule which incurs a relatively high execution overhead. A safe conclusion here is that the CRB approach and the abstract data type approach complement each other. The latter, however, represents an easier step in extending Concurrent Pascal or any similar concurrent programming language.

4. SUMMARY AND EXTENSION

In spite of the continuously increasing need for fault-tolerant concurrent programs, development of structured design aids have not caught up. The conversation scheme proposed by Randell in an abstract form seems promising as a useful aid. This chapter dealt with mechanization of the conversation scheme. Four possible mechanizations were presented in the form of feasible extensions of Concurrent Pascal. The four mechanizations were presented in the increasing order of the amount of effort that they require for extending Concurrent Pascal. Of the four, the abstract data type approach and the CRB approach seem to offer the highest level of assistance to the programmer in proper structuring of recoverable interacting sessions.

The synchronization of participant processes required at the test line of a conversation is a logical requirement which can be met without much loss of computational parallelism. That is, each participant process that has passed its portion (acceptance test) of the test line can be allowed to look ahead past the test line as long as provisions are made for such process to roll back to the recovery line in case the conversation acceptance test becomes a failure.[5,6,13] This means that a process which has left a conversation keeps its portion (RP) of the recovery line intact until the conversation acceptance test is completed. If the conversation acceptance test becomes a success, then each participant discards its RP belonging to the recovery line. Therefore, facilitating the asynchronous exit of processes from a conservation in the form of lookahead is an implementation option; its justification depends upon the affordable complexity of implementation and the amount of exploitable parallelism.

An entirely different approach to the backward recovery of interacting processes, called programmer-transparent coordination (PTC) scheme, has been studied by this author.[6,8] The motivation of the PTC scheme is to relieve the programmer of the burden of coordinating recovery structures of interacting processes, i.e., to allow the programmer to design backward recovery capabilities into a process in a manner independent of recovery structures of other processes. The scheme relies on an intelligent processing system which is capable of executing the interacting processes in such a manner that a domino effect cannot occur. However, as pointed out in references 7 and 8, this scheme is not a replacement of, but rather a complement to, a programmer-dependent coordination scheme such as the conversation scheme. Therefore, combining the PTC scheme and the conversation scheme into a unified powerful scheme for facilitating cooperative error detection and recovery is believed to be a worthwhile subject for future research.

Fault-tolerant concurrent programming is a relatively young branch of software engineering. Much more study, especially experimental study, is needed to obtain a better understanding of programming principles. Experimentation with the conversation mechanizations presented in this chapter is considered a worthwhile effort.

REFERENCES

1. Brinch Hansen, P., *The Architecture of Concurrent Programs*, Englewood Cliffs, NJ: Prentice-Hall, 1977.
2. Chandy, K. M. and C. V. Ramamoorthy, Rollback and recovery strategies for computer programs, *IEEE Trans. Comput.*, vol. C-21, pp. 546–556, June 1972.
3. Hecht, H., Fault-tolerant software for real-time applications, *Comput. Surveys*, pp. 391–407, Dec. 1976.
4. Horning, J. J., H. C. Lauer, P. M. Melliar-Smith, and B. Randell, A program structure for error detection and recovery, in *Lecture Notes in Computer Science*, vol. 16. New York: Springer-Verlag, 1974, pp. 171–187.
5. Kim, K. H., D. L. Russell, and M. J. Jenson, *Language Tools for Fault-Tolerant Programming*, Electron. Sci. Lab., Univ. of Southern California, Tech. Memo. PETP-1, Nov. 1976.

6. Kim, K. H., An approach to programmer-transparent coordination of recovering parallel processes and its efficient implementation rules, in *Proc. 1978 Int. Conf. on Parallel Processing*, Aug. 1978, pp. 58–68.
7. Kim, K. H., Error detection, reconfiguration, and recovery in distributed processing systems, in *Proc. 1st Int. Conf. on Distributed Computing Systems*, Oct. 1979, pp. 284–295.
8. Kim, K. H., You, J. H., and Abouelnaga, A., A scheme for coordinated execution of independently designed recoverable distributed processes, in *Proc. FTCS-16*, July 1986, pp. 130–135.
9. Lee, P. A., *A Reconstruction of the Recovery Block Scheme*, Univ. of Newcastle upon Tyne, England, Tech. Rep. 119, Jan. 1978.
10. Ramamoorthy, C. V. and T. Krishnarao, *The Design Issues in Distributed Computer Systems*, Infotech. Rep. on Comput. Syst., 1978, pp. 377–399.
11. Randell, B., System structure for software fault tolerance, *IEEE Trans. Software Eng.*, vol. SE-1, pp. 220–232, June 1975.
12. Randell, B., P. A. Lee, and P. C. Treleaven, Reliability issues in computing system design, *Comput. Surveys*, pp. 123–165, June 1978.
13. Russell, D. L. and M. J. Tiedeman, Multiprocess recovery using conversations, in *Proc. FTC-9*, 1979, pp. 106–109.

9. A Formal Model of Crash Recovery in a Distributed System

DALE SKEEN

and

MICHAEL STONEBRAKER

ABSTRACT

A formal model for atomic commit protocols for a distributed database system is introduced. The model is used to prove existence results about resilient protocols for site failures that do not partition the network and then for partitioned networks. For site failures, a pessimistic recovery technique, called *independent recovery*, is introduced and the class of failures for which resilient protocols exist is identified. For partitioned networks, two cases are studied: the pessimistic case in which messages are lost, and the optimistic case in which no messages are lost. In all cases, fundamental limitations on the resiliency of protocols are derived.

1. INTRODUCTION

In this chapter we present a formal model for transaction processing in a distributed database and then extend it to model several classes of failures and crash recovery techniques. These models are used to study whether or not resilient protocols exist for various failure classes.

Crash recovery in distributed systems has been studied extensively in the literature.[2,4–6,9,11,13,15,16] Many protocols have been designed that are resilient

This work was supported by the U.S. Air Force Office of Scientific Research under grant 78-3596, the U.S. Army Research Office under grant DAAG29-76-G-0245, and the Naval Electronics Systems Command under contract N00039-78-G-0013.

in some environments. All have an "ad hoc" flavor to them in the sense that the class of failures they will survive is not clearly delineated.

The purpose of this chapter is to formalize the crash recovery problem in a distributed database environment and then give some preliminary results concerning the existence of resilient protocols in various well-defined situations.

Consequently, in the next section we will give a brief introduction to transactions in a distributed database. In Section 3 we indicate the assumed network environment and our model for transaction processing. In Section 4 we shall extend the model to include the possibility of site failure and give results concerning the existence of resilient protocols in this situation. Section 5 turns to the possibility of network failure and shows the class of failures for which a resilient protocol exists. Section 6 summarizes the results in the previous two sections.

2. BACKGROUND

A distributed database management system supports a database physically distributed over multiple sites interconnected by a communications network. By definition, a *transaction* in a distributed database system is a (logically) atomic operation: it must be processed at all sites or at none of them. Designing protocols resilient to various failures, including arbitrary site failures and partitioning of the communications network, is a very difficult task.

Preserving transaction atomicity in the single-site case is a well-understood problem.[4,7] The processing of a single transaction is viewed as follows. At some time during its execution, a "commit point" is reached where the site decides to commit or to abort the transaction. A *commit* is an unconditonal guarantee to execute the transaction to completion, even in the event of multiple failures. Similarly, an *abort* is an unconditional guarantee to back out the transaction so that none of its effects persist. If a failure occurs before the commit point is reached, then immediately upon recovery the site will abort the transaction. Both commit and abort are *irreversible*.

In the multiple site case, it is the task of a *commit protocol* to enforce global atomicity. Assuming that each site has a recovery strategy that provides atomicity at the local level, the problem becomes one of ensuring that the sites either unanimously abort or unanimously commit the transaction. A mixed decision results in an inconsistent database. In the absence of failures, a unanimous consensus is easily obtained by a simple protocol. The challenge then is to find protocols ensuring atomicity in the presence of inopportune and perhaps repetitive failures.

A basic assumption within this chapter is that, during the initial phase of distributed transaction processing, any participating site can unilaterally abort the transaction. A site may choose to abort for any of the following reasons:

Site 1 (coordinator)	Site 2 (slave)
(1) Transaction is received. "Start Xact" is sent.	
	"Start Xact" is received. Site 2 responds: "yes" to commit, "no" to abort. The response is sent to Site 1.
(2) Site 2's response is received. If response = "yes" and Site 1 agrees, then "commit" is sent; else, "abort" is sent.	
	Either "commit" or "abort" is received and processed.

Fig. 9.1. The two-phase commit protocol (two sites).

1. one or more sites fail,
2. the network fails,
3. the transaction deadlocks with another transaction, or
4. the user aborts the transaction.

Clearly, before any site can commit the transaction, all sites must relinquish their right to unilaterally abort it. Once a site has relinquished that right, it can abort the transaction only in concordance with the other sites.

Let us now examine a commit protocol allowing sites to unilaterally abort. One of the simplest, and certainly the most renowned, is the *two-phase commit protocol*[4,6] illustrated in Fig. 9.1 for two sites.* It is a centralized protocol with a single coordinator (Site 1) and with the remaining sites acting as slaves.

In the first phase, the coordinator receives the transaction and forwards it to the slave (Site 2). The slave then partially executes the transaction, and indicates its readiness to commit ("yes") or its intent to unilaterally abort ("no"). The commit decision is made by the coordinator after receiving a response from the slave, and a "commit" message is sent only if both agree to process the transaction. For a transaction to commit, three messages are exchanged: "start transaction" is sent to Site 2; "yes" is sent to Site 1; and finally "commit" is sent to Site 2. Although the protocol is illustrated for only one slave, any number of slaves may participate.

*The two-phase commit protocol depicted is an optimized version of the standard two-phase commit protocol. The standard protocol includes "ack's" following the receipt of messages for commit or abort by the slaves. These messages are convenient for bookkeeping purposes, but add nothing to the fault tolerance of the protocol, and thus have been deleted.

Clearly, the protocol is correct in the absence of failures. Its fundamental weakness is its vulnerability to site failures, especially failure of the coordinator. When the coordinator fails, the remaining sites must block transaction execution until it recovers.

It is always an option for a distributed database system to block whenever a failure occurs. Even though blocking preserves consistency, it is highly undesirable because the locks acquired by the blocked transaction cannot be relinquished, rendering the data inaccessible by other requests. Consequently, the availability of data stored at reliable sites can be limited by the availability of the weakest component in the distributed system. For this reason, we postulate that blocking protocols are unacceptable to many applications.

In this chapter, we will confine our interests exclusively to *nonblocking protocols*—protocols in which operational sites never suspend because of a failure. We say that a commit protocol is *resilient* to a class of failures only if the protocol enforces transaction atomicity and is nonblocking for any failure within that class. The nonblocking constraint guarantees that a resilient protocol will always terminate irrespective of the frequency of failures. A necessary but not sufficient condition for nonblocking behavior is a strict bound on the number of messages sent by a resilient protocol.

3. THE TRANSACTION MODEL

In this section, we introduce the model, ignoring the effects of failures. Sites failures and network failures are introduced into the model in Sections 4 and 5, respectively.

3.1. The Network Assumptions

The network provides point-to-point communication between any pair of sites. It is assumed to have the following characteristics: 1) it delivers a message within a preassigned time period T, or 2) it reports a ''time-out'' to the sender.

When a timeout occurs, the sender can safely assume that the network or the recipient or both have failed. In the case of a network failure, it is not known whether the recipient received the message.

Notice that we are assuming a somewhat idealized environment by precluding the possibility that a time-out is caused by a slow but correctly executing site. However, by adjusting T and by providing low-level protocols for verifying failures, we can build systems that differentiate between failures and slow responses with an arbitrarily high degree of confidence.

3.2. Specifying a Protocol

Reasoning about commit protocols requires a well-defined notion of the ''state'' of the transaction at each participating site. Broadly speaking, this abstract state is a concise summary of transaction history and, hence an indicator of the options available to a recovery protocol. In the above description of transaction processing, we informally discussed three such states: the initial state where sites have the right to unilaterally abort; the abort state; and the commit state. We now formalize the notion of the state by borrowing from classical automata theory.

The formal specification of a protocol consists of a collection of nondeterministic finite state automata (FSA)—one for each site. The automaton executing at Site i is called the *local protocol* for Site i. The state of this automaton is the *local transaction state* (or, more succinctly, the local state) for Site i. The network is modeled as a completely passive device. It is an unbounded buffer that serves as a common read/write medium for all local protocols. A local state transition consists of reading one or more messages, performing some local processing, and sending zero or more messages. Fig. 9.2 illustrates four sites participating in a distributed transaction. Similar models have been used for network communication protocols.[1,3]

There are several restrictions on this collection of FSA's.

1. The FSA's are nondeterministic. The behavior of each FSA is not known *a priori* because of the possibility of deadlocks, failures, and user aborts. Moreover, when multiple messages are addressed to a site, the order of receiving the messages is arbitrary.
2. The final states of the FSA's are partitioned into two sets: the "abort" states A and the "commit" states C.
3. There are no transitions from a state in A to a state not in A. Similarly, there are no transitions from a state in C to a state not in C. Therefore, once a site enters an "abort" state ("commit" state), the site remains in such a state. This corresponds to the requirement that abort and commit are irreversible operations.
4. The state diagram defining an FSA is acyclic. This suffices to guarantee that a protocol sends a bounded number of messages.

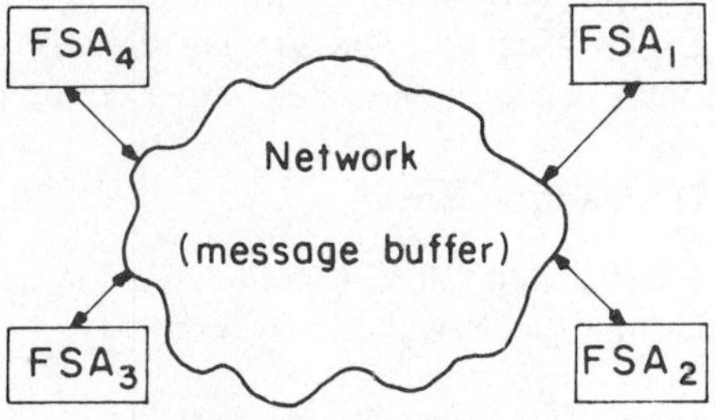

Fig. 9.2. The model with four sites.

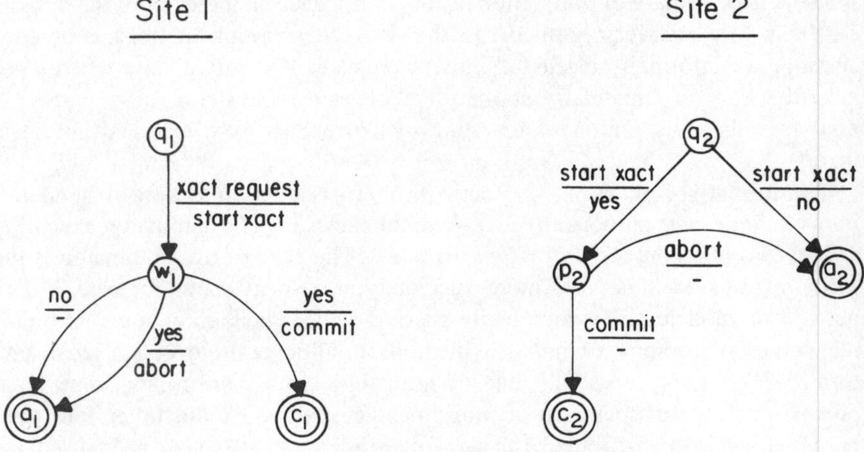

Fig. 9.3. The local protocols for the two-phase commit.

State transitions are assumed to be asynchronous among the sites and, in the absence of failures, atomic. It is convenient to consider a transition to be an instantaneous event.

The local protocols for the two-site, two-phase commit protocol (Fig. 9.1) are illustrated in Fig. 9.3.

The state diagram illustrates the conventions used in the remainder of the chapter. The states for Site i are subscripted by i, and final states are doubly circled. Messages received during a state transition are shown above the horizontal line; messages sent are shown below the line.

Both local protocols begin processing in their initial states (q_1 and q_2). A transaction begins when a *request* message is received from the application program. The receipt of the request by the coordinator (Site 1) causes a state transition to state w_1 (the wait state) and the sending of the transaction to Site 2. Upon receipt of the transaction, Site 2 nondeterministically chooses one of two possible replies. Either it replies with a "yes," accepting the transaction and moving into p_2 (the prepared or precommit state), or it replies with a "no," unilaterally aborting the transaction and moving directly to a_2. The protocol continues until both sites occupy final states: either commit (c) or abort (a).

3.3. The Global Transaction State

The *global state* of a distributed transaction is defined to consist of: 1. a global state vector containing the states of the local protocols, and 2. the outstanding messages in the network.

The global state defines the complete processing state of a transaction.

A global state is a *final state* if all local states contained in its state vector are final states. It is said to be *inconsistent* if its state vector contains both a commit state and an abort state.

A *global state transition* occurs whenever a local state transition occurs at a participating site. Barring failures, this is the only time that global state transitions occur. Since local state transitions are viewed as instantaneous and hence mutually exclusive events, exactly one local transition occurs during a global transition.

If there exists a global transition from global state G to global state G', then G' is said to be *immediately reachable* from G. A global state, together with the definition of the protocol, contains the minimal information necessary to compute all of its immediately reachable states. Starting with a unique initial global state and taking the transitive closure of the immediately reachable states, we obtain all of the reachable states. The reachable global state graph for the (2-site) two-phase commit protocol are illustrated in Fig. 9.4. In the graph, the descendants of a state are its immediately reachable successors.

The global state graph is an invaluable tool in both analysis and verification of the protocol, graphically rendering all possible actions of the protocol. A path from the initial state to a terminal state (i.e., a state without a successor) corresponds to a possible execution sequence of the protocol. The graph itself is easy to generate automatically, but can be quite large (exponential in N, the number of sites). Fortunately, a small N usually serves to illustrate a protocol, and proofs seldom require the generation of the entire graph.

A protocol is *operationally correct* only if its reachable state graph contains no inconsistent states and all terminal states are final states. When a graph contains terminal states that are not final states, then it is possible for some sites to never commit or abort the transaction. Applying these definitions to the state graph of Fig. 9.4, we can quickly verify the correctness of the two-phase protocol.

3.4. The Concurrency and Sender Sets

Two local states are said to be *potentially concurrent* if there exists a reachable global state containing both local states. Thus, for at least one possible execution of the protocol, the first state is occupied by one site at the same time that the second state is occupied by another site.

We now define two sets that will be used extensively in subsequent proofs. Both sets are easily constructed from the global state graph.

Definition: Let s be an arbitrary local state. The *concurrency set* of a local state s is the set of all local states that are potentially concurrent with it. We denote this set by $C(s)$.

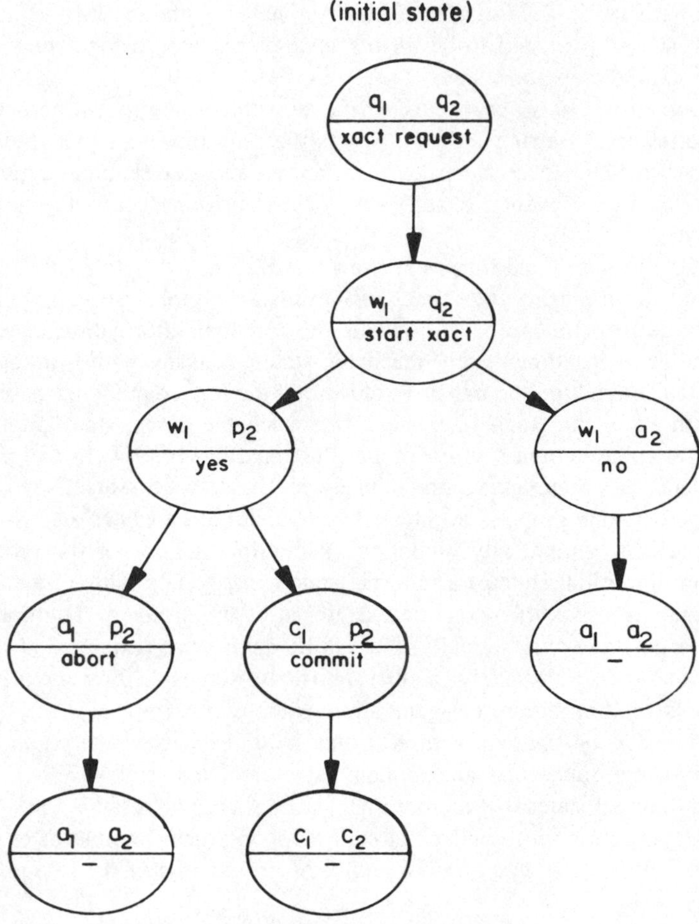

Fig. 9.4. Reachable state graph for the two-phase commit.

From the reachable state graph given in Fig. 9.4, we observe that the concurrency set for w_1 consists of $\{q_2, a_2, p_2\}$.

When a site makes a transition from state s to state t, it is convenient to consider the messages received and sent during the transition as being "received" and "sent" by state s. For example, in the two-phase commit we would say that the coordinator's wait state w_1 sends commit messages that are received by the slave's wait state p_2. We will be interested in the set of local states sending messages to a given state s.

Definition: Let s be an arbitrary local state, and let M be the set of messages that are received by s. The *sender set for* s, denoted $S(s)$, is $\{t \mid t$ "sends" m and $m \in M\}$.

Again referring to Fig. 9.4, we observe that $S(w_1)$ is $\{q_2\}$.

4. SITE FAILURES

This Section examines existence questions on nonblocking protocols for site failures. Here, we assume that the network never fails—an assumption that is relaxed in the next section.

4.1. Modeling Site Failures

A failure of any type is normally detected by the absence of an expected message. We assume that each site has at its disposal an interval timer allowing it to bound the time it waits for the receipt of a message. When the timer expires, the site is said to have "timed out" and may take appropriate action. This is modeled by *time-out* messages that are received like any other message and can cause a state transition.

Site failures are modeled by a *failure transition*, which is a special kind of local state transition.[10] Such a transition occurs *at the failed site* the instant that it fails. The resulting local state is the state initially occupied by the failed site upon recovering. An underlying assumption is that a site can detect when it has failed.

Let us temporarily assume atomic state transitions even in the presence of failures. Hence, a failure cannot occur during the middle of a transition and interrupt the sending of messages. In this case, a failure transition can be simply defined—it reads all outstanding messages and sends a *time-out* message to all participants.

In real systems, state transitions are not atomic and sites can fail after sending only a few of the messages associated with a transition. This can be modeled simply by allowing a failure transition to send any prefix of the messages normally sent by a valid transition from the same state. These messages are sent in addition to the time-out messages sent by the failure transition. We shall also allow failure transitions from the same state to terminate in different states. This generalization of failure transitions is sufficiently powerful to accurately model the behavior of any implementation of an FSA.

4.2. Independent Recovery

Independent recovery refers to a scheme where a recovering site makes a transition directly to a final state without communicating with other sites. Only local state information is used in the recovery protocol, hence recovery is independent of any event occurring after the site's failure. Independent recovery is modeled by requiring that all failure transitions terminate in a final state. This final state is assumed by the site immediately upon recovering.

Independent recovery is interesting for several reasons. First, it is easy to implement and leads to simple protocols. One need not be concerned with messages to a failed site being queued in the network or at another site that may be down when the failed site attempts to recover. This recovery strategy is of theoretic interest because it represents the most pessimistic recovery strategy. Proving the existence of a class of resilient protocols using independent recovery implies the existence of resilient protocols in all of the more sophisticated strategies of site failures. Its most important practical aspect is that it qualifies the usefulness of local state information during recovery. If the local state proves to be insufficient for resilient recovery, then those sites remaining operational during the duration of the transaction must maintain the transaction's outcome for the inoperative sites. This history will have to be maintained indefinitely until all sites have recovered and completed the transaction. In this regards, independent recovery provides the only true nonblocking recovery strategy—any strategy requiring a history mechanism will necessarily block when the history becomes temporarily unavailable due to failures.

When discussing independent recovery, we will restrict our attention to the two site case. All of the results are easily extended to the multisite case. The general case is not presented here because additional notations are required and the resulting protocols are of little practical importance.

4.3. Failure of a Single Site

Let us first consider the simple case where at most one site fails during a transaction. Our goal is to develop rules for assigning failure and timeout transitions to existing protocols to form protocols resilient to single site failures.

Not all protocols can be made resilient, as the next Theorem demonstrates.

Theorem 1: If a protocol contains a local state with both abort and commit in its concurrency set, then under independent recovery it is not resilient to an arbitrary single failure.

Proof: This follows directly from the definition of "concurrency set." Consider a local state s_i, and its concurrency set $C(s_i)$. Let $C(s_i)$ contain both an abort state and a commit state. Clearly, s_i cannot have a failure transition to the commit state, since the other site may be in the abort state. Similarly, s_i can not have a failure transition to the abort state, since the other site may be in the commit state. Hence, when Site i is in s_i, it cannot safely and independently recover.

If a protocol has no local states violating the necessary condition in the above lemma, then failure transitions can be assigned according to the following rule.

Rule 1: For every intermediate state s in the protocol: if $C(s)$, contains a commit, then assign a *failure* transition from s to a commit state; otherwise, assign a *failure* transition from s to an abort state.

The two-phase commit protocol does not satisfy the condition in Theorem 1: the concurrency set of the slave's prepared state (p_2) contains both c_1 and a_1. However, p_2 is the only local state violating this rule. This occurs because the coordinator moves into the commit state before the slave acknowledges committing the transaction. If, instead, the coordinator moves to a *prepared* state while it is waiting for the acknowledgment from the slave and moves into a commit state only after the acknowledgment is received, then it is possible to assign a failure transition to p_2. This "extended" two-phase commit protocol is shown in Fig. 9.5 and its (reachable) global state graph is shown in Fig. 9.6.

From the graph, it is easy to verify that the concurrency set for each state, including the *prepared* state, contains only one kind of final state. Hence, failure transitions satisfying Rule 1 can be defined for each state. The assignment of failure transitions is depicted in Fig. 9.7 (time-out transitions, to be discussed subsequently, are also illustrated).

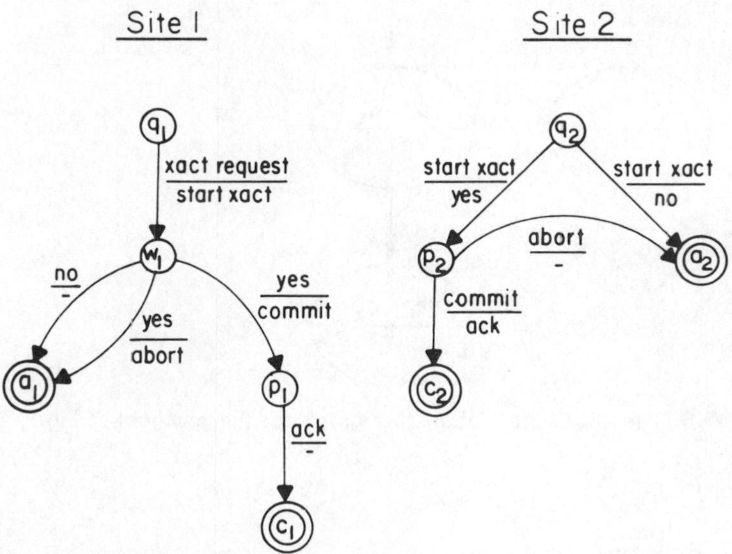

Fig. 9.5. The two-phase commit protocol extended with an *ack* message.

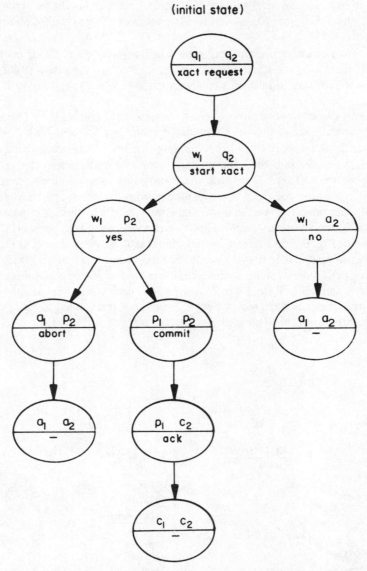

Fig. 9.6. The reachable global state graph for the protocol of Fig. 9.5.

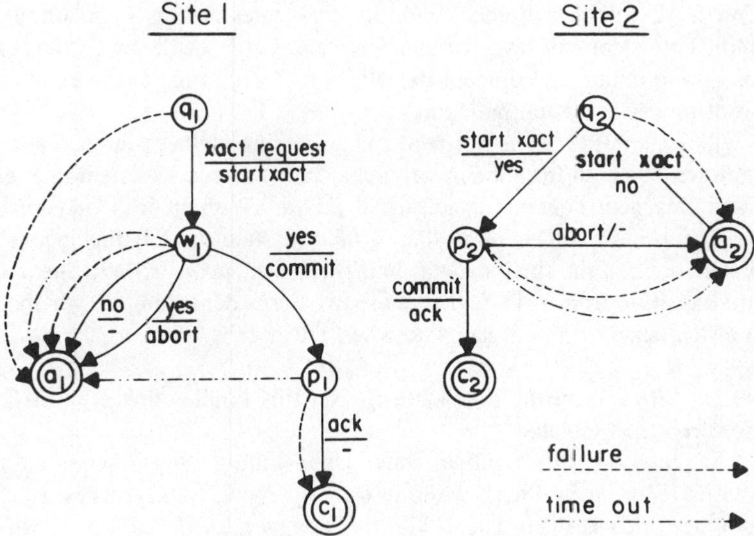

Fig. 9.7. The protocol with failure and timeout transitions obeying Rules 1 and 2.

The second rule deals with timeout transitions.

Rule 2: For each intermediate state s_i: if t_j is in $S(s_i)$ (the *sender set* for s_i) and t_j has a failure transition to a commit (abort) state, then assign a time-out transition from s_i to a commit (abort) state.

This rule is less obvious than the previous one. A "time-out" can be viewed as a special message sent by a failed site in lieu of a normal message. Like any other message received by state s_i, it must have been "sent" by a state in the sender set for s_i. Moreover, the failed site, using independent recovery, has made a failure transition to a final state. Hence, the receiving state must make a consistent decision. Time-out transitions for the extended commit protocol are illustrated in Fig. 9.7.

The protocol displayed is resilient to a single failure by either site. This can be verified by examining its reachable state graph. In fact, the rules always yield a resilient protocol under independent recovery.

Theorem 2: Rules 1 and 2 are sufficient for designing protocols resilient to a single site failure.

Proof: Let P be a protocol with no local states having a concurrency set containing both a commit state and an abort state. Let P' be the protocol resulting from assigning failure and timeout transitions to P according to the above rules. The proof proceeds by contradiction.

We will assume that P' is not resilient to all single site failures. Therefore, there must exist a path from the initial global state to an inconsistent final global state, and this path contains exactly one failure. Without loss of generality, assume Site 1 fails, and assume that it fails in state s_1. Let the inconsistent global state contain the final states f_1 and f_2. Hence, upon failing, Site 1 made a failure transition from s_1 to f_1. There are two cases depending on whether Site 2 is in a final state or a nonfinal state when Site 1 fails.

Case 1: Site 2 is in the final state f_2. But this implies that f_2 is in $C(s_1)$. Therefore rule 1 is violated.

Case 2: Site 2 is in a nonfinal state. Upon failing, Site 1 sends a "timeout" that is received by Site 2 while in state s_2. Now, Site 2 makes a timeout transition to f_2 that is inconsistent with f_1. However, by definition, s_1 is in the sender set of s_2. Therefore, Rule 2 has been violated.

4.4. Two Site Failures

The rules given above are sufficient for protocols resilient to a single failure; however, such protocols are not necessarily resilient to the failure of two sites. This can be demonstrated for the protocol of Fig. 9.3. Double failures occurring when Site 1 is in state p_1 and Site 2 is in state p_2 results in an inconsistent final state. Unfortunately, this is the only possible assignment of failure and timeout transitions satisfying both rules; hence, this protocol cannot be made resilient to two failures using only Rules 1 and 2.

Recall that the addition of a single state to the two-phase commit resulted in the above protocol, which enjoys a marked increase in resiliency over its progenitor. Can this protocol be extended with additional states to deal with double failures? The next theorem yields a negative answer.

Theorem 3: There exists no protocol using *independent recovery* that is resilient to arbitrary failures by two sites.

The double failures that are impossible to handle are "concurrent failures"—failures occurring close enough together such that neither site detects the failure of the other before itself failing. Although we will not prove it, concurrent failures are the only class of double failures from which it is impossible to recover. We now briefly sketch the nonexistence argument assuming double concurrent failures. In the discussion, we use the shorter term "*j* independently recovers to state s from G" instead of the more precise term "Site j independently recovers to state s after failing while the global state is G."

Let P be a commit protocol, and consider an execution of P resulting in global commit. This execution corresponds to some path, $G_0, G_1, \cdots, G_m$, in the global state graph for P. Clearly, from the initial global state G_0, all sites independently recover to the abort state, and from the global commit state G_m, all sites independently recover to the commit state. Let G_k be the first global state where a site recovers to a commit state, and let j be such a site. Since j independently recovers to the abort state in G_{k-1} (by assumption) but not in G_k, j must have changed states in the global state transition from G_{k-1} to G_k. Moreover, j was the only site to make a state transition (see Section 3.3). Hence, the other sites occupy the same states in G_k as they did in G_{k-1}, and each must therefore recover independently to the same state in both G_k and in G_{k-1}, namely, the abort state. Consequently, the failure of j coupled with any other failure while the global state is G_k results in an inconsistent state.

The above argument applies not only to the two-site case but to any number of sites. The complete proof for $N (N > 1)$ sites appears in the Appendix.

Several conclusions can be drawn from these results. Since a site cannot determine concurrent failures from its local state, it cannot determine when independent recovery can be safely used. For a two site protocol, this means that in all cases a recovering site must block until it can communicate with its cohort. Moreover, the cohort must maintain a record of the transaction's outcome if the transaction was completed.

Although it is not possible to design a protocol that allows nonblocking recovery, it is possible to design commit protocols that never require an operational site to block. (Here "operational site" refers to a site that has not failed since the beginning of the transaction.) Such protocols are of great practical importance: examples include the four-phase protocol of SDD-1[5] and the family of three-phase protocols.[12] All of these protocols require that a recovering site poll the other sites about the status of any outstanding transaction.

5. NETWORK PARTITIONING

A network failure results in at least two sites that cannot communicate with each other. We model such a partition in two ways. The first model is a pessimistic model where all messages are lost at the time partitioning occurs. The second model is an (overly) optimistic model where no messages are lost at the time partitioning occurs; instead, undeliverable messages are returned to the sender. While the pessimistic model is more realistic, the optimistic model is theoretically interesting since it yields upper bounds on the achievable resiliency.

A *simple partitioning* occurs when the sites are partitioned into exactly two sets with no communication possible between the sets. A *multiple partitioning* occurs when the sites are partitioned into $k(k > 2)$ sets. A multiple partitioning can be viewed as simultaneous occurrences of two or more simple partitionings.

A protocol is *resilient* to a network partitioning only if it is *nonblocking*, that is, the protocol must ensure that each isolated group of sites can reach a commit decision consistent with the remaining groups. Since the commit decision within a group is reached in the absence of communication to outside sites, this problem is very similar to the independent recovery paradigm presented in the previous Section.

Unless otherwise stated, we assume that partitions are caused by link failures rather than site failures.

5.1. Partitioning With Loss of Messages

In this pessimistic case, a network partitioning is modeled as a special type of global state transition. Until now, all global state transitions have been triggered by one local state transition. However, a network partitioning is modeled as a global state transition that changes the network state while leaving all local states unchanged. Specifically, a partitioning erases all outstanding messages and substitutes time-outs in their place. As before, upon reading a time-out message, a site may make a ''time-out'' transition.

Let us first examine the simplest type of partitioning: a simple partitioning where each partition contains exactly one site. This situation is analogous to a double site failure in a two site protocol using independent recovery. The difference is that when a double failure occurs, sites make ''failure'' transitions; whereas, when a partitioning occurs, sites make ''time-out'' transitions. It can be shown that a solution to the double failure problem implies a solution to the simple partitioning problem. An immediate consequence of this observation is the next theorem.

Theorem 4: There exists no protocol resilient to a network partitioning when messages are lost.

This applies to multiple partitionings as well as simple partitionings. The Appendix contains a proof outline that uses the proof of Theorem 3 as a paradigm.

Any time that a partitioning results in lost messages or there is the possibility of lost messages, a blocking protocol must be used. Unfortunately, this is the normal situation, especially for wide area networks. In the worst case, only a single partition can continue processing.

Finally, let us consider the possibility of site failures in conjunction with network partitioning. If all participants can differentiate between site failures and partitioning, then there is no problem. On the other hand, if a group of communicating sites cannot determine conclusively the type of failure that has occurred, then they must assume the worst, which is a partitioning. In the special case when there are only two sites, it is senseless to run any protocol more elaborate than the two-phase commit unless both sites can frequently differentiate between a site failure and a network failure. When they cannot differentiate, one site (presumably the slave) will be forced to block anyway.

5.2. Partitioning with Return of Messages

In this environment, we assume that the network can detect the presence of a partition and return undeliverable messages to their senders. This appears to represent the most optimistic model for partitions, while the loss of messages is the most pessimistic one.

In this optimistic case, a partition causes a global state transistion that redirects all undeliverable messages back to their senders and writes timeout messages to the recipients of undeliverable messages. A site may make a transition whenever an undeliverable message is returned to it or a timeout is received.

5.3. The Optimistic Two-Site Case

To study this optimistic situation, we now define two design rules that the resilient protocols must satisfy.

Rule 3: For a state s_i: if its concurrency set, $C(s_i)$, contains a commit (abort) state, then assign a *time-out* transition from s_i to a commit (abort) state.

Here, Site i in state s_i was expecting a message when the partition occurred. Instead, it received a "time-out." This site will then make a decision to abort or commit the transaction consistent with the state of the sender of the undeliverable message. At this time the site can infer that any message it sent arrived at its destination but any reply to that message was returned undelivered.

The second rule deals with a site sending an undeliverable message. It must make a commit decision consistent with the decision of the intended receiver.

Rule 4: For state s_i: if t_i is in $S(s_j)$, the sender set for s_j, and t_i has a *time-out* transition to a commit (abort) state, then assign an *undeliverable message* transition from s_i to a commit (abort) state upon the receipt of an undeliverable message.

An observant reader will note that these rules are equivalent to the rules given for independent recovery of failed sites. In fact, the two models are isomorphic. To illustrate the equivalence, consider the information conveyed by a "time-out" message from a failed site. The following is true when the operational site i receives the "time-out" indicating a failure of the other site:

1. the last message sent by Site *i* was not received (the other site failed prior to its receipt),
2. communication with the other site is impossible (it is down),
3. the other site will decide to commit using independent recovery.

Exactly the same conditions hold when an undeliverable message is returned to Site *i*.

Applying the above design rules to the protocol of Fig. 9.5 yields the protocol illustrated in Fig. 9.8. As expected, the protocol is isomorphic to the protocol of Fig. 9.7.

In light of this isomorphism, Theorem 5 is not surprising.

Theorem 5: Design Rules 3 and 4 are necessary and sufficient for making protocols resilient to a partition in a two-site protocol.

Sketch of Proof: We can make use of the proof of Theorem 2. In that proof, substitute "undelivered message" for every occurrence of "time-out" and substitute "time-out" for every occurrence of "failure." Finally, substitute "Rule 3" for "Rule 1" and "Rule 4" for "Rule 2." The result is a proof for Theorem 5.

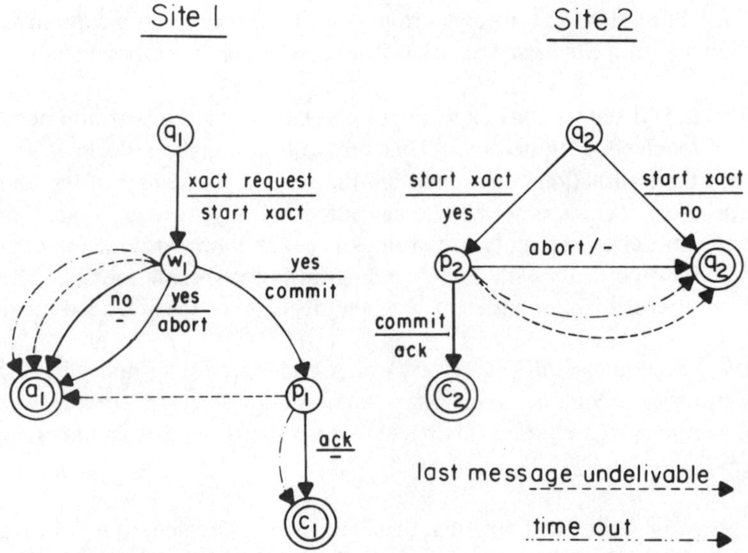

Fig. 9.8. The extended two-phase commit protocol (of Fig. 9.5) augmented with *time-out* transitions and "undeliverable message" transitions according to Rules 3 and 4.

An implicit assumption made above is that a site can distinguish between a time-out resulting from a site failure and a time-out resulting from a partitioning. Comparing the protocol in Fig. 9.8 to the protocol in Fig. 9.6, we note that the coordinator's behavior in state p_1 is dependent on the cause of the timeout. Hence, for this protocol, knowing the cause of the failure (at least for the coordinator) is crucial. It is not hard to show that this is always the case. Of course, within this model, detecting the cause of a time-out is easy to finesse: If a site is uncertain as to the reason for a time-out, then it can send another message to the same site. Presumably, if the network is down, then it will return the message "undelivered" rather than a "time-out."

5.4. The Optimistic Multisite Case

In the absence of site failures, the multisite case is very similar to the two-site case, since preserving consistency within a connected group of operational sites is not difficult. Thus, design rules 3 and 4 can be extended to multisite protocols in a straightforward way. This leads to the following result.

Corollary 1: There exist multisite protocols that are resilient to a *simple* partition when undeliverable messages are returned to the sender.

This result is the complement of the results obtained from the pessimistic model discussed earlier. The models differ in their handling of outstanding messages when the network fails: in the pessimistic model, they are lost; whereas, in the optimistic model, they are returned to their sender. Since this is the only difference between the two models, the next result is implied.

Corollary 2: Knowledge of which messages were undelivered at the time the network fails is necessary and sufficient for recovering from simple partitions.

We now turn to multiple partitions. Since we are dealing with an optimistic situation, we assume that time-outs and undeliverable messages are unaffected by additional partitions. This, in effect, is an assumption that the network is partitioned into all subsets simultaneously.

Even in this (overly) optimistic model, our results are negative, which implies negative results for all realistic partitioning models.

Theorem 6: There exists no protocol resilient to a multiple partition.

Therefore, even complete information about message traffic during a partition, and in particular, information about which messages are undeliverable, is sufficient for recovering from multiple partitions.

The proof of this theorem is similar to the proof of Theorem 3, but it is somewhat more complicated since the network state in addition to the local transaction states must be examined. The proof appears in the Appendix.

6. CONCLUSIONS

The major contribution of this chapter is the formal model for atomic commit protocols based on a nondeterministic finite state machine. Nondeterminism is used in modeling unpredictability in the environment, including the order of message deliveries and failures. Herein, we have used the model to study the existence of nonblocking protocols for site and network failures. Companion papers have used it for specifying and verifying several families of very resilient protocols.[11,12] It has been our experience that the model provides a convenient conceptual framework for reasoning about protocols.

The results in Sections 4 and 5 define fundamental limitations on the robustness of protocols with respect to both site failures and network partitions. Many of the limitations have been part of the accepted folklore on fault-tolerant distributed computing. For this reason, the results tend to be more illuminating than surprising. However, we believe that this is the first formal, systematic treatment of such existence questions. The approach is extensible to problems in related areas, such as existence results for atomic broadcast.

The only truly nonblocking site recovery strategy, independent recovery, uses local state information available at failure time. Hence, recovery does not depend on messages to down sites being queued in the network or on operational sites maintaining a log of completed transactions. This strategy is resilient to a single failure but no more. From the nonexistence proof for the case of two failures, it is clear that concurrent failures are the most difficult failures to handle: in general, the database is left in an inconsistent state if independent recovery is attempted after concurrent failures. Since a site cannot deduce from its local state whether another site's failure was concurrent with its failure, *a recovering site cannot determine when it is safe to use independent recovery.*

The results on robust network protocols are more discouraging than the independent recovery results. In realistic network environments, where a partition can result in lost messages, there exists no nonblocking protocols—not even for ''simple'' partitions. Therefore, in the worst case, the best protocols allow no more one group of sites to continue while the remaining groups block.

APPENDIX

Herein, the complete proofs for Theorems 3, 4, and 6 are given.

Theorem 3: There exists no protocol using *independent recovery* of failed sites that is resilient to two-site failures.

Proof: Let P be a protocol that always preserves consistency in the absence of failures. Let i and j be two sites. We will show: for every failure-free execution of P that commits the transaction, there exists a point in the execution where a failure of i followed by a failure of j leads to an inconsistency.

A failure-free execution of P corresponds to a path in the global state graph, $G_0, G_1, \cdots, G_m$ where G_0 is the initial global state and G_m is a final global state. We are assuming that G_m is a final *commit* state. A global state consists of a local state vector and a network state; however, for the remainder of this proof, we will ignore the network state. Hence, we view the global state G_k as a vector $\langle s_{k1}, s_{k2}, \cdots, s_{kN} \rangle$, where s_{ki} is the local state for Site i when transaction execution is in state G_k. N is the number of participating sites.

Let $f(s)$ be the result of making a failure transition while in state s. Let F_k be the global state resulting from the double failure of i and j when transaction processing is in G_k. F_k is equal to G_k except that the s_{ki} and s_{kj} are replaced by $f(s_{ki})$ and $f(s_{kj})$.

Let us now examine the sequence $F_0, \cdots, F_m$ and, in particular, the local states for i and j in this sequence. The pair $(f(s_{0i}), f(s_{0j}))$ must be equal to (a_i, a_j), since a site will always abort the transaction when it fails in the initial state. Similarly, the pair $(f(s_{mi}), f(s_{mj}))$ must equal (c_i, c_j) since we have assumed that the transaction was committed. Let k be the smallest k such that either $f(s_{ki})$ or $f(s_{kj})$ yields a commit state. This situation is depicted below:

Commit Sequence (G_l)	Global State (F_l) Resulting from the Failure of i and j
$\langle \cdots, s_{0i}, \cdots, s_{0j}, \cdots \rangle$	$\langle \cdots, a_i, \cdots, a_j, \cdots \rangle$
$\vdots$	$\vdots$
$\langle \cdots, s_{k-1,i}, \cdots, s_{k-1,j}, \cdots \rangle$	$\langle \cdots, a_i, \cdots, a_j, \cdots \rangle$
$\langle \cdots, s_{ki}, \cdots, s_{kj}, \cdots \rangle$	F_k where either $f(s_{ki})$ or $f(s_{kj})$ is a common state
$\vdots$	$\vdots$
$\langle \cdots, s_{mi}, \cdots, s_{mj}, \cdots \rangle$	$\langle \cdots, c_i, \cdots, c_j, \cdots \rangle$

Since each global transition reflects one local state transition, two adjacent global states differ by exactly one local state. Therefore, either $s_{k-1,i} = s_{ki}$ or $s_{k-1,j} = s_{kj}$, and therefore, either $f(s_{k-1,i}) = f(s_{ki})$ or $f(s_{k-1,j}) = f(s_{kj})$. This implies that $f(s_{ki})$ or $f(s_{kj})$ is an abort state. By assumption, the other one is a commit state. Hence, F_k is inconsistent.

Theorem 4: There exists no protocol resilient to a network partitioning when messages are lost.

Without loss of generality, we will restrict our attention to only two sites. Hence, the partitioning must be simple.

Sketch of Proof: Let $f(s)$ represent the result of a *time-out* transition from state s. Since messages are lost when the partitions occur, we can ignore the message state portion of a global state. Let $G_0, \cdots, G_m$ be a partition-free execution of the protocol that commits the transaction. Define F_i to be the global state resulting from a network partition occurring in state G_i. Using the notation of the previous theorem, $F_i = \langle f(s_{i1}), f(s_{i2}) \rangle$. As above, we can find the smallest k such that F_k contains a commit state. (Recall that F_0 contains only abort states.) Now, the difference between F_{k-1} and F_k is one local state. Therefore, F_k must contain an abort state as well, which makes the state inconsistent.

Theorem 6: There exists no protocol resilient to a multiple partition.

In the proof of this theorem we will only consider protocols in which each state transition reads at most one message (however, a transition can still send an arbitrary number of messages). It is shown in reference 12 that these protocols are equivalent in power to more general protocols reading an arbitrary number of messages per state change. This assumption allows a simpler proof. The proof follows the same form as the previous nonexistence proof.

Proof: Let P be a three-site protocol that is correct in the absence of failures. We will assume that P is resilient to multiple partitions. Let $G_0, \cdots, G_m$ be a failure free path in the global state graph for P that commits the transaction. Now, $G_i = (S_i, M_i)$ where $S_i = \langle s_{i1}, s_{i2}, s_{i3} \rangle$ is the vector of local states and M_i is the outstanding messages. We will consider M_i to be the union of three sets: M_{i1}, M_{i2}, and M_{i3}, where M_{ij} is the set of messages addressed to Site j.

Let G_i' be the global state resulting from a partitioning occurring during the global state G_i. Without loss of generality, we assume that all outstanding messages are returned to their senders. The recipients will receive only "time-outs." Let M_i' be the resulting set of messages. Thus, $G_i' = (S_i, M_i')$. Now, let f_j denote the transition function that moves Site j to a final state during a partitioning, i.e., $f_j(s_{ij}, M_{ij}')$ is Site j's resulting final state when a partitioning occurs during G_i.

Let k be the smallest k such that a multiple partitioning occurring while the transaction is in G_k still results in the transaction being committed. Since we have assumed that the protocol is resilient to such a partitioning, we have $f_j(s_{kj}, M_{kj}')$ equals commit for $j = 1, 2, 3$. Moreover, by our choice of k, we have $f_j(s_{k-1,j}, M_{k-1,j}')$ equals abort for $j = 1, 2, 3$. Now from G_{k-1} to G_k one state transition occurred, and let us assume that Site 1 made that transition. Furthermore, Site 1 read at most one message, and if so, let this be a message from Site 2.

Notice that we have $s_{k-1,3} = s_{k,3}$ and $M'_{k-1,3} = M'_{k,3}$ since, between G_{k-1} and G_k, Site 3 did not make a transition and none of its messages were read. Therefore, $f_3(s_{k-1,3}, M'_{k-1,3}) = f_3(s_{k,3}, M'_{k,3})$. But this is a contradiction.

ACKNOWLEDGMENT

The authors wish to thank K. Birman, K. Keller, and L. Rowe for their useful comments and for valuable discussions.

REFERENCES

1. Aho, A. V., J. D. Ullman, and M. Yannakakis, Modeling communications protocols by automata, in *Proc. 20th Annual Symp. Foundations Comput. Sci.*, Oct. 29–31, 1979, pp. 267–273.
2. Alsberg, P. and J. Day, A principle for resilient sharing of distributed resources, in *Proc. 2nd Int. Conf. Software Eng.*, San Francisco, CA, Oct. 1976.
3. Bochmann, G. V. Finite state description of communication protocols. *Comput. Networks*, vol. 2, pp. 361–372, Oct. 1977.
4. Gray, J. N., Notes on database operating systems, in *Operating Systems: An Advanced Course.* New York: Springer-Verlag, 1979.
5. Hammer, M. and D. Shipman, Reliability mechanisms for SDD-1: A system for distributed databases, *ACM Trans. Database Syst.*, vol. 5, pp. 431–466, Dec. 1980.
6. Lampson, B. and H. Sturgis, *Crash Recovery in a Distributed Storage System*, Tech. Rep., Comput. Sci. Lab., Xerox Parc, Palo Alto, CA, 1976.
7. Lindsay, B. G., *et al.*, *Notes on distributed databases*, IBM Res. Rep. RJ2571, San Jose, CA, July 1979.
8. Lorie, R., Physical integrity in a large segmented data base, *ACM Trans. Database Syst.*, vol. 2, Mar. 1977.
9. Menasce, D. A. and R. R. Muntz, Locking and deadlock detection in distributed databases, *IEEE Trans. Software Eng.*, vol. *SE-5*, pp. 195–202, May 1979.
10. Merlin, P. M., A methodology for the design and implementation of communication protocols, *IEEE Trans. Commun.*, vol. COM-24, pp. 614–621, 1976.
11. Rothnie, Jr., J. B. and N. Goodman, A survey of research and development in distributed database management," in *Proc. IEEE 3rd Int. Conf. Very Large Databases*, Tokyo, Japan, Oct. 6–8, 1977.
12. Skeen, D., Nonblocking commit protocols, presented at the ACM-SIGMOD Int. Conf. Management of Data, Ann Arbor, MI, 1981.
13. Schapiro, R. and R. Millstein, "Failure recovery in a distributed database system, in *Proc. 1978 COMPCON Conf.*, Sept. 1978.
14. Skeen, D., *Crash Recovery in a Distributed Database Management System* (Ph.D. diss.) Dep. Elec. Eng. Comput. Sci., Univ. Calif., Berkeley, 1982.
15. Stonebraker, M., Concurrency control and consistency of multiple copies in distributed INGRES, *IEEE Trans. Software Eng.*, vol. SE-5, pp. 188–194, May 1979.
16. Svobodova, L., Reliability issues in distributed information processing systems, in *Proc. 9th IEEE Fault Tolerant Comput. Conf.*, Madison, WI, June 1979.

10. Resilient Concurrency Control in Distributed Database Systems

BHARAT BHARGAVA

ABSTRACT

This chapter presents the resiliency features of the optimistic approach to concurrency control and demonstrates how it lends itself to a design of a reliable distributed database system. The validation of concurrency control, integrity control, and atomicity control has been integrated. This integration provides a high degree of concurrency and continuity of operations in spite of failures of transactions, processors, and the communication system.

1. INTRODUCTION

To provide continuity of operations in automated systems, we need to investigate principles that can provide robustness. Many systems, such as those used in space program, air traffic control, nuclear plant monitors, and ballistic missile defense demand nonstop operation. Recently, research efforts have focused on the design and implementation of distributed systems in such applications.[7]

A distributed system consists of a set of computers located in different sites connected by a communication network. Different programs can run on each of these computers and the programs can access local or remote resources such as databases. The programs can be viewed as transactions which consist of a sequence of atomic operations. The resources can be partially replicated or partitioned.

Though it has become feasible for computers to communicate at high speed

---

This work has been partially supported by the U.S. Department of Transportation, contract DTRS 5680-C-0026.

with each other and share their resources, a failure can occur in a distributed system. Some of these causes also exist in a centralized environment, but for completeness we present them as follows.

Incorrect input data. There are two sources of incorrect data: accidents, such as mistyping of input by the user or incorrect output from sensory devices or instruments (such as terminals). If incorrect data are input into the system, they can easily contaminate the database. The *external data integrity control (XDIC)* subsystem can provide a barrier against incorrect input data.

Incorrect transaction. Since transactions are executions of programs written by users and the programs can neither be fully proven correct or tested for all possible cases, incorrect transactions are a reality. The *transaction correctness control (PCC)* subsystem can ensure the correct execution of a transaction.

Incomplete transaction execution. It might not be possible to complete the execution of a transaction due to many reasons. For example, a hardware failure, deadlock problem, or violation of database security can cause the system to abort a transaction in the middle of its execution. The *transaction atomicity control (PAC)* subsystem can ensure that either none or all updates of a transaction are executed.

Incorrect concurrency control. Several transactions can run in parallel and not maintain consistency. For example, they may read incorrect data or write in the database in an incorrect order. The *concurrency control (CC)* subsystem can provide consistency via enforcement of serializability of concurrent transactions.

Site failure. A particular processor can cease operations due to software or hardware problems. The contents of the memory of the system can be lost or even the contents of secondary storage can be affected. A site failure could be local to the transaction or it could be remote. A local site failure will halt the transaction processing. A remote site can affect the completion of the transaction because a data value to be updated by the transaction resides on that site.

Communication system failure. If the communication links between two sites are broken, they no longer communicate. In addition, due to malfunction of the communication facility, messages can be lost or delivered in wrong order. Maintenance of database consistency in spite of site crashes and system partitions can be the task of the *site crash/partition treatment (SCPT)* subsystem.

Included in the above list is one more subsystem, called *internal data integrity control (IDIC)* that can check the integrity of the database before its use by a transaction, and/or check periodically or on demand the integrity of the current database state. Complete discussions on the design of a reliability control system are in references 2 and 8.

This chapter presents a framework that can help combine the functions of each of these subsystems. This framework is based on the optimistic approach that requires transaction validation, as compared to locking, as its basis for concurrency control. Some components of this approach have already been discussed.[3,4,6]

2. BASIC TERMINOLOGY AND CONCEPTS

The distributed database is modeled by a set of *logical database entities* which can have one or more *physical copies* at different sites.

A distributed database is *consistent* if it satisfies some predefined assertions on the data values. For a replicated distributed database, the physical copies of the same database entity on different sites must be identical

The user operations on a distributed database consist of a sequence of atomic operations.

Definition 2.1. An *atomic operation* is represented by $\sigma_i = A_i^j[x]$, where i is a unique identification for a transaction, j is a unique identification for a site, A is either R or W representing a read or write operation, and x is one or more logical database entities.

Definition 2.2. Atomic operations are grouped into logical units called *transactions* that preserve the database consistency if executed alone.

Definition 2.3. Two atomic operations σ_i, σ_j *conflict* if: 1. they belong to different transactions; 2. both access the same database entity at the same site; 3. at least one of them is a write operation.

Definition 2.4. The concurrent activities of a distributed database system can be modeled as a sequence of all atomic operations called the *history* of the system. The history is represented by a quadruple $h = \langle D, T, \Sigma, \pi \rangle$, where D is a distributed database, T is the transaction set, Σ is the atomic operation set, and π is a *permutation function* which gives *the permutation indices for atomic* operations σ in $h(\sigma \in \Sigma)$.

For example, if a history h is the following sequence:

$$\alpha\beta\gamma \ldots \omega$$

then $\pi(\alpha) = 1, \pi(\beta) = 2, \ldots, \pi(\omega) = |\Sigma|$.

An atomic operation in a history can be freely rearranged in the history, as long as the order of conflicting accesses is preserved.

A site projection represents the operations that are performed on a site.

Definition 2.5. A site projection g^j is obtainable from the site projection h^j through *conflict preserving exchange* (cp-exchange) if and only if there exist σ_1 and $\sigma_2 \in \Sigma^j$ such that σ_1 and σ_2 do not conflict, and the site projections are of the form:

$$h^j: \theta_1 \sigma_1 \sigma_2 \theta_2; \qquad g^j: \theta_1 \sigma_2 \sigma_1 \theta_2,$$

where θ_1 and θ_2 are strings of atomic operations. The only difference between h^j and g^j is that the order of σ_1 and σ_2 is reversed.

Since only adjacent nonconflicting operations are cp-exchanged, cp-exchange necessarily generates equivalent histories. Let $h^j \sim g^j$ mean that g^j is derived from h^j through a single cp-exchange, and let $\sim *$ be the transitive closure of cp-exchange operator.

Definition 2.6. Two histories are *equivalent* (indistinguishable) if they transform a given initial state of the same final database state. The notation $\equiv$ denotes the equivalence relation between histories.

Proposition 2.1. If $h^i \sim * g^j$ for all $j \in N$, then $h \equiv g$.

Proof: The proof is in reference 14.

Definition 2.7. A *serial history* is one in which each transaction runs to completion before the next one starts.

Definition 2.8. A history h is *serializable* if and only if there exists a serial history g such that $h^j \equiv g^j$ for every site j.

A history can be serialized according to the order of several events in the progress of a transaction. The instance when the transaction reads the first entity in the database is called α and the instance when the transaction writes on the first entity is called the event ω. The order of transactions in the serial history can also be established based on some other event in between α and ω, such as the instance when a transaction arrives for validation.

Definition 2.9. A concurrency control algorithm is correct if all of its allowed histories are serializable.

The concurrency controller represents the software module of the system which manages the concurrent access of the database by transactions issued by users. The purpose of the concurrency control is to guarantee that the concurrent activity does not result in an inconsistent database state.

2.1. Design of Concurrency Control

There are two generic approaches that can be used to design concurrency control algorithms. The synchronization can be accomplished using two types of actions:

1. *Wait.* If two transactions conflict, the conflicting operations of the new transaction must wait until the operations of the other transaction are completed. The wait can be enforced by using locks on database entities or checking timestamps[16] that can be assigned to transactions. One simple protocol that ensures serializability using locks is: *2-phase locking* (2PL).[10] The protocol requires that, in any transaction, all locks must precede all unlocks. The idea of waiting based on timestamps has been used in reference 20. The order of conflicting transactions in the serial history is established by the order of α event. This approach is *pessimistic* because some transactions could be blocked before knowing their write set and the conflict type.

2. *Validate after computaton.* Transactions can proceed freely in the system and be validated for correct concurrency control just before their commitment. If two transactions conflict, some operations of a transaction are undone or rolled back, or else one of the transactions is restarted. This approach is called *optimistic* because it is hoped that only a few transactions will be rolled back. Since recovery and roll-back facilities (including logs representing histories) are already provided in most systems, a concurrency control algorithm can take advantage of them. Locking and pessimistic time-stamp ordering provide a low degree of concurrency.[14]

2.2. Design of Atomicity Control

An atomicity control system requires that a transaction is either committed on all sites of a distributed system or is aborted on all sites. Several transaction atomicity control protocols have been discussed.[21] They extend the two-phase commit protocols[12] for distributed systems where multiple failures of sites can occur, e.g., a three-phase commit protocol. Multiple failures of a site might require several additional rounds of messages before deciding to commit or abort.

2.3. Design of Integrity Control

An integrity control system can ensure that no erroneous values (generated due to an incorrect transaction processing) are written in the database. Reference 8 presents a short survey of integrity control algorithms and reference 17 discusses some performance issues. The integrity assertions are expressed as predicates on database values and they must be true for the database to be in an integral state.

3. BASIC STEPS IN OPTIMISTIC CONCURRENCY CONTROL

The six steps in the execution and completion of a transaction are:

1. *Read.* The transaction reads the values for the required database entities into a private work space. This work space could be defined by a set of variables that correspond one to one with the entities. The set of variables representing the entities that have been read is called the read set, S(Ri).
2. *Compute.* The transaction executes by computing on the values of the variables in the private workspace and obtains a new set of values for its variables.
3. *Write in workspace.* The new values are written on local variables in the workspace. The variables correspond to the entities that will be updated by this transaction. The set of such entities is called the write set, S(Wi).
4. *Validate on the initiating site.* The site to whom the transaction is submitted is called its initiating site and all other sites in the distributed system are referred to as remote sites. The transaction validates against the set of concurrent transactions that have already validated on the initiating site. If the transaction is validated on the initiating site, it is put into the semicommit state.
5. *Validate globally.* The transaction is sent to all other sites for validation. The validation process on each site is identical.
6. *Commit and write in database.* If the transaction is validated, it is put into the commit state. The local values of the variables in the workspace become the values of the corresponding entities in the database. If the transaction wants to read some entities and then wants to compute before reading additional entities, the read, compute, write local steps of the transaction can be interleaved. The validation step on each site is done in the critical section.

3.1. General Comments on Validation

Since the transactions are isolated from each other before they reach the validation stage, while a transaction *Ti* is still computing another transaction *Tj* could commit or semicommit and update the read set of *Ti*. Hence *Ti* must validate against all such *Tj*.

If only the write sets of the semicommitted or committed transactions are kept in the database,[15] the concurrency provided by the algorithm will be the same as the locking algorithm. On the other hand, if the read set and write sets of the committed transaction are available in the validation, the degree of concurrency provided by the algorithm will be higher.[3,4] A theorem[3] shows that in a two-step transaction model (where all reads precede writes), a roll-back in the optimistic approach corresponds to a deadlock when locking is used.

4. VALIDATION ON THE INITIATING SITE

First, the integrity assertions are verified against the write set. If successful, the transaction validates against all committed and semicommitted transactions on the site for correct concurrency control. The validation step considers both the read set and the write set of all transactions. A conflict graph (CG) as defined below is constructed and is checked for cycles. If a cycle exists, the validating transaction is rejected else it is included in the set of semicommitted transactions and sent for global validation.

Definition 4.1. A *Conflict Graph* (CG) for a history $h = \langle D, T, \Sigma, \pi \rangle$ is a digraph $\langle V, E \rangle$ where V is the set of vertices representing T, the set of transactions; E is the set of edges, where $\langle i, j \rangle$ is an edge if and only if there exist conflicting atomic operations, σ_i, σ_j for which $\pi(\sigma_i) < \pi(\sigma_j)$.

Instead of the order of individual atomic operations, the edges can also be obtained by considering the order of α or ω events for each transaction.

Lemma 4.1. The CG of a serial history is acyclic.

Proof: The proof is in reference 3.

Based on the CG and the conflict (dependency) relation, a serializability class of histories for distributed database systems has been defined.

Definition 4.2. The class DCP contains all histories that are *distributed conflict-preserving*.

Definition 4.3. A history h is distributed conflict-preserving if and only if there exists a serial history g such that $h^j \sim^* g^j$ for all $j \in N$.

For a history h in DCP, the site projection h^j is serializable, since it can derive an equivalent serial site projection through a sequence of cp-exchanges, and all site projections are mutually consistent because the equivalent serial counterparts follow the same serialization order of transactions. The serializability of the histories in the class DCP can be easily tested by constructing and examining a graph that can be constructed for each DCP history.

Theorem 4.1. A history h is in DCP if and only if the CG of h is acyclic.

Proof: The proof is in reference 3. The class DCP contains the locking class.[14]

Corollary. For a history with an acyclic CG, the topological sort order of the vertices is the order of transactions in the equivalent serial history.

5. GLOBAL VALIDATION

When a transaction is validated on the initiating site, it is put into the semicommit state on that site. Next, it is sent to all the other sites for global validation. This step is combined with the first phase of the commit protocol of the atomicity control. A validation similar to that performed at the initiating site is performed at each remote site. If the transaction fails either the integrity tests or creates a cycle in the conflict graph, a reject message is sent to the initiating site. Otherwise, the transaction enters into the semicommit state and an accept message is sent to the initiating site.

When the initiating site receives an acceptance message from all sites, it commits the transaction and sends this information to all sites. This step coincides with the second phase of the commit protocol of the atomicity control subsystem.

When a site receives a message that a transaction has been committed, it changes the state of the transaction from semicommit to commit. For a rejected transaction, a global cycle will occur at least at one of the sites, because all transactions are sent to all sites for validations. Exception cases are discussed in reference 4. The transaction is either committed on all sites or rejected at all sites.

Figure 10.1 shows the states of the transaction and the transitions.

Due to variable transmission delays, transactions from two different sites can reach other sites in a different order. Since it is not desirable to block transactions from progressing, the following rule should be followed.

Rule: A transaction cannot be rejected at a site due to the validation of some newly arrived transaction after a site has agreed to semicommit the transaction and sent this message to other sites. A semicommitted transaction can only be committed or rejected by the initiating site.

There is a difficulty with this rule. Assume that T_i semicommits on site A and T_j semi-commits on site B. If T_i and T_j create a cycle in the conflict graph, then it is possible that in global validation T_i is rejected on site B and T_j is rejected on site A. Thus both transactions are rejected.

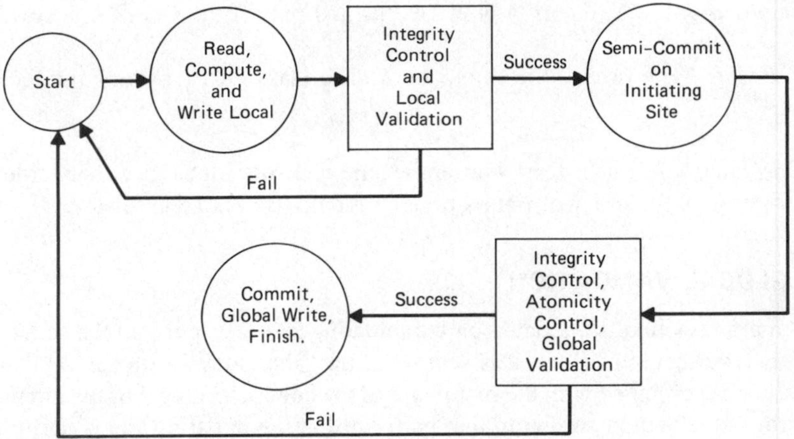

Fig. 10.1. States of a Transaction.

To reduce the rejection of all transactions involved in a cycle, the system must set a criterion for rejection which is independent of the delays in the message transmission and is independent of when a transaction reached a site.

For example, a weight can be assigned to each transaction. This weight can be a function of the age (based of the value of the α) of a transaction, the cost of rolling back or restarting a transaction, the number of times a transaction has been rejected, etc. If both transactions have the same weight, both can be rejected or else the older one can be accepted. The implementation and performance issues are in reference 4.

6. THE OPTIMISTIC CONCURRENCY CONTROL ALGORITHM

A complete optimistic concurrency control algorithm is in reference 4.

7. RESILIENCY FACILITIES DUE TO OPTIMISTIC CONCURRENCY CONTROL

The design of optimistic concurrency control as discussed in the previous sections provides several resiliency features. This section discusses the treatment of failures discussed in the introduction.

7.1. Resiliency to Transaction Failure

If partial updates of an uncommitted transaction are posted in the database and the transaction fails, the recovery procedures must be invoked. One recovery procedure using UNDO and REDO logs has been recommended.[13] The execution of UNDO actions and roll-back of individual transactions can be expensive. In this system, the executing transactions are transparent to other transactions. A failure prompts the system to initialize the values of read set and write set variables and to inform the user. Thus transaction failures are handled fast and without any cascade effects.

7.2. Resiliency to Site Failure

The system can detect that either a local (initiating) site or a remote site for a transaction has failed. The failure can occur due to either a hardware or a software failure.[19] A failure can change the values of the contents in the memory or any other volatile storage to null. The site can also refuse to accept any new transactions or might not respond to messages from other sites. In our approach, the system changes the state of the transactions on the failed site, as shown in Table 10.1.

If a remote site fails, the local site can assume that the remote site has rejected the transaction. But an optimistic solution will be to hope that the transaction will validate on the remote site. The local site can either wait for the remote site to recover (causing blocking the transactions) or assume that the remote site will validate the transaction successfully. Table 10.2 shows these cases.

The message sent to the failed remote site can be handled by the communication system, or else spoolers can be used at each site to store messages sent by other sites. The failed site is required to update itself with all committed transactions from other sites before it may start to accept new transaction for validation. If the recovered site finds that its spooler also crashed during its failure, it requests the other sites to send information about transactions that were committed during its failure. Many interesting protocols for terminating a transaction have been proposed.[21] Another approach to site failures and recovery has been presented.[1]

Table 10.1. Local Site Failure.

Local Site Failure	System's Decision at Local Site
After committing/aborting a local transaction	Do nothing. (Assume: Message has been sent to remote sites)
After semicommitting a local transaction	Abort transaction when local site recovers. Send abort message to other sites.
During computing/validating a local transaction	Abort transaction when local site recovers. Send abort message to other sites.

Table 10.2. Remote Site Failure.

Remote Site Failure	System's Decision at Local Site	System's Decision at Failed Site
Before receiving the remote transaction	a. Pessimistic: Wait for failed site to recover and validate.	a. Pessimistic: Read messages on spooler. If spooler failed reject the transaction.
	b. Optimistic: Commit the transaction based on information from other sites and send message to failed site's spooler. (Assume failed site will semi-commit the transaction.)	b. Optimistic: Semicommit the transaction before processing new transactions. If spooler failed, request other sites to send transactions that were committed or aborted during its failure.
After semicommitting the remote transaction	Same as b. above.	Same as b. above.
After aborting the remote transaction	Abort the transaction.	Do nothing.

7.3. Resiliency to Communication System Failure

When one or more of the following types of problems occur, the communication system has failed.

Network partition. A network partition occurs when the sites are separated into two or more partitions and the partitions are unable to communicate with each other. The sites in one partition can communicate with each other. A partition might consist of only one site.

Lost messages. This type of failure occurs when the messages sent by one site do not reach the designated site.

Message order messed up. This occurs when the messages are not delivered in the same order as they were sent. This can happen due to variable transmission delays.

7.3.1. Network Partition

When a network partitions, the system could decide to proceed as follows:

Do not process any transactions that want to update the database. Allow only retrievals from the database. This alternative is not very attractive except for special applications.

Process transactions in only one partition. This partition can be chosen based on some criterion such as containment of important nodes (that must not halt their operations) or containment of a majority of sites etc.. The updates of committed transactions will be sent to the other partitions when they join the active partition.

These two approaches tend to be pessimistic. Our approach is based on the optimism that few transactions in different partitions will be involved in a cyclic conflict. There are several alternatives to allow transaction processing in all partitions.

Alternative 1. The system will allow transaction processing in all the partitions, but transactions will remain in the semicommit state and will be subject to validation at unavailable sites when the partitions merge. A conflict graph CGi is maintained for each partition i. The results of transactions in the semicommit state can be made available to the user with proper warnings and can also be used by other transactions in the same partition. The merger of semicommitted transactions from several partitions can proceed as follows:

Combine CG1, CG2, . . . , CG*n* on one of the sites. If no cycle exists, then commit all transactions. Minimize roll-back if a cycle exists. Unfortunately, this minimization is NP-complete because the problem reduces to a "Feedback Vertex Problem."[9,11]

Assign a weight to each transaction in all partitions. Determine the CGi with maximum weight. Select transactions that do not create a cycle from other CGj's

$(j \neq i)$ one at a time. There are two ways to deal with transactions that create a cycle:

1. Abort the transaction that creates the cycle.
2. Consider each transaction that creates a cycle one at a time and break the cycle by aborting the transaction that minimizes transaction abort. This minimization can be done in computational complexity $\mathbf{O}(n^3)$, but will not be necessarily optimal if a global CG was formed. The minimization of abort can be based on several criteria. For example, reduce the number of transactions that are aborted, or reduce the loss of transaction processing cost. The processing cost can be a function of the parameters such as I/O cost or CPU cost. Some algorithms to reduce the number of nodes that must be removed from a graph to break a cycle are in reference 9. The performance of a protocol based on our ideas is in reference 5.

Alternative 2. Until now, the granularity of database partition has been considered at the site level. A network partition can be defined based on the partitioning of the entities in the database. One copy of each entity in the database is designated as the primary copy (or the true copy). Each primary copy has a token.

The system allows a transaction to be processed and commited in a partition if the partition has a primary copy token for all the database entities needed. Thus, transaction processing can continue in more than one partition. How the true copy tokens are maintained determines which transactions can be processed in which partition. A concurrency control algorithm that maintains tokens is in reference 18. Since no transactions in different partitions can use the same entity, the database remains consistent.

Semantic Considerations. Semantics of the operations of the transactions can be used to decrease the amount of transaction abort and to increase processing in spite of failures.

Commutative Operations: Two operations σ_i and σ_j are commutative if $\sigma_i \sigma_j \equiv \sigma_j \sigma_i$. For commutative operations, value-based updates are not allowed. A simple example of commutable operations is "Give Rupees 500 bonus to every employee, and increment John's Salary by Rupees 100." If the bonus was 5% of the salary, the operations are not commutable. Two adjacent read operations are also commutable.

The commutable operations of transactions can continue to execute in different partitions and after the merge of the partitions the values of the database entities can be set to the consistent state. This can be accomplished by remembering the value of the entity at the time of partition and applying the cumulative changes in the database values from each partition.

For example, if the value of the certain entity was x at the time of partition and at the time of partition merge, the values due to commutative actions of transactions in two different partitions are y and z. The correct value of the database entity at merge of the partitions can be set to $y + z - x$.

If the commutative property of the transaction can not be determined in advance, the system might be able to determine it at run time. For example, the system could recognize absolute increments and decrements in the database values. Every time the transaction issues an update, the system can check whether the transaction is value based.

The system can maintain a log of commutative and noncommutative operations. When the partitions merge, it can be checked if operations in different partitions were conflicting and at the same time noncommutative. If so, the transactions will have to partially roll-back up to the point where they started the noncummutative operations and will restart from such a point.

Compensating Operations: An operation σ_c is compensating for the history $\sigma_2.\sigma_3. \ldots .\sigma_n$ if and only if $\sigma_1.\sigma_2.\sigma_3. \ldots \sigma_n.\sigma_c \equiv \sigma_1$. With the facility of an UNDO log and compensating operations, the system might be able to allow the transactions to commit in the different partitions.

When partitions merge, if there is a cycle in the global graph, the system can check if the cycle can be broken by removing some semicommitted transactions. If the cycle in the global conflict graph contains only committed transactions, the system will be required to undo or compensate a committed transaction. If any committed transaction remains invisible to the environment, i.e., its updates were never seen by any transaction or user, then it could be selected to break the cycle. The other possibility is that the results of the transaction have been read by other transactions which might themselves have stayed invisible to the environment (transitive invisibility). In such related cases, all such transactions can be aborted. If the results of a committed transaction have been made available to the environment, depending on the application, the system can issue a compensating transaction. If none of the transactions involved in the cycle can be compensated, the system should be programmed to pay a penalty (such as free airfare for overbooked passengers or an insufficient funds charge to a customer's account by a bank).

The solutions range from keeping all transactions in the semicommit state to committing transactions in one partition or more. The commitment of all the transactions is possible with the necessity of a roll-back or compensating transactions.

7.3.2 Lost Messages

A transaction remains in a semicommit state unless it has been validated at all other sites. Absence of the decision of a remote site will only delay the decision on the transaction. A time-out mechanism can be used at each site, and if a transaction has been in the semicommit state for a long time due to the nonreceipt of the decision of a remote site, a request for the decision can be repeated. If the decision of a site is also sent to other sites, a site might be able to get it indirectly from other sites. A lost message can thus block only the processing of a transaction, but can not affect the system consistency.

7.3.3. Message Order Reversal

Some times the requests for global validation for two transactions arrive in a different order than that of their sending. A site will only send requests for validation for two transactions in the semicommit state if they do not cause a cycle in the conflict graph at that site. If they do not create a cycle in the conflict graph on the remote site, the order of their arrival does not matter. If both of them create a cycle they will both be rejected, and so once again their order does not matter.

ACKNOWLEDGMENT

Thanks are due to Dr. Cecil Hua for the "DCP class" and Prof. Errol Lloyd for "complexity" in 7.3.1.

REFERENCES

1. Bhargava, B. and Z. Ruan, Site recovery in distributed database systems with replicated data, in *Proc. IEEE 6th Int. Conf. on Distributed Computing Syst.*, Cambridge, May 1986 (Chapter 11, this book).
2. Bhargava, B., Reliability issues in distributed systems, *IEEE Trans. Software Eng*. vol. SE-8, Guest Editorial, May 1982.
3. Bhargava, B., Resiliency features of the optimistic concurrency control approach for distributed database systems, in *Proc. IEEE 2nd Symp. Reliability in Distributed Software and Database Syst.*, Pittsburgh, July 20–21, 1982.
4. Bhargava, B., Performance evaluation of the optimistic concurrency control approach to distributed database systems and its comparison with locking, in *IEEE Int. Conf. Distributed Computing Syst.*, Miami, Florida, Oct. 18–22, 1982.
5. Bhargava, B., Performance evaluation of reliability control algorithms for distributed database systems, *J. Systems and Software*, vol. 4, pp. 239–264, July 1984.
6. Bhargava, B., Concurrency control and reliability in distributed database system, in *Software Engineering Handbook*, C. V. Ramamoorthy and C. R. Vick, eds., New York: Van Nostrand Reinhold, 1984.
7. Bhargava, B., ed., *Concurrency and Reliability in Distributed Systems*, New York: Van Nostrand Reinhold, 1987.
8. Bhargava, B. and L. Lilien, A review of concurrency and reliability issues in distributed database systems, in *Concurrency and Reliability in Distributed Systems*, B. Bhargava, ed., New York: Van Nostrand Reinhold, 1987.
9. Davidson, S. B., *Evaluation of an Optimistic Protocol for Partitioned Distributed Database System*, Tech. Rep. #299, Princeton Univ. 1982.
10. Eswaran, E. *et al*, The notions of consistency and predicate locks in a database system, *CACM*, vol. 19, pp. 624–633, Nov. 1976.

11. Garey, M. R. and D. S. Johnson, *Computers and Intractability: A Guide to the Theory of NP-Completeness*, San Francisco: W. H. Freeman and CO., 1979.
12. Gray, J. N., Notes on database operating systems, in *Lecture Notes in Computer Science*, vol. 60, Goos and Hartmanis, eds., Berlin: Springer Verlag, 1978, pp. 393–481. Also available as IBM Res. Rep. RJ 2188.
13. Gray, J. N., The transaction concept: Virtues and limitations, *Proc. VLDB Conf.*, Cannes, France, Sep. 9–11, 1981.
14. Hua, C. and B. Bhargava, Classes of serializable histories and synchronization algorithms in distributed database systems, in *Proc. IEEE Int. Conf. Distributed Computing Syst.*, Miami, FL, Oct. 18–22, 1982.
15. Kung, H. T. and J. T. Robinson, On optimistic methods for concurrency control, *ACM Trans. Database Syst.*, vol. 6, pp. 213–226, June 1981.
16. Lamport, L., Time, clocks, and the ordering of events in a distributed system, *CACM*, vol. 21, pp. 558–564, July 1978.
17. Lilien, L. and B. Bhargava, A scheme for the verification of database integrity, *IEEE Trans. Software Eng.*, vol. 6, pp. 654–680, Nov. 1984.
18. Minoura, T. and G. Wiederhold, Resilient extended true-copy token scheme for a distributed database systems, *IEEE Trans. Software Eng.*, vol. SE-8, pp. 173–189, May, 1982.
19. Randell, B., P. A. Lee, and P. C. Treleaven, Reliability issues in computing systems design, *ACM Comput. Surveys*, vol. 10, pp. 123–165, June 1978.
20. Rothnie, J. *et al*, Introduction to a system for distributed databases (SDD-1), *ACM Trans. Database Syst.*, vol. 5, pp. 1–17, Mar. 1980.
21. Skeen, D. A decentralized termination protocol, in *Proc. IEEE Symp. on Reliability in Distributed Software and Database Syst.*, Pittsburgh, PA, July 1981, pp. 21–22.

11. Site Recovery in Replicated Distributed Database Systems

BHARAT BHARGAVA

and

ZUWANG RUAN

ABSTRACT

A solution to the problem of integrating a recovering site into a distributed database system is presented. The basic idea used for the correct recovery is to maintain a consistent view of the status (up or down) of all sites. This view need not be the exact current status of the sites, but is the status as perceived by other sites. The *session number* is used to represent the actual state of a site, while the *nominal session number* is used for the session number as perceived by other sites. The consistent view of the nominal session numbers is maintained by control transactions, which run concurrently with user transactions. This approach provides a high degree of availability. A data item is available to a transaction as long as one of its copies is in an operational site and the transaction knows the site's session number. The recovery procedure allows the recovering site to resume its normal operations as soon as possible.

1. INTRODUCTION

Site recovery is the problem of integrating a site into a distributed database system (DDBS) when the site recovers from a failure. There are two different problems under the term "site recovery" in the literature. The first concerns the resolution of transactions. That is, upon recovering, the site should commit

*Reprinted from the *Proc. 6th IEEE Intl. Conf. on Distributed Computing Syst.*, Cambridge, MA, May 1986.
This work is supported in part by a grant from Sperry Corporation and by David Ross Fellowship.

or abort the transactions that were being processed when the failure occurred, consistently with the decisions made by other operational sites in the system. Termination protocols in conjunction with commit protocols make it possible for the recovering site to make correct decisions on these transactions.[9, 10] The second problem deals with the recovery of the database. This problem is caused by attempts to increase database availability. In a distributed database system with replication, we would like user transactions to proceed even if some sites are unavailable due to failures. When a failed site recovers and rejoins the system, the consistency of the entire database is threatened because the data items at the recovering site may have missed some updates. The recovery algorithm should hide such inconsistency from user transactions, bring the recovering site up-to-date with respect to the rest of the system, and enable the recovering site to start processing transactions as soon as possible. This chapter discusses only the second problem.

There are two main approaches to this problem. The first is to redo all missed updates at the recovering site. The use of multiple *message spoolers*[6] is one practical solution using this approach. All update messages addressed to an unavailable site are saved reliably in multiple spoolers, and the recovering site processes all of its missed messages before resuming normal operations. However, scheduling the missed operations is a nontrivial problem if there is no global clock available. Moreover, this method is not suitable for systems in which sites may be down for quite a long time.

The second approach takes advantage of data replication. In this approach, the data items at the recovering site are brought up-to-date by special transactions, called *copiers*, which read the corresponding replicas at operational sites and refresh the out-of-date copies. An advantage of this approach is that copier transactions can run concurrently with user transactions so that the recovering site can start processing user transactions as soon as possible. However, since data items are brought into the database separately by independent copiers, special mechanisms are required to ensure that the database keeps its consistency while the individual data copies are merging into it. Roughly speaking, the algorithm must guarantee that no user transaction can read a copy at the recovering site before the copy is renovated, and once a copy has been included in the database all transactions writing to the logical data item must update this copy as well. Algorithms using this approach have been proposed in references 1 and 2.

It should be noted that a recovery procedure alone cannot ensure a correct recovery. Without proper conventions for user transactions, the situations left by site failures may not be recoverable at all. The following example illustrates the problem. In this example, write operations are interpreted as writing to all currently available copies and transactions can be committed as long as all write operations succeed.

EXAMPLE:
Transaction T_a reads X and writes Y; transaction T_b reads Y and writes X. Both X and Y have two copies at site 1 and 2, called x_1, x_2 and y_1, y_2, respectively. A history

$$R_a[x_1]\ R_b[y_1]\,(site\ 1\ crashes)\ W_a[y_2]\ W_b[x_2]$$

is acceptable to a concurrency control algorithm that concerns only the serializability of physical operations. Because both T_a and T_b have written to all currently available copies, they are committed. When site 1 recovers, x_1 and y_1 may be updated by copier transactions $T_c = R_c[x_2]W_c[x_1]$ and $T_d = R_d[y_2]W_d[y_1]$. No matter how the copiers are scheduled, the database cannot be brought up to a consistent state and the history becomes nonserializable.

The solution in reference 1 does not specify its model for user transactions, hence it is unclear how such anomalies are prevented from happening. The solution proposed in reference 2 uses *directories*. Briefly, each data item is associated with a directory that keeps the status of the data item, i.e. where the copies of the data item are available. User transactions read the directories to decide how to interpret their read and write operations. Directories are manipulated by status transactions, including the copiers, called INCLUDE transactions in reference 2. User transactions and status transactions are synchronized by the two-phase locking protocol so that user transactions can have a consistent view of the status of each individual data item.

In this chapter we present a new solution, that also belongs to the class of the second approach. The solution is motivated by the following considerations. First, the conventions for user transactions should not degrade the performance of normal operations too much. Hence we try to identify the necessary information that the user transactions need to know in order to avoid unrecoverable situations. We have determined that a consistent view of the status of all sites is sufficient as far as site failures are concerned. Keeping track of the status of sites turns out to be much less expensive than maintaining the status information for individual data items. Next, the recovering site is expected to start processing transactions as soon as possible. Therefore, one of our goals is to reduce the work that must be done before the recovering site resumes its normal operations. In our algorithm, as soon as the recovering site has successfully informed the other operational sites of its new status, it becomes fully operational. The recovery of the data items proceeds concurrently with user transactions. Finally, in order to eliminate unnecessary work, it is important to identify precisely the data items that have missed updates and need to be refreshed. Rather than having a mechanism built into it, our algorithm can choose many different methods for identifying the out-of-date items and make recovery efficient.

This algorithm works with a large group of concurrency control algorithms and provides considerable implementation freedom. It is resilient to multiple site failures, even if a site crashes while another site is recovering. A failed site can recover as long as there is at least one operational site in the system. Though we foresee that a similar method can be applied to the problem of the merging of network partitions, the algorithm presented in this chapter does not handle partition failures.

The next section serves as a background. Section 3 presents our basic algorithm. Section 4 sketches the correctness proof. Section 5 discusses its refinements. Finally, the last section concludes this chapter and outlines further work.

2. BACKGROUND

In this chapter, the users' view of an object is called a *logical data item*, or *data item*, denoted X. A data item is stored in the DDBS as a set of *physical copies* or *copies*. The copy of X stored at site k is denoted x_k, and the fact that X has a copy at site k is denoted $x_k \in X$. We assume that the information regarding where the copies of data item X are located is available at least at the resident sites of X.

Users manipulate the database via *transactions*. A transaction is a program that accesses the database by issuing *logical operations READ* and *WRITE* on logical data items.

There are two major functional modules running at each site on behalf of the DDBS. The *transaction manager* (TM) supervises the execution of transactions and interprets logical operations into requests for *physical operations*. The *data manager* (DM) carries out the physical operations on the copies stored at the site. We assume that the DDBS runs a correct *concurrency control algorithm* which ensures *serializable* (SR) execution of transactions. We do not discuss transaction resolution upon site failures and recoveries in this chapter, but assume that there is a correct protocol to take care of it. Hence, in the following discussions all transactions are atomic, i.e., they either meet their specifications or have no effect on the database at all.

Whether a transaction meets its specification depends on the interpretation of logical operations. For example, the strict *read-one/write-all* (ROWA) strategy can be described as

$$READ(X) = \vee\{read(x_k),\ x_k \in X\},$$

$$WRITE(X) = \wedge\{write(x_k),\ x_k \in X\}.$$

where $OP = \vee\{op\}$ means that OP is interpreted as at least one of the op's, and OP fails if no op succeeds; and $OP = \wedge\{op\}$ means that OP is interpreted as all the *op*'s, and *OP* fails if any one of the *op*'s fails. Note that these notations are informal descriptions of the semantics of the logical operations, especially in presence of failure. They imply no implementation hints, such as parallel or sequential executions of *op*'s, or the order of *op*'s in case of sequential executions.

In a system using the strict ROWA scheme, site failures never result in inconsistent data. Consequently, the site recovery (in the sense of recovery of the database) is unnecessary. However, the degraded availability for write operations makes the strict ROWA scheme impractical. In this chapter we introduce a revised scheme *read-one/write-all-available* (ROWAA). Intuitively, if a transaction knows that site *k* is down, it should not try to read a copy from site *k*, or send an update to site *k*. ROWAA not only saves the time otherwise wasted because of waiting for responses from an unavailable site, but also reduces the possibility of aborting or blocking transactions. As mentioned in the introduction, however, without some additional conventions, user transactions may create an unrecoverable state as they write to the ''available'' copies perceived by themselves. In the next section, we specify the conventions for user transactions in our ROWAA scheme, and a recovery algorithm for this scheme.

3. BASIC ALGORITHM

3.1. Session Numbers and Nominal Session Numbers

As far as recovery is concerned, a site can be in three distinguishable states. We say a site is *down* if no DDBS activity is going on at the site. A site is *recovering* if it is in an early stage of its recovery procedure. Its TM and DM may have been turned on (for processing control transactions as described below) but are not yet ready to accept user transactions. The site is *operational* or, simply, *up* if both TM and DM at the site work normally. We also say a site is *not operational*, meaning that the site is either down or recovering.

The dividing point at which a site goes from down to recovering, or from up (or recovering) to down, is very clear. The point at which it goes from recovering to up depends on the recovery algorithm. We will define this point precisely later in this section. Note that, in our algorithm, some data copies may still be out-of-date when the recovering site enters the operational state. However, the out-of-date copies in an operational site must have been marked as unreadable, and will eventually be updated by copiers or user transactions.

An *operational session* of a site is a time period in which the site is up. Each operational session of a site is designated with an integer, *session number*, which is unique in the site's history, but not necessarily unique systemwide. If a site is not in an operational session, its session number is undefined. For simplicity of description, however, we say that the site has session number 0 if it is not operational (assuming 0 is never used as a session number for an operational session). The session number of site k is denoted as $as[k]$, for the actual session number.

Because sites are up and down dynamically, it is not always possible for a site to have precise knowledge about the session number of another site. In order to have a consistent view of the session number of a particular site i in the system, we augment the database with additional data items, called *nominal session numbers*. We use the notation $NS[k]$ for the data item indicating the nominal session number of site k, and NS for the vector composed of $NS[1]$, . . . , $NS[n]$. Note that the nominal session number of site k may differ from the actual session number $as[k]$, but the difference should be kept as small as possible.

The session number $as[k]$ can be implemented as a variable shared by the TM and DM at site k. That is, the TM and DM know the local session number precisely, and use it to control their services. For example, when a site starts recovery from an earlier failure, it turns on the TM and DM and loads its session number with 0 automatically. User transactions cannot be processed at site k while $as[k]$ is 0. After the site finishes some necessary work (described in Subsection 3.4), it loads a new session number into $as[k]$ and the site becomes fully operational. The current session number must also be saved in a stable storage, so that the next time the site recovers, a new session number can be assigned correctly. In practice, session numbers can be recycled. Two different sessions can have the same session number as long as no single transaction is alive in both sessions.

In contrast, the nominal session numbers are data items similar to those in the database. They are readable by user transactions, and writable only by control transaction (described in Subsection 3.3). These read and write operations on nominal session numbers are under concurrency control like other data items. Because the nominal session numbers are read very frequently (by user transactions) but only updated occasionally (when sites fail and recover), we assume that they are fully replicated at all n sites. Since we use the capitalized letters to name logical data items and the corresponding lowercased names with subscripts for their physical copies, the copy of $NS[k]$ at site i is denoted $ns_i[k]$, and the vector composed of $ns_i[1]$, . . . , $ns_i[n]$ is denoted ns_i. The value of ns_i is the status of the system as currently perceived by site i.

3.2. User Transactions

In the ROWAA scheme, user transactions must obey the following convention. Each user transaction implicitly reads the local copy of the nominal session vector prior to any other operations. This gives the transaction a view of "current" configuration of the system, which is used by the transaction throughout its execution. More precisely, if a transaction initiated at site i reads the nominal session vector ns_i, its logical operations are interpreted by the TM at site i as:

$$READ(X) = \vee\{read(x_k),\ x_k \in X \text{ and } ns_i[k] \neq 0\},$$

$$WRITE(X) = \wedge\{write(x_k),\ x_k \in X \text{ and } ns_i[k] \neq 0\}.$$

Each request for reading or writing a physical copy at site k carries $ns_i[k]$, the session number of site k perceived by the transaction. The DM at site k first checks this number against its actual session number, $as[k]$. If they are not equal, the request is rejected. Otherwise, the DM carries out the request. For a data copy marked as unreadable, a write operation upon it removes the mark when the transaction commits, while a request for reading it triggers a *copier transaction* that renovates the physical copy. The user transaction can either be blocked until the copier finishes, or may read some other copy instead. We consider this decision as an implementation issue rather than a part of the convention for user transactions, and hence leave it unspecified.

A copier transaction is responsible for refreshing a particular unreadable data copy. It reads (a copy of) the nominal session number, locates a readable copy, uses its content to renovate the local copy and removes the unreadable mark. If the copier cannot find a readable copy of this data item among the currently operational sites, this item is considered *totally failed*. A separate protocol is needed to resolve this problem, which is not discussed in this chapter. Copier transactions may be initiated by the recovery procedure one by one for individual unreadable data copies, or on a demand basis, i.e., triggered when the DM receives read requests for them. Such choices may influence performance, but not correctness. In any case, copier transactions are executed concurrently with all other transactions after the recovering site has entered the operational state. They follow the concurrency control protocol like all other transactions.

3.3. Control Transactions

Now we will discuss the possible transitions of nominal session numbers. We impose the restriction that any changes to the nominal session numbers must be done by special transactions, named *control transactions*.

There are two types of control transactions. A control transaction of Type 1 claims that a site is nominally up. It can only be initiated by the recovering site itself when it is ready to change its state from recovering to operational. For example, when site k is ready to claim it is operational, it initiates a control transaction, that reads an available copy of the nominal session vector, say, $(ns_i[1], \ldots, ns_i[n])$, and refreshes its own copy of the nominal session vector $(ns_k[1], \ldots, ns_k[n])$, then it chooses a session number to be used for the next operational session and writes it to $ns_k[k]$ as well as $ns_j[k]$ for all $1 \leq j \leq n$

such that $ns_k[j]$ is non-zero. A control transaction of Type 2 claims that one or more sites are down. Any site can initiate this type of transactions, as long as it is sure that the sites being claimed down are actually down. This requirement can be satisfied in systems where site failures are the only possible failures. A transaction of this type reads a copy (likely the local copy) of the nominal session vector, and writes 0 to all available copies of the nominal session numbers for the sites to be claimed down.

Control transactions, like all other transactions, follow the concurrency control protocol and the commit protocol used by the DDBS. A control transaction may be aborted due to a conflict with another one, or due to a write failure (e.g. another site failure occurs during the execution of the control transaction). One difference between control transactions and user transactions is that user transactions can be processed only by sites that are operational, while control transactions can be processed by recovering sites as well.

3.4. Site Recovery Procedure

The site recovery procedure proceeds as follows:

1. When a site k gets up, it turns on its TM and DM and loads its actual session number $as[k]$ with 0, meaning that the TM and DM are ready to process control transactions but not user transactions.
2. The recovering site marks all data copies at its own site unreadable. Actually, only the data copies that have missed updates since the site failed need to be marked. There are different ways to identify such out-of-date items. We briefly discuss this issue in Section 5. Details are given in reference 5.
3. After Steps 1 and 2, the site initiates a control transaction of Type 1. Note that the control transaction writes a newly chosen session number into $ns_i[k]$ for all operational sites i, but not $as[k]$.
4. If the control transaction in Step 3 commits, the site is nominally up. The site can convert its state from recovering to operational by loading the new session number into $as[k]$. If Step 3 fails due to a crash of another site, the recovering site must initiate a control transaction of Type 2 to exclude the newly crashed site, and then try Step 3 again. Note that the recovery procedure is delayed by the failure of another site, but the algorithm is robust as long as there is at least one operational site in the system.

4. CORRECTNESS

4.1. Correctness Concepts

One-serializability (1-SR) has been used as the correctness criterion for transaction executions in distributed database systems with replication. In this subsection, we briefly define the fundamental concepts that are necessary for the correctness proof presented in the next subsection. These concepts are based on references 3 and 8, but presented in an exstensible way.

An *execution history* of a set of transactions $T = \{T_a, T_b, \cdots\}$ is a partially ordered set containing all operations of these transactions. An *augmented execution history* is a history with an initial transaction that writes to all data copies and a final transaction that reads from all data copies. Two augmented execution histories are *equivalent* if and only if they have the same *read-from* relations. To simplify our arguments in this chapter, we consider only augmented execution histories. The relation T_b *reads-x-from* T_a is denoted as $T_a \Rightarrow_x T_b$. A *serial* history is a history with total order such that the operations from different transactions are not interleaved. A history H is *serializable* if there exists a serial history, H_s, equivalent to H.

A *serializability testing graph*, STG, of a history H is a graph $(T, \rightarrow)$ with the following properties:

1. if $T_a \Rightarrow_x T_b$, then there exists an edge $T_a \rightarrow T_b$ (i.e., the graph contains all read-from edges);
2. there is an edge between any two transactions that write to the same data copy (called the *write-order* edge, and an edge between two transactions writing to x is denoted as $\rightarrow_x$); and
3. if $T_a \Rightarrow_x T_b$ and $T_a \rightarrow_x T_c$, then there is an edge $T_b \rightarrow T_c$ (called the *read-before* edge).

Intuitively, to construct an STG for a history H, we start with the *read-from* relation graph of H, and arbitrarily add edges until the resulting graph satisfies the above properties. It is easy to see that the STGs are functionally equivalent to the bigraphs used in reference 8, and the main theorem of serializability theory can be stated as:

Theorem 1. A history H is serializable if and only if H has an acyclic STG.

One example of an STG is the *conflict graph* (CG), in which all transactions with conflicting operations (read-write or write-write on the same data copy) are $\rightarrow$ related according to the order in which their conflicting operations actually take place. Obviously, the CG of a history is one of its STGs, hence the histories with acyclic CGs are serializable. The set of histories with acyclic CGs are called DCP in reference 4 and DSR in reference 8.

If we modify the definition of STG by replacing the word "edge" by "path" in 2 and 3, the Theorem is still correct. We use the notation $T_a \rightarrow^* T_b$ for the fact that there is a path from T_a to T_b.

Now we generalize these concepts to distributed databases with replication. First, we define the *READ-FROM* relations. Transaction T_b *READS-X-FROM*

T_a, denoted $T_a \Rightarrow_X T_b$, if there is some $x_i \in X$ such that $T_a \Rightarrow_{x_i} T_b$. Two histories are *equivalent* if they have the same *READ-FROM* relations. A *one-copy serial* history is a serial history with all physical operations replaced by corresponding logical operations. A history H is *one-serializable* (1-SR) if there exists a one-copy serial history, H_{1s}, equivalent to H.

A *one-serializability testing graph*, 1-STG, of a history H is a graph $(T, \rightarrow)$ with the following properties:

1. if $T_a \Rightarrow_X T_b$, then there exists an edge $T_a \rightarrow T_b$ (read-from);
2. there is an edge between any two transactions that writes to copies of the same data item X (write-order, denoted as as $\rightarrow_X$); and
3. if $T_a \Rightarrow_X T_b$ and $T_a \rightarrow_X T_c$, then there is an edge $T_b \rightarrow T_c$ (read-before).

As in STG, the word "edge" in 2 and 3 can also be replaced by "path." However, the CG of a history is not necessarily a 1-STG. The main theorem of one-serializability can be stated as:

Theorem 2. A history H is one-serializable if and only if H has an acyclic 1-STG.

In the presence of copier transactions, however, the conditions for 1-SR, in general, cannot be satisfied if we treat copier transactions in the same way as user transactions. For example, if we consider a copier T_c that refreshes a copy x_j as a writer to X, the requirement 3 will rule out many correct executions. In order to include such correct histories in the class of 1-SR, we must modify the definition of 1-STG by taking the semantics of copiers into consideration.

First, we define *READ-FROM* as a relation between a transaction and a non-copier transaction. That is, a transaction T_b *READS-X-FROM* a non-copier transaction T_a either directly, i.e. $T_a \Rightarrow_{x_i} T_b$ for a copy $x_i \in X$; or indirectly, i.e., there exists a copier transaction T_c such that $T_a \Rightarrow_X T_c$ and $T_c \Rightarrow_{x_i} T_b$ for a copy $x_i \in X$. Next, the one-copy serial history is defined as a serial history of the transactions, excluding copiers, with their physical operations replaced by logical operations. Finally, we modify the definition of 1-STG. In 1, we replace $T_a \Rightarrow_X T_b$ with $T_a \Rightarrow_x T_b$, because *READ-FROM* relations now do not reflect the *read-from* relations of copiers. In 2, we change the word "transaction" to "non-copier transaction," because we are concerned only with the write order among non-copier transactions. Note that an indirect *READ-FROM* relation is now a path rather than an edge. But adding a *READ-FROM* edge will not change the acyclic nature of the graph. Under these modifications, we find that the "if" part of Theorem 2 is still valid. That is,

Corollary. A history H is 1-SR if H has an acyclic 1-STG (under the revised definition).

It should be noted that all concepts in the theory of serializability are relative to the *database*, i.e. the domain containing all data items that transactions operate on. For example, the abstraction of a transaction in serializability theory is a sequence (or, more generally, a partially ordered set) of read/write operations upon the data items in the database. All other activities are ignored by this abstraction. Therefore, we can consider abstract transactions with respect to a particular subset of the database, meaning that only the operations upon data items within this subset are of concern. Similarly, we can consider all serializability concepts with respect to this subset. In our algorithm, the database, *DB*, is augmented by the nominal session numbers, *NS*. Hence, we can consider the abstract transactions with respect to *DB*, *NS*, and $DB \cup NS$. For example, with respect to *NS*, all but control transactions are read-only transactions. Note that a correct concurrency control algorithm ensures serializability with respect to $DB \cup NS$, but what we really want is one-serializability with respect to *DB*.

4.2. Correctness Proof

The correctness of our algorithm can be presented by the following theorem.

Theorem 3. Based on the algorithm stated in the Section 3, the conflict graph (CG) with respect to $DB \cup NS$ is a 1-STG with respect to *DB*.

Intuitively, the theorem implies that our algorithm, together with a concurrency control algorithm within the class of DCP, ensures correct executions of transactions.

Proof. We prove the theorem in two steps. First, we show that the CG with respect to $DB \cup NS$ embodies the write-order and read-before paths with respect to *NS*. Then, we use the result to prove that the CG also embodies the write-order and read-before paths with respect to *DB*.

Write-order and read-before with respect to NS. Recall that a control transaction of Type 1 initiated by site k writes to all available copies of $NS[k]$ and brings the local copies of other nominal session numbers up-to-date. This control transaction is treated as a writer only to $NS[k]$, because to the other session numbers this transaction acts as a copier. The read-from relations are defined accordingly. That is, we consider that a transaction reads $NS[k]$ from the control transaction that assigned the session number originally, rather than from the one that renovates the local copy of the session number. Under this interpretation, we can verify that any two control transactions writing to the same $NS[k]$ are connected via a CG path in which each pair of two contiguous vertices (control transactions) have intersected write sets, assuming that the system always has at least one site operational. Similarly for read-before relations. We omit the details here.

Write-order with respect to DB. Consider two transactions T_a and T_b, both writing to X. If their write sets intersect, the two transactions are connected by a CG edge. Otherwise, if T_a writes x_i but T_b does not write to x_i, they must read $NS[i]$ from different control transactions, say, $T_c \Rightarrow_{NS[i]} T_a$ and $T_d \Rightarrow_{NS[i]} T_b$. Because the CG embodies write-order and read-before paths with respect to NS, we can assume, without loss of generality, that $T_c \rightarrow^* T_d$, and conclude that $T_a \rightarrow^* T_d \rightarrow T_b$ ($\rightarrow^*$ stands for a path in CG).

Read-before with respect to DB. Consider the following cases. (a) $T_a \Rightarrow_{x_i} T_b$ and $T_a \rightarrow^*_{x_i} T_c$. Obviously, $T_b \rightarrow T_c$ because CG is a STG. (b) $T_a \Rightarrow_{x_i} T_b$ and $T_a \rightarrow^*_X T_c$, but T_c does not write to x_i. In this case, we assume $T_d \Rightarrow_{NS[i]} T_a$ and $T_e \Rightarrow_{NS[i]} T_c$, where T_d and T_e are different control transactions. Based on our results with respect to NS, T_d and T_e are $\rightarrow^*_{NS[k]}$ related, and the only possibility is $T_d \rightarrow^*_{NS[k]} T_e$ (otherwise CG is cyclic). Since T_b reads x_i directly, T_b must see the same session number as T_a, hence T_b also reads from T_d. Then we have $T_b \rightarrow^* T_e \rightarrow T_c$. (c) $T_a \Rightarrow_X T_b$ indirectly via copier transactions. For example, $T_a \Rightarrow_{x_i}$ a copier CP and $CP \Rightarrow_{x_i} T_b$, and $T_a \rightarrow^*_X T_c$ where T_c writes to some copy of X. We can apply the arguments in (a) and (b) to the triples of T_a, CP, T_c, and CP, T_b, and T_c, and conclude that $T_b \rightarrow^* T_c$. Similarly for the cases in which multiple copies are involved.

5. REFINEMENTS

In the basic algorithm described in Section 3, we ignored the problem of identifying the data items that have missed updates due to site failure, and simply assume that all data at the recovering site are out-of-date. No particular mechanism has been built into our algorithm, but the algorithm is able to work with various methods to eliminate this unnecessary work.

One way to identify the data items that have missed updates is to use *fail-locks*.[5] Similar to a lock on a data item used in concurrency control algorithms to specify that the locked object is being used by a transaction, a fail-lock is used in recovery algorithms to record the fact that the data item was updated when a site was down. Our recovery algorithm can work with the fail-lock mechanism. When a site is recovering, it collects the fail-locks set during its failure, and marks its copies of fail-locked data items as unreadable.

Another practical mechanism is to use *missing list* (ML). Conceptually, a missing list is a two-dimensional array ML: $\{item\} \times \{site\} \rightarrow \{1, 0\}$, where $ML[X, i] = 1$ means x_i has missed updates. In order to save storage space, an ML can be implemented in various ways, for example, as a list of pairs (X, i) for non-zero elements in the ML. The elements of the ML can be seen as data items augmented to the database, but they need to be stored in volatile storage only. Access to elements should be under concurrency control. Each site maintains an ML. Unlike NS, MLs at different sites are considered as different data items, rather than copies of the same logical data. A pair (X, k) in ML at site i means that $x_i \in X$, $x_k \in X$, and x_k have missed an update which is done to x_i. Our algorithm can work with MLs as follows. A write operation *WRITE*(X) writes to x_i for all $i \in X$ such that site i is nominally up. It removes (X, i), if any, from the MLs at the sites to which it writes a copy of X successfully, and adds (X, j) into these MLs for all j such that $x_j \in X$ and site j is not available for the transaction. When site i is recovering, it looks up the MLs at all operational sites. If (X, i) appears in an ML, site i removes the entry (X, i) from all MLs of nominally operational sites, and marks its own copy x_i as unreadable. Site i also forms its own ML using the entries (X, j), $i \neq j$, seen in the MLs at other operational sites. It should be noted that, under this mechanism, as long as a site has an up-to-date copy of a data item, the ML of this site has the precise information on where the copies of the data item have missed updates. We will discuss further details in a future work.

It should be noted that there is a tradeoff between the costs of the recovery procedure and the increased cost of normal operations caused by the use of mechanisms for identifying the out-of-date data items. In systems using version numbers or timestamps, even without identifying the out-of-date copies our basic recovery algorithm is not very expensive. This is because a copier can compare the version numbers or timestamps of the two copies first, then decide whether copying of the data is necessary.

6. CONCLUSION AND FURTHER WORK

In this chapter, we introduced a new algorithm for site recovery, including the conventions for user-transactions (ROWAA), and the recovery procedures.

This scheme provides a very high degree of availability. A logical read or write operation on a data item can succeed as long as one of its copies is in an operational site, and the site's session number is known by the transaction.

In this approach, the extra cost to user transactions is negligible. Although all user transactions are required to read the local copies of the nominal states, there is little overhead because these reads do not conflict with each other. The control transactions which update the nominal session numbers are only necessary when sites fail or recover.

The ideas presented in this chapter deal with the problem of failed site integration. We believe that the solution to the site failure problem and the concept of nominal session numbers are applicable to the merging of network partitions. Full details have not been worked out, but the direction of the research is outlined as follows.

The distinction between the problems of network partition and site failure is clear. In a site failure problem, the operational sites in the system can assume that no activity occurs at the failed site. Thus the failed site needs to integrate with the rest of the system and obtain updates missed during its failure. This means that the integration is only required in one direction (from the failed site to the operational sites). In a network partition problem, the system may allow updates on different data items in different partitions. For example, updates can be allowed on data items holding true-copy tokens.[7] When two partitions merge, each partition needs to obtain missed updates from the other partition. This can be accomplished by integrating the sites of a partition one by one with the other partition. When a site obtains all updates from another partition, it is considered integrated in one direction. A site is fully integrated with another partition if the integration in both directions has been completed. Two partitions are fully integrated when all sites in each partition have fully integrated. The integration in either direction follows a protocol similar to the failed site integration protocol discussed in this chapter. The granularity at which the integration takes place is up to the implementation.

REFERENCES

1. Attar, R., P. A. Bernstein, and N. Goodman, Site initialization, recovery, and backup in a distributed database system, *IEEE Trans. Software Eng.*, vol. SE-10, pp. 645–650, Nov. 1984.
2. Bernstein, P. A. and N. Goodman, An algorithm for concurrency control and recovery in replicated distributed databases, *ACM Trans. Database Syst.*, vol. 9, pp. 596–615, Dec. 1984.
3. Bernstein, P. A. and N. Goodman, The failure and recovery problem for replicated database, *Proc. of the second ACM Symp. on Principles of Distributed Computing*, pp. 114–122, Aug. 1983.
4. Bhargava, B. and C. T. Hua, A causal model for analyzing distributed concurrency control algorithm, *IEEE Trans. Software Eng.*, vol. SE-9, pp. 470–486, July 1983.
5. Bhargava, B., Transaction processing and consistency control of replicated copies during failures, to appear in *J. Information Mgmt.*
6. Hammer, M. M. and D. W. Shipman, Reliability mechanism for SDD-1: A system for distributed databases," *ACM Trans. Database Syst.*, vol. 5, pp. 431–466, Dec. 1980.
7. Minoura, T. and G. Wiederhold, Resilient extended true-copy token scheme for a distributed database system, *IEEE Trans. Software Eng.*, vol. SE-8, pp. 173–188, May 1982.
8. Papadimitrou, C. H., Serializability of concurrent updates, *JACM*, vol. 26, pp. 631–653, Oct. 1979.
9. Skeen, D. and M. Stonebraker, A formal model of crash recovery in a distributed system, *IEEE Trans. Software Eng.*, vol. SE-9, pp. 219–227, May 1983.
10. Skeen, D., Nonblocking commit protocols, *Proc. 1981 ACM-SIGMOD Conf. Management of Data*, ACM, New York, pp. 133–147.

12. The Byzantine Generals

DANNY DOLEV, LESLIE LAMPORT, MARSHALL PEASE,

and

ROBERT SHOSTAK

ABSTRACT

Reliable computer systems must handle malfunctioning components that give conflicting information to different parts of the system. This situation can be expressed abstractly in terms of a group of generals of the Byzantine army camped with their troops around an enemy city. Communicating only by messenger, the generals must agree upon a common battle plan. However, one or more of them may be traitors who will try to confuse the others. The problem is to find an algorithm to ensure that the loyal generals will reach agreement. It is shown that, using only oral messages, this problem is solvable if and only if more than two-thirds of the generals are loyal, so a single traitor can confound two loyal generals. With unforgeable written messages, the problem is solvable for any number of generals and possible traitors. The solution for a general distributed system requires connectivity of more than twice the number of traitors, while in the case of unforgeable written messages, connectivity larger than the number of traitors suffices. Applications of the solutions to reliable computer systems are then discussed.

1. INTRODUCTION

A reliable computer system must be able to cope with the failure of one or more of its components. A failed component may exhibit a type of behavior that is often overlooked—namely, sending conflicting information to different

This work was supported in part by the National Aeronautics and Space Administration under contract number NAS1-15428 Mod. 3, and the Ballistic Missile Defense Systems Command under contract number DASG60-78-C-0046, and the Army Research Office under contract number DAAG29-79-C-0102.

parts of the system. The problem of coping with this type of failure is expressed abstractly as the Byzantine Generals Problem. We devote the major part of the chapter to a discussion of this abstract problem, and conclude by indicating how our solutions can be used in implementing a reliable computer system.

We imagine that several divisions of the Byzantine Army are camped outside an enemy city, each division commanded by its own general. The generals can communicate with one another only by messenger. After observing the enemy, they must decide upon a common plan of action. However, some of the generals may be traitors, trying to prevent loyal generals from reaching agreement. The generals must have an algorithm to guarantee that:

CONDITION A. All loyal generals decide upon the same plan of action.

The loyal generals will all do what the algorithm says they should, but the traitors may do anything they wish. The algorithm must guarantee Condition A regardless of what the traitors do.

The loyal generals should not only reach agreement, but should agree upon a reasonable plan. We therefore also want to insure that:

CONDITION B. A small number of traitors cannot cause the loyal generals to adopt a bad plan.

Condition B is hard to formalize, since it requires saying precisely what a bad plan is, and we will not attempt to do so. Instead, we consider how the generals reach a decision. Each general observes the enemy and communicates his observations to the others. Let $v(i)$ be the information communicated by the ith general. Each general uses some method for combining the values $v(1)$, . . . , $v(n)$ into a single plan of action, where n is the number of generals. Condition A is achieved by having all generals use the same method for combining the information, and Condition B is achieved by using a robust method. For example, if the only decision to be made is whether to attack or retreat, then $v(i)$ can be General i's opinion of which option is best, and the final decision can be based upon a majority vote among them. A small number of traitors can affect the decision only if the loyal generals were almost equally divided between the two possibilities, in which case neither decision could be called bad.

While this approach may not be the only way to satisfy Conditions A and B, it is the only one that we know of. It assumes a method by which the generals communicate their values $v(i)$ to one another. The obvious method is for the ith general to send $v(i)$ by messenger to each other general. However, this does not work because satisfying Condition A requires that every loyal general obtain the same values $v(1)$, . . . , $v(n)$, and a traitorous general may send different values to different generals. For Condition A to be satisfied, the following must be true.

CONDITION 1. Every loyal general must obtain the same information $v(1)$, . . . , $v(n)$.

Condition 1 implies that a general cannot necessarily use a value of $v(i)$ obtained directly from the ith general, since a traitorous ith general may send different values to different generals. This means that, unless we are careful, in meeting Condition 1 we might introduce the possibility that the generals use a value of $v(i)$ different from the one sent by the ith general—even though the ith general is loyal. We must not allow this to happen if Condition B is to be met. For example, we cannot permit a few traitors to cause the loyal generals to base their decision upon the values "retreat", . . . , "retreat" if every loyal general sent the value "attack." We therefore have the following requirement, for each i:

CONDITION 2. If the ith general is loyal, then the value that he sends must be used by every loyal general as the value of $v(i)$.

We can rewrite Condition 1 as the condition that, for every i (whether or not the ith general is loyal):

CONDITION 1′. Any two loyal generals use the same value of $v(i)$.

Conditions 1′ and 2 are both conditions on the single value sent by the ith general. We can therefore restrict our consideration to the problem of how a single general sends his value to the others. We phrase this in terms of a commanding general sending an order to his lieutenants, obtaining the following problem.

Byzantine Generals Problem: A commanding general must send an order to his $n - 1$ lieutenant generals such that:

CONDITION IC1. All loyal lieutenants obey the same order.
CONDITION IC2. If the commanding general is loyal, then every loyal lieutenant obeys the order he sends.

Conditions IC1 and IC2 are called the *interactive consistency* conditions. Note that if the commander is loyal, then IC1 follows from IC2. However, the commander need not be loyal.

To solve our original problem, the ith general sends his value of $v(i)$ by using a solution to the Byzantine Generals Problem to send the order "use $v(i)$ as my value," with the other generals acting as the lieutenants.

2. IMPOSSIBILITY RESULTS

The Byzantine Generals Problem seems deceptively simple. Its difficulty is indicated by the surprising fact that, if the generals can send only oral messages, then no solution will work unless more than two-thirds of the generals are loyal. In particular, with only three generals, no solution can work in the presence of a single traitor. An oral message is one whose contents are completely under the control of the sender, so that a traitorous sender can transmit any possible message. Such a message corresponds to the type of message that computers normally send to one another. In Section 4, we will consider signed, written messages, for which this is not true.

We now study that, with oral messages, no solution for three generals can handle a single traitor. For simplicity, we consider the case in which the only possible decisions are "attack" or "retreat." Let us first examine the scenario pictured in Fig. 12.1, in which the commander is loyal and sends an "attack" order, but Lieutenant 2 is a traitor and reports to Lieutenant 1 that he received a "retreat" order. For Condition IC2 to be satisfied, Lieutenant 1 must obey the order to attack.

Now consider another scenario, shown in Fig. 12.2, in which the commander is a traitor and sends an "attack" order to Lieutenant 1 and a "retreat" order to Lieutenant 2. Lieutenant 1 does not know who the traitor is, and cannot tell what message the commander actually sent to Lieutenant 2. Hence, the scenarios in these two pictures appear exactly the same to Lieutenant 1. If the traitor lies consistently, then there is no way for Lieutenant 1 to distinguish between these two situations, so he must obey the "attack" order in both of them. Hence, whenever Lieutenant 1 receives an "attack" order from the commander, he must obey it.

However, a similar argument shows that if Lieutenant 2 receives a "retreat" order from the commander, then he must obey it even if Lieutenant 1 tells him

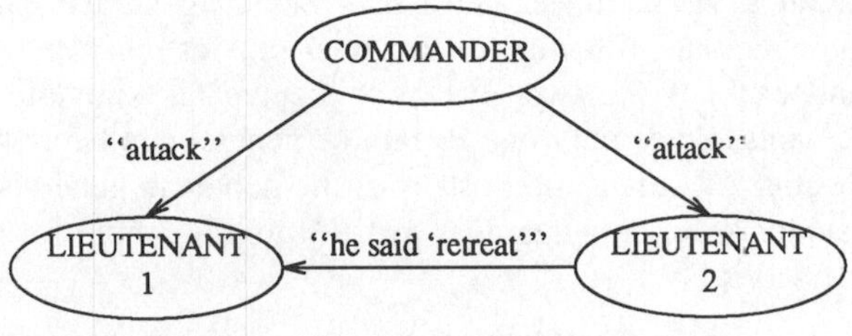

Fig. 12.1. Lieutenant 2 a traitor.

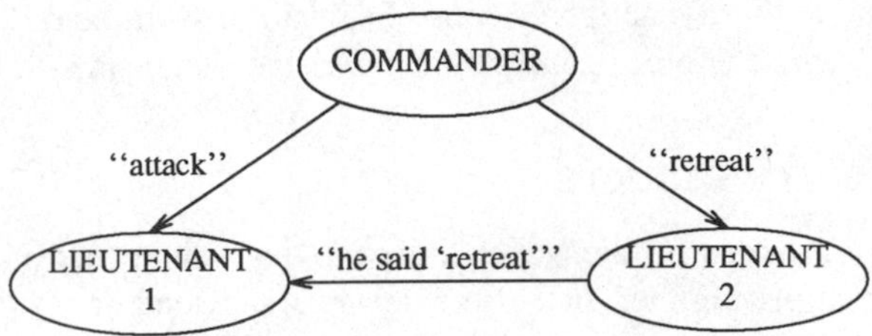

Fig. 12.2. The commander a traitor.

that the commander said "attack." Therefore, in the scenario of Fig. 12.2, Lieutenant 2 must obey the "retreat" order while Lieutenant 1 obeys the "attack" order, thereby violating Condition IC1. Hence, no solution exists for three generals that works in the presence of a single traitor.

This argument may appear convincing, but we strongly advise the reader to be very suspicious of such nonrigorous reasoning. Although this result is indeed correct, we have seen equally plausible "proofs" of invalid results. We know of no area in computer science or mathematics in which informal reasoning is more likely to lead to errors than in the study of this type of algorithm. For a rigorous proof of the impossibility of a three-general solution that can handle a single traitor, we refer the reader to reference 12.

Using this result, we can show that no solution with fewer than $3m + 1$ generals can cope with m traitors.* The proof is by contradiction—we assume such a solution for a group of $3m$ or fewer generals, and use it to construct a three-general solution to the Byzantine Generals Problem that works with one traitor, which we know to be impossible. To avoid confusion between the two algorithms, we will call the generals of the assumed solution Albanian generals, and those of the constructed solution will be called Byzantine generals. Thus, starting from an algorithm that allows $3m$ or fewer Albanian generals to cope with m traitors, we will construct a solution that allows three Byzantine generals to handle a single traitor.

The three-general solution is obtained by having each of the Byzantine generals simulate approximately one-third of the Albanian generals, so that each Byzantine general is simulating at most m Albanian generals. The Byzantine commander simulates the Albanian commander plus at most $m - 1$ Albanian lieutenants, and each of the two Byzantine lieutenants simulates at most m Albanian lieutenants. Since only one Byzantine general can be a traitor, and he simulates at most m Albanians, at most, m of the Albanian generals are traitors. Hence, the assumed solution guarantees that IC1 and IC2 hold for the Albanian

*More precisely, no such solution exists for three or more generals, since the problem is trivial for two generals.

generals. By IC1, all the Albanian lieutenants being simulated by a loyal Byzantine lieutenant obey the same order, which is the order he is to obey. It is easy to check that Conditions IC1 and IC2 of the Albanian generals solution imply the corresponding conditions for the Byzantine generals, so we have constructed the required impossible solution.

One might think that the difficulty in solving the Byzantine Generals Problem stems from the requirement of reaching exact agreement. We now demonstrate that this is not the case by showing that reaching approximate agreement is just as hard as reaching exact agreement. Let us assume that instead of trying to agree on a precise battle plan, the generals must agree only upon an approximate time of attack. More precisely, we assume that the commander orders the time of the attack, and we require the following two conditions to hold:

CONDITION IC1′. All loyal lieutenants attack within ten minutes of one another.

CONDITION IC2′. If the commanding general is loyal, then every loyal lieutenant attacks within ten minutes of the time given in the commander's order.

(We assume that the orders are given and processed the day before the attack, and the time at which an order is received is irrelevant—only the attack time given in the order matters.)

Like the Byzantine Generals Problem, this problem is unsolvable unless more than two-thirds of the generals are loyal. We prove this by first showing that if there were a solution for three generals that coped with one traitor, then we could construct a three-general solution to the Byzantine Generals Problem that also worked in the presence of one traitor. Suppose the commander wishes to send an "attack" or "retreat" order. He orders an attack by sending an attack time of 1:00, and orders a retreat by sending an retreat time of 2:00, using the assumed algorithm. Each lieutenant uses the following procedure to obtain his order.

1. After receiving the attack time from the commander, a lieutenant does one of the following:
   If the time is 1:10 or earlier, then attack.
   If the time is 1:50 or later, then retreat.
   Otherwise, continue to Step 2.
2. Ask the other lieutenant what decision he reached in Step 1.
   If the other lieutenant reached a decision, then make
   the same decision he did.
   Otherwise, retreat.

It follows from IC2′ that, if the commander is loyal, then a loyal lieutenant will obtain the correct order in Step 1, so IC2 is satisfied. If the commander is loyal, then IC1 follows from IC2, so we need only prove IC1 under the assumption that the commander is a traitor. Since there is at most one traitor, this means that both lieutenants are loyal. If follows from IC1′ that, if one lieutenant decided to attack in Step 1, then the other cannot decide to retreat in Step 1. Hence, they will both either come to the same decision in Step 1, or at least one of them will defer his decision until Step 2. In this case, it is easy to see that they both arrive at the same decision, so IC1 is satisfied. We have therefore constructed a three-general solution to the Byzantine Generals Problem that handles one traitor, which is impossible. Hence, we cannot have a three-general algorithm that maintains IC1′ and IC2′ in the presence of a traitor.

The method of having one general simulate m others can now be used to prove that no solution with fewer than $3m + 1$ generals can cope with m traitors. The proof is similar to the one for the original Byzantine Generals Problem, and is left to the reader.

3. A SOLUTION WITH ORAL MESSAGES

We have shown above that, for a solution to the Byzantine Generals Problem using oral messages to cope with m traitors, there must be at least $3m + 1$ generals. We now give a solution that works for $3m + 1$ or more generals. However, we first specify exactly what we mean by "oral messages." Each general is supposed to execute some algorithm that involves sending messages to the other generals, and we assume that a loyal general correctly executes his algorithm. The definition of an oral message is embodied in the following assumptions which we make for the generals' message system.

A1. Every message that is sent is delivered correctly.
A2. The receiver of a message knows who sent it.
A3. The absence of a message can be detected.

Assumptions A1 and A2 prevent a traitor from interfering with the communication between two other generals, since by A1 he cannot interfere with the messages they do send, and by A2 he cannot confuse their intercourse by introducing spurious messages. Assumption A3 will foil a traitor who tries to prevent a decision by simply not sending messages. The practical implementation of these assumptions is discussed in Section 6. Note that assumptions A1–A3 do not imply that a general hears any message sent between two other generals.

The algorithms in this section and in the following one require that each general be able to send messages directly to every other general. In Section 5, we describe algorithms which do not have this requirement.

A traitorous commander may decide not to send any order. Since the lieutenants must obey some order, they need some default order to obey in this case. We let **RETREAT** be this default order.

We inductively define the Oral Message algorithms as OM(m) for all non-negative integers m, by which a commander sends an order to $n - 1$ lieutenants. We will show that OM(m) solves the Byzantine Generals Problem for $3m + 1$ or more generals in the presence of at most m traitors. We will find it more convenient to describe this algorithm in terms of the lieutenants "obtaining a value" rather than "obeying an order."

The algorithm assumes a function *majority* with the property that, if a majority of the values v_i equal v, then *majority* $(v_1, \cdots, v_{n-1})$ equals v. (Actually, it assumes a sequence of such functions—one for each n.) There are two natural choices for the value of *majority* $(v_1, \cdots, v_{n-1})$:

1. The majority value among the v_i if it exists, otherwise the value **RETREAT**.
2. The median of the v_i, assuming that they come from an ordered set.

The following algorithm requires only the aforementioned property of *majority*.

Algorithm OM(0):

1. The commander sends his value to every lieutenant.
2. Each lieutenant uses the value he receives from the commander, or uses the value **RETREAT** if he receives no value.

Algorithm OM(m), $m > 0$:

1. The commander sends his value to every lieutenant.
2. For each i, let v_i be the value Lieutenant i receives from the commander, or else be **RETREAT** if he receives no value. Lieutenant i acts as the commander in algorithm OM($m - 1$) to send the value v_i to each of the $n - 2$ other lieutenants.
3. For each i, and each $j \neq i$, let v_j be the value Lieutenant i received from Lieutenant j in Step 2 (using Algorithm OM($m - 1$)), or else **RETREAT** if he received no such value. Lieutenant i uses the value *majority* $(v_1, \cdots, v_{n-1})$.

To execute 3, every processor must know when to apply the majority function, in other words, when to stop waiting for more values to come. To do this, one can use some sort of time-out technique, as we will discuss in Section 6. Note that recently, Fischer, Lynch, and Paterson[8] proved that there is no way to reach any agreement unless we assume some bound on the time at which a reliable processor responds.

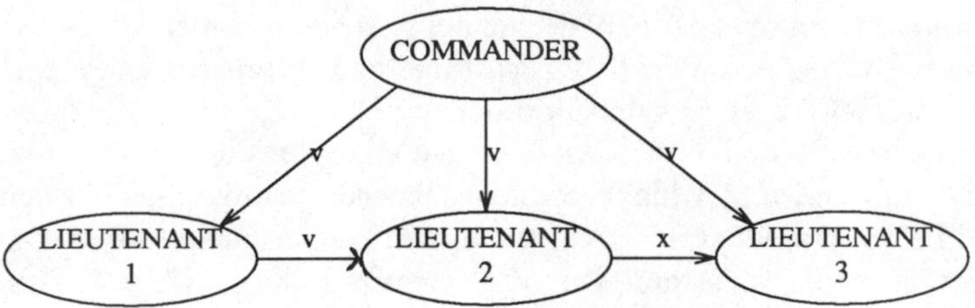

Fig. 12.3. Algorithm OM(1)—Lieutenant 3 a traitor.

To understand how Algorithm OM(m) works, we consider the case $m = 1$, $n = 4$. Figure 12.3 illustrates the messages received by Lieutenant 2 when the commander sends the value v and Lieutenant 3 is a traitor. In the first Step of OM(1), the commander sends v to all three lieutenants. In the second Step, Lieutenant 1 sends the value v to Lieutenant 2, using the trivial algorithm OM(0). Also in the second Step, the traitorous Lieutenant 3 sends Lieutenant 2 some other value x. In Step 3, Lieutenant 2 then has $v_1 = v_2 = v$, and $v_3 = x$, so he obtains the correct value $v = majority\ (v, v, x)$.

Next, we see what happens if the commander is a traitor. Figure 12.4 shows the values received by the lieutenants if a traitorous commander sends three arbitrary values x, y, and z to the three lieutenants. Each lieutenant obtains $V_1 = x$, $V_2 = y$, and $V_3 = z$, so they all obtain the same value *majority* (x, y, z) in Step 3, regardless of whether or not any of the three values x, y, and z are equal.

The recursive algorithm OM(m) invokes $n - 1$ separate executions of the algorithm OM($m - 1$), each of which invokes $n - 2$ executions of OM($m - 2$), etc. This means that for $m > 1$, a lieutenant sends many separate messages to each other lieutenant. There must be some way to distinguish between these different messages. The reader can verify that all ambiguity is removed if each

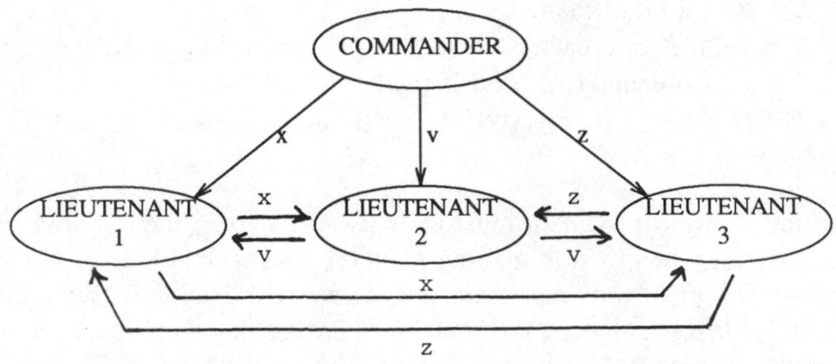

Fig. 12.4. The algorithm OM(1)—The commander a traitor.

lieutenant i prefixes the number i to the value v_i that he sends in Step 2. As the recursion "unfolds," the algorithm $OM(m - k)$ will be called $(n - 1)$, . . . , $(n - k)$ times to send a value prefixed by a sequence of k lieutenant's numbers. This implies that the algorithm requires sending an exponential number of messages. There exist algorithms which require only a polynomial number of messages,[4] but they are substantially more complex than the one we present.

To prove the correctness of the algorithm $OM(m)$ for arbitrary m, we first prove the following lemma.

Lemma 1: For any m and k, Algorithm $OM(m)$ satisfies Condition IC2 if there are more than $2k + m$ generals, and at most k traitors.

Proof: The proof is by induction on m. Condition IC2 only specifies what must happen if the commander is loyal. Using Al, it is easy to see the trivial algorithm OM(0) works if the commander is loyal, so the lemma is true $m = 0$. We now assume it is true for $m - 1$, $m > 0$, and prove it for m.

In Step 1, the loyal commander sends a value v to all $n - 1$ lieutenants. In Step 2, each loyal lieutenant applies $M(m - 1)$ with $n - 1$ generals. Since by hypothesis $n > 2k + m$, we have $n - 1 > 2k + (m - 1)$, so we can apply the induction hypothesis to conclude that every loyal lieutenant gets $v_j = v$ for each loyal Lieutenant j. Since there are at most k traitors, and $n - 1 > 2k + (m - 1) \geq 2k$, a majority of the $n - 1$ lieutenants are loyal. Hence, each loyal lieutenant has majority $(v_1, \cdots, v_{n-1}) = v$ in Step 3, proving IC2.

The following theorem asserts that Algorithm $OM(m)$ solves the Byzantine Generals Problem.

Theorem 1: For any m, Algorithm $OM(m)$ satisfies Conditions IC1 and IC2 if there are more than $3m$ generals, and at most m traitors.

Proof: The proof is by induction on m. If there are no traitors, then it is easy to see that $OM(0)$ satisfies IC1 and IC2. We therefore assume that the theorem is true for $OM(m - 1)$ and prove it for $OM(m)$, $m > 0$.

We first consider the case in which the commander is loyal. By taking k equal to m in Lemma 1, we see that $OM(m)$ satisfies IC2. Condition IC1 follows from IC2 if the commander is loyal, so we need only verify IC1 in the case that the commander is a traitor.

There are at most m traitors and the commander is one of them, so at most $m - 1$ of the lieutenants are traitors. Since there are more than $3m$ generals, there are more than $3m - 1$ lieutenants, and $3m - 1 > 3(m - 1)$. We may therefore apply the induction hypothesis to conclude that $OM(m - 1)$ satisfies conditions IC1 and IC2. Hence, for each j, any two loyal lieutenants get the same value for v_j in Step 3. (This follows from IC2 if one of the two lieutenants is Lieutenant j, and from IC1 otherwise.) Hence, any two loyal lieutenants get the same vector of values $v_1, \cdots, v_{n-1}$, and therefore obtain the same value *majority* $(v_1, \cdots, v_{n-1})$ in Step 3, proving IC1.

4. A SOLUTION WITH SIGNED MESSAGES

As we saw from the scenario of Fig. 12.1 and 12.2, it is the traitors' ability to lie that makes the Byzantine Generals Problem so difficult. The problem becomes easier to solve if we can restrict that ability. One way to do this is to allow the generals to send unforgeable signed messages. More precisely, we add to A1–A3 the following assumption.

A4.(a) A loyal general's signature cannot be forged, and any alteration of the contents of his signed messages can be detected.
(b) Anyone can verify the authenticity of a general's signature.

Note that we make no assumptions about a traitorous general's signature. In particular, we allow his signature to be forged by another traitor, thereby permitting collusion among the traitors.

Having introduced signed messages, our previous argument that four generals are required to cope with one traitor no longer holds. In fact, a three-general solution does exist. We now give an algorithm that copes with m traitors for any number of generals. (The problem is vacuous if there are fewer than $m + 2$ generals.)

In our algorithm, the commander sends a signed order to each of his lieutenants. Each lieutenant then adds his signature to that order and sends it to the other lieutentants, who add their signatures and send it to others, and so on. This means that a lieutenant must effectively receive one signed message, make several copies of it, and sign and send those copies. It does not matter how these copies are obtained—a single message might be photocopied, or else each message might consist of a stack of identical messages which are signed and distributed as required.

Our algorithm uses a function *choice*, which is applied to a set of orders to obtain a single one. It is defined as follows:

If the set V consists of the single element v,
then *choice* $(V) = v$,
otherwise *choice* (V) = **RETREAT**

In the following algorithm, we let $x{:}i$ denote the value x signed by general i. Thus, $v{:}j{:}i$ denotes the value v signed by j, and then that value $v{:}j$ signed by i. We let general 0 be the commander. In this algorithm, each lieutenant i maintains a set V_i, containing the set of properly signed orders he has received so far. (If the commander is loyal, then this set should never contain more than a single element.) Do not confuse V_i, the set of *orders* he has received, with the set of messages that he has received. There may be many different messages with the same order. We assume the existence of a bound on the time it takes correct processors to sign and relay a message. Thus, it implies the existence of some phases such that, if a message with r signatures arrives after phase r, then only faulty processors relayed it, so it can be ignored. This assumption does not necessarily mean complete synchronization of the processors.

Algorithm SM(m)
Initially $V_i = \phi$.

1. The commander signs and sends his value to every lieutenant at phase 0.
2. For each i:
   A. If Lieutenant i receives a message of the form $v:0$ from the commander at phase 0, and he has not yet received any order, then: (i) He lets V_i equal $\{v\}$. (ii) He sends the message $v:0:i$ to every other lieutenant.
   B. If Lieutenant i receives a message of the form $v:0:j_1:\cdots:j_k$ at k, $1 \leq k \leq m$, V_i contains at most one value, v is not in the set V_i, and the signatures belong to the different lieutenants, then: (i) He adds v to V_i. (ii) If $k < m$, then he sends the message

      $v:0:j_1:\cdots:j_k:i$ to every lieutenant
      other than $j_1, \cdots, j_k$.

3. For each i: At the end of phase m he obeys the order *choice* (V_i).

Observe that the algorithm requires $m + 1$ phases of message exchange. Note that in Step 2, Lieutenant i ignores any message containing an order v that is already in the set V_i, and accepts at most two different orders originated by the commander.

Moreover, Lieutenant i ignores any messages that do not have the proper form of a value followed by a string of different signatures. If packets of identical messages are used to avoid having to copy messages, this means that he throws away any packet that does not consist of a sufficient number of identical, properly signed messages. (There should be $(n - k - 2)(n - k - 3), \ldots (n - m - 2)$ copies of the message if it has been signed by k lieutenants.)

Figure 12.5 illustrates algorithm SM(1) for the case of three generals, when the commander is a traitor. The commander sends an "attack" order to one lieutenant and a "retreat" order to the other. Both lieutenants receive the two

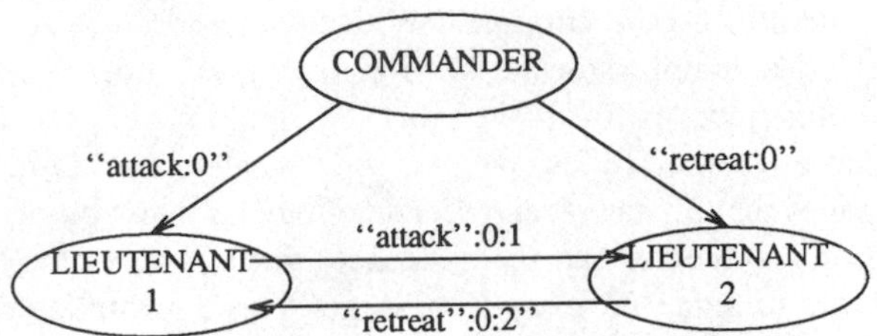

Fig. 12.5. Algorithm SM(1)—The commander a traitor.

orders in Step 2, so after step 2 $V_1 = V_2 = \{$"attack," "retreat"$\}$, and they both obey the order *choice* ({"attack," "retreat"}). Observe that here, unlike the situation in Fig. 12.2, the lieutenants know the commander is a traitor because his signature appears on two different orders, and A4 states that only he could have generated those signatures.

In algorithm SM(m), a lieutenant signs his name to acknowledge his receipt of an order. If he is the mth lieutenant to add his signature to the order, then that signature is not relayed to anyone else by its recipient, so it is superfluous. (More precisely, assumption A2 makes it unnecessary.) In particular, the lieutenants need not sign their messages in SM(1).

We now prove the correctness of our algorithm.

Theorem 2: For any m: Algorithm SM(m) solves the Byzantine Generals Problem, if there are at most m traitors.

Proof: We first prove IC2. If the commander is loyal, then he sends his signed order v:0 to every lieutenant in Step 1. Every loyal lieutenant will therefore receive the order v on time in Step 2A. Moreover, since no traitorous lieutenant can forge any other message of the form v':0, a loyal lieutenant can receive no additional order in Step 2B. Hence, for each loyal lieutenant i, the set V_i obtained in Step 2 consists of the single order v, which he will obey in Step 3 by property 1 of the *choice* function. This proves IC2.

Since IC1 follows from IC2 if the commander is loyal, to prove IC1 we need only consider the case in which the commander is a traitor. Two loyal lieutenants i and j obey the same order in Step 3 if the function choice applied to the sets of orders V_i and V_j that they receive in Step 2 induces the same value. Therefore, to prove IC1 it suffices to prove two parts: one, if a loyal lieutenant i puts exactly one order v into V_j in Step 2, then every loyal lieutenant will put exactly the same order v into V_j in Step 2; two, if V_j has two elements for some loyal lieutenant j, then V_k has two elements for any other loyal lieutenant k.

To prove the first part, we must show that j receives a properly signed message containing that order. If i receives the order v in Step 2A on time, then he sends it to j in Step 2A(ii), so that j receives it on time (by A1). If i adds the order to V_i in Step 2B, then he must receive a first message of the form $v:0:j_1:\cdots:j_k$. If j is one of the j_r, then by A4 he must already have received the order v. If not, we consider two cases:

1. $k < m$: In this case, i sends the message $v:0:j_1:\cdots:j_k:i$ to j, so j must receive the order v.
2. $k = m$: Since the commander is a traitor, at most $m - 1$ of the lieutenants are traitors. Hence, at least one of the lieutenants $j_1, \cdots, j_m$ is loyal. This loyal lieutenant must have sent j the value v when he first received it, so j must, therefore, receive that value.

Similar arguments prove that if any loyal lieutenant i decides to put two orders in V_i, then every other loyal lieutenant will decide to do so.

This completes the proof.

During the algorithm, every loyal lieutenant relays to every other lieutenant at most two orders. Therefore, the total number of messages exchanged is bounded by $2n(n - 1)$, where n is the total number of generals. By using more phases and more sophisticated algorithms, one can reduce the total number of messages to $O(n + m^2)$ as shown in reference 5.

5. MISSING COMMUNICATION PATHS

Thus far, we have assumed that a general (or lieutenant) can send messages directly to every other general (or lieutenant). We now remove this assumption. Instead, we supposed that physical barriers place some restrictions on who can send messages to whom. We consider the generals to form the nodes of a simple,* finite, undirected network graph G, where an arc between two nodes indicates that those two generals can send messages directly to one another. We now extend algorithms OM(m) and SM(m), which assumed G to be completely connected, to more general graphs.

The commander sends his value through routes in the network. For simplicity, assume that every message contains the information about the route through which it is supposed to be delivered. Thus, before sending a message, the commander chooses a route and sends the message containing the route. The receiving lieutenant, however, does not know in advance the route through which it is going to receive the message. Notice that a traitor may also change the routing through which the message is supposed to be delivered. Moreover,

*A simple graph is one in which there is at most one arc joining any two nodes, and every arc connects two distinct nodes.

a traiter may also produce many false copies of the message it is supposed to relay, then send them through various routes of its own choice.

A traitor may change the record of the route to prevent the receiving lieutenant identifying it as the source of faulty messages. To ensure the inclusion of traitors' names in the routes, assume that, after a loyal lieutenant receives a message to relay, he makes sure the lieutenant from which the message has arrived is supposed to relay it to him. Only then does he relay the message to the next lieutenant along the route to the receiving lieutenant.

A network has *connectivity* k if, for every pair of nodes, there exists k node-independent paths connecting them.

To extend our oral message algorithm OM(m), we need the following definition, where two generals are said to be *neighbors* if they are joined by an arc.

Definition: Let $\{a_1, \cdots, a_r\}$ be the set of copies of the commander's value received by Lieutenant i. Let U_i be a set of lieutenants that does not contain the commander himself. A set U_i is called a set of *suspicious* lieutenants determined by lieutenant i if every message a_j that did not pass through lieutenants in U_i carries the same value.

Algorithm Purifying $(m, a_1, \cdots, a_r, i)$

1. If a set U_i of up to m suspicious generals exists, then the *purified* value is the value of the messages that did not pass thorugh U_i. If no message is left, the value is **RETREAT.**
2. If there is no set U_i of cardinality up to m, then the purified vlaue is **RETREAT**.

Notice that if more than one set of suspicious generals exists, then there may be many purified values, but because of the way the algorithm will be used, a plurality of possible values will pose no problem. Before proving that the Purifying Algorithm actually does the right filtration, consider application of the Purifying Algorithm to the network shown in Fig. 12.6.

The network contains 10 generals, and at most 2 traitors. Assume that s and u are the faulty generals. The commander s sends the value a to Lieutenants 1 and 2, and the value b to the other lieutenants. Assume that Lieutenant 1 receives s's value through the following paths:

1. a: $s1$
2. a: $s21$
3. a: $su1$
4. b: $s741$
5. b: $s851$.

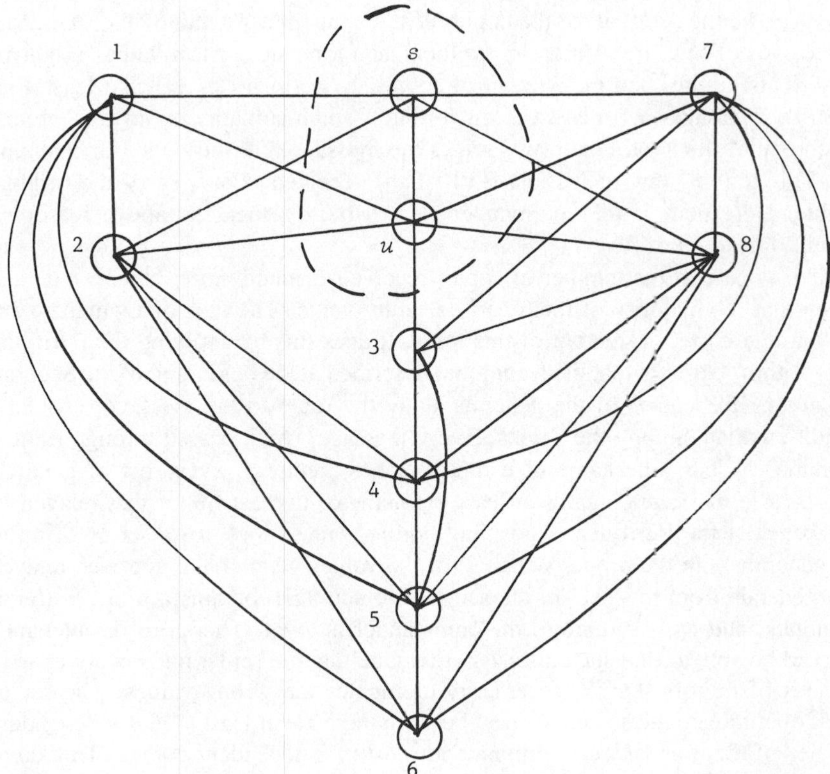

Fig. 12.6. Ten generals with two traitors, *s* is the commander.

The Purifying Algorithm provides the purified value *a* to Lieutenant 1, by choosing {7, 8} as the set of suspicious generals. Similarly, Lieutenant 2 obtains the value *a*. But the rest of the network obtain the value *b* by choosing {1, 2} as the set of suspicious generals.

The following theorem proves that, with sufficient connectivity, all of the loyal lieutenants obtain the same value if the commander is loyal.

Theorem 3: Let *G* be a network of generals which contains at most *t* traitors, and the connectivity of which is at least $2m + 1$. If a loyal commander sends $2m + 1$ copies of its value to every lieutenant, through disjoint paths, then, by use of the Purifying Algorithm, every loyal lieutenant can obtain the commander's value.

Proof: The loyal commander sends every lieutenant $2m + 1$ copies of a value, through disjoint paths. It sends the same value to all lieutenants. Let a_1,

$\cdots$, a_r be the set of all of the copies of the commander's value that Lieutenant i receives. There are at most m traitors; therefore, at most m values might be lost. This implies that the number of copies, r, is at least $m + 1$. At least $m + 1$ of the messages are relayed through routes which contain only loyal generals; each one of the loyal lieutenants relays the message faithfully without changing it. This implies that at least $m + 1$ of the received copies carry the original value. Note that, if the commander were a traitor, then the above reasoning would fail to hold.

It may be that the number of copies received is much more than $m + 1$, and even that the majority of them carry a faulty value. The task of Lieutenant i is to find the correct value out of this mess. It does this by applying the Purifying Algorithm. Observe that the technique, described at the beginning of the Section, of adding the names of the generals along the route to the message, enables i to differentiate among the values. Every message which passed through traitors contains at least one name of a traitor; more precisely, every list of generals added to a message contains at least the name of the last traitor that relayed it.

Step 1 of the Purifying Algorithm requires one to look for a set U_i of up to m generals with the property that all of the values which have not been relayed by generals from this set are the same. The network contains at most m traitor generals, and by assumption, the commander is loyal. Therefore, Lieutenant i should be able to find such a set U_i; it may be that the set he finds is not exactly the set of traitors, but U_i necessarily eliminates the wrong values. The set U_i cannot eliminate the correct values, because there are at least $m + 1$ independent copies of them and U_i can eliminate at most m independent copies. This completes the proof of the theorem.

In the case where the commander is a traitor, Theorem 3 does not ensure the ability to reach a unique agreement on a value. But the way we will use it in algorithm OM(m) will overcome the faultiness of the commander.

To obtain Byzantine Agreement in a network with connectivity k, $k \geq 2m + 1$, we improve algorithm OM(m) as follows: whenever a general sends a message to another, he sends it through $2m + 1$ disjoint paths; whenever a lieutenant has to receive a message, he uses the Purifying Algorithm to decide on a purified value. Call the improved algorithm OM′(m).

To prove the validity of the algorithm OM′(m), observe that the same general can be used again and again as a relay in the disjoint paths between pairs of generals, even if he was a commander in previous recursions. Moreover, even being a traitor does not matter for the simple reason that the total number of independent paths that would be affected by traitors will never exceed m.

Theorem 4. Let G be a network of n generals with connectivity $k \geq 2m + 1$, where $n \geq 2m + 1$. If there are at most m traitors, then Algorithm OM′(m) (with the above modifications) solves the Byzantine Generals Problem.

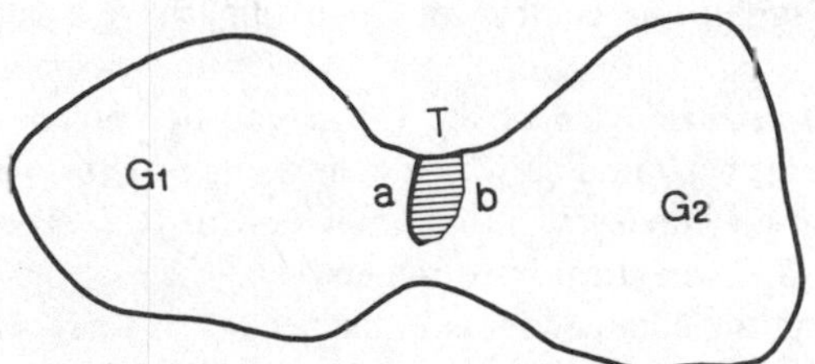

Fig. 12.7. T is the set of traitors.

Proof. The proof is essentially the same as the proof of Theorem 1, using Theorem 3 everywhere to show that, when a loyal lieutenant sends a value, every other loyal lieutenant agrees on it. The fact that we use the whole network to relay the information again and again eliminates any loss of connectivity, and enables us to obtain the desired result. The details are left to the reader.

To show that Theorem 4 is the best possible, we prove that the connectivity of $2m + 1$ is necessary for solving the Byzantine General Problem.

The case in which the number of traitors is not less than half of the connectivity is easier to visualize, and is proved in Lemma 2. Figure 12.7 describes the case schematically. The basic idea is that, if the traitors are not less than half of the bottleneck, then they can prevent the loyal generals from reaching an agreement by behaving as a filter. Every message that passes from right to left would be changed to carry one value, and every message in the reverse direction would carry another value. This behavior can cause all of the generals on the right side to agree on a different value from those on the left side.

Lemma 2: The Byzantine General Problem cannot be solved in a network of n generals if the number of traitors is not less than half the connectivity of the network.

Proof: Let G be a network with connectivity k, and let $s_1, \cdots, s_k$ be a set of generals which disconnect the network into two non-empty parts, G_1 and G_2. Assume that the subset $s_1, \cdots, s_m$ is the set of traitors, where $m \geq k/2$. Consider the following cases for the various locations in which the commander can be.

Assume the commander s is in the subnetwork G_1, and that he sends the value a to all of the lieutenants in the network. The traitors can follow the doctrine: change every message which passes from G_1 to G_2 to carry the value b; and leave every other value as a. Change the messages passing back from G_2 to G_1 to carry the value a. In this situation, every lieutenant in G_1 can consider s to be a loyal general, and thus agree on a. Similarly, the processors $s_{m+1}, \cdots, s_k$ choose a. But every receiver in G_2 cannot consider s a traitor.

They are able to ignore the conflicting values they have received by ignoring either the set $s_1, \cdots, s_m$ or $s_{m+1}, \cdots, s_k$. On the other hand, they cannot agree on a value, because each of the values can be correct, depending upon what the commander has said and which generals are traitors. Since $m \geq k$, the lieutenants in G_2 will choose b, in contradiction to IC2. The case where the commander is in G_2 is identical by symmetry.

Assume now that the commander is in the set $s_1, \cdots, s_k$. If the commander is loyal and sends the same value a to every lieutenant, then by reasoning, similar to the previous case, the traitors can prevent agreement. If the commander is a traitor, he can send the value a to G_1 and b to G_2. Thus, similarly to the previous case every decision implies violation of IC2. For a more rigorous proof see reference 3.

Our extension of Algorithm OM(m) requires that the graph G be $2m + 1$ connected, which is a rather strong connectivity hypothesis. In contrast, Algorithm SM(m) is easily extended to allow the weakest possible connectivity hypothesis. Let us first consider how much connectivity is needed for the Byzantine Generals Problem to be solvable. IC2 requires that a loyal lieutenant obey a loyal commander. This is clearly impossible if the commander cannot communicate with the lieutenant. In particular, if every message from the commander to the lieutenant must be relayed by traitors, then there is no way to guarantee that the lieutenant gets the commander's order. Similarly, IC1 cannot be guaranteed if there are two lieutenants who can only communicate with one another via traitorous intermediaries.

The weakest connectivity hypothesis for which the Byzantine Generals Problem is solvable is that the subnetwork formed by the loyal generals be connected. We will show that, under this hypothesis, the algorithm SM$(n - 2)$ is a solution, where n is the number of generals—regardless of the number of traitors. Of course, we must modify the algorithm so that generals only send messages to where they can be sent. More precisely, in Step 1, the commander sends his signed order only to his neighboring lieutenants; and in Step 2B, lieutenant i only sends the message to every neighboring lieutenant not among the j_r.

We prove the following more general results, where the *diameter* of a network is the smallest number d such that any two nodes are connected by a path containing at most d arcs.

Theorem 5: For any m and d, if there are at most m traitors and the network of loyal generals has diameter d, then Algorithm SM$(m + d - 1)$ (with the above modification) solves the Byzantine Generals Problem.

Proof: The proof is quite similar to that of Theorem 2, and will just be sketched. To prove IC2, observe that, by hypothesis, there is a path from the loyal commander to a lieutenant i going through $d - 1$ or fewer loyal lieutenants. Those lieutenants will correctly relay the order until it reaches i. As before, assumption A4 prevents a traitor from forging a different order.

To prove IC1, we assume that the commander is a traitor and must show that all loyal lieutenants have received a unique order, or every one decides on **RETREAT**. The idea is exactly as above. Suppose i receives an order $v:0:j_1: \cdots :j_k$ not signed by j. If $k < m$, then i will send it to every neighbor who has not already received that order, and it will be relayed to j within $d - 1$ more steps. If $k \geq m$, then one of the first m signers must be loyal, and must have sent it to all of his neighbors, whereupon it will be relayed by loyal generals and will reach j within $d - 1$ steps.

Corollary. If the network of loyal generals is connected, then SM$(n - 2)$ (as modified above) solves the Byzantine Generals algorithm for n generals.

Proof: Let d be the diameter of the network of loyal generals. Since the diameter of a connected graph is less than the number of nodes, there must be more than d loyal generals, and fewer than $n - d$ traitors. The result follows from the theorem by letting $m = n - d - 1$.

Theorem 5 assumes that the subnetwork of loyal generals is connected. Its proof is easily extended to show that, even if this is not the case, if there are at most m traitors, then the algorithm SM$(m + d - 1)$ has the following two properties: 1) Any two loyal generals connected by a path of length at most d passing through only loyal generals will obey the same order; and 2) If the commander is loyal, then any loyal lieutenant connected to him by a path of length at most $m + d$ passing only through loyal generals will obey his order.

6. RELIABLE SYSTEMS

Other than using intrinsically reliable circuit components, the only way we know for implementing a reliable computer system is to use several different "processors" to compute the same result, and perform a majority vote on their outputs to obtain a single value. (The voting may be performed within the system, or externally by the users of the output.) This is true whether one is implementing a reliable computer using redundant circuitry to protect against the failure of individual chips, or a ballistic missile defense system using redundant computing sites to protect against the destruction of individual sites by a nuclear attack. The only difference is in the size of the replicated "processor."

The use of majority voting to achieve reliability is based upon the assumption that all the nonfaulty processors will produce the same output. This is true so long as they all use the same input. However, any single input datum comes from a single physical component—e.g., from some other circuit in the reliable computer, or from some radar site in the missile defense system—and a malfunctioning component can give different values to different processors. Moreover, different processors can get different values even from a nonfaulty input unit, if they read the value while it is changing. For example, if two processors read a clock while it is advancing, then one may get the old time and the other the new time. This can only be prevented by synchronizing the reads with the advancing of the clock.

In order for majority voting to yield a reliable system, the following two conditions should be satisfied: 1) All nonfaulty, processors must use the same input value (so that they produce the same output); and 2) If the input unit is nonfaulty, then all nonfaulty processes use the value it provides as input (so that they produce the correct output).

These are just our interactive consistency conditions IC1 and IC2, where the ''commander'' is the unit generating the input, the ''lieutenants'' are the processors, and ''loyal'' means nonfaulty.

It is tempting to try to circumvent the problem with a ''hardware'' solution. For example, one might try to insure that all processors obtain the same input value by having them all read it from the same wire. However, a faulty input unit could send a marginal signal along the wire—a signal that can be interpreted by some processors as a 0 and by others as a 1. There is no way to guarantee that different processors will get the same value from a possibly faulty input device except by having the processors communicate among themselves to solve the Byzantine Generals Problem.

Of course, a faulty input device may provide meaningless input values. All that a Byzantine Generals Solution can do is guarantee that all processors use the same input value. If the input is an important one, then there should be several separate input devices providing redundant values. For example, there should be redundant radars as well as redundant processing sites in a missile defense system. However, redundant inputs cannot achieve reliability; it is still necessary to insure that the nonfaulty processors use the redundant data to produce the same output.

In case the input device is nonfaulty but gives different values because it is read while its value is changing, we still want the nonfaulty processors to obtain a reasonable input value. It can be shown that if the functions *majority* and *choice* are taken to be the median functions, then our algorithms have the property that the value obtained by the nonfaulty processors lies within the range of values provided by the input unit. Thus, the nonfaulty processors will obtain a reasonable value so long as the input unit produces a reasonable range of values.

We have given several solutions, but they have been stated in terms of Byzantine Generals rather than in terms of computing systems.

REFERENCES

1. DeMillo, R. A., N. A. Lynch, and M. Merritt, Cryptographic protocols, in *Proc. 14th ACM SIGACT Symp. on Theory of Computing*, pp. 383–400, May 1982.
2. Diffie, W. and M. E. Hellman, *New directions in cryptography*, *IEEE Trans. Inform. Theory IT-22*, pp. 644–654, Nov. 1976.
3. Dolev, D. The Byzantine generals strike again, *J. Algorithms*, vol. 3, pp. 14–30, Jan. 1982.
4. Dolev, D., M. Fischer, R. Fowler, N. Lynch, and R. Strong, Efficient Byzantine agreement without authentication, *Info. and Control*, vol. 3, pp. 257–274, 1983.
5. Dolev, D. and R. Reischuk, Bounds on information exchange for Byzantine agreement, *JACM*, vol. 32, pp. 191–204, 1985.
6. Dolev, D., R. Reischuk, and H. R. Strong, 'Eventual' is earlier than 'immediate,' *Proc. 23rd Annual IEEE Symp. on Foundations of Computer Science*, pp. 196–203, 1982.
7. Dolev, D. and H. R. Strong, Authenticated algorithms for Byzantine agreement, *SIAM J. on Comp.*, vol. 12, pp. 656–666, 1983.
8. Fischer, M., N. Lynch, and M. Paterson, Impossibility of distributed consensus with one faulty processor, *JACM*, vol. 32, pp. 374–382, 1985.
9. Lamport, L. and P. M. Melliar-Smith, *Synchronizing Clocks in the Presence of Faults*, Tech. Rep., Computer Science Lab., SRI International, 1984.
10. Lamport, L., R. Shostak, and M. Pease, The Byzantine generals problem, *ACM Trans. on Programming Languages and Systems*, vol. 4, pp. 382–401, July 1982.
11. Lynch, N. and M. Fischer, A lower bound for the time to assure interactive consistency, *Information Processing Letters*, vol. 14, pp. 182–186, 1982.
12. Pease, M., R. Shostak, and L. Lamport, "Reaching Agreement in the Presence of Faults," *J. ACM 27*, vol. 2, pp. 228–234, Apr. 1980.
13. Rivest, R. L., A. Shamir, and L. Adleman, A method for obtaining digital signatures and public-key cryptosystems, *CACM*, vol. 21, pp. 120–126, Feb. 1978.

13. The Fail-Stop Processor Approach

FRED B. SCHNEIDER

1. INTRODUCTION

Programming a computer system that is subject to failures is a difficult task. A malfunctioning processor might perform arbitrary and spontaneous state transformations, instead of the transformations specified by the programs it executes. Thus, even a correct program cannot be counted on to implement a desired input-output relation when executed on a malfunctioning processor. On the other hand, it is impossible to build a computer system that always operates correctly, in spite of failures in its components, by using (only) a finite amount of hardware.* Fortunately, most applications do not require complete fault tolerance; it is sufficient that the system work correctly provided no more than some predefined number of failures occur within some time interval, or provided certain types of failures do not occur. This more modest goal is attainable.

In this chapter we will present an approach to designing fault-tolerant computing systems based on the notion of a *fail-stop processor*, a processor with well-defined failure-mode operating characteristics. Briefly, our approach is as follows: first, software is designed assuming the existence of a computing system composed of one or more fail-stop processors. The number of processors required is dictated by the desired degree of fault-tolerance and any response-time constraints that must be satisfied by the system; then, a computing system is designed that implements the requisite fail-stop processors.

We proceed as follows. Section 2 defines the operating characteristics of a fail-stop processor. Section 3 concerns the problem of programming fail-stop processors, including axiomatic proof rules for a new programming construct we describe. The methodology described in Section 3 is illustrated by two examples in Section 4. The implementation of fail-stop processor approximations is discussed in Section 5. Section 6 contains a discussion of related work.

This work is supported, in part, by NSF grant MCS-8103605.

**Sed quis custodiet ipsos Custodes*? (Who shall guard the guards themselves?).[8]

Some of the insight that led to the development of fail-stop processors is discussed in Section 7. Section 8 contains some conclusions.

2. FAIL-STOP PROCESSORS

A *fail-stop processor* satisfies the following properties:

Halt on failure property. The processor halts instead of performing an erroneous state transformation that will be visible to other processors.

Failure status property. The processor can detect when any other processor has failed and therefore halted.

Stable storage property. Processor storage is partitioned into *stable storage* and *volatile storage*. The contents of stable storage are unaffected by any failure and can always be read by any fail-stop processor. The contents of volatile storage are not accessible to other fail-stop processors and are lost as a result of a failure.

A fault-tolerant computing system is constructed from a collection of fail-stop processors, interconnected so that each can read the stable storage of the others. The failure status property allows one fail-stop processor to determine that another has halted (due to a failure). This allows tasks that were being run by the halted processor to be continued, so that real-time constraints can be met. The halt on failure property prevents a failure from causing erroneous state information to be visible to other fail-stop processors. Finally, the stable storage property ensures that the state of a task that was running on a halted processor is available to the fail-stop processor that is to continue the task. To construct a fault-tolerant computing system that can tolerate up to k failures for an application requiring t processors assuming there are no failures, $t + k$ fail-stop processors are employed. Whenever a fail-stop processor in this system halts, the other fail-stop processors detect this and partition its work among themselves by reading from its stable storage.

3. PROGRAMMING A FAIL-STOP PROCESSOR

3.1. Recovery Protocols

A program executing on a fail-stop processor is halted when a failure occurs. Execution may then be restarted on a correctly functioning fail-stop processor. When a program is restarted, the internal processor state and the contents of volatile storage on the fail-stop processor on which it was running are unavailable. Thus, some routine is needed that can complete the state transformation that was in progress at the time of the failure and restore storage to a well-defined state. Such a routine is called a *recovery protocol*. Note that, because the code for a recovery protocol must be available after a failure, it must be kept in stable storage.

Clearly, a recovery protocol (i) must execute correctly when started in any intermediate state that could be visible after a failure and (ii) can only use information that is in stable storage. We associate a recovery protocol *R* with a sequence of statements *A*, called the *action statement*, to form a *fault-tolerant action FTA* as follows:

```
FTA: action
       A
     recovery
       R
     end.
```

Execution of *FTA* consists of establishing *R* as the recovery protocol to be in effect when *A* is executed, and then executing *A*. If execution of *FTA* is interrupted by a failure, upon restart execution continues with the recovery protocol in effect. Subsequent failures cause execution of *FTA* to be halted and execution of the recovery protocol in effect to begin anew when the program is restarted. Execution of *FTA* terminates when execution of either *A* or *R* is performed in its entirety without interruption. At that time, either the recovery protocol in effect when *FTA* started is reestablished, or if another fault-tolerant action *FTA'* follows *FTA*, then the recovery protocol for *FTA'* is established.

The following syntactic abbreviation will be used to denote that *A* serves as its own recovery protocol:

```
FTA: action, recovery
       A
     end.
```

Such a fault-tolerant action is called a *restartable action*.*

A program running on a fail-stop processor must, at all times, have a recovery protocol in effect. This will be the case if the program itself is a single fault-tolerant action. Alternatively, a program can be structured as a sequence of fault-tolerant actions, assuming that establishment of a recovery protocol can be done in such a way that at all times either the old recovery protocol or the new one is in effect. This is achieved by storing the identity of the recovery protocol in effect in stable storage.

---

*As we shall see, any fault-tolerant action can be converted to such a restartable action simply by omitting the action statement.

3.2. Axioms for Fault-Tolerant Actions

Following the Floyd-Hoare axiomatic approach,[7] an *assertion* is a Boolean-valued expression involving program and logical variables. The syntactic object

$$\{P\}\ S\ \{Q\},$$

where P and Q are assertions and S is a programming language statement, is called a *triple*. The triple $\{P\}\ S\ \{Q\}$ is a *theorem* if there exists a proof of it in a specified formal deductive system, usually called a *programming logic*. A programming logic consists of a set of axioms and rules of inference that relate assertions, programming language statements, and triples. Of particular interest are those logics that are sound with respect to execution of programming language statements on the program state—i.e., deductive systems that are consistent with the operation of a "real" machine. Then, the notation $\{P\}\ S\ \{Q\}$ is usually taken to mean:

> If execution of S begins in a state in which P is true, and terminates, then Q will be true in the resulting state.

It is often more convenient to write a *proof outline* than a formal proof. A proof outline is a sequence of programming language statements interleaved with assertions. Each statement S in a proof outline is preceded directly by one assertion, called its *precondition* and denoted $pre(S)$, and is directly followed by an assertion, called its *postcondition* and denoted $post(S)$. A proof outline is an abbreviation for a proof if:

PO1: For every statement S, the triple $\{pre(S)\}\ S\ \{post(S)\}$ is a theorem in the programming logic.

PO2: Whenever $\{P\}$ and $\{Q\}$ are adjacent in the proof outline, Q is provable from P.

Let *FTA* be a fault-tolerant action formed from action statement A and recovery protocol R. We wish to develop an inference rule that will allow derivation of

$$\{P\}\ FTA\ \{Q\}$$

as a theorem, while preserving the soundness of our programming logic with respect to execution on a fail-stop processor.

First, assume

F1: $\{P'\}\ A\ \{Q'\}$ and $\{P''\}\ R\ \{Q''\}$

have been proved. Then, for execution of A to establish Q, we will need

F2: $P \Rightarrow P'$ and $Q' \Rightarrow Q$.

Similarly, for the recovery protocol R to establish Q, the following (at least) must hold:

F3: $Q'' \Rightarrow Q$.

Recall that R is invoked only following a failure. By definition, the contents of volatile storage are undefined at that time. Therefore, any program variables needed for execution of R must be in stable storage. Thus, we require

F4: All program variables named in P'' must be in stable storage.*

We must also ensure that whenever the recovery protocol receives control, stable storage is in a state that satisfies P''. This will be facilitated by constructing a *replete proof outline*, a proof outline that contains assertions describing (only) those states that could be visible after a failure. Then, we will require that the precondition of the recovery protocol be satisfied in those states.

A replete proof outline is a proof outline in which certain assertions have been deleted so that:

RPO1: No assertion appears between adjacent fault-tolerant actions.
RPO2: Every triple $\{P\}\ S\ \{Q\}$ in the replete proof outline satisfies either
(a) S is a sequence of fault-tolerant actions, or
(b) $P \vee Q$ is invariant over execution of S.

RPO1 and RPO2(a) capture the fact that the program state between the execution of two fault-tolerant actions FTA_1 and FTA_2 is never visible to the recovery protocol of an enclosing fault-tolerant action—either the recovery protocol for FTA_1 or the recovery protocol for FTA_2 will receive control. RPO2(b) follows because if $P \vee Q$ remains true while S is being executed, then either P or Q will be true of the state visible to the recovery protocol should a failure occur, and both $\{P\}$ and $\{Q\}$ already appear as assertions in the replete proof outline.

For example, if

$$\{P\}\ FTA_1\ \{P_1\}\ FTA_2\ \{P_2\}, \ldots, FTA_n\ \{P_n\}$$

---

*If P'' is stronger than $wp(R, Q'')$,[1] then variables may appear in P'' that need not be stored in stable storage. Thus, in the interest of minimizing the amount of stable storage used, proofs should be in terms of the weakest assertions possible.

is a proof outline, then

$$\{P\}\ FTA_1;\ FTA_2;\ \ldots\ ;\ FTA_n\ \{P_n\}$$

is a replete proof outline. As another example, if assignment of an integer value to a variable is performed by executing a single, indivisible, (store) instruction—as it is on most machines—then

$$\{x = 3\}\ x := 6\ \{x = 6\}$$

is also a replete proof outline. This is because either the precondition or the postcondition of $x := 6$ is true of every state that occurs during execution of the assignment. Even if assignment is not implemented by execution of a single instruction, the proof outline

$$\{val = 3\}\ x := val\ \{x = 3 \wedge val = 3\}$$

is replete because the assertion $val = 3$ is not destroyed by assignment to x; it is true before, during, and after execution of $x := val$.

In addition to F1–F4, correct operation of a recovery protocol requires:

F5: Given a fault-tolerant action with action statement A and recovery protocol R satisfying F1, let $a_1, a_2, \ldots, a_n$ be the assertions that appear in a replete proof outline of $\{P'\}\ A\ \{Q'\}$ and $r_1, r_2, \ldots, r_m$ be the assertions that appear in a replete proof outline of $\{P''\}\ R\ \{Q''\}$. Then:

(i) $(\forall\ i\colon 1 \leq i \leq n\colon a_i \Rightarrow P'')$

(ii) $(\forall\ i\colon 1 \leq i \leq m\colon r_i \Rightarrow P'')$.

F5 states that P'' is an invariant of A and R. Thus, P'' will be true of any state visible after a failure.

Lastly, it must be guaranteed that failures at processors other than the one executing *FTA* do not interfere with (i.e., invalidate) assertions in the proof outline of *FTA*. Suppose an assertion a in *FTA* names variables stored in the volatile storage of another fail-stop processor *FSP*.* Then, should *FSP* fail, a would no longer be true since the contents of volatile storage would have been lost. Hence, we require that:

---

*This is often necessary when the actions of concurrently executing processes are synchronized. For example, if it is necessary to assert that a collection of processes are all executing in the same "phase" at the same time, then each would include assertions about the state of the others. See reference 19 for an example of such reasoning.

F6: Variables stored in volatile storage may not be named in assertions appearing in programs executing on other processors.

Given a fault-tolerant action, a restartable action that implements the same state transformation can always be constructed from the recovery protocol alone. (The proof of this follows from F3 and F5.) Thus, in theory, the action statement is unnecessary. In practice, the additional flexibility that results from having an action statement different from the recovery protocol is quite helpful. Presumably, failures are infrequent enough so that a recovery protocol can do considerable extra work in order to minimize the amount of (expensive) stable storage used. Use of such algorithms for normal processing would be unacceptable.

It is natural to ask whether F1–F6 are too restrictive. In that case, there would exist fault-tolerant actions that would behave correctly, but for which no proof would be possible. While we have not proved the relative completeness of the proof rule, the success we have had with its application and the way in which it was derived, suggest F1–F6 are not too restrictive to allow proof of any "correct" fault-tolerant action.

3.3. Termination and Response Time

Most statements in our programming notation are guaranteed to terminate, once started. However, loops and fault-tolerant actions are not. Techniques based on the use of variant functions or well-founded sets can be used for proving that a loop will terminate.[1] Unfortunately, without knowledge about the frequency of failures and statement execution times, termination of a program written in terms of fault-tolerant actions cannot be proved. This is because if failures occur with sufficiently high frequency, then there is no guarantee that the component fault-tolerant actions will terminate; neither the action statement nor the recovery protocol of a fault-tolerant action can be guaranteed to run uninterrupted, and so the recovery protocol could continually restart. Moreover, such properties cannot even be expressed in a programming logic like the one above. Thus, we must resort to informal means to argue that a program will terminate in a timely manner when fail-stop processors and fault-tolerant actions are used. Presumably, at some point in the future it will be possible to formalize such arguments.

For a given execution of a program S on a fault-free processor, let $t(s)$ be the maximum length of time that elapses once execution of a component statement s is begun until the execution of the next fault-tolerant action in S is started. Define

$$T_{\max} = \max_{s \in S} t(s).$$

For an execution of S to terminate at all, it is sufficient that there be (enough) intervals of length T_{max} during which there are no failures. Then, no fault-tolerant action will be forever restarted due to the (high) frequency of failures.

Of course, this gives no bound on how much time will elapse before S completes. Rather, we have argued that S is guaranteed to terminate if the elapsed time between successive failures is long enough, often enough. This should not be surprising. However, it does provide some insight into how to structure a program in terms of fault-tolerant actions if frequent failures are expected: one should endeavor to minimize T_{max}. This can be achieved by making entry into a fault-tolerant action a frequent event—either by nesting fault-tolerant actions, or composing them in sequence.

4. EXAMPLES

4.1. Updating Two Variables

In addition to allowing partial-correctness proofs of programs written in terms of fault-tolerant actions, F1–F6 permit a programmer to develop a fault-tolerant program and its proof hand-in-hand, with the proof leading the way, as advocated in references 1 and 5. F4 allows variables that must be stored in stable storage to be identified in a mechanical way from the proof; construction of a replete proof outline provides a mechanical way to determine the intermediate states that could be visible following a failure.

To illustrate the use of rules F1–F6 as an aid in developing a recovery protocol, we consider the following (artificial) problem.

> Periodically, variables x and y are updated based on their previous values. Thus, given a function G, a routine called *update* is desired that runs on a fail-stop processor and satisfies the following specification:
>
> $$\{P\text{: } x = X \wedge y = Y\} \ \mathit{update} \ \{Q\text{: } x = G(X) \wedge y = G(Y)\}.$$

Logical variables X and Y represent the initial values of x and y, respectively.

If the possibility of failure is ignored, the following program will suffice:

$$
\begin{aligned}
S1\text{: } & \{\mathrm{P}\text{: } x = X \wedge y = Y\} \\
& S1a\text{: } x := G(x);\ \{P1a\text{: } x = G(X) \wedge y = Y\} \\
& S1b\text{: } y := G(y);\ \{P1b\text{: } x = G(X) \wedge y = G(Y)\} \\
& \{Q\text{: } x = G(X) \wedge y = G(Y)\}.
\end{aligned}
$$

Note that this is a replete proof outline, provided assignment is implemented as an atomic operation: $P \vee P1a$ is invariant over the execution of $S1a$ and $P1a \vee P1b$ is invariant over the execution of $S1b$.

Things become more complicated when the possibility of failure is considered. In particular, *S1* could not be the action statement of a restartable action because F5 is violated (assuming G is not the identity function): both $P1a \Rightarrow P$ and $P1b \Rightarrow P$ are false. In order to construct a restartable action, we must find a way to make progress—compute $G(X)$ and $G(Y)$—but without destroying the initial values of x and y until both values have been updated. One way to do this is to modify *S1* so that the new values are computed and stored in some temporary variables, giving the following restartable action:

U1: **action, recovery**
$\{P: x = X \wedge y = Y\}$
U1a: $xnew := G(x);\ \{x = X \wedge xnew = G(X) \wedge y = Y\}$
U1b: $ynew := G(y);\ \{x = X \wedge xnew = G(X) \wedge y = Y \wedge ynew = G(Y)\}$
end
$\{Q': x = X \wedge xnew = G(X) \wedge y = Y \wedge ynew = G(Y)\}.$

Note that in order to satisfy F4, x and y must be stored in stable storage; variables used in computing G need not be. Having established Q', it is a simple matter to establish Q:

S2: $\{Q'': xnew = G(X) \wedge ynew = G(Y)\}$
S2a: $x := xnew;\ \{x = xnew = G(X) \wedge ynew = G(Y)\}$
S2b: $y := ynew;\ \{x = xnew = G(X) \wedge y = ynew = G(Y)\}$
$\{Q: x = G(X) \wedge y = G(Y)\}.$

This is a replete proof outline, and provided *xnew* and *ynew* are stored in stable storage, F1–F6 are satisfied. So

U2: **action, recovery**
$\{Q'': xnew = G(X) \wedge ynew = G(Y)\}$
U2a: $x := xnew;\ \{x = xnew = G(X) \wedge ynew = G(Y)\}$
U2b: $y := ynew;\ \{x = xnew = G(X) \wedge y = ynew = G(Y)\}$
end
$\{Q: x = G(X) \wedge y = G(Y)\}$

is a restartable action. Since $Q' \Rightarrow Q''$, the desired program is:

update: *U1*; *U2*.

4.2. A Process-Control Program

We now turn to a more substantial illustration of the application of the methodology: development of a fault-tolerant process control program. First, a correct program for a fault-free computing system is developed. The program is then extended to run on a system of fail-stop processors by defining the requisite fault-tolerant actions.

> Given are *sensors* to determine the state of the environment and *actuators* to exert control over the environment. Correct operation of a process-control system requires that:
>
> PC: The values written to the actuators are related to the values read from the sensors according to a given application-specific function.*

4.2.1. Assuming No Failures

Our process-control system will be structured as a collection of cyclic processes that execute concurrently. Each process p_i is responsible for controlling some set of actuators act_i. To do so, it reads from some sensors and updates $state_i$—a vector of *state variables* that reflects the sensor values p_i has read and the actions it has taken. Interprocess communication is accomplished by the disciplined use of shared variables; a process can read and write its state variables, but can only read state variables maintained by other processes. For the moment, we will ignore the problems that arise from concurrent access to state variables.

As is typical in process-control applications, each process will consist of a single loop. During execution of its loop body, process p_i: (i) reads from some sensors, (ii) computes new values for the actuators it controls and state variables it maintains, (iii) writes the relevant values to act_i, and (iv) updates $state_i$. Presumably, we are given application-dependent routines to compute values to be written to the actuators and values to be stored in the state variables.

Without loss of generality, assume that each state variable and sensor is read at most once in any execution of those routines.** Let $state_j[i, t]$ denote the value of $state_j$ read by p_i during the tth execution of its loop body, $sensors[i, t]$ denote the values read by p_i from sensors during the tth execution of its loop body, and $act_i[t]$ denote the values written to act_i by p_i during the tth execution of the loop body.

Behavior satisfying PC is characterized by the following, for each process p_1, p_2, . . . , p_n. First, the values in $state_i$ must correctly encode past actions

*It is likely that correct operation also involves a liveness property, like "sensors are read and actuators are updated often enough." We will make no attempt to argue that our program satisfies such real-time response constraints, although informal arguments could be used if timing data were available.

**Code that satisfies this restriction can be written by using local variables to store state variables and sensor values: each state variable and sensor value is stored in a local variable when it is first read; subsequent references are then made to the local variable.

performed by p_i. That encoding will be denoted here by the function E. Therefore, at the beginning of the t + 1st execution of the loop body at p_i:*

$$Istate(i,t)\colon t = 0 \textbf{ cor } state_i = E(sensors[i,t], state_1[i,t], \ldots, state_n[i,t]).$$

Secondly, values written to actuators by p_i must be computed according to the application-specific function, here called A, based on the sensor values read and the past actions of processes. Therefore, after p_i updates act_i for the tth time,

$$Iact(i, t)\colon t = 0 \textbf{ cor } act_i[t] = A(E(sensors[i,t], state_1[i,t], \ldots, state_n[i,t])).$$

must be true.

Let T_i be an auxiliary variable** defined such that, at any time, $T_i - 1$ executions of the loop body have been completed. Thus, T_i is initialized to 1 and (implicitly and automatically) incremented immediately after the loop body is executed. Then, the correctness criterion PC is satisfied if:

$$I(i)\colon Istate(i,T_i - 1) \wedge Iact(i,T_i - 1)$$

is true at the beginning of each execution of the loop body, for each process p_i.

In order to construct the loop, local variable *newstate* is introduced. This is necessary so that values used to update $state_i$ and the actuators are consistent with each other. Thus,

$$Vnewstate(i,t)\colon newstate = E(sensors[i,t], state_1[i,t], \ldots, state_n[i,t]).$$

The loop at process p_i, which has $I(i)$ as its loop invariant, is:

```
p_i: process
       do true → {I(i)}
          calc: newstate := E(sensors, state_i, . . . , state_n);
             {Vnewstate(i,T_i) ∧ Istate(i,T_i − 1) ∧ Iact(i,T_i − 1)}
          up_act: act_i := A(newstate);
             {Vnewstate(i,T_i) ∧ Istate(i,T_i − 1) ∧ Iact(i,T_i)}
          up_st: state_i := newstate;
             {Vnewstate(i,T_i) ∧ Istate(i,T_i) ∧ Iact(i,T_i)}
       od
     end.
```

*We use the notation "A **cor** B" to mean "if A then true else B".

**An *auxiliary variable* is one that is included in a program solely for purposes of performing a correctness proof. The value of an auxiliary variable never influences execution.

Because processes execute asynchronously, access to state variables must be synchronized. Otherwise, a process might read state variables while they are in the midst of being updated, which could cause the process to perform the wrong actions. To avoid this problem, the state variables maintained by each process p_i are assumed to be characterized by CC_i, called the *consistency constraint* for $state_i$. CC_i is kept true of $state_i$ except while p_i is updating those variables—i.e. performing *up_st* above. We assume that the code to compute the application-dependent functions A and E works correctly as long as values that satisfy the consistency constraints are read. To ensure that only values satisfying the consistency constraints are read, read/write locks[4] can be used to implement reader-writer exclusion on the state variables maintained by each process. A process trying to read variables in $state_i$ must first acquire a read lock for $state_i$. Such a lock will not be granted if a write lock is already held for those state variables, hence that process will be delayed if $state_i$ is being updated. A process about to update $state_i$ will be delayed if other processes are reading those values. Such lock operations are not explicitly included in our programs to simplify the exposition; they are part of the routine to compute E in *calc* and *up_st*.

Similarly, we assume that the code to compute A and E requires that sensor values used be consistent. The natural laws that govern our physical world ensure that the values of the sensors are consistent at all times. Thus, if a process read all the sensors simultaneously, consistent values would be obtained. Such a simultaneous read operation is not implementable, however. We therefore assume that sensors change values slowly enough and that processes execute quickly enough so that a consistent set of values is obtained by reading each of the sensors, in sequence, at normal execution speed.

4.2.2. Allowing Failures

We shall deal with failures by attempting to mask their effects. Thus, we shall endeavor to preserve:

PC′: At no time do state variables or actuators have values that they could not have had if the failure had not occurred.

Recall that $I(i)$ characterizes values of the state variables and actuators that satisfy PC. Consequently, if it is possible to modify the loop body so that $I(i)$ is true of every state that could be visible after a failure, then PC′ will be satisfied as well. Our task, therefore, is to modify the loop body so that it constitutes a restartable action.

$I(i)$ is true except between the time execution of statement *up_act* begins and when *up_st* completes. Thus, we must either mask intermediate states during execution of *up_st* and *up_act*, or devise a way to execute *up_st* and *up_act* together as an atomic action. This latter option is precluded by most hardware. Thus, to implement the former, we construct a single fault-tolerant action that updates the actuators and state variables based on the value of *newstate*:

$$\{Vnewstate(i,T_i)\}$$
$$upall$$
$$\{Vnewstate(i,T_i) \wedge Istate(i,T_i) \wedge Iact(i,T_i)\}.$$

As long as *newstate* is saved in stable storage, the following replete proof outline satisfies F1–F6 and accomplishes the desired transformation.

```
upall: action, recovery
       { Vnewstate(i,T_i)}
       up_act: act_i := A(newstate);
       { Vnewstate(i,T_i) ∧ Iact(i, T_i)}
       up_st: state_i := newstate;
       { Vnewstate(i,T_i) ∧ Istate(i, T_i) ∧ Iact(i, T_i)}
       end
```

A replete proof outline for the code executed at p_i is:

```
p_i: process
     action, recovery
          do true → {I(i)}
                   calc : newstate := E(sensors,state_i, . . .,state_n);
                   { Vnewstate(i,T_i) ∧ Istate(i,T_i−1) ∧ Iact(i,T_i−1)}
                   upall: action, recovery
                          up_act: act_i := A (newstate);
                          up_st: state_i := newstate;
                          end
          od
     end
```

Notice that, following a failure, a process might attempt to acquire a given read/write lock that had already been granted to it. For example, if a failure occurred while *up_st* were being executed, the recovery protocol would attempt to acquire the write lock on $state_i$, which might already be owned by p_i. Clearly, repeated requests by a given process for the same lock, without intervening release operations, should not delay the invoker. Implementation of read/write locks with this property (binary semaphores do not suffice) is possible and is described in reference 16.

5. IMPLEMENTING FAIL-STOP PROCESSOR APPROXIMATIONS

Real processors do not satisfy the halt on failure, failure status, or stable storage properties. In fact, most real processors are not even good approximations of fail-stop processors. Consequently, we now address the problem of implementing a fail-stop processor approximation. We must be content with only an approximation because it is possible to tolerate only a finite number of failures with a finite amount of hardware.

Our approximation is for a *k-fail-stop processor*—a computing system that behaves like a fail-stop processor unless $k + 1$ or more failures occur within its components. Choice of a value for k depends on the reliability desired. Obviously, as k approaches infinity, a k-fail-stop processor becomes closer to the ideal it approximates.

5.1. In Terms of Processes

A k-fail-stop processor *FSP* is implemented by a collection of real processors, each with its own storage, that are interconnected by a communications network. Failures that could result in another fail-stop processor reading the results of an erroneous state transformation are detected by voting; the effects of other failures are masked. The implementation consists of:

- $k + 1$ *p-processes* (p for program), each running on its own processor. Let $p(FSP) = \{p_1, p_2, \ldots p_{k+1}\}$ be this set of processes.
- $2k + 1$ *s-processes* (s for storage), each running on a different processor. Let $s(FSP) = \{s_1, s_2, \ldots s_{2k+1}\}$ be this set of processes.

The question of allocating processors to processes is discussed in Section 5.2.

A program running on *FSP* is run by each of the $k + 1$ p-processes in $p(FSP)$. Failures that should cause *FSP* to halt are detected by the s-processes in $s(FSP)$. This is done by comparing results when each p-process in $p(FSP)$ writes to stable storage in *FSP*, since subsequent reads to that stable storage would be the only way the effects of a failure could be visible. Because p-processes run on different processors, they fail independently. Provided fewer than $k + 1$ failures occur in the processors running p-processes, if any failure that should cause *FSP* to be halted occurs then there will be a disagreement in the write requests made by its p-processes. This disagreement will be detected by its s-processes.

A copy of the contents of the stable storage of *FSP* is stored by each of the s-processes in $s(FSP)$. Since there are $2k + 1$ s-processes, each running on a different processor, after as many as k failures in these processors, a majority of them will still be able to access correct values. Of course, this presupposes that each correctly functioning s-process updates its state whenever a write is performed to stable storage; a protocol for this is described below.

The only way a p-process can access stable storage is by sending messages to s-processes. Each of these messages m contains the following information:

m.time	The time this request was made according to the local clock on the processor running the requesting p-process.
m.rectime	The time this request was received according to the local clock on the processor running the s-process receiving the request.
m.type	"read" or "write," depending on the request.
m.var	the variable in stable storage to be written if *m.type* = write; the variable in stable storage to be read if *m.type* = read.
m.val	the value to be written if *m.type* = write.

We assume the following about the communications network.

Network reliability assumption: Messages are delivered uncorrupted and the process $orig(m)$ originating a message m can be authenticated by its receiver.

In theory, satisfying this assumption requires that there be $2k + 1$ independent and direct communication links between each p-process and s-process. Independent channels allow the majority value to be taken as the value of the message—this value will be correct provided fewer than $k + 1$ failures occur; direct channels allow authentication of message origin. In practice, a packet switching network can be made to approximate the network reliability assumption. Checksums and message retransmission are used to ensure that with high probability messages are delivered uncorrupted; digital signatures implement authentication (with high probability).

Each s-process in $s(FSP_i)$ for a k-fail-stop processor FSP_i in a system with up to N k-fail-stop processors FSP_i, FSP_2, . . . , FSP_N executes the program in Fig. 13.1. There,

choose(m, M) stores an arbitrary element from M into m, and CLOCK evaluates to the current time according to the processor's local clock. *Stable*[· · ·] is the copy of stable storage maintained by this s-process.

In addition, we require that when a p-process p_j makes a request to stable storage of FSP_i, it disseminates the request in a way that satisfies:

IC1: If p_j is non-faulty, then every non-faulty s-process s_u in $s(FSP_i)$ receives the request within δ seconds (as measured on s_u's clock).

IC2: If s-processes s_u and s_v in the same k-fail-stop processor are non-faulty, then both of them agree on every request from p_j.

```
owner := FSP_i; failed := false;
do true → /* major loop */
   for s := 1 to N
      T := CLOCK;
      D := bag of requests m delivered such that:
              orig(m) ∈ p(FSP_s) ∧ (m.type=read m.type=write)
      do D ≠ ϕ →
         minT := minimum value of m.time in D;
         minRecT := minimum value of m.rectime such that:
            m ∈ D ∧ m.time = minT
         if minRecT < T−δ →
            M := bag of requests m such that m ∈ D ∧ m.time=minT;
            D := D − M;
            if (∀m: m ∈ M: m.type=read) →
               do M≠ϕ → choose(m,M); M := M− {m};
                        send Stable[m.var] to orig(m)
               od
            [] (∀m,m' : distinct m,m' ∈ M:
               m=m' ∧ m.type=write ∧ orig(m)≠orig(m')) ∧
               |M|=k + 1 ∧ FSP_s=owner ∧ ¬ failed) →
                          choose (m, M);
                          Stable [m. var] := m. val
            [] otherwise → if FSP_s = owner ∧ ¬ failed →
                          failed := true;
                          forall d ∈ p(owner) send "halt " to d
                        [] otherwise → skip
                        fi
            fi
         [] otherwise→ skip
         fi
      od
   rof
od
```

Fig. 13.1. Program for s-process in FSP_i.

Condition IC1 ensures that all s-processes receive a message within a bounded length of time δ whenever a request is made by a non-faulty p-process. Condition IC2 ensures that all s-processes will agree on a request, even if the p-process making the request is faulty. IC2 is necessary because if a p-process fails, it might make different requests to two different s-processes. The copies of stable storage maintained by these s-processes could then become inconsistent if one s-process performs an update and another doesn't.

Finally, we require:

IC3: For each k-fail-stop processor *FSP*, the clocks of all processors running p-processes in $p(FSP)$ are synchronized.

IC3 ensures that if a request is made by one non-faulty p-process in $p(FSP)$ at time T on its clock then, since all processes in $p(FSP)$ are running the same program, the same request is made by each other non-faulty p-process at time T on its local clock.

A number of protocols to establish IC1 and IC2–called *interactive consistency* or a *Byzantine Agreement*—have been developed.[2,12,13,14] In those protocols, δ is based on message delivery time and the maximum difference in the clock speeds of any two correctly functioning processors running s-processes. At least $f + 1$ processors are required to handle up to f faults when messages can be authenticated.[3] Since our implementation of a k-fail-stop processor need tolerate at most k failures and involves $2k + 1$ processors for running s-processes, IC1 and IC2 can be achieved.

A protocol to achieve clock synchronization, as required by IC3, is described in reference 6. The protocol also requires at least $f + 1$ processors to handle up to f faults when messages can be authenticated. As described above, for a single k-fail-stop processor, IC3 requires the $k + 1$ processors running p-processes to have synchronized clocks. Thus, IC3 can be achieved.

5.1.1. Stable Storage Property

To show that the stable storage property holds for our implementation, we must show three things:

1. A majority of the copies of stable storage are correct and identical as long as k or fewer failures occur.
2. A non-faulty fail-stop processor can write to its stable storage.
3. Any fail-stop processor can read from the stable storage of any fail-stop processor *FSP* (including its own) regardless of whether *FSP* has halted in response to a failure.

The proof that our implementation satisfies part 1 of the stable storage property is as follows. All p-processes run the same program, so all non-faulty p-processes make the same requests to stable storage. Since, by IC3, the clocks of all of the non-faulty p-processes are synchronized, the non-faulty p-processes will all make requests at the same time according to their local clocks. By IC1 and IC2, if a non-faulty s-process s_u receives the first such request by time T_r on its clock, it will receive all such requests by time $T_r + \delta$ on its clock.

Thus, no request made at time T and received by an s-process at time T_r will be added, to D after $T_r + \delta$, and all s-processes will have the same request (of time T) in their respective D bags by time $T_r + \delta$. No request made at time T will be copied from D to M by an s-process before $T_r + \delta$ (on its clock), because of the way the s-process program is coded. Thus, the contents of M at each non-faulty s-process will be the same as at every other non-faulty s-process. Execution of the s-process program of Fig. 13.1 is completely determined by the contents of M. Consequently, each non-faulty s-process executes identically, so the non-faulty s-processes will update their copies of stable storage in the same way. Since there are $2k + 1$ s-processes, at least $k + 1$ will be nonfaulty. Therefore, a majority of the s-processes will update their copies of stable storage.

We now turn to part 2 of the stable storage property. Above, we argued that all non-faulty s-processes perform the same changes to stable storage and therefore a majority of the copies of stable storage and correct and identical. From the program in Fig. 13.1, it is clear that a write operation attempted by fail-stop processor FSP_i is not performed by an s-process unless all $k + 1$ p-processes in $p(FSP_i)$ request it. Moreover, write operations requested by other fail-stop processors are ignored because of the $s = owner$ conjunct in the guard. Clearly, if all $k + 1$ p-processes request an operation, then either none or all have failed in a way that makes erroneous state information—the value being written—visible to other processes. If all have failed then arbitrary behavior is permitted because there have been $k + 1$ failures. If none have failed then the write will be performed by the non-faulty s-processes.

Finally, for part 3, it suffices to note that a read operation attempted by FSP_i should result in identical responses being sent by non-faulty s-processes to each p-process in $p(FSP_i)$. If fewer than $k + 1$ failures occur, then at least $k + 1$ correct values (of a total of $2k + 1$) will be received. Thus, by taking the majority value of the responses, a p-process can obtain the correct value for the variable being read.

5.1.2. Halt on Failure Property

To detect a failure, during each (major) loop iteration it suffices for each s-process to check the write requests it has received, since spurious writes are the only way that the effects of a failure could be made visible to another process. If 1) exactly one write request from each of the $k + 1$ p-processes has been received, and 2) all the requests are identical, then (either all or) none of the $k + 1$ p-processes that make up FSP are malfunctioning. (Again, the case where all $k + 1$ p-processes are faulty need not concern us here because the definition of a k-fail-stop processor allows it to display arbitrary behavior under these circumstances.) If write requests from only some of the $k + 1$ p-processes in $p(FSP)$ are received, then the p-processes in that fail-stop processor are all sent a "halt" message and the stable storage variable *failed* is set true. (Correctly functioning p-processes will halt upon receiving a "halt" message from at least $k + 1$ s-processes.) Once *failed* is true, the values of the variables in the non-faulty s-processes don't change, since the conjunct "$\neg$*failed*" guards the assignment statement.

5.1.3. Failure Status Property

The failure status property is implemented by variable *failed*. Any process can obtain the value of *failed* at any time by reading it in stable storage. Thus, *FSP* can determine if FSP_i has halted due to a failure, by reading *failed* from FSP_i's stable storage.

This completes our implementation of a k-fail-stop processor approximation. The interface between the s-processes and the p-processes is summarized in Table 13.1.

5.2. Assigning Processes to Processors

Consider an application that requires N fail-stop processors to meet its response-time constraints, if no failures occur. For this implementation to be able to tolerate up to k failures, $N + k$ independent k-fail-stop processors are required. Use of independent fail-stop processors ensures that a single failure will cause at most one fail-stop processor to halt. Thus, provided k or fewer failures occur, there will always be at least N fail-stop processors available to run the application.

A naive implementation of such a computing system will use $3k + 1$ processors—$k + 1$ processors for p-processes and $2k + 1$ processors for s-pro-

Table 13.1. Interface Between *s*-Process and *p*-Process.

For p-process p_j in FSP_i to write to stable storage in FSP_i:

Initiate a Byzantine Agreement for the write request with all the s-processes in $s(FSP_i)$.

For p-process p_j in FSP_i to read from stable storage in *FSP*:

1. Broadcast the read request to all the s-processes in $s(FSP)$.
2. Use the value received from at least $k + 1$ different s-processes.

For a p-process p_j in FSP_i to determine if *FSP* has halted due to a failure.

Read the variable *failed* from the stable storage in *FSP*.

cesses—for each k-fail-stop processor, resulting in a total of $(N + k) \times (3k + 1)$ processors. However, recall that programs for fail-stop processors will be structured to make minimal use of stable storage. Therefore, it would be wasteful to dedicate an entire processor to running an s-process for a single k-fail-stop processor.

Suppose a single processor is able to run S s-processes without delaying any of the p-processes that interact with those s-processes. Now, we require only $\lceil (N + k)/S \rceil \times (2k + 1)$ processors to run the s-processes and $N \times (k + 1)$ processors for p-processes. Clearly, this is a substantial decrease in the number of processors over that required for the naive implementation. However, now the $N + k$ k-fail-stop processors are not independent—s-processes of different fail-stop processors share processors. Fortunately, this is not a problem because s-processes are replicated $2k + 1$-fold. Even if $S = N + k$, so there are only $2k + 1$ processors running the s-processes for all $N + k$ k-fail-stop processors and all of the failures occur in these processors, there will still be $k + 1$ s-processes running on non-faulty processors for each of the $N + k$ k-fail-stop processors. Thus, a majority of the s-processes will be running on non-faulty processors.

When a fail-stop processor halts, all of the non-faulty processors running its p-processes—up to $k + 1$ processors—halt. It is unlikely that all of these processors are, in fact, faulty. In order to recover non-faulty processors that were associated with a fail-stop processor in which there was a failure, the following scheme can be used.

> *Processor recycling scheme*: Processors are partitioned into three groups: *active*, *unavailable*, and *available*. All processors are initially assigned to the available group. As fail-stop processors are configured, processors are removed from the available group and placed in the active group. Whenever a fail-stop processor halts, those processors that were running its p-processes are assigned to the unavailable group. These processors run diagnostics and any processor that passes its diagnostics is reassigned to the available group.

The processor recycling scheme reduces the cost of a failure. Without it, a failure causes loss of all of the processors running p-processes for the fail-stop processor in which the failure was detected. With the processor recycling scheme, only processors that are unable to pass their diagnostic tests remain unavailable. The others are reconfigured into new fail-stop processors.

5.3. Other Ways to Approximate Fail-Stop Processors

There are undoubtedly other ways to approximate fail-stop processors. For example, disks are sometimes considered acceptable approximations of stable storage; a triple-redundant bus can be used to approximate IC1 and IC2 when disseminating requests to disks; and, a voter can be used to detect failures among processors running p-processes. These approximations are based on engineering data about how components usually fail; the approximation above made no assumption about the nature of failures. On the other hand, our approximation is quite expensive—perhaps too expensive for all but the most demanding applications. This suggests that it might be worthwhile to pursue investigations into other ways to implement fail-stop processor approximations, both with and without assumptions about failure modes.

6. RELATED WORK

6.1. Recovery Blocks

Despite the apparent similarity between the recovery block construct developed at the University of Newcastle-upon-Tyne[15] and our fault-tolerant actions, the two constructs are intended for very different purposes. A *recovery block* consists of a *primary block*, an *acceptance test*, and one or more *alternate blocks*. Upon entry to a recovery block, the primary block is executed. After its completion, the acceptance test is executed to determine if the primary block has performed acceptably. If the test is passed, the recovery block terminates. Otherwise, an alternate block—generally a different implementation of the same algorithm—is attempted and the acceptance test is repeated. Execution of each alternate block is attempted in sequence until one produces a state in which the acceptance test succeeds. Execution of an alternate block is always begun in the recovery block's initial state.

Recovery blocks are used to mask programming errors; fault-tolerant actions are used in constructing programs that must cope with failures in the underlying hardware (and software). Not surprisingly, the use of recovery blocks to cope with operational failures can only lead to difficulties. For example, a recovery block has only a finite number of alternate blocks associated with it, and therefore a large number of failures in the underlying system can cause the available alternatives to be exhausted. Also, the recovery block model does not admit the possibility of using stable storage for program variables.

6.2. State Machine Approach

Few general techniques have been developed to aid in the design of programs that must cope with operational failures in hardware. One approach, based on the use of state machines, was pioneered by Lamport[9] and was later extended for environments in which failures could occur, in references 10, 11, and 17. The implementation of a *k*-fail-stop processor described in Section 5 is an application of this technique.

In the state machine approach, a program is viewed as a state machine that receives input, generates actions (output), and has an internal state. Given any program, a distributed version that can tolerate up to k failures can be constructed by running that program on $2k + 1$ processors connected by a communications network in which message origins can be authenticated.* Byzantine agreement is used to ensure that each instance of the program sees the same inputs; majority voting is used to determine the output of the computation.

Consider an application that requires N processors to run and meet its real-time constraints. To implement a version of this application that can tolerate up to k faults, a total of $N \times (2k + 1)$ processors are required if the state machine approach is used, and each additional "k-fault-tolerant processor" costs $2k + 1$ real processors. It is instructive to contrast this with the cost when the fail-stop processor approach is used where S s-processes can share a single processor. A total of $(N + k) \times (k + 1) + \lceil (N + k)/S \rceil \times (2k + 1)$ real processors are required and each additional k-fail-stop processor costs (approximately) $(k + 1) + (2k + 1)/S$ processors. Thus, there are cases where, to achieve the same degree of fault-tolerance, the fail-stop processor approach requires fewer processors than the state machine approach.

However, the state machine approach has other advantages over the fail-stop processor approach. They include:

- When using the state machine approach, there is no need to divide the program state between volatile and stable storage. Also, there is no need to develop recovery protocols that reconstruct the state of the program based on the contents of stable storage.
- When using the fail-stop processor approach, additional response time is incurred when a task is moved from one fail-stop processor to another. Such delays are not incurred when the state machine approach is used, since all failures are masked. Thus, it might not be possible to use the fail-stop processor approach for applications with tight timing constraints.
- When using the fail-stop processor approach, an expensive Byzantine Agreement must be performed for every access to stable storage; with the state machine approach, Byzantine Agreement need only be performed for every input read. Thus, if reading input is a relatively infrequent event, the state machine approach will expend less resources in executing Byzantine Agreement protocols.

7. WHENCE FAIL-STOP PROCESSORS

The fail-stop processor approach can be viewed as a formalization of a well-known technique: checkpoints are taken during the course of a computation,

*If authentication is not possible, then $3k + 1$ processors are required.

and after a failure the computation is restarted from the last checkpoint. Our formulation of the approach was not based on this, but actually followed from our desire to extend Hoare-style programming logics for use in understanding fault-tolerant programs. In a fail-stop processor, all failures are detected and no incorrect state transformation due to a failure is ever visible. Thus, if execution of a statement terminates, by definition the transformation specified by that statement has occurred—the effect of execution is consistent with a partial-correctness programming logic. On the other hand, failure, by definition, prevents statements from terminating. Thus, the partial correctness (as opposed to total correctness) nature of the programming logic subsumes the consequences of failures.

If a failed processor can perform arbitrary state transformations, then the programming logic will no longer be sound with respect to the computer on which the program is being run. Thus, to ensure soundness in light of the possibility of failures, it is necessary to prohibit failures from causing arbitrary state transformations. Hence, fail-stop processors.

8. CONCLUSIONS

Constructing a reliable computing system involves two things (i) writing programs that run correctly assuming the hardware does what it is supposed to do, and (ii) constructing hardware that, with high probability, is well-behaved. Using assertional reasoning to aid in the construction of programs addresses (i); approximating fail-stop processors addresses (ii).

A methodology for developing provable correct programs to run on fail-stop processors was described in Section 3. The methodology has been successfully applied to a number of small examples, including the two-phase commit protocol[16] and a process control application.[18]

A way to approximate fail-stop processors was described in Section 5. The approximation is based on the construction of a reliable kernel (using the s-processes) that supports stable storage and detects failures. The kernel is reliable because it is replicated $2k + 1$-fold so that the effects of up to k failures are masked. Applications to be run on a k-fail-stop processor approximation are replicated only $k + 1$-fold, which is cheaper but sufficient only to detect errors and not to mask them.

Fail-stop processors simplify, but do not completely solve, the problem of building fault-tolerant computing systems. The problem is simplified because it is unnecessary to cope with arbitrary behavior and corrupted state information. However, it is still necessary to design programs that make infrequent references to stable storage, which is likely to be expensive and slow, while saving enough state information there so that a task can be continued by only accessing stable storage.

Another argument for studying fail-stop processors is that most protocols for implementing fault-tolerant systems assume processors are fail-stop or equivalent to fail-stop processors. In some models, instead of the failure status property, "time-outs" are used to detect failures. However, use of time-outs requires another assumption: that processor clocks run at the same rate. Otherwise, two processors might not agree that a third has halted, which can have disastrous consequences if the third processor has not. In other models, the stable storage property is not assumed; instead, state information is replicated at other processors. However, this turns out to be just an approximation of the stable storage property.

ACKNOWLEDGMENTS

The proof system for fault-tolerant actions was developed in collaboration with R. D. Schlichting; discussions with B. Alpern, O. Babaoglu, L. Lamport, and R. D. Schlichting were helpful in the design of the fail-stop processor approximation. D. Gries and D. Skeen read drafts of this chapter and earlier papers describing fail-stop processors and provided helpful comments.

REFERENCES

1. Dijkstra, E. W., *A Discipline of Programming*, Englewood Cliffs, NJ: Prentice-Hall, 1976.
2. Dolev, D., The Byzantine generals strike again, *J. Algorithms*, vol. 3, pp. 14–30, 1982.
3. Fischer, M., and N. Lynch, A lower bound for the time to assure interactive consistency, *IPL*, vol. 14, No. 4, pp. 182–186, 1982.
4. Gray, J., Notes on data base operating systems, in *Lecture Notes in Computer Science*, vol. 60, pp. 393–481. Berlin: Springer-Verlag, 1978.
5. Gries, D., *The Science of Programming*, New York: Springer-Verlag, 1981.
6. Halpern, J., B. Simons, and R. Strong, An Efficient Fault-Tolerant Algorithm for Clock Synchronization, IBM Res. Rep. RJ 4094, San Jose Research Laboratory Nov. 1983, San Jose, CA.
7. Hoare, C. A. R., An axiomatic basis for computer programming, *CACM*, vol. 12, 10, pp. 576–580, Oct. 1969.
8. Juvenal (Decimus Junius Juvenalis, c.50-c.130), *Satires* VI, line 347.
9. Lamport, L., Time, clock and the ordering of events in a distributed system, *CACM*, vol. 21, pp. 558–565, July 1978.
10. Lamport, L., The implementation of reliable distributed multiprocess systems, *Computer Networks*, vol. 2, pp. 95–114, 1978.
11. Lamport, L., Using Time Instead of Timeout for Fault-Tolerant Distributed Systems. Tech. Rep. 59, SRI International, Menlo Park, CA, June 1981.
12. Lamport, L., R. Shostak, and M. Pease, The Byzantine generals problem, *TOPLAS*, vol. 4, 3, pp. 382–401, July 1982.
13. Lynch N. A., M. J. Fischer, and R. Fowler, A Simple and Efficient Byzantine Generals Algorithm. Tech. Rep. GIT-ICS-82/02, School of Information and Computer Science, Georgia Institute of Technology, Atlanta, Georgia, Feb. 1982.
14. Pease, M., R. Shostak, and L. Lamport, Reaching agreement in the presence of faults, *JACM*, vol. 27, 2, pp. 228–234, Apr. 1980.
15. Randell, B., P. A. Lee, and P. C. Treleaven, Reliability issues in computing system design, *Comput. Surveys*, vol. 10, 2, (June 1978), 123–165.

16. Schlichting, R. D., *Axiomatic verification to enhance software reliability*, Ph.D. diss., Dept. of Computer Science, Cornell University, Ithaca, NY, 1982.
17. Schneider, F. B., Synchronization in distributed programs, *TOPLAS*, vol. 2, pp. 125–148, Apr. 1982.
18. Schneider, F. B., and R. D. Schlichting, Towards fault-tolerant process control software, in *Proc. 11th Annual Int. Symp. on Fault-Tolerant Computing*, IEEE Computer Society, Portland, Maine, pp. 48–55, June 1981.
19. Schlichting, R. D., and F. B. Schneider, Understanding and using asynchronous message passing, in *Proc. ACM SIGACT-SIGOPS Symp. on Principles of Distributed Computing*, ACM, Ottawa, Canada, pp. 141–147, Aug. 1982.

14. Nested Transactions: An Introduction

J. ELIOT B. MOSS

1. OVERVIEW

What are nested transactions? What are they good for? How might they be implemented? These are some of the questions that I will attempt to answer in this introduction. The discussion will be informal, in the interest of space and to appeal to a wider audience. I will assume you are comfortable with concepts such as two-phase commit, two-phase locking, etc. If not, the references can be used to gain such background.

Nested transactions are an extension and enhancement of atomic transactions. Hence I am going to present nested transactions largely by contrasting them with atomic transactions. To start on familiar ground, particularly simple locking and recovery methods are described. This concrete explanation is followed by examples to help bring the ideas home. Next, I generalize the concepts, pointing the way to more realistic schemes. At that point, you will have a good feeling for how nested transactions would work in a centralized system. I then state some ways in which nested transactions are a valuable improvement over atomic transactions.

Once the idea of nested transactions is grasped, I will expand the discussion to distributed systems. First, I shall describe a way of embedding nested transactions in a distributed system. After this, I describe a nested transaction management algorithm for distributed systems. Then, through the use of some particularly cogent examples (remote procedure call and update of replicated data) I will argue the special significance of nested transactions to reliable distributed software.

Deadlock control for nested transactions is treated next. I am going to include algorithms for distributed deadlock detection and resolution, as well as deadlock avoidance for nested transactions.

Lastly, I shall report on the current state of affairs (doubtless my information is out of date, even as I write this).

2. ATOMIC TRANSACTIONS

For purposes of this discussion, a transaction is a related set of actions that accepts inputs, modifies the system state, and produces outputs. The traditional transaction consists of a single thread of execution, having a definite beginning and end. For the discussion to be interesting, transactions must be processed concurrently (multiprogrammed or multiprocessed), and there must be some overlap in the parts of the system state that they access. Further, it is assumed that transactions may fail, for a variety of reasons, including bad inputs, hardware failure, deadlock, etc.

Atomic transactions guarantee to "hide" the effects of concurrent processing and failure. First, an atomic transaction is run in its entirety or not at all. Never is a transaction left only partly executed. This property is called *failure atomicity*. Second, concurrently executed transactions are guaranteed not to interfere with each other so as to produce inconsistent or invalid results. A lack of interference can most easily be guaranteed by promising that the system *appear* to have run transactions one at a time, each to its entirety. This property is called *serializability* and it provides *concurrency atomicity*.

3. NESTING TRANSACTIONS

An *atomic transaction* groups together a sequence of *primitive actions* (such as reads, writes, inputs, outputs) and guarantees that the package is executed as a whole (or not at all) without interference from other transactions or events in the system. A *nested transaction* consists of *either* a group of primitive actions *or* a group of nested transactions—it is a recursive concept.

The following analogy holds up fairly well. If primitive actions are like the instructions of a computer, than an atomic transaction is like a block of code: a grouping together of related instructions intended to achieve a particular goal. Nested transactions are analogous to the generalization of such blocks of code to subroutines. It is even conceivable that nested transaction could be recursive. This analogy will find later application when we discuss remote procedure calls.

While the analogy with subroutines gives some flavor of the control flow possibilities of nested transactions, it does not begin to explain how to nest failure atomicity and concurrency atomicity. In fact, at first the nesting of atomicity appears to be somewhere between impossible and absurd. This is because something that is atomic cannot be further split down into components, yet I am saying that there are atomic transactions nested within atomic transactions.

The paradox is resolved in the following way. When I say a transaction is atomic, all I mean is that the transaction's internal structure is not visible from outside the transaction. An atomic transaction might have a rich and complex internal structure, but when viewed from the outside (that is, when viewed from other transactions), it is an indivisible unit of action.

Nesting fits in with this notion of atomicity without difficulty. Each nested transaction provides a universe of execution within which actions may be performed without regard to system failure or concurrent execution of other transactions. Atomic transactions provide a similar universe. The extension made by going to nested transactions is that the universe includes the create-transaction operator. Thus, the protected universe of a nested transaction can contain subtransactions. Such subtransactions will also exhibit failure and concurrency atomicity within the universe provided by the containing transaction. Specifically, failure of one subtransaction does not affect others; each subtransaction is run entirely or not at all; subtransactions must be serializable with respect to each other; etc.

The nesting of transactions consists only of strict containment of a subtransaction in a containing transaction. This implies that nested transactions form hierarchies, and their relationships can be represented with trees. Hence, I will use tree terminology and also that of familial relationships (parent, child, ancestor, etc.). Let me run through some terms I use frequently when talking about transactions. Figure 14.1 illustrates most of my terminology.

A group of nested transactions forms a *forest* (set of trees). A particular transaction of the traditional kind corresponds to a single tree. Each nested

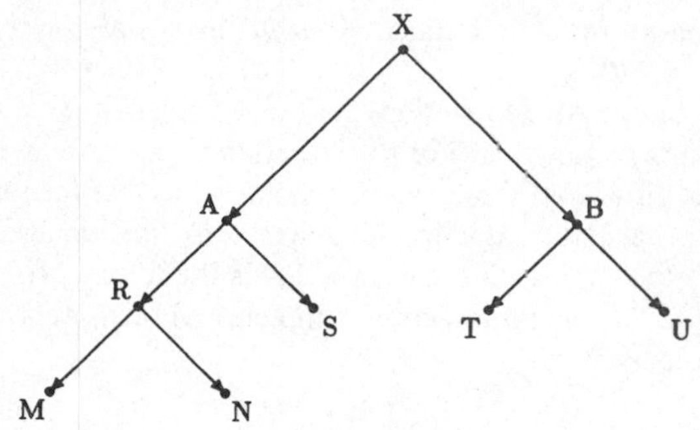

X is a *root* or *top-level* transaction.
A and B are *children* of X.
A and B are *siblings*.
X is the *parent* of A and B.
R and S are children of A (and grandchildren of X).
M, N, S, T, and U are *leaf* transactions.
M's *ancestors* are X, A, R, and M.
M's *superiors* are X, A, and R.
A's *descendants* are M, N, R, S, and A.
A's *inferiors* are M, N, R, and S.
A transaction's *universe* or *environment* consists of its inferiors.

Fig. 14.1. A transaction tree.

transaction corresponds to a node of a transaction tree. The root of the tree is called a *root* or *top-level* transaction. The root may have one or more *children*. Such children claim the root as their *parent*. Similarly, the children of the root may have children of their own. This nesting can continue to arbitrary depth. All transactions except roots have parents. *Leaf* transactions are those transactions with no children.

The parent-child relationship is generalized to *ancestor-descendant*, implying zero or more levels between the two transactions in question. Thus, each transaction is an ancestor and descendant of itself. When I need to restrict the relationship to *one* or more levels of difference, I will use the terms *superior* and *inferior* in place of ancestor and decendant (respectively).

4. CONCURRENCY CONTROL

Let me try to sharpen your possibly vague conception of nested transactions by offering one concrete way of providing concurrency control for nested transactions. Generalizations and alternatives to this method will be discussed later.

4.1. Atomic Transaction Exclusion Locking

Consider the simplest possible locking scheme: mutual exclusion locks. Concurrency control for atomic transactions via exclusion locks follows these rules:

1. Uniformity: All transactions follow the rules.
2. Meaning of Locking: For a transaction to perform an operation, the transaction must hold the lock corresponding to that operation.
3. Exclusion: If a transaction requests a lock, the request can be granted only if no other transaction currently holds the lock.
4. Release: When a transaction completes (aborts or commits), it releases all of its locks.

The exact relationships between locks, operations, and data are unimportant for our discussion with one exception: the holding of a lock must guarantee exclusive access to the data it protects.

The above scheme is called two-phase locking, because transactions have a lock acquisition phase (while they are running) and a lock releasing phase (in this case, when they complete). A slightly more general scheme is examined in some detail in reference 3. There it is shown that two-phase locking guarantees *serializability*. An execution of a set of transactions is serializable if and only if it is equivalent to some serial, one at a time execution of the same transactions. Loosely speaking, executions are equivalent if they produce the same results and leave the database in the same state when done. It is generally assumed that any transaction, if executed serially in isolation, will preserve consistency of the system state. Hence, serializability provides a promise of consistency (assuming, of course, that the system starts in a consistent state). In some cases, consistency might be realized without serializability, but there is good evidence for the general appropriateness of serializability.[14]

Note that different orders of execution of transactions may give different results. Serializability merely says that there is *some* equivalent serial execution. Note also that serializability is most easily understood and generally described in an "after the fact" way. That is, all transactions being considered are assumed to have completed successfully. Thus the issues of aborted transactions and deadlock are avoided by assuming that they have already been resolved.

How can two-phase exclusion locking be extended from atomic transactions to nested transactions? First, I make a simplifying assumption: the only nested transactions that directly invoke operations on the system state are leaf transactions. This assumption can be made without loss of generality, as I will now explain. Suppose that we have a transaction *T*. It is desired that *T* perform operations directly and that *T* have inferior transactions. The desired effect can be achieved by providing *T* with an extra child transaction that performs the operations that *T* was supposed to do directly. In this way, it can be guaranteed that only leaves manipulate the system state directly, while their superior transactions play only a controlling role in transaction processing.

4.2. Nested Transaction Exclusion Locking

Here, then, are locking rules for nested transactions:

1. Uniformity: All transactions follow the rules.
2. Meaning of Locking: For a transaction to perform an operation, the transaction must hold the lock corresponding to that operation. (Only leaf transactions may perform operations, but other transactions may hold locks, as described below.)
3. Exclusion: If a transaction requests a lock, the request can be granted only if all holders of the lock (if any) are ancestors of the requesting transaction.
4. Inheritance: When a transaction succeeds (commits), its locks are given to its parent, if any, or discarded if the transaction is top-level.
5. Release: When a transaction fails (aborts), its locks are released (discarded).

Some discussion may help in understanding these rules. Consider first the exclusion rule. Another way of stating this rule is that the requesting transaction must be *within* all environments currently holding the lock (if any). Recall that each transaction provides an environment for its inferiors. Only its inferiors are within that environment; all other transactions are outside of it. Obviously, the exclusion rule works if the requested lock is not held at all, or is already held by the requesting transaction. If the lock is held by one or more superior transactions, then several facts together imply the correctness of the exclusion rule. First, no transaction can be performing operations controlled by the lock. This is because only leaf transactions can perform operations, and superior transactions (the only holders of the lock) are obviously not leaves. Second, while a leaf possesses a lock, no other transaction can modify the locked object. Finally, the inheritance rule prevents early release of modifications from a containing environment.

Now consider the inheritance rule. By inheritance I mean the propagation of locks from child transactions to their parents when the child transactions complete successfully. (I will consider transaction failure in more detail later.) In the universe of the parent, when a child completes, the locks held by the child are released. This is so because the exclusion rule permits another inferior of the parent to obtain the lock since the child no longer holds it, and the parent is necessarily superior to its inferiors. However, no transaction not inferior to the parent can acquire the lock. From the point of view of transactions outside the parent's universe, the lock appears to be held by the parent. This is true from the time the lock is first acquired by the child until the parent commits.

Note that a lock can be held on several levels simultaneously. Note also the distinction between what happens to a transaction's locks when the transaction commits and when it aborts. Release of locks on abort gives better performance than inheritance; it allows more transactions to proceed, and requires fewer transactions to be aborted to resolve actual or potential deadlocks. This point should become more clear later. Additionally, it is hard to satisfy inheritance on abort when site crashes can occur in a distributed transaction system. It is just simplier to permit an abort to release locks, since a crash has that effect anyway. Note that, since all a transaction's effects are assumed to be undone when the transaction aborts, no consistency problems arise from discarding the locks.

A transaction can commit even if one or more of its children aborts. This will be discussed in more detail later, but briefly, the advantage is that a transaction can retry a necessary action, use a different but satisfactory method of achieving its end, or, if the aborted actions were nonessential, commit without further corrective action. Thus the handling of locks when a transaction aborts is relevant.

One other point should be clarified. Locks are propagated up the tree, from the leaves toward the root. Lock requests are *not* sent up from the leaves to higher levels of the tree, and then granted locks propagated downwards. If locks were inherited on abort as well as commit, then the two concepts would be equivalent, but since locks are discarded on abort, they are not the same. Furthermore, since locks can be held at several levels, it is not correct to think of one lock moving up and down the tree and being possessed by different transactions at different times.

In sum, the locking rules make a lock *appear* to be held from outside any transaction holding the lock, while the lock appears free inside the innermost lock holder. Acquistion of a lock makes the lock look held in more environments; inheritance of a lock makes it free in the parent's environment (and in all subordinate environments). In this way, the holding of a lock has become a relative concept: it is relative to a transaction's position in the transaction tree.

4.3. Locking Examples

Let us see how nested transaction locking works by means of a simple example. Let there be two top-level transactions *A* and *B*. Transaction *A* has two children, *AA* and *AB*. Transaction *AA* also has two children, *AAA* and *AAB*. This situation is illustrated by Fig. 14.2a. The example uses a single lock, *L*. In the figures, I have bracketed holders of *L*, and written a "+" by transactions that could hold *L*, and a "−" by ones that could not.

Initially, *L* is not held by any of the transactions. It could be acquired by any one of the leaf transactions: *AAA*, *AAB*, *AB*, or *B*. Suppose *AAA* requests *L* and is granted it. This is shown in Fig. 14.2b. At this point, no transaction other than *AAA* may be granted *L*: *AAA* exclusively holds the lock. If *AAA* fails (aborts), *L* will be released (Fig. 14.2c). However, if *AAA* commits, then *L* is inherited by *AA* (Fig. 14.2d). Now *AAB* can be granted *L*, but *AB* and *B* cannot. Note the differences between Fig. 14.2c and Fig. 14.2d.

5. RECOVERY MANAGEMENT

To make the discussion clear and brief, highlighting the differences between atomic transaction and nested transactions, I am presenting a very simple-minded recovery scheme. Other possibilities will be mentioned later. As with concurrency, I shall review recovery for atomic transactions. The method I will describe is called *shadow file* or *double copy* updating.

5.1. Shadow Recovery for Atomic Transactions

Here are the rules for atomic transactions:

1. When a transaction acquires a lock on some data, a copy of the data is made, and all work is performed on that copy. The copy is known as a *shadow*.
2. When a transaction succeeds (commits), its shadows are installed in favor of the original versions.
3. When a transaction fails (aborts), its shadows are discarded, and the original versions are left intact.

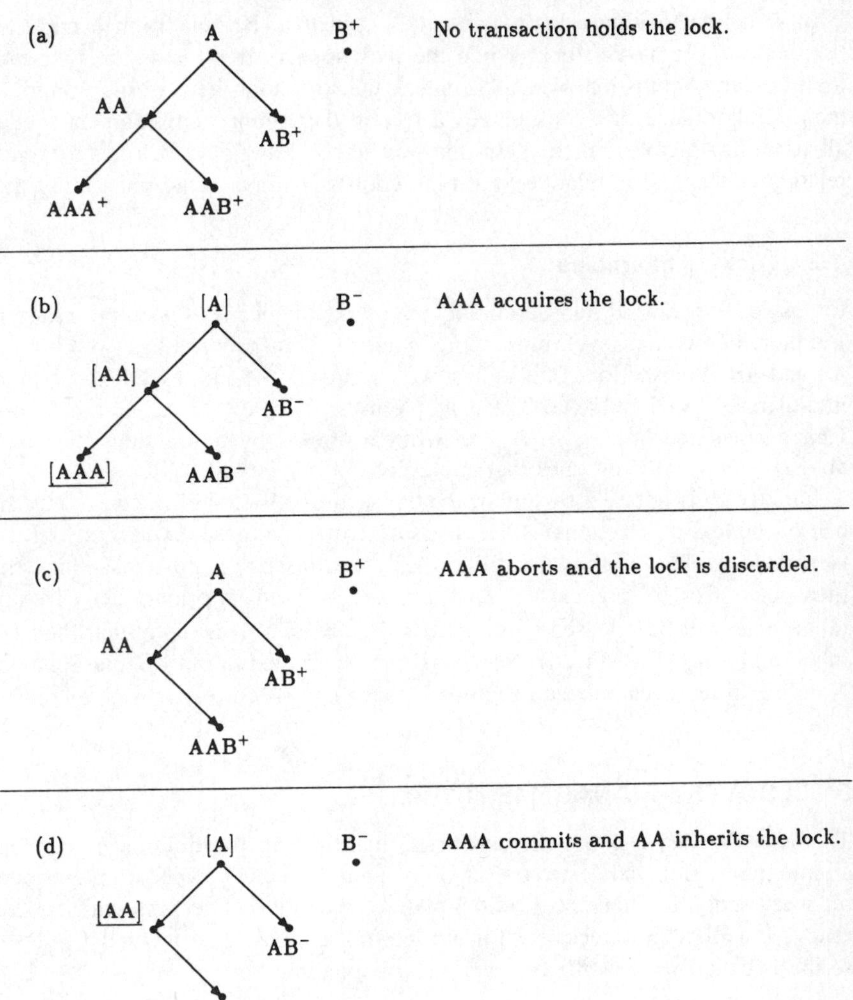

Legend: T^+ indicates T can acquire the lock
T^- indicates T cannot acquire the lock
[T] indicates T appears to hold the lock
[T] indicates T actually holds the lock

Fig. 14.2.

Provided that the installation of shadows can be made to appear atomic, the above rules make the transactions all-or-nothing, guaranteeing failure atomicity. Stable storage techniques[7] provide one way of installing shadows atomically. A closely related recovery method is to operate on the originals instead of the shadows, install the shadows on abort, but leave the originals on commit. That method probably performs better in the commit case by reducing delay. Restoring shadows on abort is very similar to logging. Log-based recovery involves writing a sequential record of all changes made, and scanning the record in case of an abort, undoing the operations performed. For more details on logging see references 5 and 11; for more about shadow methods, see reference 17.

I hope that the simplicity of the above rules makes their correctness obvious. Below are the corresponding recovery rules for nested transactions.

5.2. Shadow Recovery for Nested Transactions

1. When a transaction acquires a lock on some data, a copy of the data is made, and all work is performed on that copy. The copy is known as a shadow.
2. When a transaction succeeds (commits), its shadows are inherited by its parent, in favor of any versions the parent may hold for the same data. When a top-level transaction commits, its shadows are installed in the database.
3. When a transaction fails (aborts), its shadows are discarded, and all other versions are left intact.

The first rule may need to be clarified. The current view of the data (i.e., the data from which a copy is made) is the shadow held by the youngest (most inferior, i.e., most deeply nested) transaction holding a shadow for the data at the time; or, if no transactions hold shadows of the data, the original. This notion of current value, together with the shadow inheritance rules, insures that updates are visible within all environments where the updates have been committed. The locking rules prevent updates from being visible too widely.

Recovery for atomic transactions needs at most two copies of any data: the old and the new versions. Where the two versions reside and their representations are the concern of the various recovery mechanisms. Recovery for nested transactions may require many copies of a data item: up to one copy for each level of nesting of transactions that modify the item, plus the original. This is because the state of the item must be available whether or not each of the transactions commits or aborts, and each environment may have a different starting state for the item (because of changes previously made in the enclosing environments).

Note that shadows are created and propagated up the transaction tree in exactly the same manner as the corresponding locks.

5.3. Recovery Example

Suppose a top-level transaction T has two children T_1 and T_2, and database variable x starts with value 0. This is illustrated by Fig. 14.3a. T_1 modifies x, setting it to 1 (Fig. 14.3b). Note the shadow "$x = 1$" next to T_1 in the drawing. T_1 then commits (Figure 3c), and T inherits the shadow. T_2 then sets x to (Fig. 14.3c). Now there are two shadows: one held by T, one by T_2.

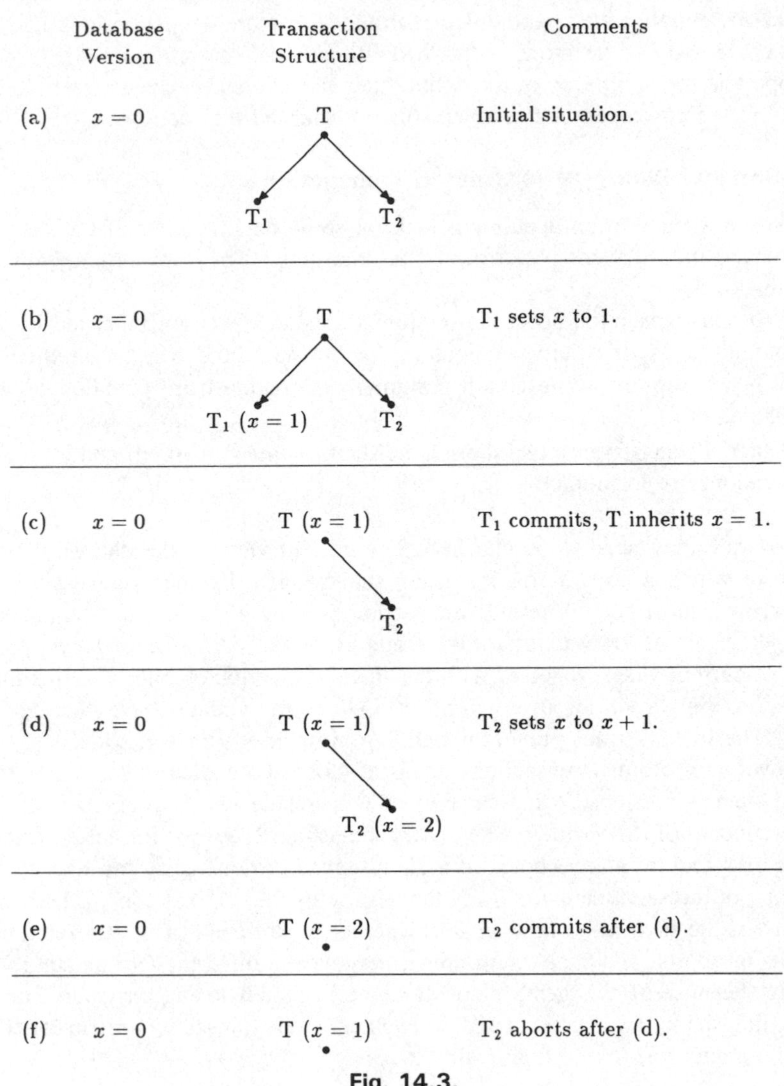

Fig. 14.3.

There are three possible outcomes of this situation:

1. T_2 commits (Fig. 14.3d) and then T commits, leaving x set to 2. Note how T inherited T_2's shadow in the figure.
2. T_2 aborts (Fig. 14.3e) and then T commits. x will be set to 1.
3. T aborts (it does not matter if T_2 commits or aborts). x is left with its original value, 0.

This example generalizes to as many levels as one likes. Note that a transaction will possess a shadow only if it possesses a lock on the corresponding data. Because there can be at most one lock per level of the transaction tree (a consequence of the locking rules), there can be at most one shadow per level of the tree. It is not too hard to construct examples where there is exactly one shadow per level, so the bound on the number of shadows is tight.

6. GENERALIZATIONS

Exclusion locking and shadow file recovery serve to illustrate the differences between single-level atomic transactions and nested transactions. But as I pointed out before, nested transactions are a more general concept, not restricted by specific concurrency and recovery control techniques. Let me now point out some of the ways in which nested transactions are easily generalized.

6.1. Nested Transaction Read-Write Locking

First, exclusion locking may be extended to read-write locking very easily. Here are the rules:

1. Uniformity: All transactions follow the rules.
2. Meaning of Locking: For a transaction to perform a read (non-modifying) operation, the transaction must hold either a read or write lock for the data to be accessed. For a transaction to perform a write (modifying) operation, the transaction must hold a write lock for the data to be modified.
3. Exclusion: If a transaction requests a read lock, the request can be granted only if all holders of write locks for the same data are ancestors of the requesting transaction. If a transaction requests a write lock, the request can be granted only if all holders of either read or write locks for the same data are ancestors of the requesting transaction.
4. Release: When a transaction commits, its locks are inherited by its parent (if any). When a transaction aborts, its locks are released.

We have omitted the two-phase rule since inheritance actually embodies it. Note also that two-phase-ness is not always sufficient for reliable concurrency control. Not only must lock holding be two-phase, but no locks can be released until the transaction has either committed or aborted. Otherwise, results would be released early and there would be problems undoing transactions that aborted after releasing some locks. It would be possible to implement such a scheme only if transactions that accessed the released data could also be tracked down and aborted, etc. For a particular scheme, see reference 16. Davies[2] covers these concepts in a more general framework; I will not pursue the matter further.

The crucial part of the extension from exclusion locks to read-write locks (also known as share and exclusion locks) is the third rule, which states the conditions under which a lock can be granted. The methods generalize to, for example, the intention locks of reference 5. However, I will not present such extensions here.

Note that the locking methods I have discussed do not prevent deadlocks. Deadlocks and their resolution will be covered in detail later.

Along other lines, nested transaction concurrency control can also be done with timestamps instead of locks. Reed[12] presents such a design. His design is more general than is required, for he allows the system to keep multiple versions for (essentially read-only) reference by old transactions. Generalization of other timestamp schemes (e.g., SDD-1[1]) to nested transactions has not been done.

Turning to recovery, it is easy to generalize logging to nested transactions; see reference 11 for the details. Checkpoint/restart should not be instrinsically more complicated for nested transactions. However, nested transactions encourage concurrency within transactions, and such concurrency might be a problem, especially in a distributed system. This is because a distributed system checkpoint/restart algorithm must guard against the domino effect.[15] When one site in a system rolls back, other sites may be forced to roll back, too, in an attempt to maintain consistency across the system. However, if checkpoints are not properly coordinated, the original site may be forced to roll back farther. This can keep up indefinitely, hence the term domino effect. Distributed checkpoint/restart requires further research. However, it may be that nested transactions can simplify the problem in some way.

7. WHY NESTED TRANSACTIONS?

There are two basic reasons why nested transactions are desirable: they provide safe concurrency *within* transactions, enhancing both performance and modularity; and they provide for finer grained recovery, permitting better control over transaction execution, simplifying the programming of reliable transaction systems. I will consider each reason in turn.

With single-level transactions, concurrency within a transaction could be as dangerous as concurrency without a transaction mechanism at all. For example, suppose I had two transactions I wished to have executed together as one transaction. Further suppose that the two transactions generally would not interfere with one another. For higher throughput, I might be tempted to run the two old transactions concurrently within a new transaction. But if the two old transactions shared data in a way I did not understand, inconsistencies could result. This problem would be especially insidious if the transactions' behaviors changed substantially in different situations.

Nested transactions provide a simple solution to the problem: just run the two old transactions as separate children of a new top-level transaction. The children could run in parallel. In cases where there was no conflict on data items, the full benefits of concurrency would accrue. When there was conflict, the transactions would be automatically serialized: no inconsistencies could result, while considerable overlap of execution might still occur. Proper handling of concurrency within transactions can thus simplify programming and make a system more robust.

Nested transactions also provide better control over recovery. When a part of a transaction is considered more than usually likely to fail (such as a lock request or an interaction with a remote computer or operator), that part can be made a child transaction. This permits the rest of the transaction's work to be preserved even when one part fails. It also permits the transaction to handle the failure by either retrying the failed operation or taking another approach. Of course, this is useful only if a retry might succeed, if there is an alternative action to be taken, or the operation was not essential in the first place.

The ability to recover from failure of a remote operation is a strong advantage for nested transactions in distributed systems. Later I will show how simple some things become if you have a nested transaction mechanism in a distributed system. Part of the simplicity comes from being able to handle failure in the first place; another part comes from the clean semantics of failure: any work done by a failed transaction will automatically be undone (by the recovery manager). This leads to a trade-off: a nested transaction recovery manager will necessarily be somewhat more complicated than a recovery manager for atomic transactions. But the benefits are great, and the added complexity is not severe. I will sketch a distributed transaction management algorithm for nested transactions in a later section.

8. DISTRIBUTED SYSTEMS

Up to this point I have discussed nested transactions without regard to whether or not they are embedded in a centralized or distributed system. The concepts are general enough for distributed systems, but there might be many ways to build distributed nested transactions. I will suggest one way that I think is best because it is the simplest yet very powerful. Perhaps someone will find a better way to do distributed nested transactions.

First, in my model neither data objects nor individual transactions are distributed. Another way of putting it is: each data object and each transaction has a single site of the distributed system called its home. The home site of a data object has complete control over that object and its manipulation, following the concurrency and recovery rules presented in previous sections. This means that locks and shadows (or logs) are entirely local and need never be copied across the computer network. However, as will be seen later, a transaction can effectively hold locks and shadows at other sites.

The main implication of my rule that each object has a single home is that any replication or movement of objects is explicit in my model. It does not mean that replication or migration cannot be implemented. In fact, one of the examples I offer later is the reading and updating of replicated data objects.

Just as each object has a single home, so does each transaction. However, a transaction's children need not have the same home as the parent or each other. A transaction accomplishes remote actions through its inferior transactions, which run at other sites on the superior's behalf. In this way, the restriction of transactions to single sites is not really a limitation of functionality. It does simplify system design and implementation, though. This is because the abort/commit decision of each transaction can be made locally, without negotiation between multiple sites. There is one exception: a top-level transaction must coordinate using a two-phase commit protocol of some sort. Only top-level transactions need a two-phase commit because only they make permanent changes to the database.

My model does not specify the relationship of any user- or application-level message passing (communciation) mechanism to the nested transaction mechanism. If applications may freely communicate, care must be taken not to violate serializability through the early realease of tentative information. Ill-disciplined communication can destroy consistency just as easily as ill-disciplined object manipulation. For a number of applications, it may be sufficient to have communication modeled after a procedure call. A child transaction is provided parameter information from its parent when the child is created (even if the child is at a different site from the parent). Similarly, a child transaction can provide result data back to its parent if and when the child commits. This rather simple mechanism may not be convenient for all applications. More work is needed in this area.

Let me make a few comments concerning assumptions I make about distributed systems. I assume that sites alternate between periods in which they run correctly and periods in which they are *crashed*. A crash causes a site (effectively) to halt, losing information in volatile storage, but retaining (perfectly) all information in stable storage. I do assume that no site stays crashed forever, but that assumption can be overcome by using more sophisticated two-phase commit procedures combined with appropriate data replication. Appropriate replication could also overcome some losses of permanent storage.

The communications medium used for transferring messages from site to site is not assumed to be reliable. Messages may be lost, corrupted (effectively the same as lost), duplicated, or delivered out of order. However, messages may not be spontaneously created. A delivered message may not differ from the sent message, unless the message is obviously corrupted (has a bad checksum). That is, any message received with a good checksum is assumed to be good. I also assume that repeated transmission of a message from one site to any other particular site will eventually work. This does not permit sites to fail permanently. More complicated protocols, such as Byzantine agreement, might overcome this objection, but the expense could be great.

All together, my assumptions about sites and communication are rather weak, if not minimal. Still, in the real world they can only be achieved in a probabilistic sense. The assumptions do have the property that the investment of additional resources (redundancy, time, etc.) will decrease the probability of system failure below any fixed positive quantity. My assumptions, and their implications and justifications are discussed in more detail in references 8 and 10.

9. DISTRIBUTED NESTED TRANSACTION MANAGEMENT

First, let me describe the data structures necessary for distributed nested transaction management. It is assumed that each transaction's *transaction identifier* (abbreviated *tid*) is unique over the entire distributed system, and that given a tid, the transaction's home node can be easily derived. A simple way of acheiving this property is to append the node number of the creating node to a locally unique identifier. Uniqueness of local identifiers over time can be achieved through using a counter that is saved to stable storage periodically. For example, the counter could be saved once every 1000 transactions. Then the saved value must be 999 or fewer transactions behind the real value. Hence, adding 1000 to the saved value on crash recovery will preserve uniqueness (this technique is not original). Note that, since the creating node and home node need not be the same (e.g., when a foreign child is being created), two node numbers may need to be included in a tid, one for the creator, and one for the home.

In addition to being able to derive a transaction's home from its tid, I also assume that it is easy to derive a transaction's superiors from its tid. One way to do that is to make tids variable in length, and include all superiors' ids as a part of each new tid. This is similar to giving the entire path to a file from the root in hierarchical directory system (e.g., /users/ebm/papers/nested/manuscript). To simplify local manipulation, tids could be handled as indexes into a local table, but must be translated to their full form before being communicated to another site. Such a scheme allows tid's to be referenced using fixed length codes (the indexes).

In addition to the tids and their implicit relationships resulting from nesting, concurrency and recovery control information must be maintained. Such information is associated with each transaction, and the associations change upon transaction abort and commit, as well as when new resources are touched and processed by a transaction. The changes made in a distributed system are pretty much the same as those made in a centralized system. The primary difference is that some changes to the data structures are instigated by other sites, rather than all causes being local. I will now outline the various events that may occur and the appropriate responses to them.

The touching and processing of objects is a purely local phenomenon and is managed as discussed in previous sections. Differences arise in transaction creation, abort, and commit.

Let us consider transaction creation first. Creation of top-level transaction is a local action, with no particular difference from a centralized system. Creation of local children proceeds as described before. It is only the creation of foreign children that is new. A record of the children should be kept with the parent: it is useful to know the identities and status (aborted, committed, running, questionable) of a transaction's children. Grandchildren and lower inferiors are not of direct interest.

The steps required to create the child transaction at the foreign node are more complicated. In order to handle later commitment properly, and to provide for the possibility of requests for later child transactions from the same parent, the foreign node needs to enter the parent and all other superiors of the new transaction in its transaction management tables. I call these entries *transaction images*: they are a kind of shadow of the real transactions. The purpose of images is to permit correct bookkeeping of concurrency and recovery information at the foreign node. When the request to create the child transaction arrives, the foreign node insures that images exist for all superiors of the new transaction, and if they do not exist, it creates them. Then the new child is created, in essentially the same manner as a local child.

Let us now consider transaction commitment. For the moment I will not discuss commitment of top-level transactions, which is somewhat different because of the requirement to update the permanent database. When a transaction commits, the concurrency and recovery information is passed up the transaction tree; i.e., it is inherited by the local image of the parent transaction. In this way, images prevent the sending of such information across the network. The information is of only local relevance anyway, since it deals only with local objects.

In addition to updating the local tables, which occurs as in a centralized system, the transaction's parent is notified of the commitment. This requires a message to be sent if the parent's home is a different node. In order to take care of lost messages, etc., the parent's node should periodically query the child's node concerning the child's status. Querying allows the system to detect lost requests, lost commitment notifications, and crashes of the child's node. Similarly, the child's node should periodically query the parent's node, to check for crashes, or the abort of any of the child's superiors (which requires abort of the child; more on this later). The frequency of queries required for good performance depends on the desired response time, the message passing and handling overhead, and the reliability of the networks and the processors. In many cases, queries and responses to them could be "piggy-backed" onto other message traffic between the nodes in question.

If the transaction that is committing had any inferiors, their sites should also be notified of the commitment. Such notifications permit the relevant nodes to propagate concurrency and recovery information in their local transaction tables in order to reflect the current abort/commit status of transactions. In particular, commitment notices can cause lock propagation, which in turn can free locks and permit blocked transactions to make progress. In order to permit such notifications to be sent, each transaction needs to gather a list of its successful inferiors. For sending notices, a list of the nodes would be sufficient, but we will need the list of transactions later. It could also be useful to keep a list of known aborted inferiors, or at least the nodes on which they were run. This will also play a role later.

In sum, upon transaction commitment, local bookkeeping information is propagated as for a centralized system, a notice is sent to the parent indicating commitment and including a list of successful and known unsuccessful inferiors of the committing transactions, and similar notices of commitment are sent to all other nodes where the committing transaction is known to have had inferiors.

When a transaction aborts, the same actions are taken except that an aborting transaction has no successful inferiors (by definition), so the lists sent with the abort notice contain only lists of known unsuccessful inferiors.

When an abort or commit notice is received, a node updates its tables appropriately. Note that the node can learn of the abort or commit of transactions other than the one that is the subject of a message. The list of successful inferiors allows the local records of any of those transactions to be updated. Suppose there is a transaction T that is an inferior of the subject S of the abort or commit notice. Further suppose that T is not on the list of successful inferiors of S. Then T should be aborted, whether or not it is on the list of unsuccessful inferiors of S. The node should update its tables to reflect the abort of such transactions.

To summarize, in addition to performing local table updates, transaction creation, abort, and commit can require requests or notices to be sent to other nodes. Abort and commit require notification of the transaction's parent and all of the transaction's inferiors. Such notices must contain a list of all of the transaction's successful inferiors.

Note that it is not required that a transaction wait for all of its children to complete before committing. This does introduce some problems (see the later discussion of "orphans"), but gives better performance when crashes or communications failures prevent determination of the status of children. Of course, a transaction should never commit unless ''enough'' of its children are known to have committed. The ''enough'' means that the transaction's specification will be met, although the ideal may not have been attained. My scheme, as descibed here, will eventually abort all in-doubt or status-unknown children. With slight additional complexity, one could indicate which unknown or in doubt children are ''desirable'' but not essential—the ones that it would be good to have commit, but are not necessary in order to commit the parent.

10. TOP-LEVEL TRANSACTION COMMITMENT

Up to this point, I have described how to deal with non-top-level transactions. Committing top-level transactions requires a *two-phase commit* protocol, such as that described in reference 5 and elsewhere. The exact protocol used is not dictated by the use of nested transactions: many different protocols are feasible. I will briefly describe a simple one that you might have seen before.

The home node of the top-level transaction plays the role of the *coordinator* of the protocol. All nodes known to have run inferiors of the transaction to be committed are *participants*. It does not matter whether the inferiors were successful or unsuccessful. The coordinator's node is included as a participant in order to simplify the description. The coordinator requests each participant to *prepare* to commit. This is the first phase of the protocol. The prepare request includes a list of the successful inferiors of the committing transaction. This permits each participant to insure that its information concerning the transaction and its inferiors is up to date. As a result, a participant may need to update its tables to reflect transaction aborts and commits of various inferiors for which the participant's information was old. In most cases, the situation is all right and the participant can get its stable storage ready and tell the coordinator to go ahead. (The stable storage preparation involves getting all changes into stable storage such that the change can either be performed, in case the transaction is committed, or removed, in case the transaction aborts.)

However, if the top-level transaction believes a particular inferior committed, and the participant sees that the inferior either aborted, or was local to the participant and the participant has no record of it, then the top-level transaction cannot be committed. Such a situation will arise if an inferior transaction commits and the node on which it was run crashes after the inferior commits but before the top-level transaction commits. Some sort of checkpointing mechanism would be required in order to avoid this problem.

In any case, the coordinator tallies the responses from the participants. If any participant says it cannot commit (or if the coordinator times out and decides to give up), the transaction can be aborted; otherwise the transaction can be committed. If the transaction is committed, a permanent record of the committment is made before the coordinator notifies any participants. This deals with the case in which the coordinator crashes.

The participants should probably be notified in case of abort, but it is not required, since they can query the top-level transaction's node and find that there is no record of the transaction. This method requires keeping a record of each committed transaction until we are sure every participant knows that the transaction is committed. Unfortunately, it is impossible to record only the aborted transactions. This is because a transaction is implicity aborted by a crash, and in such case no record of it may exist. Such records could be kept, but slow down transaction creation, since a permanent record must be made before each transaction can actually start.

In short, top-level transactions are committed through the use of a two-phase commit protocol, which insures that either all changes made by the transaction are permanently recorded, or none are. The usual two-phase commit protocol is extended to use the list of successful inferiors to resolve differences in transaction table information, and to detect certain crashes and force transaction abort.

11. ORPHANS

Distributed nested transactions introduce the possibility of discrepancies between a transaction's actual state (running, committed, aborted) and its state as known at another node. This is inherent in any distributed system. The distributed transaction management algorithms discussed in the previous sections automatically handle most of these discrepancies well. However, node crashes do introduce the possibility of inferior transactions that continue running even after one or more of their superiors has aborted or committed. Such inferiors are known as *orphans*.

Orphans arise when a transaction aborts without informing its inferiors appropriately. Most often this would occur because of node crashes, but sometimes loss messages might create orphans. Orphan creation can be restricted to crashes by requiring a transaction definitely complete (abort or commit) all of its children before its own completion. Such a protocol could be expensive, however, in terms of delay and message traffic. (It is similar to two-phase commit.) Avoiding orphans as a result of crashes requires saving the identity of foreign child transactions in stable memory before sending the creation request to the foreign node. This might also be expensive and time consuming.

The automatic querying of parent transactions will cause orphans to detect the abort of their parents eventually. Once an orphan detects that it is in fact an orphan, it can abort. Note also that orphans cannot have any permanent effect on the database, *provided* that all appropriate locking and recovery rules are in fact enforced, with no loopholes. Thus, if one is strict in the application of the theory to practice, orphans are not dangerous. Their only harm is the needless consumption of resources, and eventual detection is moderately cheap (the querying previously described).

If one is not entirely strict concerning the actions that can be performed by inferior transactions, then orphans can be more of a problem. The difficulty is that a subtransaction, like a procedure, can be written in such a way that it assumes certain conditions hold in its input data. In technical terms, the specification of the subtransaction includes a *precondition*. Such a precondition would generally be obtained by running a prior subtransaction whose postcondition implies the required precondition. A typical example is screening input data for validity in some way. However, because of crashes, a precondition can fail to hold, the required prior effects having been (implicitly) undone by the reload after the crash. When a program's precondition fails to hold, its behavior can be arbitrary. That is the problem.

I can think of only three solutions to the potential problem of orphans: first, one can be strict and guarantee no permanent effects; second, one can devise a way of checkpointing, and thus avoid the effects of crashes at the appropriate junctures; and third, one can pass around appropriate information so that the nonserializable situations that would cause orphans to misbehave are detected before the misbehavior can occur. The Argus project at MIT has been working on the last approach; it is based on tracing the information flow between transactions in the transaction tree and guaranteeing that prior transactions' effects have not been wiped out. That approach is somewhat intricate and hard to understand, but may work at acceptable cost. Checkpointing would be a simpler method to handle non-strict system designs, but the details have not been worked out. For checkpointing to be acceptable in terms of performance, high-speed stable storage would be required. That also might be feasible through a clever interface to fast (e.g., semiconductor) memory set up to survive power failures.

Finally, orphans may not be much of a problem in practice. I thought it was important to point out that they might present some difficulties, and that some systems might have to take them into account.

12. DISTRIBUTED EXAMPLE 1: REMOTE PROCEDURE CALL

Now that I have described how to imbed nested transactions in distributed systems, and described a set of protocols that can be used for their management, I will present two examples to demonstrate the usefulness of nested transactions to distributed processing. The message I wish to deliver is: nested transactions permit simple and elegant implementation of reliable applications in distributed sytems. While all of the results are not yet in, I believe that nested transactions will achieve the stated objective with competitive performance.

My first example is remote procedure call. A remote procedure call is a request made of another node to perform an action and/or return results. It requires the ability to send procedure arguments (input variable values) and obtain results (output values). The idea is that a remote procedure call will boil down to a request/response message pair when everything is working well. It is desirable that remote procedure calls be performed either exactly once (by appropriate retry and duplicate detection) or at most once (skipping retry). It is also nice if the foreign node, as part of its actions in handling a remote procedure call request, can make remote procedure calls of its own, to request assistance in fulfilling its specification.

Nested transactions provide a very natural way of implementing remote procedure calls: each call is an inferior transaction run at the target node. However, it is useful to add an extra layer of nesting. A remote call then works as follows. The caller creates a *local* child transaction to handle the remote call attempt. This child creates a *remote* grandchild to run at the foreign node, and transmits the call request. The local child may hear from the foreign grandchild that the grandchild has aborted or committed. In the case of commitment, the child commits and the call was successful. In the case of an abort, the child can retry by creating another grandchild; or the child can abort (perhaps after a certain number of failed attempts), indicating failure to the original caller.

It is also possible for the child not to hear anything and then time out. In that case, the child can abort. This will cause any actions at the foreign node to be undone, whether or not the grandchild was created, aborted, running, or committed. Lost messages or foreign node crashes could result in call timeout. In case of a failure, extra communication will be required before the nodes are in step with each other (appropriate transactions aborted/committed), but the definitions of nested transaction locking and recovery guarantee good behavior. The two levels of nesting just described can guarantee at-most-once execution of remote calls when a local timeout is used. For exactly-once execution, the caller can loop retrying the at-most-once protocol until it succeeds.

Some very nice properties result from building remote procedure calls with nested transactions. First, at-most-once or exactly-once execution can be guaranteed regardless of the semantics of the call. This is in contrast to the remote procedure call scheme developed in reference 7, where only certain kinds of actions are permitted. Granted, my scheme requires concurrency and recovery control, but reliability requires such features somewhere in the system. I believe that straightforward and uniform application of the simple semantics of nested transactions makes programming easier and reduces the likelihood of errors in programs. Another feature of the nested transaction-based remote procedure call is that the procedure calls nest to any depth with no problems, even when the calls are to sites already visited. Again, reference 7 cannot make the same claim. Communications and node failures are handled simply and uniformly by the distributed nested transaction management protocols—no additional data structures or communication is required. Finally, multiple calls may proceed in parallel.

13. DISTRIBUTED EXAMPLE 2: REPLICATED DATA

In this example, I will show how nested transactions can make it extraordinarily simple to access and update a distributed database in which logical objects can be replicated. The techniques I will present are very flexible and can achieve a wide range of policies allowing considerable control over the possible tradeoffs involved.

First, I assume that a fixed, known number of copies of some object exist, and that the location of the copies is known. The number and location of copies of a logical object would be maintained by a directory system, the details of which it is not necessary to discuss. Such a directory scheme could use the same algorithms I will describe below. However, the copies of the directory should be in known locations (or available from a known name server, etc.).

Based on the ideas presented in reference 4, each copy of a replicated object is given a number of *votes*. Each lock mode has a *quota*. To acquire a lock on the logical object in a given mode requires locking individual copies in the same mode. The sum of votes of the copies successfully locked must equal or exceed the established quota. For correctness, the quotas and votes must follow this rule: if two lock modes conflict, then the sum of their quotas must exceed the sum of the votes of all of the copies. If that rule is followed, it is impossible to lock the logical object in simultaneously conflicting modes. Note that some modes, e.g. exclusive mode, conflict with themselves. Hence the exclusive mode quota must exceed half the total votes.

Here is a simple example. Assume that the lock modes are the traditional exclusive and share modes (read and write locks). Say there are five copies of the logical object and each has a single vote. Then the write quota must be at least 3 ($2 + 2 = 4 \leq 5$ but $3 + 3 = 6 > 5$), and the read quota must be at least 6 minus the write quota. Even in this simple case, we could opt for single copy read (which would require locking all copies for write), majority read and write (both read and write quotas set to 3), or an intermediate policy (read quota of 2 and write quota of 4). This reflects flexibility in the trading off of read vs. write overhead and delay. It also reflects a robustness tradeoff: if all copies must be locked to write, then all sites must be up to write.

Note that the algorithm works in the face of the permissible failures in my system model. Network partition, for example, will not cause incorrect results (but it may not permit some operations to proceed). The *weighted voting* approach just outlined can also model more interesting situations when the votes are not even. There are additional policy options attainable if copies are locked in particular orders. One might achieve effects similar to centralized locking during normal system operation, while still providing simple recovery from failure (if the primary copy is unavailable, just proceed to the secondary, etc.).

It is easy to implement replicated object access using nested transactions. When it is desired to access a logical object that is replicated, a local access manager child transaction is created. It performs remote procedure calls to each of the copies requesting the appropriate locks. These remote calls could be done in sequence or in parallel. The manager transaction sees how many of its remote calls succeed and tallies their votes. It can retry in case of some failures. The manager can also abort after a timeout, if that is desired. In any case, the nested transaction management system does the appropriate bookkeeping at the remote sites. If the manager gets sufficient votes, it can commit, otherwise it must abort. Note that the manager can go ahead and request that changes be performed at the remote sites. If such optimism proves to be unfounded, everything is still all right, because the changes will be undone automatically when the manager aborts.

Again I argue that a nested transaction mechanism provides a uniform and simple way to program interesting tasks reliably. I believe that it is better to build replications, remote procedure call, and many other application level protocols, on top of nested transactions. The powerful common mechanism provided by nested transactions should simplify other aspects of a distributed system.

14. NESTED TRANSACTION DEADLOCK

As previously mentioned, nested transaction concurrency control is not immune to deadlock. Nested transactions can deadlock in ways similar to top-level transactions, with a few new twists that I will now discuss. The essence of deadlock analysis is the *waits-for* relation among transactions. A deadlock exists if and only if the waits-for relation has a cycle. Hence, to understand nested transaction deadlock requires an understanding of the difference between traditional waits-for relations and those for nested transactions.

A direct wait occurs when one transaction requests a lock in conflict with a lock held by another transaction. The lock requestor is said to wait for the lock holder. In atomic transaction systems, this is the only kind of waits-for relationship possible. Nested transactions, however, introduce new possibilities.

First, suppose a transaction T_a is in a direct wait for transaction T_b. (See Fig. 14.4 for an illustration of this example.) It is possible that commitment of T_b will not permit T_a to proceed. In fact, this will always occur if T_b is not a sibling of T_a or one of T_a's ancestors. The point is that certain superiors of T_b must commit (in addition to T_b) before access can be granted to T_a. Let $T_{b'}$ be the

T_a is waiting directly for T_b.

$T_{a'}$ is the oldest ancestor of T_a that is not an ancestor of T_b. It is possible that $T_a = T_{a'}$.

$T_{b'}$ is the oldest ancestor of T_b that is not an ancestor of T_a. It is possible that $T_b = T_{b'}$.

$T_{a'}$ and $T_{b'}$ are either distinct top-level transactions or siblings.

T_a indirectly waits for $T_{b'}$.

$T_{a'}$ indirectly waits for T_b and $T_{b'}$.

(a) T_a and T_b are descendants of different top-level transactions.

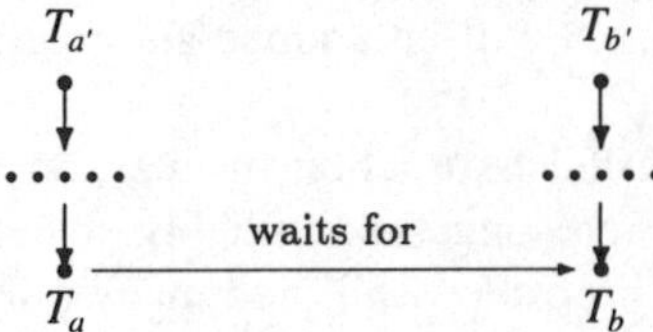

(b) T_a and T_b are descendants of the same top-level transaction T.

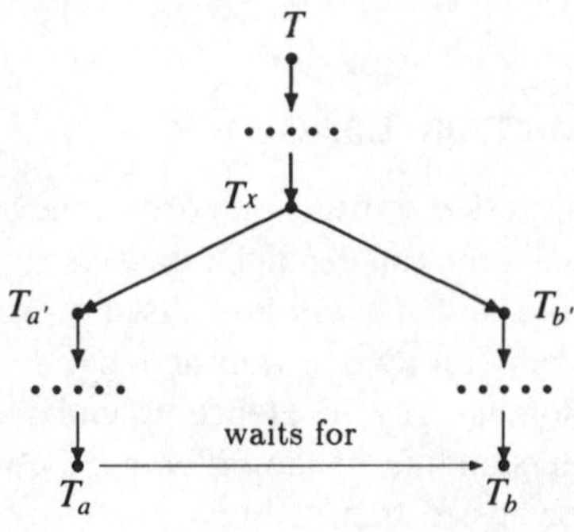

Fig. 14.4.

oldest ancestor of T_b that is *not* an ancestor of T_a. Then T_a must wait until $T_{b'}$ commits. I would say that T_a waits indirectly for $T_{b'}$ (and all ancestors of T_b inferior to $T_{b'}$).

Another effect is that the parent of T_a cannot commit until T_a does. This is also an indirect wait. Returning to the example of the previous paragraph, let $T_{a'}$ be the oldest ancestor of T_a that is not an ancestor of T_b. Then $T_{a'}$ indirectly waits for T_a, T_b, and $T_{b'}$, etc. Note that the "real" waits-for situation is represented by the siblings (or top-level transactions) $T_{a'}$ and $T_{b'}$.

Once the above-described indirect wait conditions have been taken into account, deadlocks take the same form as in an atomic transaction system: they are cycles in the waits-for relation. Note, though, that because a transaction can achieve parallelism through the action of its children, all of its progress need not cease when it is in a deadlock. However, progress will eventually stop.

In the next section, I will describe an algorithm for detecting and resolving nested transaction deadlock in distributed systems. I will suggest two improvements to the basic algorithm, which could substantially reduce the number of messages required to detect deadlocks. In the section after that, I will describe nested transaction deadlock avoidance techniques, which can be used if one prefers to avoid the additional complexity of deadlock detection, or if the application domain is such that deadlock avoidance is more efficient than detection.

14.1. Distributed Deadlock Detection and Resolution

Detecting nested transaction deadlock in a centralized system is conceptually simple: maintain a data structure representing the waits-for relation (including the indirect waits implied by nested transaction relationships), and check that data structure for cycles when new waits-for edges are added. The method I suggest for detecting nested transaction deadlock in a distributed system is somewhat different; I call it *edge chasing*. I will first describe the simplest form of edge chasing, and then offer two performance improvements.

Suppose a transaction attempts to acquire a lock and finds it cannot proceed because one or more other transactions hold conflicting locks. The requesting transaction will start to wait directly for those other transactions. For each such blocking transaction T_b, the requesting transaction T_a determines the oldest ancestor of T_b that is not an ancestor of T_a; call this ancestor transaction $T_{b'}$. Note that $T_{b'}$ is the transaction that is "really" blocking T_a. T_a sends a message to the transaction manager for $T_{b'}$ indicating that T_a is waiting for T_b, an inferior of $T_{b'}$. This transmission of a message because of a new wait is called the *initiation* of deadlock detection.

When a transaction manager receives a message describing waits, it can determine the awaited transaction (in this case, $T_{b'}$). The notice is forwarded to each of child of $T_{b'}$; the children forward it to their children, etc. In this way, the notice is propagated to all inferiors of $T_{b'}$. Now, if any descendant of $T_{b'}$ is currently waiting to acquire a lock, deadlock detection is *continued* by forwarding a new message to the awaited transaction. For example, let $T_{b''}$, an inferior of $T_{b'}$, be awaiting T_c directly, and $T_{c'}$ indirectly. Then, when the notice concerning T_a and T_b reaches $T_{b''}$, a notice listing both the T_a/T_b wait and the $T_{b''}/T_c$ wait is sent to $T_{c'}$. This notice is forwarded to the inferiors of $T_{c'}$, and so on.

Any leaf transaction that receives a wait notice and is not waiting simply discards the wait notice. However, if there is a deadlock, the notices will follow the waits-for relationship, and eventually some transaction manager will find that one of its transactions is waiting (directly or indirectly) for one of the transactions in the list in a just-received wait-notice. In sum, the wait notices trace out the waits-for graph and record a path through that graph in the messages. Since the messages are propagated along all edges in the graph, if there is a cycle it will be detected. Also, there is no false detection of deadlocks, as might occur if waits-for information were periodically gathered and joined together in a centralized or hierarchical fashion. For the moment, I will assume that wait notice messages are never lost.

The deadlock detection algorithm I have just described is perfectly feasible, and straightforward to implement. However, some simple techniques can substantially reduce the number of messages required. Let us assign each transaction a unique *priority*. Priorities are most appropriately assigned based on time of entry into the system, but limited exceptions to that can be tolerated without introducing the possibility of continually aborting a transaction because higher priority transactions keep entering the system. The priorities can be made unique by using a locally unique timestamp with the number of the generating node appended. Note that the same method can be used to generate tid's, so in fact a transaction's tid, interpreted as an unsigned number, can be its priority. In such a case, higher numbers indicate lower priorities. For reasonable comparisons between transactions created at different nodes, the priorities should be based on global system time. It is not necessary to absolutely synchronize all sites; approximate algorithms for maintaining globally consistent times are well known.

The first improvement I shall suggest to the basic algorithm is the initiation of edge chasing only when a higher priority transaction waits for a lower priority one. (The converse condition could be used if there were some good reason, but the system must uniformly apply a single rule.) Note that a cycle of transactions cannot exist without such a drop in priority, since all priorities are distinct. Wait messages must be propagated as before. However, this small change should reduce the number of messages by half (if waiting is entirely random), or more possibly even more (higher priority transactions are more likely to be older and possess more locks, hence they are more likely to be awaited than to wait).

Suppose that T_a is directly waiting for T_b, using the example discussed a few paragraphs previously. Do not compare the priorities of T_a and T_b: those priorities are irrelevant. One must compare the priorities of $T_{a'}$ (the oldest ancestor of T_a that is not an ancestor of T_b) and $T_{b'}$. The comparison must be done at the level in which the cycle would occur for my arguments concerning drops in priority to be valid.

The second improvement I offer is this. When, in propagating a wait notice, a drop in priority is found that goes to a transaction of lower priority than that causing initiation of this wait notice, this wait notice need not be propagated. This rule causes cycles to be detected only as a result of the wait for the lowest priority transaction in the cycle. Again, it could reduce the number of wait messages by a factor of two. Using the example mentioned earlier, we would stop propagating the message initiated by the drop in priority at $T_{a'}$ to $T_{b'}$ if a drop were encountered having priority even lower than $T_{b'}$.

Transaction wait notices must be retransmitted periodically, for two reasons. First, retransmission makes the algorithm robust in the face of lost messages. The second reason is best explained by giving a simple example. Suppose that T_a starts to wait for T_b, and T_a has a higher priority. Then T_a will send T_b an initiation message. At this point, assume that T_b is not waiting for any transaction. T_b would then just discard the message. If T_b later starts to wait for T_a, we have a deadlock. But because of the relative priorities, T_b will not initiate. Even if we had *any* new waiter (regardless of relative priorities) send up to n initiation messages, all n could still be lost and a deadlock would still not be detected. However, periodic retransmission of initiation by T_a solves the problem: the deadlock will be detected as soon as one of the message is received by T_b after T_b begins its wait for T_a.

Since retransmission is required to overcome communications failures anyway, we might as well use the initiation and propagation enhancements to the basic deadlock detection algorithm. I do not believe that schemes that attempt to save waits-for information and give acknowledgements to wait notices would offer better performance than the retransmission scheme. Among other things, acknowledgements double the number of messages in cases where retransmissions do not actually occur.

When a cycle is found, the lowest priority transaction in the cycle should be notified. Then it, or an appropriate inferior, should be aborted, to break the cycle and allow progress. Note that the whole transaction need not be aborted—only the inferior that, by holding the lock, is preventing progress. This is one way in which the finer granularity of recovery provided by nested transactions might improve system performance.

It has been conjectured that almost all deadlock cycles that occur in practice are of length two, and I have heard of measurements that seem to support the conjecture.[6] If it is true that cycles are mainly of length two, then it could be that most distributed deadlocks would be found and resolved using just one message. In the case of larger cycles, the extra messages used by my edge chasing algorithm might be negligible, because of the rarity of the situation in the first place. Thus, it could be that nested transaction deadlock detection in distributed systems would be very cheap.

14.2. Nested Transaction Deadlock Avoidance

There might be systems in which deadlock detection is not appropriate and deadlock avoidance is better. Avoidance prevents deadlocks by aborting transactions in situations that can lead to deadlock. Detection waits for an actual deadlock to exist.

Avoidance might be better in some systems for at least two reasons. First, if deadlocks are very rare, the extra cost of detection (in terms of system code, etc.) might not be justified. Another possibility is that detection could cause system bottlenecks (such as high traffic locks) to back up too much during the time it takes to detect and resolve a feedback. In such circumstances it is conceivable, but by no means definite, that avoidance would increase overall throughput by increasing average utilization, even if more transactions are aborted.

In a nested transaction system, the schemes for avoidance proposed in reference 13 will work just fine. There are two basic procedures that can be followed, known as *wound-wait* and *wait-die*. Both procedures involve the assignment of unique priorities to transactions and the comparison of these priorities. The priority assignment can be performed as described in the previous section. The comparisons should also be performed as explained there. In particular, the priorities of the directly waiting transactions should not be compared, but rather the priorities of their oldest distinct ancestors. Those ancestors will either be siblings or two different top-level transactions.

As before, let us assume that T_a is about to wait for T_b, and that $T_{a'}$ and $T_{b'}$ are the appropriate ancestors of T_a and T_b, respectively. Here is a description of each of the two procedures. Note that any given system must uniformly follow either wound-wait or wait-die, but not both or a mixture.

Wound-Wait:

If priority $(T_a) >$ priority (T_b), T_a *wounds* T_b, causing T_b to abort.
If priority $(T_a) <$ priority (T_b), T_a *waits* for T_b.

Wait-Die:

If priority $(T_a) >$ priority (T_b), T_a *waits* for T_b.
If priority $(T_a) <$ priority (T_b), T_a *dies* (aborts itself) rather than wait for T_b.

In each scheme, higher priority transactions will make more progress. The schemes work by preventing either drops in priority along waits-for edges (wound-wait), or increases in priority along such edges (wait-die). The two schemes can be expected to have different performance. For example, if older (higher priority) transactions hold more locks and request fewer locks, then wound-wait will probably abort fewer transactions.

In sum, well-known deadlock avoidance schemes can be used for nested transactions, once it is understood how to take the extra indirect waits of a nested transaction system into account.

15. SUMMARY AND COMMENTS

In this chapter, I have presented the concept of nested transactions and sketched their implementation. This includes concurrency control via locking, and recovery control via shadow pages. I have also described how to use and implement nested transactions in distributed systems, including some particularly relevant examples: remote procedure call and replicated databases. In addition, I have presented deadlock detection and avoidance mechanisms that apply to both centralized and distributed systems. The implementations I have suggested for nested transactions, deadlock detection, and deadlock avoidance in distributed systems are quite robust and work in the face of a variety of failures. I believe that nested transactions are a promising tool for structuring reliable distributed systems and reducing the complexity of applications software for such systems, without sacrificing reliability or performance.

Before closing I am going to mention ongoing work of which I have knowledge. Throughout the chapter, I have mentioned a few topics that I have researched, to include log-based recovery and checkpointing. I have also done some investigation of formalizing nested transactions, e.g., stating what serializability is for nested transactions, etc. Nancy Lynch at MIT has been working on proof techniques for nested transactions and nested transaction management algorithms. The Argus project, with which I was involved in earlier stages, is working on a distributed nested transaction system under the direction of Barbara Liskov, also at MIT. While much of their approach is similar to my presentation, there are many differences in detail. They have also put considerable work into designing linguistic mechanisms to support distributed computing and nested transactions.

The Eden system group at the University of Washington is using nested transaction concepts in a distributed operating system. In that design, a child transaction acts on its parent as if the parent is a data object. In this way, the concurrency and recovery information is directly attached to each transaction and effects occur by updating the permanent database or by updating an enclosing transaction (which later updates the permanent database). I think this shows an interesting relationship between the ideas of *transaction* and *object*.

Another distributed operating system incorporating nested transactions is the Clouds project at the Georgia Institute of Technology. Their approach is to provide the system implementor with sufficient primitives, but not to overly restrict their use. This is in slight contrast to my work, which is directed more towards the applications programmer's environment, but many of the concepts and problems are the same. The two are at different points in the tradeoff between freedom and safety. Also at Georgia Tech, Nancy Griffeth is working on performance simulations and comparisons of concurrency control algorithms and policies. She intends to examine nested transactions in those studies.

Nested transactions have also been explored by Alfred Spector, Peter Schwarz, and others, at Carnegie-Mellon in the TABS and Camelot projects.

There must be other people working on nested transactions in one way or another. For those of which I am unaware, there is little I can do. If I have forgotten anyone, I apologize.

As you can see, there is considerable interest in nested transactions and I expect that much work will be done with them in the near future. It is even possible that they will become a standard, classic technique, used widely in distributed systems and transactions processing.

The concepts seem to have been recognized first by Davies.[2] My thesis[8,9,10] built substantially on those concepts and presented a comparatively detailed model of distributed computing, and nested transactions and their implementation. Perhaps the first implementation of nested transactions, albeit not a very general one, was internal to System R as developed at the IBM San Jose Research laboratories. I am grateful to Davies and others for pointing the way, particularly Professor Saltzer at MIT for leading a graduate seminar on atomicity, concurrency, and recovery; Dr. Jim Gray, for his *Notes on Database Operating Systems* and other works, and to my thesis supervisor, Professor Barbara Liskov, for her continuing support. Many unnamed persons have assisted through their research work or personal encouragement. They have not been forgotten.

REFERENCES

1. Bernstein, P. A., J. B. Rothnie, N. Goodman, and C. A Papadimitriou, The concurrency control mechanism of SDD-1: A system for distributed databases (The fully redundant case), *IEEE Trans. Software Engineering*, vol. SE-4, pp. 154–167, May 1978.
2. Davies, C. T. Recovery semantics for a DB/DC system, in *Proc. ACM Nat'l. Conf. 28*, 1973, pp. 136–141.
3. Eswaren, K. P., J. N. Gray, R. A. Lorie, and I. L. Traiger, The notion of consistency and predicate locks in a database system, *ACM*, vol. 19, pp. 624–633, Nov. 1976.
4. Gifford, David K. Weighted voting for replicated data, in *Proc. 7th Symp. Operating Systems Principles*, Pacific Grove, CA, Dec. 1979, pp. 150–162.
5. Gray, J. N., Notes on database operating system, in *Lecture Notes in Computer Science*, vol. 60, R. Bayer *et al.* (eds.), Berlin: Springer-Verlag, 1978, pp. 393–481.
6. Gray, J. N., photocopies of transparencies for a talk concerning experience with System R, 1980.
7. Lampson, Butler and Howard Sturgis, *Crash Recovery in a Distributed Data Storage System*, Xerox Palo Alto Research Lab., Res. Rep., unpublished.
8. Moss, J. Eliot B., *Nested Transactions: An Approach to Reliable Distributed Computing* (Ph.D. diss.), MIT Dept. of Elec. Eng. and Comp. Sci., 1981; also available as Tech. Rep. 260, MIT Lab. for Comp. Sci.

9. Moss, J. Eliot B., Nested transactions and reliable distributed computing, in *Proc. 2nd Symp. on Reliability in Distributed Software and Database Systems*, Pittsburgh, PA, July 1982, pp. 33–39.
10. Moss, J. Eliot B., *Nested Transactions: An Approach to Reliable Distributed Computing*, Cambridge, MA: MIT Press, 1985.
11. Moss, J. Eliot B., *Log-Based Recovery for Nested Transactions*, Tech. Rep. 86–61, Dept. of Comp. and Info. Sci., Univ. of Mass. (Amherst), Dec. 1986.
12. Reed, David P., *Naming and Synchronization in a Decentralized Computer System* (Ph.D. diss.), M.I.T. Dept. of Elec. Eng. and Comp. Sci., 1978; also available as Tech. Rep. 205, M.I.T. Lab. for Comp. Sci.
13. Rosenkrantz, D. J., R. E. Stearns, and P. M. Lewis II, System level concurrency control for distributed systems, *ACM Trans. on Database Systems*, vol. 3, pp. 178–198, June 1978.
14. Rosekrantz, D. J., R. E. Stearns, and P. M. Lewis II, *Consistency and Serializability in Concurrent Database Systems*, Tech. Rep. 80-12, Dept. of Comp. Sci., State Univ. of New York at Albany, Aug. 1980.
15. Russell, David L., State restoration in systems of communicating processes, *IEEE Trans. on Software Engineering*, vol. SE-6, pp. 183–194, Mar. 1980.
16. Takagi, Akihiro, Concurrent and Reliable Updates of Distributed Databases, Tech. Memo 144, M.I.T. Lab. for Comp. Sci., Nov. 1979.
17. Verhofstad, J. S. M., Recovery techniques for database systems, *ACM Comput. Surveys*, vol. 10, pp. 167–195, June 1978.

15. True-Copy Token Scheme for a Distributed Database System

TOSHIMI MINOURA, SUSAN S. OWICKI,

and

GIO WIEDERHOLD

ABSTRACT

A concurrency and resiliency control scheme for a distributed database system with replicated data is discussed. The scheme, *true-copy token scheme*, uses *true-copy tokens* in order to designate the physical data copies (*true copies*) that can be identified with the current logical data that are globally unique, and then it realizes consistent execution of transactions by the locking on these true copies. If subsystem failures occur and if some true copies are lost, the scheme regenerates lost true copies so that their continuity is preserved.

In analyzing the true-copy token scheme, we established a precise relationship between physical transactions and their corresponding logical transactions by *data* and *time abstraction*. We will then show that continuity of logical data is preserved if continuity of true copies is preserved.

1. INTRODUCTION

Distributed database systems, where data are stored at multiple sites, are gaining importance because of the recent advances in hardware and computer communications technologies. Among the expected advantages of the decentralization of data, more specifically, *partitioning* and *replication* of data, are more efficient local processing and higher reliability. However, it is desirable that data parti-

This work was partially supported by Air Force Office of Scientific Research under contract F49620-77-C-0045, by the Joint Services Electronics Program under contract DAAG29-79-C-0047, and by the Defense Advanced Research Projects Agency under contract N00039-80-G-0132.

tioning and replication are hidden from the users of a distributed database system. Also, when multiple transactions are processed concurrently, their effects on the users must be as if they were processed one at a time. Further, the system must provide logically continuous operation even if some subsystems fail. Without reasonable concurrency and resiliency control, the application of distributed database systems will be limited.

This chapter presents a new concurrency and resiliency control scheme that handles replicated data. The scheme first establishes *logical data* by hiding the replication of *physical data*. At the highest level, a distributed database system is perceived as a collection of logical data that are not bound to particular sites. These logical data are then represented by physical data that are bound to sites. The main feature of the new scheme is the use of *true-copy tokens* which designate the physical data that can be identified with the current logical data. (Physical data copies that can be identified with the current logical data are called *true copies*.) The concept of logical data is crucial in making the new scheme resilient, since *resilient system operation* can only be realized if the continuity of the logical data is preserved in the face of subsystem failures.

One way of guaranteeing the uniqueness of a logical datum is to let its single copy circulate in the system like the ''control token'' in reference 14 or the ''hopping permit'' in reference 13. Another way is to designate a primary site for each logical datum that is represented by multiple physical copies.[1,27] The new concurrency control scheme extends these ideas and allows, for each logical datum, either one *exclusive copy* that can be accessed for read-write purposes or multiple *share copies* that can be accessed for read-only purposes (multiple share copies for the same logical datum must possess the same content). An exclusive copy can be split into multiple share copies, and these multiple share copies can be revoked to create a single exclusive copy again. Then, in order to realize consistent transaction processing, two-phase locking is applied on these exclusive or share copies (true copies) after transferring them to the sites where they are accessed.

One of the correctness proofs of the new concurrency control scheme is performed by using a technique of data abstraction analysis. The approach is basically the one developed for sequential programs.[9,10,30] First, that logical data are correctly implemented by the true-copy token mechanism is shown. Then, the correctness of the scheme is discussed solely at the logical data level. One new aspect of our proof is that execution timings of logical (*abstract*) operations are pinpointed on the time axis. (This technique is called *time abstraction*.) Thus, we establish a precise relationship between physical transactions and their corresponding logical transactions.

Migration of exclusive copies may allow efficient local processing of transactions in a batch. Multiple share copies are useful for data that are occasionally updated but are mostly used for read-only purposes by many users. However, the main benefit of migrating true copies is that the resiliency problem can be discussed within this framework. That is, logically continuous system operation can be realized as long as continuity of true copies is preserved.

Based on the above principle, a simple resiliency scheme that combines a reliable storage mechanism and a reliable message transmission mechanism is designed. One unique feature of the scheme is that once true copies are reliably transferred between sites, each site can employ the same reliable storage subsystem as one for a centralized database system in order to support the true copies residing at that site, including those brought in from other sites.

A model of a distributed database system is given in Section 2. The concurrency control part of the new scheme is discussed in Section 3. Section 4 establishes the relationship between physical transactions and their corresponding logical transactions. The resiliency control part of the new scheme is discussed in Section 5. Section 6 concludes this chapter.

2. DISTRIBUTED DATABASE SYSTEM MODEL

In this section, we will discuss the model of a distributed database system used in this chapter. The key aspect of the model is the notion of *logical objects*.

2.1 LOGICAL OBJECTS, PHYSICAL OBJECTS, AND SITES

In our model, a *distributed database system* consists of a set of *logical objects*, a set of *physical objects*, a set of *sites*, and a set of *transactions*.

Each logical object X, to which an independent value can be assigned, is represented by multiple (*replicate*) physical objects $x_1, \ldots, x_k$ for some k that assumes the same value except during the transitional periods while update operations on them are in progress.

An *object* is a data container that can store a *data value*. An object can be characterized by read and write operations applied to it.

Definition: Object. The data value of an object can be changed only by a write operation, and when a write operation is applied to it, the data value specified by the write operation will become the *current* data value of the object. When a read operation is applied to an object, the current data value of the object will be returned.

In other words, a read operation applied to an object returns the data value written by the latest write operation applied to the object. However, there are some subtle points about logical objects, and they will be more precisely discussed in Section 4.

Each site of a distributed database system accommodates a subset of the set of physical objects in the system, and each physical object belongs to exactly

DDBS = {X, Y, Z}

LOGICAL OBJECTS:	SITES:
$X = \{X_1, X_2, X_3\}$	$H = \{X_1, Y_1, Z_1\}$
$Y = \{Y_1, Y_2\}$	$I = \{X_2, Y_2\}$
$Z = \{Z_1\}$	$J = \{X_3\}$

Fig. 15.1. A distributed database system.

one site. An example of a distributed database system is shown in Fig. 15.1. The system DDBS consists of three logical objects *X*, *Y*, and *Z*. *X* is *fully replicated* at all sites *H*, *I*, and *J*; *Y* is *partially replicated* at sites *H* and *I*; and *Z* has a single physical representation at site *H*.

Here, the terms "logical" and "physical" are used to indicate only a relative degree of abstraction. "Physical" does not mean direct implementation by hardware; a "physical object" may be a "logical object" at another level of abstraction. The important fact, however, is that in our model logical objects are globally unique entities and they are not bound to any particular sites.

In this chapter, we will sometimes denote a distributed database system by its set of logical objects, and a site by its set of physical objects.

2.2. Transactions and Operations

A *transaction* is a set of *operations*. An operation is an activity that manipulates data or that coordinates the execution of other operations. We consider four types of operations, namely, *read operations*, *write operations*, *local computations*, and *synchronization operations*.

Read and write operations, either logical or physical, are used to access objects, either logical or physical. Local computations of each transaction can transform the data read by read operations and supply the transformed data to write operations. Furthermore, data may be passed in the form of *messages* between two physical operations that occur at different sites.

A physical read operation $read(x_i)$ returns the current data value of physical object x_i, and a physical write operation $write(x_i)$ updates the current data value of physical object x_i. Further, we will show in Section 4 that a logical read operation $read(X)$ returns the current data value of logical object *X*, and that a logical write operation $write(X)$ updates the current data value of logical object *X*.

At this point, we will mention the following relationship between logical operations and physical operations. A logical read operation $read(X)$ corresponds to a physical read operation $read(x_i)$, some i, and a logical write operation $write(X_i)$ corresponds to the set of physical write operations $\{write(x_1),$

write(x_2), . . .}, each of which writes the same data value as *write*(X). Now, the reader is cautioned that we are postponing a precise definition of the execution timings of logical operations until we introduce the true-copy token scheme in later Sections.

A physical write operation applied to a physical object at a site other than the one where it is created is called a *remote update*. Usually a transaction creates physical write operations at the site where most of its local computations are performed.

Execution of read and write operations may be delayed by the *system scheduler* in order to avoid unacceptable intermixing of read and write operations of different transactions. A *concurrency control scheme* is the specification of the behavior of such a system scheduler. Synchronization operations (e.g., *lock-seize* and *lock-release* operations) may be used to coordinate the execution of other operations. Note that synchronization operations are used by transactions when part of the responsibility of the system scheduler is relegated to transactions.

In Fig. 15.2, we give an example of a transaction which runs on the distributed database system shown in Fig. 15.1. The transaction is described in two ways, as a logical transaction and as a physical transaction.

Concurrency control problems can be discussed either at the physical object level or at the logical object level. This differentiation must be made in terms of operations. Treatment at the logical object level gives direction to the handling of replicate physical objects, especially in the presence of subsystem failures.

Data values created for logical (and hence physical) objects can be identified as *versions*. Each logical object must initially contain version zero, and each

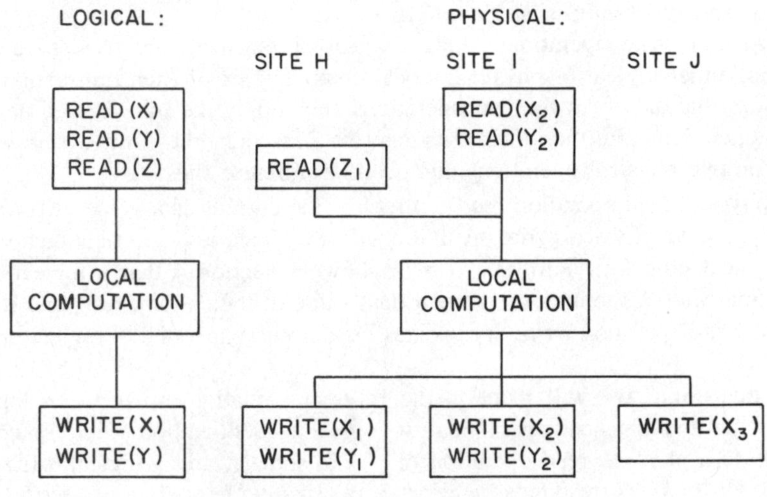

Fig. 15.2. Transaction.

time a logical object value is updated, its version number must be incremented by one. This version number can be assigned to each of the updates sent to the replicate physical objects associated with the logical object.

A write operation (typically a remote update to a replicate physical object) is *redundant* if the data value written by it is overwritten by another write operation without being read by any read operation. Redundant write operations may be omitted. By properly ignoring redundant physical write operations, the intersite traffic can be reduced, and efficiency of system operation can be enhanced. Redundant physical write operations are often automatically eliminated if only the latest version of each logical object is transferred between sites.

2.3. Execution Sequences and Consistency Condition

The execution of an operation A, either logical or physical, is characterized by the occurrences of its initiation event a and its termination event $\underline{a}$, which we call *operation events*. In fact, defining these events for a logical operation is not trivial, as we discuss in Section 4. However, at this point we will assume that they are given *a priori*.

Definition: Execution Sequence $\ll$. An execution sequence $\ll$ for a set of transactions is a total ordering on the set of operation events caused by the execution of these transactions: for two operation events a and b, $a \ll b$ if a precedes b according to global time.

Now we discuss a criterion for correct system operation. Subsystem failures are not considered until Section 5. The definitions in this section are applicable either at the physical or at the logical object level. Informally, an execution sequence of transactions is *serializable* if the effects on the users are as if transactions were processed one at a time. Papadimitriou has given a precise condition that characterizes the maximal set of serializable execution sequences for a set of transactions.[23] He has also shown that the serializability test of an execution sequence in general is NP-complete.

Other authors[5, 19, 24, 25] have used a stricter condition (class CPSR in reference 3 or class DSR in reference 23) that can be tested in polynomial time. We will use this stricter condition in our proofs.

Before we proceed, we need some definitions.

Definition: CONFLICT. The binary relation CONFLICT on a set of operations, either logical or physical, is defined as

$$\text{CONFLICT} = \{ (A, B) \mid \text{operations } A \text{ and } B \text{ belong to different transactions and access the same object, and furthermore one of them is a write operation} \}.$$

We say that operations A and B conflict over an object x, either logical or physical, when (A, B) is in CONFLICT and x is accessed by A and B. Further, we say that two transactions conflict when they contain conflicting operations. Conflicting operations will induce the following ordering on the set of transactions.

Definition: D-Precedence $\lll$. Given an execution sequence $\ll$ for a set of transactions, the D-precedence $\lll$ on the set of transactions is defined as

$$\lll \; = \left\{ (R, S) \mid (A, B) \text{ is in CONFLICT and } a \ll \underline{b} \text{ for some operations } A \text{ of transaction } R \text{ and } B \text{ of transaction } S \right\}.$$

We now define the consistency condition used in our proofs.

Definition: Consistency Condition C. Consistency condition C is true if D-precedence $\lll$ is acyclic.

Intuitively, this definition means that in an execution sequence that satisfies consistency condition C, conflicting operations must define a consistent (non-circular) ordering on the transactions to which they belong. The condition that conflicting operations cannot occur concurrently is implicit in the above definition. In this chapter, a *consistent execution sequence* is one that satisfies consistency condition C, and *a concurrency control scheme is consistent* if any execution sequence allowed by the scheme is consistent.

In a consistent execution sequence, conflicting operations are generally not allowed to occur concurrently. Therefore, in later sections we use the following shorthand notation: we write $A \ll B$ instead of $\underline{a} \ll b$ for two conflicting operations A and B.

2.4. Subsystem Failures

We further assume that each site of a distributed database system consists of a *mainframe* and a *secondary storage subsystem*. Data at each site are held either on the *main memory* within the mainframe or in the secondary storage subsystem. The exact locations of site data are irrelevant while the site is operating normally. If the mainframe fails, the data on the main memory will be lost. The data held by the secondary storage subsystem may be damaged when the secondary storage subsystem fails. Further, the data held by the secondary storage subsystem may be damaged also when the mainframe fails. The extent of tolerable damages to site data is discussed in Section 5.

We assume that a message can be sent from one site to another only when the *message-link* connecting them is normally functioning. When message link failures occur to a distributed database system, the system may be divided into multiple *partitions.* Each partition is the largest group of sites such that bidirectional communication is still possible between any pair of sites in it. That is, bidirectional communication may be impossible for two sites that belong to different partitions.

3. CONCURRENCY CONTROL

In this section, we shall describe, without considering subsystem failures, the concurrency control part of the true-copy token scheme, and then we prove that any execution sequence allowed by the scheme satisfies consistency condition C at the physical object level.

3.1. General Description

We first give an intuitive description of the true-copy token scheme. The new concurrency control scheme first establishes *true copies* that can be identified with the logical objects, and then performs locking on these true copies.

One way of guaranteeing the uniqueness of each logical object is to designate a unique physical copy (*true copy*) that can be identified with the logical object. In the "primary site" scheme,[1,26] a physical copy at the primary site of each logical object is the true copy of that logical object. In the "hopping permit" scheme,[13] the "hopping permit" designates the current true copy of the single logical object in the system. In reference 14, a "control token" which itself is a globally unique entity is used to issue "tickets" that uniquely order transactions. The true-copy token scheme extends these ideas.

Consider a particular logical object. When the logical object is used for read-write purposes, consistency will be violated if more than one physical copy is *independently* accessed at a different site. However, when the logical object is used for read-only purposes, multiple physical copies can be allowed at different sites as long as their contents are the same. Considering these two cases, we can switch between a single read-write copy (*exclusive copy*) and multiple read-only copies (*share copies*) according to the need.

Figure 15.3 shows how an exclusive copy or multiple share copies can occur for a logical object at each given time. At times t_1, t_3, and t_4, only one exclusive copy exists in the system; however, at time t_2 two share copies, and at time t_5 three share copies exist in the system.

A physical object can contain either an *exclusive copy*, *share copy*, or a *void copy*. Exclusive copies and share copies are called *true copies*, and we will show in Section 4 that their data values are identical to the current data values of their associated logical objects. The content of a void copy may be obsolete. Read-write accesses are allowed to have exclusive copies and read-only accesses are allowed to share copies, but void copies are not accessed for normal transaction processing. To visualize the transfer of time-dependent access rights, we

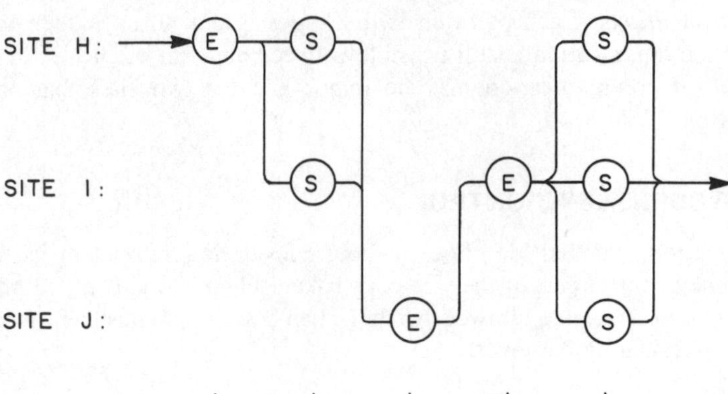

Fig. 15.3. True copies.

assume that a true copy possesses a *true-copy token*, i.e., either an *exclusive-copy token* or a *share-copy token*.

True-copy tokens handle replicate physical objects that cannot be handled efficiently by a locking mechanism alone. We can conceive that exclusive-copy tokens and share-copy tokens are spatial extensions of exclusive locks and share locks.

Two types of locks, namely *share locks* and *exclusive locks*, are used over the true copies to realize consistent transaction processing. A transaction accessing a logical object needs to lock one of its replicate physical objects that contains a true copy. An exclusive copy can be exclusively locked and a share copy can be share locked; furthermore, locking must be two-phase. Although two-phase locking is used, it is not a complete locking at the physical object level. Write operations to physical objects at remote sites are performed without locking.

A transaction issues a *lock-seize* request in order to set a lock in a desired mode. A lock can be reset by a *lock-release* request. A lock once set is *active* until it is reset. Now two-phase locking can be defined as follows.[5]

Definition: Two-Phase Locking. A transaction is *two-phase locked* if no lock-release requests are issued by the transaction before all lock-seize requests of that transaction are issued.

Remote updates can be performed either 1) by carrying the current data value of each logical object with its true-copy token(s), or 2) by letting the exclusive-copy token issue a series of version numbers that are unique relative to each logical object and by performing remote updates according to these version numbers.

Updates for a logical object originate only from its exclusive copy, and they can be uniquely ordered by their version numbers. Also, although a remote update to a replicate physical object formally belongs to some transaction, it is more appropriate to consider that remote updates are carried out by the system when one of the above two methods is employed. When remote updates are performed by the system, a transaction need only submit one data value in order to update the set of replicate physical objects belonging to a logical object.

3.2. Concurrency Control Scheme

We will now state the true-copy token scheme more precisely. The new scheme allows several variations, so we are going to state only the basic rules that must be observed in any implementation. Note that we are not giving an algorithm that describes every required procedure, and that we are instead giving a set of constraints that are necessary to prevent inconsistent system operation. A positive aspect of this approach is that any implementation that satisfies the basic rules given in this section will possess the properties discussed in Subsection 3.3 and Section 4. Two different remote update mechanisms and various true-copy token transfer methods are discussed in reference 20.

We assume that, if a deadlock occurs, one or more of the transactions causing the deadlock are preempted in such a way that the preempted transactions do not leave any effect to the system. In order to avoid the "domino effect" of transaction abortion, the structure of each transaction may have to be restricted.[2,20] Further discussions concerning deadlocks in the true-copy token scheme can be found in reference 20.

As we stated in the preceding subsection, a true copy is assumed to possess a true-copy token that specifies the type of the true copy, either an exclusive copy or a share copy. When a true-copy token is "transferred" from a physical object x_i to another physical object x_j, x_i ceases to contain a true copy, and then x_j starts to contain a true copy specified by the true-copy token. (In an actual implementation this time precedence can be established by passing a descriptor representing the true-copy token between the sites where those two physical objects reside.) A true copy is said to be *free* if it is not locked by an transaction.

Now we will state the basic rules of the true-copy token scheme.

T1. Each physical object contains either an *exclusive copy*, a *share copy*, or a *void copy* of the logical object to which the physical object belongs.

T2. At the point of system creation, there exists exactly one free exclusive copy for each logical object.

T3. At any given time, either one exclusive copy or only share copies exist for each logical object.

T4. When a physical object obtains a true-copy token, all remote updates created thus far for the physical object must have been completed before the content of the physical object becomes a true copy. Remote updates to each physical object must follow the order of their creation.

T5. A transaction that wants to make read-write accesses to a logical object X must exclusively lock the exclusive copy of X. An exclusive lock can be set only on a free exclusive copy. Once the exclusive copy is exclusively locked, the transaction can read from or write to it. When the transaction writes to the exclusive copy of X, it must also create the remote updates for other physical objects belonging to X; the same data value must be supplied for all of the replicate physical objects of X. An exclusive-copy token cannot be transferred to another physical object or changed to a share-copy token while an exclusive copy is exclusively locked.

T6. A transaction that wants to make read-only accesses to a logical object X must share lock a share copy of X. A share lock can be set only on a share copy, which may have already been share locked. Once a share copy is share locked by a transaction, the content of the share copy can be read by the transaction. A share copy cannot be revoked until all share locks on it are released.

T7. Locking on true copies by a transaction must be *two-phase*.

Rule T3 may be replaced by the following three rules.

T3a. An exclusive-copy token can be transferred to another physical object belonging to the same logical object.

T3b. An exclusive-copy token can become a share-copy token. A share-copy token can create other share-copy tokens, and the newly-created share-copy tokens can be granted to other physical objects belonging to the same logical object.

T3c. When an exclusive copy of a logical object for which there currently exist multiple share copies is required, all of these share copies must be revoked except the one that becomes the exclusive copy.

Note that the invariant specified by rule T3 is not invalidated by any of the operations specified in the above three rules.

Rules T5 and T6 may be modified so that share locks can be applied to an exclusive copy. Then, an exclusive copy can be revoked only when it is neither exclusively nor share locked, and an exclusive copy that is only share locked can be changed to a share copy. This modification does not affect the set of transactions that can be executed concurrently.

Redundant remote updates may be discarded to reduce the intersite traffic, as we mentioned in Subsection 2.2. If more than one remote update occurs to the same physical object at some remote site before the physical object obtains a true copy, remote updates other than the last one are redundant, for the data values written by them will never be accessed.

Figure 15.5 shows which combination of transactions shown in Fig. 15.4 can be processed concurrently. A transaction is "active" if it is being executed by using a local data, and a transaction is "blocked" if it cannot be executed by using local data.

In Fig. 15.5(a), transaction *P* can proceed because x_1 contains an exclusive copy, and y_1 contains a share copy. Note that *P* makes read-write accesses to logical object *X* and a read-only access to logical object *Y*. The remote update to x_2 by *P* can be discarded because it will be overwritten by the remote update by transaction *Q*; it is redundant.

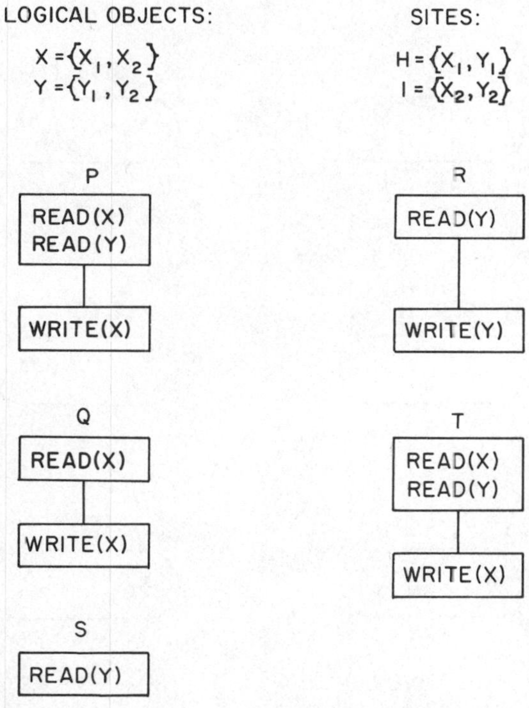

Fig. 15.4. Sites and transactions.

Also in Fig. 15.5(a), transaction *R* tries to make read-write accesses to logical object *Y*. However, physical object y_2 contains a share copy and not an exclusive copy, so *R* cannot exclusively lock y_2, and is blocked.

Once *P* is completed at site *H* and transaction *Q* starts its execution using the exclusive copy in x_1, the share-copy token of y_1 can be released and the content of y_2 can become an exclusive copy; then *R* can proceed. In Fig. 15.5(b), both *Q* and *R* are running concurrently. The remote update to x_2 created by *Q* must be sent to site *I* before the content of x_2 becomes an exclusive copy and is accessed by transaction *T*.

In Fig. 15.5(c), transaction *S* introduced at site *H* is blocked because the

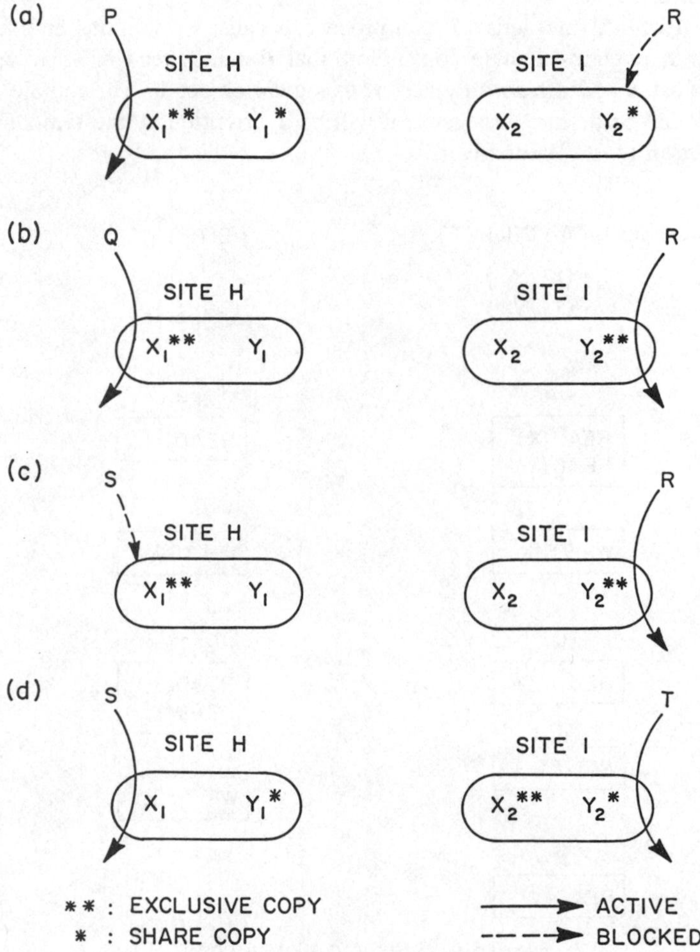

Fig. 15.5. True-copy token scheme.

content of y_1 is not a share copy. In Fig. 15.5(d), however, two share copies, those in y_1 and y_2, exist for logical object Y at the same time, and both transactions S and T are active.

Now we shall briefly state how to perform remote updates so that they satisfy rule T4 given above. A straightforward method is to transfer true copies themselves among physical objects, i.e., to carry the latest data value created for each logical object within its true-copy tokens and to update each physical object to the value specified by the true-copy token when it is visited by a true-copy token. In this method, a remote update addressed to each remote physical object is not created. Therefore, assume that remote updates are carried by true copies and that a remote update carried by a true copy is applied to its target physical object when the true copy arrives at the physical object for the first time after the remote update is created. Further assume that remote updates carried by a true copy are overwritten before they arrive at their target physical objects by their successive remote updates when newer values are created for the true copy.

The obvious disadvantage of this method is that we have to carry a lot of data when a logical object is large, even when the modified part is small. Another disadvantage is that replicate physical objects are not kept up-to-date. Some advantages of this method are that it is easy to understand, that remote updates need not be addressed to individual physical objects, and that redundant remote updates are automatically ignored.

Another method to perform remote updates, a ''sequenced update mechanism,'' is described in reference 20. This method can eliminate the two disadvantages associated with the previous method.

3.3. Correctness Proof

In this Subsection we will prove that the true-copy token scheme presented in the preceding subsection is consistent, by directly showing that any execution sequence allowed by it satisfies consistency condition C at the physical object level.

An immediate consequence of the two-phase locking rule (rule T7) is that all locks set by each transaction are active at some point during the execution of the transaction. We define the *lock peak point* R_p of a transaction R as the first point in time at which all locks set by transaction R are active.

Definition: Lock-Peak-Point Ordering $\ll_p$. The binary relation $\ll_p$ on a set of transactions that use two-phase locking is defined as follows: $R \ll_p S$ if $R_p \ll S_p$, where R_p and S_p are the lock peak points of transactions R and S, respectively.

As R_p and S_p are not operation events, we have extended the execution sequence $\ll$ to include lock peak points. Obviously, $R \ll_p S$ means that the lock peak point of R precedes that of S. Note that $\ll_p$ is acyclic because $\ll_p$ is a total ordering.

We are now going to prove that any execution sequence allowed by the true-copy token scheme satisfies consistency condition C at the physical object level. We will show that, in any execution sequence, D-precedence $\lll$ defined on the set of transactions can be embedded in the lock-peak-point ordering $\ll_p$, i.e., that if $R \lll S$ for any pair of transactions R and S, then $R \ll_p S$. In the following proof, operations are physical ones, and the execution timings of remote updates are those times when they are actually applied to physical objects. Also, a true copy is either an exclusive copy or a share copy, and an access is either a read operation or a write operation.

Theorem 1. The true-copy token scheme is consistent.

Proof. Assume that, for a pair of transactions R and S, $R \lll S$. Then, some operation A of transaction R and some operation B of transaction S conflict over some physical object x_k, and $A \ll B$. Accesses made by A and B to x_k are either local accesses performed under locking while x_k holds a true copy, or remote updates.

First, if x_k is locally accessed by both A and B, $R \ll_p S$ because local accesses are made with x_k being locked.

Second, if A is a local access and B is a remote update, then the remote update B must be preceded in S by a local write operation C that writes the same data value as B to some physical object x_i $(i \neq k)$ that contains an exclusive copy when C is applied to it (Fig. 15.6(a)). Now if $C \ll A$, then $B \ll A$ because B must be applied to x_k before x_k obtains the true copy accessed by A (rule T4). Therefore, $A \ll C$, and hence $R \ll_p S$ because x_i can seize the exclusive copy accessed by C only after the true copy accessed by A is released.

Third, if A is a remote update and B is a local access, A must be preceded in R by a local write operation C that accesses x_i writing the same value as A (Fig. 15.6(b)). As C precedes A and A precedes B, C precedes B and hence $R \ll_p S$. Note that S can exclusively or share lock x_k only after the exclusive lock on x_i is released by R.

Finally, if accesses by both operations A and B are remote updates (Fig. 15.6(c)), the ordering rule of remote updates (rule T4) guarantees that these remote updates are performed in their order of creation. Hence, transaction R exclusively locks some physical object x_i and creates the remote update A before transaction S exclusively locks some physical object x_j and creates the remote update B. Consequently, $R \ll_p S$.

We have shown that conflicting operations are performed according to the lock-peak-point ordering $\ll_p$ defined for the transactions to which they belong,

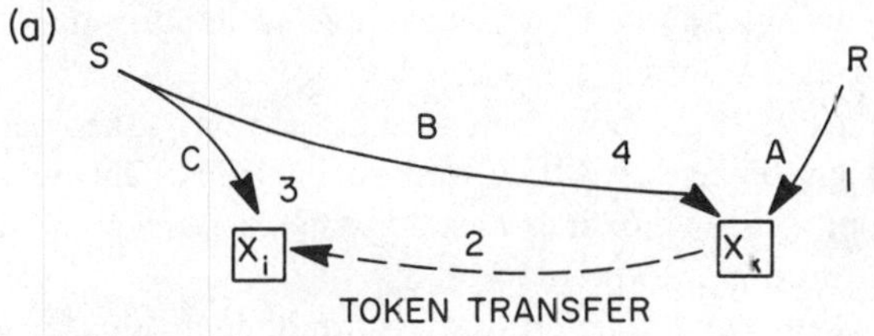

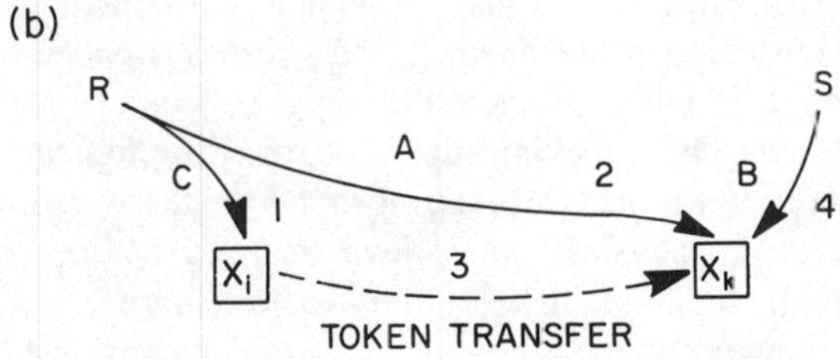

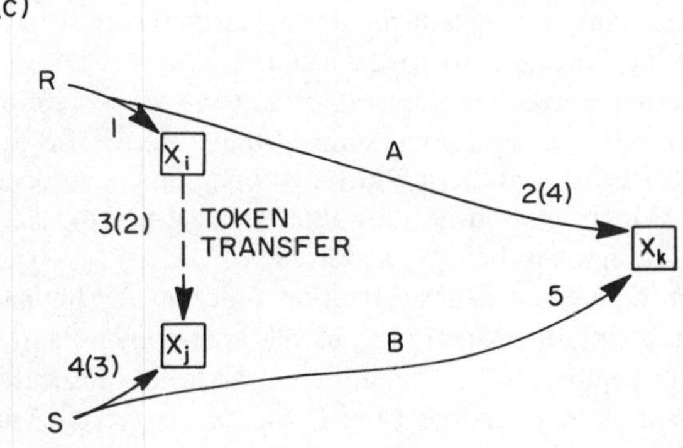

Fig. 15.6. "$\lll$" and "$\ll_p$".

i.e., that if $R \lll S$ for transactions R and S, then $R \ll_p S$. Since $\ll_p$ is acyclic, $\lll$ is acyclic, and hence consistency condition C is satisfied.

Numbers in Fig. 15.6 indicate the event ordering. In Fig. 15.6(a) (Fig. 15.6(b)), the true-copy token that is transferred from x_k (x_i) to x_i (x_k) may be used at other sites after it leaves x_k (x_i) and before it reaches x_i (x_k). In Fig. 15.6(c), that $x_i = x_j$ is allowed.

4. LOGICAL OBJECTS AND LOGICAL OPERATIONS

In the preceding section, we have shown that the true-copy token scheme maintains consistency condition C at the physical object level. From the standpoint of system structuring, however, it is desirable to assume that logical objects themselves hold data values.

In this section, we shall show that, in the true-copy token scheme, transactions access logical objects as if they were real entities. Our discussion follows the standard approach of handling abstract data in sequential programs,[9,10,30] except that our proof is informal.

First, a *data abstraction function* for the current data values of logical objects is defined. Then, we show that logical operations cause the expected effects on the logical object values. A new aspect of our proof method is that logical operations are considered instantaneous, and (*abstract*) execution timings are defined for them. Once logical objects and logical operations are established, it is shown that the two-phase locking rule is observed by logical operations.

Before we proceed, we need a minor abstraction step. Assume that an execution sequence at the physical object level realized by the true-copy token scheme is given. In order to make our discussion simple, we reinterpret the given execution sequence in the following way. 1) Each physical operation takes place instantaneously at the point when the actual physical operation is initiated; and 2) Each true-copy token transfer occurs instantaneously at the point when the new holder of the true-copy token receives it.

Note that these changes are applicable only to our perception of the system operation and not to the actual operation of the system. The first interpretation is allowable because no conflicting physical operations can occur concurrently, and the second interpretation is allowable because no transactions can access true copies while they are being transferred.

Now we can define the data abstraction function for logical object values. The following definition states that, in the true-copy token scheme, logical objects and true copies can be "identified." Note that logical objects are (fictitious) entities at the logical object level, whereas true copies are entities at the physical object level.

Definition: Logical Object Value. The current data value of each logical object is specified by the current content of either an exclusive copy or a share copy associated with the logical object.

Lemma 2. The current data value of each logical object is uniquely defined at any time.

Proof. When there is a single exclusive copy for a logical object, obviously its data value is uniquely defined. When a share copy creates other share copies, these share copies reflect all past updates created for them, and hence their contents are the same. Furthermore, the contents of share copies will not change until they are revoked and an exclusive copy is created. Hence, even when there are multiple share copies, their contents are the same.

We now want to show that, in the true-copy token scheme, logical read and write operations access logical objects as if they were real entities. In order to make the definition of logical objects meaningful (the definition of an object was given in Subsection 2.1), an access ordering must be specified on the logical read and write operations applied to each logical object.

We now define the execution timings of logical operations. In the case of physical operations, we have conceived that they are activities that actually take place on the hardware and that their execution timings can be defined unambiguously. The definition of the execution timings of logical operations, on the other hand, requires discretion.

As we stated in Subsection 2.2, a logical read operation *read*(X) is represented by a physical read operation *read*(x_i) for some x_i. Therefore, it is natural to identify the execution timing of *read*(X) with that of *read*(x_i).

The problem is not so simple for a logical write operation *write*(X) because in our model *write*(X) is represented by the set of physical write operations $\{$*write*(x_1), *write*(x_2), . . . $\}$. However, the underlying concept of the true-copy token scheme is to identify true copies with logical objects. Thus, it is natural to identify the execution timing of a logical write operation *write*(X) with that of the physical write operation *write*(x_i) that is applied to the physical object containing the exclusive copy of logical object X. In the true-copy token scheme, only one operation in the set of physical write operations representing *write*(X) is applied to an exclusive copy. Therefore, the execution timing of *write*(X) is also uniquely defined. The reader is cautioned that this definition is applicable only when the true-copy token scheme is used. That is, different definitions must be given for other schemes.

Definition: Execution Timings of Logical Operations. Given a physical level execution sequence of transactions realized by the true-copy token scheme, the execution timings of logical operations are defined as follows:

L1. Assume that logical read operation *read*(X) occurs when its corresponding physical read operation *read*(x_i), some i, occurs.

L2. Assume that logical write operation *write*(X) occurs when one of its corresponding physical write operations is applied to the exclusive copy of X.

L3. Assume that the execution timing of a lock-seize or lock-release operation on a logical object is that of its corresponding lock-seize or lock-release operation applied to a true copy associated with the logical object.

Now we show that the logical execution sequence thus defined is a consistent way of viewing the physical one.

Lemma 3. When transactions are executed by using the true-copy token scheme, transactions will not see any difference, even if physical objects and physical operations are replaced by their logical counterparts, i.e., logical objects and logical operations.

Proof. First, the data value returned by the physical read operation *read* (x_i), representing a logical read operation *read* (X), is the data value of a true copy for X, and is by definition the current data value of logical object X. Hence, *read* (x_i) can be replaced by *read* (X) without affecting the transaction issuing it.

Second, when a logical write operation *write* (X) is assumed to occur, one of its corresponding physical write operations is applied to the exclusive copy of X, and consequently the current data value of X changes as specified by *write* (X). Hence, *write* (X) is correctly implemented.

Third, we show that the data values of the logical objects are not changed by other physical operations. Remote updates have no effects on the current data values of logical objects because they are applied to void copies. Further, transfer of a true-copy token has no effect on the current data value of the logical object associated with the true-copy token, since two physical objects between which a true-copy token is transferred possess the same content when the true-copy token transfer occurs. This is because all past remote updates are applied to a physical object when it obtains a true copy (rule T4).

Consequently, in the true-copy token scheme we can assume that logical objects are accessed as if they were real objects.

Lemma 4. In the true-copy token scheme, two-phase locking is realized over logical objects.

Proof. First, we show that conflicting lock instances are mutually excluded at the logical object level. If a logical object is exclusively locked by some transaction, the exclusive copy of the logical object is exclusively locked at some site. Then no other transactions can lock a true copy belonging to the same logical object, for the exclusive copy that is exclusively locked is the only true copy of the logical object. On the other hand, if a logical object is share locked, a share copy of the logical object is share locked at some site. Then, only share copies can exist for that logical object, and no transaction can exclusively lock the logical object because share copies cannot be exclusively locked.

Second, by definition, the timing of the locking on logical objects is identical to the timing of the two-phase locking applied to true-copies (rule T7).

It is well known that two-phase locking applied to a centralized database system preserves consistency condition C.[3,5,23] Hence, from Lemmas 3 and 4 we can conclude the following theorem:

Theorem 5. Any execution sequence allowed by the true-copy token scheme satisfies consistency condition C at the logical object level.

5. RESILIENCY CONTROL

In this section, we will first give a definition of *resilient system operation*. Then, we shall show that the true-copy token scheme can be made resilient by employing a reliable storage mechanism and a reliable message transmission mechanism. Finally, the system partitioning problem is discussed. The resiliency scheme discussed in this section can handle site crashes and message link failures as long as each site can always restore its own data. However, the scheme fails when some sites cannot restore their own data.

Resiliency schemes that can tolerate complete failures of some sites in distributed database systems are described in references 21 and 22. Since the resiliency scheme discussed in this section is simpler and more efficient than those schemes, a sensible approach would be to employ those schemes only when the scheme discussed in this section fails.

5.1. Resilient System Operation

So far, we have not considered site or message-link failures. When such subsystem failures occur, *continuity* of data may be lost. However, when the true-copy token scheme is employed, continuity of logical object values can be preserved by preserving continuity of true copies.

Lemma 6. Logical operations will not be affected if true copies are regenerated with the values possessed by lost true copies.

Proof. If a true copy is regenerated with the value possessed by the lost true copy, then the proof of Lemma 3 is still valid. The combined process of the loss and the regeneration of a true copy of logical object X preserves the value of X. Note that logical objects whose true copies are lost are not accessed until those lost true copies are regenerated.

When the mainframe at a site fails, some transactions being executed at that site may not be completed. Then, these transactions must be *aborted*, and their effects must be nullified. Transactions that are not aborted must be *committed*. The effect of a committed transaction must be complete.

We will now give the definition of *resilient system operation.*

Definition: Resilient System Operation. System operation is *resilient* if the following three conditions are satisfied:

R1. Each transaction submitted to the system is either *committed* or *aborted*. Each logical write operation issued by a committed transaction updates the value of its target logical object, and no logical write operations issued by aborted transations affect the logical object values.
R2. Each read operation issued by a committed transaction returns the current value of its target logical object.
R3. The execution sequence defined for committed transactions is *serializable* at the logical object level.

When condition R1 is satisfied, we say that *atomicity* of each transaction is preserved. Condition R2 does not impose any requirement on the values read by aborted transactions.

5.2. Reliable Storage Mechanism

In implementing a reliable distributed database system, we assume that each site is equipped with a *reliable storage* subsystem. A site that is guarded by a reliable storage subsystem can restore its own data even if its mainframe and part of its secondary storage fail. A site equipped with a reliable storage subsystem will be called a *reliable site*.

We assume that the reliable storage subsystem employed by each site possesses the following properties:

S1. Data written to the reliable storage will never be lost.
S2. A set of data can be *atomically* written to the reliable storage at each site.
S3. An individual write operation to reliable storage is relatively expensive. Therefore, it is impractical to move to reliable storage every piece of data generated by the mainframe.

A conventional method for making a centralized database system resilient against mainframe and disk failures is to use *checkpoint dumps** and *log records*, which effectively provide reliable storage.[6,7,8,15,26,28,29] A reliable storage subsystem can also be implemented by duplicating a storage subsystem that uses the ''intentions-list'' mechanism[11,12,18] or the shadow mechanism.[17] Results of

*A checkpoint dump is a complete copy of a database state. In reference 8, such a copy is called an archive, and the term ''checkpoint'' is used for a different purpose.

performance simulations of a simple reliable storage subsystem are reported in reference 16.

5.3. Reliable Token Transfer

We will now consider the problem of connecting reliable sites, in order to realize a reliable distributed database system. Since reliable sites will never lose their data, a reliable distributed database system can be constructed if true copies can be reliably transferred between these sites.

However, if a message link fails, true-copy tokens being transferred over the message link may be lost. When a site crash occurs, there is a possibility of losing messages on the crashed site; these messages may have been generated by the crashed site itself, or they may have been sent from other sites. Further, as we assume that true-copy tokens and locks are kept in main memory while a site is operating normally, they may be lost or released if a mainframe failure occurs.

We can realize reliable token transfer by retransmitting possibly lost messages (message retransmission is widely practiced in communication networks[4]). In implementing a reliable token transfer mechanism, we make the following assumptions:

- M1. A damaged message can always be detected as damaged.
- M2. If the same message is sent repeatedly some finite number of times, it will eventually reach its destination site.
- M3. Duplicate messages can be detected.

Assumption M1 is based on the fact that the probability of an occurrence of undetectable error is extremely small when an appropriate error detection code is used. Assumption M2 implies another assumption, that a failed message link will eventually be restored. Since relevant messages are associated with true-copy tokens, version numbers can be used to detect duplicate messages.

In order to transfer a true-copy token from a *sender* site to a *receiver* site, both of which are operating normally, the following procedures must be used by reliable sites.

- X1. Before the sender site releases the true-copy token, it must write to its reliable storage a *Token-Release* record remembering to which site the true-copy token is being sent, and then it must delete the *Token-Seize* record for the true-copy token. Once these operations are complete at the sender site, the true-copy token can be sent to the receiver site by a *Token-Grant* message.
- X2. When the receiver site receives the *Token-Grant* message, it must write to its stable storage a *Token-Seize* record before the site begins to use

the true copy associated with the true-copy token. Then, the receiver site must send a *Token-ACK* message to the sender site acknowledging the receipt of the true-copy token.

X3. When the sender site receives the *Token-ACK* message from the receiver site, the *Token-Release* record at the sender site must be deleted.

Figure 15.7 shows the normal interaction of the sender site and the receiver site.

In the procedure above, a true-copy token held by a site is remembered by the *Token-Seize* record written on the stable storage at that site, and a true-copy token being tranferred is remembered by the *Token-Release* record written on the stable storage at the sender site. Step X2 can be modified so that the *Token-ACK* message is effectively returned to the sender site by returning the true-copy token itself after its use. This modification can reduce the number of required messages.

Now we will state the additional procedures that are required when the system is restored from subsystem failures.

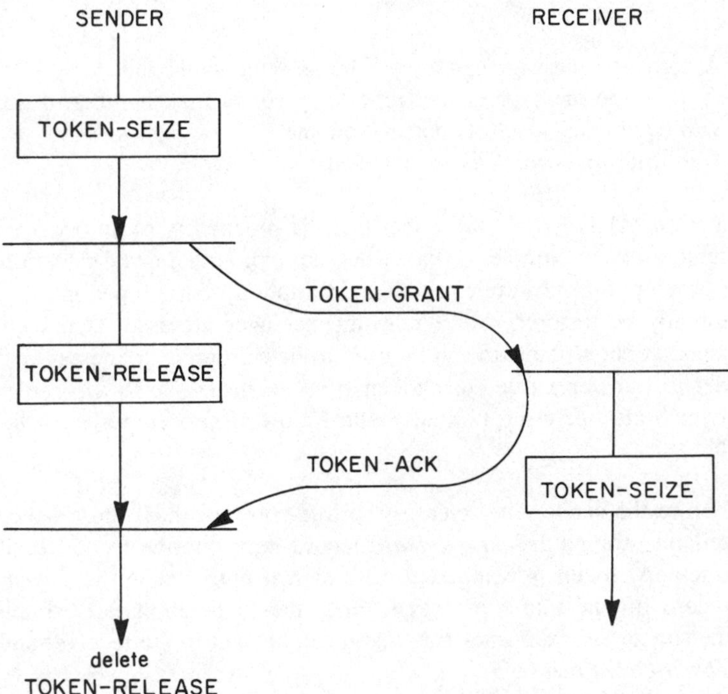

Fig. 15.7. Reliable token transfer.

X4. When a site is restored from a site failure, it must take the following action. If a *Token-Seize* record is found at that site and if no *Token-Release* record for the same true-copy token is found, then the true-copy token indicated by the *Token-Seize* record must be regenerated at that site.

X5. If a *Token-Release* record is found at some site and if the true-copy token associated with the *Token-Release* record may have been affected by the subsystem failures, then the *Token-Grant* message for the true-copy token indicated by the *Token-Release* record must be sent again to the receiver site. A true-copy token sent over a message link may be affected if any of the sender site, the message link, and the receiver site fails.

X6. When a redundant *Token-Grant* message is received for the true-copy token that has already been received, the message must be ignored except that a *Token-ACK* message must be sent back to the sender site, even if it has already been sent.

X7. If a *Token-ACK* message whose matching *Token-Release* record does not exist is received, the message must be ignored.

When a *Token-Release* record is found at a site, a true-copy token has been sent to another site as indicated by the *Token-Release* record, but its acknowledgment has not been returned to the sender site yet. The true-copy token may have been lost while it was being transferred to the receiver site. Therefore, the true-copy token must be sent to the receiver site again. However, if the true-copy token has already reached the receiver site, the *Token-Grant* message must be ignored. Also, note that if both *Token-Seize* record and *Token-Release* record for the same true-copy token are found at a site, then the *Token-Release* record prevails.

5.4. Transaction Processing

We have shown that true copies can be reliably transferred between sites. If every true copy required by a transaction is transferred to the site where the transaction is executed, then the transaction can be executed as if it is executed by a centralized database system, and each site can use the reliable storage subsystem in order to support the true copies at that site.

As we have mentioned, a transaction is a collection of operations, and a transaction as seen by its user is like an ordinary program with write operations intermixed with other operations. However, we restrict the transaction structure seen by the system in order to support our resiliency scheme. The main features of our restricted transaction structure is a *transaction buffer* that supports the abortion of a partially executed transaction without causing any ill effect to the system.

A transaction buffer is provided for each transaction. Until a transaction issues a *Transaction-End* command, updates created by the transaction are kept in its transaction buffer, and they are not applied to the reliable storage. This restriction allows transaction abortion at any time before the transaction issues the *Transaction-End* command. A transaction can be aborted simply by discarding its transaction buffer.

Once the *Transaction-End* command is issued, the updates in the transaction buffer must be written into the reliable storage. Therefore, all write operations of each transaction are effectively collected at the end of the transaction. A transaction cannot be aborted once the *Transaction-End* command is issued.

We will now state how transactions can be executed by each site.

E1. In order that a transaction can be executed at a site, all of the true-copies accessed by the transaction must be available at that site. Therefore, some true copies must be brought in from other sites. If a physical object to accommodate a true copy does not exist at a site, a *tentative* physical object can be created in order to accommodate the true copy. Whenever a true copy is obtained by a site, the content of the true copy must be written to reliable storage before the true copy is used by the transactions at that site.

E2. Updates* created by each transaction must be *atomically* applied to the reliable storage at that site where the transaction is executed.**

E3. If a site failure occurs, the reliable storage subsystem at the failed site must restore a "transaction-consistent"[8] state.

As we discussed, the continuity of true copies is preserved when they are transferred between sites. If the reliable storage subsystem at each site works correctly, true copies at each site will be effectively manipulated only by committed transactions (rules S1, S2, E2, and E3). Further, two-phase locking applied on true copies guarantees that the resultant execution sequence is serializable if aborted transactions are excluded. Consequently, conditions R1, R2, and R3 for resilient system operation are satisfied even if subsystem failures occur.

5.5. System Partitioning

While the system is operating normally, all sites in the system belong to one partition, and a true-copy token of each logical object can be transferred to any site where it is required.

---

*The output of the transaction must be included in these updates. It can be released once the updates are moved to reliable storage. On the other hand, the output must always be produced if the updates are reflected on reliable storage.

**Updates of transactions must be moved to reliable storage according to the "U-precedence" defined for those transactions.[16,22] This requirement can be automatically satisfied when exclusive locks are held until reliable storage is updated.

When the system is partitioned, each partition will possess a subset of the true copies that exist in the system. System partitioning can be supported without any consistency problem by letting each transaction access only those true copies that are available within the partition where the transaction is executed. Note that a transaction cannot be executed if some true copies required by the transaction are not available within the partition where the transaction is executed, and that the set of transactions that are executable within each partition is partly decided by chance. Remote updates to physical objects at the sites within other partitions must be delayed until message-links are restored.

6. CONCLUSION

A new concurrency and resiliency control scheme, the true-copy token scheme, was developed for a distributed database system with replicated data. The scheme first establishes logical objects by hiding replication of physical objects and then applies locking on these logical objects in order to preserve consistency. The behavior of the logical objects was precisely discussed by using the concept of data abstraction. In doing so, execution timings of logical operations were explicitly defined. This technique was called *time abstraction*.

The new concurrency control scheme supports, for each logical object, either one read-write copy or multiple read-only copies at one time. Multiple read-only copies that can be updated by revoking them will be useful, because many files in real systems are used in this way.

We have also shown that the true-copy token scheme can be made resilient by combining a reliable true-copy transfer mechanism and a reliable storage mechanism; the latter has long been used by centralized database systems. The resiliency scheme discussed in this chapter cannot handle complete site failures. Resiliency schemes that can restore a failed site by using redundant data stored at other sites are discussed in references 21 and 22. Even when those schemes are employed, the scheme discussed in this chapter can be used as the first level recovery scheme.

REFERENCES

1. Alsperg, P. A., G. G. Belford, J. D. Day, and E. Grapa, *Multi-copy Resiliency Techniques*. Center for Advanced Computation, Urbana-Champaign: Univ. of Illinois, May 1976.
2. Bayer, R., H. Heller, and A. Reiser, Parallelism and recovery in database systems, *ACM Trans. Database Systems*, vol. 5, pp. 139–156, June 1980.
3. Bernstein, P., D. Shipman, and W. Wong, Formal aspects of serializability in database concurrency control, *IEEE Trans. Software Engineering*, vol. SE-5, pp. 203–216, May 1979.
4. Edge, S. W. and A. J. Hinchley, A survey of end-to-end retransmission techniques, *SIG Computer Communications Rev.*, vol. 8, pp. 1–16, Oct. 1978.
5. Eswaran, K., J. Gray, R. Lorie, and I. Traiger, The notions of consistency and predicate locks in a database system, *CACM*, vol. 19, pp. 624–633, Nov. 1976.

6. Fossum, B. M., Data base integrity as provided by a particular data base management system, in *Data Base Management*, J. W. Klimbie and K. L. Koffeman (eds.), Amsterdam: North-Holland, 1974, pp. 271–288.
7. Gray, J., Notes on data base operating systems, in *Lecture Notes in Computer Science*, vol. 60, New York: Springer-Verlag, 1978, pp. 393–481.
8. Gray, J., P. McJones, M. Blasgen, B. Lindsay, R. Lorie, T. Price, F. Putzolu, and I. Traiger, The recovery manager of the System R database manager, *Comput. Surveys*, vol. 13, pp. 223–242, June 1981.
9. Guttag, J. V., E. Horowitz, and D. R. Musser, Abstract data types and software validation, *CACM*, vol. 21, pp. 1048–1064, Dec. 1978.
10. Hoare, C. A. R., Proof of correctness of data representations, *Acta Informatica*, vol. 1, pp. 271–281, 1972.
11. Lampson, B. W. and H. E. Sturgis, *Crash Recovery in a Distributed Data Storage System*, Res. Rep. Xerox Palo Alto Research Center, Apr. 1979.
12. Lampson, B. W., Atomic transactions, in *Distributed Systems—Architecture and Implementation*, (*Lecture Notes in Computer Science*, vol. 105), Berlin: Springer-Verlag, 1981, pp. 246–265.
13. Lee, C. H., Queueing analysis of global locking synchronization schemes for multicopy databases, *IEEE Trans. Computers*, vol. C-29, pp. 371–384, May 1980.
14. Le Lann, G., Algorithms for distributed data-sharing systems which use tickets, in *Proc. 3rd Berkeley Workshop on Distributed Data Management and Computer Networks*, San Fransisco, CA, Aug. 1978, pp. 259–272.
15. Lindsay, B. G., Single and multi-site recovery facilities, in *Distributed Data Bases*, I. W. Draffan and F. Poole (eds.), Cambridge University Press, 1980, pp. 247–284.
16. Liu, C. and T. Minoura, Effect of update merging on reliable storage performance, in *Proc. 2nd Intl. Conf. on Data Engineering*, Los Angeles, Feb. 5–7, 1986, pp. 208–213.
17. Lorie, R. A., Physical integrity in a large segmented database, *ACM Trans. Database Systems*, vol. 2, pp. 91–104, March 1977.
18. Menasce, D. A. and O. E. Landes, On the design of a reliable storage component for distributed database management systems, in *Proc. 6th Intl. Conf. on Very Large Data Bases*, Montreal, Canada, Oct. 1–3, 1980, pp. 365–375.
19. Minoura, T. Maximally concurrent transaction processing, in *Proc. 3rd Berkeley Workshop on Distributed Data Management and Computer Networks*, San Francisco, CA, Aug. 1978, pp. 206–214.
20. Minoura, T., *Resilient Extended True-Copy Token Algorithm for Distributed Database Systems* (Ph.D. diss.), Stanford University, May 1980. Available from University Microfilms International, 300 N Zeeb Road, Ann Arbor, MI 48106. Also as Tech. Rep. TR-197, CSL, Stanford University (microfiche only).
21. Minoura, T. and G. Wiederhold, Resilient extended true-copy token scheme for a distributed database system, *IEEE Trans. Software Engineering*, vol. SE-8, pp. 173–189, May 1982.
22. Minoura, T., S. Owicki, and G. Wiederhold, Consistent distributed database state maintenance. TR-83-60-2, Dept. of CS, Oregon State Univ., July 1983.
23. Papadimitriou, C. H., The serializability of concurrent database updates, *JACM*, vol. 26, pp 631–653, Oct. 1979.
24. Schlageter, G., Process synchronization in database systems, *ACM Trans. Database Systems*, vol. 3, pp. 248–271, Sept. 1978.
25. Stearns, R., P. Lewis, and D. Rosenkrantz, Concurrency control for database systems, in *Proc. IEEE Symp. on Foundations of Comp. Sci.*, Oct. 1976, pp. 19–32.
26. Stonebraker, M., Wong, E., and P. Kreps, The design and implementation of INGRES, *ACM. Trans. Database Systems*, vol. 1, pp. 189–222, Sept. 1976.

27. Stonebraker, M. Concurrency control and consistency of multiple copies of data in distributed INGRES, *IEEE Trans. Software Engineering*, vol. SE-5, pp. 188–194, May 1979.
28. Verhofstad, J. S. M., Recovery techniques for database systems, *ACM Comput. Surveys*, vol. 10, pp. 167–195, June 1978.
29. Wiederhold, G., *Database Design, 2nd edition*, New York: McGraw-Hill, 1983.
30. Wulf, W. A., R. L. London, and M. Shaw, An introduction to the construction and verification of Alphard programs, *IEEE Trans. Software Engineering*, vol. SE-2, pp. 253–265, Dec. 1976.

16. Performance Evaluation of Reliable Distributed Systems

HECTOR GARCIA-MOLINA

and

JACK KENT

1. INTRODUCTION

In the early decades of the computer age, the most important characteristic of a computer system was its speed. Thus, computers were usually judged by how fast they could perform a given task, and naturally, techniques were developed to predict this.[13] These techniques relied on queueing models, analysis, and (or) simulation. With them, it became possible to evaluate and compare designs or ideas without actually implementing them. For example, a systems manager could select a scheduling strategy for an operating system without long delays or inconveniences.

Now that relatively fast computers have become affordable and widespread, other aspects of computers are becoming important also. For instance, it may not suffice for a computer to be fast, it may also have to be *reliable*. To achieve reliability, the resources of computers (e.g., processors, memory, disks) are being replicated and distributed, and algorithms to manage and coordinate these resources are being developed. A number of these algorithms are presented in other chapters of this book. (Emphasis is also turning to other aspects, like ease of use. However, we will not consider these in this chapter.)

With the emergence of reliable computing systems, a need for improved evaluation techniques has clearly arisen. These techniques should be able to predict not just how fast the reliable system can perform a specified task, but also how well the system satisfies the reliability requirements, however these are defined. It might also be possible to evaluate and compare not only the hardware, but also the new coordination algorithms that make the reliable system possible. Without such tools, it may be impossible to rationally select a failure recovery strategy or to measure the progress that is being achieved.

Unfortunately, evaluating the reliability of a system is more difficult than simply evaluating its speed or performance. The main reason is that speed and performance are well defined terms, while reliability is not. To evaluate performance, one typically measures the time it takes the system to complete a given task, or how many tasks of a type can be performed per unit of time. There are also a limited number of secondary measures that are commonly studied. Examples of these are the size of queues, the wait time in these queues, the number of deadlocks, the number of aborted transactions, and the number of messages transmitted over a network.

In the case of "reliability," it is not clear what the term means precisely, let alone how one measures or evaluates it. Intuitively, at least, reliability has two aspects. First, a system is said to be reliable if its outputs or results are *correct*. For example, if the system is computing the number Π, the output should indeed be Π. If the system is managing accounts at a bank, no money should be lost.

The second aspect of reliability has to do with *availability*. A reliable system should tolerate failures and should be able to continue operation, even if in a degraded fashion. For example, in the banking system, customers at the branch offices should be able to obtain their account balance at the local computer, even if the bank's central computer is down.

How is a reliable system evaluated? We could measure the speed of the reliable system, but notice that the speed could vary as failures occur. Should we measure the rate at which useful work is done when all the system components are operational? Or when some are failed? Or should the measures somehow be averaged? We could even try to measure the availability of the system, for instance, the fraction of the time the system is operational. But, such a measure is complicated by the fact that the system may have different operational levels, not just one. In each level, the system may be available, however, with different capabilities or performance. We could also evaluate the correctness of the system. For example, consider a system which is performing a Monte Carlo simulation, where runs are performed in parallel on independent processors. Under normal circumstances, the confidence interval may be 1%, but if processors fail, the interval can grow. So, in this sense we may evaluate the accuracy of the system as a function of the failures that occur. Of course, no one measure will be totally adequate, so we will probably want to combine mulitple measures in some way. But how is this done?

Our objective in this chapter is to study the evaluation of reliable systems in order to "resolve" some of these questions, most of which do not have definitive answers. To do this, we will present a collection of models and measures that have been proposed (to evaluate reliable systems) and then show samples of the results obtained. We will not discuss the mathematical analysis of these models in any great detail, our primary intent is to illustrate the range of options that are available. Further, the analyses are usually complex and cannot all be reviewed in a single chapter.

In the following section, we start by discussing how the failures of the hardware components of a system can be modeled. In Section 3, we will model a complete system, made up of failure-prone components. In that Section, we shall assume that the system as a whole is either fully operational or inoperative. Such a simple view is inadequate in many cases, especially when we wish to evaluate gracefully degrading systems or compare algorithms. In Section 4, we are going to look at more refined models and measures for those cases.

In this chapter, when we speak of a system, we will usually refer to a distributed computing system. To be truly reliable, systems must have replicated resources and independent control units, hence they are "distributed." However, from our point of view, it is not important if the resources are geographically distributed (or not), or whether the system is loosely coupled (or not).

2. THE COMPONENTS

Any computing system can be viewed as a collection of interacting components. A first step in any reliability evaluation is to decide how the system will be broken down into components, how each of these components can fail, and how often it will fail. In this decomposition and modelling process, the desired accuracy of the evaluation and the complexity of the resulting model must be carefully considered. Accuracy improves as more components are considered, but the resulting model may become impossible to analyze mathematically, or even to simulate. If we assume that some components do not fail, or that they fail in simple ways, we can simplify the analysis considerably. However, this occurs at the expense of accuracy.

For example, consider a distributed computing system consisting of three computers and a network. We might model the system as being comprised of these four components. To enhance the accuracy of our model, we could separate each computer into a processor and a permanent storage device, and decompose the network into a set of communication lines. If we wished to model software failures (e.g., bugs), we could model each processor as a collection of processes. This decomposition can continue ad infinitum.

For each component, we must decide how it fails. In designing reliable systems, one usually considers many types of failures. For instance, a network may lose some messages, may deliver them out of order, may delay them excessively due to congestion, etc. However, considering all of these failure types in an evaluation is seldom practical. Instead, components are simply assumed to have two states: functioning properly or not functioning at all. Thus, a network (or a communication line) will either transmit all messages properly (the transmission time may be modeled by a probability distribution), or will not transmit any messages. A processor will either execute the algorithms that it has been provided (and nothing else), or will execute nothing at all.

For each component, we must model how often it fails, and if it is repaired, when this occurs. Depending on the complexity of our model, we may not require the actual distribution of failures and repairs; less elaborate measures may suffice. Among these are the expected time until failure (repair) of a component and the probability a component fails (is repaired) in a fixed time interval. The latter measure is used in discrete time Markov models. We will see an example of such a model in Section 4a.

At times, we need the failure and repair distributions. We can use probability distribution functions to model the inter-failure time $F(t)$ and inter-repair time $R(t)$. If the system is in a repaired (failed) state, $F(t)$ ($R(t)$) represents the probability that the system fails (is repaired) before time t.

A variety of distributions have been used to model (computer) failure. By far, the most frequently used in any reliability modelling is the exponential distribution. "It is especially appropriate to model computer failures; as the number of components is large and, if we assume each component is stochastically independent and is replaced immediately upon failure, the sequence of failure times is simply the sequence of all individual component failures. Under fairly weak conditions on the component failure distribution, the sequence of computer failures after a long time is approximately a Poisson process. . . . Because the time between successive events in a Poisson process is exponential and these times are independent, this result is often invoked to support the assumption of an exponential failure law."[2]

Besides being a reasonably accurate model of failures, the exponential distribution facilitates analysis due to its *memoryless property*. A random variable X is said to have this property if:

$$P[X > T + S \mid X > T] = P[X > S] \text{ for } S, T > 0$$

That is, assume a component has an exponentially distributed inter-failure rate and has not failed up to time T. The probability it will last at least S time units longer is exactly the same as the probability that a new component will last for at least S time units. Thus, when evaluating the time until the next computer failure, we need only consider how long the computer has been up since the most recent failure and can ignore its prior history.

Other distributions have been proposed as failure models. These are the gamma, weibull, normal, and lognormal distributions. For further information on these distributions, we refer the reader to references 2, 5, and 21. We want to emphasize that choosing failure models other than the exponential distribution often leads to intractable analyses. Thus, our distribution choice depends not only on how realistically it models failures, but also on the resulting complexity of the analysis.

The literature on repair distributions has been far less extensive. According to Barlow *et al.*, the log-normal distribution seems to most reasonably approximate inter-repair times. And although it is generally agreed that repairs do not form a Poisson process, the exponential distribution is often used to model repairs, again, because it simplifies the analysis.

3. THE STANDARD MEASURES

In classical reliability modelling, we assume that the system under consideration can only be in one of two states: up or down. When the system is up, user requests can be processed at a fixed rate, and when it is down, no requests can be processed. In this model, we consider only a single type of user request.

Although the model is very simple, it is useful in some cases. A number of basic reliability measures have been defined in terms of this model. We will discuss them shortly.

First, let us formalize the up/down system model. Consider a distributed system consisting of a number of components; these components might be processors, computers, or communication links. As per Section 2, we assume that the state of each component is operational or inoperative. The state of the system is the collection of the individual states. In general, if there are n components, there will be 2^n system states (e.g. one state may be computer 1 is operational, computer 2 is not, network is operational, . . .). Each system is classified as operational (up) if the system can perform the user requests while its components are in the specified state, otherwise it is classified as inoperative (down).

Let X^+ be the set of operational system states. Let X^- be the set of inoperative system states. These are some of the measures we can obtain (along with a description of their relevance):

(a) K-resiliency[1]: This is the minimum number of component failures the system can tolerate before entering a state in X^-. It gives us a rough approximation of the system reliability, and is usually a straightforward measure to obtain.
(b) Steady State Availability of X^+ (A): This is the probability of being in X^+ in the time interval $[0, t]$ as t goes to ∞. Often, if the tasks are small, availability can be used to approximate system throughput (the number of requests processed per unit period of time). That is, if x is the average time for the system to process a task, then *throughput* $= A/x$.
(c) Mean Time To First Failure: Starting from a state $S \in X^+$, this is the average time elapsed until the system changes to a failed state. This

measure gives an idea of how much work the system can accomplish before entering a failed state.

(d) Mean Cycle Time: The average time elapsed between 2 consecutive encounters of X^+.

To evaluate (a), we enumerate states. Specifically, we are looking for the smallest i, such that a combination of $i + 1$ component failures will shut down the system.

We must resort to other techniques to evaluate (b), (c), and (d). If the model is a continuous time Markov chain, then standard techniques can be used to evaluate the measures (the model is Markovian if the probability that a transision occurs between *adjacent* system states S_1 and S_2 before time t is exponentially distributed. States S_1 and S_2 are adjacent if the system can change directly from S_1 to S_2 without entering another state). If the model is non-Markovian, we have two options. We can approximate the non-Markovian model via a Markovian one,[21] or we can attempt an analysis of the original model, sometimes suceeding.

As an example of the above, let us consider two systems. System one is a distributed database with replicated data. We model this system as a Markov process and derive all four measures. System two is a transaction-oriented database equipped with a checkpoint-crash recovery mechanism. Modelling this system as a non-Markovian process, we compute the availability measure.

Let us describe the first system. There are two computers connected via a very reliable network, with users attached to either machine. Users of both computers access the same data, so there are two copies of the database, with each user managing his own copy (refer to Fig. 16.1).

Users of system one run only update transactions, i.e. transactions that modify the data. These update transactions must be synchronized, otherwise problems of inconsistency or divergence of data may occur.[12,20] Also, the system's update algorithm must cope with these problems in the event of site failures.[4,17,20] This system maintains consistency by allowing updates to complete only if both computers are up.

We model the system as a Markov process by enumerating all possible system states and determining the interstate transition rates. Since there are two com-

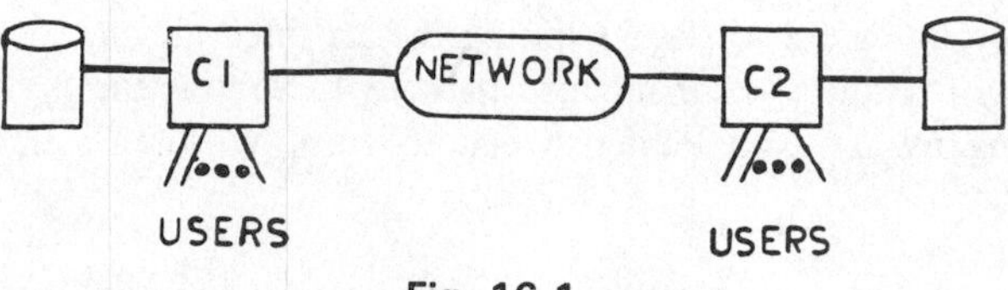

Fig. 16.1.

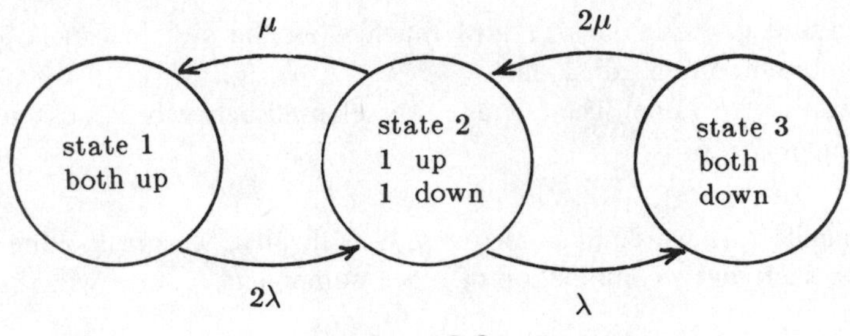

Fig. 16.2.

ponents, there are four states. However, since both components are identical, we can combine the states where one computer is up and the other is down into a single state. The resulting three states are shown in Fig. 16.2. Implicit in the model are three assumptions:

1. The rate at which components fail is λ (i.e., the mean time between failures is $1/\lambda$). Therefore, the rate from state 1 to 2 is 2λ (there are two computers that may fail).
2. The rate at which components are repaired is μ.
3. Components cannot change state in the same instant of time, e.g. there is no edge from state 1 to state 3 in Fig. 16.2.

Since the system requires both computers to process user requests, only state 1 is operational.

Notice that we have embedded many assumptions in the model, both about the hardware and the software. Revising these assumptions will yield a different model.

Let's evaluate the measures for the model above. Firstly, the system is zero-resilient, as one failure will prevent updates from completing.

To evaluate availability, we pose equations which describe the transitions between states. Let $p_i(t)$ be the probability that the system is in state i at time t. For state 1 we have (by the properties of continuous time markov chains):

$$p_1(t + \Delta t) = p_1(t)(1 - 2\lambda\Delta t) + p_2(t)(\mu\Delta t).$$

Here, Δt represents a small interval of time, $\mu\Delta t$ is the probability that the system goes from state 2 to state 1 during the Δt interval, and $(1 - 2\lambda\Delta t)$ is the probability that the system remains in state 1. Subtracting $p_1(t)$ from both sides, dividing by Δt, and letting Δt go to zero, we obtain the differential equation:

$$p_1'(t) = -2\lambda\Delta t p_1(t) + \mu\Delta t p_2(t) \quad \text{where} \quad (p_1(0) = 1).$$

Similarly, we can obtain the equations for state 2 and state 3:

$$p_2'(t) = -(mu + \lambda)\Delta t p_2(t) + \mu \Delta t p_2(t)$$
$$+ p_3(t) 2\mu \Delta t \quad \text{where} \quad (p_2(0) = 0)$$
$$p_3'(t) = -2\mu \Delta t p_3(t) + \lambda \Delta t p_2(t) \quad \text{where} \quad (p_3(0) = 0).$$

We can solve these equations for $p_1(t)$, $p_2(t)$, and $p_3(t)$. By letting t go to ∞, we obtain the availability.*

$$\textit{Availability} = p_1 = \left(\frac{\mu}{\lambda + \mu}\right)^2.$$

The *MTTF* (Mean Time to Failure) from state 1 is easy to derive. It is the average time until a departure from the state.

$$MTTF_1 = \frac{1}{2\lambda}.$$

Let $MTTO_i$ be the mean time until an operational state is reached from state i, $i \in X^-$. We can compute the MCT (Mean Cycle Time) by solving the system of equations:

$$MCT = \frac{1}{2\lambda} + MTTO_2$$

$$MTTO_2 = \frac{1}{\lambda + \mu} + \frac{\lambda}{\mu + \lambda} MTTO_3$$

$$MTTO_3 = \frac{1}{2\mu} + MTTO_2$$

For example, with respect to the second equation, $\frac{1}{\lambda + \mu}$ is the average time we spend in state 2 before a transition. The probability that the next transition from state 2 leads to state 3 is $\frac{\lambda}{\lambda + \mu}$. Once we enter state 3, the mean time until we reach state 1 is $MTTO_3$, thus we have derived the second term. There is no third term as $MTTO_1 = 0$; so $\frac{\lambda}{\lambda + \mu} MTTO_1 = 0$.

*For another method to solve for the steady-state probabilities, refer to reference[18] for a discussion of local-balance.

We now consider the second example. Chandy *et al.*[7] and Young independently measured the availability of a transaction-oriented database system equipped with a crash recovery mechanism. The mechanism works as follows: In the event that a media failure is detected (and thus the database is lost), the system log is searched for the most recent *checkpoint*. Events occurring after the checkpoint are reenacted, making use of other information available on the system log. Chandy *et al.* call this the *audit trail*.

Transaction processing must be suspended during checkpoints and recoveries. The time required to checkpoint the database is fixed. The recovery time is a function of the length of the audit trail, which in turn depends on the time between checkpoints. Our goal is to find a fixed intercheckpoint interval T which minimizes the number of suspended transactions, that is, maximizes system availability.*

In accordance with our up/down assumption, the system has three states: it is either processing, checkpointing, or recovering; the first state is the only up state. Note that if the system is in a recovery state, the time until transition to the processing state is not independent of previous events. The recovery time is directly dependent upon how recently the system was checkpointed. Thus, as we mentioned earlier, the system model is not Markovian.

The authors describe their model of a crash recovery mechanism:

1. The time between media fault detections is exponentially distributed.
2. The time required to recover is directly proportional to the size of the audit trail since the most recent checkpoint.
3. Transactions arriving during a checkpoint or recovery are queued for later processing. The time to process these queued transactions (after recovery) is small compared to the mean time between failures.
4. Errors do not occur during checkpoint or recovery.
5. The transaction arrival rate is fixed.

We can outline the analysis of the model. Again, the problem is to find a fixed interval T (the time between successive checkpoints) that maximizes system availability. T is a function of the system's parameters:

a. λ: the failure rate of the system;
b. F: the expected time required to checkpoint the database;
c. μ: arrival rate of transactions that modify the database (update transactions); and
d. b: the rate at which update transactions on the audit trail can be reprocessed.

*There are other factors involved. For instance, there is a space premium for frequent checkpointing as the audit trail need only cover the time since the most recent checkpoint.

How do we measure the system availability? Let K represent how much quicker it is to redo an update transaction via the audit trail rather than restarting the transaction. From (c) and (d) we have that:

$$K = \frac{\mu}{b}.$$

Define $V(T)$ as the expected time to recover between two successive checkpoints separated by time T. $O(T)$ is the *overhead time* incurred from checkpointing and recovery, given an intercheckpoint time T. Thus:

$$O(T) = F + V(T).$$

$r(T)$ is the fraction of time the system spends checkpointing and recovering.

$$r(T) = \frac{O(T)}{T},$$

and finally we have an equation for availability, based on an intercheckpoint time T.

$$A(T) = 1 - r(T).$$

After posing a differential equation, the authors determine T_{opt}, the intercheckpoint time that maximizes availability.

$$T_{opt} = \left(\frac{2F}{\lambda K}\right)^{1/2}$$

In Fig. 16.3, we see T_{opt} graphed as a function of F and λK. For instance (holding F and K constant), as failures occur more frequently, λK increases and T_{opt} decreases. Thus, checkpoints should be taken more often when failures increase, supporting our intuition.

4. ADDITIONAL MEASURES

In many cases, a simple up/down model may be inappropriate for evaluating complex reliable systems. Thus, we need to consider more detailed models, as well as additional measures of reliability. To illustrate this, let us consider some examples.

Our first example is a distributed transaction system. A network partition of this system can force some operational sites to suspend processing, while other

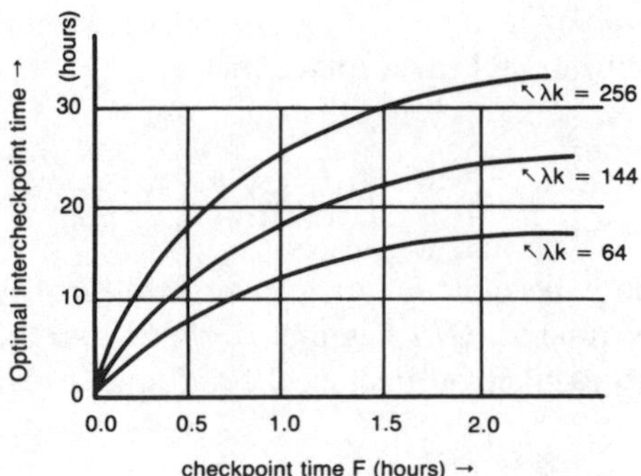

Fig. 16.3.

operational sites continue processing.[22] During the partition, the system is available (up) for some tasks and not available (down) for others. Furthermore, one task may be performable in only ''half'' of the system. The standard measures cannot be readily applied to this system, as it is not consistent with the up/down model.

We will now describe a second system. Unlike the previous system, if system two can process one type of task, it can process all tasks; however, the rate at which system two processes tasks varies. When all components are operating, the system can process a task T in one second. If one of the components fail, the same task requires five seconds to complete. The up/down model does not take into consideration different computational speeds for various operational states and thus is not an accurate model of this second system.

In the third system we shall consider, tasks are being run interactively. A user in this system is especially concerned with the response time of his request (task), i.e. the clock time elapsed from the request initiation until its completion. If the tasks are relatively small, we can model the system as up/down and possibly get an approximation of system throughput (refer to Section 2). But as the task duration grows, the probability that the task encounters a failure and is in some way delayed also grows. An evaluation of the response time must take this into account, and again, the up/down model and measures are not fully adequate.

The limitations of this model suggests that we look for other ways to evaluate reliable-distributed systems. In the next Subsection, we review some of the new approaches that have been taken.

4.1. A Modified Availability Measure

As in Section 2, Martella *et al.*[19] also examine a distributed database. However, their system differs from the previous one in two important ways.

1. Data is only *partially* replicated.
2. Queries (read-only transactions) are executed, as well as updates.

This system cannot be modelled as up/down; there are states of the system where some transactions can be processed and not others. We must take into account the different transaction types and their resource requirements when evaluating availability.

The authors describe a modified availability measure A_T. This is the probability that a transaction T, run from site C, with read set R and write set W, can complete in the distributed system. The measure is especially useful when we know the composition of different transactions in the system. For instance, assume there are n transaction types, and a user runs a transaction of type T_i with probability p_i. We can compute the standard *system availability* as

$$\textit{system availability} = \sum_{1}^{n} (A_{T_i})(p_i)$$

To illustrate the model, consider a distributed database system composed of four computers C_1, C_2, C_3, and C_4. Let w, x, y, and z represent entities accessed by the computers. To increase availability, some of the entities are partially replicated. Let us assume (as per the authors' example):

1. C_1 contains (w, x, y)
2. C_2 contains (x)
3. C_3 contains (x, y)
4. C_4 contains (z)

Martella's model considers the communication topology, as well as the location of data, i.e. whether C_i can communicate with C_j. In the example above, we will assume there is a (symmetric) communications link between each site.

A transaction T is run from C_2. T has read set $R_T = (y, z)$ and write set $W_T = (x)$.

T must access R_T. It can read y from C_1 or C_3 as there are communications links connecting C_2 to both computers. Entity z is available only at C_4.

T must write W_T. As in the previous example, consistency constraints demand that all copies of the entity *eventually* have identical values. We can guarantee that failed computers will eventually receive the updates using a majority-based voting scheme.[23] As x is replicated at C_1, C_2, and C_3, an update can occur if the originating site is up and at least half of the other copies (C_1 or C_3) can be accessed.

We can represent the conditions for T to run successfully. In our notation, $L_{i,j}$ implies the link between C_i and C_j is up and U_i means computer C_i is up.

The following equation is thus a necessary and sufficient condition for T to successfully read.

$$((L_{2,1} \text{ and } U_1) \text{ or } (L_{2,3} \text{ and } U_3)) \text{ and } (L_{2,4} \text{ and } U_4)$$

A similar equation can be derived to express the conditions for a successful write by T. We can combine the conditions to describe when the entire transaction will run. Figure 16.4 shows the combined conditions for the transaction T in what Martella *et al.* call a *search graph* (assuming all components are operational initially). Transaction T can run successfully if there is a path from the source node to the destination node. The leftmost edge in Fig. 16.4 signifies that C_2 must be up for T to run. Next follows the conditions for a read (refer to the previous section). The rightmost three parallel edges represent the conditions for a successful write.

As the last step in the modelling procedure, we construct a discrete Markov chain from the search graph. Let us assume that there are n components (links and computers) that sometimes (or always) participate in the execution of T. There are 2^n system states in the Markov model of T. A state s is operational if, using only operational components in s, we can find a path from the source to drain in the search graph for T.

To finish constructing the discrete Markov chain, we need to label the transition probabilities between states. Transitions occur when components fail or are repaired. For every pair of states s_1 and s_2, $p(s_1, s_2)$ is the probability that the system changes from s_1 to s_2 in a fixed time interval. After adding these

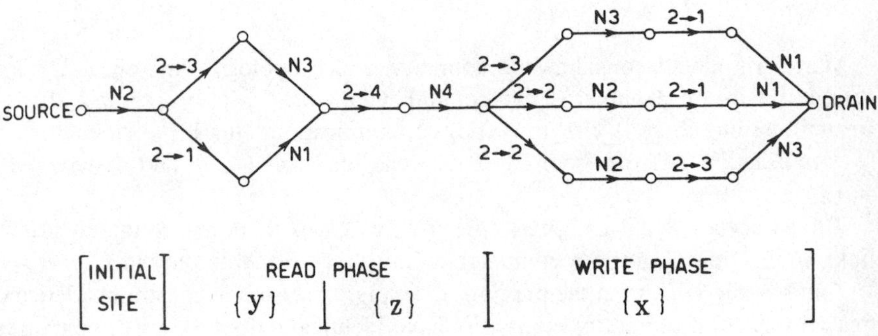

Arc $i \rightarrow j$ in the graph corresponds to $L_{i,j}$
Arc Ni corresponds to U_i

Fig. 16.4. The search graph for transaction T.

probabilities to the model, we can use standard techniques to compute the steady state probabilities, and thus A_T.

Using this technique (and making some assumptions on the probability of a link or computer failure), the authors compute the time-specific availability of transaction T (described earlier). (The time-specific availability is the probability that the system is operational at time $t + u$, given that it was in a specific state at time t.) Their results are plotted in Fig. 16.5. As entity z appears to be the availability bottleneck (it appears at only one site), the authors replicate z at another site and then recompute the time-specific availability. Figure 16.6 represents this new scenario; copying z allows a 3.6% improvement in the (steady state) availability.

4.2. Mean Number of Blocked Sites

In a distributed transaction system, all sites processing on behalf of a transaction T must agree on the direction of T (commit/abort). A *commit protocol* C is used for this purpose. A *termination protocol* for C, TP_C, is executed by operational sites to terminate a transaction, when C cannot complete due to a component failure.

A slave S holds locks on behalf of transaction T if, due to a component failure, C cannot complete and TP_C cannot determine the status of T. When this happens, we say *S blocks* on behalf of T. The number of slaves that block is determined by the states of the slaves (which is a function of the time of failure and of the commit protocol) and the termination protocol TP_C. *Blocking* prevents other transactions from executing, as they cannot obtain needed resources.

For systems with reliable networks, there is a commit protocol C and termination protocol TP that never force operational sites to block.[22] For systems with unreliable networks, the above assertion is false; for all C and TP_C, there is a partition that will block some sites.

Clearly, blocking should be avoided whenever possible, so a natural measure of system reliability is the number of blocked sites. That is, in a distributed transaction system with an unreliable network, what is the average number of sites that block T, when the sites use C and TP_C? Cooper[9] and Chin *et al.*[8] try to answer this question.

Cooper looks at five different commit protocols, combining each with a straightforward termination protocol. Should a network failure occur before C has completed, a slave S_i will terminate the transaction if S_i can communicate with an *informed* slave or the coordinator (an informed slave is a slave that has reached a commit or abort state).

The commit protocols Cooper examines are:

1. Noncooperating two-phase commit[16]—under this protocol, slaves can communicate only with the coordinator.

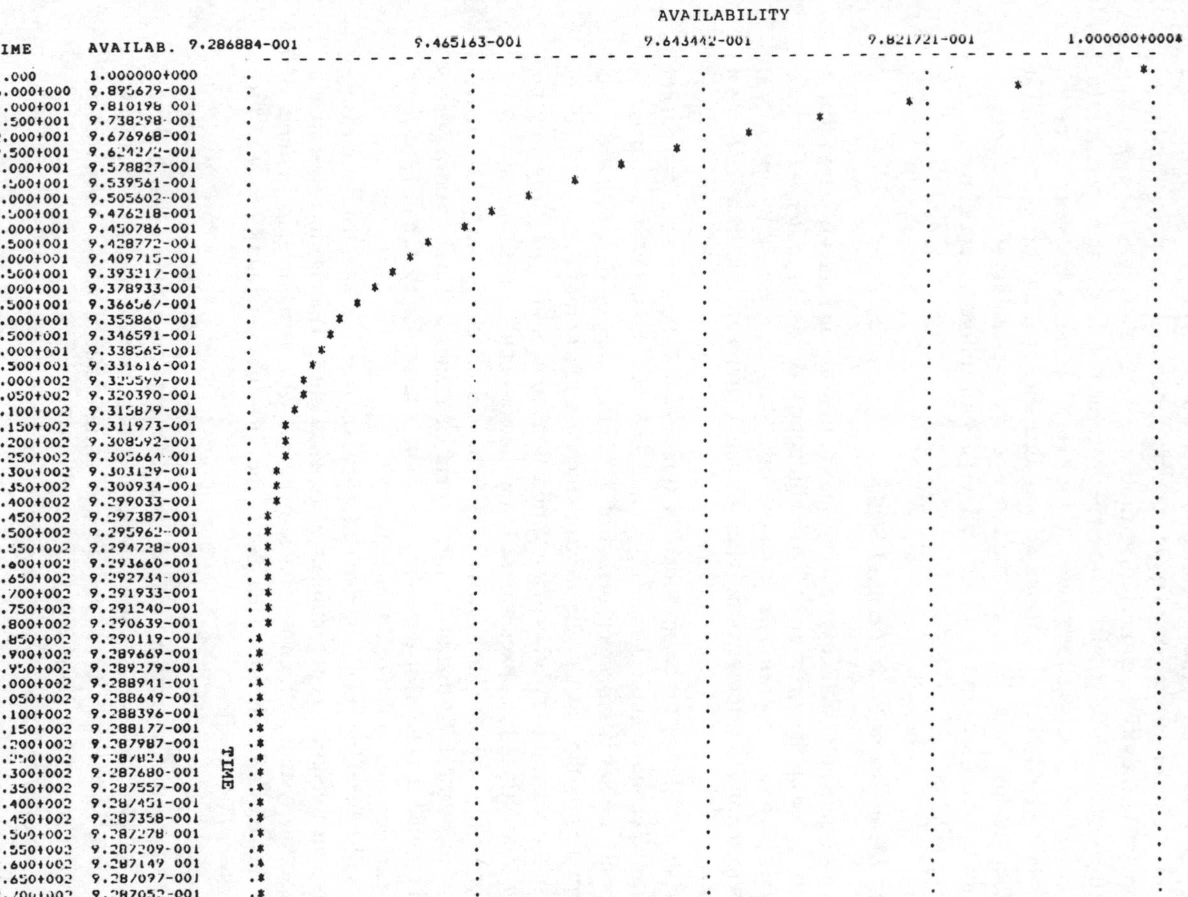

Fig. 16.5. Plot of availability vs. time for the example distributed database.

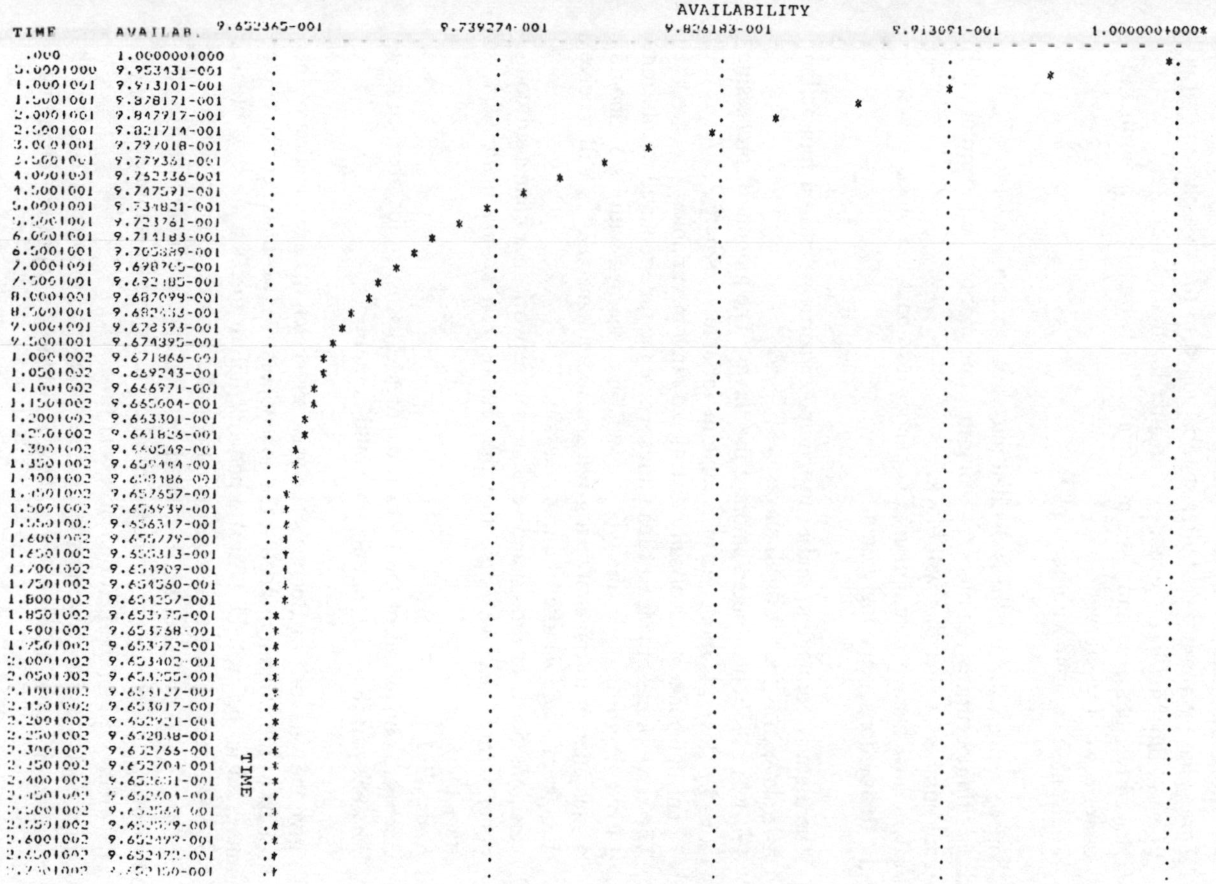

Fig. 16.6. Same as Fig. 16.5 but with duplication of (z).

2. Cooperating two-phase commit—slaves can communicate with each other for information about the transaction status.
3. Three-phase commit[22]—a buffer state is added to the two-phase commit to avoid blocking in the event of computer failure.
4. Nested two-phase commit[16]—a modification of two-phase commit that requires fewer messages.
5. Four-phase commit with backups.[22]

In Cooper's model, the system is divided into separate components* by a network partition occurring at time τ.** Using this information, he determines the expected number of sites that will block.

We will now list the assumptions Cooper makes about the physical system and the transactions executing therein.

a. There are N computers, and every computer participates in a transaction as a slave. S is the set of all slaves, $|S| = N$.
b. Work is evenly distributed amongst the slaves. The amount of processing done by slave j is modelled by a random variable T_j, where $T_1, T_2, \ldots, T_N$ are independent, identically distributed random variables.
c. The network has broadcast capabilities where the time required to transmit a fixed length message (the type we will be concerned with) is δ. Should n sites attempt to transmit to a given site s simultaneously, s will receive the last message $n\delta$ after the transmission.
d. Partitions occur at time τ and separate the network into connected components (note that we imply that the relation *can communicate with* is transitive).
e. $\delta \ll E[T_i]$.
f. Each site obtains all of the locks it requires. That is, in the absence of a network partition, the transaction would commit.

To give the "flavor" of Cooper's analysis, we sketch his examination of the least robust of the commit protocols, the noncooperative two-phase commit. We are interested in the probability that a network failure forces a slave to block, or as Cooper says, "that a partition occurs while a slave is in its *window of uncertainty*."[9] To evaluate the likelihood of blocking, we must quantify the window of uncertainty; $w(s)$ is the probability that slave s (running at site s) is in its window when the partition occurs at time τ.

Using a noncooperative two-phase commit, slaves can communicate only with the coordinator. Thus, in order for a slave s to block, a partition separating s

*As Cooper's model is independent of the system topology, he does not consider the likelihood of a given partition in his model.
**τ is not a random variable, it is fixed.

from the coordinator must occur after s voted yes (to the first phase message) but before s received the commit message.

If slave s sends its yes vote at time T_s, the last slave will send its message at

$$M = \max_{\sigma \in S} (T_\sigma).$$

The coordinator will receive the last yes vote at time $M + \delta$, and the slave will receive the commit message at time $M + 2\delta$. Therefore,

$$\begin{aligned} w(s) &= P(\textit{slave s is in its window of uncertainty}) \\ &= P[T_s \leq \tau \leq M + 2\delta]. \end{aligned}$$

We are interested in the expected number of sites that will block (let this be a random variable B) after the partition occurs. Let us introduce some notation; G_i represents the slaves that slave i can communicate with (including itself) at time τ. G_c represents the slaves that can communicate with the coordinator at time τ (one slave will be resident at the same site as the coordinator, thus $|G_c| \geq 1$).

Sites that cannot communicate with the coordinator (there are $N - |G_C|$ of them) are blocked. Thus

$$E[B] = [N - |G_c|]\, w(s).$$

Now let's look at the expected number of sites that will block using the cooperative scheme. In the event of a network partition, an uninformed slave can ask other slaves in the same group if they know the direction of the transaction. Understandably, slaves will block less frequently than before. For s to block, not only must s be detached from the coordinator, but every other slave in s's group (including s itself, of course) must be uninformed.

Thus, to evaluate the probability that slave s blocks, we should evaluate the probability that s's group, G, blocks. At time

$$M_g = \max_{\sigma \in G} (T_\sigma),$$

the last slave in G will send its yes vote, so that all sites in G will block if the partition occurs between this time and the time when the commit message arrives. The probability that G blocks then, is

$$w(G) = P[M_g \leq \tau \leq M + 2\delta],$$

and, similarly, we can compute the expected number of blocked sites for group G.

Using a three-phase commit, we can narrow the window of uncertainty even further by synchronizing the slaves. We do not describe the analyses of the remaining commit protocols, but proceed directly to a numerical example. Cooper evaluates $E[B]$ for each commit protocol, assuming that:

1. Processing time is exponentially distributed with parameter $\lambda = 10$;
2. $\delta = \frac{1}{2}$;
3. $N = 12$;
4. $|G|$, the size of the partition groups, equals 3; and
5. τ varies from 2.5 to 40.

In Fig. 16.7, Cooper plots the expected number of blocked sites as a function of the partition time. These results (and others obtained by him) give us a useful way to evaluate and compare commit protocols.

Chin *et al.* examines the behavior of commit-termination protocols in a network partition. However, their approach is different from the above work. Cooper

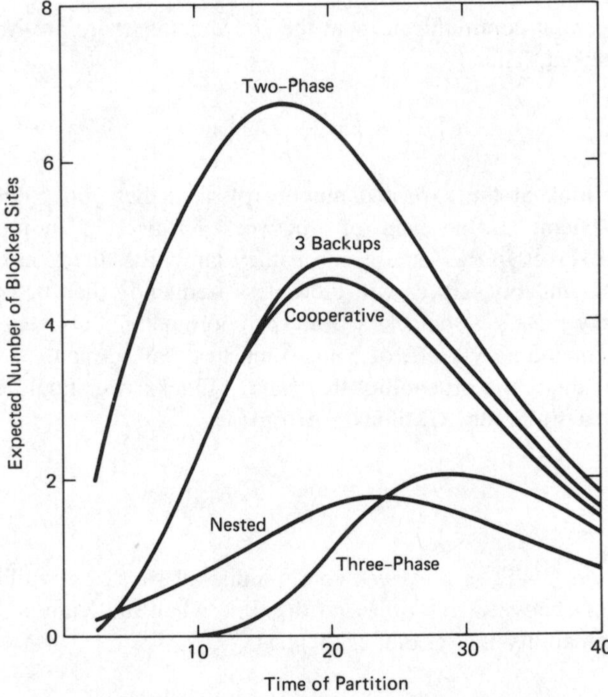

Fig. 16.7. Partition into 4 groups of 3 sites each.

evaluated previously existing commit protocols coupled with a straightforward termination protocol *TP*. If a group (partition) *G* contained an informed site or the coordinator, then *TP*, executing at sites in *G*, would direct these sites to the appropriate final state; otherwise *G* (all sites in *G*) would block. Chin *et al.* pose a more general question: For an arbitrary commit protocol *C*, what is the termination protocol TP_C that performs "best" (according to two different performance measures) in a network partition? To answer this question, they first describe the properties of TP_C. Then, using combinatorial arguments, they determine an optimal TP_C based on each measure.

A termination protocol executing at sites in *G* for commit protocol *C*, TP_C, has one function. It instructs sites in *G* to commit, abort, or wait until further repairs, while guaranteeing that no two sites will enter different final states.

Let us examine the possible termination protocols for a two-phase commit. We will modify the notation used earlier; a group *G* will now contain information about the states of slaves in *G*. Firstly, if a group *G* contains a site in the commit/abort state, *TP* will instruct all other sites in *G* to commit/abort. If *G* does not have such a site, then all sites in *G* must necessarily block until they can be sure of the transaction status. They cannot safely terminate until either *G* grows to G^1 (via a repair), where G^1 includes an informed site, or the system is completely repaired.

The termination protocols for every *blocking*[22] commit protocol are equally straightforward. (Skeen defines a blocking commit protocol as a protocol that can block, even if the network never fails.) As Chin *et al.* point out, only the *nonblocking* protocols are candidates for interesting termination protocols. They consider many such protocols in their paper; we will limit ourselves to Skeen's decentralized three-phase commit[22] (refer to Fig. 16.8). As a review, this commit protocol has two nonfinal states, *Wait* and *Prepare*. The *Wait* state is adjacent to the *Abort* state, the *Prepare* state is adjacent to the *Commit* state.

We want to construct an optimal termination protocol TP_{d3pc} for each of two measures. "Measure (1) is the number of components that would be left waiting over all possible partitions. It is relevant when most of the possible partitions (groups) are equally probable, for instance, in tree structured or ring structured network topologies."[8]

$$m_1 = \left| (G \mid G \textit{ is a group in a possible partition and } G \textit{ blocks}) \right| .$$

(Note that a so-called "nonblocking" protocol can still block if partitions occur.) The second measure represents the average number of sites that wait, not the number of groups.

$$m_2 = \sum_{G \textit{ blocked}} |G| .$$

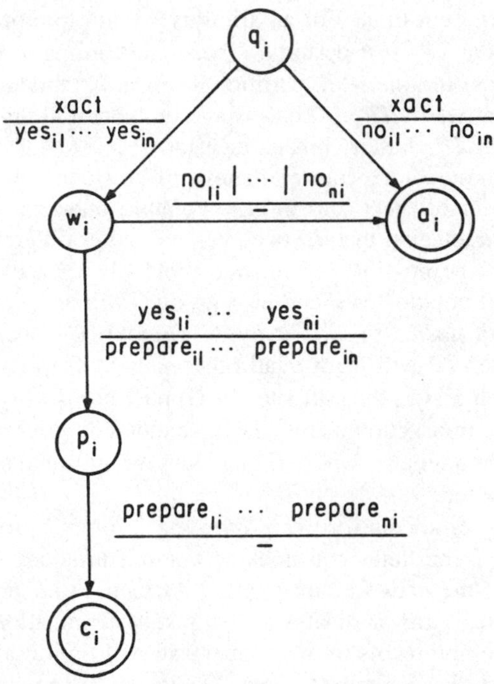

Fig. 16.8. The decentralized three-phase commit protocol.

Call termination protocols that perform best in the first sense *weakly optimal* and in the second sense *site optimal*.

Chin *et al.* determine a lower bound on the first performance measure for TP_{d3pc}. We refer the reader to reference 8 for details. Specifically, the authors show that $m_1 \geq 2^n - 2$, where n is the number of sites in the system. Can we construct a termination protocol, TP_{d3pc}, that achieves this lower bound? The answer, as we will soon see, is yes.

Let us describe this protocol. First, we must choose two non-negative numbers c and a, respectively termed the "commit quorum" and the "abort quorum." A group G will decide to commit, abort, or wait as follows: If G contains a site in the *Prepare* state and $|G| \geq c$, then G will commit (i.e., G has formed a commit quorum). Failing this, if G contains a site in the *Wait* state and $|G| \geq a$, then G will abort. Failing both of the above, G will wait (block) until further repairs. If we choose $a + c \geq n + 1$, then (using the above termination protocol) we can guarantee that no two groups in a network partition will reach different final states.

Let us evaluate m_1 and m_2 for the above protocol when $a = 1$, $c = n$, and $n = 4$. We need only consider groups not containing a final state (those containing a final state will not block, and thus do not contribute to m_1 or m_2). Thus, every group can only contain sites in the *Prepare* or *Wait* state. A group can contain from one to three sites. (A group with zero sites or with four sites does not correspond to a partition of the network.) For a group with i specific sites (slaves), there are 2^i different possible state combinations (each slave can be in the *Wait* or *Prepare* state). Further, there are $\binom{n}{i}$ different ways to pick the i slaves. To evaluate m_1 and m_2, we must consider the termination decisions of Q different groups (according to the quorum-based protocol described above) where:

$$Q = \sum_{i=1}^{3} \binom{n}{i} 2^i = 64.$$

The 64 groups and their termination decisions are illustrated in Fig. 16.9. A hyphen in column j indicates that slave j is not part of that particular group; otherwise the column contains the state of the slave. The letter to the right of a group is the group's decision; y is abort and w is wait. Also, at the bottom of Fig. 16.10, are the corresponding values for m_1 and m_2.

For arbitrary n, the quorum-based protocol with $a = 1$ and $c = n$ will block $2^n - 2$ sites. Thus, the termination protocol achieves the lower bound for m_1 (and is necessarily *weakly optimal*).

Using similar combinatorial arguments, Chin *et al.* derive a *site optimal* TP_{d3pc}. Can TP_{3pdc} be both *weakly optimal* and *site optimal*? The answer, as Chin *et al.* show, depends on n, the number of sites. Referring the reader to reference 8 for proofs, they show that: 1) for $n \geq 9$, there is no TP_{d3pc} which is both *weakly optimal* and *site optimal*; and 2) for TP_{d3pc} that is optimal in either sense, there is a partition of the network in which all groups must wait.

4.3. Number of Backed-out Transactions

Beyond causing sites to block, a failure may also force transactions to be backed-out or undone. Backing our transactions clearly wastes resources and slows down the system, so measuring (and minimizing) the number of backed-out transactions is important.

In a partitioned system with replicated data, backing out transactions is particularly costly. In such systems, the decision to backout a transaction is usually delayed until the partition is repaired, which may occur a considerable amount of time after the transaction was submitted. As the time between submission

1	2	3	4	
-	-	-	w	y
-	-	w	-	y
-	w	-	-	y
w	-	-	-	y
-	-	w	w	y
-	w	-	w	y
w	-	-	w	y
-	w	w	-	y
w	-	w	-	y
w	w	-	-	y
-	w	w	w	y
w	-	w	w	y
w	w	-	w	y
w	w	w	-	y

1	2	3	4	
-	-	-	p	w
-	-	p	-	w
-	p	-	-	w
p	-	-	-	w
-	-	p	p	w
-	p	-	p	w
p	-	-	p	w
-	p	p	-	w
p	-	p	-	w
p	p	-	-	w
-	p	p	p	w
p	-	p	p	w
p	p	-	p	w
p	p	p	-	w

1	2	3	4	
w	p	-	-	y
p	w	-	-	y
w	-	p	-	y
p	-	w	-	y
w	-	-	p	y
p	-	-	w	y
-	w	p	-	y
-	p	w	-	y
-	w	-	p	y
-	p	-	w	y
-	-	p	w	y
-	-	w	p	y
w	w	p	-	y
w	p	w	-	y
p	w	w	-	y
p	p	w	-	y
p	w	p	-	y
w	p	p	-	y
w	w	-	p	y
w	p	-	w	y
p	w	-	w	y
p	p	-	w	y
p	w	-	p	y
w	p	-	p	y
w	-	w	p	y
w	-	p	w	y
p	-	w	w	y
p	-	p	w	y
p	-	w	p	y
w	-	p	p	y
-	w	w	p	y
-	w	p	w	y
-	p	w	w	y
-	p	p	w	y
-	p	w	p	y
-	w	p	p	y

number of groups = 64
y = abort
w = wait

Fig. 16.9. Tabular representation of the quorum-based TP with a = 1, c = n for n = 4.

$$m_1 = \{s \mid f(s) = w\} = \text{number of waiting components} = 2^n - 2 = 14$$

$$m_2 = \sum_{f(s)=w} |s| = \text{number of waiting sites} = \sum_{k=1}^{n-1} k\binom{n}{k} = 28$$

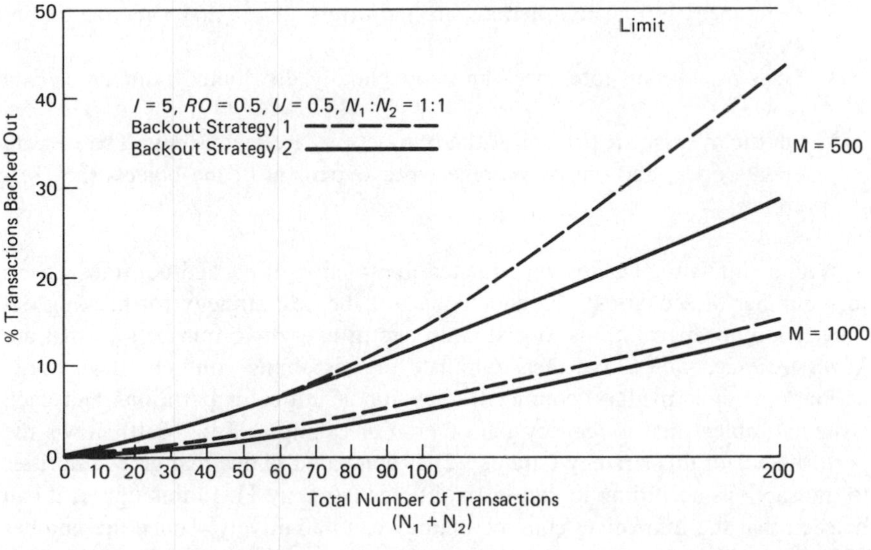

Fig. 16.10.

and backout grows, the inconvenience to the user also increases (he must wait longer to be sure of the outcome of his transaction). Thus, in this environment, it is especially important that we minimize the number of backouts.

For example, consider a car rental database which (for reliability) has been duplicated at two computers. A customer calls the company to reserve a car at the London airport, but at that time the link between the two computers is down (the system is partitioned). Not wanting to lose this customer, the company issues a tentative reservation, assuming that the number of cars at London will be sufficient to satisfy the reservations made independently during the partition. When the link between the computers is repaired, the system will check to see if there are enough cars. If there are not, some reservations will be canceled (backed-out), and this may be inconvenient to the affected customers. Thus, it is important to reduce the number of backouts, both by reducing the frequency and duration of partitions, and by intelligently backing out transactions at repair time.

S. Davidson[10] has studied this measure and has used it to compare backout strategies for partitioned, replicated database systems. Her model includes the following assumptions and parameters:

1. There are a fixed number, M, of data objects, and each is duplicated at two sites.
2. The first site processes N_1 transactions during the partition, and the second one N_2.

3. References by the transactions are uniformly distributed over the M objects.
4. Each transaction references an exponentially distributed number of data objects.
5. On the average, R percent of the transactions are ready-only. The rest are update ones, and on the average write U percent of the objects they reference.

With a simulator, Davidson computed the fraction of backed-out transactions in a number of scenarios. She concluded that the best strategy for backing out transaction at repair time is to first undo one of every two transactions that are in *immediate conflict*, and then eliminate the remaining conflicts. Two transactions are in immediate conflict if they run in different partitions and each writes an object that is read by the other. For example, Fig. 16.10 shows the performance of this strategy (strategy 2) as compared to one that gives priorities to transactions according to their arrival times (strategy 1). In this figure, it can be seen that the immediate conflict strategy can definitively reduce the number of backouts in some cases. Although we do not cover them here, Davidson also discusses how the minimal number of transactions can be selected to break all immediate conflicts, and other factors which may reduce the number of backouts.

4.4. Mean Computation Before Failure

MCBF (Mean Computation Before Failure)[3] is the average amount of work that the system can perform before failing. When the system as a whole can either be up or down, the mean time to failure (MTTF) is a useful measure of reliability. However, in gracefully degrading systems, a better measure may be the mean amount of useful work (computation) that can be performed before a failure occurs (MCBF). Such a measure is proposed by Beaudry. "Measures such as MTTF are appropriate for ultra-reliable systems; however, they may not be sufficient for evaluating gracefully degrading systems. In contrast to the ultra-reliable architectures, gracefully degrading systems may use redundancy in computing resources to gain performance as well as to increase system reliability. Gracefully degrading systems retract to a detected failure by reconfiguring to a state which may have a decreased level of performance. For example, if a single processor of a multiprocessor system fails, the system may continue to operate without the faulty processor, but has a lower level of performance until the processor can be repaired and reconfigured into the system again."[3]

We have computed MTTF in Section 2, and computing MCBF is similar. Firstly, we model the system as a continuous-time Markov chain. Failure and repair rates are thus approximated by an exponential distribution. Next, we associate with each state a number α. This is a measure of the state's computational capacity; a large α indicates that work can be done quickly. "Many factors can influence α. For example, system overhead due to dynamic testing, error detection recovery, an increase in the transaction arrival rate, a change in operating system functions, all can decrease the computation capacity of the system."[3]

Let us illustrate the computation of MCBF by an example. We will consider a computer with n processors, running software designed for parallel computation of differential equations (the application is not important). The program solves an equation slower with only one working processor than it does with n processors. That is, if α_i is the working capacity of a state with i computers operational, then $\alpha_i > \alpha_{i-1}$.

We shall model the system above using a Markov chain (refer to Fig. 16.11). The inter-failure and inter-repair times are exponentially distributed, respectively with mean λ and μ. Let $MCBF_i$ be the mean computation before failure given that the system is in state i. Figure 16.11 also shows how $MCBF_3$ can be expressed in terms of $MCBF_2$ and $MCBF_4$. In general, for $0 < i < n$,

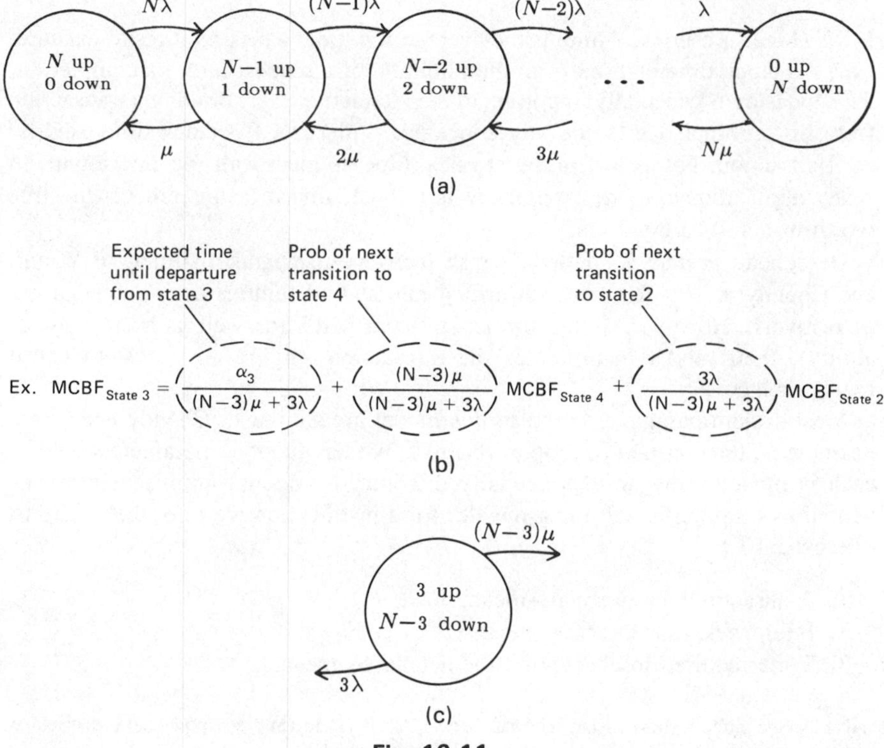

Fig. 16.11

$$MCBF_i = \frac{1}{i\lambda + (n-i)\mu}\alpha_i + \frac{(n-i)\rho}{i\lambda + (n-i)\mu} MCBF_{i-1}$$
$$+ \frac{i\lambda}{i\lambda + (n-i)\rho} MCBF_{i+1}.$$

If $i = 1$ or $i = n$, the terms for $MCBF_0$ and $MCBF_{n+1}$ are dropped from the equation, and, after solving a system of $n + 2$ equations, we have the desired values.

Beaudry describes some other performance measures related to her model. For instance, *computational availability* is the average amount of computation that can be done by the system per unit time (in the steady state).

$$\textit{Computational Availability} = \sum_{i \in X^+} \alpha_i p_i(\infty)$$

where (as before), $p_i(t)$ is the probability that the system is in state i at time t.

4.5. Mean Response Time

MRT (Mean Response Time) is the average *real* time a task requires to execute, i.e., the clock time elapsed from the initiation of a request until its completion. This measure is especially important to the interactive user, running a transaction from his terminal. He is not only concerned with the CPU clock time used by the transaction, but also with the physical time he must wait for turnaround. In many applications where expediency is critical, this measure reflects the true worth of a software system.

Derochette *et al.*[11] modelled a crash recovery mechanism similar to Young and Chandy *et al.*, i.e., constant arrival rate and no failures during checkpoint or recovery. However, as the former measure MRT (as well as system availability), their model incorporates the transaction surge after a system pause (crash or recovery).

Most system parameters used in this model are similar to Chandy *et al.* (for example K, the constant of proportionality). We list the other parameters below; each is modelled by an exponentially distributed random variable. The exponential assumption is not unreasonable; for a justification we refer the reader to reference 10.*

1. Transactions interarrival—mean: $1/\lambda$.
2. Intercheckpoint interval—mean: T
3. Time required to checkpoint the database—mean: Z

*Actually the authors show (using renewal theory) that if (1) to (5) are exponentially distributed and γ is small, then (6) is necessarily exponentially distributed.

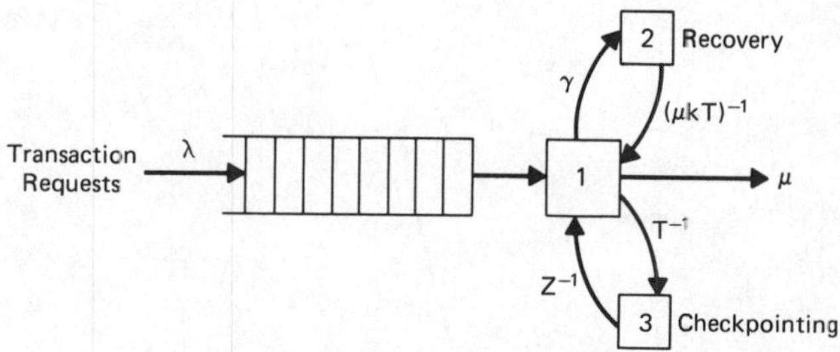

Fig. 16.12.

4. Transaction interprocessing—mean: $1/\mu$
5. Inter-failure time—mean: $1/\gamma$
6. Time required to recover—mean: μKT

Let us motivate the derivation of (6). In the event of a failure, T time has elapsed, on average, since the last checkpoint. μT is the average amount of processing done since the last checkpoint. μKT corresponds to the average time needed to reprocess the transactions interrupted by a failure. K takes into account the percentage of transactions that modified the database and the speed at which these transactions can be redone.*

Now that we have described the system parameters, we can state more formally the authors' objective. They wish to determine optimal checkpoint intervals T^0 and T^1. T^0 is the expected value of an intercheckpoint interval that maximizes availability, similarly T^1 minimizes *MRT*.

The authors describe the system via a queueing model (refer to Fig. 16.12). Transactions enter the system at rate λ. There, they are either processed, or suspended due to checkpoint or recovery. From the figure, we see that the system (server) can be in three different states. In state 1, the system processes transactions at rate μ. In state 2, the system is checkpointing the database, and in state 3 the system is recovering from a computer failure.

Using queue-theoretic techniques to analyze the model, the authors evaluate T^0 and T^1. Summarizing their main result, "the value of T^0 can be a very bad choice for average intercheckpoint interval, if we are interested in minimizing *MRT* to transactions."[11] To illustrate this, in Fig. 16.13 we see MRT (W) and availability (A) plotted against average intercheckpoint interval *T*. The optimum for *MRT*, T^1, clearly differs from the optimum for availability, T^0.

Garcia et al.[14] also use *MRT* as a measure of availability, describing a technique for evaluating the mean response time of a user request in a distributed system. They define the computational needs of a task *T* as the amount of time

*The speed at which transaction are redone depends upon the logging mechanism used.

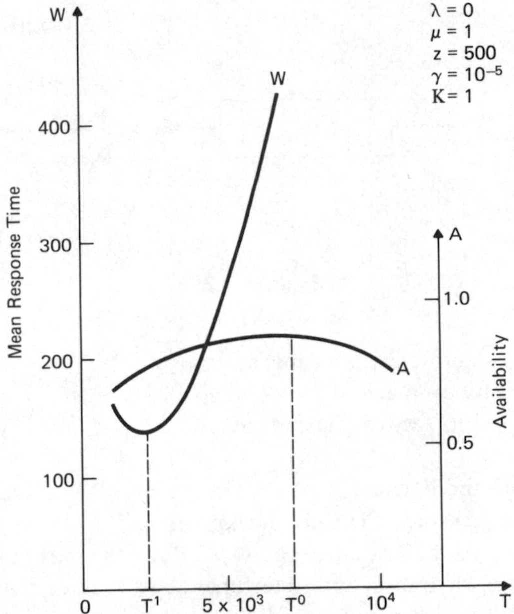

Fig. 16.13. Average intercheckpoint interval.

T requires to execute in the distributed system, given that no failures occur and that there is no interference from other tasks (this particular scenario is later referred to as a reference state). The authors determine, via this modelling technique, the expected time T requires to run in this distributed system, given that failures occur.

To describe the distributed system, Garcia *et al.* use a model similar to Beaudry (previous section), but with extra information. As in Beaudry, every operational state has associated with it a number α; this number measures how quickly a transaction can be processed in the state. The alphas are input parameters to the model and can either be measured or obtained through simulation.

Consider the distributed system we modelled in the example of Section 2. Figure 16.14 shows the model for the system of Fig. 16.1 running a certain update algorithm which does reconfigurations after failures or repairs. In this case, the task is an update transaction T, and let us assume that T is submitted by a user at computer C1. State 1 represents the system when both the computers are in normal operation. Since work can be done in this state, $\alpha(1) > 0$. This state is called a *working state*, as work can be performed on the task in this state and no work is ever lost upon entry.

When computer C2 fails, the system does not go directly into state 2 (C1 =

up, C2 = down) as reconfiguration is necessary. State 7 models the reconfiguration phase of C1 where no updates are processed.[15] Work cannot be done in this state, but no work was lost upon entry. For this reason, we call state 7 a *pause state*. C1 may fail or C2 may be repaired, so that in state 7 there are not only transitions into state 2 but also state 4 (C1 = down, C2 = up) and state 5 (C1 and C2 reconfiguring together). For the same reasons as above, state 4 is a working state and state 5 is a pause state. The observant reader will notice that $\alpha(2) < \alpha(1)$. This occurs because, in state 1, updates require a two-phase commit protocol,[16] involving at least two rounds of messages between computer C1 and C2. In state 2 however, computer C1 processes updates by itself, so messages are not needed. That is, in state 2, computer C2 cannot interfere and slow C1 down.

Now, let us consider the events that would transpire (according to our update algorithm) when C1 fails (Remember that T is submitted to C1). As C2 reconfigures and processes updates, C1 cannot continue processing transactions in progress during the failure. Instead, these transactions must be aborted. As all work accomplished by T is lost upon entry to state 1, it is termed a *crash state*.

We shall model the time required for C1 to 'catch up' (get an up-to-date copy of the data) by adding the pause state 5.

As in Beaudry, the authors model the system (both hardware and software) by a Markov process. Each state i contains not only transition information but also a constant indicating how quickly work can be performed in i (if at all) and whether entry into i causes work to be lost.

It is important to note that inherent in the model of Fig. 16.14 are many assumptions about the algorithm for processing updates. Clearly, using different assumptions yields different models. For example, Fig. 16.15 models an algorithm with no reconfigurations. Here, a lone computer never processes updates.

After modelling the system, we can evaluate its performance and the expected time the system will require to complete transaction T (submitted at C1). Suppose that T is submitted when the system is in state 1. If the transaction needs X seconds to complete in the reference system, and the system stays in state 1 more than $\alpha(i)X$ seconds, the request completes in 1. But several other sequences of events might occur. For example, consider the following scenario: C1 crashes before the user request is completed, C1 is eventually repaired, and the system returns to state 1. Here, the request is restarted and completes before any further failures. The above sequences contribute to the expected duration of a user request according to the probability that the sequence occurs and the expected duration of the sequence.

By considering all possible sequences of events, we can compute the expected duration of a user request. Since there are an infinite number of sequences, we only consider those that contribute "significantly" to the expected value.

We now give a brief example to illustrate the use of our evaluation technique

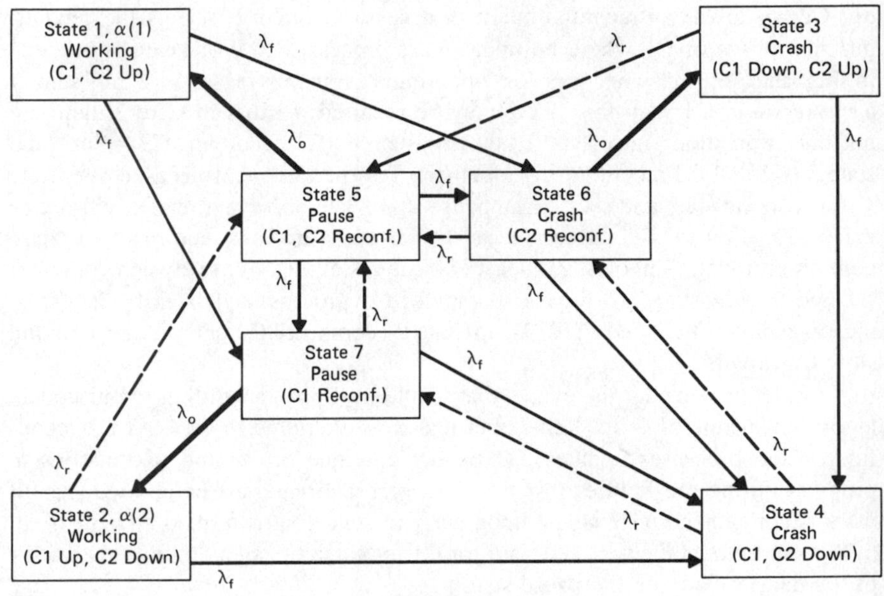

Fig. 16.14.

and the results that it can produce. Suppose that we wish to compare the two options (that we have presented) for managing dual copies of a database in a distributed computing system. Option 1 allows reconfigurations while option 2 forces updates to be processed only when both computers are up.

Let us assume that after studying the hardware and the algorithms, we come up with the following values:

1. The average time between computer failures is 10 hours ($= 1/\lambda_f$);
2. The average time to repair a computer is 0.5 hours ($= 1/\lambda_r$);

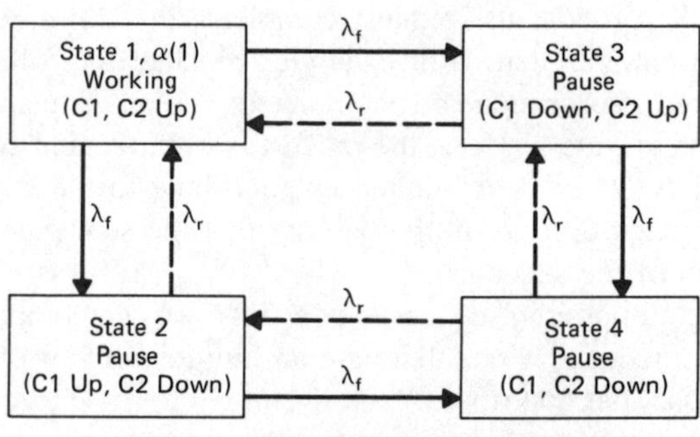

Fig. 16.15.

Table 16.1. Expected Durations of User Requests

Computing Requirements	Duration With Reconfigurations			Duration Without Reconfigurations	
	starting in node1	starting in node2	starting in node1 given failure occurred	starting in node1	starting in node1 given failure occurred
0.25	0.265	0.151	0.533	0.276	0.775
0.50	0.534	0.331	0.852	0.551	1.04
0.75	0.807	0.536	1.16	0.827	1.30
1.00	1.08	0.761	1.47	1.10	1.57
3.00	3.54	3.06	4.19	3.31	3.68
5.00	8.49	5.99	7.36	5.51	5.81
8.00	12.1	11.6	13.2	8.82	9.03

3. The average reconfiguration time is 0.01 hours ($= 1/\lambda_o$);
4. In both alternatives, the power of state 1 is $\alpha(1)$;
5. In the reconfiguration alternative, $\alpha(2) = 0.5$.

Table 16.1 presents some of the results that can be obtained by analyzing the two work graphs. Variable X is the time it takes to execute the user request on the reference system. As expected, as X decreases, the expected time to complete the request approaches $\alpha(i)X$, where i is the starting node. As X grows and the probability of encountering a failure grows, the expected duration increases. (With the reconfiguration alternative, the requests started when the system is in state 2 take less time to execute, because of the reduced overhead for processing update requests.) Notice that for small X, the reconfiguration alternative is better because work can be performed while computer C2 is down. However, as X grows, the no reconfiguration strategy is best. In this case, the benefits of performing work when C2 is down are outweighed by the risk of losing work when C1 crashes.

Table 16.1 also gives the expected duration of a user request given that a failure occurs. As can be expected, this measure is more sensitive to variations in crash recovery strategies.

5. CONCLUSION

In this chapter, we have surveyed models and measures that have been used to evaluate reliable systems. We want to emphasize that, while we included several systems for each measure, it is especially advisable in reliability-performance modelling to try different measures for a given system.

Let us consider the analysis of Cooper as an example. Based on his measure (the expected number of blocked sites in a network partition) and sample data, three-phase commit and nested two-phase commit perform the best. But there are other aspects of commit protocols we should consider.*

Suppose we measure the number of messages sent out by a commit protocol. Too many messages can congest the communication network and cause processing delays. The three-phase commit examined by Cooper requires $5N$ messages, where N is the number of sites involved in the protocol. The nested two-phase commit requires only $2N$ messages. Evaluating protocols solely on the basis of this measure would rule out the three-phase commit and strongly favor the nested two-phase commit.

What if we measure a commit protocol's end to end delay, i.e., the number of message rounds required to complete a commit protocol. This measure directly relates to the MRT of a transaction, as transactions use commit protocols during their execution. The nested two-phase commit requires $2N$ message rounds, more than any of the other commit protocols. Certainly we would not choose it if we ranked commit protocols only by end to end delay.

We can see from the above that there rarely is one measure that tells us all about a system; whenever possible we should combine measures to better appraise a system's worth. Note that Gelenbe evaluates the availability and mean response of a crash recovery system. Chin *et al.* describe alternate ways of measuring blocked sites. Beaudry uses four measures to evaluate gracefully degrading systems, we discussed only two.

We do not want to imply that combining analytical measures is a performance evaluation panacea. When we cannot accurately model even very restrictive measures, we must consider other options.

Often simulation is a viable alternative. Using simulations, we can more closely approximate the behavior of the real system than with analytical techniques. And for many applications, a few carefully chosen graphs generated by a simulation are sufficient to describe the interaction of the system parameters.

How do we choose between simulation and analytical modelling? How intricately do we model the system, e.g., what parts of the system can be considered irrelevant to the model? In evaluating reliable systems, as in any type of performance evaluation, we are confronted with these tradeoffs between accuracy and complexity. To resolve them, we must determine when the extra resources (e.g. computer time, man-hours) required by a "complex" analysis justify expanding a simpler analysis.

---

*Cooper mentioned some of these other aspects in his paper. But his analysis dealt only with the expected number of blocked sites.

As an example, Chandy *et al.* elaborate on their model in Section 3 to describe a more realistic crash recovery mechanism. This newer model describes a system where the transaction arrival rate varies cyclically (thus they omit assumption 5 of Section 3). Is it superior to the old model? In a case study the authors did for the Nuclear Ordinance Logistics System, using the old model they obtained an optimum availability of $\frac{17}{18}$ by spacing the checkpoints every 12 hours. The newer model was able to exploit the cyclic nature of the transaction arrivals. With it, the authors discovered that one checkpoint at lunch and another at the end of the shift would maximize availability at $\frac{23}{24}$.*

REFERENCES

1. Alsberg, P. A. and J. D. Day, A principle for sharing of distributed resources, *Proc. 2nd Int. Conf. on Software Engineering*, San Francisco, CA, Oct. 13–15, 1976, pg. 558.
2. Barlow, R. E. and F. Proschan, *Mathematical Theory of Reliability*, New York: Wiley, 1965.
3. Beaudry, M. D., Performance-related reliability measures for computing systems, *IEEE Trans. Computers*, vol. C-27, pp. 540–547, June 1978.
4. Bernstein, P. A. and N. Goodman, Concurrency control in distributed database systems, *ACM Comput. Surveys*, vol. 13, pp. 185–221, June 1981.
5. Boes, D., F. Graybill, and A. Mood, *Introduction to the Theory of Statistics*, New York: McGraw-Hill, 1974.
6. Buzacott, John, Markov approach to finding failure times of repairable systems, *IEEE Trans. Reliability*, vol. 4, pp. 128–133, Nov. 1970.
7. Chandy, K. M., J. C. Browne, C. W. Dissly, and W. R. Uhrig, Analytic models for rollback and recovery strategies in database systems, *IEEE Trans. Software Engineering*, vol. SE-1, pp. 100–110, March 1975.
8. Chin, F., and K. V. S. Ramarao, Optimal Termination Protocols for Network Partitioning, *Tech. Rep.*, Dept. of Comp. Sci., University of Alberta, Canada, Oct. 1982.
9. Cooper, E. C., Analysis of distributed commit protocols, in *ACM Int. Conf. on Management of Data*, June 1982, pp. 175–183.
10. Davidson, S., *Evaluation of an Optimistic Protocol for Partitioned Distributed Database Systems*, Tech. Rep. 299, Department of Electrical Engineering and Computer Science, Princeton University, May 1982.
11. Derochette, D. and E. Gelenbe, Performance of rollback and recovery systems under intermittent failures, *ACM Operating Systems*, vol. 21, pp. 493–499, June 1978.
12. Eswaran, K. P., J. N. Gray, R. A. Lorie, and I. L. Traiger, The notions of consistency and predicate locks in a database system, *ACM*, vol. 19, pp. 624–633, Nov. 1976.
13. Ferrari, D., *Computer Systems Performance Evaluation*, Englewood Cliffs, NJ: Prentice-Hall, 1978.
14. Garcia-Molina, H. and J. Kent, A technique for evaluating the performance and reliability of distributed computing systems, Tech. Rep. 291, Princeton University, Dec. 1981.
15. Garcia-Molina, H., Reliability issues for fully replicated databases, *Computer*, pp. 31–42, Sept. 1982.
16. Gray, J. N., Notes on database operating systems, in *Operating Systems: An Advanced Course*, R. Bayer *et al.* eds., Berlin: Springer-Verlag, 1979, pp. 393–481.

*Note that the actual checkpoint times must be specified in the new model as the arrival rate varies.

17. Kohler, W., A survey of techniques for the synchronization and recovery in distributed computing systems, *ACM Comput. Surveys*, vol. 13, pp. 149–183, June 1981.
18. Kleinrock, L., *Queueing Systems (Vol. 1: Theory)*, New York: John Wiley, 1975.
19. Martella, G., B. Ronchetti, and F. A. Schreiber, *Availability Evaluation in Distriubted Database Systems, Performance Evaluation*, Amsterdam: North Holland, pp. 1, 3, 1981.
20. Rothnie, J. B. and N. Goodman, A survey of techniques of research and development in distributed database management, in *Proc. 3rd VLDB Conf.*, Tokyo, Japan, 1977, pp. 48–62.
21. Singh, C. and R. Billinton, *System Reliability Modelling and Evaluation*, Hutchinson Company, 1977.
22. Skeen, D., *Crash Recovery in a Distributed Database System* (Ph.D. diss.), University of California at Berkeley, UCB/ERL M82/45, 1982.
23. Thomas, R. H., A. solution to the concurrrency control problem for multiple copy databases, in *Proc. IEEE Compcon*, San Francisco, CA, Spring 1978, pp. 56–62.
24. Young, J. W., A first order approximation to the optimum checkpoint interval, *ACM*, vol. 17, pp. 530–531, Sept. 1974.

17. Names and Name Resolution

DOUGLAS E. COMER

and

LARRY L. PETERSON

ABSTRACT

Naming is an important issue in any programming system, especially when the system spans multiple computers. In this chapter, we will survey the naming mechanism in several distributed systems, and we describe the underlying principles of names and name resolution in distributed systems. We also define familiar concepts and terminology involved in naming, and we describe the role of name servers in name resolution.

1. INTRODUCTION

A significant characteristic of any computing system is the way in which objects in the system are named. The mapping of names into the objects they represent is the responsibility of the computing system's *name resolution mechanism*. Because the naming mechanism supports references to objects, it directly influences both the ease with which users refer to objects, and the degree of object sharing allowed in the system. Although, in practice, a distributed system's name resolution mechanism is tied to other components of the system (e.g., the protection mechanism), we will focus on only those issues directly related to naming in this chapter.

We are going to characterize distributed systems as consisting of multiple processing components that are physically distributed and that interact through a communications network. In addition, a set of services unifies the distributed system and provides access to the resources comprising the system.[20] In practice,

This work was supported in part by grants from the National Science Foundation (MCS-8219178) and SUN Microsystems Inc.

distributed systems range from tightly coupled distributed operating systems, to very loosely coupled mail systems. We shall survey the naming mechanism supported by several distributed systems in the rest of this section, and we will discuss existing models of naming in Section 2. We are then going to present an alternative model that describes the underlying principles of naming in Section 3, look at an example naming system in Section 4 and explore the types of names found in distributed systems based upon the model in Section 5. Finally, we shall investigate the role of name servers in name resolution in Section 6, explore naming in computer networks in Section 7, and discuss the relationship between object relocation and name resolution in Section 8.

1.1. Distributed Operating Systems

Distributed Operating Systems (*DOS*) such as the Newcastle Connection,[5] LOCUS,[37] Accent,[27] TILDE,[9] EDEN,[2] and the V-System,[6] consist of a collection of computers connected by a local area network. The *DOS* provides users of the system with access to the same types of objects as centralized operating systems: files, compilers, printers, etc. Users identify objects as though they are local, even if they are implemented on remote computers; the *DOS* hides the distributed nature of the environment by providing transparent access to the component resources.

For example, consider several implementations of a naming mechanism for a UNIX-like file system.[28] On a single processor system, each file is named by possibly many high-level *path* names described by a tree structure, a single unique identifier called an *i-number*, and a low-level name consisting of the disk at which the file can be found. In a distributed system that does not support location transparency, users identify a file with both a path name for the file, and the computer (*host*), on which the file resides (e.g. *host*:*file*). The Newcastle project incorporates the host name into the path name, resulting in a file name of the form */. . ./host/path*. (The Newcastle approach also allows for multiple levels of hosts within the hierarchy.)

In the LOCUS system, however, users name files with standard UNIX path names. Also associated with each file is a low-level name that specifies where in the system the file currently resides. The lower-level name consists of a *file system* name (roughly corresponding to a host), and a *file descriptor* that identifies the file within the file system. The file system name in turn maps into the network address(es) of the host(s) on which the file can be found. We schematically depict LOCUS names in Fig. 17.1.

The LOCUS naming mechanism not only allows users to name files in the same way they do on a single-processor system, but it also hides the physical location of the file, thus allowing the system to relocate the file without the user's knowledge.

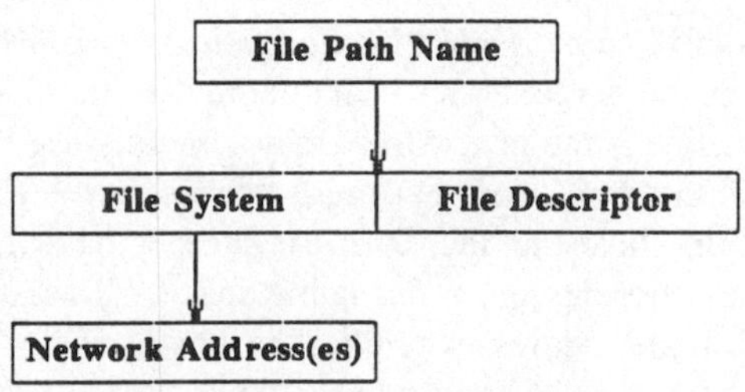

Fig. 17.1. LOCUS names.

The TILDE system also supports location transparency, but unlike LOCUS, it uses a different approach to high-level names for files. Instead of arranging files in a single tree structure, TILDE organizes names into a forest of tree structured directories. The TILDE scheme supports location transparent names for files across the entire *DARPA* Internet, rather than in only the local distributed system.

Finally, we consider the V-System's naming mechanism for processes. First, an identifier called a *logical-id*, is associated with each service offered in the system (i.e., there exists a logical-id for the file server, another for the name server, etc.) Each logical-id is in turn bound to a process-id (*pid*) that identifies both a network address for the host on which the process executes, and a local process-id for the process. Like location transparent file names in LOCUS and TILDE, logical-ids for processes can be rebound to a different location without affecting the users or application programs.

1.2. XEROX Internet

On the larger scale, XEROX interconnects individual local area networks to form an internet. Users work on workstations connected to the internet, and request services from server processors that are also connected to the internet. *GRAPEVINE*,[3] for example, provides a mechanism for users to send messages to each other by implementing a message service and a registration service. Users register themselves with a certain registry. Programs running on behalf of message senders access the registration service to locate a message server willing to accept the message for the recipient. Users identify each other for the purpose of sending mail with names of the form *F.R*, where *R* identifies a registry, and *F* denotes a user that is registered at that registry. *F* is bound to the network address of a mail server willing to accept the user's mail.

1.3. DARPA Internet

Even though the distributed system supported by XEROX is physically larger than those that implement *DOS*, it is still under the auspices of a single authority.

The *DARPA* Internet is an example of a distributed system in which the component processors have a large degree of autonomy. In the *DARPA* Internet, the primary shared resource is the host. Users may remotely log into a remote host, access files on a remote host, and send mail to a user on a remote host.

From its inception, hosts in the *DARPA* Internet have been identified by alphanumeric names chosen from a *flat* name space. The database of bindings of host names to Internet addresses (called the *host table*), is maintained by a central authority that oversees changes to the table, and distributes copies of the table to every host in the Internet. Because the table must be distributed to all hosts in the Internet whenever changes are made, the centralized host table approach assumes that changes happen infrequently, and that the number of hosts remains relatively small.

As the number of hosts in the *DARPA* Internet has grown larger in recent years, the flat name space has become impractical. The domain name project offers a solution by replacing the flat name space with a hierarchical one[21,22,26] (i.e., names are described by a tree-like structure). Structuring the name space in a hierarchy allows the central authority to delegate responsibility over the collection of name to address bindings; the single host table is partitioned and distributed over multiple databases, thus making the name space more manageable.

Domain names are resolved into Internet address by a hierarchy of naming authorities, called *domains*, each of which defines an interpretation of a set of simple names. That is, each domain partially resolves a full domain name. The top level of the hierarcy is initially partitioned into five categories: education, government, commercial, military, and other organizations. Additional levels of the hierarchy are defined as needed, with no limit on the height of the domain-name tree. For example, a host named *arthur* in the Computer Science Department at Purdue University might be named *arthur.CS.Purdue.EDU* in the domain-name scheme. Notice that domain names, when read right to left, specify a path in a conceptual tree of domains from the root to a leaf.

The conceptual naming graph is implemented by partitioning the set of domains into *zones*, such that the bindings contained in the domains of a given zone are managed by a *name server*.* That is, the name servers that implement the hierarchical naming system are themselves hierarchically distributed throughout the Internet. To resolve a domain name, a *resolver* program running on the behalf of a user might first contact the root name server (i.e., a name server that implements the bindings in the root domain), which in turn contacts a name server that implements a lower-level zone. Eventually, a name server is contacted that returns the appropriate Internet address.

---

*For efficiency, name servers cache information from other zones, and for reliability the bindings in a given zone may be contained in multiple name servers.

1.4. Computer Mail

While processors in many distributed systems cooperate so that all resources in the system can be accessed by all users in the system, processors in computer mail systems only cooperate to the degree necessary to exchange mail. That is, the only nameable resource is the computer *mailbox*. The underlying computer mail system consists of a confederation of interconnected delivery systems. Users on a single computer system share a *local* mail delivery system. If computer systems communicate through shared protocols they may cooperate to form a *network-wide* delivery system. When computer systems are connected to more than one network, network delivery systems overlap to form a *global* mail system.[1] Hosts that connect networks and pass mail from one to the other are called *mail bridges* or *relays*.

On networks like the *DARPA* Internet,[25] mailbox address contains information identifying a user on a specific host. For example, a sender might identify John Doe, a computer scientist at the National Laboratory, as *jxd@nlabs*, where *jxd* is John Doe's login identifier, and *nlabs* is the official *DARPA* host name for the computer he uses.

On networks like *UUCP*,[23] however, the mailbox address must specify all the intermediate computers through which the message must travel to reach the destination computer. For example, if the sender's computer is connected to a computer named *host1*, which is connected to another computer named *host2*, which is in turn connected to *nlabs*, the sender might specify John Doe's *UUCP* mailbox address as *host1!host2!nlabs!jxd*. *UUCP* style addresses are called *source-route* address[35] because the route through the network is specified at the source computer. *UUCP* names are also called *relative* names because they must be interpreted relative to the starting point.

When the recipient's mailbox exists on a remote network, the address must identify the mail bridges that the message needs to cross. For example, if we consider *nlabs* to be a mail bridge between the *UUCP* and *DARPA* Internet networks, and John Smith is a user with login identifier *jxs* on the *DARPA* host *stateu*, then the sender in the previous example might address John Smith at State University as *host1!host2!nlabs!jxs@stateu*, meaning that the message must be passed from *host1* to *host2* and then to *nlabs*, where *nlabs* acts as a relay and forwards the message to *stateu*.

Finally, just as many *DOS*s support high-level names that hide the location of objects, there exist name servers for computer mail that allow users to name mailboxes with high-level names. For example, work on the *CSNET* project by Denning and Comer,[13] and Solomon, Landweber, and Neuhegen,[34] allows users to identify a recipient with a set of *attribute-value* pairs. A name server then returns the *unique identifier* for the recipient, as well as maps the identifier into a mailbox address so that delivery can be performed. The model divides the binding of a high-level name for a recipient into a mailbox address into two

Human-Readable-Name

↓

Unique Identifier

↓

Object's Address

Fig. 17.2. *CSNET* naming scheme.

separate steps, thus allowing the unique identifier to be rebound to a different address if the user's mailbox moves to a new location. Fig. 17.2 depicts the three level naming scheme by the *CSNET* name server.

The naming scheme developed by the *IFIP* Working Group 6.5 also replaces mailbox addresses with hierarchical *human-oriented names*.[10] The top level of the hierarchy partitions the world into countries and international organizations. The next level further divides names into geographical and organizational partitions. Individual names reside at the lowest level of the hierarchy. Since the hierarchy does not fix the meaning of each level, each level is composed of two parts: the level *type* (e.g., country or organization), and a *discriminator* (e.g., USA or UK). With the *IFIP* scheme, a sender might identify John Doe as

⟨*country, USA*⟩ ⟨*organization, National Labs*⟩ ⟨*personal name, John Doe*⟩

2. REVIEW OF EXISTING WORK

We now review current work that models and explains names and name resolution in distributed systems. First, Watson[39] proposes that an *identifier* for an object is mapped into a lower level identifier for the object, with subsequent mappings eventually yielding the object itself (see Fig. 17.3). Watson also describes a specific naming scheme that involves both high-level, human-readable, identifiers, and low-level identifiers that specify objects' locations.

In another model, Shoch[32] distinguishes between the nature of different levels with the following definition:

The *name* of a resource indicates <u>what</u> we seek,
an *address* indicates <u>where</u> it is,
and a *route* tells us <u>how to get there</u>.

In a *DOS*, for example, the named resource might be a file, the address is the current location of the file in the distributed system, and the route is the sequence of network connections through which a request must travel to reach the file.

In work on the *IFIP* directory service for computer mail, Sirbu and Sutherland[33] discuss the relationship between the process of resolving the name of a recipi-

Identifier$_{level\,n}$

Identifier$_{level\,n-1}$

.

.

.

.

.

Identifier$_{level\,1}$

Object

Fig. 17.3. Multi-level mapping of identifiers to objects.

ent's mailbox, and the process of delivering the message to the mailbox. In *absolute* name resolution, the recipient's name is completely resolved into the address of a mailbox and the message is then delivered to that address, while in *incremental* resolution, the message is moved towards the destination in conjunction with name resolution.

Oppen and Dalal[24] construct a naming model that describes how *clients* refer to *objects*. They represent each client and object in the distributed system by exactly one vertex in a directed graph. If vertex u has an outgoing edge labeled i, then $u[i]$ denotes the vertex at the end of the edge. In addition, if $u[i_1] \ldots [i_k] = v$ then $i_1 > \ldots > i_k$ denotes a *path* from u to v. The model characterizes the nature of various types of names, including *absolute* names, *relative* names, and *hierarchical* names.

Based on their abstract model, Oppen and Dalal describe the Clearinghouse name server that implements a universal name resolution service. The Clearinghouse provides a coherent naming system that supports uniform and transparent access to all objects, independent of the object's type. It resolves names for objects into information that the client uses to access the object (i.e., the address of the object's manager).

A significant characteristic of the Clearinghouse is that, although the name server database is distributed, the name server is logically centralized. Cheriton and Mann,[7] describe an alternative approach to naming in a distributed system in which the name server service is logically distributed across the managers for the object type. In their view, the name of an object is resolvable by the manager that implements the object; the approach uses a centralized name server only to locate the manager that completes the name resolution. Terry[36] presents a general model for analyzing the name server mechanism for a given naming convention.

Finally, we can gain experience from studies of names in programming languages and operating systems. For example, Johnston[18] defines the contour model for resolving names in Algol-like languages. Daley and Dennis,[11] Fabry,[15] Denning,[12] Henderson,[16] and Ritche and Thompson[28] describe various paradigms for referencing and sharing segments and files in operating systems.

To summarize, we observe the following four characteristics of naming systems in distributed environments: (1) multiple levels of names exist for objects, where high-level names are mapped into low-level names; (2) there exist kinds of names, such as hierarchical, absolute, and relative; (3) names contain information used to locate the computer on which remote objects are implemented; and (4) naming systems are implemented by name servers.

3. A COMPREHENSIVE NAMING MODEL

The discussion to this point provides an intuitive understanding of name resolution mechanisms in distributed systems. In this Section, we shall define a comprehensive model for naming that captures the important principles of name resolution. We present our model in three steps. First, we define a model of computation in distributed systems that ignores issues of synchronization and protection, and focuses instead on the components of a distributed system that play a role in name resolution. Second, we define the basic model for name resolution that translates names for objects into the objects they denote. Finally, because the objects in a distributed system are implemented on multiple computers connected by network hardware, we describe the role of name resolution in actually locating objects in the distributed system.

A point of clarification regarding syntax and semantics. While names are generally thought of in semantic terms—they denote objects—our view is that process of resolving a given name into the object it denotes is a syntax-directed operation. That is, just as compilation is a syntactic process (program semantics are defined by assigning actions to syntactic constructs), name resolution is also a syntactic process; a name's meaning is specified by a name to object binding. This chapter concentrates on the syntactic aspects of naming (i.e., name resolution), and it ignores questions of semantics (i.e., the establishment of bindings).

3.1. Computations in a Distributed System

We conceptually view the underlying distributed system in terms of an *object model*,[19] in which the system is said to consist of a collection of *objects*, denoted O. An object is either a physical resource (e.g., a disk or a processor), or an abstract resource (e.g., a file or a process). Objects are further characterized as being either *passive* or *active*, where passive objects correspond to stored data, and active objects correspond to processes that act upon passive resources. For the purposes of our discussion, we use the term object to denote only passive objects, and we treat the behavior of processes separately. The objects in a distributed system are partitioned into *types*, Associated with each object type is a *manager* that implements the object type, and presents *clients* throughout the distributed system with an interface to the object. The interface is defined by the set of *operations* that may be applied to the object.

Because clients and managers that invoke and implement operations are physically implemented in terms of a set of cooperating processes, they can be described by models of distributed processing and concurrent programming (e.g., *remote procedure calls* (*RPC*), and *interprocess communication* (*IPC*).[4,38] However, because we are not concerned with process synchronization and data protection in this chapter, we will not limit our view of distributed systems to either the *RPC* or the *IPC* approach. Instead, we shall think of all the processing involved in carrying out an operation on behalf of a client as a single *computation* that encompasses both the work involved in actually performing the operation, as well as the overhead incurred by the system in locating the manager and identifying the object. Furthermore, we view all of the processors that comprise a distributed system as forming a single virtual processor, and we think of a computation as being implemented in terms of a single process, called an *operation-process*, that runs on the virtual processor. We will now consider the distributed nature of objects in the distributed system.

First, we view a distributed system as being composed of a finite set of *environments*, denoted E, where an environment defines the subset of objects currently available or accessible to a computation (i.e. O is partitioned across E). Although no inherent relationship exists between environments and physical processors, a single physical processor and the locally implemented objects could be represented by a single environment. If we view environments as corresponding to *address spaces* (roughly equivalent to a process in the V-System), then several environments would be associated with a single processor. An operation-process executes in a single environment at any given time. In other words, we view a computation as being defined by an operation-process and the set of objects accessible to the operation-process, where we let $\epsilon \in E$ denote the environment in which a given operation-process currently executes. Also, we ignore the possibility of operation-processes interfering with each other.

Second, the environments in the system are connected by a set of directed *links*, denoted L, such that an operation-process is allowed to move from its current environment to a new environment, if and only if a link leads from the current environment to the new environment. We visualize the relationship between environments and links with a directed graph, denoted $D = (E, L)$, where the vertices of D correspond to the environments in the system, and the edges represent links that connect environments. Because a link does not necessarily exist between all environments, we say that a path in D represents a *route* from one environment to another. (We let R represent the set of all possible routes in D.) Figure 17.4 schematically depicts a distributed system, where the vertex containing ϵ marks the current environment of some computation.

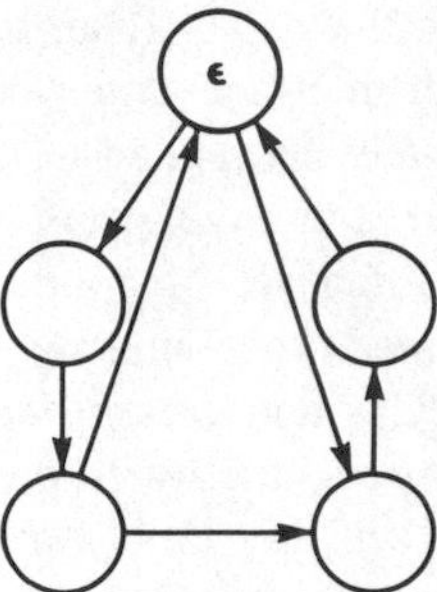

Fig. 17.4. Schematic view of a distributed system.

Thus, instead of viewing a distributed system in terms of the physically distinct processors, we think of a distributed system as containing a set of environments and a single virtual processor, and we view the computation encompassing an operation as a single process that moves from environment to environment over links, thereby gaining access to needed objects. When a client invokes an operation of an object, in effect it initiates an operation-process that executes in some starting environment, while the manager completes the operation-process by performing the operation on the object in a possibly remote environment. Because managers implement abstract objects in terms of other objects, we say that a set of environments in which the manager implements the object is associated with each object type. Now consider how clients reference objects. Informally, an object is identified with a *name*, where a name is a *string* composed of a set of *symbols* chosen from a finite *alphabet*. We represent the general form of names used to identify objects with a *language*, denoted N, which defines names to be composed of a sequence of one or more *simple names* separated by delimiters. (A name that contains more than one simple name is said to be *compound name*.) For example, the compound name *host1!user@host* consists of the five tokens "*host1*", "*!*", "*user*", "*@*", and "*host2*", where "*user*" is the second simple name component.

We think of N as being partitioned into three sets: a set of names that are assumed to be *resolvable*, a set of *unresolved* names, and a set of *unresolvable* names. We assume that the set of resolvable names, dentoed $\Omega \subseteq N$, does not require any further interpretation, and that the manager for each object type is able to access the appropriate object, given its resolvable name. Thus, if we let $\omega \in \Omega$ denote a resolvable name for object $o \in O$, such that o is implemented in environment $e \in E$, then we can say that ω is resolvable and understood in environment e.

Finally, the distributed system provides a *name resolution mechanism* that translates the arbitrary name specified by the client into both a resolvable name that the manager understands, and a route from the client's environment to the environment in which the manager implements the object. That is, we can formally express the resolution mechanism as performing the following mapping

$$N \rightarrow \Omega \times R.$$

Although this mapping functionally describes a distributed system's name resolution mechanism, we choose to represent the resolution mechanism with a different function, denoted Φ, that maps an arbitrary name into a resolvable name, and has the *side-effect* of moving the process along the route to the manager's environment. In other words, if a client identifies object o with an unresolved name ν while executing in environment e_{client}, such that o is implemented in $e_{manager}$ and ω is a resolvable name for o in $e_{manager}$, then Φ translates ν into ω and moves the process from e_{client} to $e_{manager}$.

We will discuss the translation of arbitrary names into resolvable names in Section 3.2, while describing the movement of operation-processes from an initial environment to the environment that implements the object in Section 3.3.

3.2. Name Resolution

We now present a model for name resolution that extend Saltzer's model of names in operating systems[29] and computer networks,[30] in which we focus on the resolution of arbitrary names for objects into resolvable names for objects by assuming a distributed system that contains only one environment.*

Recall that we express a distributed system's name resolution mechanism with a partial function, denoted Φ, that maps arbitrary names into resolvable names; i.e., it performs the mapping

$$\Phi: N \rightarrow \Omega.$$

Our model does not distinguish between ''names'' and ''addresses'' as defined by Shoch. Instead, it treats various ways of identifying an object as different *forms* of names, and it describes the bindings between forms in a hierarchy. At each level in the hierarchy, names are defined by a uniform set of rules; we assume that a name is resolvable, given a representation of the name and the set of rules for a level. In other words, we say that names are purely syntactic entities, and name resolution is a syntax-directed operation.

Informally, Φ is defined by three components: a finite set of *contexts*, each of which defines an interpretation of a set of names, a universal function that *resolves* names relative to an interpretation, and a mechanism that defines the

*In a system modelled by a single environment, resolvable names are commonly called *universal* names.

closure of a name and a context. Because we view all names as being resolved relative to a given context, we say that a context and a name pair form a *qualified name*. To translate an unresolved name into a resolvable name, Φ first forms a qualified name from the given name and a selected context, where the closure mechanism selects the initial context based upon the current *state* of the operation-process that invoked Φ. The universal resolution function then translates the initial qualified name into a resolvable name by successively interpreting a name according to a context, where a context interprets a name to be either another qualified name or a resolvable name, (i.e., given an arbitrary name as an argument, a context either returns a new name and a new context to interpret that name, or it returns a resolvable name).

Formally, let $C = \{c_i | i > 0\}$ denote the set of contexts available in a distributed system, such that each context in C is a partial function that performs the mapping

$$c_i\colon \mathrm{N} \rightarrow \Psi,$$

where Ψ represents the set of all qualified names, and each $\psi \in \Psi$ is a pair $\langle c_i, \nu\rangle$ for $c_i \in C$ and $\nu \in \mathrm{N}$. (Recall that we assume $\Omega \subseteq \mathrm{N}$. We also allow the context component to be undefined, denoted $\perp$.) Furthermore, let f_R denote the universal resolution function that performs the mapping

$$f_R\colon \Psi \rightarrow \Omega,$$

and let $S = \{s_i | i > 0\}$ denote the finite set of possible states that may be assumed by an operation-process, such that the closure mechanism is defined by the function

$$f_C\colon S \rightarrow C.$$

Finally, define the name resolution mechanism Φ as follows

$$\Phi(\nu) = \begin{cases} \nu & \text{if } \nu \in \Omega \\ f_R(\langle f_c(\sigma), \nu \rangle) & \textit{otherwise} \end{cases},$$

where $\sigma \in S$ represents the current state of the operation-process that invoked Φ. The rest of this Section describes the three components of a distributed system's name resolution mechanism in detail.

First, a context defines an interpretation of a set of names, where by "interpretation" we mean a mapping of arbitrary names into qualified names. We think of the mapping performed by a context in two stages: it first calls a *translating* function to select a simple name from a given name, and then it looks up the simple name in a table of simple name to qualified name *bindings*.

Formally, let f_T^i denote the translating function associated with context c_i. It performs the mapping

$$f_T^i: \nu \rightarrow \langle \nu_s, \nu' \rangle$$

for arbitrary names ν and ν', and simple name ν_s. That is, the function takes a name in N as an argument, and returns a pair of names: the first is a simple name and the second is an arbitrary name. Also, let $\beta = \langle \nu_s, \psi \rangle$ denote a single binding of simple name ν_s to qualified name ψ, where a finite set of bindings are associated with each context c_i. (Fig. 17.5 depicts the table of bindings associated with a context, where ν_s is a simple name, c_j is a context, and γ is an arbitrary name.)

We think of f_T^i as building a *parse tree* out of the simple name and delimiter tokens that comprise a given name, and then based on the parse tree, returning a simple name and an arbitrary name. We identify two possibilities: the translating function either extracts a simple name from the tree, and returns a pair consisting of the selected simple name and the name corresponds to the rest of the tree (e.g., f_T^i returns the pair ⟨*host1*, *host2!user*⟩ when applied to the name *host1!host2!user*), or it returns a pair consisting of an arbitrary simple name (i.e., not necessarily a simple name component of the inputted name), and the original name (e.g., f_T^i returns the pair ⟨*DARPA*, *user@host*⟩ when applied to the name *user@host*).

Thus, while the language N defines the sequence of simple name and delimiter tokens that comprise names throughout the entire naming system, the tokens are parsed on a context by context basis, according to the precedence assigned to delimiters by each context's translating function (i.e., the delimiters behave like operators). Clearly, the translating function is a very powerful mechanism; we assume that the model is applied to a system based on an intuitive understanding of delimiters and simple names.

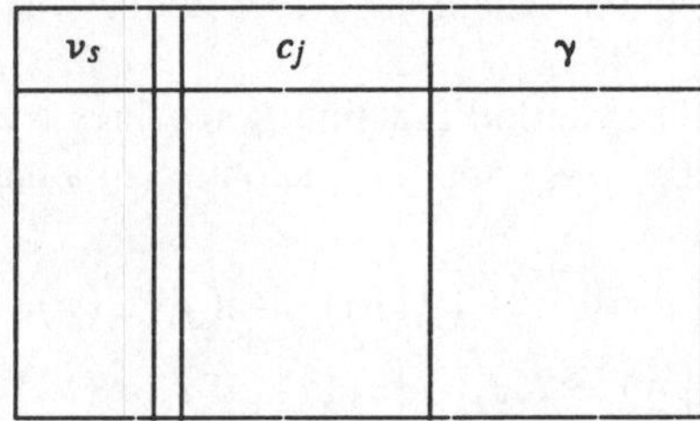

Fig. 17.5. Context viewed as a table.

To complete the arbitrary name to qualified name mapping, c_i looks up the simple name returned by its translating function in the table of bindings, and retrieves the corresponding qualified name. Because not all of the bindings in the table contain fully specified qualified names, the context may augment the retrieved qualified name before returning it. Specifically, there exist two types of bindings: *complete* bindings, in which the qualified name components of the binding contains both a name and a context (where the qualified name component of the binding is returned), and *partial* bindings, in which the qualified name component of the binding contains only a context (where the qualified name returned contains the context and the arbitrary name returned by the translating function). Formally,

Definition: For context $c_i \in C$ applied to the arbitrary name ν, suppose that the translating function returns the pair $\langle \nu_s, \nu' \rangle$, and $\beta = \langle \nu_s, \psi \rangle$, where $\psi = \langle c_j, \gamma \rangle$, is a binding in c_i.

1. If $\gamma \in \mathrm{N}$, then β is a *complete* binding and c_i returns $\langle c_j, \gamma \rangle$.
2. If $\gamma = \perp$, then β is a *partial* binding and c_i returns $\langle c_j, \nu' \rangle$.

We let a qualified name of the form $\psi = \langle \perp, \omega \rangle$ denote a special case of complete binding, called a *final* binding, in which the context component of the qualified name is undefined. Final bindings signify that the name component of the qualified name is a resolvable name.

Second, consider the closure function f_C that maps the state of a process into a context in C. Although we could equate states with environments (where environments represent address spaces), for the purpose of this chapter we will let environments correspond to hosts, and we define states as follows. Let U denote the set of all users in the distributed system. Each state $s_i \in S$ is defined by the pair $\langle e_k, u_x \rangle$, where $e_k \in E$ is the current environment of the process, and $u_x \in U$ is the user on who's behalf the process is executing (i.e., the user that invoked the client). We will discuss the mapping performed by f_C in detail in Section 5; for now, we shall think of the function as being implemented by a table of state/context pairs, where each user defines his or her own entry in the table.

Finally, the universal resolution function f_R resolves a qualified name into a resolvable name by successively applying a context to a name. Formally stated.

$$f_R(\langle c_i, \nu \rangle) = \begin{cases} f_R(c_i(\nu)) & \text{if } f_1(c_i(\nu)) \in C \\ f_2(c_i(\nu)) & \text{if } f_1(c_i(\nu)) = \perp \\ \perp & \textit{otherwise} \end{cases}$$

where f_i denotes a *selector* function that returns the ith component of a given tuple.

From an operational perspective, f_R translates one qualified name into another, based on the interpretation of the name in the specified context, where a qualified name with an undefined context component signifies a resolvable name. That is, we think of the function as moving from one context to another until encountering a resolvable name.

Although we think of Φ as representing the name resolution mechanism for a given distributed system, f_R is a general function that resolves names in any distributed system; it is the set of contexts and the closure function that uniquely define names in a particular system. We say that C and f_C define the *naming system* for a distributed system.

3.3. Moving an Operation-Process Through the System

We now complete our model of a distributed system's name resolution mechanism by defining Φ in a system that contains more than one environment. In addition to mapping arbitrary names that identify objects into resolvable names for objects, Φ has a side-effect of moving a process from an initial environment to an environment that defines the object. In other words, while translating an arbitrary name into a resolvable name, Φ also translates the arbitrary name into a route through the underlying system; Φ "executes" the route (i.e., moves the process along the route) as it uncovers the individual links that comprise the route.

Specifically, we not only view the interpretation of a name defined by a context as mapping an arbitrary name into a qualified name, but we also think of the interpretation as determining what link, if any, the process should traverse. Formally, let $\beta = \langle \nu_s, \psi, l_j \rangle$ for $l_j \in L$, represent an extended binding in the contexts of C, where simple name ν_s is said to be bound to the qualified name ψ and the link l_j. (Let the triple $\beta = \langle \nu_s, \psi, \perp \rangle$ denote a binding that does not specify any movement through the system.)

Furthermore, let Φ_M represent a system mechanism that *moves* a process from one environment to another over a specified link. That is, if $\epsilon \in E$ denotes the current environment of a process, and the process applies Φ_M to link l_j, then the process is moved from ϵ to ϵ' (i.e., the state of the process changes from $\sigma = \langle \epsilon, u_x \rangle$ to $\sigma' = \langle \epsilon', u_x \rangle$), where l_j is a link that leads from ϵ to ϵ'.

Φ employs Φ_M to move a process from its current environment to a new environment, based upon the links encountered in the bindings of contexts. We operationally define the affect of Φ on the environment in which a process executes in Fig. 17.6, where *translate* is a primitive operation corresponding to f^i_T, *lookup* is a primitive operation that returns a pair containing the qualified name and link bound to a simple name, and *type* is a primitive operation that returns the type of the binding associated with a simple name.

```
ci(v) = begin
            <vs, v'> = translate(v)
            <ψ, l> = lookup(vs)
            if (l ≠ ⊥)
                  ΦM(l)
            if (type(vs) = complete)
                  return(ψ)
            if (type(vs) = partial)
                  return(< fi(ψ), v'>)
            else
                  return(⊥)
        end
```

Fig. 17.6. Operational description of context c_i.

Note that it is not our objective to fully specify the operation of Φ_M, which is an abstraction of the transport mechanism of a distributed system's underlying network. Instead, we emphasize that the name resolution mechanism and the transport mechanism are intertwined, and that in fact, the name resolution mechanism drives the transport mechanism, based on the name it is resolving.

4. AN EXAMPLE OF A NAMING SYSTEM

We illustrate our model by examining a distributed system that implements mailbox objects. Using computer mail allows us to give concrete examples for a single, intuitively obvious, object type. In addition, mail contains a rich set of names, which, unlike many low-level names, are easily readable. We will briefly consider additional examples in Section 7.

To simplify the example, we further restrict our discussion to a distributed mail system similar to the *DARPA* Internet, where we assume that the Internet contains only two hosts (*nlabs* and *stateu*), and a pair of mailbox objects, representing the location where users John Doe and John Smith receive their mail.

Recall that we can model a distributed system with a directed graph $D = (E, L)$. For our example, we represent each host as an environment in E, and we let the network connections between hosts correspond to links in L, where $l_{Addr\text{-}nlabs}$ denotes a link leading to environment e_{nlabs} (corresponding to host *nlabs*). Because the underlying network architecture of the *DARPA* Internet logically connects all hosts, we assume that D forms a completely connected graph. Finally, because files implement mailbox objects, we let $\Omega = \{$*/usr/mail/jxd*, */usr/mail/jxs*$\}$ represent the set of resolvable names for mailbox objects. Figure 17.7 schematically depicts the example distributed system D.

Now consider the names for mailbox objects supported by the system. In

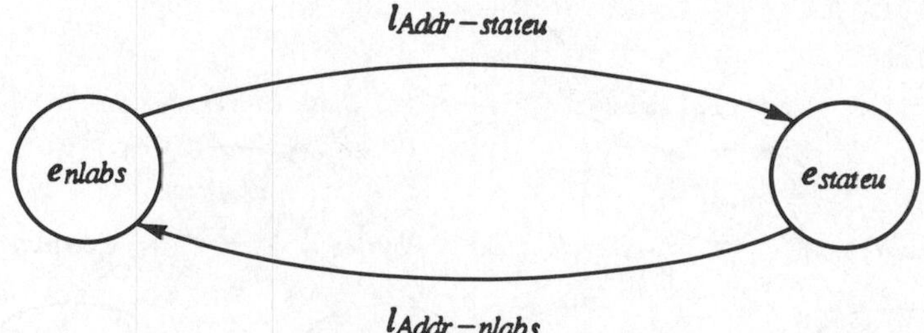

Fig. 17.7. Underlying distributed system for the *DARPA* Internet.

addition to conventional *DARPA* names of the form *user@host*, we assume that the naming system supports a set of high-level, human-oriented names for mailboxes, as well as a unique identifier for each mailbox. (Users identify recipients with a high-level name, and each unique identifier is bound to the current *user@host* name for the mailbox.) Thus, if John Doe has an account on the host *nlabs*, then his mailbox might have the high-level name *John Doe/Research/National Labs*, the unique identifier *UID-Doe*, and the low-level name *jxd@nlabs*.

We now describe the naming systems for our example. Conceptually, we view the contexts that comprise the naming system with a directed graph, denoted K, called a *naming network*. The set of vertices in K correspond to the union of the set of contexts C and the set of resolvable names Ω, where we distinguish between vertices that correspond to contexts and vertices that correspond to resolvable names with ellipses and boxes, respectively. The set of edges in K correspond to the bindings contained in the contexts of C, such that (c_i, c_j) is an edge labeled "$\nu_s \rightarrow \gamma$" if and only if context c_i contains the complete binding $\langle \nu_s, \langle c_j, \gamma \rangle \rangle$, (c_i, c_j) is an edge labeled "ν_s" if and only if context c_i contains the partial binding $\langle \nu_s, \langle c_j, \perp \rangle \rangle$, and (c_i, ω) is an edge labeled "ν_s" if and only if context c_i contains the final binding $\langle \nu_s, \langle \perp, \omega \rangle \rangle$ for resolvable name $\omega \in \Omega$. Also, we augment edge labels with links to represent bindings that specify moves through the distributed system. Figure 17.8 depicts the naming network for our example system.

It is important to understand that we describe naming in distributed systems with two distinct graphs: the conceptual naming network K that abstractly defines names, and the underlying distributed system graph D that represents the physical structure of the system. Furthermore, we think of the resolution mechanism Φ as traversing the naming network (based upon matches between the simple name components of the name being resolved and the edge labels), while routing the process through the environments of D (based upon the links encountered in K).

In our example, if a user on the host *stateu* sends a message to John Doe,

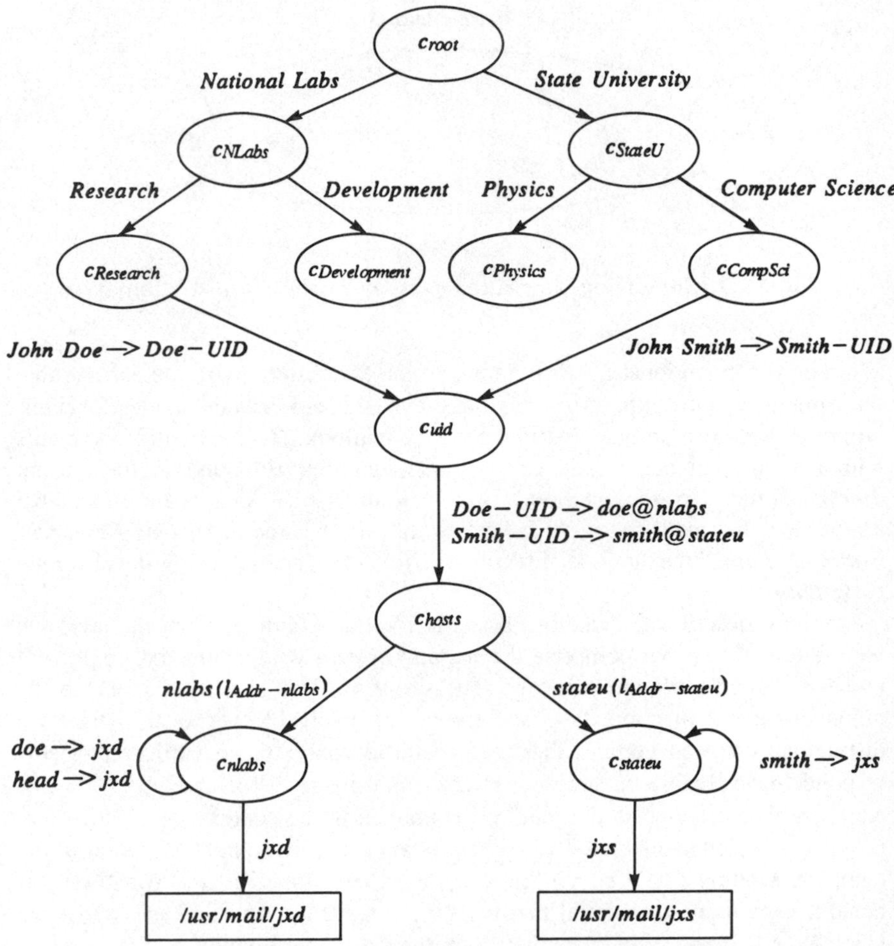

Fig. 17.8. Naming network for mailbox names.

identifying his mailbox with the high-level name *John Doe/Research/National Labs*, then Φ translates the name into the resolvable name */usr/mail/jxd*, and moves the process corresponding to the delivery operation from e_{stateu} to e_{nlabs}. Figure 17.9 traces the operation of Φ, where the intermediate qualified names represent states in the resolution of the name, and f_R represents a transition function between states. Moves through D are depicted as a side-effect.

5. NAMES IN DISTRIBUTED SYSTEMS

The model described in the previous two Sections defines names to be syntactic entities, and name resolution to be a syntax-directed operation. We now discuss

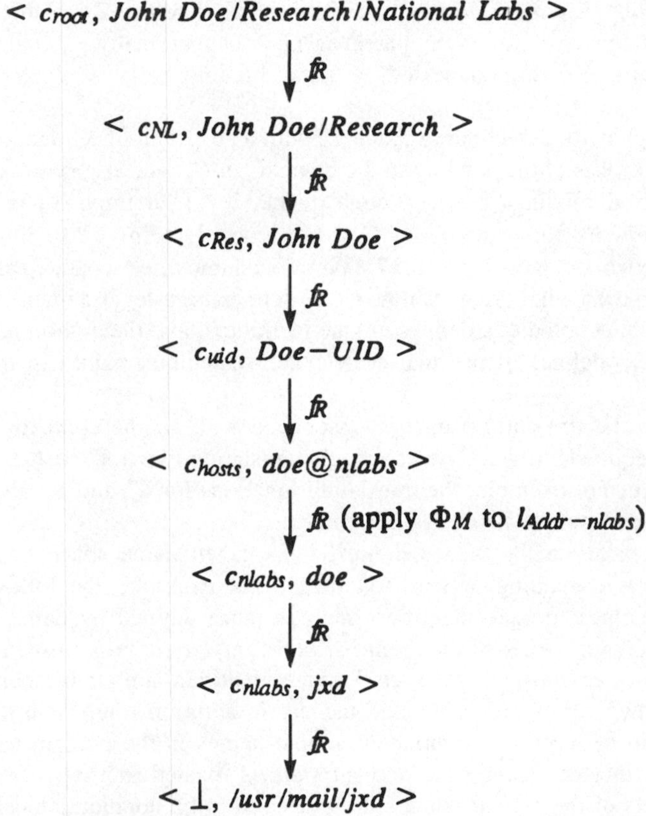

Fig. 17.9. State transition view of name resolution.

the names found in a distributed system based on the system's resolution mechanism (i.e., C and f_C). That is, we define familiar (but informally described) concepts and terminology associated with naming. Specifically, we consider the behavior of groups of contexts, and we investigate the closure function in more detail. Finally, we discuss the bindings of simple names to qualified names. (We use the example naming system described in Section 4 to illustrate our definitions.)

5.1. Name Spaces

Although the model presented in Section 3 describes the resolution of names on a context by context basis, we understand that there exists a fundamental relationship between groups of contexts that treat names in a uniform manner; we say that such a collection of contexts form a *name space*. Formally stated,

Definition: A *name space* is a partition of C, denoted C_n, such that 1. The translating functions for each context in C_n are functionally equivalent; and 2. The contexts in C_n are connected by partial bindings.

We graphically depict name space C_n with a subgraph of K, denoted K_n, that includes vertices corresponding to the contexts in C_n, and edges that correspond to the partial bindings between contexts in C_n.* (Subgraph K_n is called the naming network for name space C_n.) For example, Fig. 17.10 illustrates the naming network depicted in Fig. 17.8 partitioned into three separate name spaces; the uppermost name space, denoted C_H, defines high-level names, the middle name space, denoted C_U, defines unique identifiers, and the bottom name space, denoted C_D, defines names that correspond to mailbox names in the *DARPA* Internet.

Because the translating function associated with all the contexts in a name space are equivalent, we say that a single translating function exists for an entire name space. For example, the translating functions for C_H and C_D always select the *right-most* simple name at each context.

We characterize the names defined by a given name space based on the structure of its naming network. Consider, for example, the following three forms of names: unique identifiers such as those defined by name space C_U, *DARPA* domain names of the form *jxd.nlabs.anycity.anystate.usa*, and *UUCP* names like *host1!host2!host3!user*. Unique identifiers are simple names, while the latter two forms are compound names. In addition, there is a hierarchical relationship between the component simple names in the domain names (i.e., *anycity* is located in *anystate* and *anystate* is located in the *usa*), while the components of the *UUCP* name are understood to be nonhierarchical. (In fact, they are adjacent to each other when viewed as hosts in the underlying distributed system.) Formally, we make the following three definitions.

Definition: Name space C_n for which naming network K_n contains a single vertex is said to be a *flat* name space. Names defined in a flat name space are called *flat* names.

Definition: Name space C_n for which naming network K_n forms a directed acyclic graph with more than one node is said to be a *hierarchical* name space. Names defined in a hierarchical name space are called *hierarchical* names.

Definition: Names defined in name space C_n for which K_n and D are isomorphic (recall that $D = (E, L)$ is the directed graph representing the distributed system), are called *source-route* names.

---

*Our definition does not preclude the possibility that complete bindings may exist within a given name space. Such intraname space bindings are a special case of complete bindings called *indirect* or *recursive* bindings, that form a cycle in the corresponding subgraph of the naming network.

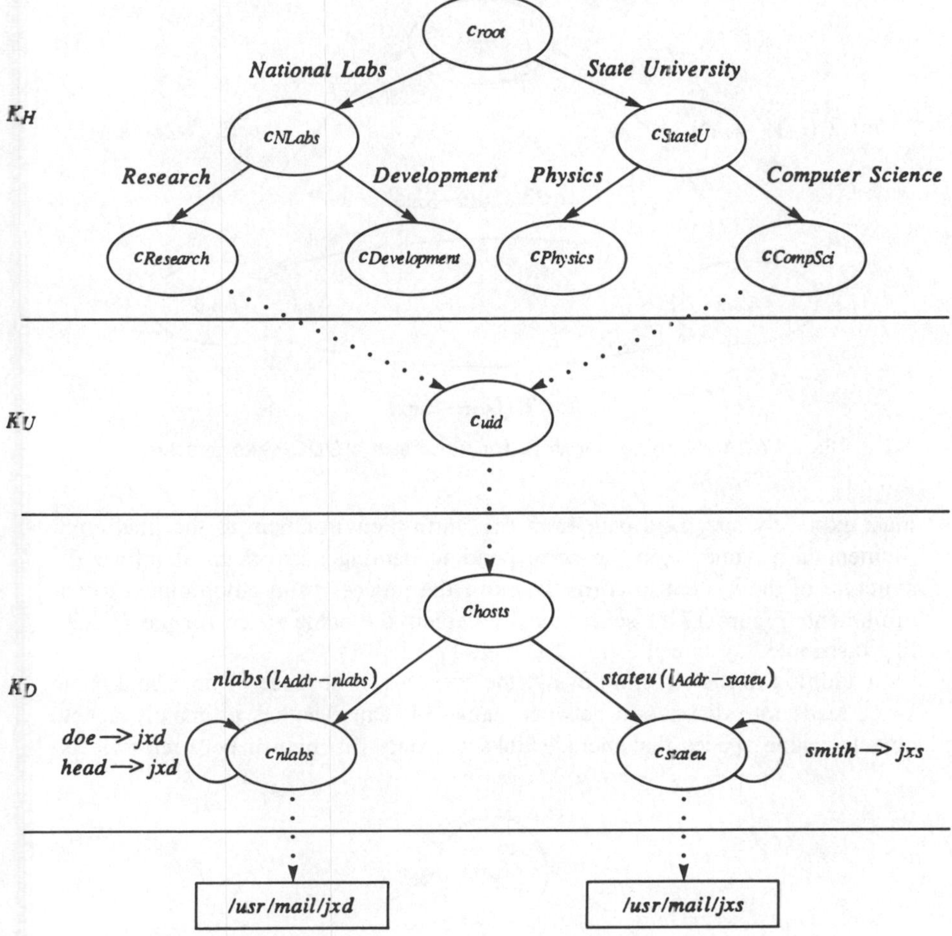

Fig. 17.10. Naming network partitioned into name spaces.

Definition: Names defined in name space C_n for which K_n and D are isomorphic (recall that $D = (E, L)$ is the directed graph representing the distributed system), are called *source-route* names.

Thus, domain names are hierarchical because they are described by an acyclic naming network, while names defined in name spaces C_H and C_D, as well as *GRAPEVINE* names of the form $F.R$, are a special case of hierarchical names that are modeled by a graph that forms a tree. In the *UUCP* name space, however, there is an intuitive relationship between the naming network that defines a set of names and the underlying distributed system; when the user

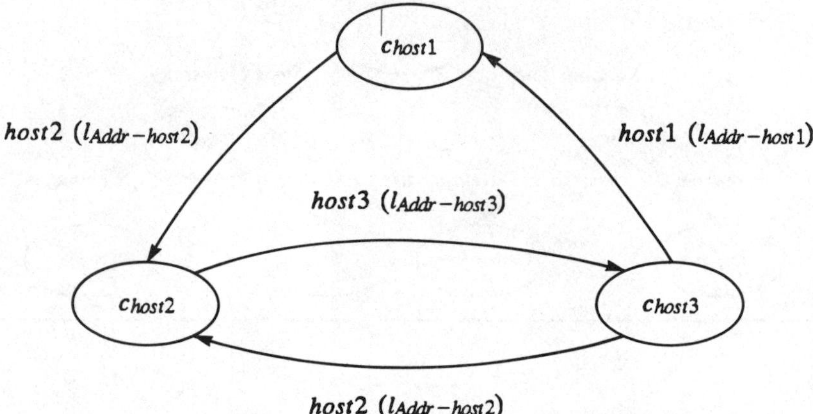

Fig. 17.11. Naming network for names in a *UUCP*-like system.

must explicitly specify a path from the starting environment to the final environment in a name, then the corresponding naming network must mirror the structure of the system to correctly move the process from environment to environment. Figure 17.11 schematically depicts the name space for the *UUCP*-like distributed system illustrated in Fig. 17.12.

In addition to the structure of K_n, the presence or absence of links in a name space leads to a distinction between names. Because names ultimately denote objects, name spaces that include links not only distinguish between objects,

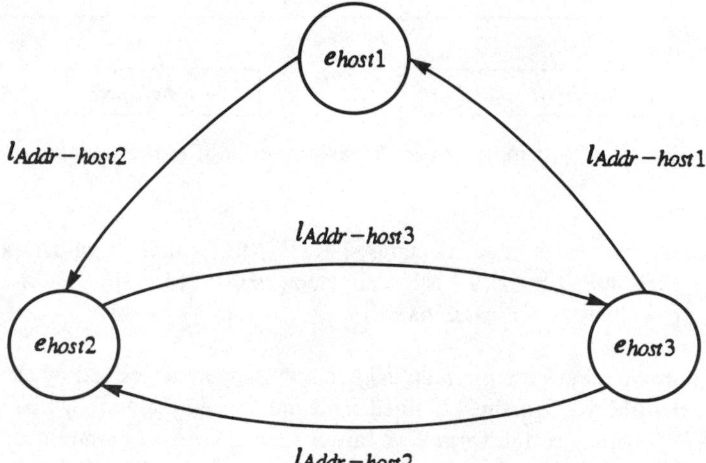

Fig. 17.12. Underlying *UUCP*-like distributed system.

but they also specify where the object is located in the distributed system. Name spaces that do not contain links, however, do not aid in locating an object; they exist for the convenience of the client that must identify the object. Thus,

Definition: Names defined in name space C_n such that for all $c_i \in C_n$, the constituent bindings are of the form $\langle \nu_s, \psi, \perp \rangle$, are called *logical* names.

Definition: Name space C_n for which there exists a context $c_i \in C_n$ that contains bindings of the form $\langle \nu_s, \psi, l_j \rangle$ for $l_j \in L$, is called a *physical* name space. Names defined in a physical name space that have simple name components bound to links are known as *addresses*.

For example, *DARPA* Internet names of the form *user@host* direct the process to the correct host and therefore constitute addresses, while names defined by C_H and C_U are logical. Note that resolving an address uncovers a route in the underlying system from the source to the destination environment and moves the process along the route, while no moves are associated with the resolution of a logical name.

5.2. Levels

In addition to partitioning contexts into name spaces, we view a collection of one or more name spaces as forming a *level*, where a level is loosely defined to be a collection of contexts that define names of a given form. Consider for example, a multinetwork mail system consisting of the *DARPA* Internet and the *UUCP* network mail systems, in which there exists names of the form *user@host*, *host1!host2!user*, and *host2!user@host1*. The first two forms are defined by name spaces that correspond to the *DARPA* Internet (depicted by K_D in Fig. 17.10), and the *UUCP* network (depicted in Fig. 17.11), respectively. The last form, however, is defined by a combination of the two name spaces. Formally,

Definition: A *level* is a collection of contexts connected by partial bindings that do not necessarily have equivalent translating functions.

In other words, for a distributed system that spans multiple network mail systems, there exists a level in the naming system corresponding to conventional "mailbox addresses." The level is composed of contexts drawn from the set of name spaces for each component network mailing system in the multinetwork system, as well as contexts that roughly correspond to mail relays (i.e., they contain bindings that connect them to contexts in separate name spaces). Figure 17.13 schematically depicts the level for a multinetwork mail system containing the *DARPA* Internet and the *UUCP* network mail systems.

Given our partitioning of naming systems into levels, we can abstractly view

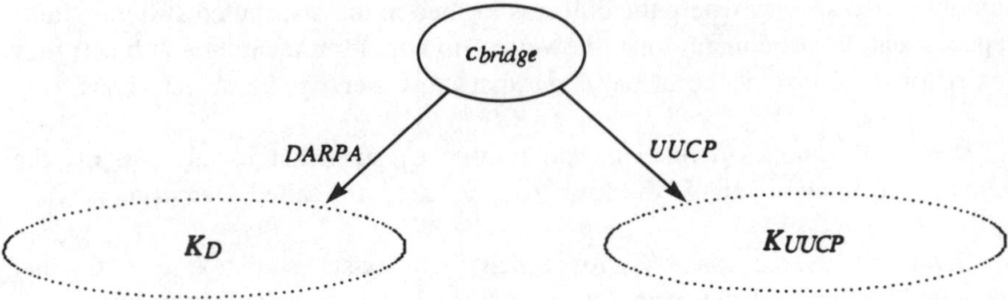

Fig. 17.13. Level composed of multiple name spaces.

the overall process of name resolution as being partitioned into two orthogonal dimensions. In one dimension, names of one form (as defined by one level) are translated into names of another form (as defined by another level), while in the second dimension, names of a given form are interpreted within a single level. That is, we visualize the subgraphs corresponding to each level in the naming network as being in separate planes, where the edges between contexts in different levels connect contexts in adjacent planes. Similarly, we think of the state transition representation of the operation of Φ as two-dimensional: involving transitions between states within a given level, and transitions between states in different levels.

5.3. Closure Function

As defined in Section 3.1, the closure function selects an initial context based on the state of a process, where the state consists of the current environment and the user on whose behalf the process is executing. We now investigate the effect of the closure function f_C upon names defined by a naming system.

First, because the bindings in a naming system are well defined, and the behavior of Φ is deterministic, if names are always resolved starting at the same context, then a given name must always resolve into the same resolvable name. If, however, resolution begins at different contexts, then different names may resolve into the same resolvable name (or a given name may resolve into different resolvable names), depending on the starting context. Formally, we make the following two definitions.

Definition: Names defined in name space C_n, such that $f_C(s_i) = f_C(s_j)$ for all s_i, $s_j \in S$, are called *absolute* names.

Definition: Names defined in name space C_n, for which there exists states s_i, $s_j \in S$ such that $f_C(s_i) \neq f_C(s_j)$, are called *relative* names.

Because the two definitions are mutually exclusive, we think of a given name space as either supporting absolute names or relative names, but not both.

Next, we consider the mapping between states and contexts in more detail.

Definition: If there exists an environment $e_k \in E$ and a user $u_x \in U$ such that $f_C(\langle e_k, u_x \rangle) = c_i$, and $f_C(\langle e_k, u_x \rangle) \neq f_C(\langle e_i, u_y \rangle)$ for all $u_x \neq u_y$ and all $e_i \in E$, then c_i is called a *private* context. Names defined by a private context are called *aliases*.

Definition: A context $c_i \in C$, such that c_i is not a private context is called a *public* context. Names defined by a public context are called *public* names.

In other words, aliases are names used by a specific user to identify objects, while public names are available to many users. Figure 17.14 illustrates a portion of the example naming system that includes a private context denoted $c_{private}$. Note that, in practice, the private contexts that define aliases are root nodes in the naming network that are connected to the rest of the naming network by complete or final bindings. Therefore, aliases are generally simple names.

Finally, we shall consider an extension to the closure function that allows it to return a set of contexts at which names resolution may begin. In the following definition, let $\hat{C}$ denote the subset of C returned by f_C.

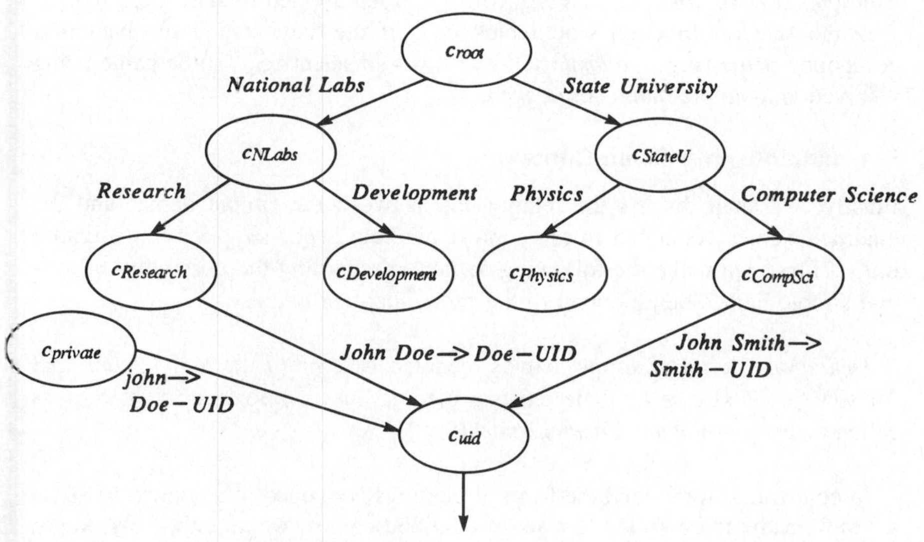

Fig. 17.14. Naming network with a private context.

Definition: A naming system for which $f_C(\sigma) = \hat{C}$, such that $\hat{C}$ contains more than one context, is said to support *multiple-relative* names. Furthermore: 1. If all of the contexts in $\hat{C}$ are in the same name space (i.e., $\hat{C} \subseteq C_n$ for some name space C_n), and the name space is hierarchical, then names resolved relative to the root of the naming network are called *full* names,* while all other names are considered *abbreviated* names; and 2. If the contexts in $\hat{C}$ are in two or more levels, the naming system is said to support *multiple-views*.

For example, f_C might return the set $\{c_{private}, c_{root}, c_{nlabs}, c_{research}, c_{hosts}\}$, in which case John Doe's mailbox is namable as *john*, *John Doe/Research/National Labs*, *John Doe/Research*, *John Doe*, and *doe@nlabs*, where the first name is an alias, the second name is a full name because it is resolved starting at the root of the naming network, and the third and fourth names are abbreviated names because they are resolved starting at interior nodes of the tree. Furthermore, because the set of starting contexts are contained in more than one level (e.g., $c_{root} \in C_H$ and $c_{host} \in C_D$), the naming system supports multiple-views of the object (i.e., a high-level view and a low-level view).

In practice, the contexts in the set $\hat{C}$ returned by f_C are either tried in order until one is found that leads to successful resolution of the name (similar to a *search path* in *UNIX*), or a selector function is associated with the naming system to pick one of the contexts based on the syntax of the name being resolved, where the selector function either counts the number of simple name components or looks for a special delimiter (e.g., "~" or "/"in *UNIX*). For example, if f_C returns the set $\{c_{hosts}, c_{nlabs}\}$ when applied to state $\langle e_{nlabs}, u_x \rangle$, then the selector function would pick c_{hosts} if the name being resolved is a compound name (e.g., *jxd@nlabs*), and it would select c_{nlabs} if the name being resolved is a simple name (e.g., *jxd*).

5.4 Bindings in a Given Context

Finally, we shall discuss the relationship between the simple names and the qualified names contained in the context bindings. (For simplicity, we ignore links.) First, we make the following definition regarding the possibility of several simple names being bound to the same qualified name.

Definition: A set of simple names, denoted $N_{syn} = \{\nu_k | k > 0\}$, such that for some context $c_i \in C$, there exists a binding $\langle \nu_k, \psi \rangle$ for each $\nu_k \in N_{syn}$, is called a set of *synonyms* (or *nicknames*).

In contrast, if we extend the form of bindings contained in a context to allow a simple name to be bound to a set of qualified names, where either any one of

*Full names are often called absolute names, but we use the term full to distinguish between a special case of multiple-relative names and absolute names.

the qualified names, or all of the qualified names may be selected (denoted by separating the qualified names in the set with "|" and "&" respectively), then the following types of names result.

Definition: A name ν defined in name space C_n, such that for some simple name component ν_k, there exists a context $c_i \in C_n$ that contains the binding $\langle \nu_k, \{\psi_1 | \cdots | \psi_n\} \rangle$, is called a *generic* name.

Definition: A name ν defined in name space C_n, such that for some simple name component ν_k, there exists a context $c_i \in C_n$ that contains the binding $\langle \nu_k, \{\psi_1 \ \& \cdots \& \ \psi_n\} \rangle$, is called a *group* or *multicast* name.

Informally, if a simple name is bound to the set $\{\psi_1 | \cdots | \psi_n\}$, and the context returns a single qualified name ψ_i from the set, where a qualified name is selected based on some factor outside the realm of name resolution (i.e., the availability or ease of access of the object it denotes), then the naming mechanism is said to support generic names. Similarly, if a simple name is bound to the set $\{\psi_1 \ \& \cdots \& \ \psi_n\}$, and the name resolution mechanism conceptually splits into n separate occurrences, each of which proceeds with one of the qualified names ψ_i from the set, then the name resolution mechanism is said to support group names. For example, name space C_H supports the group *everyone* by having the binding

$$\langle everyone, \{\langle c_{uid}, Doe\text{-}UID \rangle \ \& \ \langle c_{uid}, Smith\text{-}UID \rangle\}\rangle$$

in context c_{root}. (Alternative combinations of bindings support the same group.)

6. NAME SERVERS

In this section we use the naming model to get a handle on the implementation of naming systems by name servers. Conceptually, a name server corresponds to a context; it consists of a data structure that contains a set of bindings, and a program that returns the binding associated with a given name. In the framework for distributed systems used throughout this chapter, there exists a name server object type, denoted O_{NS}, upon which a *lookup* operation may be performed. (For simplicity, we refer to a name server object and its manager collectively as a "name server," and we let the term "name server object" denote the set of bindings implemented by a given name server.) Furthermore, a *name server service* provides a *resolve* command that is implemented by the set of name servers, in the same way as the message service is implemented by a set of mailbox objects. Thus, we think of name servers as implementing contexts, and the name server service as implementing the resolution function f_R.

6.1. Distribution of Bindings Over Name Server Objects

Each name server object employed by the name server service implements some subset of the bindings defined by the contexts of a naming system, where we consider the set of bindings in the system to be distributed over the name server objects on context boundaries. We now define the relationship between contexts and name server objects, where a limited naming system, consisting only of the name space C_H, illustrates our discussion. (For a similar discussion see reference 22.)

Formally, the set of contexts C is partitioned into a set of *zones*, denoted $Z = \{z_j \mid j > 0\}$ (i.e., each $z_j \subseteq C$), such that name server object o^j_{NS} *implements* the bindings defined in the contexts of zone z_j.* In other words, the partition of contexts defined the distribution of bindings over name server objects. (We ignore the related question of how name server objects are distributed throughout the system.)

Consider the following three partitionings of C. First, each zone z_j may contain exactly one context c_i, such that the bindings contained in each context c_i are implemented by a single name server object o^j_{NS}, and each name server object o^j_{NS} implements only those bindings contained in context c_i. Second, a single zone may contain more than one context, such that a single name server object implements the bindings defined by several contexts. Finally, there may be a single name server associated with an entire name space (or naming system). Figure 17.15 schematically depicts the first scenario in which a single name server object exists for each context in C_H. (A box represents a zone that defines the set of bindings implemented in a single name server object.)

Whether or not each name server maintains the structure of the component

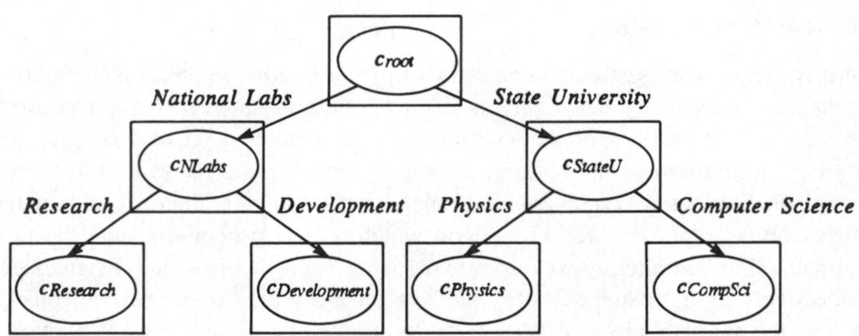

Fig. 17.15. Single context per zone partition of c_H.

*In practice, bindings may not be distributed over name servers across context boundaries (i.e., one name server object may implement a subset of the bindings from more than one context, and zones may overlap).

contexts is a question of internal representation, and does not affect our abstract view of a naming system. For example, rather than take advantage of the hierarchical relationship between the contexts, a single name server that implements an entire name space might compress the names into a flat data structure, such that instead of matching one simple name component at a time, it does a string comparison of entire compound names. Also, multiple copies of a name server object may exist in the system, in which case the name server is said to be *replicated*.

6.2. Naming Name Server Objects

We now turn our attention to the problem of naming name server objects. Recall that the name server service is implemented by a set of name servers, each of which implements some subset of the bindings that comprise the naming system. The service moves from name server to name server in the same way as we visualize the function f_R iterating over sequence of contexts. Thus, to resolve a given name, the service contacts a set of name servers, requiring that the service be able to identify each name server object with a name. For the purpose of the following discussion, we assume that each name server implements a single context, similar to the example illustrated in Fig. 17.15.

To gain an intuitive understanding of the implications of naming name server objects, consider an analogy from the *UNIX* file system. The names of files in the system are defined by *directories*, where a directory is an abstraction similar to a context. Directories, however, are implemented as files. Thus, file objects are named by entities that are themselves implemented as files, corresponding to the situation in which the names of objects in a distributed system are implemented by other objects in the system.

Our mathematical model avoids the problem by identifying the abstract version of a name server object (i.e., a context), with a meta-symbol (e.g., c_i). Thus, the binding of simple name ν_s to context c_i is represented by a binding of the form $\langle \nu_s, \langle c_i, \perp \rangle \rangle$, and implicitly depicted in the naming network with a directed edge.

When implementing contexts in name servers, however, the name of the next name server object must be explicitly supplied. In the *UNIX* file system, this is accomplished by identifying the file that implements a directory with a lower-level name for that file (called an *i-number*). Similarly, the bindings contained in name server object o^j_{NS} identify other name server objects with names that are resolvable by still other name servers. For example, if we let *UID–NS–NL* be the unique identifier for the name server object that implements context c_{NL}, then the name server that implements context c_{root} would contain a binding of the form $\langle$ *National Labs*, $\langle$ *UID–NS–NL*, $\perp \rangle \rangle$, implying that the service should next access the name server object named *UID–NS–NL*.

In addition to naming the next name server that should be queried, the name server service must also have knowledge of an initial name server that it can access, loosely corresponding to the starting context defined by the closure function f_C. That is, the name server service must know *a priori* the names of some set of name servers at which it can begin resolving a name. In our example naming system, the service might know about name server object o_{NS}^{root}, or it might know the names of a set of name server objects that it should try (e.g., $\{o_{NS}^{Research}, o_{NS}^{NLabs}, o_{NS}^{root}\}$).

6.3. Discussion

We will conclude this Section with two observations regarding the role of name servers in name resolution. First, because Φ defines a name resolution mechanism for objects that are distributed throughout the distributed system, and name server objects may themselves be distributed throughout the system, there exists a relationship between the name servers that define the name of objects, and the objects themselves. For example, name servers that implement name spaces for *GRAPEVINE*,[3] whether physically distributed over multiple environments or not, are understood to be logcally centralized because they define logical names. In contrast, if the distribution of the name server matches the distribution of objects as defined by a physical name space (e.g., name space C_D that defines names of the form *user@host*), then the objects and the name servers are located close together (i.e., in the same environment). Chertion and Mann[7] consider name servers that are associated with the object manager for which they define names to be logically distributed.

Second, because the object being named by the client, as well as the name server objects needed to resolve the name for the object, are potentially located in remote environments of the distributed system, Φ may need to employ the transport mechanism Φ_M to reach both the object and name server objects. That is, while a client initiates a process that employs Φ to direct it from environment to environment, Φ in turn becomes a client of the name server objects in the system by invoking the *lookup* operation, thereby initiating its own process. Thus, we conceptually think of the original process as moving from a starting environment to a final environment, while Φ takes "side-trips" to possibly remote name server objects to determine the next move for the original process.

7. NAMING IN COMPUTER NETWORKS

Although the preceding discussion focuses on a distributed system that supports access to computer mail, we note that the naming model is widely applicable. For example, a *DOS* that supports *UNIX*-like file names, unique identifiers, and names of the form *host*:*file* is analogous to our electronic mail example. We note, however, that the applications described so far are limited to naming mechanism for distributed systems that are similar to computer mail; we assume

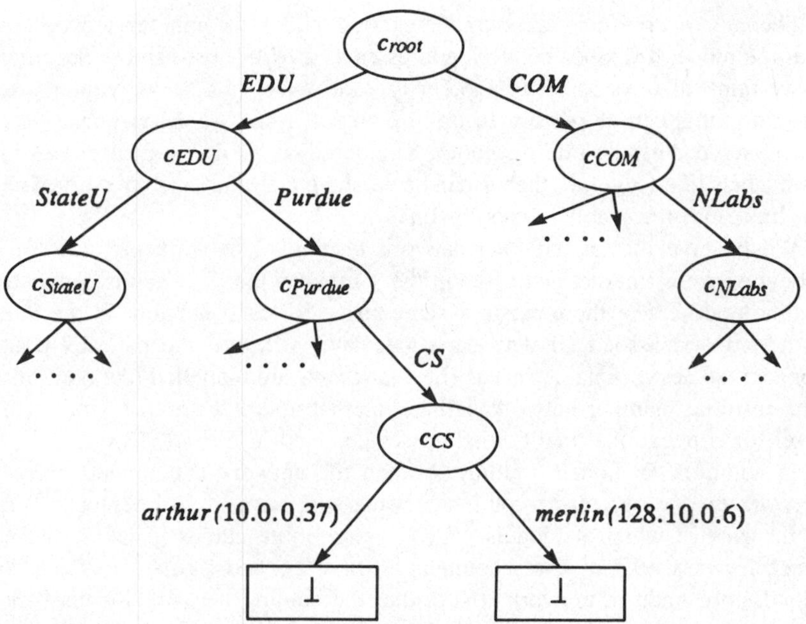

Fig. 17.16. Name space for *DARPA* domain names.

the existence of a form of name that identifies both a destination environment and an object (e.g., *jxd@labs*). In this Section, we consider applying the model to both host names (e.g., *nlabs*), and network addresses for hosts.

First, unlike computer mail in which a reply is not required, many operations in distributed systems result in a reply being returned to the operation's origin. In other words, after initially locating the destination environment, the process moves between the source and destination environments to complete the operation. For each request or reply, the naming mechanism need only locate the correct environment.

In general, the name resolution mechanism must be able to resolve a name into a route to a destination environment independent of a specific object. In such a case, the naming network includes no resolvable names for objects, but only links that define moves from one environment to another. For example, if we equate hosts with environments and Internet addresses with links, then Fig. 17.16 schematically depicts an example name space for *DARPA* Internet domain names, where 10.0.0.37 and 128.10.0.6 are Internet addresses.*

*The naming network in Fig. 17.16 is consistent with the naming networks illustrated throughout this paper. Alternatively, we could represent links as leaves in the hierarchy rather than as edge labels.

Second, we consider extending the naming model to computer networks, such that the model describes network addresses as well as host names. Specifically, if we think of links as being another type of object (where we view Φ_M as an operation that can be performed on link objects), and we assume that the links encountered during name resolution are identified by unresolved names rather than labels like l_{Addr_host}, then Φ can be employed to translates unresolved names for links into resolvable names for links.

We observe that at the inter-network level of a network architecture, our model explains internet addresses in the same way that it explains conventional mailbox addresses: there exists a name space for each network in the internet and a context associated with each gateway, such that the gateway contexts connect the network name spaces (i.e., gateways are modelled like mail relays). The resulting naming network defines internet addresses and is similar to the level for conventional mailbox addresses depicted in Fig. 17.13.

In addition, Φ models routing between the network attachment nodes in a network (as well as macro-routing between gateways in an internet),[31] similar to the way in which it models *UUCP* source-route names. That is, the name space for network addresses contains a set of contexts, each of which corresponds to a node in network. (Note that the naming network for network addresses, and the graph of the underlying network, are analogous to the graphs illustrated in Figs. 17.11 and 17.12, respectively.) Furthermore, because many networks allow implicit routing as well as explicit routing (i.e., source-routes), we note that a context that models the routing table at a given node contains a set of partial bindings, and that the arbitrary name in the pair returned by the context's translating function is the original name, thereby providing for the <u>same</u> name to be interpreted at the next context (i.e., network node).

A final note regarding the relationship between our model and routing in computer networks. Throughout this chapter we have assumed that the naming system is given and constant, and we have ignored the issue of how the bindings are defined and updated. In the name spaces like C_H, C_U, and C_D the bindings are defined by individuals and system administrators, and once defined, they remain relatively static (i.e., they only change when a mailbox is moved). In contrast, the bindings comprising name spaces that model the lowest levels of computer networks are defined and controlled by the network's *routing algorithm*; the bindings contained in the context corresponding to a given network node change to reflect the current network traffic.

The important point is that the bindings in <u>all</u> naming systems vary over time, but this variance plays a more significant role in computer networks. In other words, while our definition of a route is consistent with traditional definitions of routes, the conventional understanding of <u>routing</u> corresponds to the algorithm that define how bindings are <u>changed</u>, rather than to the resolution of an address according to the bindings defined by a context at a given instance of time.

Understanding the general principles involved in defining and changing bindings over time is a topic of future research. (We investigate changes to bindings that correspond to object relocation in the next section.)

8. OBJECT RELOCATION

As mentioned in the previous section, we have concentrated on issues involved in resolving names relative to a naming system that is assumed to exist and be static, and we have ignored the question of how the bindings that comprise a naming system are established and changed. We now briefly examine the changes to a naming system resulting from object relocation.

We begin by noting that multiple names may be defined in a single name space to identify a given object. In particular, as we describe in Section 4, there exist two types of contexts: public contexts that support names used by all users to identify objects (called public names), and private contexts that support user dependent names (called aliases). In addition, it is possible that several public names may be defined for the same object in a given name space. For example, in name space C_H, each user may name the object corresponding to John Doe's mailbox with a different alias (e.g., the alias *john* in Fig. 17.15). In addition, several public names may identify the mailbox, each of which identifies a different *role* played by John Doe (e.g., if John Doe is the head of the Research Division of National Labs, his mailbox might be namable as both *Doe/Research/Nlabs* and *Head/Research/NLabs*). A similar situation occurs in a *DOS* when a single file is assigned multiple names (i.e., several links exist to the file).

If a naming system allows multiple names for the same object to be defined in a name space (a concept directly related to object sharing), then it must insure that those names resolve to the object after changes are made to the bindings in the naming system. In particular, we are concerned with changes to bindings that occur to addresses because an object has been *relocated* to a new environment. One solution is to include information with each name ν, that identfies all qualified names that depend on ν (known as a *backward link*). Then, if ν is changed to ν' because the object has been relocated (e.g., moving John Smith's mailbox from *nlabs* to *stateu* implies that the low-level name changes from *jxs@nlabs* to *jxs@stateu*), the appropriate bindings can be changed. If a large number of names depend upon ν, however, backward links become impractical. In the rest of this Section, we shall consider two alternative solutions.

The first solution, called *forwarding*, uses an indirect binding within the same name space to link the old name ν to the new name ν'. That is, instead of replacing ν with ν' in some name space, the appropriate bindings for the new name are added to the name space. For example, if we attempt to resolve a name that depends on the name *jxs@nlabs*, in the situation where John Smith's mailbox moves from *nlabs* to *stateu*, then the delivery-process first moves to the environment corresponding to host *nlabs*, and is then forwarded to the environment corresponding to host *stateu*. Forwarding is similar to *soft* links in the UNIX file system because multiple path names for a file are bound to another path name.

A second solution is to simply limit the number of names that depend on a given physical name to one (therefore restricting the number of necessary backward links to one), and then bind the multiple names for an object to that one name; that is create an intermediate name space that defines a unique identifier for each object, and bind the multiple high-level names to that one unique-id. For example, to reflect the movement of John Smith's mailbox from *nlabs* to *stateu*, *Smith-UID* would have been bound to *jxs@stateu* instead of *jxs@nlabs* in name space C_U defined in Section 3. This technique is known as *redirection*, because the delivery-process is redirected to the correct environment. Redirection is similar to *hard* links in the UNIX file system because multiple file names are bound to a single *i-number*.

9. SUMMARY

This chapter presents a formal model for name resolution in distributed systems that views names to be purely syntactic entities, and name resolution to be a syntax-directed operation. Specifically, a distributed system's name resolution mechanism is described by a set of contexts that define interpretations of names (including moves through the environments in the system), such that the name resolution mechanism moves through a sequence of interpretations to resolve a name.

In addition to describing how names are resolved, we also formally define terminology for concepts and issues related to naming. First, we observe that when groups of contexts behave in a similar manner, they collectively form a level (or name space), each of which defines names of a given form (a view similar to Watson's model). We also identify the characteristic of levels that corresponds to Shoch's definition of names and addresses. Second, we note that the structure of the naming network that represents a name space leads to definitions for flat names, hierarchical names, and source-route names. Third, based upon the properties of the closure mechanism associated with Φ, we distinguish between absolute and relative names; abbreviated, full, and multiple names; and public names and aliases. We also define group names, generic names, and synonyms. Thus, our model both explains the partitioning of names into levels (as do Shoch's and Watson's models), as well as the nature of names corresponding to any given level (as does the Oppen and Dalal model). Finally, we describe the role of name servers in name resolution by defining the relationship between name servers and contexts, and we discuss the issue of object relocation.

A final note regarding our discussion of name resolution. Our model looks at only half of the naming problem; it considers resolution of names in a naming system that is assumed to exist, and it ignores the question of how the bindings that comprise the naming system are defined. To complete the picture, mechanisms for creating and deleting both objects and bindings should be defined.

REFERENCES

1. Allman, Eric, SENDMAIL—An internetwork mail router, in *UNIX Programmer's Manual*, vol. 2, 4.2, Berkeley Software Distribution, Aug. 1983.
2. Almes, Guy, Andrew Black, Edward Lazowska, and Jerre Noe, *The Eden System: A Technical Review*, Tech. Rep. 83-10-05, University of Washington, Seattle, WA, Oct. 1983.
3. Birrell, Andrew D., Roy Levin, Roger M. Needham, and Michael D. Schroeder, Grapevine: An exercise in distributed computing, *CACM*, vol. 25, pp. 260–273, Apr. 1982.
4. Birrell, Andrew, and Bruce Nelson, Implementing remote procedure calls, *ACM Trans. Computer Systems*, vol. 2, pp. 35–59, Feb. 1984.
5. Brownbridge, D. R., L. F. Marshall, and B. Randell, The Newcastle connection, *Software Practice and Experience*, vol. 12, pp. 1147–1162, 1982.
6. Cheriton, David and Willy Zwaenepoel, The distributed V kernel and its performance for diskless workstations, in *Proc. 9th ACM Symp. on Operating System Principles*, Oct. 1983, pp. 129–139.
7. Cheriton, David and Timothy Mann, Uniform access to distributed name interpretation, in *Proc. 4th Int. Conf. on Distributed Computing Systems*, (May 1984).
8. Comer, Douglas and Larry Peterson, A name resolution model for distributed systems, Tilde Tech. Rep. CSD-TR-491, Purdue University, Aug. 1984.
9. Comer, Douglas, The TILDE Project, Tilde Tech. Rep. CSD-TR-500, Purdue University, Nov. 1984.
10. Cunningham, I., *et al.*, Emerging protocols for global message exchange in *Proc. Fall COMPCON*, San Francisco, CA, Sept. 1982, pp. 153–161.
11. Daley, R. C. and J. B. Dennis, Virtual memory, processes, and sharing in MULTICS, *CACM*, vol. 11, pp. 306–312, May 1968.
12. Denning, Peter, Virtual memory, *ACM Comput. Surveys*, vol. 2, pp. 153–189, Sept. 1970.
13. Denning, Peter and Douglas Comer, *The CSNET User Environment*, Tech. Rep. CSD-TR-456, Purdue University, July 1981.
14. Dennis, Jack B. and Earl C. Van Horn, Programming semantics for multiprogrammed computations, *CACM*, vol. 9, pp. 143–155, Mar. 1966.
15. Fabry, R. S., Capability-Based Addressing, *CACM*, vol. 17, pp. 403–411, July 1974.
16. Henderson, D. A. The Binding Model: A semantic base for modular programming systems, Massachusetts Institute of Technology, Tech. Rep. MIT/LCS/TR-145, Feb. 1975.
17. Hopcroft, John and Jeffrey Ullman, *Introduction to Automata Theory, Languages, and Computation*, Reading, MA: 1979.
18. Johnston, John, The contour model of block structured processes, *Proc. Symp. on Data Structures in Programming Languages*, Gainesville, FL, Feb. 1971, pp. 55–82.
19. Jones, Anita, The object model: A conceptual tool for structuring software in *Lecture Notes in Computer Science: Operating Systems*, vol. 60, R. Bayer, R. M. Graham, and G. Seegmuller, eds. New York: Springer-Verlag, 1978, pp. 7–16.
20. Lampson, B. W., M. Paul, and H. J. Seigert, eds., *Lecture Notes in Computer Science: Distributed Systems—Architecture and Implementation*, vol. 105, pp. 1–9. New York: Springer Verlag, 1981.

21. Mockapetris, P., Domain names—Concepts and facilities, *Request For Comments*, 882, Nov. 1983.
22. Mockapetris, P., Domain names—Implementation and specification, *Request For Comments*, 883, Nov. 1983.
23. Norwitz, D. A. and M. E. Lesk, Implementation of a dial-up network of UNIX systems, in *UNIX Programmer's Manual*, vol. 2, 4.1, Berkeley Software Distribution, 1979.
24. Oppen, Derek and Yoger Dalal, The Clearinghouse: A Decentralized Agent for Locating Named Objects in a Distributed Environment, Res. Rep. Office Products Division, XEROX, Oct. 1981.
25. Postel, Jonathan B., Simple mail transfer protocol, *Request For Comments*, 821, Aug. 1982.
26. Postel, J. and J. Reynolds, Domain requirements, *Request For Comments*, 920, Oct. 1984.
27. Rashid, Richard F. and George Robertson, Accent: A communiction oriented network operating system kernal, *Proc. ACM Symp. on Operating System Principles*, Pacific Grove, CA, Dec. 1981, pp. 64–75.
28. Ritchie, Dennis and Ken Thompson, The UNIX time-sharing system, *CACM*, vol. 17, pp. 365–375, July 1974.
29. Saltzer, Jerome, Naming and binding of objects, in *Lecture Notes in Computer Science*, vol. 60, ch. 3, pp. 99–208. New York: Springer-Verlag, 1978.
30. Saltzer, Jerome, "On the naming and binding of network destinations, in *Proc. Int. Symp. on Local Computer Networks, IFIP/T.C.6*, Florence, Italy, Apr. 1982, pp. 311–317.
31. Schwartz, M. and T. E. Stern, Routing techniques used in computer communication networks, *IEEE Trans. Communications*, vol. COM-28, pp. 539–552, Apr. 1980.
32. Shoch, John F., Inter-network naming, addressing and routing, in *Proc. 17th IEEE Computer Society Int. Conf. (COMPCON)*, Sept. 1978, 72–79.
33. Sirbu, Marvin and Juliet Sutherland, Naming and directory issues in message transfer systems, in *Computer-Based Message Services*, H. T. Smith, Ed., pp. 15–37. New York: North-Holland, 1984.
34. Solomon, Marvin, Lawrence Landweber, and Donald Neuhegen, The CSNET name server, *Computer Networks*, vol. 6, pp. 161–172, 1982.
35. Sunshine, Carl, Source routing in computer networks, *ACM SIGCOMM Computer Comm. Rev.*, vol. 7, pp. 29–33, Jan. 1977.
36. Terry, D. B., An analysis of naming conventions for distributed computing systems, *SIGCOMM Tutorials and Symp. on Communications Architecture and Protocols*, Montreal, Canada, June 1984, pp. 218–224.
37. Walker, Bruce, Gerald Pepek, Robert English, Charles Kline, and Greg Thiel, The LOCUS distributed operating system, *Proc. 9th ACM Symp. on Operating System Principles*, Bretton Woods, NH, Oct. 1983, pp. 49–70.
38. Watson, Richard, Distributed system architecture model, in *Lecture Notes in Computer Science: Distributed Systems—Architecture and Implementation*, B. W. Lampson, M. Paul, and H. J. Siegert, eds. New York: Springer Verlag, 1981.
39. Watson, Richard, Identifiers (naming) in distributed systems, in *Lecture Notes in Computer Science: Distributed Systems—Architecture and Implementation*, pp. 191–210. B. W. Lampson, M. Paul, and H. J. Siegert, eds. New York: Springer Verlag, 1981.

18. Specification and Verification of Concurrent, Distributed Processes

JOYLYN N. REED, RAYMOND T. YEH,
and BO-SHOE CHEN

1. INTRODUCTION

This chapter describes a software specification and verification technique suitable for concurrent, distributed systems. *Specification* is a term with several meanings in the area of software engineering. It can refer to a set of general software requirements formulated at an early stage of system development. Or, it can refer to a concise mathematical characterization of the functionality of a program or program unit actually implemented with code. The specification technique described here is in the latter category. That is, it provides mathematical descriptions of functionality and behavior in such a way that (subsequent) implementations can be formally shown correct.

The specification/verification technique is based on the following three principles:

1. Structuring a large, complex program as a hierarchy of modules simplifies system design and implementation. A specification technique should be modular to reflect a hierarchical structure. Module specifications should characterize functionality and behavior, but hide nonessential detail, such as algorithms and data structures.

2. Specification techniques based on formal, i.e., mathematical, verifiability provide mechanisms to validate, before a program is executed, that it "does what it is supposed to do." To date, these mechanisms typically become prohibitively complex when applied to a large software system. However, research has demonstrated that formal verifiability of a program specification technique contributes significantly to an understanding of the programming language itself. The importance of underlying verification mechanisms for specification schemes is to foster well-designed programming languages and reliable programs.

3. A verification mechanism should allow independent verifications of modules; i.e., verification of a module specification should not require knowledge of the external environment of the module. Specifications which separate re-

quirements (directed at the environment) from commitments (by the module) support modular verification of hierarchically structured units. Consistency checks of the requirements and commitments of component modules should be part of the verification procedure for the corresponding higher level composite module.

The modular specification/verification technique outlined here deals with liveness properties of concurrent programs. The strategy is to combine an abstract specification language with an inductive-assertion based proof system for the implementation language. The technique is illustrated with the CSP of reference 9 as the implementation language. The reader is assumed to be familiar with this CSP. The abstract specification language is based on EBS.[4] The CSP proof system is an extension of the CSP proof system for safety properties of Soundararajan.[17,18]

Since a concurrent program is composed of sequential programs, it is not surprising that conterparts of inductive-assertion formal verification systems for sequential languages[5,8] exist for concurrent languages. Their inadequacy, particularly with respect to cyclic programs operating in distributed environments, stems from their inability to deal with a class of properties (informally called liveness), which are not of interest or are nonexistant for sequential programs. Intuitively, liveness properties are those that state "something (presumably good) happens (possibly repeatedly) in the future." Examples include program termination and guaranteed message deliveries. In contrast, safety properties are those that state "if something happens, then it is good." Assuming program termination, a description of program variables at termination is such a partial correctness property, as is, assuming transmission, a description of message content.

There are a number of concurrent language verification systems dealing with safety properties. Some of these include termination.[1,2,11,12,13,15,17] Inductive-assertion verification systems for liveness properties are fewer in number.[6,7,10,14] There are two aspects to formally dealing with liveness properties: their formulation and their verification. Certain liveness properties cannot even be formulated in those systems directed primarily at safety properties.

The use of abstraction serves two purposes. Besides its usual function of supporting modular specification and verification, abstraction provides a natural way to formulate liveness properties. There are two aspects to this use of abstraction. The first is the identification of abstractions suitable for describing module functionality and behavior, together with a proof system to enable meaningful interpretations and verifications. The second is the identification and abstract formulation of those attributes required of one module by another to support the latter's behavior. Formulation of these attributes, which deal with synchronization of communications, allows modular analysis of liveness properties of interacting component systems.

Section 2 presents the specification and verification technique. It firsts describes the abstract specification language. The section also describes the CSP proof system and its use in the specification and verification of programmed modules. Section 3 consists of examples.

2. AN ABSTRACT SPECIFICATION AND VERIFICATION METHOD

2.1. Preliminaries and Overview

Why do standard inductive-assertion proof systems not deal with liveness properties other than termination? To answer this question, perhaps a more revealing name for these verification methods is insertion-assertion proof systems. A correctness property is of the form $\{P\}S\{Q\}$, where S is the program, and each of P and Q is an assertion (predicate) describing a state or history of states of the program variables. For a sequential program S, $\{P\}S\{Q\}$ is verified by producing an annotated program (i.e., S interspersed with assertions) with $\{P\}$ and $\{Q\}$ as the first and last assertions, respectively. For a concurrent program, the correctness property is typically inferred by the application of certain rules to a set of individually verified correctness properties for the component sequential programs. Annotated programs are produced according to the axioms and rules of the proof system. Intuitively, the insertion of an assertion into a program means that, during execution, whenever control is at the corresponding point, the assertion describes the associated state or history of states of the variables.

Thus, unless extended, these systems can only formulate properties dealing with a finite current state or a finite number of state transitions. Referring to an infinite future is beyond their reach. Since termination is a property of a finite future, extensions of these systems with rules proving termination provide no insight into dealing with general properties of an infinite future.

2.1.1. Deducing Liveness Properties from Safety Properties

However, a preassertion (loop invariant) for an infinite cyclic statement of a nonterminating programs describes all possible ''pasts'' of the program's infinite future. The basis for the verification technique described here is a formulation of an infinite future in such a way that its description follows from verifiable descriptions of all of its finite ''pasts.''

This formulation is natural within a proof system with the ability to prove termination and whose assertions refer to finite history variables (sequences). The system is extended with an axiom which establishes an infinite history sequence for those programs containing infinite while loops. This infinite sequence is the union of a countable collection of finite histories, each of which satisfies the loop invariant and is a subset of its successor. This is the mechanism for proving liveness properties (of an infinite future) from corresponding safety properties. Owicki and Lamport,[14] in providing an inference rule with temporal operators to deduce liveness properties from safety properties, demonstrate that such a mechanism is the key to reasoning about liveness properties. The application of the axiom requires first proving a special kind of liveness property, that a given statement is an infinite while loop.

2.1.2. Abstract Specification—Procedural Implementation

The technique described here uses abstractions to capture the essence of system behavior, including ''forever live'' behaviors, and to facilitate stepwise development of modularly structured programs by hiding nonimmediate detail. The previously mentioned axiom provides the means to interpret these abstractions in a natural way. The technique includes specification and verification of terminating processes, but this chapter is concerned with the application of cyclic processes.

A concurrent program is hierarchically structured as a set of interacting modules. Each module is classified as *composite*, i.e., composed of other interacting modules, or *implementation*, i.e., implemented directly with code. At each level, the composite modules can further be decomposed into their component modules, which are themselves either composite or implementation.

A module specification consists of an external part and an internal part. The (externally known) external part, which is of the same type for both composite and implementation modules, consists of the following nonprocedural abstract descriptions:

1. behavior—input/output descriptions.
2. requirements—what is needed from the linked modules to support the specified module's behavior, and
3. commitments—what the specified module provides to linked modules to support their behavior.

The internal specification is not externally known. The type of internal specification depends on whether the module is composite or implementation. A composite internal specification consists of a list of external specifications of component modules, together with communication channel connections. An implementation internal specification is procedural. It consists of code plus explicit interpretations of the external abstractions.

Verification of a composite module requires establishing that: 1) the external behaviors of the component modules imply the external behavior of the composite module, and 2) the requirements and commitments of the component modules are mutually supportive and consistent. Verification of the implementation module requires an annotation establishing that the specified interpretation satisfies the abstract external description.

2.2. External Specification of a Module

An external specification of a module is a nonprocedural axiomatic description of abstractions (which are interpreted in internal procedural specifications of implementation modules). This abstract view of a module is an extension of that of EBS.[4]

A system consist of undefined, partially ordered (by "→") events. Events referred to in an external specification of a module belong to one of three sets: ENV (the environment of the module), SYS (internal to the module), or PORTS (a set of single direction communication channels between the module and its environment). PORT events have associated messages. With each port A of module S is associated a set of events, denoted READY(A), which is internal to S, and, hence, a subset of SYS(S). Interpretations for the abstractions must satisfy certain general axioms, which are listed below. An external specification further limits the interpretations for a specific module.

2.2.1. *General Axioms*

Axiom 1. The events of a single PORT are well-ordered.

In the next axiom, LINK refers to a composite module specification term, and is explained in the next section. Suffice it here to note that a LINK C of ports A and B equates these sequences of events, and redundantly names this sequence C. Intuitively, the axiom states that communication takes place whenever and only when two modules are simultaneously ready.

Axiom 2. Synchronization axiom—let A and B be ports of modules M and N, respectively, connected via LINK C. Then:

$$\begin{aligned}&\forall i(i \geq 1 \Rightarrow (c_i \in C \Rightarrow ra_i \rightarrow c_i \wedge rb_i \rightarrow c_i \wedge \\ &(i > 1 \Rightarrow c_{i-1} \rightarrow ra_i \wedge c_{i-1} \rightarrow rb_i)) \wedge \\ &(|\text{READY}(A)| \geq i \wedge |\text{READY}(B)| \geq i \Rightarrow |C| \geq i))\end{aligned}$$

where $C = \langle c_1, c_2, \ldots \rangle$, $\text{READY}(A) = \langle ra_1, ra_2, \ldots \rangle$, $\text{READY}(B) = \langle rb_1, rb_2, \ldots \rangle$, and $|S|$ denotes the cardinality of S.

2.2.2. *External Specification Constructs*

The external specification of a module (as shown in the EXTERNAL part of Fig. 18.2) consists of three parts. BEHAVIOR describes port events (including, perhaps both message content and order). REQUIRE and PROVIDE describe system READY events: those that are required of linked modules to support the specified module's behavior, and, those that are provided by the specified module to linked modules.

2.3. Internal Specification and Verification of a Composite Module

Figure 18.1 represents a composite module composed of two submodules. The internal specification of a composite modules (shown as the INTERNAL STRUCTURE of Fig. 18.2), consists of a list of external specifications of submodules plus channel connections. A network link connects a submodule inport to another submodule outport. An interface link connects a composite module inport [outport] to a submodule inport [outport]. For the verification procedure, a link of two ports implies that their event sequences are equal.

Verification of a composite module is two step. First, the EXTERNAL BEHAVIOR's of the submodules plus the LINK's must imply the composite BEHAVIOR. Second, the PROVIDE's and REQUIRE's must be mutually supportive and consistent. Intuitively, a PROVIDE statement is of the form "if the module linked to one port meets a certain requirement, then this module makes a certain commitment with respect to another port." Requirements directed at modules external to a given composite module may be assumed for the verification of the internal structure of this module; verification of these requirements is part of the verification procedure for the higher level module containing the composite module as a submodule. Thus, the PROVIDE's of the submodules plus the REQUIRE's referring to INTERFACE linked systems must imply the submodule REQUIRE's referring to linked submodules. Additionally, the component PROVIDE's must imply the composite PROVIDE, and the composite REQUIRE must be the conjunction of the submodule REQUIRE's referring to INTERFACE linked systems.

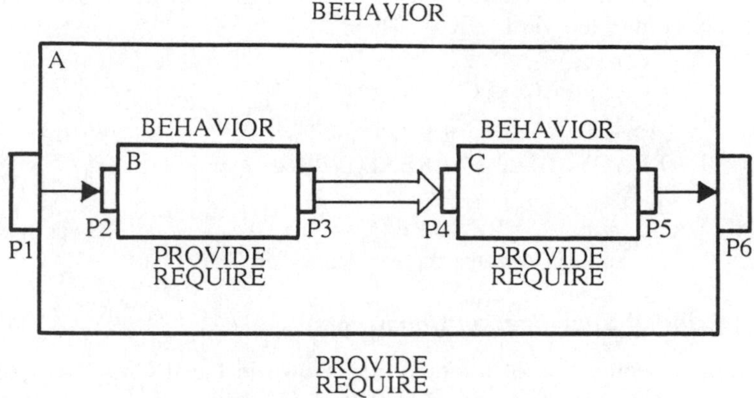

Fig. 18.1. Composite module. Composite Module: A; Submodules: B, C; Ports: P1, P2, P3, P4, P5, P6; Network Links: ═; Interface Links: —.

```
SYSTEM          (* name and port declarations *)

  EXTERNAL          (* externally seen abstract description *)

    BEHAVIOR          (* port-event descriptions *)
    REQUIRE           (* what is required from the linked systems *)
    PROVIDE           (* what is provided to the linked systems *)

  INTERNAL STRUCTURE   (* the internal composition *)
    SUBSYSTEM
      EXTERNAL
        BEHAVIOR
        REQUIRE
        PROVIDE                  (* component system
    .                               abstract external
    .                               descriptions *)

    NETWORK           (* internal channel connections *)
      LINK
              .
              .       (* <portname> = = <portname> = <portname> *)
              .

    INTERFACE         (* internal-to-external channel connections *)
      LINK
              .
              .       (* <portname> = = <portname> = <portname> *)
              .

end SYSTEM
```

Fig. 18.2. Template of a composite module specification.

2.4. CSP Proof System

The addition of two axioms to a generalized version of the safety property proof system of reference 16 provides the means to interpret the event and relation abstractions of an external specification. Soundararajan's system, similar to reference 3, is characterized by communication history sequences of messages and independent proofs of component process correctness properties. A proof of $\{p\} P_1 // \ldots // P_N \{q\}$ is two-step. First, individual proofs of properties of the form, $\{p_i\} P_i \{q_i\}$ are derived in isolation; that is, q_i represents the strongest possible description of the variables and communications (in terms of a communication history, H_i) of P_i (if and at termination) provable without knowledge of coprocess interaction (other than synchronization). Second, q is shown to follow from the conjunction of the q_i's and the predicate COMPAT defined on the H_i's. Intuitively, COMPAT describes the ordered intersections, imposed by the strict synchronization requirement of CSP, on the history sequences of messages.

Below, we provide the "flavor" of the "safety" semantics of CSP. For simplicity, these axioms and rules do not reflect the distributed termination convention; and the failure of all boolean guards of an alternative statement results in the execution of a SKIP statement. The primary difference between these rules and the systems of reference 16 is the inclusion of "ready" elements to communication histories (an idea suggested by the ready sequence mechanism of Hoare[10]). Thus, in this system, CSP I/O statements are not atomic. Not listed but included are the standard rules for SKIP, assignment, composition, conjunction, and disjunction. The assertion $P[t/x]$ represents the assertion P with t substituted for all free occurrence of x. $S/-x$ denotes the sequence x concatenated to the end of sequence S.

Axiom *Output* (for I/O not in a guard):
$\{p[H_i/-\ \langle\{(i,j,\text{ready})\},\ (i,j,y)\rangle\ /\ H_i]\}\ P_j!y\ \{p\}$

Axiom *Input* (for I/O not in a guard):
$\{\forall u(p[u,H_i\ /-\ \langle\{(j,i,\text{ready})\},\ (j,i,u)\rangle\ /\ x,H_i])\}\ P_j?x\ \{p\}$

The effect of each of these two axioms is to extend the communication history by two elements, a "ready" element and a "message" element.

The semantics of I/O statements in guards are different. We first define the transmission part of $P_j!$ $[P_j?]$ to be $P_j!!$ $[P_j??]$, with the following semantics:

Axiom *Goutput*:

$$\{p[H_i\ /-\ \langle(i,j,y)\rangle\ /\ H_i]\}\ P_j!!y\ \{p\}$$

Axiom *Ginput*:

$$\{\forall u\ (p[u,\ H_i\ /-\ \langle(j,i,u)\rangle\ /\ x,H_i])\ \}\ P_j??\ x\ \{p\}$$

Guarded statements have the following semantics:

Rule *Guarded Alternative*:

$$\begin{array}{l} p \Rightarrow q_1[H_i\ /-\ \langle\{d_k,\text{ready}\mid Bg_k\}\rangle\ /\ H_i], \\ \{q_1 \wedge B(g_k)\}\ C_t(g_k);\ S_k\ \{q\}, \\ p \wedge (\forall k(\sim B(g_k)) \Rightarrow q,\ k = 1, 2, \ldots, m \\ \hline \{p\}\ [(k=1, \ldots, m)\ g_k \rightarrow S_k]\ \{q\}. \end{array}$$

Rule *Guarded Repetition*:

$$\{p\}\ [(k=1, \cdots, m)g_k \rightarrow S_k]\ \{p\}$$
$$\text{- -}$$
$$\{p\}\ *[(k=1, \ldots, m)g_k) \rightarrow S_k]\ \{p \wedge \forall k(\sim B(g_k))\}$$

where $g_1, \ldots, g_m$, are guards, $B(g_k)$ denotes the boolean part of g_k, d_k denotes the direction part of g_k, and $C_t(g_k)$ denotes the transmission part of g_k and is of the form $P_j??x$ or $P_j!!y$.

Intuitively, the predecessor of a message element (from an I/O in a guard) in the communication sequence is a set of ready elements corresponding to the set of communications enabled in the guard.

Rule *Parallel Composition*:

$$\{I_i \wedge H_i = \{\}\}\ P_i\ \{Q_i\},\ i = 1, \ldots, N$$
$$\text{- -}$$
$$\{\wedge_i I_i\}\ P_1 // \ldots // P_N\ \{(\wedge_i Q_i) \wedge \text{COMPAT}(H_1, \ldots, H_N)\},$$

where COMPAT is defined:

COMPAT($H_1, \ldots, H_N$) = if $H_1 = H_2 = \ldots = H_N = \{\ \}$
  then TRUE
  else if $\exists i,j(i \neq j \wedge \text{first}(H_i) \ \underline{*}\ \text{first}(H_j))$
    then COMPAT($H_1, \ldots,$ rest(H_i), $\ldots,$ rest(H_j) $\ldots, H_N$)
    else FALSE.

The relation $\underline{*}$ for message elements is equality, and for ready elements is that their intersection is nonempty. Intuitively, the above rule states that whenever one process records a communication with another, the latter also recorded the communication in a way mutually consistent with all other coprocesses' histories.

2.4.1. Cyclic and Potentially Cyclic Statements

In order to prove general properties of cyclic processes, it is first necessary to prove that these processes cycle. For certain processes, it is feasible to divide this task into two steps: 1) establishing that a given statement is p-cyclic (potentially cyclic—i.e., cyclic under the assumption of blocking freedom), and 2) with assumptions about coprocesses, establishing blocking freedom.

A technique for proving that P_i p-cycles on statement $S = *[GS]$, for program

$P_i = S_o; S;$, is to produce an annotation for P_i, which establishes that: 1. S_0 contains no infinite WHILE loops, 2. $[GS]$ contains no infinite WHILE loops, and 3. Postcondition$(S) \Rightarrow$ FALSE.

Steps 1. and 2. are accomplished with Floyd's technique[5] of mapping an annotated flowchart into a well-ordered set in such a way that the assumption of an infinite WHILE loop produces an infinite decreasing sequence in the well-ordered set. For some processes, p-cycling can be established in isolation, i.e., without information about received message contents.

The establishment of blocking freedom for P_i can be accomplished by comparisons of descriptions of P_i's communication sequence corresponding to blocking situations with descriptions of coprocess communication sequences derived with no implicit assumptions about blocking freedom. If each "blocking" communication sequence for P_i is shown to be "compatible" with some coprocess communication subsequence, then blocking freedom for P_i is assumed.

The following two axioms provide the mechanism to derive these descriptions of communication histories and comparisons which ensure blocking freedom. Possibly infinite communication histories yield interpretations for the abstractions of external specifications. Final segments, which correspond to tails of execution sequences, are statically determined annotated subgraphs of a process annotated flowchart. $A \leq B\,[A < B]$ denotes that A is an [proper] initial segment of B. The variables i and j range over the set of positive integers.

Intuitively, SH, which represents the communication history of P_i, assuming proper coprocess synchronization, is composed of a monotonic collection of finite histories, each element of which represents a subhistory corresponding to an iteration of S. H^* represents the communication history of P_i, linked to arbitrary coprocesses, i.e., with no implicit assumptions of synchronization. Axiom 3 intuitively states that if the processes do not synchronize properly and P_i becomes permanently blocked, H^* is a finite sequence whose last element is a ready element.

Axiom 3. The history sequence axiom. Let P_i be a process which p-cycles on statement S. Let Q be the preassertion for S in an annotation for P_i. Then there exist communication histories, H^* and SH, and a sequence of communication histories, $H_1, H_2, H_3, \ldots$ satisfying:

I. 1. $\forall i(H_i \leq H_{i+1} \leq SH)$
   2. $\forall i(\exists X_i(Q\,[X_i, H_i \,/\, X, H]))$,
   3. $H^* \leq SH$,

where X is the set of nonhistory local variables of P_i,

II. if every final segment of P_i contains an I/O statement, then

1. $\forall i(\exists j(H_i < H_j))$,
2. $H^* < SH \Rightarrow val(\text{last}(H^*)) = \text{ready}$,

III. if P_i cycles on S, then $H^* = SH$.

Axiom 4. Let H_i^* and H_j^* be *histories for coprocesses P_i and P_j, respectively. Then:

1. $\forall k(\#r(H_i^*,i,j) \geq k \wedge \#r(H_j^*,i,j) \geq k \Rightarrow$
   $\#m(H_i^*,i,j) \geq k \wedge \#m(H_i^*,i,j) \geq k)$,
2. $\text{ready}(\text{last}(Hi^*)) \vee \text{ready}(\text{last}(H_j^*)) \Rightarrow \sim(\text{last}(H_i^*) \underline{*} \text{last}(H_j^*))$,

where $\#r(H, i, j)$ [$\#m(H, i, j)$] represents the number of elements in H of type $\{(i, j, \text{ready})\}$ [(i, j, x)], and ready(e) is a predicate stating that element e is a ready element. The analogous statement of (1.) holds for direction (j, i).

Intuitively, Axiom 4 states that two coprocesses do not block with respect to one another if they become simultaneously ready to communicate. Thus, to prove P_i is blocking free, it is sufficient to establish that H_i^*, in conjunction with coprocess *histories, does not contain a ready element as its last element.

A cyclic statement may be inside a WHILE loop, and the program may exit it several times before becoming forever in it. Thus, the previously described technique for proving p-cycling is not completely general; its applicability may serve as criteria for "well-structured" cyclic programs. If establishing that there are no infinite WHILE loops requires information about message content, a third step is necessary to prove cycling; i.e., descriptions of coprocess *histories must be shown to satisfy assumptions made about them. Although such procedures are possible, it may be that such tightly-coupled processes are not amenable to this type of modular approach.

The next section describes how these axioms provide interpretations, stated in internal specifications of implementation modules, for external abstractions.

2.5. Internal Specification and Verification of an Implementation Module

The internal specification of an implementation module (as shown in the template of Fig. 18.3), is procedural and consists of three parts. The CODE is a CSP process. The PERFORMANCE describes the *history. INTERPRET explicitly identifies ports, declared in the first line, with subsequences of the *history.

Associated with each explicit interpretation of a port A is an implicit interpretation of READY(A) as the subsequence of the *history corresponding to A. With the natural interpretation of "→", axioms A1 and A2 are satisfied.

```
SYSTEM          (* name and port declarations *)

   EXTERNAL         (* external description *)

      BEHAVIOR         (* description of port events *)
      PROVIDE          (* description of system ready events *)
      REQUIRE          (* description of the ready events
                          required of the systems in the environment
                          linked to the ports *)

   INTERNAL         (* internal implementation description *)

      CODE             (* CSP program *)
      PERFORMANCE
         terminates                  (* one of these statements *)
         cycles
         assert                      (* statement describing the *history
                                        sequence of Axiom B1 *)

      INTERPRET        (* designations of ports as subsequences
                          of the *history sequence *)
```

Fig. 18.3. Template of an implementation module specification.

The role of READY events is to formulate willingness-to-communicate attributes of component modules.

For example, an isolated analysis of a process P_i can establish that it is forever willing to alternate sending and receiving to P_j; that is, an annotation establishes that H_i^* has the following property, where ready(H_i^*, k, i, j) [mess(H_i, k, i, j)] is a predicate representing that the kth element of H_i^* is a ready [message] element with direction (i, j):

$$\exists k(\text{ready}(H_i^*,k,i,j)) \wedge \\ (\text{mess}(H_i^*,k,i,j) \Rightarrow \exists k'>k(\text{ready}(H_i^*,k',j,i)) \\ \wedge (\text{mess}(H_i^*,k,j,i) \Rightarrow \exists k'>k(\text{ready}(H_i^*,k',i,j)).$$

If ports A and B are interpreted as subsequences of H_i^* corresponding to directions (i, j) and (j, i) respectively, then the translated commitment from P_i to P_j is:

$$\exists r \in \text{READY}(A) \wedge (a \in A \Rightarrow \exists r \in \text{READY}(B)(a \rightarrow r)) \wedge \\ (b \in B \Rightarrow \exists r \in \text{READY}(A)(b \rightarrow r)).$$

If P_j makes an analogous commitment, then P_i and P_j do not block with respect to one another; the assumption that they do violates Axiom 2 (and 4).

Verification of an implementation module is two part. First, the *assert* and INTERPRET statements must imply the BEHAVIOR. Second, an annotation must establish the PERFORMANCE and the translated PROVIDE statements. The translated REQUIRE statements may be assumed in order to verify the PERFORMANCE. REQUIRE states what is required from coprocesses to ensure blocking freedom for the specified process; and, hence, that its p-cyclic statement is indeed cyclic. The PROVIDE statement must be derived without such assumptions of coprocess synchronization.

3. EXAMPLES

Example 3.1, which illustrates that two different internal implementations are possible for the same external specification, specifies and verifies a module, first as an implementation module and then as a composite module. Example 3.2 specifies and verifies an implementation module. Example 3.3 specifies and verifies a composite module, which contains the module of 3.2 as a submodule.

The following are simplifying definitions:

1. abc_i represents the ith element of sequence ABC.
2. $ER(X) == \exists r \in \text{READY}(X) \wedge (x \in X \Rightarrow \exists r \in \text{READY}(X)(x \rightarrow r))$.
3. $ERA(X,Y) == \exists r \in \text{READY}(X) \wedge (x \in X \Rightarrow \exists r \in \text{READY}(Y)(x \rightarrow r)) \wedge (y \in Y \Rightarrow \exists r \in \text{READY}(X)(y \rightarrow r))$.

ER [*ERA*] is a predicate indicating that a module is ever-ready to communicate [alternatively] via X [via X and Y]. The next two predicates defined on communication histories state that the kth element is a ready or message element, respectively.

4. $\text{ready}(P_i, P_j, H, k) == \text{elem}(H, k) = \{(P_i, P_j, \text{ready})\}$.
5. $\text{mess}(P_i, P_j, H, k) == \exists x(\text{elem}(H, k) = (P_i, P_j, x))$.

3.1. Reliable Transmission Service

Module RTS is a reliable transmission service which relays messages from one module to another. Figure 18.4 is the external specification of RTS. Section 3.1.1. specifies and verifies RTS as an implementation module, i.e., implemented directly with code. Section 3.1.2 specifies and verifies RTS as a composite module, i.e., composed of two submodules. These two different implementation for RTS are represented schematically in Fig. 18.5. Note that this specification does not indicate the buffer size of RTS.

SYSTEM RTS (A: INPORT; B: OUTPORT);

EXTERNAL

BEHAVIOR

B1 = = $\forall i(a_i \rightarrow b_i \wedge b_i$.mess = a_i.mess).

REQUIRE

(*Systems linked at A and B must be ever-ready to communicate via A and B*)

R1 = = ER(PORTLINK(A)).
R2 = = ER(PORTLINK(B)).

PROVIDE

(*Systems linked to A and B ever-ready to communicate implies RTS ever-ready to communicate via A and B*)

P1 = = R1 ⇒ ER(B).
P2 = = R2 ⇒ ER(A).

Fig. 18.4. External specification of RTS.

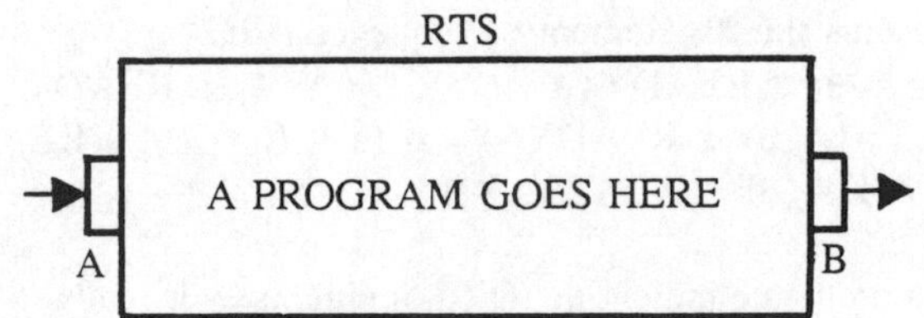

RTS implemented as a single-element buffer (Implementation Module).

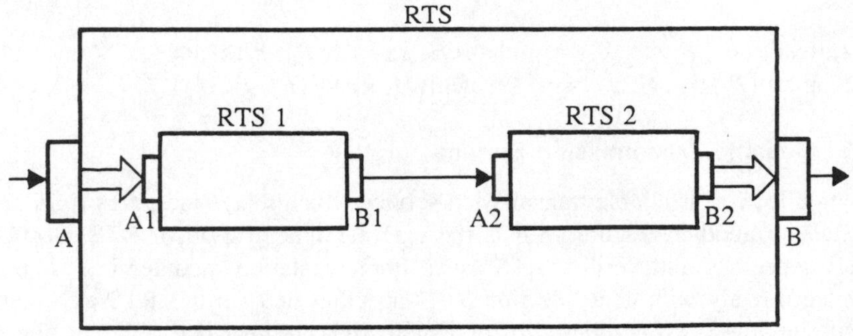

RTS implemented as a two-element buffer (Composite Module).

Fig. 18.5. Two implementations for RTS.

3.1.1. Specification and Verification of RTS as an Implementation Module

Fig. 18.6 is the specification of RTS as an implementation module.

For simplicity, RTS expects to be continually activated. The predicate FOUR (describing consecutive subsequences of four elements), defined for communication history H and positive integer i is:

$$\text{FOUR}(H,i) = \text{ready}(\text{LA},\text{RTS},H,i-3) \wedge \text{mess}(\text{LA},\text{RTS},H,i-2) \wedge \text{ready}(\text{RTS},\text{LB},H,i-1) \wedge \text{mess}(\text{RTS},\text{LB},H,i) \wedge \text{val}(H,i) = \text{val}(H,i).$$

Verification of RTS is two-part.

1. The *assert* and INTERPRET statements must imply the EXTERNAL BEHAVIOR statement. RTS.B1 follows immediately from the former statements and the implicit interpretation of "→" as ordinary sequential order.
2. An annotation for RTS must establish the PERFORMANCE and the translated PROVIDE statements. Since the PERFORMANCE statements depend on proper synchronization with coprocesses, the translated RE-

```
SYSTEM RTS (A: INPORT; B; OUTPORT:)
INTERNAL
  CODE
    RTS::
        b := TRUE;
    ST: *[b;LA?x → b := FALSE;
         ▮
           b;LB!x → b := TRUE;
         ]
  PERFORMANCE
    cyclic ST. (*RTS cycles on ST*)

    assert · (*The assertion about the *history of Axiom 3*)
       ∀i(imod4 = 1 ⇒ FOUR(H*,i)).
  INTERPRET
  (*A is the set of elements read from LA*)
  A = {c|c ∈ H* ∧ dir(c)=(LA,RTS)}.

  (*B is the set of elements written to LB*)
  B = {c|c ∈ H* ∧ dir(c)=(RTS,LB)}.
```

Fig. 18.6. Internal specification of RTS as an implementation module.

QUIRE statements may be assumed for the verification of PERFORMANCE. In contrast, verification of the PROVIDE statements, which represent commitments by RTS to an arbitrary set of coprocesses, does not assume the REQUIRE statements.

A partial annotation is shown in Fig. 18.7. The loop invariant, LI, is defined as follows (H is the communication history and last(H,2) represents the two-element tail of H):

$$LI == (\forall i (i \leq |H| \wedge i\text{mod}4 = 0 \Rightarrow \text{FOUR}(H,i)) \wedge (b \Rightarrow |H|\text{mod}4 = 0) \wedge (\sim b \Rightarrow |H|1\text{mod}4 = 2 \wedge \text{last}(H,2) = \langle\{(LA,RTS,ready)\}, (LA,RTS,x)\rangle).$$

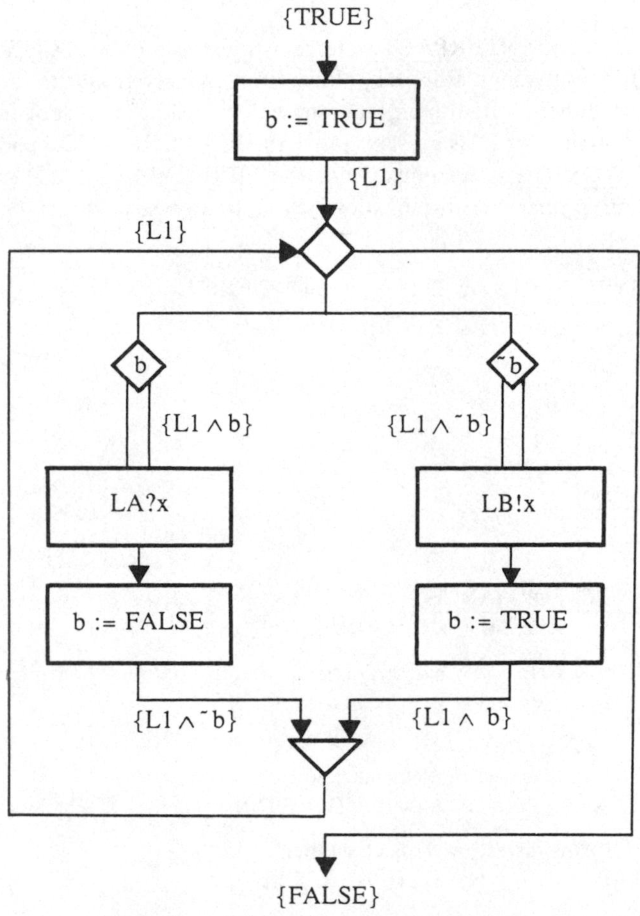

Fig. 18.7. Partial annotation of RTS.

1. Verifying that ST is cyclic requires establishing: 1) "b := TRUE;" terminates, 2) no blocking implies that the interior guarded statement terminates, 3) postcondition of ST is {FALSE}, and, 4) RTS does not block at an I/O.

   Conditions 1, 2, and 3 are obvious, and establish that ST is p-cyclic. The translated requirements R1 and R2 state that LA and LB should be forever willing to send and receive to RTS, respectively. These requirements in conjunction with Axioms 3 and 4 establish that RTS is blocking free.
2. The *assert* statement follows from Axiom 3, and that ST is cyclic and all final segments of RTS contain an I/O statement.
3. The PROVIDE statements follow from Axiom 3(I) and 3(II).

3.1.2. Specification and Verification of RTS as Composite Module

Figure 18.8 is the internal specification of RTS in terms of submodules RTS1 and RTS2. The external specification of each of these modules is simply that of the external specification of RTS (Fig. 18.4) with A_i and B_i substituted for A and B, respectively. Thus, the composite RTS is implemented as a two-place buffer.

Verification of composite module RTS is two-part. First, the BEHAVIOR must follow from the subsystem BEHAVIOR's and the port sequence equivalences designated by the NETWORK and INTERFACE links. Second, the REQUIRE's and PROVIDE's must be mutually supportive and consistent. "LINKS" is shorthand for "LINK(BA) ∧ LINK(AA) ∧ LINK(BB)."

```
SYSTEM RTS (A: INPORT; B: OUTPORT);
INTERNAL STRUCTURE (* Composite *)
   SUBSYSTEM RTS1 (A1: INPORT; B1: OUTPORT);
   SUBSYSTEM RTS2 (A2: INPORT; B2: OUTPORT);
   NETWORK
      LINK(BA) == RTS1(B1) = RTS2(A2);
   INTERFACE
      LINK(AA) == RTS(A) = RTS1(A1);
      LINK(BB) == RTS(B) = RTS2(B2);
   end SYSTEM.
```

Fig. 18.8. Internal specification of composite module RTS.

I. The following implication establishes that the BEHAVIOR of RTS follows straightforwardly from the composition of its submodules:

$$\text{RTS1.B1} \wedge \text{RTS2.B1} \wedge \text{LINKS} \Rightarrow \text{RTS.B1}$$

II.

1. The following implications establish that the subsystem REQUIRE's (i.e., by the submodules of the submodules) follow from the PROVIDE's (by the submodules to the submodules) and the REQUIRE's (by the composite module of external modules).

   i. RTS2.P2 ∧ RTS.R2 ∧ LINK(BA) ∧ LINK(BB) ⇒ RTS1.R2
   ii. RTS1.P1 ∧ RTS.R1 ∧ LINK(BA) ∧ LINK(AA) ⇒ RTS2.R1

2. The following implications establish that the composite PROVIDE follows from the subsystem PROVIDE's and the links. Clauses i. and ii. are given above.

   iii. RTS2.P1 ∧ RTS1.P1 ∧ (ii) ∧ LINKS ⇒ RTS.P1
   iv. RTS1.P2 ∧ RTS.P2 ∧ (i) ∧ LINKS ⇒ RTS.P2

3. The following implication establishes that the composite REQUIRE is the conjunction of the subsystem REQUIRE's involving systems linked via the INTERFACE:

$$\text{RTS.R1} \wedge \text{RTS.R2} \wedge \text{LINKS} \Leftrightarrow \text{RTS1.R1} \wedge \text{RTS2.R2} \wedge \text{LINKS}$$

3.2. An Implementation Module

Figures 18.9 and 18.10 contain the specification of an implementation module, FORM-F, which computes a function F from the natural numbers to {true,false}. The nature of F, which is to determine if a number is prime, is purposely not revealed in this external description. For simplicity, the module expects to be continually activated. The predicate FOUR (describing consecutive subsequences of four elements), defined for communication history H and integer i is:

$$\begin{aligned}\text{FOUR(H,i)} = {} & \text{ready}\,(U,\text{FORM}-\text{F},H,i-3) \wedge \text{mess}(U,\text{FORM-F},H,i-2) \\ & \wedge \text{ready}(\text{FORM-F},U,H,i-1) \wedge \text{mess}(\text{FORM}-\text{F},U,H,i) \\ & (val(H,i+3) = \sim(\exists j(1<j<val(H,i-2) \wedge val(H,i-2)\text{mod}j = 0))).\end{aligned}$$

3.2.1. *Verification of Implementation Module FORM-F*

Verification of FORM-F is two-part.

1. The *assert* and INTERPRET statements must imply the EXTERNAL BE-

SYSTEM FORM-F (FIN: INPORT; FOUT: OUTPORT);

EXTERNAL

BEHAVIOR

B1 == $\forall i((\text{fin}_i \rightarrow \text{fout}_i \rightarrow \text{fin}_{i+1}) \wedge (\text{fout}_i.\text{mess} = F(\text{fin}_i.\text{mess})))$.

REQUIRE

(*FIN and FOUT must be linked to the same module*)
R1 == SYS(PORTLINK(FIN)) = SYS(PORTLINK(FOUT)).

(*The linked module should be ever-ready to communicate alternatively via these ports*)

R2 == ERA(PORTLINK(FIN), PORTLINK(FOUT)).

PROVIDE

(*FORM-F is ever-ready to communicate alternatively via FIN and FOUT*)
P1 == ERA(FIN,FOUT).

(*Restatement of port declarations to aid verification*)
P2 == SYS(FIN) = SYS(FOUT).

Fig. 18.9. External specification of FORM-F.

HAVIOR statement. FORM-F.B1 follows immediately from the former statements and the implicit interpretation of "→" as ordinary sequential order.

2. An annotation for FORM-F must establish the PERFORMANCE and the translated PROVIDE statements. Since the PERFORMANCE statements depend on proper synchronization with coprocesses, the translated REQUIRE statements may be assumed for the verification of PERFORMANCE. In contrast, verification of the PROVIDE statements, which represent commitments by FORM-F to an arbitrary set of coprocesses, does not assume the REQUIRE statements.

A partial annotation is shown in Fig. 18.11. The loop invariant, LI, is defined as follows (H is the communication history):

$$\text{LI} == \forall k(1 < k \leq |H| \wedge k \bmod 4 = 0 \Rightarrow \text{FOUR}(H, k))$$

1. Verifying that ST is cyclic requires establishing: 1) FORM-F does not block at an I/O, 2) no blocking implies the interior guarded statement of ST terminates, and 3) the postcondition of ST is {FALSE}.

   Condition 3. is obvious. A mapping (à la Floyd) from the arcs of the repetitive statement into a well-ordered set of three-tuples is indicated in the annotation, and establishes Condition 2. Hence, ST is p-cyclic. R1 and R2 state that U should be forever willing to alternate sending and

```
SYSTEM FORM-F(FIN: INPORT; FOUT: OUTPORT);

INTERNAL

CODE

FORM-F::

ST: *[U?x → y := TRUE; i := 2;
          [x≤2 → b := FALSE;
           ▮
           x>2 → b := TRUE;]
          *[b ∧ i≤x/2 ∧ xmodi ≠ 0 → i := i+1;
            ▮
            b ∧ xmodi = 0 → b := FALSE; y := FALSE;
            ▮
            b ∧ i>x/2 → b := FALSE;]
          U!y]

PERFORMANCE
   cyclic ST.
   assert ∀i(imod4=1 ⇒ FOUR(H*,i)).

INTERPRET
   FIN == {c|c ∈ H* ∧ dir(c)=(U,FORM-F)}.
   FOUT == {c|c ∈ H* ∧ dir(c)=(FORM-F,U)}.

   (* The definition of F, not known externally, is specified here *)
   F == F(x) =~ (∃j(1<j<x) ∧ xmodj = 0)).

end SYSTEM
```

Fig. 18.10. Internal specification of FORM-F.

receiving to FORM-F. These translated requirements in conjunction with Axioms 3 and 4 imply that the blocking of FORM-F yields inconsistent *histories for FORM-F and U. Hence, FORM-F does not block, and 1. is established.

2. The *assert* statement follows from Axiom 3, and that ST is cyclic and all final segments of FORM-F contain I/O statements.
3. The PROVIDE statement follows from Axiom 3(I) and 3(II).

3.3. Set Example

Module SET, with ports A and B, maintains a set membership list of people. Requests for additions come in through port A, and are answered (YES or NOTELIGIBLE) though port B. A person's eligibility is determined by formulas F and G, whose exact natures are hidden within the module. The module as-

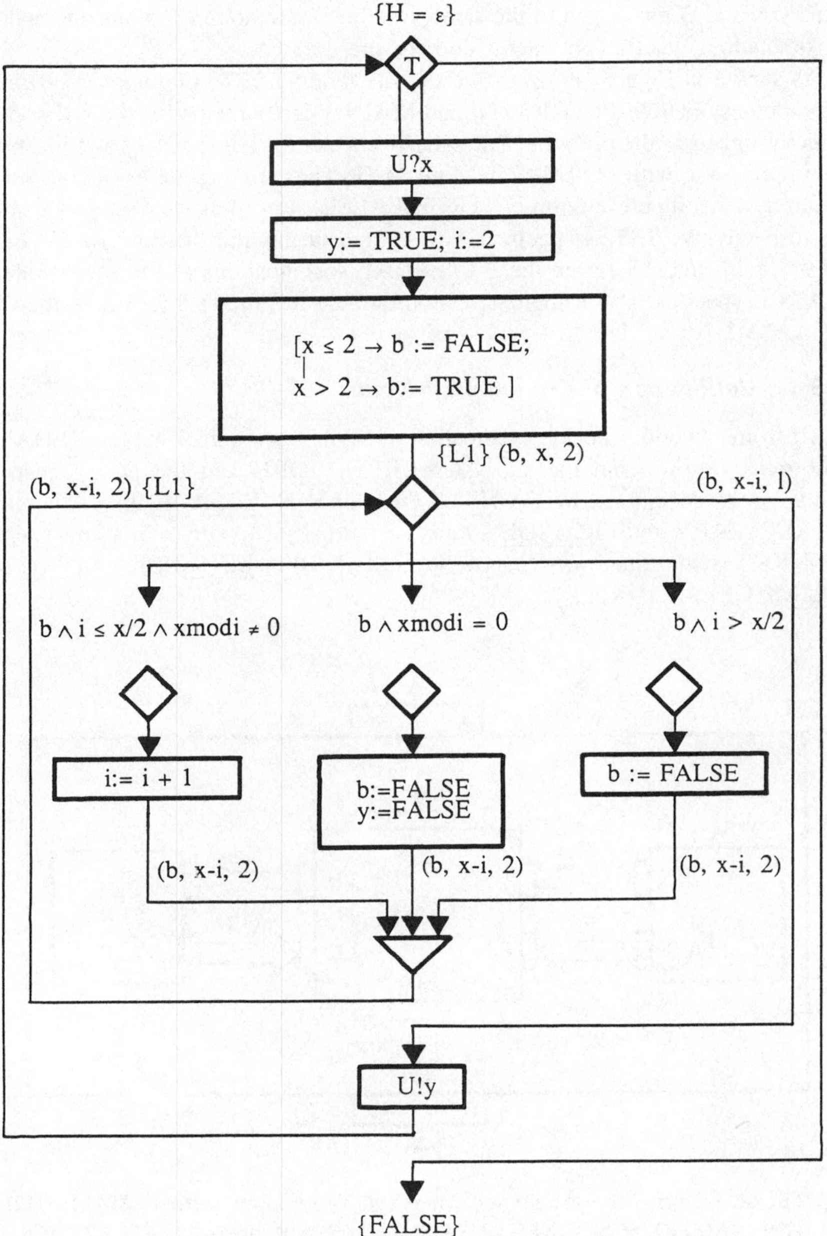

Fig. 18.11. Partial annotation of FORM-F.

sumes A and B are linked to the same system. For simplicity, other interesting tasks, such as deletion and status queries, are omitted.

As shown in Figure 18.12, the composite module SET is composed of three submodules: FORM-F, FORM-G, and MAIN. MAIN maintains the set, and is directly linked to the ports of SET. MAIN checks for eligibility of a request by communicating with FORM-F and FORM-G. These two modules operate concurrently to compute eligibility (TRUE,FALSE) according to formulas F and G, respectively. SET is specified as a composite module in Fig. 18.13. Fig. 18.9, 18.14, and 18.15 are the EXTERNAL specifications of the submodules. MAIN is specified as an implementation module in Fig. 18.16, and verified in Section 3.3.1.

3.3.1. Verification of Composite Module SET

Apart from syntactic checks, verification of SET is two-part. First the BEHAVIOR must follow from the subsystem BEHAVIOR's and the port sequence equivalences designated by the NETWORK and INTERFACE links. Second, the REQUIRE's and PROVIDE's must be mutually supportive and consistent. "LINKS" is shorthand for "LINK(A) ∧ LINK(B) ∧ LINK(FL) ∧ LINK(FR) ∧ LINK(GL) ∧ LINK(GR)."

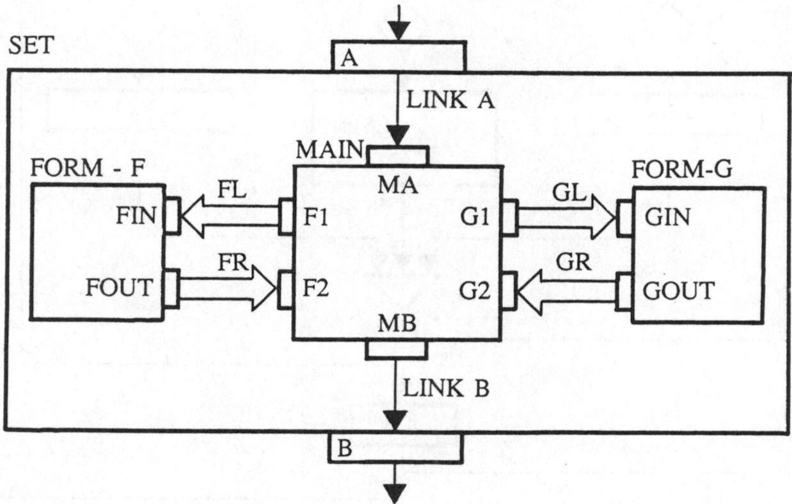

Fig. 18.12. Composite module set. Message Types: For ports A, MA, F1, FIN, G1, GIN: NAMEID = NONNEGATIVE INTEGER; For ports FOUT, F2, GOUT, G2: ELIGIBILITY = {TRUE, FALSE}; For ports MB, B: REPLY = {"ADDED", "NOTELIGIBLE"}.

```
SYSTEM SET (A: INPORT; B: OUTPORT);

EXTERNAL

BEHAVIOR
B1 == ∀i((a_i→b_i→a_{i+1}) ∧
        (F(a_i.mess.PERSON) ∧ G(a_i.mess.PERSON) ⇒ b_i.mess = "ADDED") ∧
   ((F(a_i.mess.PERSON) ∧ G(a_i.mess.PERSON)) ⇒
                                   b_i.mess = "NOTELIGIBLE")).

REQUIRE
R1 == SYS(PORTLINK(A) = SYS(PORTLINK(B)). (*A and B must be linked to
                                          same system*)
R2 == ERA(PORTLINK(A), PORTLINK(B)).

PROVIDE
P1 == ERA(A,B).

INTERNAL STRUCTURE

SUBSYSTEM MAIN (MA,F2,G2: INPORT; MB,F1,G1: OUTPORT);
SUBSYSTEM FORM-F (FIN: INPORT; FOUT: OUTPORT);
SUBSYSTEM FORM-G (GIN: INPORT; GOUT: OUTPORT);
(* Subsystem EXTERNAL specifications are in Figs. 18.9, 18.14, and 18.15 *)

NETWORK
LINK(FL) == MAIN(F1) = FORM-F(FIN);
LINK(FR) == MAIN(F2) = FORM-F(FOUT);
LINK(GR) == MAIN(G1) = FORM-G(GIN);
LINK(GL) == MAIN(G2) = FORM-G(GOUT);

INTERFACE
LINK(A) == MAIN(MA) = SET(A);
LINK(B) == MAIN(MB) = SET(B);

end SYSTEM.
```

Fig. 18.13. Specification of SET.

The following implication establishes that the BEHAVIOR of SET follows straightforwardly from the composition of its submodules: MAIN.B1 ∧ FORM-F.B1 ∧ FORM-G.B1 ∧ LINKS ⇒ SET.B1

1. The following implications establish that the subsystem REQUIRE's (by the submodules of the submodules) follow from the PROVIDE's (by the submodules to the submodules) and the REQUIRE's (by the composite module of external modules). "LINKS$(X_1 \ldots . X_N)$" is shorthand for "LINK(X_1) ∧ . . . LINK(X_N)."

SYSTEM MAIN (MA,F2,G2: INPORT; MB,F1,G1: OUTPORT);

EXTERNAL

BEHAVIOR
B1 = = $\forall i((a_i \rightarrow f1_i \rightarrow f2_i \rightarrow b_i) \wedge (a_i \rightarrow g1_i \rightarrow g2_i \rightarrow b_i)$
(fi_i.mess ∧ gi_i.mess ⇒ b_i.mess = "ADDED") ∧
(~(fi_i.mess ∧ gi_i.mess) ⇒ b_i.mess="NOTELIGIBLE")).

REQUIRE
R1 = = SYS(PORTLINK(MA) = SYS(PORTLINK(MB)).
R2 = = ERA(PORTLINK(MA), PORTLINK(MB)).
R3 = = SYS(PORTLINK(F2)) = SYS(PORTLINK(F1)).
R4 = = ERA(PORTLINK(F1), PORTLINK(F2)).
R5 = = SYS(PORTLINK(G2)) = SYS(PORTLINK(G1)).
R6 = = ERA(PORTLINK(G1), PORTLINK(G2)).

PROVIDE
(* Cooperation from certain links ensures an ever-readiness to communicate via others *)
P1 = = R3 ∧ R4 ∧ R5 ∧ R6 ⇒ ERA(MA,MB).
P2 = = R1 ∧ R2 ∧ R5 ∧ R6 ⇒ ERA(F1,F2).
P3 = = R1 ∧ R2 ∧ R3 ∧ R4 ⇒ ERA(G1,G2).

(* Restatement of port declarations to facilitate verification *)
P4 = = SYS(MA)=SYS(MB)=SYS(F1)=SYS(F2)=SYS(G1)=SYS(G2).

Fig. 18.14. EXTERNAL specification of MAIN.

SYSTEM FORM-G (GIN: INPORT; GOUT: OUTPORT);

EXTERNAL

BEHAVIOR
B1 = = $\forall i$((gin$_i$→gout$_i$→gin$_{i+1}$) ∧
(gout$_i$.mess=G(gin$_i$.mess))).

REQUIRE
R1 = = SYS(PORTLINK(GIN)) = SYS(PORTLINK(GOUT)).
R2 = = ERA(PORTLINK(GIN), PORTLINK(GOUT)).

PROVIDE
P1 = = ERA(GIN,GOUT).
P2 = = SYS(GIN)=SYS(GOUT).

end SYSTEM.

Fig. 18.15. EXTERNAL specification of FORM-G.

i. SET.R1 ∧ SET.R2 ∧ LINKS(A,B) ⇒ MAIN.R1 ∧ MAIN.R2
ii. FORM-F.P1 ∧ FORM-F.P2 ∧ LINKS(FL,FR) ⇒
MAIN.R3 ∧ MAIN.R4
iii. FORM-G.P1 ∧ FORM-G.P2 ∧ LINKS(GL,GR) ⇒
MAIN.R5 ∧ MAIN.R6
iv. MAIN.P2 ∧ MAIN.P4 ∧ FORM-G.P1 ∧ FORM-G.P2
∧ SET.R1 ∧ SET.R2 ∧ LINKS ⇒ FORM-F.R1 ∧ FORM-F.R2
v. MAIN.P3 ∧ MAIN.P4 ∧ FORM-F.P1 ∧ FORM-G.P2
∧ SET.R1 ∧ SET.R2 ∧ LINKS ⇒ FORM-G.R2 ∧ FORM-G.R2

2. The following implication establishes that the composite PROVIDE follows from the submodule PROVIDE's and the links. Clauses ii. and iii. are given above.

MAIN.P1 ∧ FORM-F.P1 ∧ FORM-F.P2 ∧ FORM-G.P1
∧ FORM-G.P2 ∧ ii. ∧ iii. ∧ LINKS ⇒ SET.P1

3. The following implication establishes that the composite REQUIRE is the conjunction of the submodule REQUIRE's pertaining to system linked via the INTERFACE.

SET.R1 ∧ SET.R2 ∧ LINKS(A,B) ⇔ MAIN.R1 ∧ MAIN.R2 ∧ LINKS(A,B)

3.3.2. Specification/Verification of Implementation Module MAIN

The EXTERNAL and INTERNAL specifications of MAIN appear in Figs. 18.14 and 18.16, respectively. The predicate TWELVE defined for communication history H and integer i is:

TWELVE(H,i) == ready(U,MAIN,H,i) ∧ mess(U,MAIN,H,$i+1$)
∧ ready(MAIN,F,H,$i+2$) ∧ mess(MAIN,F,H,$i+3$) ∧
ready(MAIN,G,H,$i+4$)
∧ mess(MAIN,G,H,$i+5$) ∧ ready(F,MAIN,H,$i+6$) ∧
mess(F,MAIN,H,$i+7$)
∧ ready(G,MAIN,H,$i+8$) ∧ mess(G,MAIN,H,$i+9$) ∧
ready(MAIN,U,H,$i+10$)
∧ mess(MAIN,U,H,$i+11$)
∧ ($val(H,i+1) = val(H,i+3) = val(H,i+5)$) ∧

```
SYSTEM MAIN (MA,FI,GI: INPORT; MB,FO,GO: OUTPORT);

INTERNAL

CODE
MAIN::
        S:={ };
ST: *[U? name →
            F!name; G!name; F?felig; G?gelig;
            [(felig ∧ gelig → S:=S U {name};
                    U!''ADDED'';
            ■

            ~(felig ∧ gelig) → U!''NOTELIGIBLE'']]

PERFORMANCE
   cyclic ST.
   assert ∧i(imod12=1 ⇒ TWELVE(H*,i)).

INTERPRET
MA = {c|c ∈ H* ∧ dir(c)=(U,MAIN)}.
MB = {c|c ∈ H* ∧ dir(c)=(MAIN,U)}.
FO = {c|c ∈ H* ∧ dir(c)=(MAIN,F)}.
FI = {c|c ∈ H* ∧ dir(c)=(F,MAIN)}.
GO = {c|c ∈ H* ∧ dir(c)=(MAIN,G)}.

end SYSTEM
```

Fig. 18.16. Internal specification of MAIN.

$$((val(H,i+7) \wedge val(H,i+9)) \Rightarrow (val(H,i+11)=\text{''ADDED''})) \\ \wedge (\sim(val(H,i+5) \wedge val(H,i+9)) \Rightarrow (val(H,i+11)=\text{''NOTELIGIBLE''})).$$

Verification of MAIN is two-part:

1. The *assert* and INTERPRET statements must imply the EXTERNAL BEHAVIOR statement. MAIN.B1 follows immediately from the former statements, and the implicit interpretation of "→" as ordinary sequential order.
2. An annotation for MAIN must establish the PERFORMANCE statements and the translated PROVIDE statements. The translated REQUIRE may be assumed for establishing the PERFORMANCE. A partial annotation is shown in Fig. 18.17. The loop invariant, LI, is defined as follows (for communication history H):

$$\text{LI} == (\forall i((|H|=1 \wedge \text{ready }(U,\text{MAIN},H,i)) \vee (1 < i < |H| \wedge i\text{mod } 12=1 \\ \Rightarrow \text{TWELVE }(H,i)))) \wedge \\ S=\{val(H,i) \; | i<|H| \wedge i\text{mod}12=1 \wedge val(H,i+11)=\text{''ADDED''}\}$$

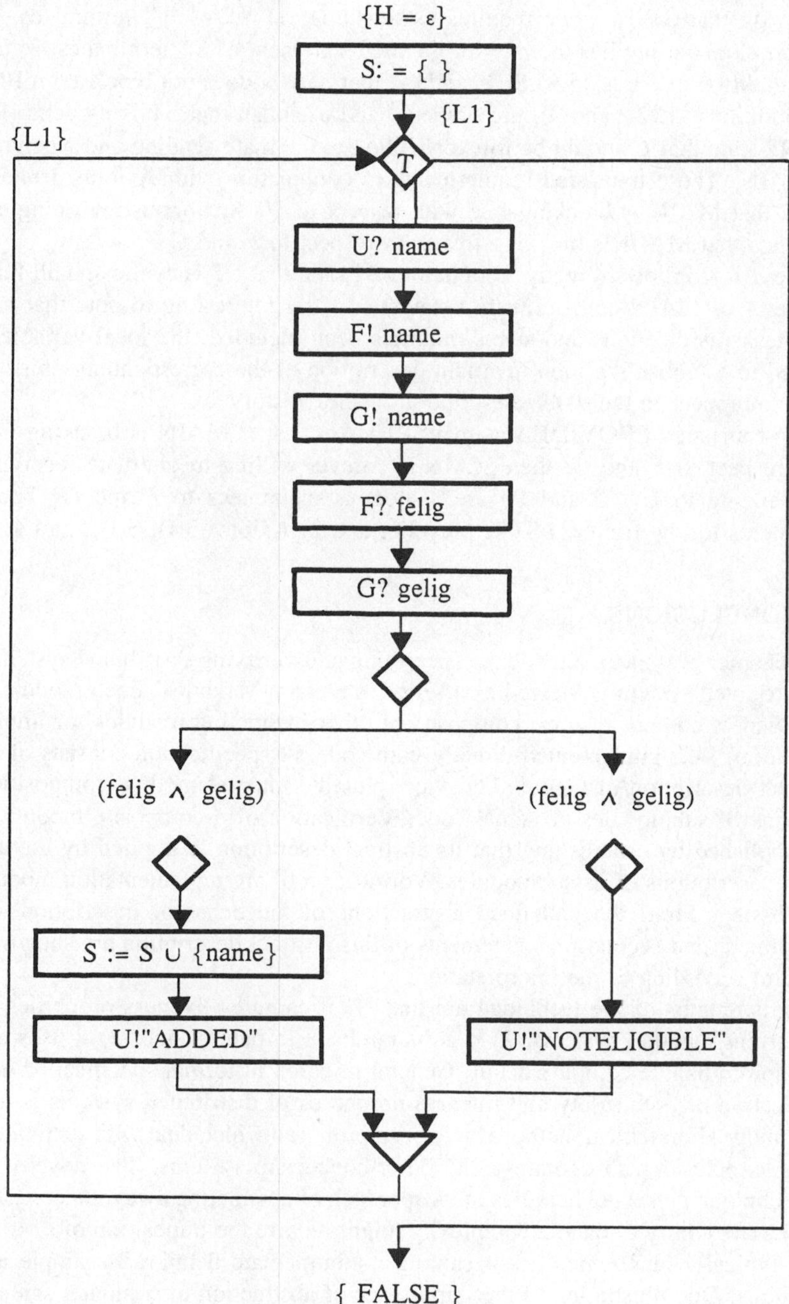

Fig. 18.17. Partial annotation of MAIN.

Verifying that ST is cyclic requires establishing: 1) "$S=\{\ \}$" terminates, 2) that no blocking implies the interior guarded statement of ST terminates, 3) the postcondition of ST is {FALSE}, and, 4) that MAIN does not block at an I/O.

Conditions 1), 2), and 3), are obvious, and establish that ST is p-cyclic. R1 and R2 state that *U* should be forever willing to alternate sending and receiving to MAIN. These translated requirements in conjunction with Axioms 3 and 4 imply that MAIN is blocking-free with respect to *U*. Analogous reasoning establishes that MAIN is blocking-free with respect to *F* and *G*.

The *assert* follows directly from axiom B1, and that ST is cyclic and all final segments of MAIN contain an I/O statement. It is interesting to note that had such tasks as deletions and status inquiries been included, the local variable *S* needed to establish the loop invariant description of the corresponding *history does not appear in the *assert* description of the *history.

The translated PROVIDE statement P1 states that if MAIN is blocking-free with respect to *F* and *G*, then MAIN is forever willing to alternate receiving and sending to *U*. P2 and P3 are analogous guarantees to *F* and *G*. These statements follow from: 1) ST is p-cyclic, and 2) Axioms 3(I), 3(II), and 4.

4. CONCLUSIONS

This chapter presents a method for specifying and verifying distributed systems. A distributed system is viewed as a set of interacting modules. Each module is classified as composite, i.e., composed of other interacting modules, or implementation, i.e., implemented directly with code. A specification consists of an abstract description of module behavior, plus the internal module composition in terms of submodules or actual code. Verification of a composite module is accomplished by establishing that its abstract description is implied by the abstract descriptions of its submodules. Verification of an implementation module is two-step. First, the undefined abstractions of the behavior description are interpreted, and second, the statements of this abstract description are shown to be valid according to the interpretation.

The strengths of the technique are that: 1) it captures liveness properties of concurrent, parallel systems, 2) it is hierarchical in nature, and, 3) it uses abstraction to handle complex detail. General research in formal specification and verification of both safety and liveness properties of distributed systems is just beginning. Hierarchical methods have been proposed which deal with such properties associated with operating and other concurrent systems. The novelty of the technique presented here lies in its approach of abstracting away unnecessary detail. The ability to handle complexity might require the imposition of a structure, typically hierarchical, representing nonimmediate detail with simple abstractions. One illustration of the importance of abstraction to computer science is the use of abstract data types to solve complex problems. The previously described method for specifying and verifying implementation modules is analogous to the specification and verification of abstract data types.

Abstract terms in combination with the CSP proof system enable reasoning about such properties not based on temporal logic constructs nor explicit mention of time or program counters. Rather, a verification resembles a standard Floyd–Hoare type verification of a sequential program. The methods used in references 7 and 14 rely on temporal logic constructs to formulate properties and proofs of liveness properties of concurrent programs. The method used in reference 6 for specifying/verifying cyclic, concurrent programs does not use temporal logic, but does require explicit variables for time and program counters. The method of Hoare for modularly specifying and verifying liveness properties of concurrent, cyclic programs[10] does not use temporal logic or time or program counters. Formal proof rules defining the semantics of a language provide the ability to derive in a formal logical system specifications of cyclic processes from code itself, or from specifications of component modules. The system includes the semantics of only send, receive, and repeat statements.

Perhaps the primary importance to date of formal verification systems for programming languages is their contribution to language and program design. The nonexistence of reasonable proof rules for general GOTO statements demonstrate the potential chaos created by such constructs. The proof rules for WHILE loops illustrate that iterations are characterized by invariant relationships. The absence of reasonable proof rules for GOTO statements demonstrates the potential chaos of such constructs.

This specification and verification method is illustrated with CSP as the implementation language. Although CSP is not generally suitable for real systems, its use here reveals some possibly fundamental concepts.

The previously described approach suggests that identifying and proving that a particular program statement is cyclic is fundamental to reasoning about liveness properties of cyclic programs. For certain program structures, proving cycling is reduced to the tractable problem of proving termination of certain program segments. A natural question to arise is whether ease of proving segment termination is a criterion for well-structured cyclic programs.

The specification/verification method provides the ability to verify modularly general liveness properties. This approach requires the formulation and external visibility of certain internal attributes of modules, i.e., those that capture cooperation to synchronize communications. This suggests that module descriptions solely in terms of externally seen input/output are not sufficient for reasoning about liveness properties of resultant composite systems.

Another key to the ability to interpret abstractions in terms of CSP is the use of history variables by the formal proof system for the language. It would seem that the formulation and verification of properties of a system's past, present, and possibly infinite future are facilitated by a sequential record of the system's behavior. Further development of this method for CSP appears in reference 17.

This method applied to a real parallel or distributed system requires the identification of suitable abstractions capturing the essential properties of the system, and a proof system for the implementation language yielding valid interpretation for the abstractions. The method would follow the lines described here applied to a system: 1) in which system properties can be described in terms based on its input/output channels, and, 2) implemented with a language axiomatically defined with history variables and with the ability to prove nontermination. A problem to be considered is the identification of abstractions and proof rules applicable to system properties not describable solely in terms of input/output channels. For example, since critical sections are strictly internal to the processes, nonsimultaneous critical section executions cannot be described exclusively with message properties of the processes.

Other proposed approaches for formulating and verifying liveness properties of concurrent systems are based on temporal logic. These methods are, or can be made, into hierarchical, modular techniques. However, the stepwise developments carry along hindering complex detail. Possibly, a hybrid method is optimal. That is, at the language level, specification utilizes temporal logic operations. The accompanying proof system is suitable for interpreting abstractions seen at a higher level. Thus, the temporal logic formulation facilitates handling immediate detail at the language level, and the abstract formulation hides this detail when it becomes nonimmediate at higher levels.

The characterization of a program with a black-box, concise specification complete enough to enable its use as a component within a complex system is a practical problem. Abstraction offers a natural way to hide nonimmediate detail. Abstraction-based specifications sufficiently characterize data types and associated procedures. Abstraction-based specifications for concurrent, interacting components must capture attributes required for synchronization. That such abstractions can be built on mathematical systems for proving correctness properties of programs is evidence that an abstract approach to characterizing component, concurrent modules is promising.

REFERENCES

1. Apt, K. R., N. Francez, and W. P. deRoever, A proof system for communicating sequential processes, *TOPLAS*, vol. 2, pp. 359–385, July 1980.
2. Ashcroft, E., Proving assertions about parallel programs, *J. Comput. Syst. Sci.*, vol. 10, pp. 110–135, Feb. 1975.
3. Brinch Hansen, P., Language Notation for Network Programs, Tech. Rep., Comp. Sci. Dept., USC, Los Angeles, CA, 1981.

4. Chen, A. B. and R. T. Yeh, Event-based behavior specification of distributed systems, in *Proc. IEEE Symp. on Reliability in Distributed Software*, Pittsburgh, PA, July 1981.
5. Floyd, R. W., Assigning meaning to programs, in *Proc. Symp. in Applied Math.*, pp. 19–32, Am. Math. Soc., 1967.
6. Francez, Nissim and Amir Pneuli, A proof method for cyclic programs, *Acta Informatica*, vol. 9, pp. 133–157, 1978.
7. Hailpern, B. and S. Owicki, Modular Verification of Concurrent Programs, Tech. Rep. RC-9130, IBM Research, 1981.
8. Hoare, C. A. R., An axiomatic basis for computer programming, *CACM*, vol. 12, pp. 171–176, Oct. 1969.
9. Hoare, C. A. R., Communicating sequential processes, *CACM*, vol. 21, pp. 666–677, Aug. 1978.
10. Hoare, C. A. R., A Calculus of Total Correctness for Communicating Processes, Tech. Mono. PRG-23, Oxford Univ. Computing Lab., Oxford, U.K., Apr. 1981.
11. Lamport, L., The Hoare logic of concurrent programs, *Acta Information*, vol. 14, pp. 21–37, June 1980.
12. Levin, G. M. and D. Gries, A proof technique for communicating sequential processes, *Acta Inform.*, vol. 15, pp. 281–302, 1981.
13. Misra, J. and K. M. Chandy, Proofs of networks of processes, in *IEEE Trans. Soft. Eng.*, vol. SE-7, pp. 417–426, July 1981.
14. Owicki, S. and L. Lamport, Proving liveness properties of concurrent programs, *TOPLAS*, July, 1982.
15. Owicki, S. and D. Gries, An axiomatic proof technique for parallel programs, *Acta Informatica*, vol. 6, pp. 319–340, 1976.
16. Reed, J. and Yeh, R. T., Specification and verification of liveness properties of concurrent, distributed processes, *TOPLAS*, (to appear).
17. Soundararajan, N., Axiomatic semantics of communicating sequential processes, *TOPLAS*, vol. 6, pp. 647–662, Oct. 1984.
18. Soundararajan, N., Correctness proofs of CSP programs, *Theoretical Computer Science*, vol. 24, pp. 131–141, 1983.

19. A Review of Current Research and Critical Issues in Distributed System Software

JOHN A. STANKOVIC, KRITHI RAMAMRITHAM,
and
WALTER H. KOHLER

ABSTRACT

A survey of current research in distributed systems software is presented. Emphasis is placed on research in distributed operating systems, programming languages for distributed systems, and distributed databases. While many references are made to existing research projects, systems, and languages, an attempt is made to identify the important issues and, where possible, to categorize current solution techniques for the individual issues. Some of the important open research questions for distributed system software are itemized.

1. INTRODUCTION

A distributed software system is one that is executed on an architecture in which multiple processors are connected via a communication network. The main issue in the design of such systems is: how are programs, data, and control to be distributed among the components of a distributed system? In this chapter, we consider this issue from the perspective of system software including distributed operating system, programming language, and database areas. The goal of this chapter is to survey the current research in these areas as well as to briefly identify some of the critical research problems for distributed system software.

Section 2 summarizes current research in distributed operating systems and

Preparation of this material was funded in part by the following: the National Science Foundation under grants MCS 82-02586, MCS 81-04203, ECS 81-20931, DCR-8403097, and DCR-8500332. This survey was written in 1984.

programming language areas. These two areas are discussed together due their symbiotic nature. Section 3 discusses distributed database research. Critical issues in the design, implementation, and evaluation of distributed system software are itemized in Section 4.

Given that distributed systems have been under investigation for a number of years now, a survey of issues in this area could have a very wide scope. We will focus only on the issues connected with those software aspects mentioned above. Our presentation here does not directly include such areas as the communication subnet, parallel algorithms, hardware architectures for distributed systems, the impact of other areas such as artificial intelligence on distributed systems, and distributed applications.

2. DISTRIBUTED SYSTEM SOFTWARE

After a brief overview of distributed operating systems and distributed programming language reasearch, this section describes the following distributed system software issues: 1) Structuring distributed systems; 2) Addressing distributed processes and resources; 3) Communication primitives; 4) Nature of communication channels; 5) Task scheduling; 6) Decentralized control; 7) Protection and security; 8) Reliability; and 9) Distributed file systems.

2.1. Overview of Operating Systems and Programming Languages

Due to the wide variety of distributed systems there is a wide variety of operating systems controlling them. For the purposes of discussion, we simplistically divide these operating systems into three classes—network operating systems (NOS), distributed operating systems (DOS) and distributed processing operating systems (DPOS).

Consider the situation where each of the hosts of a computer network has a local operating system that is independent of the network. The sum total of all of the operating system software added to each of these network hosts in order to communicate and share network resources is called a *network operating system*. The added software often includes modifications to the local operating system. In any case, each host can still act independently of the network and various degrees of sharing are possible. The most famous example of such a network is ARPANET, and it contains several NOS's, e.g., RSEXEC and NSW.[60] Such operating systems are characterized by their having been built on top of existing operating systems.

Next, consider networks where there is logically only one native operating system for all of the distributed components. This is called a *distributed operating system*. A DOS tries to manage the resources of the network in a global fashion. Since this can be done in many ways, there is a very wide spectrum of DOSs. In this chapter we will attempt to single out a particular subset of

DOSs which we will call *Distributed Processing Operating Systems* (DPOS). A DPOS is a DOS that specifically attempts to improve reliability by using decentralized control where possible to avoid central points of failure. The advantages and disadvantages of such systems are argued in references 53, 95, and 186. Some systems we list as DOSs in Table 19.1 may also use some decentralized control, but it is usually less prevalent (again, it is a spectrum) and incorporated more for performance reasons than for both reliability and performance reasons, as in DPOSs. Let us point out that this categorization is quite subjective and we believe that some researchers may not agree with our classification of some systems as being DOS or DPOS. Some may even argue whether a category such as DPOS is necessary. Nevertheless, this is our current categorization.

A DOS (including DPOSs) may be implemented in a variety of ways. The most common implementation is to replicate the OS code (or a kernel) at each host of the distributed system. One might be tempted to then consider this replicated piece as a local OS. In fact it is not, because resources are allocated in a more global fashion, there is no exclusive, local administrative control, and, in general, there is no dichotomy from the user's point of view between being on the network or not. On the other hand, there is no requirement for a DOS to be implemented by replication and many implementation designs are

Table 19.1. Categorization of operating systems for distributed computing.

Network Operating System
NSW[60]
RSEXEC[60]
XNOS[102]

Distributed Operating Systems
Accent[157]
Apollo[9]
CHORUS[84]
DCS[57]
DEMOS/MP[148]
Domain Structure[32]
LOCUS[212]
Eden[113]
RIG[12,111]
ROSCOE (Arachne)[182]
TRIX[213]
UNIX (6)
WEB[86]

Distributed Processing Operating Systems
ADCOS[187]
ARCHOS[96]
CLOUDS[129]
Fully DP System[54]
HXDP[95]
Medusa[146]
Micros[217]
StarOS[98]

File Systems
Cambridge FS[47]
DFS[201]
Felix FS[61]
LOCUS[147]
MESA[161]
ROE[59]
Violet[72]

possible. For example, see any of the DOSs or DPOSs in Table 19.1. A final point that should be made is that distributed systems with DOSs are designed and implemented with network requirements in mind from the beginning, in contrast to NOSs where the network aspects are usually afterthoughts.

Other distributed sytems such as SIFT,[131] REBUS,[10] and Tandem[16] are concerned with reliability, but primarily employ standard reliability techniques such as voting and checkpointing rather than decentralized control. These systems are not treated in this chapter.

In Table 19.1, we attempt to categorize some of the current distributed computing OS reseach. We apologize for those systems omitted and again note that the classification is subjective. For additional information, we list seven distributed file systems (also see Section 2.10)

Distributed file systems, typically, have only some of the functionality attributed to operating systems, and hence we list them separately. Notice that LOCUS is listed twice because it began as a distributed file system and then evolved into a DPOS. The (6) after UNIX indicates that there are at least 6 extensions to UNIX for distributed systems including Locus,[156] and those extensions done at Bell Labs,[126] Berkeley,[169] Purdue, and Newcastle upon Tyne.[155]

Programming Languages for distributed systems, in general, contain message-based mechanisms for process communication and synchronization. Though most extant distributed systems have been programmed using ad hoc modifications to sequential languages, concurrent languages based on shared variables for process interaction are becoming more widely available. Illustrative languages in this category have been listed under *Concurrent Programming Languages* (CPL) in Table 19.2. Such languages provide high-level constructs for the specification of processes and the interaction between processes. Process interaction is via resource sharing controlled by mechanisms based on the monitor concept.[92] A monitor is a structured mechanism which synchronizes access to shared resources.

Although the shared variable based approach is appropriate for processes with shared memory, it is not suitable for programming systems in which physically distributed processes cooperate and interact closely in order to perform a single task. For such systems, due to the presence of an underlying communication network, a message-based interaction is more appropriate. Languages designed to make this possible are called *Message Passing Languages* (MPL) and are listed in Table 19.2. However, in general, programs are written such that various modules in a progarm interact via procedure calls. In order to give users a uniform interface, irrespective of whether the program is executed on a centralized system or on a distributed system, a few languages have been designed to permit process interactions via procedure calls to remote sites. The remote procedure calls themselves would be implemented through an underlying message passing protocol. We call such languages *Remote Procedure Languages*

Table 19.2. Categorization of programming languages for distributed computing.

Concurrent Programming Languages	Remote Procedure Languages
Concurrent Pascal[28]	Distributed Processes (DP)[29]
Modula[216]	Argus[125]
Mesa[136]	Ada[48]
Message Passing Languages	**Hybrid Languages**
CSP[93]	*MOD[43]
Gypsy[78]	SR[6]
PLITS[58]	
Guardian-extended CLU[124]	
Smalltalk[76]	

(RPL). The possibility of interactions through message-passing and procedure calls is essential in order to configure tightly-coupled processes as a single logical module that executes on a single processor; processes within a module interact via local procedure calls and shared variables, whereas processes in different modules interact via message-passing or remote procedure calls. Hence, some of the proposed languages provide for interactions via both message passing and remote procedure calls. In Table 19.2, they are termed *Hybrid Languages* (HL). Details concerning these languages such as program structuring and communications primitives, can be found in subsequent sections. (For a survey of language notations for expressing the communication and synchronization in concurrent systems, see reference 7.)

For many of these issues, much of the distributed system software research is experimental work in which actual (prototype) systems are built. However, further work needs to be done in the evaluation of these systems in terms of the problem domains they are suited for and their performance. The prototype work is valuable because many individual research ideas are integrated into an actual system and it is important to know how well they coexist.

2.2. Structuring Distributed Systems

The autonomous and distributed nature of the components of distributed systems causes a qualitative and quantitative change in the problems faced in developing software for these systems: The software should not only be functionally correct, but also perform reliabily in the face of component failures, long delays, and missing data. This Section discusses how each node in a distributed system can be structured, and the next two Sections deal with communication between nodes.

A node in a distributed system is a collection of resources and processes, and is typically an autonomous entity. Processes outside a node access the processes and resources within a node via messages, whereas intra-node communication is normally through shared memory (HXDP is an exception). Definition of the structure of a node requires the specification of a name for a node, the resources and processes that constitute the node and a set of interfaces for accessing these processes and resources. The structure of a node could change with time.

The so-called *client-server model* in conjunction with *object-orientation* appears to be a conceptually attractive structuring mechanism. There has been considerable work on both centralized[99,214,219] and decentralized [97,147] object based systems in the context of operating systems and programming language levels.[76,125] Conceptually, an object is a collection of information and a set of operations defined on that information. In practice, the term object is sometimes viewed simply as a collection of information with common access characteristics. In either case, objects seem to provide a convenient and natural model for reducing the complexities in distributed operating systems. For example, moving a process, after it has begun execution, to another processor in order to balance the load in the system requires careful treatment of code, data, and environment information. Treating each of these pieces of information as objects (or possibly the combination of them as objects) facilitates their movement. Typically, when an object corresponds to a shared resource, associated with the object is a server which controls the execution of operations on the object and services requests for operations on the objects. Most DOSs and DOPSs use the object concept in their design and implementation.

Another structuring concept found in distributed operating systems is the notion of a task force.[98] A task force is a collection of concurrently executing processes that cooperate to accomplish a certain task, e.g., the file manager of a DPOS can be configured as a task force (see Medusa[146]). Processes within a task force communicate with each other as well as with other task forces. Hence, a distributed system can be viewed as a collection of task forces. We should also note that the client-server model and the concept of task forces are not mutually incompatible, and that the two may appear in the same system.

Many of the proposed programming languages for distributed systems have provided facilities for structuring distributed system software as a set of objects and processes that access the objects; operations on the objects are executed via remote procedure calls.[143] Argus[125] (where the concept of a *guardian* is introduced), SR[6] (where the term *resource* is used), and *Mod[43] (where *modules* are used for structuring systems) represent this approach. In Argus, a distributed program consists of a set of guardians. Each guardian encapsulates a set of resources, which are instances of abstract data types. Operations on these resources are controlled by the guardian, which is designed to handle concurrent access and system failure. These issues are discussed further in Sections 2.4 and 2.9. Processes and data within each guardian, resource, and module exist and run on one physical node. In SR, a resource is defined along with a set of processes, called operations, to access the resource. In *Mod, a module is defined by the data structure definitions, procedures, processes, and an external interface, and is thus similar to a resource in SR.

Considering other languages, in Mesa,[136] monitors control access to shared resources accessed by users via *entry procedures*. In DP,[29] active processes are used to implement monitors which control access to shared resources. In Ada,[48] autonomous components of the system can be programmed as Ada *packages* that encompass resources, operations on the resources, as well as the tasks that manipulate the resources.[154,177]

Only Argus addresses the issue of failures of nodes by applying concepts such as locking and atomicity, concepts traditionally applied in databases (see Section 3). The problem of structuring distributed systems is complicated by the presence of truly distributed resources such as distributed databases, wherein resources need to be partitioned and replicated for achieving reliability and availability (see Section 3).

2.3. Addressing Distributed Processes and Resources

The addressing issue [45,172,175] in distributed systems is complicated because *names* are used in the context of so many different functions and levels. For example, names are used for referencing, locating, scheduling, allocating and deallocating, error control, synchronization, sharing, and in hierarchies of names—to name a few. Names actually identify a resource in a logical way, then are mapped to an address which in distributed systems is then mapped to a route. Names used at different levels referring to the same object must also be bound together. Allowing relocation and sharing of objects causes additional problems. Ideally, names should be bound to addresses and routes dynamically for increased flexibility, but this causes a potentially large and excessive run time penalty. Broadcasting is often involved in implementing dynamic binding of names, addresses, and routes. Heterogeneous distributed systems cause additional naming problems (more mappings are required).

Addressing can also be categorized as implicit, explicit, global, or functional.[194] The simplest form of connection establishment is *implicit addressing*, where a process can only communicate with one other process in the system. This is usually the case for processes created to perform a single service and only communicate with their parent process. Though such a model is appealing in its simplicity, it is not flexible enough by itself to allow any pair of processes to communicate, a minimal requirement of a general communication facility.

Explicit addressing is characterized by the explicit naming of the process with which communication is desired.[30,93] This addressing scheme is particularly suited for process configurations in which the output of one process serves as input to another. Explicit addressing requires a global knowledge source containing the identity of each process in the system. Some systems have predefined names for processes providing system services and a user accessible table of user process ID's. A communication mechanism dependent on explicit addressing is an adequate basis for a complete communication system, as evidenced by its use in the Thoth system.[35] However, explicit addressing by itself is not flexible enough to effectively handle such common circumstances as process migration in distributed systems and multiple processes providing a single service.

Global addressing associates global names with message receptacles, or *mailboxes*. A process can declare a mailbox into which messages can be received and can specify a destination mailbox when sending a message. Such a scheme is used in Good *et al.*,[78] wherein the mailbox is global to the processes that have access to it. Gelernter and Bernstein[69] describe a communication model in which all communication takes place via distributed but globally accessible memory.

Functional addressing establishes a connection based on the need to serve or request a service. In this case, the communication path is itself a named entity of the system. For the user of a path, the identity of the process or processes on the other end of the path is insignificant. What is significant is that they are providing a service or that they are requesting that a service be provided. This scheme is flexible because an individual process is not necessarily associated with a communication path, and names of paths themselves may be passed within messages. This kind of addressing was introduced in Balzer[14] and expanded in Walden.[211] Functional addressing is the underlying concept used in many current languages, most notably in the following: PLITS[58] and *Mod,[43] where *port* denotes a path, Distributed Processes[29] and Ada,[48] where *entry* denotes a path, a SR,[6] where *operation* denotes a path. It is also used in the following message-based operating systems: Accent[157] and Gutenberg,[194] where *port* denotes a path, and DEMOS,[17] where *link* denotes a path.

Addressing in most programming languages is static in that the processes accessible to each process is fixed at compile time. However, some languages, for example Gypsy[78] and PLITS,[58] do support dynamic addressing whereby it is possible to interact with a changing environment.

It should be clear that the various forms of addressing described above need different kinds of operating system support. Implicit addressing is straightforward since a process is connected to only one other process. Translation from logical name to physical address is necessary for explicit addressing. In global addressing, access to mailboxes has to be mutually exclusive. Even here, mapping from logical mailbox names to physical mailbox addresses has to be performed. Also, implementing global mailboxes requires substantial support from the underlying communication network since, typically, there will be multiple senders and receivers associated with a single mailbox. Functional addressing requires the most operating system support. This is essentially due to the dynamic nature of path connections between servers and the served. The first element of address mapping is the determination of the process that provides the needed service followed by communication with the process along the path connected with the process.

2.4. Communication Primitives

As discussed in Section 2.1, there are two basic ways in which inter-process communication (IPC) can take place: through message-passing or through remote procedure calls (RPC). In this Section, we discuss the primitives used for these two types of communication, their semantics and the concurrency induced by them. The next Section deals with the channels along which communication takes place.

Communication primitives can be either *blocking* or *nonblocking*. For instance, with the *synchronous send*, the sender is blocked until the message is received by the destination process.[93] Thus, this blocking primitive not only transfers data but also synchronizes the sender and the receiver. Since a message is sent only if the receiver is ready, the synchronous send requires no message buffering or queueing. The *no-wait send* (or queuing send, as discussed in reference 70) is a nonblocking primitive. Using this primitive, the sender resumes execution as soon as the message is composed and buffered within the communication facility. Thus, concurrency between communicating processes is maximized.[124] However, the need for buffering introduces problems of flow and congestion control, addressed in the next section. Another form of nonblocking send is the *conditional send*, which sends a message only if the receiver is blocked and is waiting for a message to arrive. If the receiver is not blocked, a flag is returned indicating that the receiver is not ready. This form of send requires the receiver to use a blocked receive, which is discussed next.

There are two forms of receive: unconditional and conditional. The *unconditional receive*, or *blocked receive*, blocks the receiver until a message is queued on the *selected* communication channel. This primitive synchronizes the receiver with respect to the sender of messages. The unconditional receive sacrifices process concurrency by blocking the receiver when no messages are queued. It has two variations. Frequently, it is desirable to block on a set of communication channels. The first message received on any of the specified set of communication channels is forwarded to the receiver. This primitive, known as *restricted unconditional receive*, is useful for a serving process awaiting messages from a specified set of channels. A second variation is the *blind unconditional receive*. This form of unconditional receive blocks until a message arrives on one of the communication channels to which the requesting process has receive access.

The *conditional receive* (or selective receive as discussed in Rao[158]) introduces a polling capability, allowing the receiving process control over the degree of concurrency desired. The conditional receive polls a (set of) communication channel(s) for a queued message. If no message is present, control is returned with a flag indicating that no message is available, otherwise, one of the messages present is provided to the receiver. The conditional receive can be generalized to check for a more complex condition than the presence or absence of a message.[6]

When the protocols used in client-server interactions or in distributed databases are examined, it is observed that communication is initiated by a process which first sends a message requesting service to another process and then awaits response. The servicing process first receives the request and then sends the response. Such an interaction resembles a procedure invocation and was first discussed in reference 29. In the context of a distributed system, where the invoked procedure could be executed at a remote node, it is termed a *remote invocation send*[124] or a *remote procedure call* (RPC).[143]

Users execute RPCs just as they would local procedure calls. The system performs the sends and receives necessary to execute the call and to obtain the results of the call.[183] To increase the parallelism in the system, some languages permit remote procedure calls to be executed asynchronously, in which case, the call can proceed in parallel with local computations. For example, in Mesa,[136] a call is *forked* and results of the call obtained by using the *join* construct. In Ada,[48] this effect is achieved by creating a task which performs the remote procedure call. The call then executes in parallel with the creating task.

There have been different proposals regarding the implementation of a remote procedure call. In SR,[6] a cyclic process exists for each type of call, thereby serializing calls to the same procedure. In Distributed Processes,[29] *MOD[43] and Argus,[125] a new process is created to execute each call. If these processes share variables, then the processes need to be synchronized. In Ada,[48] a server process may be designed to execute more than one type of RPC. A server receives a request for a RPC via the *accept* statement, it then executes the body of the called procedure, and returns the result of the call via result parameters. The server then proceeds with its execution. Since a calling task waits until the call is completed, a *rendezvous* occurs during the execution of the call. In languages that support only message passing via send and receive, a procedure call is realized by first *sending* a message to a server and then *receiving* a response from it. In this case, the server will first *receive* input parameters to the call and then *send* the results of the call (e.g., PLITS[58]).

A server should be designed to schedule concurrent requests based on criteria such as priority and fairness. Also, conditions, reflecting different synchronization requirements and service policies, can be imposed on the execution of requests. These should be satisfied before the service is provided. For instance, operations that modify some shared resource need be executed mutually exclusively. Most programming languages permit the specification of such constraints, for example, Ada's *when* clause attached to an *accept* statement, specifies when the associated *entry* call can be serviced. Also, in Ada, calls on the same entry are scheduled according to their order of arrival. Ramamritham[154] describes schemes for structuring resource servers that satisfy different scheduling policies.

Nelson examines various remote procedure call mechanisms with respect to call semantics, concurrency, exception handling, and performance.[143] Below, we briefly analyze the communication primitives discussed so far from the viewpoint of parallelism, expressiveness, and reliability. (Also, consult Stankovic[188] for an extended comparison of message-based, i.e., via explicit send and receive primitives, and remote procedure call approaches to communication.)

Considering message-based communication primitives, blocking communication primitives can be used to realize both synchronization and communication. In this case, each process can be completely sequential and parallelism is obtained by the concurrent execution of multiple sequential processes (e.g., CSP.[93] This facilitates the understanding of the resulting programs. On the other hand, asynchronous or nonblocking communication primitives permit the explicit introduction of parallelism and can be used to achieve arbitrary multiple threads of control.

We now compare message-based communication and the RPC-based communication. While the positive features of message-based primitives discussed above can be usefully exploited in the design of operating systems to support different programming languages and applications, communication using explicit send and receive primitives does have its disadvantages in the context of programming languages. In procedural languages, interactions between modules (namely parameter passing followed by value return) are via procedure calls. Interactions between modules on different nodes using sends and receives, instead of using a procedure call, requires using two syntactically unrelated language constructs, namely send and receive, in the place of a single construct, namely a procedure call. This not only requires the addition of new constructs into procedural languages but also makes unstructured and error-prone module ineractions possible. This is in contrast with the remote procedure call-based approach which uniformly extends the use of languages designed for uniprocessors to distributed systems.

However, extending this syntactic transparency to semantic transparency is hampered by possibilities of failure of processors and communication links. In particular, it is nontrivial to satisfy the property that every procedure call will always return. Thus, it is still unclear whether message-based communication or remote procedure call based communication is appropriate for distributed system software. What is clear, however, is that since both are suitable bases for powerful communication, research on either approach will contribute to the other.

Whichever communication primitive is chosen it is essential to provide efficient implementations for them. Spector[183] describes a communication model to discuss the efficient implementations of communication between nodes in a local area network. He shows that the overheads depend primarily on the reliability semantics imposed on a primitive. Hence, we conclude our discussion of communication primitives by describing various reliability semantics in the context of the remote procedure call. They are exactly-once, last-one, at-least-once, last-of-many, and at-most-once semantics.

In the absence of failures, a remote procedure call has the same semantics as a local procedure call. These semantics are termed the *exactly-once* semantics. A remote procedure call is said to have the *last-one* semantics if the result of the call as well as the side-effects are those of the very last call that completes. Though the results of intermediate executions are abandoned the side-effects of intermediate executions may affect the final result. When machine failures are taken into account, a local procedure call has the last-one semantics.

To obtain the *at-least-once* semantics for a remote procedure call, the call is made repeatedly until it is guaranteed that the call has completed at least once. These semantics are satisfied in the presence and absence of failures and hence the caller need not be concerned with failures. The problem with this semantics is that it is not possible to know how many times the call actually executed or whether the returned results are from the final call or some previous call. The latter problem is solved in the *last-of-many* semantics, first proposed in reference 109, in which the results of a remote procedure call are those of the very last one of the many repeated calls. The last-of-many semantics is acceptable when remote operations are *idempotent*, i.e., the operations return the same results on repeated executions. If processors do not fail and if the communication channels are reliable, then an exactly-once semantics can be achieved using the scheme for the last-of-many semantics. This requires the server of a remote procedure call to retain the execution record of a completed call until the caller has acknowledged that he has received the results of the call. However, to achieve last-of-many semantics in spite of processor failures in a distributed system it is necessary to *exterminate orphaned* remote procedure calls, i.e., calls that have become unwanted due to the failure of the caller. Schemes for the treatment of orphans are described in Nelson[143] and Srivastava.[185]

In situations where nodes or communication links are unavailable over extended periods, semantics that require at least one completion of the called procedure may cause a caller to wait longer than desired. In such cases, the caller may desire to have the call ignored. Thus, the semantics considered so far are not always appropriate.

Frequently remote procedure calls are endowed with the *at-most-once* semantics,[125] making the remote procedure call an atomic action. The semantics results from the use of a built-in transaction mechanism to implement a remote procedure call. It permits the abortion of a call due to communication or processor failure and is based on the premise that, in case of failures, the caller should be given the option to proceed with the call or terminate, depending on the demands of the particular application. It should be pointed out that the relationship between the independent notions of remote procedure call and transactions is, as yet, unclear. Whereas robust applications such as airline reservation systems require atomic remote procedure calls, it appears unnecessary to make all remote procedure calls atomic.[143]

2.5. Nature of Communication Channels

In the previous Sections we have discussed the structure of processes in a distributed system, the addressing of resources and processes, and the primitives used for communication between processes. This Section discusses the issues that pertain to the communication channel, the entity along which the logical communication takes place.

The primary considerations in the design of communication channels in a distributed system are buffering (flow control) techniques, message structure, directionality, ownership, frequency of use, transference rights, and connection structure.[209]

Regardless of the buffering technique used, buffer maintenance introduces the problem of resource allocation. (In this section and those that follow, the term *port* refers to a communications link between two processes.) *Port-local allocation* assigns a fixed buffer space to each port.[157] When the buffer space is filled and a process attempts to send another message to the port, there are three alternatives. First, if a flow control option is included in the send primitive, the port can dynamically expand its size to allow an additional message. Second, the sending process can remain blocked until space is available on the port for an additional message. Third, an error flag can be returned to the sending process indicating a full port. The *process-local allocation* technique associates the buffer space with the process rather than the port.[104] This restricts the total number of outstanding messages for a process. A third resource allocation alternative is to maintain a global buffer pool (examples include Roscoe[182] and UNIX.[164]) This technique, termed *system-global allocation*, introduces a bottleneck in the system. A viable solution to the two problems mentioned above is to combine the port-local and system-global techniques. The *port-global* hybrid associates a fixed buffer space to each port while reserving buffer space with the system.

An important issue in *message structure* is the typing of data within messages. Some systems purport the benefits of stongly typed data within messages (Eden,[113] CLU,[124] and Accent.[157] Strong typing of data restricts the contents of messages being passed and thus improves reliability in general, but in a distributed system consisting of heterogeneous nodes, it is especially important in ensuring proper conversion of messages across nodes. However, heterogeneous computer networks[5,11,118] cause problems because of the different internal formatting schemes that exist. One proposed solution to the data incompatibility problem is to define a canonical representation for each type that can be used in messages. Each different implementation of the type defines a translation function between its representation and the canonical representation.[90] Further complications arise when there are precision loss and data type incompatibility, internetwork mappings (gateways), including naming,[175] and routing.

Another issue concerning message structure is the length of the messages. The Roscoe,[182] StarOS[98] and Thoth[35] systems have short, fixed length messages. This is in part due to the belief that most messages in such tightly coupled systems are short control messages. Special, synchronous communication paths are provided for large data transfer, such as reading and writing files. In systems which permit a message to contain the address of a buffer or the capability to access an object, the buffer or the object becomes accessible to the receiver. Thus, even though the actual message transferred is of fixed length, the size of information effectively transferred is of variable length. Medusa,[146] Accent,[157] and CLU[124] provide for variable length messages, and, in general, most protocols for loosely coupled systems support variable length message transfers. Variable length messages are somewhat more difficult to implement than the fixed length messages due to the buffering problems they induce.

Directionality concerns whether or not a single process has both send and receive access to single communication path. If so, the path is bidirectional (or duplex, as used in TRIX[213]). In systems providing only unidirectional paths, along which a process may send or receive messages but not both, bidirectional communication can be simulated via a pair of paths.

Ownership deals with the capability to destroy the path and terminate communication without consent of all processes with access to the path. Ownership can be associated with the directionality of communication, as in the Accent system and the Gutenberg system[194] where the allocator of a path automatically has ownership and a set of access rights to the path.

Frequency of use deals with the limitations of the number of times a path can be used. The DEMOS[17] and Roscoe[182] systems have a 'reply' path, created for the sole purpose of returning a single message. Such a path is automatically destroyed after it is used once.

Transference rights concern the ability to duplicate a path, or pass access and/or ownership rights of an established path to another process. For example, a process with ownership rights to a path can send that privilege to a receiving process, allowing it to destroy the path or change the path's characteristics. Transferring access rights can, but does not necessarily, imply loss of the transferred right.[152] The transference and access rights of processes to a path, directly affect the resulting connection structure of a path, discussed next.

Connection Structure of a path is the nature of process connections established by the path. Connection structure can take four general forms: one-to-one, one-to-many, many-to-one, and many-to-many. Communication paths that are not one-to-one can often be functionally equivalent to a set of one-to-one paths, an important issue in examining connection complex connection structures. The Process Control Language (PCL)[117] provides a complete specification of a wide variety of topological structures of unidirectional communication paths. The terms used below are introduced in the PCL description.

The *simple* path is provided for a one-to-one connection. A single queue is maintained to hold all messages. The *broadcast* and *multiple read* connections are one-to-many connections, associating a set of receivers with each sender. Every message sent on a broadcast communication path is received by every receiver and hence is suited for system wide dissemination of information; any message sent on a multiple read path is received by the first process requesting it and hence is suitable in situations where multiple servers exist for a single type of service and the service is performed equally well by any of the servers.

Many-to-one connections are provided in the *multiple-write* and *concentration* paths. A multiple-write mapping is the converse of the multiple-read mapping: every message sent by any sender is received by the receiver. This connection which is useful when multiple users are served by a single server and can be simulated by forming a set of simple paths from the sender processes to the receiver. The concentration path can be used for synchronization of the set of senders: every message received is the concatenation of the set of messages from a single send by each sender. A message cannot be received until every sender has transmitted a message. Thus a concentration path can be used to connect processes, that are solving a set of subproblems in parallel, with the process awaiting the result of the subproblems. Many-to-many paths are combinations of one-to-many and many-to-one paths.

2.6. Task Scheduling

Most of the research on scheduling for distributed systems can be considered *task assignment* research and can be loosely classified as either graph theoretic,[27,39,195-197] based on mathematical programming,[40,41,127] of heuristic.[38,39,49,50,77] By task assignment is meant that a task is considered to be composed of multiple modules and the goal is to find an optimal (or in some cases a suboptimal) policy for assigning the modules of an individual task to processors. Typical assumptions found in *task assignment* work are: processing costs are known for each module of the task, the interprocess communication (IPC) costs between every pair of modules is known, IPC cost is considered negligible for modules on the same host, and reassignment does not occur.

An example of task assignment research where reassignment does occur can be found in the *domain structure* operating system.[32] The scheduling algorithm in this system directly addresses the scheduling and dynamic movement of individual tasks. It does this by describing tasks' structure necessary to facilitate their movement during execution. However, the scheduling algorithms are completely heuristic and contain weighting factors which are left unspecified, presumably to be tuned as system parameters. Interaction between multiple tasks in the system and the necessary scheduling decisions to account for these interactions are not discussed.

Task assignment research for extremely large distributed systems has also received some attention. Micros[217] for one, has a unique scheduling algorithm called Wave scheduling. The Wave scheduling algorithm co-schedules (assigns) groups of related tasks onto available network nodes. The scheduling managers themselves are distributed over a logical control oligarchy and send waves of requests toward leaves of the control oligarchy attempting to find enough free processors. In fact more processors than required are requested because some parts of the control oligarchy may not be able to supply the necessary processors. This is a form of probabilistic scheduling.

A second form of scheduling research on distributed systems, referred to as job scheduling, can be thought of as assignment of entire jobs which are not decomposed into modules to processors. Whereas modules in task assignment could interact with one another, jobs are independent of each other. Approaches to job scheduling have included bidding,[57,153,181,191] queueing theoretic approaches,[1,38,103] the use of estimation theory,[31] and statistical decision theory.[190,192]

As an example of job scheduling, bidding schemes attempt to match specific jobs to processors based on the current ability of the processors to perform this work. These schemes are suboptimal, but are more extensible and adaptable than many of the other approaches. However, the cost of making and acquiring bids may become excessive, and the factors to use in making the bids have not been extensively studied.

The Distributed Computer System (DCS)[57] was the first system to perform a form of dynamic load balancing using a bidding technique. This system used percentage of available memory as a load indicator. Incoming jobs are then routed to processors with the most memory available. Information concerning current system status is gathered by means of a broadcast message. However, no analysis, comparisons or measurements were performed to determine the effectiveness of this scheme.

The basic bidding approach has been modified in various ways by Stankovic[191] and by Ramamritham and Stankovic.[153] For example, in the latter, bidding is used to schedule jobs with real-time constraints (such as deadlines) on a loosely-coupled network. The bidding algorithm is specifically tailored to deal with deadlines, subnet delays, scheduling overheads, and delays in the processors. The bidding algorithm is used in conjunction with a locally executed guarantee algorithm with either guarantees arriving tasks (that they will meet their deadlines) or invokes the bidding algorithm to find a suitable location for execution of the arriving task, if possible.

Distributed scheduling research known as clustering refers to scheduling highly communicating tasks on the same processor. *Highly communicating* implies that there is a large amount of data transfer between tasks of the cluster, or a high frequency of data transfer between the tasks of the cluster, or both. Two operating systems StarOS[98] and Medusa[146] both implemented on the Cm* multi-microprocessor[202] deal with clustering.

StarOS is a message-based, object-oriented multiprocessor operating system. One main idea of StarOS is the task force, a large collection of concurrently executing processes that cooperate to accomplish a single task. The structure and composition of a task force varies dynamically and it is the unit for which major resource scheduling decisions are made. Even though StarOS is designed for a multi-microprocessor, we believe that the task force concept could also be used for more loosely coupled distributed systems. In fact, as stated earlier, the task force is an important scheduling approach for distributed systems. The scheduling function itself is divided between processes which are called schedulers, and a low level mechanism called the multiplexor. The schedulers decide which environments are to be loaded and the multiplexor performs the actual loading. As far as we know only very simple scheduling algorithms were implemented.

Medusa[146] is an attempt to capitalize on the architectural features of Cm*. Medusa is implemented as a set of utilities (OS functions), each utility being a task force (task force has the same meaning as described above for StarOS). Each utility contains many concurrent, cooperating activities. Load balancing is done by automatically creating new activities within a task force to handle increased load and automatically deleting activities when the load is reduced, by coscheduling (an attempt to have different activities of the utility executing simultaneously on *different* hosts), and by pause time (a short time in which the context of a process remains loaded after an interrupt to determine if it will be reactivated). The pause time concept is supposed to reduce context swaps.

As a final note on scheduling, we note that there is a similarity between some of the above described scheduling research and research in routing algorithms. For example, both must pass state information either asynchronously or periodically, in order to cooperate in making scheduling decisions. See references 63, 130, and 178.

2.7. Decentralized Control

Distributed systems provide the potential for decentralized control which is usually advocated for increased reliability. Certain operating systems, referred to in this paper as DPOSs, use decentralized control to achieve reliability. In this regard, various forms of decentralized control of resources are appropriate to our current discussion: decentralized control that is needed for distibuted databases, decentralized control that is needed for stochastic replicated functions (see the following definition), such as routing and scheduling, and decentralized control via decomposition.

In distributed databases, concurrency control algorithms are sometimes implemented as decentralized control algorithms with increased reliability but also increased cost (number of messages required). The decentralized concurrency control algorithms must maintain database integrity. This constraint reduces potential parallelism, but is necessary. Solutions to this type of decentralized control are known (see Section 3).

The second type of decentralized control is the type used for *stochastic replicated* functions such as routing and scheduling functions. By replicated functions we mean that the decentralized controllers implementing a function are equal partners involved in the entire problem, not just a subset of the original problem created, say, by decomposing the original problem. By stochastic it is meant that there is no data integrity constraint and information is noisy and out of date. In contrast to the decentalized control problem for databases, solutions (in the most general form) to decentralized control for stochastic replicated functions are not known, e.g., Team theroy [91] and various forms of control theory all fall short in dealing with this problem.[189]

Only preliminary work has been done in the area of decentralized control for stochastic replicated functions.[115,192] Possible approaches might include the use of random graphs, decision theory,[85,123,149,190,215] and stochastic learning automata.[75,139] The complicating issues for stochastic replicated functions include the need for very low overhead solutions, the operation in the presence of noisy and delayed information, the high degree of interaction between cooperating controllers, and the fact that decisions of each controller affect the others.

The majority of the research work on decentralized control is based on extensions to centralized solutions where the entire state is known and can be more accurately described as *decomposition techniques*, rather than decentralized control.[8,33,36,62,91,94] In such work large scale problems are partitioned into smaller problems, each smaller problem being solved, for example, by mathematical programming techniques, and the separate solutions being combined via interaction variables. The interaction variables normally model very limited cooperation. See Larsen[112] for an excellent summary of decomposition-based decentalized control. Yet other surveys have appeared, including Sandell *et al.*,[174] that note the unclear meaning of optimality for decentralized control and hypothesize the need for a completely different approach. One approach for decentralized control is based on the concept of a *domule*. A domule is the combination of a decision agent (controller), its local subsystem, and interaction relations between agents.[204] Using this concept, interesting heuristics are proposed for decentralized control but these are largely based on decomposition. Many applications in distributed software may be adequately addressed by known decomposition techniques. However, to apply these techniques many of the complicating issues listed above for stochastic replicated functions would have to be absent or have minimal effect. In summary, decentralized control remains a rather perplexing issue.

2.8. Protection and Security

Protection and security have been one of the main concerns of computer systems from their inception.[79,172] The problem of achieving the desired degree of protection and security is exacerbated in distributed systems because there may (should) be no central repository of authoritative information on the connected computers, the individuals using them, or their intentions. Also, in distributed systems, a malicious user can eavesdrop and tamper with the communication channels and thus can copy, alter, and replay messages as well as emit false messages. Primarily, there are two major requirements in protected systems.

authorization: ensuring that only authorized users are permited access to protected information, and

authentication: verifying the identity of communicating entities to one another.

Thus,in distributed sytems, protocols for decentalized authorization and authentication become necessary.

Standard approaches to authorization or access control in multi-user systems are typified by those used in the Cambridge File Server (CFS)[47] and the Xerox Distributed File System (DFS).[201] In the DFS, accesses to protected files are permitted only after consulting a directory that contains *identity-based access control* lists: For each file, the directory contains a list of identities of authorized users and the operations they are authorized to perform. One of the shortcomings of this approach is the need for additional mechanisms that permit system utilities such as a directory service to have more privileges than the users of the utilities.[137] Also, the use of user identities, i.e., the identities of passive entities (as opposed to active entities such as processes), for authorization results in a system with static protection features. But, if process identities are used in access control lists, the dynamics of process creating and destruction requires continuous updating of the control lists. These shortcomings are avoided in a capability-based protection sytem.

The CFS provides access control based on *capabilities*. Only if a user is able to provide a valid capability for a file is the user permitted access to the file. The identity of the user is unimportant. The shortcomings of identity-based access control mentioned above are avoided since presenting a capability is sufficient for gaining access to a protected object and also because users are free to pass capabilities to the processes providing service.

Systems employing a capability mechanism view all protected data as strongly-typed objects which are uniquely identified. A capability consists of an object identifier and a set of access rights which allow the manipulation of the object with a subset of the operations defined by the object's type. Object-oriented systems such as CAL,[108] CAP,[141] Hydra,[219] and Intel 432[44,99] associate groups of objects with a protection domain. A protection domain consists of a (set of) process(es) and local data in addition to shared objects. A process within a domain has the right to distribute access rights to processes outside the domain.

In DEMOS,[17] ROSCOE,[182] and ACCENT[157] ports (termed *links* in the first two systems) are the primary protected entities in the system and hence processes require capabilities for accessing them. As discussed earlier, ports provide for communication and optional data sharing between tasks. Thus, in these systems, to access a protected remote object, a process should have the capability to access the port connecting the process to the remote object as well as the capability to access the remote object. In the scheme proposed in references 152 and 194, a port is created for a specific type of access to a specific object. Creation of ports is controlled by a distributed capability directory. Once a port has been created to access an object via an operation and has been appropriately typed, only access to the port need be checked, access to the object need not. This results in a reduction in the overheads incurred in accessing remote objects.

The work reported in references 4, 101, and 128 incorporate capabilities into concurrent programming languages in an attempt to increase the flexibility of controlling dynamic access to shared objects. Although this is an important extension, the use of programming languages to provide protection has inherent limitations in that the policies enforced by any language can be compromised in a number of ways. For example, the user could modify object code on secondary storage or develop programs in a different language.

Secure communication via insecure communication channels mandates the *encryption* of messages. This has taken additional importance given the extensive use of networks that connect heterogeneous computer systems. Voydock and Kent[210] survey the security mechanisms used in conjunction with high-level network protocols. Here we briefly look at two uses of encryption in authentication and authorization.

Needham and Shroeder[142] present protocols for authentication of users in a distributed environment. Their protocols are designed for secure interactions between two principals on different computers, for one-way communication such as those occurring in mail systems, and for signed communication in which an intermediary can anthenticate the contents of a communication. Their scheme is based on the presence of *authentication servers* that possess authoritative information about each user's encryption keys. According to their analysis both conventional and public key encryption algorithms[46,140] are comparable in the number of messages exchanged during authentication.

A method for authorization and authentication based on *sealing* (encrypting) an object with a key is described in reference 73. In this scheme, sealed objects are self-authenticating, and to access an object a user presents appropriate keys to unseal the object, then accesses the object, and finally reseals it. Thus, as long as keys are securely stored, users need not trust the computer system where their (sealed) information is stored. But since there are no controls over the transfer of keys between users, users should be trustworthy as far as their handling of keys is concerned.

Any *secure* system should ensure the *separation* of information belonging to different security classifications and the *mediation* of flow of information between users with different security classifications. Unlike in *security kernels*,[3] where these two functions are provided by a single mechanism, the scheme proposed by Rushby and Randell[155] for structuring secure distributed systems exploits the separation provided by physical distribution. This scheme involves interconnecting a number of small trustworthy components and larger untrusted host machines. While a host machine is associated with a single security partition, the trusted components mediate the information flow between untrusted hosts.

Given the increase in the number of applications of physically distributed computers, there is bound to be an increasing interest in and a need for ensuring security and protection of information.

2.9. Reliability

The physical separation of componets of distributed systems reduces the possibilities of simultaneous failure of multiple components and also facilitates the provision of redundant resources. These can be used to design systems that not only have better performance but also have a degree of availability and reliability. The issue of reliability transcends many of the topics considered so far, in particular, process structuring, resource structuring, inter-process communication, design of communication channels, and decentralized control. Also, the issue of reliability is addressed in distributed database systems using transactions, nested transactions, and commit and recovery protocols. Hence many of the issues relevant to reliability are dealt with in the sections that relate to these topics. In this section, we summarize the basic concepts of reliable distributed systems.

To synthesize a reliable distributed system it is necessary to implement *reliable physical processors* and *reliable storage* media. A reliable processor has provision for periodic *checkpointing* of processor states on reliable storage and for restarting a processor from a previously saved state. *Reliable storage* facilities provide atomic operations on the storage devices. Lampson's proposal[110] is based on the use of *shadow* copies of disk pages that are updated instead of updating pages *in place*. On commitment of the updates, the shadow copies replace the *current pages*. To decrease the possibility of failure, the shadow copies are maintained on a storage device that is different from the current pages.

Object-orientation provides a convenient method for structuring resources. Objects can be manipulated only via predefined operations, which, for example, are executed as *atomic remote procedure calls*. The procedures are themselves defined within processes that control access to the *atomic objects*, as in guardians.[125] This approach is attractive due to the confinement of errors within (a set of) guardians whereby rollback and restart are limited to activities within (a set of) guardians.

For its functioning, a reliable system requires techniques for detecting erroneous states in the system. Here we briefly review some of these techniques. A technique used in highly reliable systems is called *Triple Modular Redundancy*. Any computation is performed by three different processes and the result is validated by a majority vote. Also, redundant information such as parity or checksum, can be associated with the objects themselves, so that an erroneous state of an object will be reflected as an erroneous parity or checksum. Another technique is to associate consistency checks with the objects. At certain points during the use of an object these checks are used to determine whether or not the object is in a consistent state. A time-out mechanism, sometimes called a watchdog timer, can be used to detect erroneous behavior of system components, if the typical response time for the component is known. Timers can be reset by a status message indicating a positive response. All these techniques can be supplemented by diagnostic checks which determine if components of the system exhibit the expected behavior in specific situtations.

Exceptions in distributed sytems can occur due to data transmission errors as well as due to process control errors. Data transmission errors, including lost messages, the receipt of garbled messsages, duplicates, and misdirected messages should be transparent at the process level. Though it appears that the communication facility and its underlying protocols should ensure reliable, error free data transmission across communications paths between processes, according to the end-to-end argument, such functions placed at the lower levels of the system are often redundant and unnecessary.[173] The rationale for this argument is that since an application has to take into account errors introduced not only by the communication network but also by the layers that separate the application and the communication network, many of the error detection and recovery functions can be correctly and completely provided only at application level.

Process control errors take the form of processes involved in a deadlock or a livelock, and destroyed processes (including node failure). For example, the blocked receiver problem occurs when a receiver blocks on an unconditional receive and no message is even delivered to the process. Unexpected process destruction is the most likely candidate for causing a blocked receiver problem. The IPC facility must take responsibility for notifying the other processes attached to the destroyed process. The IPC facility should notify the receivers connected to the communication paths to which the destroyed process has send access. Processes with send access to a port connected to a destroyed receiver should be notified on the next attempt to send a message.

Many of the proposed recovery techniques for distributed systems have been discovered in the context of distributed databases. Sections 3.8 and 3.9 deal with these techniques.

Designers of programming languages for distributed systems have only recently started paying attention to the specification of actions to be taken in the event of a failure. An often-adopted solution to exception handling is a time-out. A sending process specifies the time within which it expects its message to be received whereas a receiving process specifies the time within which it expects the next message to arrive. When the time limit is exceeded, the process concerned is informed about the time expiration.[48,125] As discussed earlier, Argus integrates many proposals for designing reliable distributed systems. In PLITS,[58] the notion of transaction keys can be used to notify processes about errors. For instance, a process can be programmed to wait for a message by transaction key only, without specifying the source of the message. Thus, failure of a sending process can be intimated to the receiving process by using the appropriate transaction key.

2.10. Distributed File Systems

Research in distributed file systems can be considered as providing an important but only incremental step in establishing integrated distributed computing systems. Three representative distributed file systems (see Table 19.1) are now briefly described in order to illustrate what facilities current distributed file systems provide. This section then leads into a discussion of distributed database issues which subsume the issues involved here.

The Xerox Distributed File System (DFS)[201] is used as a basis for database research. Overall, DFS gives the illusion of a single, logical file system, and it runs on a local network. To support this illusion there exists a file locating facility that makes file location transparent to the user. The DFS is based on a client-server model where multiple servers (one being designated the primary) may cooperate to service a single transaction in an atomic fashion. Multiple files, located across the network, may be involved in a single atomic transaction. File replication is not supported. Users access the DFS through programs called clients that run on the user sites. DFS uses a locking mechanism between transactions that supports client caches for increased efficiency. Finally, facilities exist to deal with server crashes and aborted transactions.

The Felix file server[61] is designed to support a variety of file systems, virtual memory, and database applications by providing a simple interface. Felix is the base upon which a higher level file system is to be built. Felix is the only storage component in the system and runs on a local area network. An atomic transaction in Felix may involve single files or a set of files. A highly flexible mechanism for file sharing is supported by using six access modes specified when the file is opened (read copy, write copy, read original, write original, read exclusive and write exclusive). The level of locking granularity is the block level. Access control is based on capabilities and no file replication is supported. Felix is also based on the client-server model.

LOCUS[147] is a distributed file system that is application code compatible with UNIX.[164] In contrast to the above two systems LOCUS does support file replication. A centralized synchronization site which is dynamically chosen at the time a file is opened is used to maintain mutual consistency among replicated files as well as to synchronize multiple accesses to shared files. LOCUS continues to operate even if there is partial system failure or network partitioning (see also Section 3.9 for a discussion of version vectors). A concept based on version vectors is used to resolve conflicts at system recovery time. LOCUS is not designed as a client-server model but as a file system integrated with the rest of the operating system.

Many of the open issues for distributed file systems are the same as for distributed databases (see Section 3). These include how to maintain the atomic property in the presence of crashes and other failures, support of multiple copies, concurrency control and deadlock resolution. Other issues include directory assignment, replication and partitioning, division of the responsibility between file servers and clients, and the relationship of the distributed file system to the operating system.

3. DISTRIBUTED DATABASE MANAGEMENT

In this section we give a brief survey of the current research associated with the development of general purpose distributed database management systems (DDBMS's). Rothnie and Goodman[165] state that "distributed database management is an attractive approach . . . because it permits the database system to act conceptually as a centralized system, while physically mirroring the geographic distribution of organizations. . . ." Some of the potential advantages of distributed database management systems are: easy access to geographically distributed but logically integrated data from a single site, increased reliability and availability, faster data access, and incremental system growth.

The following are the main concepts involved in distributed database management: 1) Transaction model; 2) Data models; 3) Synchronization (concurrency control); 4) Data replication and location transparency; 5) Distributed directory/dictionary management; 6) Deadlock resolution; 7) Nested transactions; 8) Recovery (Failure handling); 9) Network partitioning; 10) Typical applications; and 11) Prototypes and testbeds.

3.1. Transaction Model

The *transaction concept* has emerged as an abstraction which allows programmers to group a sequence of actions into a logical execution unit. If executed atomically, a transaction transforms a current consistent state of the database into a new consistent state.[55] The virtues and limitations of the concept as it applies to databases are described in reference 82. The virtues are strong enough that the ideas of transactions and related concepts have also started appearing in distributed programming languages (as described in Section 2) and in distributed operating systems,[129,168,184,200] further integrating these three research areas. In the database area, it is the job of the transaction processing component of a DDBMS to preserve atomicity of transactions. In order to do this, protocols for resolving data access conflicts between transactions (concurrency control protocols) and protocols for recovering a consistent state of the database in spite of user errors, application errors, or partial system failure (processes, nodes, links, etc.) are necessary.[105]

There is general agreement that the logical structure (system architecture) of a distributed database management system can be described by Fig. 19.1. The four basic components are transactions, transaction managers (TM's), data managers (DM's), and data. Each user transaction is controlled by and interacts with the data management system through a single transaction manager (TM). The TM's may simultaneously control multiple independent user transactions. The TM in charge of a transaction forwards database access and update requests to the data manager (DM) local to the data. The local DM's are responsible for managing their own stored databases and for completing local access and update commands received from TM's on behalf of transactions. The level of the access and update commands passed to the DM's depend on the implementation. They may be low level page read and write requests or high level query and update operations requiring extensive computation as well as file input and output. A more detailed description of this logical model and how it is used as a basis for concurrency control theory can be found in reference 10.

3.2. Data Models

By restricting the choice of data model, there is more potential to optimize performance. The relational model has been the choice of researchers in DDBMS's. One reason is the opportunity for optimizing query processing by decomposing the query into subqueries which can be performed at remote sites.[24] The choice of a decomposition depends on the processing costs, the communication costs, and the data distribution. There continues to be some interest in

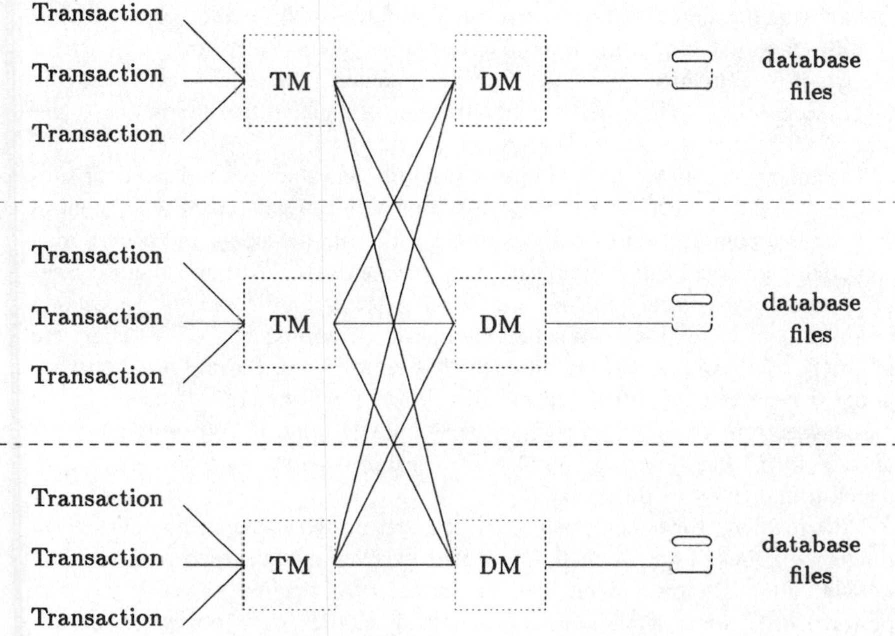

Fig. 19.1. DDBMS system structure.

developing optimal decompositions which minimize the processing and communication costs.[47] However, even with a very simplified model of the distributed database and of the cost of processing a query, the costs of computing an optimal solution are large. Experimental work is needed to test the suitability of the model and the real savings before the utility of this research can be evaluated.

Due to the large number of existing DBMS's, a very practical problem is how to map between them or how to provide a single intermediate model which will enable an application to access heterogeneous systems. The research trend seems to be towards higher level nonprocedural semantic data models.[89] There is also interest in integrating database support into the operating system.[82]

3.3. Synchronization (Concurrency Control)

Bernstein and Goodman[20–22] have developed a unified framework, called *serializability theory*, for analyzing the correctness of concurrency control algorithms.[64, 80, 114, 116, 120, 132–134, 162, 163, 199] A schedule for a group of transactions [x, y, z,. . .] with the property that all actions of any transaction, for example, y, comes before or after any actions of other transactions is a *serial schedule*.

This means that transactions are executed one at a time in some order. Serializability theory assumes that a serial execution is semantically correct. A schedule which is equivalent in its effect on the database to a serial schedule is said to be serializable. The serializability theorem[20,21] states the conditions under which a schedule is serializable.

The theory partitions the synchronization problem into two independent sub-problems: read-write and write-write synchronization. Each concurrency control scheme is a combination of policies to solve the sub-problems and each policy can be implemented using combinations of mechanisms. The three major classes of concurrency control policies are: locking (two-phase locking), timestamp ordering, and validation (also called the optimistic approach.[25,107,176] There are a variety of algorithms to support each of these policies. Several hundred variations have been identified for the distributed environment[20,21] covering the entire spectrum from centralized to decentralized control. We will make no attempt to list the very large number of research papers which have been dedicated to the study of this topic.

New methods for concurrency control are expected to be combinations and minor variations of known methods. However, even though many variations are known, little is known about how the choice of a scheme will affect system performance. Some simulation and queueing studies have compared performance, but the results are still inconclusive. In fact, since the models used in the studies have not been validated, their results should not be accepted without close scrutiny. Several experimental studies involving testbed sytems are either underway or planned. The results from these studies should be helpful in the comparative evaluation, but it is unlikely that one approach will always be the best due to the wide variety of applications and system structures. These studies should provide enough evidence to determine if the choice of concurrency control algorithm has a primary or secondary impact on performance compared with other factors.[13]

The correctness of a concurrency control algorithm is judged by the serializability of all the schedules allowed in the scheme.[19,150] That is, if all the legal schedules of a scheme are serializable, then the scheme is correct with respect to the serializability requirement.

Serializability represents the strongest degree of consistency. Some applications may require only lower degrees of consistency by allowing, for example, reads from multiple objects without concern for time consistency between the values read. Gray *et al.*[81] discuss four degrees of consistency, degree 0 through 3, where lower degrees require fewer locks to be set or locks to be held for a shorter period of time. A smaller degree of consistency may increase performance but has the disadvantage of reducing the effectiveness of system recovery after failure. Gray *et al.* suggest that the performance penalty of degree 3 consistency is small and consequently lower degrees of consistency are a bad idea.

3.4. Data Replication and Location Transparency

In order to enhance data availability and reliability, it is desirable to support the replication of critical data at multiple sites.[51,199] However, replication results in a more difficult concurrency control problem than in a database without replication. Several tranaction protocols have been suggested which maintain mutual consistency during normal operation of a distributed database with replication. The primary copy protocol[2] chooses one of the copies of a particular piece of data as a master and all requests for this data are made to this central site. The central site easily guarantees consistency through locking. More flexible voting schemes the majority consensus[205] and weighted voting[71] protocols have subsequently been proposed. These schemes avoid the bottlenecks and reliability concerns connected with the primary copy protocol.

Data replication can be implemented by defining two levels of abstraction:[207] database entity → database objects, and request → actions. Requests and entities are the elements in the higher level abstraction. Each database entity is physically represented by one or more replicated objects. Requests are implemented by actions on these objects. This separation should be supported by the systems to avoid problems of inconsistency which the user might introduce if updates were improperly done.

The high cost of replication in terms of increased delay and storage requirements makes the fully redundant case impractical in most situations.[15,65] Many applications would prefer to have those parts of the database which have a high read to update ratio replicated at the sites from which access is frequent. For the majority of data, replication is not expected to be cost effective. Where it is justified, the number of redundant copies will probably be small (two or three copies). A simple partitioned database where the sites and network are reliable should be adequate for many applications.

Knowledge of the physical location of the data should not be required by the end user. This can also be supported by the two level abstraction mechanism.[207] However, there is some disagreement over whether the application programmer or the operating system should control the placement of data at a particular site. Also, if the location of data is known, then it should be possible to use this information to improve performance.

3.5. Distributed Directory/Dictionary Management

General purpose distributed database management systems require a directory/dictionary (catalog) to help manage the database.[121] The directory/dictionary contains the definitions of the physical and logical structure for the data as well as the rules for mapping between the two. The directory also contains the local names of all resources—relations, files, programs, nodes, etc.—and the addressing rules for locating them. It can be thought of as a specialized distributed database system and as such can be implemented in a wide variety of ways: redundant vs. nonredundant copies, centralized vs. partitioned, etc.

The directory/dictionary problem is not unique to DDBMS's. The problems of defining, naming, and locating objects are central to the distributed programming environment[145] and have been discussed in Section 2.

3.6. Deadlock Resolution

Within database systems, deadlock is a circular wait-for condition which may arise when a locking scheme is used for concurrency control. It may occur among a set of transactions as a result of the decision to wait for a lock because of lock mode incompatibility between the granted lock and the request. The circular wait-for condition prevents any transaction from proceeding unless one or more of them are chosen as victims to be aborted. Most concurrency control schemes using locking with delay incorporate a deadlock resolution mechanism, but a deadlock-free locking policy can be designed using deadlock avoidance or prevention mechanisms as well.

We classify the mechanisms into three categories. More discussion of these approaches can be found in references 34, 74, 106, 133, 144, 165, 171.

Timeout. One of the simplest ways to resolve deadlock is to specify a maximum wait time, and roll back the transaction which is waiting if the time expires before the request is granted.

Deadlock Prevention and Avoidance. Deadlock can be prevented by requiring each transaction to preclaim and obtain locks to all the objects to be accessed before execution. In this case, if a lock request cannot be granted because the lock is held by a conflicting transaction, all locks preclaimed are released and the transaction is aborted.

As another more interesting example of a prevention mechanism, we discuss briefly two protocols proposed by Rosenkrantz *et al.*[165] which use timestamps to define a priority. This approach does not require transactions to preclaim objects but may rollback transactions that are not really deadlocked. The basic philosophy is that an older transaction (one with a smaller timestamp) is favored when conflicting with a younger transaction on the assumption that it may have already used more resources and thus more cost will be paid for rollback and restart. The two variations are:

1. *Wait/Die Protocol:* If the requester (of a lock) is older (smaller timestamp), then it is allowed to *wait*; otherwise, it *dies* (die means rollback and restart).
2. *Wound/Wait Protocol:* If the requester is older, then the requester *wounds* the conflicting younger transaction, otherwise, the request *waits*. *Wound* is an activity in which the requester sends messages to all the nodes the

younger transactions has visited saying that it is wounded and the scheduler will abort a wounded transaction if the transaction has not initiated termination. If the younger transaction is terminating, i.e., in two-phase commit stage, then the wound message is ignored to save some unnecessary rollback/restart.

See references 105 and 165 for more details.

Deadlock Detection. The detection mechanisms are mostly based on finding cycles in a transaction wait-for graph (TWFG). The nodes of the graph represent the waiting transactions, and the directed edges indicate for which transactions a given transaction is waiting. When cycles are detected, they are broken by choosing victims to be rolled back and restarted. This mechanism seems to have greater popularity than other mechanisms. However, in distributed systems a global transaction wait-for graph (GTWFG) must be constructed to detect deadlock involving two or more nodes. The GTWFG is maintained by exchanging messages among the nodes, causing additional communication overhead and delay. When a detection mechanism is chosen, some other decisions have to be made by the designer:

- Detector organization: centralized detector, distributed detectors, or something in between, e.g., hierarchically organized detectors with a detector for a cluster of nodes and a higher-level detector for a cluster of detectors.
- Detection initiation: is detection made periodically using a predefined time parameter, is it initiated every time a transaction has to wait, or when any suspended transaction has waited for more than a predefined time period.
- Failure resiliency: establish backup for a centralized detector and activate when centralized detector fails.

The importance of an efficient detection algorithm for performance and which is the best approach are issues which have not been adequately resolved. It clearly depends on the average frequency of deadlock in the database application environment. A study by Gray[83] showed that the frequency of deadlock goes up with the square of multiprogramming level and the fourth power of the transaction size.

Little has been written about deadlock in the context of NOS, DOS and DPOSs. One exception is the Medusa system where deadlock avoidance is used. Here functions provided by the utilities (OS functions) are divided into service classes such that (i) a single utility provides all the services in each class, and (ii) there are no circularities in the dependencies between classes. Furthermore, each utility must contain separate pools of resources so that it can provide independent service to each class. These conditions avoid the deadlock problem. More work is required for all approaches to deadlock in distributed systems.

3.7. Nested Transactions

The concept of nested transaction has been proposed as a generalization of the basic transaction model.[82,138] In this model, each transaction consists of a set of hierarchically structured subtransactions. Each subtransaction is an atomic activity with respect to the other subtransactions under the same parent. Concurrency of subtransactions within a transaction is allowed as long as they follow the concurrency control rules.

To cope with partial failures of a distributed computation, a subtransaction can be aborted independently of its parent transaction. This property is quite useful. For example, due to disk errors a subtransaction may fail while attempting to access a database file. If the database file is replicated at another node, the parent transaction can invoke a new subtransaction to work on the request without having to abort.

Other properties of nested transactions are: 1) a transaction is committed only when the root transaction, i.e., top-level transaction, commits, and 2) the abortion of a parent transaction will abort all the subtransactions rooted at that subtransaction, even if the subtransactions are *temporarily* committed under the world of its parent transaction. Thus, the atomicity of root transactions is preserved among concurrent root transactions as in the case of the basic transaction model.

Nested transactions also have been proposed as a good basis for building distributed systems because they encapsulate the synchronization and failure properties of distributed systems in a very clean and usable way and take care of the most difficult parts of reliable, concurrent, distributed computation.[138] Since complicated applications can be decomposed into independently implemented and tested subtransactions, it is expected that both programmer productivity and program structure can be improved if a distributed system supports nested transactions. The idea of nested transactions has also migrated into the distributed programming language area (see ARGUS[125]).

3.8. Recovery (Failure Handling)

It is the responsibility of the DDBMS to insure that transactions are atomic in spite of user errors, application errors, or partial system failures.[87,88] This means that if a failure occurs to prevent the successful completion of a transaction, all database entities that the transaction modified must be restored to their state prior to the transaction. The same mechanism is used by the concurrency control scheme to roll back one or more transactions to resolve deadlock. This rollback is normally achieved by using a *shadow paging* mechanism or a *write ahead log*.[206] Operating system support is needed to make these mechanisms more efficient.

Protocols for preserving transaction atomicity are called *commit protocols*.

They are used to insure the completion (commit) or rollback (abort) of the actions of a transaction at all sites. When multiple sites are involved, the question of site autonomy arises.[122] It is well known that when the common two-phase commit protocol is used, a site loses its autonomy to independently roll back once it enters the second phase of the two-phase protocol. Skeen[179] calls this a blocking protocol because a site failure under certain circumstances may leave operational sites blocked waiting for the failed site to recover. He has proposed an extension, called a three-phase commit protocol, which has the property that it is nonblocking if certain assumptions about the system behavior and failure modes are true. The nonblocking property is achieved by using additional messages and an associated termination protocol. More research is needed to evaluate whether the assumptions on system behavior are realistic, and if the performance penalty of the additional messages required by the third phase are worth it.

Failure handling mechanisms can be classified into two protocols: the termination protocol and the recovery protocol. The *termination protocol* is invoked at failure detection time to guarantee transaction atomicity. It attempts to terminate (commit or abort, depending the transaction's current state) all affected transactions at all the participating nodes. A node which has failed must execute a *recovery protocol* before it resumes communication with other nodes. The major functions of the recovery protocol are to restart the system processes, and to re-establish consistent transaction states for all transactions affected by the failure, if this is not already accomplished by a termination protocol. More research is required to address recovery issues such as failure detection, network partitioning, and node restart and integration.[66, 135, 208]

3.9. Network Partitioning

A distributed database consists of a set of data items and a set of sites connected by communication links. Under normal operation any site can communicate with any other site. A network partition of the distributed database is a maximal subset of communicating sites. A system is partitioned at time *t* if it is composed of more than one partition. Four interrelated issues associated with partitioned databases are:

- Detection of the partitioned database.
- The degree of user transaction progress permitted during the time of the partition.
- Strategies and algorithms for merging or avoiding the merging of partitioned databases (note, finding an optimal solution to the general problem of merging partitioned databases in such a way as to retain serializability is NP complete) and

- recovery schemes at the time of network partitioning and at the time of merging.

Each of the above issues is further complicated when 1) complete or partial replication of the data is allowed, and 2) multiple failures and multiple partitions are expected during the same time interval (this gives rise to multiple race conditions).

It is important to stress that the complications are not obscure theoretical problems, but arise in many situations, especially when networks are large.

The protocols used to deal with network partitioning must be evaluated at three different stages: under normal system operation, during the partitioned state, and at the time of the merging. Different protocols tradeoff performance among these different stages.

In general, there are two common approaches in dealing with the network partitioning problem: a deterministic approach and an optimistic approach. The deterministic approach avoids data inconsistencies while the optimistic approach permits data inconsistencies for the period of time that the network is partitioned, but then they are resolved upon merging. The second approach is called optimistic because is assumes that there will be a relatively small number of conflicts to resolve upon the merge.

The deterministic approach includes protocols referred to as primary copy,[2] majority consensus,[205] weighted voting and quorum based commit.[179] A number of protocols exist for the optimistic approach including the use of version vectors as typified in LOCUS,[147] the use of precedence graphs created from histories of transactions committed during the partition,[218] special automatic merging procedures based on merge rules specific to a data type,[56] and tools to help in resolving differences in files accrued during the partition.[68] The optimistic approach allows more availability than the deterministic approach since access to data is not blocked, but additional information must be retained during the partition to enable effective merging (such as version vectors or transaction histories), and *a priori* knowledge is often required (e.g., semantics about the data items being updated and the need for serialization or not). Overall, the work on network partitioning has been quite preliminary and there has been little evaluation and comparison of the approaches.

3.10. Typical Applications

Real-time, interactive transaction processing is the *typical* application for a general-purpose DDBMS. But the characteristics and requirements of these systems are vague. How much data is required in the entire database? How much data is required by a single transaction? What percent of the data is located locally vs. remotely? How many sites will a transaction need to access? What percent of transactions are read only vs. update? What is the probability of conflict with other concurrent transactions? The lack of adequate answers to these and many other questions makes it impossible to define a *typical* workload and application.

3.11. Prototypes and Testbeds

The best-known DDBMS prototypes are SDD-1[167] distributed INGRES[198] and R*.[122] However, none of these systems meet all of the goals of a DDBMS,[207] and little has been published regarding the operational performance of these systems.

In order to compare and understand the tradeoffs involved in the design of DDBMS's, a more flexible experimental approach is needed. These systems, called *testbeds*, emphasize modularity and flexibility so different algorithms and strategies can be easily *plugged in* and compared. They must also be architecturally similar to real systems in order for the experimental results to be meaningful. The DDTS project at Honeywell[52] is an example of a planned testbed system for DDBMS experimentation on a wide variety of issues: data models, multi-schema architectures, user interfaces, semantic integrity, data translation, data allocation, transaction optimization, concurrency control, and reliability and recovery. The CARAT project at UMASS[67] is an operational testbed system where the focus is on the issues of distributed concurrency control, deadlock detection, crash recovery, and network partitioning.

Distributed data management represents an important paradigm for distributed software systems research and development. All the major distributed system research issues, as discussed in the next section, are important to the successful design and implementation of DDBMS's.

4. CRITICAL RESEARCH ISSUES

The current state of the art is such that different proposals exist for solving, albeit partially, some of the problems discussed above, but not much is known about their appropriateness, efficiency and applicability in a distributed environment and the tradeoffs that they entail. Hence, there is a need for work in the following areas:

Theory: A theory of distributed systems needs to be developed in order to deal with issues such as complexity, theoretical limitations, and semantics. Formalisms for distributed computation (both for specifications and for analysis) are required. These formalisms should be able to handle failure-prone systems also, since reliability is one of the crucial aspects of distributed systems.

Specification: There is a need to design languages that provide for the specification of a number of features which were, so far, entirely the responsibility of the underlying operating system. These features include data and control distribution, choice of communication primitives, protection requirements and error-recovery schemes.

Design, Experimentation, and Evaluation: Design methodologies are needed for distributed systems. There is also a need to emphasize the *integration* of the various solutions to distributed system problems. The experiments need to build a core of knowledge pertaining to the issues that are relevant to such systems. One of the motivations behind these experiments would be to obtain performance measurements that can be used to evaluate the different proposals. Thus modelling, simulation, and proof techniques need to be developed to analyze and evaluate the experimental systems. Obviously, not every solution will be appropriate for all situations. Hence, the evaluation of the various proposals must be directed towards uncovering the assumptions under which a particular scheme performs well. This is especially important in practice, since in the future, distributed systems are bound to be used both for special-purpose as well as general-purpose applications.

We now list some of the important open questions that need to be addressed in terms of theory, specification, design, experimentation and evaluation.

Distribution of Control: Decentralized control algorithms for various functions of operating systems, such as task scheduling and resource allocation, are needed especially those concerned with a high degree of cooperation between decentralized controllers. Investigation of scheduling concepts such as bidding, clustering, co-scheduling, pause time, wave scheduling is required. The use of various mathematical models such as adaptive control, stochastic control, statistical decision theory, and stochastic learning automata for dealing with uncertainty, inaccuracies and delay in distributed systems is also necessary. Scheduling tasks with real time constraints on a loosely coupled distributed system has received little attention to date due to the difficulties involved. The interaction of the scheduling function between the programming language and operating system is also an important issue.

Distribution of processes and resources: It is an open question on how to distribute processes that cooperate to execute a given task. This would affect the topology of the resulting network of processes and the manner in which individual nodes are designed. A crucial question is whether movement of processes in execution is cost-effective and what the best means is to implement such movement. Tradeoffs between static and dynamic allocation of resources should be investigated. Directory assignment, replication, and partitioning should also be addressed. For client-server models of distributed file systems where do we divide the responsibility between file servers and clients? When should distributed file systems be embedded in the operating system and when should a file server model be used? How should the operating system itself be distributed?

Protection and Security: Specification techniques for the protection requirements within a node and between nodes are needed. Models for protection are required. The problems with revocation of access rights in a distributed environment must be solved. Schemes for implementing protection requirements in a communicating failure-prone environment are needed. Encryption of messages for secure communication and integration of security and protection must be further addressed.

Inter-process Communication: Specification of various aspects of communication paths, such as, directionality, structure of messages, reliability, ownership and access rights should be possible. Given the usefulness of different types of message primitives, users should be able to choose and specify the one appropriate for a given situation. Since there are a number of schemes for addressing processes and resources, each requiring differing operating system support and each providing differing levels of transparency and flexibility, the efficacy of the addressing schemes needs further investigation.

Reliability: A more comprehensive theory as well as realistic and practical schemes for error recovery and reliability in general are required. Overheads introduced by fail-safe systems and the trade-offs that such schemes entail must be investigated. How effective is decentralized control as an aid in providing error recovery? Is the nested atomic action the appropriate programming abstraction for the high level programmer? Can it be supported efficiently? What is the best method for implementing reliable interprocess communication? Issues related to network partitioning and slow degradation of the working of nodes in a network is a fairly recent but important research topic.

Heterogeneity: Techniques for dealing with information transfer between nodes with varying capabilities, storage schemes, and data models are needed. Efficient network interfaces for heterogenous hosts must be developed. How does heterogeneity affect the distribution of programs and data in a distributed system and vice versa?

Synchronization and Concurrency: In order to implement the atomic action abstraction, some system level mechanism for synchronizing concurrent access requests to shared data must be provided. Concurrency control theory is well developed, and there are many algorithms and approaches for solving the associated distributed deadlock problem assuming locking is used, but there is no sound basis for choosing one approach over another. Experimental studies will be required to compare the performance of alternate approaches for a variety of applications.

In summary, this chapter has attempted to provide a broad review of distributed system software issues. We again apologize for unintentionally omitting other related relevant research and fully realize that material such as this is somewhat outdated by the time it is published. Nevertheless, a lot of information has been included here and we hope that it is helpful to the researchers in the field of distributed systems.

REFERENCES

1. Agrawala, A. K., S. K. Tripathi, and G. Ricart, Adaptive routing using a virtual waiting time technique, *IEEE Trans. Software Eng.*, vol. SE-8, pp. 76–81, Jan. 1982.
2. Alsberg, P. and J. Day, A principle for resilient sharing of distributed resources, in *Proc. 2nd Int. Conf. on Software Eng.*, San Francisco, CA, 1976.
3. Ames, S. and M. Gasser, Security kernel design and implementation: An introduction, *Computer*, vol. 16, July 1983.
4. Ancilotti, P., M. Boari, and N. Lijtmaer, Language features for access control, *IEEE Trans. Software Eng.*, vol. SE-9, pp. 16–25, Jan. 1983.
5. Anderson, B., *et al.*, Data Reconfiguration Service, Tech. Rep., Bolt Beranek and Newman, Cambridge, U.K., May 1971.
6. Andrews, G. R., Sychronizing resources, *ACM Trans. Programming Languages and Systems*, vol. 3, pp. 405–430, Oct. 1981.
7. Andrews, G. R. and F. Schneider, Concepts and notations for concurrent programming, *ACM Comput. Surveys*, vol. 15, pp. 3–44, Mar. 1983.
8. Aoki, M., Control of large-scale dynamic systems by aggregation, *IEEE Trans. Automatic Control*, June 1978.
9. Apollo, Domain Architecture, Manual Apollo Computer, Inc., Feb. 1981.
10. Ayache, J. M., J. P. Courtiat, and M. Diaz, REBUS, a fault tolerant distributed system for industrial control, *IEEE Trans. Computers*, vol. C-31, pp. 637–647, July 1982.
11. Bach, M., N. Coguen, and M. Kaplan, The ADAPT system: A generalized approach towards data conversion, in *Proc. 5th Int. Conf. Very Large Data Bases*, Rio de Janeiro, Brazil, Oct. 1979.
12. Ball, J. E., J. Feldman, J. Low, R. Rashid, and P. Rovner, RIG, Rochester's intelligent gateway: System overview, *IEEE Trans. Software Eng.*, vol. SE-2, pp. 321–328, Dec. 1976.
13. Balter, R., P. Berard, and P. Decitre, Why control of concurrency level in a distributed systems is more fundamental than deadlock management, in *ACM SIGACT-SIGOPS Symp. on Principles of Distributed Computing*, Ottowa, Canada, Aug. 1982.
14. Balzer, R. M., *Ports—A Method for Dynamic Interprogram Communication and Job Control*, Tech. Rep. for an ARPA contract at RAND, Aug. 1971.
15. Barabara, D. and H. Garcia-Molina, How Expensive is Data Replication: An Example, Tech. Rep. 286, Dept. of Elect. Eng. and Comp. Sci., Princeton University, June 1981.
16. Bartlett, J. N. A non-stop operating system, in *Proc. 11th Hawaii Int. Conf. on System Sciences*, Jan. 1978.
17. Baskett, F., J. Howard, and J. Montague, Task communication in DEMOS, in *Proc. 6th ACM Symp on Operating System Principles*, pp. 23–31, West Lafayette, IN, Nov. 1977.
18. Bernstein, P. A., D. W. Shipman, and W. S. Wong, Formal aspects of serializability in database concurrency control, *IEEE Trans. Software Eng.*, vol. SE-5, pp. 203–216, May 1979.
19. Bernstein, P. A. and D. W. Shipman, The correctness of concurrency control mechanisms in a system of distributed databases, *ACM Trans. Database Systems*, vol. 5, pp. 52–68, Mar. 1980.
20. Bernstein, P. A., and N. Goodman, Concurrency control in distributed database systems, *ACM Comput. Surveys*, vol. 13, pp. 185–221, June 1981.
21. Bernstein, P. A. and N. Goodman, A Sophisticate's Introduction To Distributed Database Concurrency Control, Res. Rep. TR-19-82, Harvard University, also in *8th Intl. Conf. on Very Large Data Bases*, Sept. 1982.
22. Bernstein, P. A. and N. Goodman, Concurrency control Algorithms for multiversion database systems, in *Proc. ACM Symp. on Principles of Distributed Computing*, Ottowa, Canada, Aug. 1982.

23. Bernstein, P. A., D. W. Shipman, and J. B. Rothnie, Jr., Concurrency control in a system for distributed databases (SDD-1), *ACM Trans. on Database Systems*, vol. 5, pp. 18–25, Mar. 1980.
24. Bernstein, P., *et al.*, Query processing in a distributed databases (SDD-1), *ACM Trans. on Database Systems*, vol. 6, Dec. 1981.
25. Bhargava, B., Performance evaluation of the optimistic approach to distributed database systems and its comparison to locking, in *IEEE 3rd Intl. Conf. on Distributed Computed Systems*, Fort Lauderdale, FL, Oct. 1982.
26. Birrell, A., R. Levin, R. Needham, and M. Schroeder, Grapevine: An exercise in distributed computing, *CACM*, vol. 25, pp. 260–274, Apr. 1982.
27. Bokhari, S. H., Dual processor scheduling with dynamic reassignment, *IEEE Trans. Software Eng.*, vol. SE-5, pp. 341–349, July 1979.
28. Brinch Hansen, P., The programming language Concurrent Pascal, *IEEE Trans. Software Eng.*, vol. SE-1, pp. 199–207, June 1975.
29. Brinch Hansen, P., Distributed processes: A concurrent programming concept, *CACM*, vol. 21, pp. 934–941, Nov. 1978.
30. Britton, D. E. and M. E. Stickel, An interprocess communication facility for distributed applications, in *Proc. 1980 COMPCON Conf. on Distributed Computing*, San Francisco, CA, Feb. 1980.
31. Bryant, R. M. and R. A. Finkel, A stable distributed scheduling algorithm, in *Proc. 2nd Int. Conf. in Distributed Computing Systems*, Paris, France, Apr. 1981
32. Casey, L. and N. Shelness, A domain structure for distributed computer system, in *Proc. 6th ACM Symp. on Operating Systems Principles*, pp. 101–108, West Lafayette, IN, Nov. 1977.
33. Chandrashekaran, S. *et al.*, Stochastic automata games, *IEEE Trans. Systems, Science and Cybernetics*, Apr. 1969.
34. Chandy, K. M. and J. Misra, A distributed algorithm for detecting resource deadlocks in distributed systems, in *ACM Symp. on Principles of Distributed Computing*, Ottowa, Canada, Aug. 1982.
35. Cheriton, D. R., M. A. Malcolm, L. S. Melen, and G. R. Sager, Thoth, a portable real-time operating system, *CACM*, vol. 22, Feb. 1979.
36. Chong, C.-Y. and M. Athans, On the Periodic coordination of linear stochastic systems, in *Proc. 1975 IFAC*, Aug. 1975.
37. Chow, Y.-C. and W. Kohler, Models for dynamic load balancing in a heterogeneous multiple processor system, *IEEE Trans. Computers*, vol. C-28, pp. 354–361, May 1979.
38. Chow, T. C. K. and J. A. Abraham, Load redistribution under failure in distributed systems, *IEEE Trans. Computers*, vol. C-32, pp. 799–808, Sept. 1983.
39. Chow, T. C. K. and J. A. Abraham, Load balancing in distributed systems, *IEEE Trans. Software Eng.*, vol. SE-8, pp. 401–412, July 1982.
40. Chu, W. W., Optimal file allocation in a multiple computing system, *IEEE Trans. Computers*, vol. C-18, pp. 885–889, Oct. 1969.
41. Chu, W. W., L. J. Holloway, M. Lan, and K. Efe, Task allocation in distributed data processing, *Computer*, vol. 13, pp. 57–69, Nov. 1980.
42. Chu, W. W. and P. Hurley, Optimal query processing for distributed database systems, *IEEE Trans. Computers*, vol. C-31, pp. 835–850, Sept. 1982.
43. Cook, R. P., *Mod—A language for distributed programming, in *Proc. 1st Conf. on Distributed Computing Systems*, pp. 233–241, Huntsville, AL, Oct. 1979.
44. Cox, G., W. Corwin, K. Lai, and F. Pollack, A Unified Model and Implementation for Interprocess Communication in a Multiprocessor Environment, Tech. Rep., Intel Corporation, 1981.
45. Davies, D. W., E. Holler, and E. D. Jensen, S. R. Kimbleton, B. W. Lampson, G. Le Lann,

K. J. Thurber, and R. W. Watson, Distributed systems—architecture and implementation, in *Lecture Notes in Computer Science*, vol. 105, New York: Springer-Verlag, 1981.

46. Diffie, W. and M. Hellman, Multiuser cryptographic techniques, *Procedure AFIPS 1976 NCC*, New York: AFIPS Press, pp. 109–112, 1976.
47. Dion, J., The Cambridge file server, *ACM Operating System Rev.*, Oct. 1980.
48. Department of Defense, *Reference Manual for the Ada Programming Language*, Washington, D.C.: U.S. Govt. Printing Office, July 1980.
49. Efe, K., Heuristic models of task assignment scheduling in distributed systems, *IEEE Computer*, vol. 15, June 1982.
50. El-Dessouki, O. I. and W. H. Huan, Distributed enumeration on network computers, *IEEE Trans. Computers*, vol. C-29, pp. 818–825, Sept. 1980.
51. Ellis, C., A robust algorithm for updating duplicate databases, in *Proc. 2nd Berkeley Workshop on Distributed Management of Data and Computer Networks*, Berkeley, California, pp. 146–158, May 1977.
52. Elmasri, R., C. Devor, and S. Rahimi, Notes on DDTS: An apparatus for experimental research in distributed database management systems, *ACM SIGMOD Record*, vol. 11, pp. 32–49, July 1981.
53. Enslow, P., What is a distributed data processing system,'' *IEEE Computer*, vol. 11, Jan. 1978.
54. Enslow, P. and T. Saponas, Distributed and Decentralized Control in Fully Distributed Processing Systems, Final Tech. Rep., GIT-ICS-81/82, Georgia Institute of Technology, Atlanta, GA, Sept. 1980.
55. Eswaran, K. P., J. N. Gray, R. A. Lorie, and I. L. Traiger, The notions of consistency and predicate locks in a database system, *CACM*, vol. 19, pp. 624–633, Nov. 1976.
56. Faissol, S., *Availability and Reliability Issues in Distributed Databases* (Ph.D. diss.), Comp. Sci. Dep., University of California, Los Angeles, 1981.
57. Farber, D. J., *et al.*, The distributed computer system, in *Proc. 7th Annual IEEE Computer Society Int. Conf.*, San Francisco, CA, Feb. 1973.
58. Feldman, J. A., High level programming for distributed computing, *CACM*, vol. 22, pp. 353–368, June 1979.
59. Floyd, R. A. and C. S. Ellis, The ROE fiie system, in *Proc. 3rd Symp. on Reliability in Distributed Software and Database Systems*, Clearwater Beach, FL, Oct. 1983.
60. Forsdick, H. C., R. E. Schantz, and R. H. Thomas, Operating systems for computer networks, *IEEE Computer*, vol. 11, Jan. 1978.
61. Fridrich, M. and W. Older, The FELIX file server, ACM SIGOPS, in *Proc. 8th Symp. on Operating System Principles*, pp. 37–44, Pacific Grove, CA, Dec. 1981.
62. Fu, K.-S., Learning control systems, *IEEE Trans. Automatic Control*, Apr. 1970.
63. Gallager, R., A minimum Delay routing algorithm using distributed computation, *IEEE Trans. Communications*, vol. COM-25, Jan. 1977.
64. Garcia-Molina, H., A concurrency control mechanism for distributed databases which uses centralized locking controllers, in *Proc. 4th Berkeley Conf. on Distributed Data Management and Computer Networks*, pp. 113–124, Berkeley, CA, Aug. 1979.
65. Garcia-Molina, H., *Performance of Update Algorithms for Replicated Data in a Distributed Database* (Ph.D. diss.), Stanford University, 1979.
66. Garcia-Molina, H., Reliability Issues for fully replicated distributed databases, *Computer*, vol. 16, pp. 34–42, Sept. 1982.
67. Garcia-Molina, H., F. Germano, Jr., and W. H. Kohler, Architectural overview of a distributed software testbed, in *Proc. 16th Hawaii Intl. Conf. on System Science*, Honolulu, HI, Jan. 1983.
68. Garcia-Molina, H., T. Allen, B. Blaustein, R. Chilenskas, and D. Ries, Data-Patch: Integrating inconsistent copies of a database After a Partition. *Proc. 3rd Symp. on Reliability in Distributed Software and Database Systems*, Clearwater Beach, FL, Oct. 1983.

69. Gelernter, D. and A. J. Bernstein, Distributed communication via global buffer, *Proc. Symp. on Principles of Distributed Computing*, Ottawa, Canada, Aug. 1982.
70. Gentleman, W. M., Message passing between sequential processes: The reply primitive and the administrator concept, *Software—Practice and Experience*, vol. 11, pp. 435–466, 1981.
71. Gifford, D., Weighted voting for replicated data, in *Proc. 7th Symp. on Operating System Principles*, pp. 150–159, Pacific Grove, CA, Dec. 1979.
72. Gifford, D. K., Violet: An experimental decentralized system, *Operating Systems Rev.*, vol. 13, Dec. 1979.
73. Gifford, D. K., Cryptographic sealing for information secrecy and authentication, *CACM*, vol. 25, pp. 274–286, Apr. 1983.
74. Gligor, V. D. and S. H. Shattuck, On deadlock detection in distributed systems, *IEEE Trans. Software Eng.*, vol. SE-6, pp. 435–440, Sept. 1980.
75. Glorioso, R. M. and F. C. Osorio, *Engineering Intelligent Systems*, Bedford, MA: Digital Press, 1980.
76. Goldberg, A. *et al.*, Articles on the smalltalk system, *Byte*, vol. 6, Aug. 1981.
77. Gonzalez, M. J., Deterministic processor scheduling, *ACM Comput. Surveys*, vol. 9, pp. 173–204, Sept. 1977.
78. Good, D. I., R. M. Cohen, and J. Keeton-Williams, Principles of proving concurrent programs in Gypsy, in *Proc. 6th ACM Symp. on Principles of Programming Languages*, pp. 42–52, San Antonio, TX, Jan. 1979.
79. Graham, R. M., Protection in an information processing utility, *CACM*, vol. 11, pp. 365–369, May 1968.
80. Gray, J. N., R. A. Lorie, and G. R. Putzolu, Granularity of locks in a shared database, in *Proc. Intl. Conf. Very Large Databases*, pp. 428–451, Boston, MA, Sept. 1975.
81. Gray, J. N., R. A. Lorie, and G. R. Putzolu, Granularity of locks and degrees of consistency in a shared database, in *Proc. Modeling in Database Systems*, Nijssen, ed., Amsterdam: North-Holland, 1976.
82. Gray, J. N., Notes on data base operating systems, in *Operating Systems: An Advanced Course*, R. Bayer, R. M. Graham, and G. Seegmuller, eds., Berlin: Springer-Verlag, pp. 393–481, 1979.
83. Gray J. N., The transaction concept: Virtues and limitations, *Very Large Database Conf.*, pp. 144–154, Sept. 1981.
84. Guillemont, M. The Chorus distributed operating system: Design and implementation, in *Int. Symp. on Local Computer Networks*, Florence, Italy, Apr. 1982.
85. Halter, A. N. and G. W. Dean, *Decisions Under Uncertainty*, Chicago, IL: South-Western Pub. Co., 1971.
86. Hamilton, J., Functional Specification for the WEB Kernel, Manual Digital Equipment Corporation, R & D Group, Maynard, MA, 1978.
87. Hammer, M. and D. Shipman, An overview of reliability mechanisms for a distributed database system, in *Proc. COMPCON Spring '78*, pp. 63–65.
88. Hammer, M. and D. Shipman, Reliability mechanisms for SDD-1: A system for distributed databases. *ACM Trans. Database Systems*, vol. 5, pp. 431–466, Dec. 1980.
89. Hammer, M. and D. McLeod, Database description with SDM: A semantic database model, *ACM Trans. Database Systems*, vol. 6, pp. 351–386, Sept. 1981.
90. Herlihy, M. and B. Liskov, A value transmission method for abstract data types, *ACM Trans. Programming Languages and Systems*, vol. 4, pp. 527–551, Oct. 1982.
91. Ho, Y., Team decision theory and information structures, in *Proc. IEEE*, vol. 68, June 1980.
92. Hoare, C. A. R., Monitors: An operating system structuring concept, *CACM*, vol. 17, pp. 549–557, Oct. 1974.
93. Hoare, C. A. R., CSP: Communicating sequential processes, *CACM*, vol. 21, Aug. 1978.
94. Jarvis, R. A., Optimization strategies in adaptive control: A selective survey, *IEEE Trans. Systems, Man, and Cybernetics*, vol. SME-5, Jan. 1975.

95. Jensen, E. D., The Honeywell experimental distributed processor-An overview of its objective, philosophy and architectural facilities, *IEEE Computer*, vol 11, Jan. 1978.
96. Jensen, E. D. and N. Pieszkocm, ARCHOS: A physically dispersed distributed system, *Distributed Processing Technical Committee Newsletter*, vol. 6, 1984.
97. Jones, A. K., The object model: a conceptual tool for structuring software, in *Lecture Notes in Computer Science 60*, Berlin: Springer-Verlag, pp. 3–19, 1978.
98. Jones, A. K., R. J. Chansler, I. Durham, K. Schwans, and S. R. Vegdahl, StarOS, a multiprocessor operating system for the support of task forces, in *Proc. 7th Symp. on Operating System Principles*, Pacific Grove, CA, Dec. 1979.
99. Kahn, K. C., *et al.*, iMAX: A multiprocessor operating system for an object-based computer, in *Proc. 8th Symp. on Operating System Principles*, pp. 14–16, Pacific Grove, CA, Dec. 1981.
100. Kamoun, F., M. B. Djerad, and G. Le Lann, Queueing analysis of the ordering issue in a distributed database concurrency control mechanism: A general case, in *IEEE 3rd Intl. Conf. on Distributed Computed Systems*, Fort Lauderdale, FL, Oct. 1982.
101. Kieburtz, R. B. and A. Silberschatz, Capability managers, *IEEE Trans. Software Eng.*, vol. SE-4, Nov. 1978.
102. Kimbleton, S. R., H. M. Wood, and M. L. Fitzgerald, Network Operating Systems—An Implementation Approach, in *Proc. AFIPS Conf.*, p. 47, 1978.
103. Kleinrock, L. and A. Nilsson, On optimal scheduling algorithms for time-shared systems, *JACM*, vol. 28, pp. 477–486, July 1981.
104. Knott, A proposal for certain process management and intercommunication primitives, *Operating Systems Rev.*, Oct. and Jan. 1975.
105. Kohler, W. H., A survey of techniques for synchronization and recovery in decentralized computer systems, *ACM Comput. Surveys*, vol. 13, pp. 149–183, June 1981.
106. Korth, H. T., Edge Locks and Deadlock Avoidance in Distributed Systems, in *ACM SIGACT-SIGOPS Symp. on Principle of Distributed Computing*, Ottowa, Canada, pp. 173–182, Aug. 1982.
107. Kung, H. T. and J. T. Robinson, On optimistic methods for concurrency control, *ACM Trans. Database Systems*, vol. 6, June 1981.
108. Lampson, B. W. and H. E. Sturgis, Reflections on an operating system design, *CACM*, vol. 19, May 1976.
109. Lampson, B. W. and H. E. Sturgis, Crash Recovery in a Distributed Storage System, revised and expanded unpublished paper, Res. Rep. Computer Science Laboratory, Xerox Palo Alto Research Center, Palo Alto, CA, 1979.
110. Lampson, B., Atomic transactions, in *Lecture Notes in Computer Science*, vol. 105, B. W. Lampson, M. Paul, and H. J. Siegert, Berlin: Springer-Verlag, pp. 365–370, 1981.
111. Lantz, K. A., RIG, an architecture for distributed systems, in *Proc. ACM Pacific 80*, San Francisco, CA, Nov. 1980.
112. Larsen, R. E., *Tutorial: Distributed Control*, IEEE Catalog No. EHO 153-7, New York: IEEE Press, 1979.
113. Lazowska, E., H. Levy, G. Almes, M. Fischer, R. Fowler, and S. Vestal, The architecture of Eden system, in *Proc. 8th Annual Symposium on OS Principles*, Pacific Grove, CA, Dec. 1981.
114. Le Lann, G., Algorithms for distributed data-sharing systems which use tickets, in *Proc. 3rd Berkeley Workshop on Dist. Databases and Comp. Networks*, Berkeley, CA, Aug. 1978.
115. Le Lann, G., Distributed systems—Towards a formal approach, *Proc. IFIP Congress*, Toronto, Canada. Amsterdam: North Holland Pub., pp. 155–160, Aug. 1980.
116. Le Lann, G., A distributed system for real-time transaction processing, *IEEE Computer*, vol. 14, Feb. 1981.

117. Lesser, V., D. Serrain, and J. Bonar, PCL: A process-oriented job control language, *IEEE Trans. Computers*, vol. C-29, Dec. 1980.

118. Levine, P. H., Facilitating Interprocess Communication in a Heterogeneous Network Environment (Masters thesis), MIT, 1977.

119. Lin, W. K., Concurrency control in a multiple-copy distributed database system, in *Proc. 4th Berkeley Conf. on Distributed Data Management and Computer Network*, (Aug.)

120. Lin, W. K., Performance evaluation of two concurrency mechanisms in a distributed database systems, ACM SIGMOD Conference, 1981.

121. Lindsay, B., Object Naming and Catalog Management for a Distributed Database Manager, IBM Res. Rep., RJ2914 (36689), Aug. 1980.

122. Lindsay, B. and P. G. Selinger, Site Autonomy Issues in R*: A Distributed Database Management System, IBM Res. Rep., RJ2927 (36822), San Jose, CA, Sept. 15, 1980.

123. Lindgren, B. W., *Elements of Decision Theory*, New York: MacMillan Co., 1981.

124. Liskov, B., Primitives for distributed computing, *Proc. 7th Symp. of Operating System Principles*, Dec. 1979.

125. Liskov, B. and R. Scheifler, Guardians and actions: Linguistic support for robust, distributed programs, in *Proc. 9th Symp. on Principles of Programming Languages*, pp. 7–19, Albuquerque, NM, Jan. 1982.

126. Luderer, G. W. R., *et al.*, A distributed UNIX system based on a virtual circuit switch, in *Proc. Symp. on Operating System Principles*, Pacific Grove, CA, Dec. 14–16, 1981.

127. Ma, P. Y. R., E. Y. S. Lee, and J. Tsuchiya, A task allocation model for distributed computing systems, *IEEE Trans. on Computers*, vol. C-31, pp. 41–47, Jan. 1982.

128. McGraw, J. R. and G. R. Andrews, Access Control in Parallel Programs, *IEEE Trans. Software Eng.*, vol. SE-5, pp. 1–9, Jan. 1979.

129. McKendry, M. S., J. E. Allchin, and W. C. Thibault, Architecture for a global operating system, in *Proc. IEEE INFOCOM83*, Apr. 1983.

130. McQuillan, J. M., Adaptive Routing Algorithms for Distributed Computer Networks, BBN Report 2831, May 1974.

131. Melliar-Smith, P. M. and R. L. Schwartz, Formal specification and mechanical verification of SIFT. *IEEE Trans. Computers*, vol. C-31, July 1982.

132. Menasce, D., G. Popek, and R. R. Muntz, A Locking Protocol for Resource Coordination in Distributed Systems, Tech. Rep. UCLA-ENG-780-8, Dept. of Computer Science, UCLA, Oct. 1980.

133. Menasce, D. A. and R. R. Muntz, Locking and deadlock detection in distributed data bases, *IEEE Trans. on Software Eng.*, vol. SE-5, May 1979.

134. Menasce, D. A., G. J. Popek, and R. R. Muntz, A locking protocol for resource coordination in distributed databases, *ACM Trans. on Database Systems*, vol. 5, June, 1980.

135. Minoura, T. and G. Wiederhold, Resilient extended true-copy token scheme for a distributed database system, *IEEE Trans. on Software Eng.*, vol. SE-8, May 1982.

136. Mitchel, J. G., W. Maybury, and R. Sweet, Mesa Language Manual, Xerox PARC Report CSL-79-3, Apr. 1979.

137. Mitchel, J. G. and J. Dion, A comparison of two network-based file servers, *CACM*, vol. 25, pp. 233–245.

138. Moss, J. E. B., Nested transactions and reliable distributed computing, in *Proc. 2nd Symp. on Reliability in Distributed Software and Database Systems*, Pittsburgh, PA, July 1982.

139. Narendra, K., Learning automata—A survey, *IEEE Trans. Systems, Man, and Cybernetics*, vol. SMC-4, July 1974.

140. National Bureau of Standards, Data Encryption Standard, Federal Information Processing Standards 46, Jan. 1977.

141. Needham, R. M. and R. D. Walker, The Cambridge CAP computer and its protection system, in *Proc. 6th ACM Symp on Operating System Principles*, West Lafayette, IN, Nov. 1977.
142. Needham, R. M. and M. D. Schroeder, Using encryption for authentication in large networks of computers, *CACM*, vol. 21, Dec. 1978.
143. Nelson, B. J., Remote Procedure Call, Xerox Corperation Tech. Rep. CSL-81-9, May 1981.
144. Obermarck, R., Distributed deadlock detection algorithm, *ACM Trans. Database Systems*, vol. 7, June 1982.
145. Oppen, D. and Y. K. Dalal, The Clearinghouse: A Decentralized Agent for Locating Named Objects in a Distributed Environment, *Xero Corporation*, Office Products Div. Rep. OPD-T8103, Oct. 1981.
146. Ousterhout, J., D. Scelza, and P. Sindhu, Medusa: An experiment in distributed operating system structure, *CACM*, vol. 23, Feb. 1980.
147. Popek, G., *et al.*, LOCUS, a network transparent, high reliability distributed system in *Proc. 8th Symp. on Operating System Principles*, pp. 14–16, Pacific Grove, CA, Dec. 1981.
148. Powell, M. L. and B. P. Miller, Process migration in DEMOS/MP in *Proc. 9th Symp. on OS Principles*, Bretton Woods, NH, Oct. 1983.
149. Raiffa, H. and R. Schlaifer, *Applied Statistical Decision Theory*, Cambridge, MA: Division of Research, Graduate School of Business Adm., Harvard University, 1961.
150. Ramamritham, K., Correctness of a distributed transaction system *Information Systems*, vol. 8, 1983.
151. Ramamritham, K., S. Vinter, and D. Stemple, Primitives for accessing protected objects, in *Proc. 3rd Symp. on Reliability in Distributed Software and Database Systems*, Clearwater Beach, FL, Oct. 1983.
152. Ramamritham, K., D. Briggs, D. Stemple, and S. Vinter, Privilege transfer and revocation in a port-based system, *IEEE Trans. Software Eng.*, May 1986.
153. Ramamritham, K. and John A. Stankovic, Dynamic task scheduling in distributed hard real-time systems, *IEEE Software*, July 1984.
154. Ramamritham, K., Resource controller tasks in Ada: Their structure and semantics, in *Proc. 7th Int. Conf. on Software Engineering*, Orlando, FL, Mar. 1984.
155. Randell, B., Recursively structured distributed computing systems, in *Proc. 3rd Symp. on Reliability in Distributed Software and Database Systems*, Clearwater Beach, FL, Oct. 1983.
156. Rashid, R., An Inter-Process Communication Facility for UNIX, Tech. Rep. Carnegie-Mellon University, June 1980.
157. Rashid, R. F. and G. G. Robertson, Accent: A communication oriented network operating system kernel, in *Proc. 8th Symp. on Operating System Principles*, Pacific Grove, CA, Dec. 14–16, 1981.
158. Rao, R., Design and evaluation of distributed communication primitives, in *Proc. ACM Pacific 1980*, San Francisco, CA, Nov. 1980.
159. Reed, D. P., *Naming and Synchronization in a Decentralized Computer System* (Ph.D. Diss.), Dept. of Comp. Sci., MIT, 1978.
160. Reed, D. P., Implementing atomic actions on decentralized data, in *Proc. 7th ACM Symp. on Operating System Principles*, Pacific Grove, CA, Dec. 1979.
161. Reid, L. G. and P. C. Karlton, A file system supporting cooperation between programs, in *Proc. 9th Symp. on OS Principles*, Bretton Woods, NH, Oct. 1983.
162. Ries, D., The effects of concurrency control on the performance of a distributed data management system, in *Proc. 4th Berkeley Workshop on Distributed Data Management and Comp. Networks*, San Francisco, CA, Aug. 1979.
163. Ries, D. R. and M. R. Stonebraker, Locking granularity revisited, *ACM Trans. on Database Systems*, pp. 210–227, June 1979.
164. Ritchie, D. and K. Thompson, The UNIX time-sharing system, *CACM*, vol. 17, July 1974.
165. Rosenkrantz, D. J., R. E. Stearns, and P. M. Lewis, System level concurrency control for

distributed database systems, *ACM Trans. on Database Systems*, vol. 3, pp. 178–198, June 1978.

166. Rothnie, J. B. and N. Goodman, A survey of research and development in distributed database management, in *Proc. 3rd Intl. Conf. on Very Large Data Bases*, pp. 48–62, Tokyo, Japan, Apr. 1977.
167. Rothnie, J. B., Jr., P. A. Berstein, S. Fox, N. Goodman, M. Hammer, T. A. Landers, C. Reeve, D. W. Shipman, and E. Wong, Introduction to a system for distributed databases (SDD-1), *ACM Trans. on Database Systems*, vol. 5, pp. 1–17, Mar. 1980.
168. Rowe, L. A. and K. P. Birman, Network support for a distributed database system, in *Proc. 4th Berkeley Conference on Distributed Data Management and Computer Networks*, San Francisco, CA, Aug. 1977.
169. Rowe, L. A. and K. P. Birman, A local network based on the UNIX operating system, *IEEE Trans. on Software Eng.*, vol. SE-8, pp. 137–146, Mar. 1982.
170. Rushby, J. and B. Randell, A distributed secure system, *Computer*, vol. 16, July 1983.
171. Rypka, D. J. and A. P. Lucido, Deadlock detection and avoidance for shared logical resources, *IEEE Trans. on Software Engineering*, vol. SE-5, pp. 465–471, Sept. 1979.
172. Saltzer, J. H., Naming and binding of objects, in *Operating Systems: An Advanced Course*, Berlin: Springer-Verlag, 1978.
173. Saltzer, J. H., D. P. Reed, and D. D. Clark, End-to-end arguments in system design, in *Proc. 2nd Int. Conf. on Distributed Computing Systems*, Paris, France, Apr. 1981.
174. Sandell, N., R. Varaiya, M. Athans, and M. Safonov, Survey of decentralized control methods for large scale systems, *IEEE Trans. on Automatic Control*, vol. AC-23, Apr. 1978.
175. Schoch, J. F., Inter-network naming, addressing and routing, in *Proc. Compcon 78*, San Francisco, CA, Spring, 1978.
176. Schlageter, G., Optimistic methods for concurrency control in a distributed database system, *VLDB*, 1981.
177. Schumann, A. S., M. A. Clarke, and N. W. Nikolaou, Programming distributed applications in Ada: A first approach, in *Proc. Int. Conf. on Parallel Processing*, (Aug.).
178. Segall, A, The modelling of adaptive routing in data-communication networks, *IEEE Trans. on Communications*, vol. COM-25, pp. 85–95, Jan. 1977.
179. Skeen, D., A Quorum-Based Commit Protocol, Tech. Rep. TR 82-483, Cornell University, Feb. 1982.
180. Skeen, D. and M. Stonebraker, A formal model of crash recovery in a distributed system, *IEEE Trans. on Software Engineering*, vol. SE-9, May 1983.
181. Smith, G. R., The contract net protocol: High level communication and control in a distributed problem solver, *IEEE Trans. Computers*, vol. C-29, Dec. 1980.
182. Solomon, M. H. and R. A. Finkel, The Roscoe distributed operating system, in *Proc. 7th Symp. on Operating System Principles*, Pacific Grove, CA, Mar. 1979.
183. Spector, A. Z., Performing remote operations efficiently on a local computer network, *CACM*, vol. 25, pp. 246–259, Apr. 1982.
184. Spector, A. and P. M. Schwartz, Transactions: A construct for reliable distributed computing *ACM Operating Systems Rev.*, vol. 17, Apr. 1983.
185. Srivastava, S. K.. On the treatment of orphans in a distributed system, *Proc. 3rd Symp. on Reliability in Distributed Systems*, Oct. 1983.
186. Stankovic, J. A. and A. van Dam, Research directions in (cooperative) distributed processing, in *Research Directions in Software Technology*, Cambridge, MA: MIT Press, 1979.
187. Stankovic, J. A., ADCOS—An Adaptive, System Wide, Decentralized Controlled Operating System, Tech. Rep., Univ. of Massachusetts, Nov. 1981.
188. Stankovic, J. A., Software communication mechanisms: Procedure calls versus messages, *IEEE Computer*, vol. 15, Apr. 1982.
189. Stankovic, J. A., N. Chowdhury, R. Mirchandaney, I. Sidhu, An evaluation of the applica-

bility of different mathematical approaches to the analysis of decentralized control algorithms, in *Proc. COMPSAC 82*, Chicago, IL, Nov. 1982.

190. Stankovic, J. A. A heuristic for cooperation among decentralized controllers, in *Proc. INFOCOM 83*, Apr. 1983.
191. Stankovic, J. A. and I. S. Sidhu, An adaptive bidding algorithm for processes, clusters and distributed groups, in *Proc. 4th Int. Conf. on Distributed Computing*, May, 1984.
192. Stankovic, J. A., Simulations of three adaptive, decentralized controlled, job scheduling algorithms, *Computer Networks*, 1984.
193. Stankovic, J. A., Bayesian decision theory and its application to decentralized control of job scheduling. *IEEE Trans. on Computers*, Feb. 1985.
194. Stemple, D., S. Vinter, and K. Ramamritham, Functional addressing in Gutenberg: Interprocess communication without process identifiers, *IEEE Trans. Software Eng.*, Nov. 1986.
195. Stone, H. S., Multiprocessor scheduling with the aid of network flow algorithms, *IEEE Trans. on Software Eng.*, vol. SE-3, Jan. 1977.
196. Stone, H. S., Critical load factors in distributed computer systems, *IEEE Trans. on Software Eng.*, vol. SE-4, May 1978.
197. Stone, H. S. and S. H. Bokhari, Control of distributed processes, *IEEE Computer*, vol. 11, pp. 97–106, July 1978.
198. Stonebraker, M. and E. Neuhold, A distributed database version of INGRES, *Proc. 1977 Berkeley Workshop on Distributed Data Management and Computer Networks*, pp. 19–36, May 1977.
199. Stonebraker, M., Concurrency control and consistency of multiple copies of data in distributed INGRES, *IEEE Trans. Software Eng.*, vol. SE-5, pp. 180–194, May 1979.
200. Stonebraker, M., Operating system support for database management, *CACM*, vol. 24, pp. 412–418, July 1981.
201. Sturgis, H., J. Mitchell, and J. Israel, Issues in the design and use of a distributed file system, *ACM Operating System Rev.*, pp. 55–69, July 1980.
202. Swan, R. J., S. H. Fuller, and. D. P. Siewiorek, Cm*:A modular, multi-microprocessor, in *AFIPS Conference*, vol. 46, NCC, 1977.
203. Tenney, R. R. and N. R. Sandell, Jr., Structures for distributed decision-making, *IEEE Trans. Systems, Man, and Cybernetics*, vol. SMC-11, pp. 517–527, Aug. 1981.
204. Tenney, R. R. and N. R. Sandell, Jr., Strategies for distributed decisionmaking, *IEEE Trans. Systems, Man, and Cybernetics*, vol. SMC-11, pp. 527–538, Aug., 1981.
205. Thomas, R. H., A majority consensus approach to concurrency control for multiple copy databases, *ACM Trans. Database Systems*, vol. 4, pp. 180–209, June 1979.
206. Traiger, I., Virtual memory management for database systems, *ACM Operating System Rev.*, vol. 16, pp. 26–48, Oct. 1982.
207. Traiger, I., *et al.*, Transactions and Consistency in Distributed Database System, *ACM Trans. Database Systems*, vol. 7, Sept. 1982.
208. Verhofstad, J. S. M., Recovery techniques for database systems, *Comput. Surveys*, vol. 10, pp. 167–195, June 1978.
209. Vinter, S., K. Ramamritham, and D. Stemple, Protecting objects through the use of ports, in *Proc. Phoenix Conf. on Computers and Communications*, Phoenix, AZ, Mar. 1983.
210. Voydock, V. L. and S. T. Kent, Security mechanisms in high-level network protocols, *Comput. Surveys*, vol. 15, pp. 135–171, June 1983.
211. Walden, D. C., A system for interprocess communication in a resource sharing computer network, *CACM*, vol. 15, Apr. 1972.
212. Walker, B. G., G. Popek, R. English, C. Kline, and G. Theil, The LOCUS distributed operating system, in *Proc. 9th Symp. on OS Principles*, Bretton Woods, NH, Oct. 1983.
213. Ward, S., TRIX: A network oriented operating system, in *Proc. COMPCON*, San Francisco, CA, 1980.

214. Wilkes, M. V. and R. M. Needham, *The Cambridge CAP Computer and its Operating System*, Elsevier North Holland, 1979.

215. Winkler, R. L., *Introduction to Bayesian Inference and Decision*, New York: Holt, Rinehart & Winston, 1972.

216. Wirth, N., Modula: a language for modular multiprogramming, *Software—Practice and Experience*, vol. 7, pp. 3–35, Jan. 1977.

217. Wittie, L. and A. M. Van Tilborg, MICROS, A distributed operating system for Micronet, a reconfigurable network computer, *IEEE Trans. Computers*, vol. C-29, Dec. 1980.

218. Wright, D. D., On merging partitioned databases, *Proc. SIGMOD 83*, vol. 13, May 1983.

219. Wulf, W., E. Cohen, W. Corwin, A. Jones, R. Levin, C. Pierson, and F. Pollack, HYDRA: The kernel of a multiprocessor operating system, *CACM*, vol. 17, June 1974.

Index